Johann Wolfgang von Goethe, Karl Friedrich Zelter, Arthur Duke Coleridge

Goethe's Letters to Zelter

Johann Wolfgang von Goethe, Karl Friedrich Zelter, Arthur Duke Coleridge

Goethe's Letters to Zelter

ISBN/EAN: 9783741124860

Manufactured in Europe, USA, Canada, Australia, Japa

Cover: Foto ©Andreas Hilbeck / pixelio.de

Manufactured and distributed by brebook publishing software (www.brebook.com)

Johann Wolfgang von Goethe, Karl Friedrich Zelter, Arthur Duke Coleridge

Goethe´s Letters to Zelter

GOETHE'S LETTERS TO ZELTER.

WITH EXTRACTS FROM THOSE OF ZELTER TO GOETHE,

SELECTED, TRANSLATED, AND
ANNOTATED

BY

A. D. COLERIDGE, M.A.,
LATE FELLOW OF KING'S COLLEGE, CAMBRIDGE.

LONDON: GEORGE BELL AND SONS.
YORK STREET, COVENT GARDEN.
1887.

THE FOLLOWING VERSION OF LETTERS
SELECTED FROM
GOETHE'S CORRESPONDENCE WITH ZELTER,
IS INSCRIBED TO THE MEMORY OF
HENRY BRADSHAW, M.A.,
LATE LIBRARIAN OF THE UNIVERSITY OF CAMBRIDGE, WHOSE
WISDOM AND LEARNING
CAN BE BEST APPRECIATED BY THE WISE AND LEARNED,
BUT WHOSE LOVABLE QUALITIES WERE KNOWN BY HEART
TO HIS CONTEMPORARY AT SCHOOL AND COLLEGE,
AND FRIEND FOR MORE THAN
FORTY YEARS.

PREFACE.

ANY new light thrown upon Goethe's genius and character should be welcome to the student of German literature. The recent production of the *Jahrbuch*, and the affiliation of the English Goethe Society to the Weimar *Goethe-Gesellschaft*, have so stimulated the interest of readers in the publication of new matter affecting Goethe, that it is hoped the present volume may be opportune rather than otherwise. Many years ago, I studied the Goethe-Zelter Correspondence, with the wish to learn all I could about the tutor of Mendelssohn, the friend of Goethe, and "the restorer of Bach to the Germans." Such was the compliment paid to Zelter's memory by Abraham, the father of Felix Mendelssohn. How strenuously the son endorsed his father's opinion is a matter of common knowledge to the readers of many works which illustrate the history of the composer's life. But with us Englishmen the pupil's fame has so completely eclipsed that of the teacher, that Zelter is little more than a name. He was no ordinary man. A stonemason by trade, he became a musician by choice, and was so successful in his art-career as ultimately to conduct the *Singakademie* at Berlin. He also achieved the still higher distinction of becoming Goethe's most intimate correspondent. Beginning with mere reports of Berlin gossip, and casual interchange of criticisms on men and things, he ended by drawing out, as few did, the inmost sympathies and chosen confidences of the Weimar sage. Goethe's respect for Zelter's force of character was apparently never neutralized by his dogmatism, or the rash and mistaken opinions traceable here and there throughout the correspondence. "Excellent, but crusty," are the epithets attached to Zelter's name by his pupil, Edward Devrient,

and the publication of the Goethe-Zelter Correspondence
was harshly judged by Felix Mendelssohn, whose language
on the subject of his kith and kin, as they are discussed
throughout the work, seems to me exaggerated and unfair.
After close study, I find no "unhandsome treatment" of
any single member of the Mendelssohn family, least of all
of the brilliant Felix himself, who thus airs his suscepti-
bilities in a letter to his father:—"To return to the
much-talked-of correspondence between Goethe and Zelter.
One thing struck me on this subject: when in this work
Beethoven or anyone else is abused, or my family un-
handsomely treated, and many subjects most tediously discussed, I remain quite cool and calm, but when Reichardt
is in question, and they both presume to criticise him with
great arrogance, I feel in such a rage that I don't know
what to do, though I cannot myself explain why this
should be so."

Zelter's scientific pretensions must have been limited in
his early days, as apprentice and journeyman, to a knowledge of bricks and mortar, though later on in life, he
became a learned theorist in the nobler art of music.
With the characteristic self-confidence of an imperfectly
educated but gifted man, he is ready to lay down the law
on whatever subject the all-embracing Goethe has started
for discussion. Had I included a list of the topics mentioned in these letters, instead of limiting the index to the
names of persons, and of such works of art and literature
as are generally known, the result would have been a strange
medley. Handel and Bach alternate with Berlin play-
bills; Werner, Görres, and Byron with Teltower turnips;
pike, mixed pickles, and game are set off against anti-
Newtonian optics. Even if we attach small value to
Zelter's estimate of men and things outside his own vocation, and find Goethe adopting towards him a more
careless and familiar style than he did with Eckermann—
the Boswell of his later days—it does not follow that the
rough, and at times uncouth and unintelligible language
of Zelter should be suppressed. His music has become as
obsolete as his criticism, but it must be remembered to his
credit, that it had a charm for Goethe, Schiller, Voss, and
Tieck. He had a stray taste, too, for literature; his *Auto-*

biography, edited by Dr. Rintel, his *Life of Fasch*, accompanyist to Frederick the Great, are readable works. But England's real indebtedness to Zelter consists in the fact that it was he who trained Felix Mendelssohn to an enduring love of Sebastian Bach, the knowledge of whose music it was the younger man's mission to diffuse. "Nothing less," says Devrient, "than the absolute success of the first resuscitation of Bach's masterpiece, (the Passion Music,) on the 11th of March, 1829, could have initiated the subsequent study of this master by the leading musicians of modern times." Beyond a question, we owe to Zelter and his pupil the slow but sure appreciation of the work of that immortal master, who, if Mendelssohn is to be believed in, "is in no one point inferior to any master, and in many points superior to all." We may smile or sneer at many of the oracular utterances of the ex-stonemason, but condone his pardonable self-complacency in the boast, that he knew every note from the pen of his hero, Sebastian Bach, who, says he, '*is one of those that cannot altogether be fathomed.*"

Even if the extracts I have made from Zelter's own letters are neither "elegant" nor profound, I would fain hope that they will make Goethe's remarks intelligible. I have given as literal a version of these as it was in my power to give, but I have taken the liberty of paraphrasing Zelter's language where it was barely intelligible. My original intention was to have published in their entirety the whole of Goethe's letters contained in the six volumes of correspondence, supplementing them with quotations from Zelter's letters, interspersed here and there, as a key to the answers sent by the philosopher to the musician. From necessity rather than from choice, I abandoned the plan, and must own that in the abundant materials I had for two volumes, there was a plentiful "chronicle of small beer." Passing events and trifles which—nearly a century since—had an interest at Berlin and Weimar, for two intimate friends, are dull and insipid reading now, many of the allusions can only be guessed at, and are riddles to the Germans themselves. Many of the letters, too, are so loosely strung together, that it is a matter of great difficulty to pick up the threads of discourse and reflection,

b

dropped at intervals of several months, and then taken up again by either of the two correspondents, as if they had formed part and parcel of yesterday's discussion. For these and other reasons, I have allowed Zelter to speak for himself, and limited my selection of letters to such parts of the correspondence as I thought might be of interest to the general reader.

Of all the works I have consulted as books of reference, I have found Düntzer's *Life of Goethe*, (admirably translated and annotated by T. W. Lyster, Esq.,) the most indispensable. Since the publication of Lewes's *Life of Goethe*, the researches of modern scholars have brought to light much authentic information that was not available twenty years ago, and Düntzer's work is in many respects a running commentary on the more notable parts of this correspondence. *The Conversations of Goethe with Eckermann*, and *The Correspondence between Schiller and Goethe*, have also been of great service to me. The references throughout are to the English translations of those works by Lyster, Oxenford, and Miss D. Schmitz.

The translations of the poems, other than those made by E. A. Bowring, Esq., and the lines taken from Longfellow's translation of Dante, are by my daughter Mary E. Coleridge.

A. D. C.

October, 1886.

ERRATA.

Page 7, line 36, *for* Revel, *read* Reval.
,, 54, ,, 33, *for* Traugott Maximilian, *read* Karl.
,, 72, ,, 19, *for* Augerblicks, *read* Augenblicks.
,, 83, ,, 3, *for* to, *read* for.

GOETHE'S LETTERS TO ZELTER.

1796.

1.—GOETHE TO MADAME UNGER.*

Weimar, 15th June, 1796.

YOUR letter, dear Madam, and the enclosed songs, gave me very great pleasure. Herr Zelter's admirable compositions reached me while I was with people who first made me acquainted with his work. His melody to the poem *Ich denke Dein*† had an inconceivable charm for me, and I could not help composing that song for it, which stands in Schiller's *Musenalmanach*.‡

I am no judge of music, being without knowledge of the means it makes use of for its purposes; I can only speak of the effect it produces upon me, when I let it exercise its powers over me completely and repeatedly; and hence I can say of Herr Zelter's music to my poems, that I could scarcely have believed music capable of such heart-felt tones.

Thank him very much for me, and tell him that I should very much like to know him personally, with a view to mutual discussion. In the eighth volume of my Novel§ there will, it is true, be no space left for songs; still, the list of things left by Mignon and the old Harper is not

---

* Wife of Goethe's publisher in Berlin. Goethe's personal acquaintance with Zelter began three years later. (See Rintel's *Life of Zelter*, p. 194.)

† The song here alluded to is by Frau Friderike Brun (1765-1835), who was the authoress of a number of poems, and of several books of travel. (See Professor Buchheim's *Deutsche Lyrik*, note on p. 382.)

‡ This periodical, containing short poems and pieces, was published annually. It is chiefly famous for the *Xenien*, a collection of epigrams by Goethe and Schiller suggested by Martial's *Xenia*.

§ *Wilhelm Meisters Lehrjahre*.

B

yet exhausted, and all of it that can be allowed to see the light, I should much prefer entrusting to Herr Zelter.

Meantime, I may perhaps soon send some other poems, with the request that they may be set to music for Schiller's *Musenalmanach;* I had hoped to enclose them in this letter, which consequently has been longer in coming than it ought to have been.

Accept my thanks, dear Madam, for the trouble you have taken, and believe that I know how to appreciate the interest, which kind and enlightened minds take in me, and those of my works, by which I can even bring a part of my existence near to persons far from and unknown to me.

GOETHE.

1799.

2.—GOETHE TO ZELTER.

Weimar, 26th August, 1799.

It is with sincere gratitude that I reply to your friendly letter, by which you would fain express in words that of which your compositions themselves have long convinced me: that you take a lively interest in my works, and have a true inclination for making much of their spirit your own. The beauty of an active sympathy consists in its reproductive force, for if my poems called forth your melodies, I can well say that your melodies have stirred me to many a song, and doubtless if we lived nearer to one another, I should more frequently than at present feel myself inspired by a lyric mood. It would give me sincere pleasure to hear from you on any subject.

I enclose a production * which has rather a strange appearance. It was suggested by the question, whether dramatic ballads might not be worked out in such a manner, as to furnish a composer with material for a Cantata.

Unfortunately this particular ballad is too slight to deserve being treated on so large a scale.

Farewell. Remember me to Herr Unger.

GOETHE.

---

* *Die erste Walpurgis Nacht.* Zelter's efforts to set this ballad-poem were unsuccessful; it was reserved for Mendelssohn to redeem his master's failure.

1801.

3.—GOETHE TO ZELTER.

Weimar, 29th May, 1801.

You have accomplished a very meritorious piece of work by the monument you have raised to Fasch,* besides giving me great pleasure by what you have done.

The remembrance of a human life that has passed away is so contracted, that affection is obliged, as it were, to re-animate the ashes, and present the glorified Phœnix to our eyes. Every honest fellow may hope some day or other to be represented thus by his friend, his pupil, his brother artist.

When compared with an individuality thus lovingly resuscitated, what a poor figure is made by those necrologists, who, immediately after a man's death, sedulously balance the good and bad that has been believed in and applauded by the multitude, during the life of an eminent person, bolster up his so-called virtues and faults with hypocritical righteousness, and thereby are worse than death in destroying a personality, which can be imagined only in the living union of those opposite qualities.

I was specially delighted with your account of the origin of the Mass in sixteen parts, and the Vocal Society † to which it gave rise; how pleased I was that worthy Fasch should be so fortunate as to have lived to see such an idea realized.

In one of your last letters—for which, alas! I still owe you an answer—you ask whether there is anything among my papers in the shape of an opera?

You will find in the next number of Wilman's *Taschen-*

---

* Founder of the *Singakademie* at Berlin. He and Emmanuel Bach shared the duty of accompanying Frederick the Great's flute Concertos. His influence on musical taste in Berlin was so great, that Beethoven honoured him with two visits in the summer of 1796. "As a master of composition in many parts, Fasch is the last representative of the great school of sacred composers, which lasted so long in Italy." (See article *Fasch* in Sir G. Grove's *Dictionary of Music*.) The "monument" alluded to, is Zelter's biography of his former master.

† The *Singakademie*.

buch the first scenes of the Second Part of the *Zauberflöte*.* Some years ago I sketched a plan for a serious cantata, *Die Danaiden*, in which, after the fashion of the ancient Greek tragedy, the Chorus was to appear as the principal subject; but neither of the two pieces will, I expect, ever be finished. One ought to live with the composer, and work for some particular theatre, otherwise but little will come of such an undertaking.

Be sure to send me from time to time some of your compositions, for they give me great pleasure. Speaking generally, I do not live in a musical sphere; we reproduce throughout the year first one, then another piece of music, but where there is no production, an art cannot make itself vividly felt.

Farewell, and hold me in remembrance.

GOETHE.

* The libretto of Mozart's famous opera was adapted by Schikaneder from *Lulu, oder die Zauberflöte*, a fairy tale in Wieland's *Dschinnistan*. Eckermann tells us that Goethe, while acknowledging that it was full of indefensible improbabilities, added, "In spite of all, however, it must be acknowledged that the author had the most perfect knowledge of the art of contrast, and a wonderful knack of introducing stage effects." As early as 1796, Goethe entered into an agreement with Wranitzky to continue the libretto. This must have failed, for in 1823 Eckermann says, that Goethe has not yet found a composer to treat the subject properly.

1802.

4.—GOETHE TO ZELTER.

Weimar, 6th December, 1802.

WHEN, during these gloomy days, I thought of cheerful subjects, I then often looked back to the time of your delightful presence amongst us last year. I have but slender hope of seeing you again soon; yet it is my wish that a thread should continue to be spun between us. Therefore give a kindly welcome to *Der Graf und Die Zwerge* * (The Count and the Dwarfs), who appear herewith; they now, for the first time, as I think, show style and ingenuity. Cherish these merry imps in your true musical sense, and prepare for yourself and us some diversion for the winter evenings. But do not let the poem out of your hands; nay, if possible, keep it secret.

My whole household thinks of you affectionately and lovingly.   GOETHE.

* A ballad of Goethe's, now called *Hochzeitlied.*

1803.

5.—GOETHE TO ZELTER.
Weimar, 31st January, 1803.

ONLY a line to tell you briefly, that good Dr. Chladni* is here, and will remain in the neighbourhood till about the 9th or 10th of February. Perhaps this may partially influence your decision as to the journey. If you could meet him, while he is still here, we should have some lively discussions about music and acoustics.

Only thus much, to testify again to my eager wish to see you under my roof.   GOETHE.

6.—ZELTER TO GOETHE.
Berlin, 3rd February, 1803.

.... MADAME MARA † has arrived here, and I yearn for the divine singing of this artist, after so many years. In all that time I have heard no such singer, for with her glorious voice she can do everything, and anything she does is exactly right. Your dear kind letter of the 24th of January has almost damped my spirits. I was unwilling to come empty-handed to Weimar, and have therefore not been idle. I hoped that several quite new songs of yours would win your favour. *Die Sehnsucht, Was zieht mir das Herz so?* and *Der Sänger* are quite new, and, as I think, better than even Reichardt's. Since the First Part of *Wilhelm Meister* was published, I have had *Der Sänger* constantly in my mind, and here it is at last on paper. Reichardt's music to it is like a march, and starting rather imperiously, should at all events end as it began; I have restored the Ballad-form. Then, again, I have finished several of your songs, and have added four new strophes to *Das Blümlein Wunderschön. Der Junggesell* and *Der Mühlbach*, at the suggestion of a critic in the

---

* Author of a work on *Acoustics*. (See *Schiller and Goethe Correspondence*, vol. ii., p. 438.)

† This famous singer was born at Cassel in 1794, and died at Revel in 1833, soon after she had received a birthday poem from Goethe, *Sangreich war dein Ehrenweg.* An interesting memoir of her is to be found in Rochlitz's *Für Freunde der Tonkunst.*

Apollo, have been made rather more full-bodied. Schiller's *Hero und Leander*, *Worte des Glaubens*, *Kampf mit dem Drachen*, *Die Sänger der Vorwelt* have received the final touches; I have re-set some new Sonnets, one of Herder's amongst them, and several old German songs of the seventeenth century by Abschatz, Zinkgräf, P. Gerhard. I reckon up to you my small glories, like a child who has had Christmas presents from the Muses, and when all is told, do not know what to do with all my treasures. Could I but achieve something great! My years are waning, and —nothing comes of it. Could you not suggest something by Herder, whom I esteem most highly? I read so little, and re-read so often my old favourites, that fine things often escape me. And now, " Enough, ye Muses ! "—But pray be on your guard, that your house is not haunted ! It is my spirit which has taken up his quarters with you, and is settling down and nestling by degrees. . . . .

ZELTER.

7.—GOETHE TO ZELTER.

Weimar, 10th March, 1803.

I CAN quite understand that it requires some resolution to leave one's own circle, and to look up distant friends at this season of the year; yet I take to heart in more ways than one your letter of refusal. Apart from what we should have gained for the general and higher aims of Art by personal communication, it so happens that I am this winter busy with the organization of the Opera and Orchestra, more with a view to the future than the present; and I had thought your help in this matter was absolutely indispensable.

The importance of the old proverbial advice, " Go straight to the right smithy," * was clear enough to me long ago; but what is the good of knowing this, if the smithy is so far off, that one cannot get to it with bag and baggage ?

So as I cannot give up the hope of seeing you, I make a proposal which I trust you will take in good part.

If you could possibly find time, more or less, for a trip to us, I am at present so circumstanced as to expect that

* *Gehe vor die rechte Schmiede.*

through you great advantage would accrue to institutions I have at heart, so I feel bound, at all events, to defray your travelling expenses to and fro, and to provide for you during your stay here Now, if you feel inclined to weigh the inconveniencies of the journey, and the loss of your valuable time, against the possibility of an agreeable visit here, after all you would not have such a heavy bill against us, and perhaps we could arrange to meet more often in future, not, I dare say, to any great advantage on your part, but anyhow without your suffering any pecuniary disadvantage.

Consider this, and tell me what you think of the proposal, to which I hope you will give a favourable answer; and this the sooner, that you are in no way restricted as to the time of your visit, and we should be ready to welcome you any day between this and Whitsuntide. Your room is still unoccupied, and ready to receive you.

All your friends think of you with enthusiasm, which was yesterday rekindled by the repetition of your new compositions—the *Heiterlied* and the *Zwerge*. Schiller thanks you most sincerely.

A new Tenor * has come here; he has a very beautiful voice, but is in every sense a novice. What a thing it would be for him and for us could you give him a hint in the way of improvement! I mention but this one link in the chain of obligations we should gladly owe you. I need not tell you what a serious business is the improvement of our Theatre, and particularly of the music, for the wedding of our Crown Prince,† and the fêtes which have to be given in the last quarter of the present year, &c.—as little need I repeat the proposals and requests I have already made. I enclose the very delightful composition you asked for.‡

If you look through Herder's *Volkslieder*, published some time since, as well as his miscellaneous poems, you are certain to find much that will interest you. When my small concerts are given, I am very anxious that every one

---

* Brand of Frankfurt. (See *Schiller and Goethe Correspondence*, vol. ii., p. 445.)
† The Crown Prince was betrothed to the Grand Duchess Maria Paulowna.
‡ Zelter's music to *Die Erinnerung*.

of my friends should be astonished at himself, when he hears his works reproduced in your music.

Please tell me plainly what you think of Madame Mara?..

GOETHE.

8.—GOETHE TO ZELTER.

Weimar, 1st July, 1803.

ACCEPT, dear friend, a little present, which Herr Geh. Rath von Wolzogen* will bring you from me.

You relished Herr von Knebel's† Spanish snuff, and a further supply was discovered. Where? You shall hear, when it comes safely to hand. Fill your box with it, and sometimes think of my affection and esteem for you when you take a pinch, whether you are alone or in good company. That is always a pleasant moment.

The sower, when he has sown his seed, goes away and lets it sprout; what a pity you cannot see how much good is springing up from what you have sown among us....

GOETHE.

9.—ZELTER TO GOETHE.

Berlin, 1st July, 1803.

.... AT Dresden I met Madame Mara, who was delighted to see me; she was just going to give a concert which I attended; there as everywhere she has admirers and enemies. The thing she liked best was the unexpectedly good receipts—that's the first point with her just now.

The first thing that drew my attention in Berlin was a short biography of the late Mozart, half dedicated to you;‡ to this is appended an anything but short, and anything but æsthetic description of his works, together with any-

---

* Schiller's brother-in-law, Councillor of Legation, and recommended by Schiller to Goethe as a student of architecture. (See *Schiller and Goethe Correspondence*, vol. i., p. 402.)

† Major Karl Ludwig von Knebel, formerly tutor to Prince Constantine of Weimar. His translations from Propertius attracted the attention of Schiller and Herder. Goethe mentions him as "helping me in a very friendly way with my optical studies." (See *Schiller and Goethe Correspondence*, vol. i., p. 278, and vol. ii., p. 466.)

‡ It was dedicated jointly to Goethe and to Herr Müller, Cantor of the *Thomas-Schule* in Leipzig.

thing but a good portrait of him. Now could you find out for me, who is the Neudietendorf author of this educational work for young musicians? The Neudietendorfers may make a good thing of him. I read in the papers that my beautiful Queen* was graciously bountiful to your mother; this gave me exquisite pleasure. Here they stoutly maintain that very soon you will be with Schiller in Berlin, and in several quarters I have been questioned on the point. The possibility I had no wish to contradict, especially as your friends think, that it will soon be time to pronounce judgment on the sinful race, and that can only be done in person.

4th July. I saw for the first time a performance of Schiller's *Braut von Messina.* . . . . Iffland gave a good rendering of Bohemund, and Bethmann as Cæsar was first rate. . . . . I had rather say nothing about the choruses, for all my ideas on that subject are confused and misty. I would wager that Schiller is right, and that there is something behind which none of us as yet suspect. Perhaps I may one day write to you at greater length about this, when the piece is printed, and the play in black and white before me.

The position of the Chorus was not to my taste. I should have thought the Chorus ought to stand close to the side scenes, right and left, and as far as possible in the background, so that the largest possible interval might separate it from the chief groups. By this means the Chorus would, as it were, become a main factor of the whole, enlightening and invigorating it. . . . .

I wish you would instruct me about the tendency of the Greek Chorus. . . . .

The glorious snuff, redolent with the fragrance of all the Muses, is a real refreshment to me; no wonder now if I write something good.

ZELTER.

10.—GOETHE TO ZELTER.

Weimar, 28th July, 1803.

So often have I followed you in thought, that I have unfortunately neglected to do so in writing; to-day

* Louisa of Prussia.

only a few words, to accompany the enclosed sheet. I shall continue my reflections, and therefore only touch the main points as briefly as possible; you will yourself of course supply the details.

Of Mozart's biography I have heard nothing further as yet, but shall inquire about it, and about the author too.

Your beautiful Queen made several people happy on her journey, none more so than my mother; nothing could have given her more pleasure in her declining years.

Be sure to write to me from time to time, and please send me the play-bills month by month. Pray also give me some account of the performance of my *Natürliche Tochter*, only speak frankly and without reserve. As it is, I am inclined to shorten some scenes, which must seem long, even if they are admirably acted.

Will you give me a sketch of the duties of a *Concert-Meister?* in so far, at least, as it is necessary for one like me to know, so that I may to some extent be able to judge of a man in this position, and possibly to guide him.

Madame Mara sang last Tuesday in Lauchstädt; I have not yet heard how it went off.

Thank you heartily for myself and my friends for the songs, which I received through Herr von Wolzogen. There was no time to think of producing anything new.

I hope soon to send you the proof-sheets of my poems, with the request that you will keep them secret until they are published. . . . .

GOETHE.

ENCLOSURE.

You will by this time have before you in print the *Braut von Messina*, and be able to appreciate more accurately what the poet has achieved; you will also gather from his preface, what he thinks about the matter, and learn how far you agree with him. With reference to your letter, I will jot down my thoughts on this subject, for a few words will suffice to make us intelligible to one another.

In Greek tragedy the Chorus is seen in four Epochs.

In the first Epoch, a few characters calling up the past into the present are introduced between the singing, in which divinities and heroes are exalted, and genealogies, mighty deeds, portentous destinies, are brought before the fancy. Of this we have a proximate example in the *Seven before Thebes*, by Æschylus. This, then, was the beginning of dramatic art—the old style.

The second Epoch shows us the whole Chorus as the mystic leading character of the piece, as in the *Eumenides* and *Supplices;* these, I am inclined to think, represent the lofty style. The Chorus is independent, the interest rests upon it; it is—one might say, the republican period of dramatic art, the rulers and the gods are mere supplementary personages.

In the third Epoch the Chorus becomes supplementary; the interest is projected upon the families, their respective members and chiefs, with whose destinies the destiny of the surrounding people is but slightly connected. The Chorus is subordinate, and the figures of the Princes and Heroes step forth in their isolated majesty. This I am inclined to think the grand style. The tragedies of Sophocles stand on this level. Inasmuch as the multitude has only to watch the hero and Fate, and cannot influence Nature either in special instances or generally, it falls back upon reflection, and undertakes the office of an appointed and welcome spectator.

In the fourth Epoch, the action continues more and more to confine itself to private interests, the Chorus appears often as a wearisome tradition, as an inherited piece of the dramatic inventory. It becomes unnecessary, and therefore in a living, poetical whole is equally useless, tiresome, and disturbing—as, for example, when it is called upon to keep secrets, in which it has no interest, &c. Several examples of this are to be found in the plays of Euripides, of which I may name *Helena* and *Iphigenia in Tauris*.

You will see from the above—in order to return again to the musical thread—that any attempts must be made in connection with the first two Epochs, and this might be done by very short Oratorios.

G.

THE ENCLOSURE—continued.

Now, as Greek tragedy disengaged itself from the lyric element, so we, even in our own day, have a remarkable example of the efforts made by the Drama to disengage itself from the historical, or rather the epic element; we find this in the manner in which the story of the Passion is sung in Catholic churches, during the week before Easter. There are three individuals, one of whom represents the Evangelist, the second Christ, the third the rest of the interlocutors; these and the Chorus (turba) represent the whole, as you yourself know well enough. I will add a short quotation, that you may the sooner see what I mean.

"*Evangelist*: Then said Pilate to him:
Interlocutor: Art thou then a King?
Evangelist: Jesus answered:
Christ: Thou sayest it. I am a King. For this end was I born, and came into the world, that I might bear witness of the truth. Whoever is of the truth, heareth my voice.
Evangelist: Pilate saith unto him:
Interlocutor: What is truth?
Evangelist: And when he had so said, he went forth again unto the Jews, and saith unto them:
Interlocutor: I find no fault in him. But ye have a custom, that I should release one unto you at the feast. Will ye then that I release unto you the King of the Jews?
Evangelist: Then they cried out all together again, and said:
Turba: Not this man, but Barabbas!
Evangelist: Now Barabbas was a murderer."

Now, if you confine the function of the Evangelist merely to the beginning, so that he may pronounce a general historical introduction as a prologue, and if you make the intermediate incidents presently emanating from him useless by the coming and going, the movements and actions, of the various personages, you will have made a very good beginning for a drama.

I now remember that this course has been followed in Oratorios on the Passion; but probably something new and important might be produced, if one set to work in thorough earnest.

11.—ZELTER TO GOETHE.

7th August, 1803.

. . . . WHEN I received your dear letter of the 28th of July, I had just been leisurely reading Schiller's Preface to the *Braut von Messina*, and had already begun to try a musical arrangement of the Choruses. Thus much have I as yet divined, that thoroughly to identify myself with the new *genre*, I should need a quiet year. So soon as I have completed enough to be recognizable, I will write to you about my discovery. Your dissertation on the Chorus has been extremely useful to me, for I am more concerned about a definite view of the ancient Greek Chorus, than about my new invention. The Musician is so horribly subordinate to the Poet, and besides that he needs the whole strength of his art. Your idea of making an attempt with a small Oratorio is excellent, and for more than one reason I should like to see it carried out. It is a new way to the heart, and I constantly think of it. . . . .

ZELTER.

12.—ZELTER TO GOETHE.

Berlin, 10th August, 1803.

. . . . You ask me about the music to the second part of the *Zauberflöte*. I take you to mean by that our new re-presentation of Winter's music. It is put on the stage with great magnificence and at huge expense. . . . The score is very full, and crammed with effects, that stun and overwhelm one's ears and senses. There is a full house every time, though I see no signs of real satisfaction on the part of the public, for whom apparently the piece was written; I suppose it will come in time. . . . .

Professor Fichte, to whom I gave the enclosed letter of

the Jena advocate,* is doubly grateful, as it is rather pleasant in itself, and goes just far enough to avert any unpleasantness. Fichte is just about to write on the subject to Herr Geheimrath Voigt.† Fichte dissents from your proposal to shorten *Die Natürliche Tochter*,‡ thinking the piece so rounded and complete, that it would only suffer by abbreviation. He intends writing to Schiller about it, but specially with reference to the two Berlin representations, which he attended as an earnest listener. He is actually more pleased with them than I, who read the play twice beforehand, and then found quite unfamiliar characters, which afterwards I have to find "natural."....

Madame Mara is to arrive here to-day or to-morrow—the 14th August. They say that she was terribly put out at Lauchstädt, though her concert—owing to the help of Reichardt §—was a success. She had explained in Dresden that she wanted to regale the Electoral Prince with her talent, but as she was told that His Royal Highness was pleased to hear music during dinner, she was forced to

---

* Salzmann, a lawyer employed by Fichte about a mortgage which he had raised upon a house of his in Jena, and about which he had consulted Schiller. (See *Schiller and Goethe Correspondence*, vol. ii., p. 460.)

† Christian Gottlob von Voigt was a friend of the Duke of Saxe-Weimar, Karl August, and one of his ministers. Goethe praises his various and comprehensive knowledge of natural history. (See *Schiller and Goethe Correspondence*, vol. ii., p. 475.)

‡ Schiller expressed his admiration of this work in a letter to Humboldt:—"The high symbolism with which it is handled, so that all the crude material is neutralized and everything becomes a portion of an ideal Whole, is truly wonderful. It is entirely Art, and thereby reaches the innermost Nature, through the power of truth." Fichte declared it to be Goethe's masterpiece. G. H. Lewes observes in his *Life of Goethe*, "that a drama which is *so* praised, *i.e.* for its high symbolism, is a drama philosophers and critics may glorify, but which Art abjures."

§ Johann Friedrich Reichardt, Capellmeister and Court-composer to Frederick the Great, founder of the *Concerts Spirituels*, author of several operas, but more famous for his *Singspielen*, which are of great importance in the history of German dramatic music. Mendelssohn spoke of him with enthusiasm, and arranged for the performance of his *Morning Hymn, after Milton* at the Cologne Festival of 1835. His love of art induced him to visit the chief capitals of Europe, and his letters, like those of our own Dr. Burney, give copious details of music, politics, literature, and society.

confess that she could not sing at a banquet. By this explanation she lost a hundred ducats, and the Electoral Prince, an aria. . . . . ZELTER.

13.—GOETHE TO ZELTER.

Weimar, 29th August, 1803.

. . . . FICHTE has written a very beautiful and kind letter to Schiller about *Eugenie*.* Thank him for it, and tell him at the same time that we champion his cause very heartily; alas! a curse rests so easily on all that lawyers dabble with!

What say you to the scheme of transplanting the *Literatur Zeitung* to Halle? We others, who are behind the scenes, are never tired of wondering, that a Royal Prussian Cabinet should allow itself to be foiled by names, shams, charlatanism, and importunity, just like any other public body. As if such an institution could be conquered and transported, like the Laocoon, or any other movable work of art!

We are now continuing it as usual in Jena, and as we still have Hofrath Eichstädt, the very active editor, everything will go on in its old course. New contributors, and new methods we are just starting, will, I hope, ensure an honourable result for the business.

If you care to be one of our party, we earnestly bid you welcome. How I should like you to utilize the reviewer's path, so as to say about music what is so urgently needed just now, and bring your criticism before the public definitely and regularly. I shall share in the undertaking, giving advice, and acting also. Schiller, Voss, and Meyer †

---
* The heroine of *Die Natürliche Tochter*.
† Heinrich Meyer's *History of Art* was a favourite book with Goethe. Speaking of him to Eckermann, Goethe says: "I am ever convinced anew, how much is needed to be thoroughly great in any one thing. In Meyer lies an insight into art belonging to thousands of years." His Art-criticism, and his own paintings are constantly alluded to in the *Schiller and Goethe Correspondence*. The copy of Aldobrandini's *Wedding*, made by him in Rome, subsequently found a place on Goethe's walls. When at Florence, he edited the works of Cellini. Schiller wished him to draw a vignette on the title-page of his *Wallenstein*, for which he himself suggested a Nemesis, "as an interesting and significant illustration."

are inclined to do the same, and I hope that next year will be honourably distinguished from the present. Tell this also to Fichte, whose aid we likewise invoke; Schiller will write to him more in detail about the matter. If you know of any other able man in Berlin, it matters not what his calling may be, as long as he is opposed to the old leaven of Schütz, Bertuch, and Böttiger,* try and induce him to join our interest. In fact, you are at liberty to speak quite openly about the matter. The authorization for a society, which will undertake the contemplated continuation of the scheme, is just being drawn up; there will soon appear a preliminary public announcement, and I will shortly let you know of further details.

Tell me who is the author of *The Confessions of a Female Poisoner* †—a first-rate man in every way.

Some time ago Herr Unger wrote to me about an eighth part. I can neither accept nor refuse; on the one hand, because I should be truly glad to complete the number; on the other, because my next works are promised to Cotta, with whom I have reason to be very well satisfied. Please

---

* Hofrath Schütz was the founder and editor of the *Allgemeine Literarische Zeitung* in Jena. Goethe speaks disparagingly of him as a reviewer, in his letters to Schiller.—Bertuch, the translator of Cervantes, was the original owner of the famous *Gartenhaus* at Weimar, in which Goethe lived for seven years. The Duke, aware of Goethe's taste for gardening, forced Bertuch to part with his property. "Bertuch, for example, is very comfortable," Goethe had said, when pressed to reside at Weimar, and eager to find some excuse for leaving it; "if I had but such a piece of ground as that!" Whereupon the Duke immediately attacked Bertuch with, "I must have your garden." "But, your Highness—" "But me no buts," answered the Duke, "I can't help you. Goethe wants it, and unless we give it to him, we shall never keep him here; it is the only way to secure him." When bent on strict privacy, Goethe "would lock all the gates of the bridges which led from the town to his house, so that, as Wieland complained, no one could get at him, except by aid of picklock and crowbar." Here he made his studies for *Die Metamorphose der Pflanzen*. Lewes tells us that "a half-pay captain with us would consider the house a miserable cottage; yet it sufficed for the Court favourite and Minister."—Karl August Böttiger, a literary busybody, nicknamed by Schiller and Goethe *Ubique*. In Bertuch's *Journal of Fashion* he wrote an essay on the *Xenia* of Martial, and some translations, which were severely criticised by Goethe. (See *Schiller and Goethe Correspondence*, vol. i., p. 144.)

† Buchholz.

say a kind word to Herr Unger on the subject, to prevent him from misconstruing my silence.

I hoped beforehand that *Cellini** would have an effect upon you; what a world is opened up in such a work! The time I devoted to working it out, is one of the happiest periods of my life, and I shall continue to do a good deal more yet. If your reading of the book has in a certain sense depressed you, as I can well understand, I hope that the cheerful effect may come afterwards.

In the main I sympathize thoroughly with your complaints regarding the general matter and details. A hearty farewell. G.

14.—ZELTER TO GOETHE.

7th September, 1803.

.... As a thoroughly useful correspondent in Paris, I am inclined to recommend young Mendelssohn,† who was fortunate enough, a few years since, to have an interview with you at Frankfort-on-the-Maine. He is an excellent youth, well read, and possessed of good broad taste. He is now in Berlin, and hopes to pass through Weimar on his return to Paris. If you approve, I might give him a letter to you. Whatever else I can do for the interests of the Jena *Literarische Zeitung*, I will do gladly, as opportunity offers.

ZELTER.

15.—GOETHE TO ZELTER.

Weimar, 10th October, 1803.

.... My training-school for actors, begun in the first instance with Unzelmann,‡ has already increased to

---

* Goethe's translation of Benvenuto Cellini's *Autobiography* was published in separate numbers. Writing to Schiller in 1798, he says: "A second edition of *Cellini* will be added to Meyer's work on the *History of Art in Florence*." (See *Schiller and Goethe Correspondence*, vol. ii., p. 63.)

† Abraham Mendelssohn, banker, second son of Moses the philosopher, and father of Felix Mendelssohn.

‡ Son of Madame Unzelmann, a famous actress.

twelve. Next Thursday they are going to act their first piece, scenery and all, but with closed doors. I hope much good will result from this effort.

Could you get some reliable account of young Lauchery, son of the royal ballet-master? He has some appointment at the Military School in Berlin. We are so situated as to be more in want of a man who understands dancing, than of a dancer; someone who has an easy method of teaching, and a taste for stage-groupings and ballets. He has been recommended to us, and I should like to have a more accurate account of him from you. . . . .

· Farewell, and do not leave me long without news of you.

GOETHE.

1804.

16.—GOETHE TO ZELTER.

Weimar, 27th February, 1804.

How long have I been silent, my honoured friend, and yet how often have I longed to be with you on Mondays and Tuesdays! This winter I have heard scarcely a note, and feel what a beautiful part of life's enjoyment has thereby been lost to me.

November and December were passed chiefly in preparations for our literary campaign. January did not treat me over well, though my head kept clear, and I was not altogether inactive. In February I took up my *Götz von Berlichingen*, in order to knead it into a morsel which our German public may perhaps swallow at once. That is an unsatisfactory piece of work; as in altering an old house, you begin with little bits and end by entirely changing the whole at heavy expense, without after all having made a new building.

Now Schiller's *Tell*, which you too will soon see, is by contrast all the more fresh and unbroken. Lately we have enjoyed several pleasant visits. Professor Wolf * was here for nearly a fortnight, and Hofrath von Müller † about as long; Voss was here only for a few days. We have however been enjoying Madame de Stael's society for a month past. This strange woman is soon going to Berlin, and I shall give her a letter to you. Be sure to pay her a visit immediately; it is a very easy matter to get on with her, and she is sure to be greatly delighted

---

* Friedrich August Wolf, a great philologist, author of the *Prolegomena ad Homerum*. Eckermann describes a dinner-party given by Goethe in his honour. "The conversation was very lively. Wolf was full of witty sallies, Goethe being constantly his opponent in the pleasantest way. 'I cannot,' said Goethe to me afterwards, 'get on with Wolf at all, without assuming the character of Mephistopheles. Nothing else brings out his hidden treasures.'"

† Johannes Müller, the historian.

with your musical performances, although literature, poetry, philosophy and the like, are more in her way than the fine arts.

Herr von Müller will have brought you the large seal; a smaller one shall soon follow. I am still in difficulty about the ring. I sent a beautiful, yellow, Java cornelian to Dresden, in the hope of getting it back as a ring-stone of exquisite colour; unfortunately, on being cut, it turns out half spurious, half real, and therefore useless. But—come what may—you shall have some such keepsake from me; only please have a little more patience with the dawdler!

Our newspaper does well enough; when once the heavy square foundation stones are safely laid, the rest of the building will mount up more lightly. . . . .

GOETHE.

17.—GOETHE TO ZELTER.

Weimar, 28th March, 1804.

MANY a traveller testifies to your works and deeds, in so far as they are visible and work outwards; your refreshing letter gives me a glimpse into your inner life, worked by no steel spring, but animated by a living spirit. I think you happy in working on continuously and progressively in that element which you have yourself created, and in being able to hope that you have also achieved something that will last. At the same time, it seems to me, one must speak honourably of the great multitude which people often gird at, though after all, it supplies the plastic organs, and also the means for propagating what has been achieved. We others, in our narrow circles, work momentary wonders—magician-like—and immediately see our air-formed phantom again dissolve into air. . . . .

GOETHE.

18.—ZELTER TO GOETHE.

Berlin, 1st May, 1804.

. . . . NOTHING as yet has been seen or heard of Schiller's *Tell*. They say that Iffland, finding passages in it that were doubtful from a political point of view, forwarded the play to the Cabinet, in the first instance, for revision. Your *Götz* and the second part of *Die Natürliche Tochter* are expected all the more eagerly; do not keep us waiting too long. . . . .

Herr von Kotzebue has given a lecture in the Academy on the History of Prussia. It was highly praised, and people compare it to Tacitus. . . . .

ZELTER.

19.—GOETHE TO ZELTER.

Weimar, 13th July, 1804.

YOUR essay, my dear friend, has given me and a few of the initiated, to whom I showed it, much pleasure; nay more, it has edified and strengthened us in our convictions of what is good and right. It has sprung from the depth of your character and talent, and must very keenly affect such minds as are at all susceptible. But what will the world think of it and make out of it? A world which does not care to listen, when leading articles of complaint are formally drawn up against it, and which of course cannot dream of finding a worthy enjoyment which it does not know, but rather snatches at some fugitive joy, self-created out of itself, and therefore conformable to itself.

It is a very bad sign of our days, that every art, which after all is surely meant in the first instance only to produce an effect upon the living, should, in so far as it is excellent and worthy of eternity, find itself in conflict with the time, and that the true artist frequently lives alone and in despair, inasmuch as he is convinced that he possesses and could impart to men what they are seeking.

We agree with you in this, that music in the first instance can only be improved through hymns, and that even for a Government nothing could be more desirable in every sense, than to foster an art, whilst encouraging higher feelings, and purifying the sources of a religion, which is adapted alike to the cultivated and uncultivated. You have expressed yourself so admirably and concisely upon this point, that nothing can be added to it. But what we now wish you to take to heart, for effect's sake, is that you should, if possible, conceal the opposition in which you stand to the time, and generally that you should dwell more upon the advantages which religion and morals would derive from such an Institution, and less upon those which Art has to expect from it. We must not avail ourselves of our arguments in favour of the Good, whereby we are convinced men may be moved, but must consider what would probably be their arguments. . . . .

G.

ENCLOSURE.

SCHILLER TO ZELTER.

Weimar, 16th July, 1804.

IT is not from negligence, dear friend, that I am so late in giving you news of myself, after the happy hours we spent together in Berlin. I expected, every post-day, that I should be able to write definitely to you about the business you know of, and in which, as I dare hope, you are kindly interested. As yet however, nothing has been determined, so I cannot say whether my conditions will be accepted. Therefore no more of my affairs for the present; let us talk of yours.

The essay you sent to Goethe, I have read with real pleasure; you have written it out from your heart of hearts, and this stamp it bears on every line. But just because it so successfully attacks the diseased part, and so frankly and honestly declares war against charlatanism in Art, probably in its present form it is not altogether adapted to win the favour of those, who are to lend a hand in furthering the work. What Goethe has written to you on this point, is also my conviction. You will be obliged to keep your most striking arguments *in petto*, and to lay stress upon those that relate to the political requirements of the time.

It seems to me an extremely happy circumstance, that the interest of Art just now meets such an external want, and if no mistake is otherwise made as regards form, you could not possibly, I think, fail to interest the rulers of the state in your scheme. All will depend on the way the subject is represented. Few feel that it is high time to do something for Art, but that matters cannot remain as they are with regard to religion, can be made intelligible to all.

And as people are ashamed of having a religion themselves, and want to pass for "enlightened," they must be very glad of the possibility of coming to the aid of religion with Art.

Consequently the whole thing would immediately assume a more favourable aspect, if the first impulse were to come from the ecclesiastical and political side, if from thence one could point first of all to your *Singakademie*, as to an instrument lying ready to hand, and then first asked what you propose. You would surely not find any difficulty in inducing one or other of your theologians and Academicians to supply the incentive. It was Berlin, which in the dark days of superstition first kindled the torch of rational religious freedom; this was at the time a glory and a necessity. Now, in the days of unbelief, another glory is to be won, without forfeiting the first; now let Berlin add warmth to the light, and ennoble Protestantism, of which it is destined to be the metropolis.

I only wish I could be a Berlin Academician for six weeks, so that I might have a calling to make myself heard on this subject; but there are plenty of people for that. Do you not think that Schleiermacher, for instance, would do?

Now is the very moment for an enterprise of this kind in the Brandenburg provinces. People wish to promote the Academy and the Universities. Something must be done for spirituality and morals; nay, as Catholicism has been newly established in France, the spirit of the age demands that religion should also be thought of in Protestant countries, and even philosophy has taken this direction. All this, and similar arguments might furnish material for a deduction, by which the subject might be made more of a state affair. Only, as I must again repeat, the advantage which would thus fall to the musical side must not appear to be the main object, but only a secondary consideration.

Let us soon hear, dear friend, whether you think you can attack the subject from this point, and whose services you think of enlisting for it. If you think I can in any way be of use to you in the matter, you may count on my willingness to help you.

My wife wrote to your wife about a week ago. We

intend going to Jena in three days time, and remaining there, till my wife's confinement is over. Write and tell me something about the performance of *Tell* in Berlin ; I see from the papers that it went off fairly well. We are eagerly expecting your melodies to the latest songs. I send you a few other things out of the Swiss world.
I embrace you with all my heart.
Yours most sincerely,
SCHILLER.

20.—GOETHE TO ZELTER.

Weimar, 30th July, 1804.

THANK you very much for the play-bills which you sent me through Mademoiselle Amelang. I look forward with pleasure to your Schiller song, which we will do as well as we can, so soon as our music begins to chime round us again. I hope in a month's time to have a reading-rehearsal of my *Götz von Berlichingen;* that it is so far advanced, is entirely owing to you. I did not understand why, during a year past, I had dealt with my work like Penelope, for ever unravelling again what I had woven. Then in your essay I found the words, "What we do not love, we cannot do ; " then my eyes were opened, and I saw clearly that I had hitherto treated the work as a piece of business, which, with others, had to be got rid of ; this explained how it was done, and why it had no power of lasting. Henceforth I devoted to this subject more attention, sympathy, and concentration ; so the work—I will not say gets good—but anyhow gets finished.

Now might I ask you for a couple of small pieces of music ? First, for Georg's song, *Es fing ein Knab'ein Vögelein*, which I believe you have already set ; secondly, I want a quiet, devotional, and elevating four-part hymn, with Latin words, that would take some eight minutes to perform. It may be a bit out of some Mass, or anything else of the kind.

How much I wish we lived nearer one another, or that we were both more mobile ; the results of enduring mutual intercourse are incalculable. Anyhow, let us write to one another from time to time.

Schiller has given us an admirable work in *Tell*, one upon which we may all congratulate ourselves.
A thousand farewells.

GOETHE.

21.—GOETHE TO ZELTER.

Weimar, 8th August, 1804.

I THANK you most heartily for sending me the little song so promptly, and will now go more into detail about the Chorus in *Götz*. It is really meant to be sung at the nuptials of Maria and Sickingen. The simple Church procession passes over the stage to the sound of a hymn, an organ may perhaps be heard at a distance, and as the chapel is close by, the chanting may continue audibly, whilst a scene is being played outside. Have the goodness, then, to take some words out of a Psalm.

The character of it, as you observe, is gentle and solemn, inclining to sadness, on account of the circumstances; a prelude to the following scene, where those but just married are, so to speak, chased away by Götz. All things considered, I think you are perfectly right in saying that eight minutes are too long; we will be content with four, to fill up which is quite within my power. . . . .

Thank you very much for the melody to my Serenade; it is very pleasing, and certainly better suited to my poem, than my poem is to Reichardt's very praiseworthy melody.

The little song for Georg is quite appropriate, without instrumental music; we will see how the little fellow turns out. I am very anxious to get this new version of *Götz* out of hand. I should long ago have had it finished, but for its tiresome length; for in trying to make the play more theatrical, it became longer rather than shorter. What was diffuse has certainly been condensed, but what was transitory has become fixed; it will still take nearly four hours to play. Should it be given in Berlin, pray write to me at once about your first impressions; for with the exception of the introductory part of the first Act of the drama, and half of the second, which have been left almost entirely as they were, the piece has been altogether decomposed and recomposed.

My kind greetings to your dear wife, and thank her for the interest she takes in my sons and daughters. I am, alas! still a long way from completing the continuation of my *Natürliche Tochter*; nay, I have several times been tempted to destroy the First Part for really theatrical purposes, and to make a single piece out of the whole of the Three Parts I first intended. No doubt the situations, which according to the original plan are too long, would then appear much too sketchy. Farewell, and pray forgive my rambling letter.

G.

22.—GOETHE TO ZELTER.

Weimar, 24th September, 1804.

By Herr Levin I again send you a packet of snuff, which our dear Duchess Amalia * gave to me for you, with many kind messages. I hope it may prove as good as the last, and that more will follow.

Götz has been played; I send you the gay play-bill. Herr Levin undertakes to tell you about the play and the performance. I should myself call it good, but for its excessive length. On future occasions, I mean to have merely parts of it played, and thus ascertain what particular portions the public would most readily dispense with, and these can afterwards be entirely omitted.

Herr Levin will tell you that your Choral hymn was very charming and beautiful, and very well adapted for bringing into relief the important moment. I enclose an advertisement of our Art Exhibition of this year. I shall write again in a few days. Let me hear from you soon.

GOETHE.

---

* Amalia, the Dowager-Duchess of Weimar, was a niece of Frederick the Great. Schiller speaks of her intellect as " extremely limited," though she learned Greek enough from Wieland to read Aristophanes, translated Propertius, talked politics with the Abbé Raynal, and set Goethe's *Erwin und Elmire* to music. Her correspondence with Goethe's mother shows how little she cared for the dignities of her state, and even Schiller owned that this pleasure-loving Duchess had " at any rate the merit of throwing aside all the stiffness of ceremony."

23.—GOETHE TO ZELTER.

24th November,* 1804.

. . . . IN return for your description of the picture of Judas Iscariot, you shall in my next page have a description of an old picture, which unfortunately is lost to us, and contrasts *e Diametro* with yours. In order to shorten the reflections which force themselves upon my mind, I will give you a design on the other side of this page, showing how we, the latest philosophers, are wont, by signs and abbreviations, to express ourselves to one another. I am convinced that it will be as clear to you as daylight.

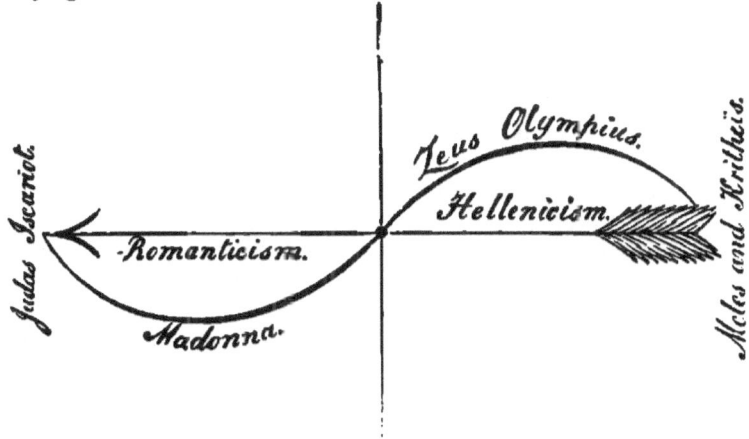

With all good wishes,

G.

MELES AND KRITHEÏS.

The Fable.

Kritheïs, the nymph of the fountain, is in love with the river-god Meles; from these two, who are of Ionic origin, Homer is born.

* On the 15th November, Zelter had described in a letter from Berlin, a picture by Carl Ludwig, called " The Damnation of Judas Iscariot." In Letter 24 Goethe sends the description back to him for reference.

The Picture.

Meles is represented in the flower of early youth. The nymph, though she thirsts not, drinks from his spring, which is visibly running into the sea; she scoops the water up, and seems to be chatting with the babbling fountain, while her fond tears are falling into it. But the river loves her in return, and is enjoying the sweet tribute.

The chief beauty of the picture lies in the figure of Meles. He is reposing upon crocuses, lotus flowers, and hyacinths,—a lover of flowers, as befits youth. His figure is youthful and tender, though perfectly developed; one might say his eyes were dreaming of some poetic thing.

But one of the most graceful features is, that no torrent of water flows forth, but that, by passing his hand over the surface of the earth, he causes the gently rising water to gurgle through his fingers, so that it seems a river suited to call forth the dreams of love. But it is no dream, Kritheïs! thy silent wishes are not in vain. Soon the waves will begin to surge up, and favouring your loves, they will hide thee and the god beneath their emerald and purple canopy. How lovely the girl is! How delicate and Ionic her form! Modesty adds grace to her figure; and the flush on her cheeks is just sufficient. Her hair is gathered under her ears and adorned with a purple fillet. But she looks so sweet and simple, that her tears even do not affect the tenderness of her expression. Her neck is even more beautiful, as it is unadorned, and on looking at her hands, we see soft long fingers, as white as the forepart of the arm, which, as seen through the white robe, appears whiter still; the rounded bosom shows itself.

But what have the Muses to do here? At Meles' spring they are no strangers; for before this, in the form of bees, they guided the fleet of the Athenian colonies hither.

But as in this picture they lead their light dances, they appear as joyous Fates, celebrating the approaching birth of Homer.

24.—GOETHE TO ZELTER.

Weimar, 16th December, 1804.

HEREWITH the letter you ask for, but please let me have it back again at your convenience. I can well believe that Judas Iscariot was not very successful in Berlin. Only a Sunday's-bairn could appreciate the merits of such a subject. On the other hand, in the catalogue of the Berlin Exhibition, many a page—nay, pages may be found, containing a written account of what is not to be seen in the picture—nay, what cannot be seen in it.

I am very sorry that I am unable to attend your lectures. To be sure, it is in accordance with my nature to live in a small place; but the worst is, that one has next to nothing to relish there, except what one dishes up for oneself, whereas in big places one can often and comfortably dine out.

Talking of dining out, reminds me of an earthly need, which you can very well satisfy. Please send me by the mail half a bushel of genuine Moravian turnips, only take care that they are well packed, so that they may not be instantly frost-bitten. In return I will send you one day soon some Greek fruit, which has the great advantage of refreshing at the same time both body and soul.

A thousand farewells.

J. W. GOETHE.

1805.

25.—GOETHE TO ZELTER.

Weimar, 29th January, 1805.

TURNIPS and fish have arrived safely, the former beautifully dry, the latter well frozen. . . . .
The new version of *Götz von Berlichingen* was sent to Iffland * as early as the beginning of last December, but it is his way to remain dumb in such cases, to cook and brew things in his own mind, till he thinks them at last done enough to come out with. So take no notice of it. In a man of his merits one must excuse an oddity, and all the more, as such behaviour is perhaps a necessity in his position. So much for to-day. Thank your dear wife for the parcel; her recipe was carefully followed, and the dish was capital. You shall soon hear again of phenomena of opposed polarity, Greek pictures and Tarentine snuff. Cheer up, and think of me.

GOETHE.

26.—GOETHE TO ZELTER.

Weimar, 1st June, 1805.

SINCE the time I left off writing to you, I have had few good days. I thought to lose myself,† and now I lose a friend, and in him the half of my existence. In truth, I ought to begin a new mode of life, but at my age there is no longer a way. Now therefore I only look straight be-

---

* " Very significant to me was the observation I made, that he almost invariably had it in his power to command the purest and most appropriate state of mind in his audience, which, of course, is possible only by a union of genius, art, and study."—Goethe to Schiller, vol. ii., p. 85. Schiller preferred Iffland's comic to his tragic acting.

† On the 2nd April, Zelter had written from Berlin : " Your illness has made quite a remarkable sensation here, and everyone is rejoiced at your recovery; I myself shall not be free from anxiety, till I get a line from you again." Schiller died on the 9th May, while Goethe was still weak and enfeebled from another relapse.

fore me at each day as it comes, and do what is nearest to me, without looking further afield.

But as, notwithstanding, people try to turn every loss and misfortune into some diversion for themselves, I am being urged by our actors, and many others, to honour our departed friend's memory by a stage-performance. I shall say nothing further about this, except that I am not disinclined, and all I should like to ask you just now is, whether you would be willing to assist me in this, and first of all— if you would be so kind as to let us have your Motett, *Der Mensch lebt und bestehet*, of which I see a notice in the 27th number of the *Musikalische Zeitung;* will you either compose something else in the solemn style, or look out and hand over to us compositions, the character of which I would specify to you, in order that suitable words may be added? As soon as I know your private opinion, you shall hear further particulars.

Your admirable series of short essays on the arrangements of the Orchestra, I have hitherto kept by me, really because they contained a sort of satire upon the state of affairs here. Reichardt now wishes to have them for the *Musikalische Zeitung.* I have looked them up and read them over again, and I find that I cannot possibly withhold them from the intelligence-sheet of our *Literatur Zeitung,* where they will very soon make a capital figure under the line. Some of our affairs have undergone alteration, and in the end we may perhaps blame even that which we allow to happen.

Geheimrath Wolf of Halle is at present here. Could I but hope to see you too this year! Is there no likelihood of your coming to Lauchstädt at the end of July, to assist in preparing and carrying out the above-mentioned work? Think this over, and tell me only of the possibility; the means would be an after-consideration. How about your store of snuff? Meanwhile I have been fortunate enough to get another packet of the genuine article. How shall I send it you? Farewell, and let me hear from you soon.

G.

27.—ZELTER TO GOETHE.

11th June, 1805.

.... THE unexpected death of our beloved Schiller has called forth a general and profound sensation here in Berlin; Iffland's conduct, (though the underlying motives are not yet clear), is honourable. He seems to be planning something, or else to be working with peculiar energy for some plan, that has been formed already. This evening a very brilliant and earnest performance of *Die Räuber* took place; the whole strength of our company and resources were employed; the house was densely packed. Iffland played Franz, and was unmistakably determined to do his utmost; Karl and Amalie were equally well played by Mattausch and Madame Fleck. Our public, with whom this play is a great favourite, received it in the old way, but with redoubled enthusiasm. *Kabale und Liebe* is announced for next Friday. It seems as if the Directors wished by a series of performances of all Schiller's plays, given at short intervals, partly to fête the public, which worships Schiller, and to sustain its zeal, partly to make patent the great merits of the departed, and thus finally to do something for Schiller's memory. Nor does the Treasury suffer by this, for just now, whenever Schiller is played, the house is always full—an unusual thing at this season of the year.

Then let us too do something in this matter, something which shall be in lasting connection with a lasting subject. (This between ourselves, of course.) If you are not too much over-wrought, it might be a soothing, healing employment for you, and I will pull myself together, and do what I can—all the more, as really there exists nothing of the kind that would be appropriate for a stage. Perhaps our work might to this extent be universal, that it might be used on any solemn occasion, as a regular stock piece. . . . .

Yours,
ZELTER.

28.—GOETHE TO ZELTER.

Weimar, 19th June, 1805.

MY best thanks for your prompt despatch of the music I asked for. I will try, as soon as possible, to hear the best they can make of it. On the whole I am of your opinion, that we should have no patchwork on this occasion, but cut something out of the whole piece. Unfortunately, I have never been so lucky as to have a first-rate musician by me, with whom I might have worked in common, so in cases like this, I have always been obliged to keep to cobbling and patching, and so once again I thought it would be my fate in the present instance.

You shall now however hear of my scheme as soon as possible, and let me know what you think of it. But our plan, as well as our work, must be kept a secret, till we are ready, and can step forward with an easy mind.

While working at *Rameau's Neffe*, and things connected with it, I often thought of you, and wished for only a few hours' talk with you. I know music more by reflection than by enjoyment, and hence only in the general sense. I am glad this little volume amused you; the dialogue too is a genuine masterpiece.

I am in your debt for *Wilhelm Meister*, as for much else besides. Meantime a fresh box of Spanish snuff, which I trust will arrive in good condition.

Iffland is perfectly right in taking advantage of the pathological interest of the public for his purposes. If the Germans are not touched realistically, it is difficult to touch them ideally. If he carries out his series of representations, and leads them up to a first-rate performance for the benefit of the children that are left, he will deserve praise. I enclose the Frankfort absurdity. It is said in that paper, that Schiller did not die rich, that he left four children; yet it offers the blessed public free admission to the funeral ceremony! Priests and monks contrive to make the funeral ceremonies of their saints of greater benefit to the survivors. The deep feeling of loss is the prerogative of friends. The Frankfort gentlemen, who as a rule cannot appreciate anything but money, would have done better to express their sympathy more realistically, considering that, (between ourselves be it said), they never paid our excellent friend for a single manuscript, during his lifetime, though he worked hard enough, but always waited, till they could get the printed piece for twelve *groschen*. Pardon my being so discursive. I could add much more, if I wished to say all that there is to say on this subject. Geheimrath Wolf of Halle was with me for a fortnight. The presence of this very able man has strengthened me in every sense. I am daily expecting Jacobi.* Why may I not also hope to see you this year?

Farewell, and write to me again soon, in order that such long pauses may not arise. Otherwise some day or other we may unawares pause ourselves into life everlasting.

G.

29.—GOETHE TO ZELTER.

Lauchstädt, 4th August, 1805.

UP to to-day, I have been flattering myself, though with only a faint hope, that we should see you here. It is one of the saddest conditions under which we suffer, that not only death, but even life separates us from those we most esteem and love, and whose co-operation could best help us on our way.

That this letter may be despatched at once, I pass forthwith from such sorrowful reflections to a request. I am going to give a dramatic representation of Schiller's *Glocke*, and beg you to help me with it. Read the poem through, and send me an appropriate Symphony for it, by any master. Then, in the middle of the fifth verse, declaimed by the Master, after the line:

Say a holy word,

I should like a short Chorale, for which the words:

In all we strive to do,
Thy grace, O Lord, be near us!

might form the text. Thereupon, the following four lines, as far as *With waves of fiery brown*, would be spoken again,

---

* Friedrich Heinrich Jacobi, a philosophical writer, then well known, and author of a work on *The Teaching of Spinoza*. It was almost thirteen years since he and Goethe had met. They had been intimate in youth, though their friendship was often interrupted by differences of opinion. (See Goethe's *Early Letters*, p. 128, and *passim*.) Jacobi's harsh criticism of *Wilhelm Meister* brought Schiller into the field, as Goethe's apologist. It is difficult to reconcile the conflicting opinions of Lewes and Düntzer, as to the pleasure which Goethe, still smarting from the recent loss of Schiller, derived from the present visit.

but the Chorus would then have to be repeated, or, if you like, further developed musically.

In the final Chorus, I should like to hear the words: *Vivos voco. Mortuos plango. Fulgura frango.* in a Fugue, which, as far as possible, should imitate the pealing of bells, and, as befits the occasion, lose itself in *Mortuos plango.**

If a happy thought should strike you, do me the favour to work it out, and send me the scores direct to Weimar, whither I shall soon go.

If it were possible for your gift to reach me by the 19th or 20th, it would come very opportunely; for I should like to start in Weimar with this representation.

I then hope to send you the other poem, or at all events a sketch of it, and it might be given on the 10th of November, in honour of our friend's birthday. More in a few days' time.

G.

30.—GOETHE TO ZELTER.

Lauchstädt, 1st September, 1805.

I AM once more in Lauchstädt, and am dictating this, in the rooms where your presence made me so happy. I have been to Magdeburg with Geheimrath Wolf, and from thence to Helmstedt, where I found many very interesting persons and things; afterwards, we went by way of Halberstadt, past the Harz, and returned by way of Aschersleben to Halle.

Here I am, again quite alone, after sending my son Augustus, who has accompanied me so far, back to Weimar, and I am recapitulating all the good that has befallen me during the last eight weeks, and trying by degrees to evoke what we agreed upon.

An ancient work which fell into my hands, almost accidentally, will be useful for this purpose. You will receive herewith my translation of a translation. As soon as I can

---

* The performance took place at Lauchstädt, on the 10th August. Goethe added an Epilogue to the poem. Zelter's music has been set aside for Romberg's, which may perhaps be superseded by that of Max Bruch.

revise it in accordance with the original, the words will, of course, sound quite differently, but I dare say you will find no more food for thought in it then, than you will now, though here and there the expressions still halt. Do write, and send your letter soon to Weimar. Before I leave these parts, you shall hear more from me. In particular, I am now dictating something about the underlined passage in that old mystic.* A thousand farewells, and thanks for your visit, which made me glad to live again, and increased my gladness.

G.

Enclosure.

"As we are convinced, that he who contemplates the intellectual world, and is conscious of the beauty of real intellect, can also take note of the Father of them, who is exalted above all sense, let us endeavour to acquire insight, to the best of our powers, and for ourselves express, in so far as such things can be made clear, the way in which we can intuitively perceive the beauty of the mind and of the world.

"Suppose then two blocks of stone placed beside one another, one of which was left in the rough, without any artistic work on it, while the other was shaped by Art into a statue of some man or deity. If the latter, it might represent a Grace or a Muse; if the former, it need be no man in particular, but rather one put together by Art out of everything beautiful. To you, however, the stone brought by Art into a lovely form, will forthwith appear beautiful, though not because it is a stone—for else the other mass would likewise pass for beautiful—but because it has a form which Art gave it.

"Yet the material had not such a form; that was in the inventor, before it reached the stone; it was, however, in the artist, not because he had eyes and hands, but because he was gifted with Art.

"Therefore, there was a still greater beauty in the Art. For it is not the form, resting in Art, which reaches the stone, but it remains there, and another inferior form goes

* Plotinus, *Ennead. V.*, lib. viii., c. I., p. 541, ed. Marsil. Ficinus. Basil. MDCXV.

forth, which neither continues in its own purity, nor even as the artist wished it, except in so far as the material obeyed the Art.

"But when Art produces also that which it is and possesses, and the beautiful, according to reason, her constant guide; then of course that Art which possesses more, and more truthfully, a greater and more excellent beauty of Art, is more perfect than anything else which comes to outward expression.

"For inasmuch as the form, advancing into material, gains extension by that very act, it becomes weaker than that which continues undivided. For that which endures separation, steps aside from itself, strength from strength, warmth from warmth, force from force, beauty too from beauty. The motive power must be more excellent than the result. For it is not the unmusical which makes the musician, but music, and the super-sensuous music produces music in sensuous tones.

"But should any one despise the Arts, because they imitate Nature, let him take this for an answer, that natures also imitate much besides—nay, more—that the Arts do not precisely imitate what we see with our eyes, but go back to that rational element, of which Nature consists, and in accordance with which she acts.

"Further—the Arts produce much out of themselves, and on the other hand, add much that falls short of perfection, whilst they have beauty in themselves. Thus Phidias could create the god, though he actually imitated nothing perceptible to his senses, but he grasped such a divinity in his mind, as Jove himself would appear, should he ever meet our eyes."

31.—GOETHE TO ZELTER.

Weimar, 18th November, 1805.

MY thanks for your kind thought of my bodily welfare must no longer be delayed, especially as the products of Brandenburg and England have come safe to hand. The turnips are all the more welcome, as there are no chestnuts on the Rhine or Maine this year. So we do not eat them as a separate dish, but served up with cabbage, they are very effective. On the 9th of November, as the day on which we too wished to commemorate Schiller in our Theatre, his Imperial Majesty of Russia was content with a performance of *Wallenstein's Lager;* so soon as you kindly send us your work, we will make up for lost time.

How fares it with your music lessons? I too have set aside one morning in every week, on which I lecture to a small circle, on my experiences and convictions, relative to natural history. This opportunity enables me for the first time to realize what I possess—what I do not possess.*

Demoiselle Jagemann † too has at last arrived. The play-bills have come to hand, and were very welcome, as they were a proof of your kind remembrances. Let me soon hear from you again. The results of my quiet work will, ere long, give you some pleasure.

So much for to-day; with best wishes,

G.

---

* "He (Goethe) delivered lectures on Natural Science, on Colour, Magnetism, Elasticity, every Wednesday morning before a select circle, consisting of the Princess (Caroline) and her governess, Charlotte von Stein and her sister-in-law; and in these lectures he sought to interweave ethical considerations. His delivery, the result of careful thought and practice, pleasant to hear, and instinct with feeling, charmed the ladies, notwithstanding the habit of often passing his hand over his forehead, in which he resembled Gall." (See Lyster's Translation of Düntzer's *Life of Goethe*, vol. ii., p. 235.)

† Caroline Jagemann, a famous actress, mistress of the Grand Duke Karl August, who created her Baroness von Heygendorf. She was very jealous of Goethe's influence over him, and headed an intrigue, with a view of forcing Goethe to resign his post, as *Intendant* of the Weimar Theatre; this he finally did, in consequence of his annoyance, when the Grand Duke invited a comedian, named Karsten, to exhibit his poodle on the stage, in the well-known drama of *The Dog of Aubry.* Goethe, who loathed dogs, declared he would have nothing more to do with the Theatre, and Karl August, who refused to give way, offensively dismissed him. Caroline Jagemann is also said to have been the only woman, to whom Schopenhauer, the pessimist philosopher, was deeply attached.

1806.

32.—GOETHE TO ZELTER.

Weimar, 5th March, 1806.

..... I HAVE felt tempted several times lately, to pay you and Berlin a visit, but once more so many things chain me to the spot, that I really do not see my way to a happy determination. But as I feel the pressing need, not only of hearing from you, but also of vividly realizing your circumstances, and of bringing mine more clearly before you, it has occurred to me to send you my son,* so that he may take my kindest greetings to you, and that also, in his early days, when worldly things still make a jovial impression, he may absorb, and also vividly recall for my enjoyment, the image of the great city.

Now though he is already a steady boy, and able to take care of himself, I had rather not think he was quite alone, and left to himself in that whirlpool of a town. Let me ask then, if you could get him lodgings near you, and at first provide him with what he wants. I send you a letter of credit, so that he may not have all the money he may need, in his pocket at once. I shall say no more about this; all else must depend on circumstances. The main point is: whether such a visit would not bore you? I shall give him letters and cards to my other friends in Berlin, and he is sure to make friends, but before all things I should like to know that he was safely established. His visit ought not to extend beyond a fortnight or three weeks; he might arrive the week before Easter. A thousand greetings, and please let me have an answer soon.

G.

33.—GOETHE TO ZELTER.

Weimar, 26th March, 1806.

SCARCELY had I sent my letter, telling of the postponement of Augustus' journey, when yours arrived, with

---

* Julius August Walther Goethe, Goethe's only son; he married Ottilie von Pogwisch, and died at Rome on the 28th October, 1830.

this unexpected and distressing news,* which has utterly
upset me. At the very time when Berlin is more than ever
before my eyes, when with a map before us, we are looking
for the new *Münzstrasse*, and I am hoping to get a clearer
idea of yourself and your surroundings from my boy, just
as last year he brought me back the picture of my mother,
—you are experiencing a violent wrench—one which I feel
with you in every sense. I must now think of you as
lonely, with the cares of a large household upon you, and with
much difficult business to attend to—or else my thoughts
revert to my own self, and I imagine a like terrible event
in my own case. Unfortunately, the obstacle which detains
my deputy, cannot be set aside, otherwise I should send
him at once, for the presence of a new, friendly, and affectionate being, would perhaps be a comfort to you, and the
good to which it would give rise, would probably counter-
balance the inconvenience it might occasion. It would
also be consoling to me, to know that a representative of
my affection, and of my heartfelt sympathy, was with you;
but even this is not to be, and all this happens at a time,
when I too have many burdens to lift and drag after me.
No more! Pray, let me have further news of you soon.

G.

34.—Zelter to Goethe.

11th June, 1806.

. . . . I have just come home from the new Romantic
play, which you have probably heard of, as it is being so
much discussed: *Die Weihe der Kraft*. The author is Herr
Werner,† the same who wrote *Die Söhne des Thals*. Very
conflicting criticisms I expect will be made on the play, for
one part of the public expects something great, whereas the
other is prejudiced against it, because it turns the Reforma-

---

* Zelter had written to tell Goethe of his wife's death in childbirth, on
the 16th March.

† Zacharias Werner, author of *The Sons of the Valley*, and *Wanda*, a
play greatly admired by Goethe, who had it performed at Weimar the
following year. Goethe (who humorously calls him "Dr. Luther"),
was infected for the time being with Werner's passion for writing
sonnets, but owing to his extravagant mysticism, his influence over the
poet soon wore off.

tion into a subject for mirth and amusement. So at least I apprehend, for the police took precautions for the first performance, which necessarily presupposes some public excitement.

The play is quite good enough for us, and would have to be much better, to please the multitude less. I judge it, as I do a Sonata by a young composer: it has everything in it, like Noah's Ark. The author, it seems, tried to bind up high aspirations with his subject, and then, his bundle getting too heavy, in the fifth Act, after the destruction of image-worship and feeling for Art, he lets it fall on the middle of the high road. People pray and sing—by note —and the general impression on my mind was—repulsive religiosity. It ceases to be a play, it is the parody of a serious and sacred crisis of the Church; whilst endeavouring to make itself intelligible, it profanes itself. Nothing worth speaking of is left for meditation. Luther alone has every advantage, and the Papacy, in contrast to him, cuts an awkward, nay, stupid figure; a vulgar piece of devilry, with no charms, nothing to stimulate, pique, nor impose upon the multitude. Unbelief, (the Emperor and the Kingdom), stands between, with no will, no influence. Allegory does not face history, as a looking-glass does an object; it stands by its side, reproducing, ruminating on itself. Needless to say, our *soi-disant* clergy are fain to fly into a passion, when their flocks had rather go to the Theatre than the Church, for their sermons, anthems and prayers. . . . .

Z.

35.—ZELTER TO GOETHE.

2nd August, 1806.

. . . . On the 23rd July we had a very merry sledging-party. Several officers of the Royal *Gendarmerie* had had a sledge built with covered wheels, and after 10 o'clock at night, drove through the streets of Berlin, with lots of torch-bearers, and making a great noise. In the sledge sat Doctor Luther with an immense flute, and opposite him, his friend Melancthon; on the back-seat of the sledge was Catherine von Bora, holding a whip, which she cracked as they went past, and wearing a huge train, ten yards long. On cavalry horses sat the nuns of the Augustine convent, carrying torches, led by their prioress; they also had long trains and wore ugly masks. The procession paraded the streets for several hours, to the delight of the pleasure-loving public. There are many different explanations of this undergraduate joke; the most likely, as I think, is this, that the dramatic tendency of Luther is nearly synonymous with what we call a summer sledging-party *—a mere craze for a daily novelty. Iffland is so much annoyed, that they say he personally complained of this indecency to the King. The result is, that one of these officers has been removed from Berlin, and the others are under arrest, having been warned that they would be cashiered, if they tried anything of the kind again. Thus the matter stands at present, and since then, the play has not been acted again. However, the culprits show few signs of repentance, and—it is said—are only waiting for the expiration of their term of arrest, to make it hot again for Iffland. . . . .

Z.

36.—Goethe to Zelter.

Jena, 15th August, 1806.

. . . . On my return from Carlsbad, I found several things that pleased me extremely, in addition to your letter; e.g. the opinions of a young painter on colour, which are definite and circumstantial. One part of his short essay is almost word for word the same in my *Farbenlehre*. The commentary on another part of his work will be found in mine, and there are certain passages, which I shall ask the author to make over to me, inasmuch as my own convictions could not be expressed better. To find this agreement of opinions in a cotemporary, who has hitherto known absolutely nothing about me and my endeavours, gives me fresh inclination to go on and finish my task. So much for to-day. . . . .

G.

---

* A proverbial expression for any artificial amusement, to which people have recourse, merely for the sake of change.

37.—GOETHE TO ZELTER.

Weimar, 26th December, 1806.

THANKS a thousand times, dear friend, for having at last broken the painful silence. Since the 14th October * I have been with you daily in thought, and even while writing this, a sealed letter, addressed to you, is lying on my desk, but I had not the courage to send it off. For what have we to tell one another? On the 12th December I kept your birthday in silence; and in the future too, I suppose, we shall only be able to celebrate in silence, what is good in silence. Anyhow I have got through these bad days without much harm. There was no need for me to take part in public affairs, as they were sufficiently well attended to by able men; and thus I could keep in my cell, and brood over my inmost thoughts. During the worst hours, when one could not but be anxious about everything, my greatest fear was that of losing my papers, and from that time onwards, I have been sending everything I can to the printers. My *Farbenlehre* makes brave progress. My ideas and fancies about organic Nature too are gradually being revised, and thus I shall endeavour to rescue all I can of my intellectual being, as no one can tell what may be the fate of the rest.

Some proof-sheets of my works, published by Cotta, have come to hand. Some of the poems of the first volume will, I hope, call forth melodies from you, so that we may feel and see, that we are still the same as of old. I congratulate you upon having found your musical treasures unharmed. I am sorry that you are involved in the Administration, as for much besides that Herr Schmidt tells me of. However, nowadays, it is not in our power to say, in which direction we should prefer being active. Your good spirit will never forsake you; may your good courage likewise never fail you. Let me occasionally hear something of you; I will write also. A hearty farewell!

GOETHE.

* The date of the battle of Jena. On the 15th October Napoleon came to Weimar, on the 16th he ordered that the plundering should cease, and on the 17th he left the town. On November 3rd Goethe writes to F. A. Wolf: " I have had first General Victor, then Marshals Lannes and Augereau in the house, with adjutants and suite." On the very day that he wrote to Zelter, (December 26th), Goethe re-opened the Theatre.

1807.

38.—GOETHE TO ZELTER.

Wiemar, 4th May, 1807.

Best thanks for your music to my verses. Just now it is most refreshing to take refuge, if only for a short time, in a light and easy mood.

The company game you ask me about, is played thus: Take a thin shaving of wood, or a taper, light it, and let it burn a little, then blow out the flame, and while it is left smouldering, repeat, as fast as you can, the following adage:—

"Dies the fox, the skin's a treasure,
Length of days means loss of youth;
If he lives, why, let him live,
If he dies, why, let him die.
Never bury him with his skin,
That survives to honour him."

Then pass the glimmering taper quickly on to your neighbour, who has to repeat the same stanza, and this goes on, till the last spark is extinguished; the person, in whose hand it goes out, must pay a forfeit.

Our Duchess Dowager is a great loss,* at a time when so much is topsy-turvy, and out of joint. We must reflect no further on this subject, nor on anything else at the present time. We must live on from one day to another, and do and accomplish what is still possible. . . . .

G.

39.—GOETHE TO ZELTER.

Weimar, 7th May, 1807.

. . . . I am very glad to hear that you liked my *Elpenor*,† and the object of those pages has now been at-

---

* The Duchess Amalia died April 10th, 1807, and Goethe's brief account of her life and influence was read aloud from all the pulpits in the country, at the solemn service held in her memory, nine days afterwards.

† This fragment of a tragedy had been begun as far back as 1781. In 1798 Goethe sent it to Schiller, who wrote thus: "If it is not by the

tained. Perhaps, however, your affection for me personally must be looked upon, as influencing you in the praise you bestow on my fragment: for I willingly own, that I am no longer able to judge this work myself. When anything comes to a standstill, one never knows whether it is one's own fault, or that of the subject. Generally, however, one entertains an aversion for what one cannot finish, as for a thing that resists one, and which one cannot master. In fact, while publishing my works, I have felt very keenly, how strange these things have become to me, nay, that I scarcely feel any more interest in them. This goes so far, that unless I had had continued, loyal, friendly assistance, those twelve little volumes would never have been put together. However, we have now got through most of them, and, with the exception of one volume, they will all be in Cotta's hands, within the next few days. Then come what may to us, this much at any rate will be safe. I am anticipating with joy your diversion over the continuation of my *Faust;* it contains, too, things which will interest you from a musical point of view.

You would do me a great favour, if you could procure me a catalogue of the works of Art, which have been taken away from Berlin; if only we know where they are kept, they will not be lost to us.

Farewell, and write again before Whitsuntide, and then send me news of yourself to Carlsbad.

G.

40.—GOETHE TO ZELTER.

Carlsbad, 27th July, 1807.

IT is a long time, my very dear friend, since you heard from me. I will now shortly tell you what I have been doing in the meantime. I came to Carlsbad in a very poor state of health, which was at first so aggravated by a

hand of a woman, still it suggests a certain womanliness of sentiment, even in so far as a man might possess this feature of character." Goethe, who had accidentally omitted to tell Schiller the real authorship of the work, was delighted with the clearness and justice of his remarks upon it, and said that they explained, why he himself had never cared to finish it. (See *Schiller and Goethe Correspondence,* vol. ii., pp. 106, 107.)

careless use of the waters, common indeed, but not suitable for me, as I then was, that I sank into a miserable condition. By the change of cure, and by the use of other means, prescribed by Dr. Kappe of Leipzig, things suddenly took a turn for the better; as this has lasted for six weeks, I gladly let my friends know of it. It is eight weeks now since I came here, and I have been occupying myself in different ways at different epochs: first of all in dictating short fairy-tales and stories, which I have long carried about in my head; then for a time, I took to drawing landscapes, and illuminating, and am now engaged in classifying my geological opinions relating to the district round about, and in briefly commenting on a collection of rock specimens, which is on view here.

I have become acquainted with interesting people of all kinds; amongst whom, Reinhard, the French resident, who but lately held an appointment in Jassy, and whose fortunes you are sure to have heard of, probably ranks first. As a rule however, I am very much alone, for in the world one meets with nothing but Jeremiads, which although they are called forth by great evils, appear nevertheless to be mere hollow phrases, as you hear them in society. When anyone laments over what he and those around him are suffering, what he has lost and fears to lose,—I listen with sympathy, and am glad to discuss the matter and to comfort him. But when people lament over the whole thing that is supposed to be lost, but which no one in Germany has ever in his life seen, and much less cared about,—I have to conceal my impatience, in order not to appear impolite, or an egotist. As already said, it would be inhuman not to sympathize with a man, who feels the loss of his living, the destruction of his career; but if such a man thinks that the world has in the smallest degree suffered in consequence, I cannot possibly agree with him.

Write and tell me, dear friend, how you are getting on. I have thought of you a thousand times, and of what you have accomplished as a private person, without the support of the wealthy and powerful, and without any special encouragement. Perhaps what we have most to regret from political change, is mainly this, that under its old constitution, Germany, and especially the Northern part, allowed the individual to cultivate himself, as far as possible, and that it permitted everyone to do what was right in his own eyes, without, however, there ever being any special interest shown in him by the community.

To these general, and certainly inadequate reflections, which I should like some day to discuss further with you personally, I wish to add a special request, which I beg you will kindly comply with soon.

Although we have both voices and orchestra in Weimar, and in addition to that, I am the master of such ceremonies, still I never could secure musical enjoyment with any certain regularity, because the odious relations of life and the Theatre invariably destroy the higher element, for which alone they exist, or ought to exist. Schleswig has again sent us two new people, a very good Tenor, and a kind of assistant rehearser; I have not yet made their personal acquaintance, but they seem to be good and intelligent people. Our Opera, as at present constituted, I do not care to interfere with, particularly as I do not thoroughly understand these musical matters. I should therefore prefer leaving the Secular to itself, and withdrawing into the Sanctuary. Now I should like once a week to have sacred part-songs performed at my house, in the same way as at your *Singakademie*, though it were but the most far-off reflection of it. Help me to this, and send me some part-songs for four voices, not too difficult, and with the parts already written out. I will gratefully reimburse you for any expense you may incur. Let me know whether I could get such things, with notes printed or engraved. Canons too, and whatever you may think useful for the purpose. You shall always be in our midst, in spirit, and heartily welcome whenever you care to appear in person. Let me have a few lines, for I shall remain another month here, and send me a parcel to Weimar, that I may begin at once, when I get home. Farewell, and rest assured of my lasting friendship.

G.

41.—GOETHE TO ZELTER.

Carlsbad, 30th August, 1807.

. . . . There is really something Promethean in your nature, which I can only wonder at and esteem. While you were calmly and patiently bearing what is hardly to be borne, and forming plans ahead for happy and creative activity, I have been acting like one who has already crossed Cocytus, and has at least tasted the waters of Lethe. Otherwise, in so far as I still feel myself a denizen of this earth, I have done what I could after my fashion, taking in many an experience, reading a good deal, learning, making notes, working things out, &c. . . . .

G.

42.—GOETHE TO ZELTER.

Weimar, 15th September, 1807.

You really are a good friend! When I returned home, I found the songs, and we have already started our little *Singschule*. We shall by degrees attract our stage-singers and Chorus, besides people from the Town; then we shall see how we get on. We have plenty of room in our Theatre.

Your renewed invitation makes my heart heavy. It is unpardonable, that I should still be unacquainted with your Institution, but for several years past, I have felt a certain clinging to the place I live in; this has mainly arisen from the many interests awakened, but as yet undeveloped within me. Thus I am busy throughout the year, merely in trying to get things cleared up here and there, independently of the circumstances of my health and time. The latter, however, would be less likely to prevent my coming, were it not for the former. But on a closer survey, I feel a dread of new influences and excitements, and therefore, of my own free will, deny myself many a pleasure.

The praise given to our Theatre by Leipzig, inspires me with energy and heart, once more to devote myself eagerly to the business of this winter. We have, in this instance, been rewarded for our perseverance, and shall go on in the old way, with confidence and hope; and thus, even the basest detraction and opposition, such as we once had to experience from Berlin, will be of no avail. Your perseverance too, my worthy friend, is ever before my eyes. I am only afraid, that if you do go to Italy, the glorious bond of so many years will be dissolved. It is pleasant and natural, that some of the grains of seed, scattered broadcast by you, should have fallen upon the tea-tables.* Please get me some songs of that kind; they might be the very thing for birds of our feather!

I shall not tell you anything about my other doings, but hope soon to be able to send you some of the fruits of my quiet industry. Farewell, and let me too have a song now and then. I could the more readily enjoy such little things just now, as I have several guitars at hand, if you would set them to an easy accompaniment for that instrument.

G.

43.—GOETHE TO ZELTER.

Jena, 16th December, 1807.

FIRST of all, dear Friend, I could not ask enough of you; now it was one thing, now another; I plagued you with my commissions, though you have enough to do without them, and now that everything has come, songs, pricelist, and turnips, I am like those, whose prayers have been answered, and with no more thanks, turn from the giver to the gifts. I will not excuse this, for there is always time to send a few lines to a friend; but since my return home from the baths, I have felt strangely oppressed by the Present, as though I had to pay another penalty for those four months, which I spent upon the unclouded mountain-heights, like a retired Gymnosophist. To be sure, nothing disagreeable has happened to me; but yet so much that I liked and disliked forced itself upon me, that neither my physical, nor my moral powers, were quite sufficient for the task.

I thought I should at last be able to send you the second

---

* In allusion to the small vocal societies in Berlin, called *Singe-Thees*. There were about fifty of them, and Zelter viewed them with some suspicion, as being "the most dangerous enemies of the *Singakademie*," though it owed its origin to one of them.

batch of my works, but it has not even reached me yet,—not so much as a complete set of proof-sheets; otherwise I should have sent these in the meantime, in so far as they contain anything new.

My small Choir, which, it is true, consists as yet of hardly more than four voices, is educating itself quite nicely, and even already shows its influence upon the Theatre. Shortly before I left home, it was greatly improved by the acquisition of a young female voice, which might almost pass for a Counter-Tenor. Might I ask you, at your convenience, to let me have Schiller's *Punschlied?* Unfortunately I have but one voice-part left; the others have been mislaid.

Werner, "the Son of the Valley,"* has been with us in Jena, for the last twelve days; we find him interesting and agreeable. He reads us portions of his printed and unprinted works, and thus we are enabled to look beyond the strange, outward shells of these phenomena, into the kernel, which is toothsome and strong.

So much, my dearest friend, for the present. I am packing up to return to Weimar. I have been very happy here, and—you would never guess it, I have been drawn into Sonnetteering. I shall send you a dozen some day soon, on the one condition that no one sees them, and that they are not copied. But should you care to set one of them to music, I should be very much pleased; I am only too glad to see my productions floating in your element. Write to me again, if only a line or two. A word from a friend is doubly enjoyable, in these short, dark days.

Geheimrath Wolf has given us an excellent number on the study of antiquity, which is rich in thought, and reminds us of everything we know, pointing out in a friendly way, what else we ought to know, and how we should deal with the whole matter. Once more, farewell!

G.

* See Note on Werner, Letter 34.

1808.

44.—GOETHE TO ZELTER.

Weimar, 22nd January, 1808.

"OUT of the eater came forth meat, and out of the strong came forth sweetness"—so said I, when your well-filled hamper was unpacked. Everything came safely, and the jar was so well squeezed in, that nothing ran out of it, though it had had a good shaking. The housekeeper thanks you, but Augustus is particularly grateful—it is he, who is in a condition to make the largest inroads on your present; we others help ourselves more moderately.

The music has already been handed over to our little School; your first consignment is still the best thing we have had for some time past. The greater part of it was performed yesterday before our Princesses, who were much pleased.

You once told me something about a *Stabat Mater;* pardon me for reminding you of it. My little Institution gets on well; but the young people, as you well know, are very fond of stepping out of the rut, and each one fancies himself better off, when he is singing some pitiful or mournful lament of unrequited love, as a Solo. I allow such things, towards the end of each Session, and at the same time execrate men like Matthisson, Salis, Tiedge, and the Clergy in a body, who show us heavy Germans—even in songs—a path beyond the world, which we leave quickly enough, as it is. Add to this, that musicians themselves are often hypochondriacal, and that even joyous music may dispose to melancholy. I praise what springs from you, dear friend. Again yesterday, during the *Niemals erscheinen die Götter allein,* and in the *Liebe Freunde, es gab bessre Zeiten,** it seemed just as if everyone was shaking from his head the dust and ashes of the century. So much good I owe

* Poems by Schiller.

to you; perhaps some day I shall be able to repay you. May you be happy!

GOETHE.

45.—GOETHE TO ZELTER.

Weimar, 20th April, 1808.

HERE are the songs, dearest Friend. Just glance at them! Perhaps you will make some remarks in red ink, and say generally what you think of the young man's * gift, and in particular, let me know how far he seems to have gone in this difficult art. I shall perhaps send him to you about Michaelmas, as next winter, he may possibly become the Conductor of my small musical parties. As I was not fated to revel, at ease, at the rich table of a great city, I must cultivate and plant on a small scale, and produce and accomplish what is possible, at the time, and under the circumstances.

Pray tell me, when you have time, something about Church music in Constantinople, which, with the Greek Church, seems to have spread in the East, and to have influenced the Sarmatian peoples. Whence comes, do you think, the universal tendency towards minor-tones, which can be traced, even in the Polonaise?

This Easter, eight Choristers have passed through here, on their way from St. Petersburg to Paris, to join the Choir of the Russian Ambassador's Chapel. They sang in the Greek Church here, on both feast days, when—as his Royal Highness told me—they perform nothing but genuine, ancient Church compositions. The nearest thing that I have heard to it, is the *Canto fermo* of the Italians, and the way in which the Passion is given in the Papal Chapel, in the actual words of the Evangelists. . . . .

G.

---

* Traugott Maximilian Eberwein, who afterwards conducted the little concerts, given at Goethe's house, on Sunday mornings, before a select audience, who were always invited to breakfast.

46.—ZELTER TO GOETHE.

Berlin, 1st May, 1808.

.... AMONGST Herr Eberwein's songs, which I herewith return, with the first sheets of *Faust,—Am Neujahrstage* pleases me most; one recognizes a definite sentiment in it, and what is still more, this sentiment is homogeneous throughout....

The faults of a master are always the outcome of mastery, and therefore do no harm; filigree-work, on the other hand, only veils the disgrace of bungling.....

You ask, whence comes the universal tendency towards minor-tones, traceable even in the Polonaise. I have had the same experience, but musical historians give no satisfactory information on the subject..... I think I first met with the almost universal bias in favour of the minor keys, in the songs of Northern nations, especially of dwellers in the Islands, and on the Coasts. The history of the art of music says next to nothing about the songs of the far North; travellers, who may have dabbled with musical knowledge, have given such unsatisfactory descriptions of them, that we are more impressed with the meagreness of their knowledge, than with the true spirit of the songs, for none but good musicians can describe such things correctly. The hunting and fishing songs of Russia, Curland, and Livonia, Norway, and Scotland, are the first that lead us to draw some conclusion, as to a free indication of character; still more the *dances*, which are capable of more outward expression than the songs, which demand inward cultivation. This is why the Scotch, Russian, and Polish dances are so beautiful, and so truly national, that they are imitated, though clumsily enough, amongst all cultivated nations. But these very dances, so far as I thought them genuine, were always set to minor keys, the best of them anyhow. It is well known that the Russians and Poles love dancing, and that they dance beautifully, with grace, agility, and expression, showing much more dignity and life, than one would ever suppose from their ordinary habits. The Russian songs and dances which I have heard, were, without exception, in minor keys, though at the same time

very lively, consisting of numbers of quick notes and short
metres. Had these dances been in major keys, I should
have thought them extravagant and wild in their mirth;
whereas in the minor key, they become serious, tender,
nay, yearning, whilst they seem to strain after cheerfulness,
which is hindered by a damp, cold atmosphere, and the use
of austere diet.

The genuine Polonaise inclines already to the South, a
more luxurious passion seems to awake in it. . . . .

Now, if we pass at a bound, from the North to Italy, the
minor keys are found, especially in the best days of music,
only in temples and churches, where they were indispensable, on account of the so-called Greek or Ecclesiastical
modes. In songs and dances, there prevails a light, flexible
melody, even in the expression of the fiercest passion, (with
few exceptions,) and in more recent times, the Italians
have gone so far, that to an air such as this:

> Tu mi da me dividi,
> Barbaro! tu m'uccidi!
> Tutto il dolor ch'io sento,
> Tutto mi vien da te.
> Non son nelle selve Ircane
> Tigre di te piu feroce.

the brightest melodies are set, to prevent the appearance of
anything doleful, and these airs are the most famous of all.
On the whole, the Opera Buffa is found in far greater perfection than the serious Opera, for which no better poems
yet exist, than those of Metastasio, Apostolo Zeno, and the
like. Yet in the Opera Buffa, minor keys are used to
heighten the comic situation, and, as it were, to bid defiance to seriousness.

According to this, one might look for a minor key tendency in Climate. Now, there stand the North-Germans
in the centre, straining laboriously towards every point of
the compass, in order to enrich their flat territory. They
learn to make everything, but, in the end, all that they long
for is a spice of something to fire the blood, and that they
call passion. It is another matter with shepherd-folk and
mountaineers. These seem to take their scales from their
bugle-horns, for they know no other instrument, so their

songs and dances are either major or minor, as the horn gives it out. Such a dance is the Scotch hornpipe, to the following melody:—

This dance is in a major key, but I have met with Swiss songs, also in minor keys, which for the moment have escaped my memory.

As for music in Constantinople, I know as much as my historians, *i.e.* nothing at all. An Oriental Emperor, Constantine IX, surnamed Porphyrogenitus, made emperor at seven years old, and poisoned in the year 959, is said to have been a great musician. Then Nicolai * tells me, a Greek Emperor, Constantinus, wrote a work in the tenth century on the Court ceremonies at Constantinople, which was printed at Leipzig in 1751, in two folio volumes of Greek and Latin, and, according to him, must certainly be in the Weimar Library. Perhaps this book may contain something about music in Constantinople. You may possibly get further information in the Abbot Gerbert's Latin work, *De cantû et musicâ sacrâ*, which however ·I do not possess. The same author also published a work, called, *Scriptores ecclesiastici de Musicâ sacrâ potissimum. Ex variis Italiæ, Galliæ, et Germaniæ codicibus manuscriptis collecti.* . . . .

Yours,
ZELTER.

* Presumably "the Berlin Aristarchus," author of a parody on *Werther*, in which Werther shoots himself with chicken's blood, and marries Charlotte afterwards. Goethe answered with a burlesque poem, called *Nicolai at Werther's Grave*. (See Lewes's *Life of Goethe*, p. 156.)

47.—GOETHE TO ZELTER.

Carlsbad, 22nd June, 1808.

YOUR dear letter of the 6th of April did not reach me till I got here. I at once sent back Eberwein's songs, and afterwards, a copy of your obliging criticism. What a good thing it would be for that young man, to study under you for a good spell! Just now, however, he is experiencing the fate of all beginners; they go astray like sheep, and each takes his own line.

My best thanks for what you have said, to my comfort and instruction, in reply to my questions; only as to your theoretical statements, which, as I well know, square with the convictions of the physical and musical world, I have something in my own way to remind you of. How I should like to talk with you on this subject, which is so closely connected with others I am ruminating upon; then some of the chief knots would surely be unravelled for me. I enclose a sheet of paper, on which your statement is repeated, followed by my doubts, objections, and questions, in so far as I was able to concentrate my thoughts upon so complicated a subject. As I have numbered the points of argument, and kept a copy of them, you might, as a friend, answer each number separately, and I should be able to keep your explanations, together with my draft.

I have now been here since the 15th of May, and, for the first fortnight, when we had most beautiful weather, spent my time busily enough; after that, some pleasant company arrived, bad weather set in, and my mode of life changed. A third epoch is in prospect, fine weather and a number of people, when once again, perhaps, I may turn my solitary hours to profit.

I suppose you have not yet received your copy of my last eight volumes; but I hope, even though it comes rather later, you will give it a kind welcome. The fragments of an entire life-time, when placed in juxtaposition, certainly present a strange and disjointed appearance, so that reviewers find themselves in quite a peculiar dilemma, when, either with good or evil intentions, they endeavour to treat what is printed together, as if it belonged together. A friendly intelligence knows best, how to throw life into these fragments.

If Voss's Sonnet is objectionable to you, we are completely agreed upon that point likewise. We have had in Germany several instances of very gifted men, losing themselves at last in pedantry, and it is the same in his case. From sheer prosody, his poetry has entirely vanished. And what is the meaning of persecuting with hate and rage an individual rhythmical form,—the Sonnet, for example? when after all it is only a vessel, into which every one who has brains, can put what he likes. How ridiculous it is, to be for ever chewing the cud of that Sonnet of mine,* in which I spoke rather unfavourably of Sonnets, to make a party question of an æsthetic subject, and to drag me also forth, as a member of a party, without considering, that one may quite well jest and joke about a thing, without despising or denouncing it on that account.

I hope therefore, that the accompanying poems of this class will meet with all the better reception from you; only I urgently beseech you, not to let them out of your hands.

I have nothing further to write to you from here, except that I am in good health, and as industrious as I can be. If the two first numbers of the Vienna *Prometheus* have reached you, you have, I daresay, bestowed a kindly glance on my *Pandora*. In the fifth or sixth number, you will become more intimately acquainted with that pretty child. Be sure and read Friedrich Schlegel's article *On the Language and Wisdom of the Indians*, and admire the way in which he has contrived to weave in a perfectly crude Roman Catholic confession of faith, with the grandest views of the world, mankind, and the history of culture. This little volume may thus be regarded, as a declaration of his having joined the only saving Church.† All this hocus-pocus,

---

* This alludes to an epigram called *Das Sonnet*, published in 1806. It is found at the head of the cycle called *Epigrammatisch*, and the last six lines of it are directed against the Sonnet form, though Goethe afterwards continued to write Sonnets himself.

† In a previous letter, Zelter had spoken as follows, of Schlegel's conversion to Roman Catholicism: " The only saving Church has

however, whatever its effect may be, will not help him in the main. The true mode of thought is too widely spread, and is no longer in danger of being destroyed, however much it may be modified by individual things.

G.

A Simile as Postscript.

All the Arts, seeing that they could only work themselves upwards, by exercise and thought, practice and theory, seem to me like towns, the ground and soil of which, the foundations in fact, can no longer be made out. Rocks have been blasted, and these same stones hewn into shape, and made into houses. Caves were found very convenient, and converted into cellars. Where the earth gave way, it was intrenched and walled up; perhaps by the very side of the primary rock, a bottomless piece of swamp was met with, where stakes and pile-work had to be driven in; when all is at last completed and made habitable, what part of it can be called Nature, and what, Art? Where is the foundation, and where are the accessories? Where the substance, where the form? How difficult it is then, to give reasons, if we would assert, that in the earliest times, had they overlooked the whole at once, all the arrangements might have been made more in accordance with the objects of Nature and of Art. If you consider the piano, or organ, you might imagine you had the town of my simile before you. Would to God I too might for once pitch my tent by your side, and attain the true enjoyment of life! I should then be heartily glad to forget all questions about Nature and Art, theory and practice.

1. You say—" The minor key is distinguished from the major, by the minor third."

Is it not also distinguished, by diminishing or narrowing the other intervals?

2. "Which takes the place of the major third."

This expression can only hold good, if we start from the major key. A theorist of Northern nationality, when

caught a good fish in him, but I am annoyed about it, because I once had a considerable opinion of him."

speaking of the minor tones, might as well say, that the major third takes the place of the minor third

3. " Our present diatonic (natural) scale."

That the diatonic scale should be the only natural one— it is against this, that my opposition is properly directed.

4. " Originates in the way the string is divided. If it were divided in half," &c., &c.

That the division of the string into different parts should produce sounds harmonious to the ear, is a very pretty experiment, which might even be made the foundation of a certain scale ; but, if it cannot be accomplished in this way, might it not be possible in some other manner ?

5. " The string may, however, be divided into as many parts as you please, and yet this will never produce a minor third, although by so doing, you can always get nearer to it."

You ask too much of an experiment, when you require it to do everything. Was not electricity at first produced only by friction, whereas its grandest manifestations are now produced by mere touch. Our aim should be an experiment, by which one could represent the minor tones also as original.

6. "Accordingly, this minor third is no immediate *donum* of nature, but a work of more recent art."

I deny the conclusion, as I do not admit the premises.

7. " And it must be regarded as a diminished major third."

This is a subterfuge, of which theorists usually avail themselves, when they have established something which restricts Nature : for they are then obliged to recall and annihilate what they formerly maintained, in a very paradoxical fashion. If a major third is an interval which Nature gives us, how can we diminish it, without destroying it ? How much and how little can it be diminished, and not be a major third, and still be a third ? And, generally, at what point would it cease to be still a third ? My imaginary Northern theorist might quite as justly affirm, that the major third is an augmented minor.

8. " And so—even by the strictest composers—it has been treated as a consonant interval."

We have an evident instance here, of what so often

happens both in Art and in *technique*, that the practical sense knows very well, how to save itself from theoretical limitation, without making much fuss about it.

9. " That is—it may, like the major third, be introduced everywhere, freely and without preparation, which, in a pure style, is not allowed to any dissonance."

" If it is treated as a consonant interval, it is consonant, for such things cannot be established at first hand by convention. If it may be introduced freely and without preparation, then it is no dissonance; it is by nature harmonious, and so also is everything which springs from it."

Here intervenes a very remarkable consideration, in respect of all physical inquiry,—one which has been already touched upon before. Man in himself, in so far as he makes use of his sound senses, is the greatest and most perfect physical apparatus that there can be. And it is, in fact, the greatest evil of the more modern physics, that experiments are, as it were, separated from man himself, and that Nature is recognized only in that which artificial instruments demonstrate—nay, they want to prove and limit her capability by these. It is precisely the same with calculation. There is much that is true, that will not admit of being computed, just as there is a great deal that cannot be brought to the test of definite experiment. On the other hand, however, man stands so high, that what otherwise defies representation, finds its representation in him. What then is a string and all its mechanical divisions, compared with the ear of the musician? Nay, it may be said, what are the elementary phenomena of Nature herself, compared with man, who has first to control and modify them all, before he can in any way assimilate them to himself. However, I do not intend to lose myself in these considerations just now; I shall take an early opportunity of speaking of this again, as well as of asking you for further information on a few other points.

48.—GOETHE TO ZELTER.

Weimar, 30th October, 1808.

ACCEPT my best thanks, dear Friend, for all that you are doing, and all you mean to do for young Eberwein.

The world of Art has certainly gone too much to the bad, for a young man to perceive so easily, upon what things depend. They always look for something in some quarter, other than that whence it proceeds; and even if they once catch a glimpse of the source, they are unable to find their way to it.

For this reason, some half-dozen of our younger poets put me into a state of despair; in spite of their extraordinary natural gifts, they will scarcely manage to write much that I can like. Werner, Oehlenschläger, Arnim, Brentano, and others work and toil away; but all they produce is absolutely wanting in form and character. No one will understand, that the highest and sole operation of Nature and of Art is *Formation*, (*Gestaltung*,) and in Form, *Specification*, so that each thing may be and remain something special, something significant. It is not Art, to allow one's talent to act capriciously, according to one's individual convenience; something should always arise out of it, as from the scattered seed of Vulcan, there arose a marvellous serpent-boy.

It is very bad, at the same time, that the Humoristic, owing to its not possessing any solidity or law in itself, degenerates sooner or later into melancholy and moroseness; we have the most frightful examples of this in Jean Paul, (see his last production in the *Damenkalender*,) and in Görres, (see his *Schriftproben*.) *

However, there are always plenty of people who marvel at and glorify such things, for the public is ready to thank anyone, who tries to turn its head.

Have the kindness, dear friend, whenever you have a quarter of an hour to spare, to give me a brief sketch of the errors of young musicians: I should like to compare them with the blunders made by painters, for one must, once for all, calm oneself about these matters, denounce the whole system, not think about the culture of others, and devote the short time that remains, to one's own works.

But while expressing myself in so ungracious a manner upon these points, I must nevertheless, as good-natured

* A publication issued by Görres in 1808, at Heidelberg, under the pseudonym of Peter Hammer

grumblers are wont to do, at once recall my words, and beg of you to continue devoting your attention to Eberwein, at all events till Easter, as I shall send him back to you again. He feels great confidence in you, and great respect for your Institute; but even this, unfortunately, does not mean very much with young men, for secretly, they still think that what is extraordinary may just as well be produced in their own silly manner. A good many men have an idea of the goal, only they would like to reach it, by sauntering along on labyrinthine ways.

You will have been more than enough reminded of us this month, by the newspapers. It was worth a good deal, to be a personal witness of these events. I too have experienced a favourable influence from such a strange constellation. The Emperor of France was very gracious to me.* Both Emperors presented me with stars and ribbons, which therefore, we, in all modesty, gratefully acknowledge.

How much I wish, that you and your fellow-citizens might likewise find comfort and tranquillity in this epoch, for your sufferings have hitherto gone beyond the limit of what is bearable. You are then, it seems, still personally engaged in public affairs? Write and tell me in what way. My kind regards to Herr Geheimrath Wolf; we expect to have his little daughter with us soon.

Pardon me for not writing at greater length, about the latest events. You will be astonished, I know, on reading the newspapers, that this flood of the mighty and the great ones of the earth has rolled as far as Weimar, and on to the battle-field of Jena. I cannot refrain from enclosing a remarkable engraving. The point where the Temple stands, is the farthest point, reached this time by Napoleon, towards the North-East. If you pay us a visit, (which Heaven grant you may!) I will place you on the very spot, where the little man here, is pointing to the world with his stick.

No more to-day. I have so many debts in the way of letters, that I do not know where to begin cancelling them.

G.

---

* For Napoleon's conversations with Goethe in October, 1808, see Düntzer's *Life of Goethe*, vol. ii., pp. 266, 267, (in Lyster's translation.)

49.—ZELTER TO GOETHE.

Berlin, 12th November, 1808.

. . . . WHAT you say in your letter about Specification of Formation, Form and Character, is perhaps truer of music, (anyhow, they are more difficult of attainment in music), than of the imitative arts. For each of the poetic spirits named by you, I could name a musical counterpart, and so confirm your judgment: one sees with admiration and terror, false lights and streaks of blood on the horizon of Parnassus. Men so brilliantly gifted as Cherubini, Beethoven, and several others, steal the club of Hercules— to smash flies with; at first one marvels, and then directly afterwards, one shrugs one's shoulders at the amount of talent wasted, in making trifles important and lofty methods common. I really could despair, when it occurs to me that the new music *must* perish, if an art is to come out of music.

No art can exercise a beneficent influence, which wanders about in endless space, shameless and shapeless, like the more modern music, laying bare isolated fragments of its highest and most secret charms, to the public gaze of the common and vulgar, like an anatomical cabinet, or a collection of anecdotes about love-secrets, and over-satiating common curiosity. Let people object as they will, to the composers of earlier centuries, (for who has not got to learn more than he knows?) they never threw art away, nor exposed the inner Sanctum; had we contrived to build on their foundation, we might have an art, and we should be very different people in our own estimation.

50.—ZELTER TO GOETHE.

Berlin, 26th December, 1808.

. . . . IN honour of the King's return, I have instituted a *Liedertafel*—a society, formed of twenty-five men, the twenty-fifth of whom is chosen Master; it assembles once a month, at a supper of two courses, enlivened by jovial German songs. The members must be either poets,

singers, or composers. The writer or composer of a new
song, reads or sings, or has it sung before the whole table.
If it is applauded, a box is passed round the table, into
which everyone, (if he likes the song,) puts a *groschen* or
two, as he pleases. The money is counted out on the table;
if it comes to so much, that a silver medal, of the value of
a good *Thaler* can be purchased with it, the Master hands
over the medal to the winner, in the name of the *Liedertafel*,
they drink the health of the poet or composer, and discuss
the beauty of the song. If a member can show twelve silver
medals, he has a supper at the expense of the community,
he is crowned with a wreath, he can ask for any kind of
wine he chooses, and is presented with a gold medal, worth
five-and-twenty *Thalers*. All other arrangements are mentioned in the plan, which is just now being put into circulation. Anyone blurting out words, that are compromising
or offensive, to a single member, or to the whole body, pays
a forfeit. Satirical verses on individuals are not sung;
everyone has full liberty to be himself, provided only that
he is liberal. We only permit twelve rules; there may be
fewer, not more. Now, do give me a sketch for a pretty
scroll, rather a big one, with the word "Welcome" on
it,—and one for a *small*, and one for a *gold* medal; I must
press you in the matter, for we must strike when the iron
is hot. The members are all enthusiastic, and can hardly
wait for the King's arrival. . . . .

We are just now expecting here the Roman Humboldt,*
who has become *Staatsrath des Cultus der Akademien und
Theater*. If he is still the same man that he was, before
he went to Italy, I shall be very glad of him. Here, which-
ever way things tend, he may do good service, for in these
matters, we have long led a sinful life. . . . .

Z.

* Karl Wilhelm, Freiherr von Humboldt.

1809.

51.—GOETHE TO ZELTER.

Jena, 1st June, 1809.

.... I ENCLOSE a small poem;* perhaps you may yourself be inclined to accompany it with the necessary musical declamation; or perhaps you will give it to Eberwein, to try his hand on. I was induced to write it by the good people of the Lauchstädt district, who, in an all-devouring age, wished to preserve the memory of a pure act of humanity.

As it was not yet advisable for me to go to Carlsbad, I have come to Jena, where I am trying to finish a novel,† which I sketched and began a year ago, among the Bohemian mountains. It will probably come out this year, and I am all the more anxious to hurry on with the work, as it will be a means of thoroughly re-establishing an intercourse with my friends at a distance. I hope you will think it is in my old way and manner. I have stored away much in it, hidden many things in it; may this open secret give you also pleasure!

Since Eberwein left, and all the actors took to quarrelling, I have kept rather aloof from music. I hope in future to have all the more enjoyment of it through him—echoes from your heaven, which, alas! I am destined never to enter, a thought which often grieves me. In these warlike days, we see for the first time, how clumsily and awkwardly we behaved in times of peace. Let the little Ballad—when you have set it to music—be as widely known as you like, and do not leave me too long, without a word of encouragement. Unfortunately, I have spent this winter with very little joy or profit. Since the spring, I have again begun revising my *Farbenlehre*, and am having it

---

* The dramatic Ballad, *Johanna Sebus*.
† *Die Wahlverwandtschaften*.

printed; in my own story, I have got to the end of the seventeenth century, and, taking it altogether, am close upon the sixtieth sheet. It is a strange thing, to see on paper so large a mass of one's own, and other people's life, and yet it seems not worth the reading. What has been written, as well as what has been actually done, shrivels up and does not become worth anything, till it has again been taken up into life, again been felt, thought, and acted upon.

Herr Hirt has sent me his great work upon Architecture. I am highly delighted to see so important a task, one that has taken over twenty years to accomplish, successfully finished at last.

Farewell, and remember me!

G.

52.—GOETHE TO ZELTER.

Weimar, 30th October, 1809.

In place of reiterated thanks, I send you to-day nothing but a friendly greeting, by one who is about to leave us, Herr Lorzing, a brother of our actor. I have followed you to Königsberg with my thoughts and wishes, though they only referred to your own welfare. The fools of Germans are still for ever bawling against egotism, would to Heaven, they had long ago honestly looked after themselves and their belongings, and then again, after those nearest, and again nearest to them! then perhaps everything might have looked different. Now, we will not allow ourselves to be led astray, but will keep to the old road.

Anyhow, I am still continuing my own way in Weimar and Jena; two tiny places, which God has still preserved to us, though the noble Prussians would, not long since, have liked, in more than one way, to destroy them. A thousand thanks for having again done all you could for our edification, in training a good fellow, and returning him to us, as a helpful brother-citizen. Though I know but few details, I can nevertheless, in my own way, see into your whole life, i.e. the life of your State, and its prospects and hopes; and so I certainly wish, that so noble and dear a friend may, after so many trials, be blessed at least with better prospects. If I had a clear idea of your sphere of activity, your deeds and actions, I might be more easy in my mind about your circumstances: for, at a distance, one usually sees only what is wanting, and what is missing. Hope and fear are two hollow entities.

With these few words you will receive my novel. Do as if the greater part had been dedicated to you, and for the rest, pardon my silence and stagnation. It is getting almost impossible to speak to an individual about individual things. But if one could grasp broader relationships, one might still, I suppose, represent and express much.

No more to-day! the turnips arrived safely. Our thanks shall be renewed for every fresh dishful.

G.

53.—GOETHE TO ZELTER.

Weimar, 21st December, 1809.

I REALLY forget when and what I last wrote to you; for with me, the days perform the valuable service of a sponge, as they wash the immediate past clean out from my memory. My feeling remains intact, and this tells me that I am indebted to you for all sorts of things. When I remember this, I think first of those delicious turnips, which it would be hard indeed for me to forget, because, before I am aware of it, there they are on the table again, as good as ever! On Thursdays and Sundays, Eberwein lets us hear much of the music he has brought back with him, and whatever he can impart to us, on the strength of what you have sent us with your benediction. Schiller's things have been most admirably conceived. The music supplements them, for really no song is perfect, until it has been set to music. Here, however, there is something quite peculiar. The meditative or meditated enthusiasm is now for the first time raised, or I should rather say, melted into the free and lovely element of sensuousness. One thinks and feels, and is carried away by it.

You can also imagine that the mirthful pieces do not fail to produce their effect, as I have more affection for such things, and in fact everybody is glad to be, or to be made, merry. . . . .

During these winter months, I am working as busily as I can, in order to be rid of my work on Colours; after that, however, I intend to turn my back, even upon the rainbow, which will, in any case, through this malicious attitude, be annihilated for my individual self. With the first breath of Spring, I shall go to Carlsbad, intending, if possible, to live there in my old way.

Write and tell me something, when you have the opportunity, about yourself; and send me something pleasant. It is true, we have plenty of the old, the unfathomed, but after all, the immediate moment is the most charming.

G.

1810.

54.—ZELTER TO GOETHE.

Berlin, 17th February, 1810.

.... It is our custom to print the words of songs, which we sing on high days and holidays at the *Liedertafel*. As I look upon your song* as our property, I shall allow it to be printed with the rest, unless you expressly forbid it; please therefore, if you do not wish it, let me know in the course of the month. . . . .

Z.

55.—GOETHE TO ZELTER.

Weimar, 6th March, 1810.

YOUR music to *Johanna Sebus* I have, to be sure, only heard as yet imperfectly, but sufficiently for me to assure you, that I think it quite excellent. I should have to be very discursive, were I to try and tell you of everything that flitted through my mind on this occasion. Only one thing I will say,—that you have made very important use of something for which I have no name, but which is called imitation, painting, and I know not what besides, —something which becomes very defective in others, and degenerates into incongruity.

It is a kind of symbolism for the ear, whereby the subject, in so far as it is in motion, or not in motion, is neither imitated nor painted, but produced in the imagination, in a way, that is quite peculiar, and impossible to grasp, inasmuch as the thing described and the describer appear to stand in scarcely any sort of relation to one another.

It is a matter of course that in music, thunder can roll, and waves roar quite naturally. But it is surprising, how

---

* The song is now called *Rechenschaft*, but see the following letter.

well you have expressed the negation, *Kein Damm, Kein Feld*, by a disjointed, interrupted execution, as also the anticipation of delight before the passage, *doch Suschen's Bild*. Do not let me ramble on, as I should have to speak of the whole, as well as the details. I hope soon to hear it again and again, and to enjoy it thoroughly, which is better than reflection and criticism. Your corrections arrived safely, and have been inserted.

As for the song, it might be called *Duty and Pleasure*, (*Pflicht und Frohsinn*.) Go on as you are, and as often as it is sung, let some genial fellow insert a new verse, or sing it, instead of some other one. I have not yet heard the melody; latterly, I have really had too much stress put upon me, from all quarters.

Now good-bye, and let me have Voss's *Trommellied*, for Eberwein did not bring it with him. Our little Society gave a musical entertainment the other day, in the Theatre, when your *In Flammen nahet Gott*, and the *Gunst des Augenblicks*, and other things, were most effective.

G.

56.—Zelter to Goethe.

Berlin, 4th April, 1810.

For some weeks past, I have not been up to my usual mark; perhaps it was the withering March wind, or some other outside influence, that made me, not exactly ill, but low, and out of spirits. I eat without relish, and instead of feeling glad to be alive, am rather the reverse.

So yesterday afternoon I took no wine, as I did not want it, and went to sleep after dinner on the sofa. Meantime my sensible letter-carrier laid your blue envelope on my breast, and I joyfully recognized it on awaking. Before I broke the seal, I called for a glass of wine, that I might be as jolly as possible. As my daughter was pouring it out, I broke open the letter, and shouted, "*Ergo bibamus!*" The child started, so that she let the bottle fall; I caught it up, —once more I was bright and cheery, and the wine, from gratitude for its salvation probably, did its part.

That the first impression might not ebb away, I sent for pen and ink, so as to set your poem to music there and then. Looking at the clock, I found it was time to go to the *Singakademie*, after which, to-day, there was a meeting of the *Liedertafel*. Forty members were present. I read the poem aloud; at the end of each strophe, they one and all shouted of their own accord in unison, as though in a double chorus, "*Bibamus!*" laying such portentous stress on the long vowel, that the floors rang again, and the vault of the great hall seemed to shake. This gave me the melody at once, and here you have it, just as it composed itself; if it is the right thing, I claim no part in it, it is all yours, and yours alone. . . . .

Z.

57.—GOETHE TO ZELTER.

Weimar, 18th November, 1810.

. . . . AT the end of this week, we are to hear Paer's* *Achilles* in Italian; Brizzi has arrived, and will act the hero for us. Our other singers are either practising their Italian, or beginning to learn the language; come what may, we shall have a pretty performance. . . . .

In conclusion, let me tell you of a curious enterprise we have in prospect, that is, a performance of *Faust*, in his present condition, as far as it is practicable. Perhaps you could help us with some music, more especially for the Easter Song and the Slumber Song, *Schwindet ihr dunklen Wölbungen droben*. . . . .

GOETHE.

* Ferdinando Paer, an Italian composer, and one of the leading representatives of the Italian operatic school, at the close of the last century. He was at one time Maître-de-chapelle to Napoleon, whom he had accompanied to Warsaw and Posen in 1806. The subject of one of his operas, *Eleanora, ossia l'Amore Conjugale*, was the same as that of Beethoven's *Fidelio*.

1811.

58.—GOETHE TO ZELTER.

Weimar, 28th February, 1811.

I HAVE read of the illustrious Oldenburg, first Secretary of the London Society, that he never opens a letter, till he has placed pen, ink, and paper before him, but thereupon he writes his answer, immediately after the first reading. And thus, it seems, he gets through an immense amount of correspondence in comfort. Could I have imitated this virtue, fewer people would have had to complain of my silence. But now the arrival of your dear letter, recalling all the wealth of our summer life, excites in me such a desire to answer it, that I address these lines to you, if not indeed at the first reading, at all events, on my awakening, the morning after.

First then, I pity you for being obliged to write, when you ought to be doing and working. But business-matters, all the world over, and especially with you, have long been transacted on paper, and business-people do not reflect that acts, (derived from the Latin *actu*,) mean as much as something *done*, and that therefore nothing should be stitched up in them, which we are only about to do, or wish to do. If I still amuse myself sometimes by stitching together a *fasciculus*, it is only when I am occupied with a thing that is hastening to its end.

I thought I could prophesy, that the good *Pandora* would linger a little, when she got home again. The life in Töplitz was much too favourable for this task, and your thoughts were so continuously and thoroughly occupied with it, that an interruption must necessarily cause a standstill also. But do not be disheartened; so much has already been done to it, that the rest will doubtless come of itself in good time.

I cannot quarrel with you, for declining to compose the music to *Faust*. My proposal was rather frivolous, like the undertaking itself. So this too may be set aside for yet another year, for the trouble I have had in managing *The Constant Prince*, has pretty well exhausted the zest, which one must bring to such things. This piece has certainly turned out well, beyond all expectation, and has given myself and others much pleasure. It means a good deal, to have conjured up a work, nearly two centuries old, one written for quite another latitude, for a race of perfectly different manners, religion, and culture, so that it should appear fresh and new to a spectator. For nowhere is the antiquated, or that which does not speak to one directly, more quickly felt, than on the stage.

As for my works, you shall certainly have the thirteenth volume, both in vellum and in the ordinary binding. You have done well, in throwing a sprat to catch a salmon. Another copy will soon be found for you.

It is very good of you, not to have neglected my *Farbenlehre*; taken in small doses, it will have a very good effect. I know very well, that my way of treating the subject, natural as it is, is very different from the usual method, and I cannot expect, that everyone should immediately recognize and adopt its advantages. Mathematicians are foolish people, and so far from possessing even a notion of the main point, that one has to be indulgent to their conceit. I am very curious to see, who will be the first to understand the thing, and behave honestly about it: for they are not all wooden-headed, nor all maliciously inclined. Moreover, I have, in this instance, become more and more conscious of the fact, which I had quietly recognized long ago, that the training given to the mind by mathematics is extremely one-sided and limited. Voltaire even ventures to say somewhere, "*J'ai toujours remarqué que la Géométrie laisse l'esprit où elle le trouve.*" Franklin also has a peculiar aversion to mathematicians, and expresses this plainly and clearly, in reference to social intercourse, when he speaks of their spirit of littleness and contradiction, as being intolerable.

As regards the actual Newtonians, they are like the old Prussians, in October, 1806. They thought they might yet win by tactics, although they had long been vanquished by strategy. When once their eyes are opened, they will be surprised to see, that I have already been to Naumburg and Leipzig, while they are still rummaging about, in the vicinity of Weimar and Blankenhayn. That battle was lost beforehand, and it is the same here too. That doctrine is already extinguished, though these gentlemen still think they may despise their adversary. Pardon my big way of talking; I am as little ashamed of it, as those gentlemen are of their littleness.

I have been most strangely misconstrued by Kügelgen,* as by many others. I thought I spoke most kindly to him; for the picture and the frame really turned out all that could be desired, and now the good man takes offence at an outward form of politeness, which, after all, we certainly ought not to neglect, as many people feel hurt, if it is not used. People have often been annoyed with me, for a certain heedlessness in these things, and now I am vexing good men by my formality. Never lay aside any old fault, dear friend, for either you will fall into some new one, or your new virtue will be regarded as a fault; and take up what position you please, you will never satisfy yourself, or other people. However, I am glad to know this, for I should like to be on friendly terms with this excellent man.

As for the antique bull,† I propose that you should pack it carefully, in a strong box, and send it to me for inspection. There were many replicas of such things in old times, and the copies differ very much in value. Herr Friedländer, (to whom my kindest regards,) might tell me at the same time about his collections, and how one could serve him in return, for it would be difficult to give a good bronze in exchange, as there are hardly any duplicates of such things, and such as do exist, become doubly interesting, on account of their resemblance or non-resemblance. In the meantime, I could offer him this. I have a very fine collection of medals, the greater part in bronze, dating from the middle of the fifteenth century, up to the present day. It was made, chiefly in order to bring before friends and connoisseurs, the course pursued in Plastic

* The painter, Kügelgen, had complained to Zelter, of Goethe's coldness, in addressing him as *Hochwohlgeborner Herr.*
† The property of David Friedländer, a Jewish friend of Zelter's.

Art, the reflex of which can always be traced in medals. Now, I have some beautiful and important duplicates of these, so that I probably could arrange and hand over an instructive series. Any amateur, not yet in possession of anything of the kind, would thus obtain a good foundation, and have sufficient inducement to proceed further. A collection of this kind would likewise offer a good opportunity for very interesting observations, as in the case of a series of Greek and Roman coins; nay, more—it would complete the idea, which these give us, and would enable us to trace it up to more modern times. Let me add, that the bull must be very perfect, if I am not to be the loser by the exchange proposed. Let me hear some further particulars.

As I have plenty more room in my letter, I will add, that I have been highly gratified lately by a present from the Empress of Austria, of a handsome gold snuff-box, with a wreath of brilliants in the centre, on which stands the name *Louise* in full. I know you will be interested in this, as so unexpected and inspiriting a piece of luck is no every-day occurrence. Now farewell, dear Sun, and continue to give forth warmth and light.*

G.

SICILIAN SONG.

Ye black and roguish eyes,
 If ye command,
Each house in ruins lies,
 No town can stand.
And shall my bosom's chain,—
 This plaster wall,—
To think one moment, deign,—
 Shall it not fall?

FINNISH SONG.

If the loved one, the well-known one,
Should return as he departed,
On his lips would ring my kisses,
Though the wolf's blood might have dyed them;
And a hearty grasp I'd give him,
Though his finger-ends were serpents.

---

* In this letter are enclosed three songs, Sicilian, Finnish, and Swiss, copied by F. W. Riemer.

Wind! Oh, if thou hadst but reason,
Word for word in turns thou'dst carry,
E'en though some perchance might perish
'Tween two lovers so far distant.

All choice morsels I'd dispense with,
Table-flesh of priests neglect too,
Sooner than renounce my lover,
Whom, in Summer having vanquish'd,
I in Winter tam'd still longer.

Swiss Song.

Up in th' mountain
I was a-sitting,
With the bird there
As my guest,
Blithely singing,
Blithely springing,
And building
His nest.

In the garden
I was a-standing,
And the bee there
Saw as well,
Buzzing, humming,
Going, coming,
And building
His cell.

O'er the meadow
I was a-going,
And there saw the
Butterflies,
Sipping, dancing,
Flying, glancing,
And charming
The eyes.

And then came my
Dear Hansel,
And I show'd them
With glee,
Sipping, quaffing,
And he, laughing,
Sweet kisses
Gave me.

(E. A. BOWRING.)

59.—ZELTER TO GOETHE.

Undated.

.... At last I too have seen and heard the newly-crowned Parisian Opera, *Die Vestalin*.* It is a downright good joke, for the gentlemen of the Paris Conservatoire, who could not make up their minds, to which of two excellent people they should award the prize, because they really have no critical standard, and trilling and chirping is all they are up to, are forced to see the Emperor putting his finger into the pie, and giving a prize to a young artist, who, when he is once past twenty-five, will never do anything much. The libretto is loosely enough constructed, for an Opera, and there is room for music. Herr Spontini has used it like a boy, whose hands have just been set free from swaddling-bands for the first time, and he lays about him with both fists, so violently, that the pieces fly about one's ears.

Bettina † wanted to be married last Sunday week. But both parties had forgotten a few trifles, *e.g.* the calling of the banns, the hiring of lodgings, and similar preparations. I fancy, therefore, the affair must remain *in statu quo*, until after Lent.

Z.

60.—GOETHE TO ZELTER.

Weimar, 18th March, 1811.

A THOUSAND thanks, my dear Friend, for your suggestion, that that Bull should be sent off to me. It has latterly stimulated me and my circle to new thoughts on Art, and I only wish I could sum them all up again with you. If Herr Friedländer tells you what I wrote to him, you will see that my first suspicion, in calling this creature

---

* This famous Opera, finished by Spontini in 1805, long remained a favourite with the Parisians, having, by the year 1824, reached its two hundredth performance. Napoleon had founded a prize, to be given every ten years, for the most successful Opera, written within that period. This was the prize won by Spontini.

† Bettina married the Baron von Arnim.

of Art a Tragelaph (Goat-Stag) of ancient and modern times, has been confirmed. I should have had to be much more prolix, had I wished to go to the root of the matter, and to say everything that forces itself into consideration in this instance. A small box of interesting bronze medals has been sent to Herr Friedländer, and, as his son is a collector and a connoisseur, I hope it will be favourably received.

I am very sorry for Herr Weiss' own sake, that he has taken to storming against my *Farbenlehre;* impotent hate is the most horrible of feelings, for, properly speaking, we should hate no one whom we cannot annihilate. But as I am—above all things—fond of genetic observations, I will explain to you, whence this worthy man's indignation has really arisen. See my *Farbenlehre*, I. Polem. § 422. I will here quote the passage, for the sake of convenience:—

"We anticipate here an observation, which properly belongs to the history of the *Farbenlehre*. Haüy, in his manual on Physics, repeats the above assertion, with Newton's decisive words; but the German translator is compelled to add in a note, ' I shall take occasion to say further on, to which kinds of light of the Colour-spectrum, as tested by my own experiments, this actually applies, and to which it does not.' This then, on the absolute assertion of which the correctness of the Newtonian theory alone depends, holds good, and does not hold good. Haüy expresses unconditionally the Newtonian theory, and accordingly, in the lectures of the Lycées, it is unconditionally impressed upon the mind of every young Frenchman. The German must come forward with conditions, and yet the theory, which is at once destroyed through conditions, continues to be the one that holds good; it is printed, translated, and the public, for the thousandth time, has to pay for these myths."

Now the translator is, in fact, Herr Weiss himself, whom I did not mention by name in the quoted passage, because I knew how to value him as a man, who spared himself no trouble, and inspired good hopes, and whose books I had been able to make good use of. I am, as I said before, sorry for him; for when anyone who devotes himself to the study of Nature, and is still vigorous mentally, refuses to acknowledge, what I have more or less achieved in my

1811.] TO ZELTER. 81

Farbenlehre, he will find, nevertheless, that it will often come home to him, and he does not gain by it morally; he will be standing in his own light, and spite of this, he will, in the end, be obliged—for his own purposes—to make use of what he learns from me, and to disavow the source, from whence he got it. However, such tergiversations and malversations are met with so frequently in the history of the sciences, that it would create astonishment, if they did not repeat themselves in our own times.

May you succeed in every way, in all you do, and in all you write! I see, as in a picture, how you fare in your *Singakademie*. Let anyone but educate a certain number of pupils, he will thereby be educating almost as many adversaries. Every genuine artist must be looked upon, as one who is guarding something that is acknowledged to be sacred, which it is his wish to propagate with earnestness and care. But every century, in its own way, tends towards what is secular, striving to make what is sacred, common, what is difficult, easy, what is serious, amusing: and nothing could be said against this, were it not for the fact, that earnestness and humour are thereby utterly destroyed. So much for to-day! Let me often hear from you. *Johanna Sebus* is often enough asked for, at our musical gatherings on a Sunday, and goes charmingly; I might almost hope that you yourself would be satisfied. We have not yet had it performed with instruments. Eberwein is doing admirably; I wish he could have the good fortune, to enjoy another six months of your society and teaching. Our *Capellmeister*, Müller, keeps his orchestra and chorus, as well as the solo singers, capitally together, and we certainly have been well off, in the way of musical enjoyment this winter. And herewith, from my heart, farewell! I am busy in various ways, and am quietly getting rid of things, so that I may soon be able to set out again on my summer tour.

G.

ENCLOSURE.

GOETHE TO HERR DAVID FRIEDLÄNDER.

Weimar, 8th March, 1811.

THE Bull you so kindly sent me, has arrived safely, and I am much obliged to you for it. Whilst offering you

G

my best thanks, I will, at the same time, tell you what I think about this work of art.

Towards the end of the sixteenth century, a skilful worker in bronze may have come into the possession of the fragment of an antique bull, and, moreover, of the uninjured fore-part of the same; this is the more likely, as figures of this kind were cast in two parts, and soldered together in the middle. The artist may have perceived the value and dignity of this fragment,—modelled it accordingly, and restored the hinder part, after the fashion of his own art. Over this renovated model, he then made the necessary form, cast the entire figure, and worked it out afresh. Hence the discordance of the parts, which strikes one, on looking at this creature. The fore-part has the imposing, tasteful, and intellectual quality of ancient art; the hinder part, on the other hand, has certain excellencies belonging to more modern times, e.g. something natural and elaborate in the parts; but the actual meaning of the antique has not been grasped, either as regards the position, or movement of the limbs, and so the result is a work with a double meaning, which only interests us rightly for the first time, when it has been divided into two parts, as I have divided it. But I should not have been able to maintain this distinctly, were it not, that I myself already possess a bull of the same size, which is a genuine antique; this has enabled me to make the comparison. This, moreover, is the very reason, why this new specimen is so valuable to me, for of course, in such cases, it is mainly a question of one's insight and judgment, one's knowledge of the epochs in Art, and ability to distinguish periods of time.

So I packed up my best duplicates at once, and am sending them with this, carefully secured, in the hope that the little box will arrive safely. I do not add any catalogue, as your son, who is a connoisseur, and the possessor of so considerable a collection, and who moreover has every other means at his command, will easily be able to criticise and arrange the things I have forwarded. There is little necessity for me to add anything about their value. I only hope, that the collection may be welcome, if not as a whole, at all events in part. I sometimes receive a contribution to my art treasures, from Rome, and should I find any duplicates among these, I will not fail to let you know.

Last year's programme to the *A. L. Z.* was written by our great connoisseur, Herr Hofrath Meyer; it was to have been continued this year, but has not been printed yet. Meanwhile, I enclose a proof impression of the plate, which was to have accompanied the continuation. I have in my possession all the medals given in the engraving, and I reckon them among my treasures. May I ask you to let me have a few lines, announcing the safe arrival of the little box?—while wishing to hear that it has been kindly received, I would fain hope, that the connection formed between us may be continued in future. With every good wish for your welfare, and commending myself to your kind remembrance,

GOETHE.

61.—GOETHE TO ZELTER.

Carlsbad, 26th June, 1811.

.... I TRUST you may in some way be rewarded, for what you are doing for *Pandora*. Could I have foreseen your interest in this work, I should have treated the subject differently, and tried to free it from what is at present difficult of fusion with music and representation. But now it cannot be otherwise. Go on with it, as is most easy to you, and I will see if I can manage to complete the Second Part.* I have planned and sketched out everything, but the figures themselves have got rather far away from me, and I am even somewhat astonished at their Titanic shapes, when, (as it chanced, yesterday,) I happen to read aloud something out of it.

May all harmonious spirits attend you on your journey to Silesia, and may your active perseverance be rewarded by adequate results!—for truly, when one reflects how little the World has responded to your fair and noble achievements, one may well say, that the response has been inadequate.

---

* The Second Part was never written; Goethe found that he had planned the First on too large a scale for continuation. Frau von Levezow was the prototype of Pandora.

You certainly will not find me here on your proposed homeward journey through Bohemia. The last four, nay, the last five months of the year, promise to be very lively for Weimar, and happy too, please God! In August, we expect Her Highness's confinement, in September, Iffland's return, and in October, Brizzi. Alas! in all such cases I seem to myself like a double Hermes, one mask of which resembles Prometheus, neither of which—because of the eternal fore and after—can at the moment summon up a smile.

Carlsbad is just now lively enough; it has looked quite different to me this time. As my wife was here and had her own carriage, I have got further out into the open country than in the last few years, and have taken fresh pleasure in the neighbourhood, and what is to be found there, because I have been able to wander through it with new companions, who were justly astonished and delighted with a great deal that they saw.

Himmel has been here for some days, and, though suffering, is still the same as of old, cheerful and sympathetic, and improving even the roughest instruments by his playing. I have all along heard and seen too little of him, and we do not meet very often, owing to his gay way of life; yet it has occurred to me latterly, whether I might not be able to edit the maxims, convictions, impulses, or whatever you like to call them, by which he steers in his musical settings of lyric poems, or by which he is guided. This does not seem to me impossible, and I think I am fairly on the way; still I have too many deficiencies to be able to get quit of my task so easily. If, at your leisure, you will enlighten me on this point, you would be doing me a kindness. Now farewell, and should you care to let me have a word, before you leave Berlin, send it direct to Weimar.

G.

1812.

62.—GOETHE TO ZELTER.
Weimar, 8th April, 1812.

.... As the work of my little musical Institute has been broken in upon this winter,* I have not had so much pleasant interchange of thought with you as usual. I have been very busy at the Theatre, and have brought out upon the stage a concentrated *Romeo*.† You will probably soon see the play in Berlin; take the opportunity of letting me hear what you think of it, what others think of it, and how it was acted. I like so much to have your frank reports and criticisms.

I have been working at the second volume of my biographical effort,‡ in thought and memory, much more than on paper; if I come to Carlsbad, I dare say it will get on quicker. The contents of this volume are not over favourable; we must first cross a valley, before we regain a favourable and cheerful height; meanwhile, let us see how we can stroll through it with our friends, pleasantly and profitably.

Two friends, Herr von Einsiedel and Riemer, § have conferred a benefit on the Theatre, by translating and remodelling Calderon's play, *Life's a Dream*. Our actors devoted much industry and care to the performance, as I—with the technical spirits of the Theatre—did to the arrangement; so we have got hold of a good play, which will last.

* Owing to the intrigues of Caroline Jagemann, the actress.
† Goethe's version of this play, first acted at Weimar, January 31st, 1812, kept the stage in Berlin, up to our own time, though it was severely criticised at first.
‡ *Dichtung und Wahrheit.*
§ Court-page and ultimately chamberlain to the Duchess Amalia. He was something of a poet and musician, was known everywhere as *L'Ami* Riemer, and entered Goethe's house, as tutor to his son, having previously served the Humboldt family in that capacity; he remained with Goethe as secretary and companion.

Our friend Riemer was this Easter appointed Professor at the Gymnasium here; and, sorry as I am to lose him, I am glad to know that he is active, and, moreover, in a way suited to his powers and talents. Nay, he is up to much more than is here demanded of him, so he cannot but feel at home in his business. . . .

G.

63.—ZELTER TO GOETHE.

Berlin, 14th April, 1812.

As regards your concentrated *Romeo*, I suppose you will have seen from the newspapers, the hostile criticisms of certain blatant critics. I understand too little about the matter, to determine accurately the rights and wrongs of it. Many of our learned patrons would be only too glad to pose, as the gossips, or University-chums of genius, and then, before we know where we are, back comes Schröder's *Hamlet*, and no one so much as grumbles. On the other hand, there are people who insist on getting over everything, so long as *you* have had a hand in it, and, so I have been revelling once more in the vision of true passion, which has none of the taint of virtue, so-called. And that is my barometer, or measuring-rod, for taking in the whole crew at a glance.

I am heart and soul one of those, who are averse to losing a single word of Shakespeare; the parts omitted often belong to my favourite passages,—but I am also satisfied with a claw of him. More than that, I care little for the reconciliation of the Capulets and the Montagues, after what has gone before, and only in so far as Shakespeare says it with his own words. From a moral point of view, everyone is bright enough to know, what must naturally arise out of such a family feud; so in my judgment, you were perfectly right in finishing the play, where it really ends.* The new friendship is either a matter of course, or follows, because the old people would like to die in peace. . . . . The way the poet is blamed, and Mlle.

* In Goethe's version, the play ends with a short soliloquy of the Friar after Juliet's death.

Maas extolled in our newspaper, can be no enigma to you, as you know both. For this artist, (as we call such an one here,) is still just what she always was—a good *reservoir*. She speaks her part glibly, one may say, inoffensively, and the spectator can make his Juliet for himself. . . . .

ZELTER.

64.—GOETHE TO ZELTER.

Weimar, 17th April, 1812.

. . . . I HAVE made up my mind to send you a little thing I wrote last year,* so that we may have a new subject for regular discussion.

I wrote this Cantata, or Scena, if you prefer to call it so, for Prince Friedrich von Gotha, who wanted something of the kind, to show off his good and well-trained tenor voice.

Capellmeister Winter of Munich has set it to music very successfully, with ability, taste, and fluency, so that the Prince's talent is displayed in its best light. He is now however keeping the score in his own hands, for which I do not blame him. But why should I not show the poem to you, and thus throw some new life into our communications? Farewell, and continue to love me!

G.

65.—ZELTER TO GOETHE.

Berlin, 25th April, 1812.

. . . . YOUR *Rinaldo* will be no easy matter, if the full meaning hidden in it is to be brought out,—its enchanting lightness, grace, and charming smoothness! He who is not too old should take a lesson from the Italian School, but in some happy hour, we will try our hand at it. . . . .

A little time ago, I found in Voltaire's works, (the Gotha edition of 1785,) a musical Opera, *Samson*, which Rameau actually set to music, though it has never yet been brought out. I rather liked Voltaire's treatment, and the subject,

* *Rinaldo.*

assuming some necessary alterations, would be thoroughly suitable for an Opera.

An Opera, in my judgment, should not have more than three Acts; two long and one short, or better still, one long, between two short Acts. Here is my plan. . . . .

Act I. Choruses of Israelites lament their defeat, but encouraged by Samson, conquer the Philistines.

Act II. Triumphal entry of the Israelites. Reconciliation of Samson with Delilah. Recognition of the son, (supposed to have been born to Samson and Delilah.) Treachery practised on Samson.

Act III. Imprisonment and death of Samson, the well-known story; very brilliant.

Now what do you say to this? Would there not be field enough there, for treatment and dramatic action? I thought you might set to, and anyhow rectify this plan; at all events I will have the verses made for me here. . . . .

ZELTER.

66.—GOETHE TO ZELTER.

Carlsbad, 19th May, 1812.

YOUR dear letter of the 8th of May finds me in Carlsbad on the 18th, so I intend to send you a reply at once, as I think you will read it within ten days.

Your kind words about *Rinaldo* are not only very pleasant to me, but will, I hope, prove fruitful, for they have raised me to the consciousness of that, which by Nature and inclination, I have done, and should like to do, particularly for music on the stage. When you say—"Everything is freely and lightly hinted; the words are not encroaching, and the musician has actually to do with the subject itself"—this is giving me the greatest praise I could wish for; for in my opinion, a poet ought to draw his sketch, upon a very widely-woven canvas, in order that the musician may have ample space for working out his embroidery with greater freedom, and with coarse or fine threads, as he thinks fit. The libretto for an Opera should be a cartoon, not a finished picture. This is certainly our opinion, but most of our good Germans are completely wanting in any idea of these things; yet hundreds would fain try their hand at it. How great, on the contrary, is our admiration of many of the Italian works, where poets, composers, singers, and stage decorators, can all agree about a certain adequate *technique*. One new German Opera after another fails for want of appropriate words, and the good Viennese, who do not in the least know where the shoe pinches, offer a hundred ducats for the best Opera, which anyone in Germany may produce, whereas they might double the amount at the right smithy, and thereby themselves be the gainers.

The matter is, in fact, more difficult than people suppose; one would have to spend a cheerful existence on the spot itself, among all those who are contributing to the performance, and then, year after year, one ought to produce something new. One thing would lead to another, and perfection might spring, even from a failure.

Just now I should have no faith in *Samson*; it is one of the most monstrous of the old myths. A perfectly bestial passion of a supernaturally strong, divinely-gifted hero for the most accursed wretch, that the earth has ever seen,— the mad desire, that ever leads him back to her, though, owing to repeated acts of treachery, he is each time conscious of his danger—this lustfulness, which itself springs from the danger—the mighty conception one must form of the overweening *savoir faire* of this gigantic woman, who is capable of fettering such a bull! On looking at all this, dear friend, it will at once become manifest to you, that we should have to annihilate it, if only to get at names in accordance with the proprieties of our time and stage. It would be much more advisable at once to choose a subject with fewer specific difficulties, if not indeed, one that would of itself float upon the element of the day. Look at the *Schweizerfamilie*,* and things of that stamp.

I must mention one other consideration. Subjects from the Old Testament produce a very strange effect here; this was brought before my notice, when Robert's *Jephtha*, and Alfieri's *Saul* were given. They do not excite any disfavour, but still it is not favour; not disinclination, but uninclination.

* An Opera by Winter.

Those myths, truly grand as they are, present a respectable appearance in the solemn distance, and our youthful devotion remains attached to them. But when these heroes step forward into the present, it occurs to us, that they are Jews, and we feel a contrast between the ancestors and the descendants, which confuses and jars upon us. This is the way I explain it to myself hurriedly, whilst closely watching the effect of both pieces. This last consideration would be set aside, were the myths transferred to other nations. But other difficulties would then arise; I shall think further about this.

In conclusion, I must beg of you not to withhold those compositions, and at the same time, for our old love's sake, to give our correspondence new life.

And pray, no such long pause again!

G.

67.—GOETHE TO ZELTER.

Carlsbad, 2nd September, 1812.

.... I MADE Beethoven's acquaintance in Töplitz. His talent astounded me; but unfortunately, his natural temperament is wholly uncontrolled, and although, indeed, not at all wrong in thinking the world detestable, still, in so doing, he does not make it pleasanter, either for himself or for others. However, he is greatly to be excused, and much to be pitied, for he is losing his hearing, which perhaps affects the musical, less than the social part of his being. As it is, he is laconic by nature, and is now becoming doubly so through this defect. And now a hearty farewell!

G.

68.—ZELTER TO GOETHE.

Berlin, 13th September, 1812.

.... JUST now Milder-Hauptmann* is with us. I have heard her in Gluck's *Iphigenia*, the *Schweizerfamilie*,

---

* Pauline Anna Milder-Hauptmann, a famous singer, for whom the part of Fidelio was written. Thayer relates the hard fights she had with the master, about some passages in the Adagio of the great Scena in E major, described by her, as "ugly, unvocal, and inimical to her and the *Zauberflöte*, in which she sings the part of Tamino. The voice, figure, and style of this young artist are so free, powerful, and graceful, especially in the part of Emelina, that we have seen nothing like it for a long time here. They blame her vocalization, as inartistic, and that kind of thing, but I find much to praise, *e.g.* warmth, truth, solid and equal singing, and a kind of Swiss sturdiness, most naïvely expressed; anyhow, I have never seen passions represented so chastely and effectively. . . . .

Z.

69.—ZELTER TO GOETHE.

Berlin, 14th September, 1812.

. . . . We have lost our very clever Italian Capellmeister, Righini,* who died at his native place, Bologna, on the 19th of August. He was to us much what Salieri was to Vienna; fresher than Salieri perhaps, but pretty equal in breadth and height. . . . .

What you say of Beethoven is quite natural; I too admire him with awe. His own works seem to cause him a secret shudder—a feeling which, in the new culture, is set aside much too lightly. His works seem to me like children, whose father might be a woman, or whose mother, a man. The last work of his that I became acquainted with, (*Christus am Oelberge,*) seems to me an unchaste thing, the ground and aim of which is an eternal death. The musical critics, who seem to be more at home in anything, than in what is natural and individual, have poured themselves out in the oddest fashion, in praise and blame of this composer. I know musical people, who formerly, on hearing his works, were alarmed, nay, indignant, and are now seized with a

organ." (See Thayer's *Life of Beethoven*, vol. ii. p. 290, and the article "Milder-Hauptmann," in Sir G. Grove's *Dictionary of Music and Musicians*.) Her splendid, but unwieldy voice was heard to great advantage in the leading parts of Gluck's classical Operas. Haydn once said to her, "Dear child, you have a voice like a house." Goethe wrote some lines in her honour, after hearing her in *Iphigenia in Tauris*, presenting her at the same time with a copy of his own drama on the same subject.

* Vincenzo Righini, a second-class composer. One of his twenty Operas, *Il Convitato di Pietra, ossia Il Dissoluto*, was the forerunner of Mozart's *Don Giovanni*, which came out ten years afterwards.

passion for them, like the devotees of Grecian love. How thoroughly one can enjoy them, is conceivable, and what may come of it, you have shown clearly enough in the *Wahlverwandtschaften*. . . . .

Z.

70.—GOETHE TO ZELTER.
Weimar, 3rd November, 1812.

YOUR letter, my beloved Friend, announcing the great misfortune * which has befallen your house, has greatly afflicted—nay, bowed me down, for it came to me, when I was in the midst of very serious meditations on life, and it was only through you yourself, that I was enabled to rise again. On the black touchstone of death, you have proved yourself genuine, refined gold. How glorious a character appears, when it is penetrated with mind and soul, and how beautiful must that talent be, which rests on such a basis! As to the deed or misdeed itself, I can say nothing. When the *tædium vitæ* seizes a man, he is only to be pitied, not blamed. That all the symptoms of this strange disease, as natural as it is unnatural, at one time raged furiously through my own innermost being, no one who reads *Werther* will probably doubt. I know full well what resolutions and efforts it cost me in those days, to escape from the waves of death; just as with difficulty I saved myself, to recover painfully, from many a later shipwreck. And so it fares with all sailors' and fishermens' stories. After the storm at night, the shore is reached again, the drenched man dries himself, and the following morning, when the glorious sun once more breaks forth over the glittering waves, "the sea has once more an appetite for figs." †

* The suicide of Zelter's son, minutely described in a previous letter. Here, for the first time, Goethe uses the familiar *Du*, instead of the formal *Sie;* not even Schiller was ever thus addressed by him.

† A play upon the Greek proverb, the origin of which is explained by Zenobius, *Prov rb.*, cent. v. 51 :—

'Ο Σικελὸς τὴν θάλασσαν.
Σικελὸς, φασὶν, ἔμπορος σῦκα ἄγων
ἰναμάγησεν· εἶτα ἐπὶ πέτρας καθήμενος,
καὶ ὁρῶν τὴν θάλασσαν ἐν γαλήνῃ
ἔφη, Οἶδα ὃ θέλει· σῦκα θέλει.

When one sees how the world in general, and the young world in particular, is not only given over to its lusts and passions, but how, at the same time, what is nobler and better in it is abused and perverted by the serious follies of the time, so that everything which should have led to its blessedness, becomes its curse, not taking into account the inexpressible pressure from without, one is not astonished at the misdeeds, by which man rages against himself and others. I could trust myself to write a new *Werther*, which would make the nation's hair stand more on end than the first one. Let me add one other remark. Most young persons, conscious of some merit in themselves, make more demand upon themselves than is fair. To this, however, they are urged and driven, by their gigantic surroundings. I know half-a-dozen such persons, who are certainly being ruined and whom it would be impossible to help, even if one could enlighten them as to their real advantages. No one easily arrives at the conclusion, that reason, and a brave will are given us, that we may not only hold back from evil, but also from the extreme of good.

Now let us pass on to other things in your letters, which have done me good, and first of all, accept my thanks for your remarks on the pages of my biography. I had already, in a general way, heard many kind and friendly things said about them; you are the first and only one, who has entered into the matter itself. I am glad that the description of my father produced a favourable effect upon you. I will not deny, that I am heartily tired of these German *patres familiarium*, these *Lorenz Starks*,* or whatever they are called, who yield with gloomy humour to their Philistine natures, and who, by their uncertainty, obstruct and destroy the desires prompted by their good nature, and the happiness of those around them. In the next two volumes my father's portrait will be still further developed; if—on his part, as well as on the son's—one grain of conscious understanding had entered into that estimable family relationship, much might have been spared to both. This however

---

* *Lorenz Stark* is the title of a novel by J. J. Engel (1741-1802). It was first published in *Die Horen*. The hero is a strict, somewhat pedantic father.

was not to be, and in fact, it does not seem to belong to this world. The best of plans for the journey is destroyed by a silly mischance, and one never goes further, than when one does not know whither one is going.

Pray, be kind enough to continue your remarks: for as— in accordance with the requirements of the representation— I go slowly, and keep a great deal *in petto,*—(at which many readers are already getting impatient, who would, I suppose, be very glad to have the whole meal—from beginning to end—served up to them, boiled and roast at one sitting, that the following day they might be entertained at some other refreshment-stall, or eating-house, better or worse as their luck might be,) as I therefore, as aforesaid, keep behind the hill. so as to advance, at the right moment, with my lancers and cavalry; it is exceedingly interesting to me, to hear what you—as an experienced campaigner— notice in the advanced guard.

I have not yet read any reviews of this little work; this I intend doing, once for all, when the next two volumes are out. For many years past, I have observed, that those, whose duty and wish it is, to speak about me in public, whether well or ill disposed towards me, seem to feel themselves in a painful situation; at all events, I have scarcely met with a reviewer, who has not, in some passage, assumed the famous look of Vespasian,* and presented a *faciem durum.*

If some day or other, you could send me *Rinaldo* unawares, it would be a grand thing. I have no connection with music, except through you, for which reason, let me thank you heartily for the *Invocavit* and the *Three Kings,* though I have as yet only feasted upon them with my eyes.

We live here, spending quite disproportionate sums on music, and yet we are really quite songless and soundless. The Opera, with its old stock pieces, and the novelties that are dished up, and slowly enough produced for a small Theatre, cannot be a compensation to anyone. Meanwhile, I rejoice that both Court and Town are made to believe, that there is some kind of enjoyment to be had. The inhabitant of a great city must be deemed fortunate in this respect;

---

* See Suetonius' *Life of Vespasian,* chapter xxii.

1812.]

for after all, it attracts many remarkable foreign artists. I should indeed have liked to hear Madame Milder.

You aimed a good shot at Alfieri; he is more remarkable than enjoyable. His plays are explained by his life. He torments readers and listeners, as he tormented himself as an author. His disposition was out and out that of a Count, *i.e.* aristocratic to the core. He hated tyrants, because he was conscious of a tyrannical vein in himself; and Fate had conferred a very appropriate affliction upon him, in punishing him tolerably well, at the hands of the *Sans-culottes*. This same aristocratic and courtly nature in him becomes very amusing at the end, when he cannot find any better way of rewarding himself for his merits, than by getting an Order made for himself. Could he show more clearly, how incarnate these forms were in him?

In the same way, I cannot but agree with what you say about Rousseau's *Pygmalion*. This work is certainly of the monstrous order, and extremely remarkable, as a symptom of the main disease of those days, when State and morals, Art and talent, together with a nameless article, which however was called Nature, had to be stirred, nay, were actually stirred and whipped up into a kind of pap. This operation, my next volume will, I hope, bring into view; for was I not myself seized by the epidemic, and was it not beneficently guilty of the development of my being, which is now inconceivable to me in any other way?

And now I have still to reply to your inquiry about the *Erste Walpurgis Nacht*. The matter stands thus. Amongst historical inquirers, there are some men, and moreover men whôm we cannot but respect, who look for a real foundation for every fable, every tradition, however fantastic and absurd it may be, and always expect to find a kernel of fact, beneath the legendary husk. We owe a great deal of good to this mode of treating the matter; for the study demands great knowledge, nay, it is even necessary to have mind, wit, and imagination, to convert poetry into prose in this way. Thus, one of our German antiquarians has endeavoured to rescue, and to give an historical foundation for the story of the witches' and devils' ride on the Brocken, a legend which has been current in Germany, from time immemorial. His explanation is, that the heathen priests and patriarchs of Germany, when they were driven from their sacred groves, and when Christianity was forced upon the people, used to retire—at the beginning of spring—with their faithful followers, to the wild, inaccessible heights of the Harz mountains, in order, according to the ancient custom, there to offer prayer and flame to the unembodied god of heaven and earth. And further, in order to be safe from the armed spies and converters, he thinks, they may have found it well, to disguise a number of their own people, so as to keep their superstitious foes at a distance, and that thus, protected by the antics of devils, they carried out the purest of services.

I found this explanation somewhere, a few years ago, but cannot remember the name of the author. The idea pleased me, and I have turned this fabulous story back again into a poetical fable.

And now, my very kindest farewell! How much I wish that I could go to you, in place of this letter!

G.

71.—GOETHE TO ZELTER.

Weimar, 12th December, 1812.

THE mail-coach will bring you a strange work, which is certain to afford you some amusement. It is written by a remarkable, though certainly rather a strange man, and contains a new series of symbols for musical notation. Instead of the lines, intervals, heads and tails of notes, hitherto in vogue, he employs numerical signs, maintaining that this method is a much simpler one. I am no judge of this, for in the first place, I have been accustomed to the old style of musical notation, from my youth upwards, and in the second, no one could have a greater horror of figures than I have;—again, I have ever avoided and fled from all numerical symbols, from those of Pythagoras, up to our latest mathematico-mystics, as from something shapeless and comfortless.

The author, who calls himself Doctor Werneburg, is certainly a born mathematician, but with this peculiarity, that while simplifying matters for himself, he makes them difficult for others; consequently, he has never been able to carry anything out, and I hardly think he will ever be happy and contented, either as a citizen, or as a man of science.

Let me have a few lines about this little book; for you will see at a glance what speaks in its favour, or the reverse.

A few days ago, while meditating—as one is apt to do on winter evenings—on many a thing gone by, it struck me, that Herr Friedländer, last year, offered me in exchange a small bust of Jupiter, in red marble. If it is still to be had, and he has not changed his mind, I should be glad, if it could be packed up and sent to me. I would then, as before, let him know frankly what I think of it, and offer him the best thing I have to give in return. I have, for instance, two medallions of Moses, by Cellini, with the inscription *ut bibat populus*, which I certainly ought to value highly, as I hunted for one in vain, for thirty years, and then, by a strange coincidence, got them both in one year.

Perhaps the possessor of the bust has some other pet fancy, which I can meet half-way. . . . .

We actually expect Iffland before the New Year. I am greatly delighted at the prospect of seeing him again, after so long, and of admiring the great consistency of his acting, by which he contrives to ennoble every part he plays. It is probably one of the rarest of phenomena, and one, I think, that has never occurred with any other nation, that the greatest actor should generally select for himself parts, which are intrinsically unworthy of him, though, by his acting, he knows how to invest them with the highest momentary value. Carefully examined, such conduct has a most unfavourable influence on the taste of the people; for to be forced, under a given condition, to prize that which one does not esteem otherwise, creates a discord in our feelings, which, with the multitude, generally adjusts itself in favour of what is paltry and despicable, inasmuch as it has crept in under the cloak of excellence, and now asserts that it is excellent itself.

However, let us keep these observations to ourselves; they are of no use to the world, which prefers its own chaotic course.

H

In working at the Third Part of my Biography, I am coming to the first effects of Shakespeare in Germany. Is there anything new to be said on this subject? I hope so. Shall I express myself in accordance with what everyone thinks? This I very much doubt. And moreover, as the Germans have ever been in the habit of insisting that they understand the thing, better than the man whose profession it happens to be, that they understand it, better than he who has spent his whole life upon the subject, this time, too, they will make wry faces, for which however, they shall be forgiven, in consideration of their other defects.

But, dearest friend, pardon me also, if I too sometimes appear a little sour in my letters. "Old churches, dark windows," says the German proverb, and the short days do not make them clearer. I mostly reserve my cheerfulness for my biographical hours, so that nothing gloomy and impure may mingle with the reflections, which must be put in train anyhow.

Now, good-bye. Let me soon hear from you.

G.

72.—ZELTER TO GOETHE.

Berlin, 24th December, 1812.

My sweet friend and master! My beloved, my brother! What shall I call him, whose name is ever on my tongue, whose image is reflected on all that I love and honour? When the Weimar envelope wanders up my steps, all the suns rise on my house. The children, who know it well, tear each other to bits, for the privilege of bringing me the letter, and seeing their father's radiant face, and then I hold it long unopened, to see if it is really what it is, to squeeze it and kiss it. . . . .

I too have lately acquired a treasure, for I have bought an original picture by Denner, a portrait of the highly esteemed composer, Hasse,* who died in Italy, in the year

---

* Johann Adolph Hasse, *Il caro Sassone*, the rival of Porpora and Gluck, was the most popular dramatic composer of his age. His last Opera, *Ruggiero*, was performed at Milan in 1774, on the same occasion as a dramatic Serenade, *Ascanio in Alba*, by Mozart, who was then only seventeen years of age. Hasse is said to have exclaimed, "This boy will

1783, aged seventy-eight, after an artistic life that was rich in results. The picture was painted in 1740; it is two and a half feet high, and two feet broad, painted in oil, and in good preservation; it represents the artist, as a handsome man, in the fulness of his strength, and the zenith of his fame in Germany, but especially in Italy, where he was famous under the name of *Il Sassone*. Eyes, mouth, chin, and nose are beautifully chiselled and rounded, and the bearing of the man, with his expression and colour, confirm his character as an artist, who could only feel quite happy in Italy,—for in Italy he learnt, loved, pleased, married, and died, and he also adopted the religion of that country. His wife was the famous singer, Faustina. . . . .

Z.

throw us all into the shade." Two airs from his *Artaserse* were sung by Farinelli, every evening for ten years, to Philip V of Spain. (For a charming, idealized account of his influence at Dresden, and of his wife, Faustina, see the modern novel of *Alcestis*.) Faustina, Cuzzoni's famous rival, was for many years the *prima donna* of Dresden, and Sebastian Bach himself came to hear her, on a holiday trip from Leipzig.

1813.

73.—GOETHE TO ZELTER.

Weimar, 15th January, 1813.

I MUST enclose a few lines to you in my parcel to Herr Friedländer, which, even though they may reach you a little later, you will, I hope, affectionately welcome. I wish above all things to thank you, for having so promptly informed our artistic friends of my wish, and to beg you at the same time, to thank these worthy men, for having so promptly forwarded to me their parcel, just at the New Year. Once again it is a problematical work, and serves the rest of us in the North, who, alas! live rather in criticism than in contemplation, as a topic for manifold discussion. You will, probably, when you have an opportunity, get them to show you the letter, in which I have expressed my opinion about it. But belonging—as I surely do—to the school of Identity, nay, having been born to it, here too the heavy task is laid upon me, of uniting merciless criticism with irrational enthusiasm.

Iffland's presence was a great delight to me. I gave myself up to the pure enjoyment of his talent, endeavoured to understand everything *as* he gave it, and did not trouble myself about *what* he gave. Listen patiently to the following remark. If we care sincerely for the welfare of Art, we must wish that it should deal with great and worthy objects; for when the last artistic touches have been given, we look, from a moral point of view, for the greatest perfection in the subject dealt with. It was for this reason, because we were still under the delusion, that it was possible to exercise a genetic influence on men, that we, the Weimar Friends of Art, continued to discuss those *objects* with sincerity, in the *Propyläen*,* and it was this that we aimed

---

* A periodical, "through which Goethe hoped to work for ideal plastic art, as Schiller worked for the drama." So few copies were sold, that the publication was discontinued. There are frequent allusions to it in *The Correspondence between Schiller and Goethe.*

at in our prize-essays. Our efforts were however of no avail, for since that time, the saint and legend fever has spread on all sides, and has banished all that is truly joyous from Plastic Art. I only complain of this in passing, for I wished to follow up my first remark by saying, that Art, as it is represented by the greatest masters, creates a form so vital in its strength, that it ennobles and transfigures everything it touches.

For this very reason, a worthy substratum stands to some extent in the way of the eminent artist, because it ties his hands, and checks the freedom, in which, as a plastic artist and an individual, he would like to expatiate. Musicians have frequently been upbraided for liking bad librettos, and it has been said in jest, that one of them offered to set a poster* to music; if the song were not independent of the words, how could the Good-Friday music in the Sistine Chapel possibly have ended with the word *Vitulus?* and there may be other instances. Many a playbill would make a better Opera than the libretto itself, if it were properly arranged. Thus I have greatly admired Iffland's way of throwing life into dead plays,—nay, his creation out of nothing. The multitude, however, always realistically minded, is distressed about the great, and—in their opinion—wasted outlay.

The effect produced by *Don Ranudo* was remarkable. The utter worthlessness of the piece, the immoral demand, that nobility of birth should ignobly renounce its treasure, stood out like a ghost, and nearly a thousand people, in one small house, were put out of humour; for even ordinary human intelligence must feel, that the man, whose natural disposition cannot and will not allow him to submit to degradation, does not deserve to be degraded. No one could get up a laugh, from pure compassion.

This was to me a remarkable phenomenon, because I regarded it as a symptom, that Sans-culottism is already antiquated, and that the different ranks of Society are just now absorbed in quite other cares and passions, than those of tormenting and fighting and irritating one another.

In addition, I thought it remarkable, that Iffland, who,

---

* Telemann of Hamburg.

in his written plays, aims at the most ample breadth, in his acting, conjures up again the conciseness and terseness of plays that are extemporized. How different our stage would seem, if he had not been forced to take this roundabout way, and how different it would seem to all of us, if the direct ways to salvation did not remain a secret to every human being. . . . .

I was glad to have a little friendly talk with Herr Pfund, though only for a short time; what recommended him specially to me, was his attachment to you. I first loved his *fiancée*, when she was a child of eight years old, and when she was sixteen, I loved her more than was fair. You may be all the more friendly to her for that, if she comes to you.

And now a hearty farewell!

G.

74.—ZELTER TO GOETHE.

Berlin, 21st February, 1813.

. . . . YESTERDAY, matters were rather serious at our Court in Berlin. Out of a number of Cossacks, estimated at about three hundred, some hundred and fifty assembled on the heights before the town, and dashed through the gates, cutting and shooting down a number of Frenchmen, whom they found in the streets. This was towards noon. I was at the Academy. When I wanted to stroll home, about two o'clock, the bridges were already barred by the French, and planted with cannon, so that I was forced to make a very long *détour*, and finally reached home, past three o'clock. There had been lively work in my street. The houses opposite mine were riddled with balls. Several citizens are killed, and my neighbour, a merchant, is mortally wounded. At five o'clock the Cossacks had found their way out to the gate again. If these bold fellows had quietly penetrated, in full force, into the house of the French Governor, the Duke of Castiglione, instead of busying themselves with cutting down Frenchmen, one by one, in the streets, and alarming the whole city, the *coup* might have succeeded; and, on the other hand, if the French, who appeared to be taken by surprise, had barred the gates at once, not a single Russian would have escaped with his skin. I and my house are still undamaged; my eldest son has gone to join the king at Breslau, as a cavalry *Jäger*. At this moment, (ten o'clock at night,) they say the French intend to leave the town after midnight; I doubt it, for they have been reinforced by 2,000 infantry.

22nd February.

Morning. Seven o'clock. The French have not withdrawn; the whole garrison bivouacked throughout the night, in the streets. An ominous calm prevails; nobody knows what to be about,—meantime I am revising my earlier compositions.

24th February.

All is quiet. The Cossacks are swarming before the gates. The Viceroy and General St. Cyr have arrived with cavalry, and the town is now occupied by some 12,000 men. It is an anxious state of things, but it is long since I have slept so well, as I have since last Saturday. It is so quiet, that of an evening you can hear the footsteps of a dog. . . . .

27th February.

The day before yesterday, I heard a capital performance of Beethoven's Overture to *Egmont*. Every important theatrical work on the German stage ought, by rights, to have its own music. The profit, which would thence accrue to poet, composer, and public, is incalculable. The poet has the composer on his own field, and can guide him, and teach him to understand, nay, learn to understand him; the composer works, imbued with an idea of the whole, and knows for a certainty, what he must avoid, without being limited, and it must be a happiness, for each to recognize himself beside, and explain himself through the other. . . . .
You will see from the papers, that the French have left Berlin. . . . .

Z.

75.—GOETHE TO ZELTER.

Töplitz, 3rd May, 1813.

The enclosed, my dearest Friend, was intended for you long ago; I delayed forwarding it, for at last one scarcely knew, what connections one still had in the world, what not; a good opportunity now occurs of sending it to Berlin. Though at first anxious on your account, I was soon able to feel calm; now, I am anxious about myself and my property, and perhaps I shall not feel calm again so soon. On the 17th of April, I left Weimar, more owing to the persuasion of my immediate relatives and friends, than from any determination of my own. By means of a Prussian passport, I had just succeeded in crossing the lines, when, on the 18th, the French again took possession of Weimar, not without using force. Of this, however, I myself know nothing more than what is generally reported; for since that time, I have had no tidings thence, and no letter of mine has been able to get there.

In Dresden, Dr. Sibbern told me he had seen you, that you had wished him to take charge of something for me, but that you had refrained from so doing, as he would probably not come to Weimar. He certainly will not get there, but I should have been delighted to hear something about you in Dresden. I enclose a small poem, a parody of one of the most wretched of all German poems—*Ich habe geliebt, nun lieb' ich nicht mehr*. If poetizing were not an inward and necessary operation, independent of any outward circumstances, these strophes certainly could not have arisen at the present time; but as I imagine that one day or other, you will all be playing and singing again, I dedicate this unseasonable joke to you.

Farewell, and let me hear something about you soon.

GOETHE.

76.—GOETHE TO ZELTER.

Töplitz, 23rd June, 1813.

As an opportunity offers for sending you a few words, my dearest Friend, I shall not let it pass, for in the present distracted state of the world, one knows no longer, whom one belongs to. I have been here for the last eight weeks, leading a solitary life, peacefully working at my third volume, which I hope to have ready at Michaelmas. May Heaven grant us peace, for a thousand and again a thousand reasons, that we may find readers too! On the 3rd of May, I sent you a report of myself by Herr von Lützow, with an enclosure. How much I have thought of you; wherever we turn our thoughts, we see friends in danger.

My people are well, and resolutely bear up through all; I am well, and can work. What more could I wish for? I trust that things are going on pretty well with you, and that I may soon hear.

G.

77.—GOETHE TO ZELTER.

Weimar, 29th October, 1813.

PROFESSOR KIESEWETTER promises me, that this note shall reach you soon. He will tell you how matters stand with us, and how the monster passed us by, with quite a lenient step. I and mine have nothing to complain of,— nay, we may even consider our fate as fortunate, compared with that of so many others. Tell me something pleasant about yourself. In the midst of so much trouble, it is a great consolation, not to be completely cut off from those we love. All blessings be yours! inwardly, if not outwardly.

G.

78.—GOETHE TO ZELTER.

Weimar, 26th December, 1813.

AT last, my good old Friend, I see your dear handwriting again! You kindly warn me about the vegetables, and a great comfort it is, for I perceive from this, that the most monstrous Fate cannot destroy even the cycle of turnips. So let it be with all our other possessions.

First of all, then, you will very much oblige me, by setting the words, *In te, Domine, speravi, et non confundar in æternum,* as a vocal quartet, as charmingly as you alone can; your name shall be highly extolled thereby. When you have refreshed me thus, I will send you some *quodlibets* for your *Liedertafel*, where all of you, I suppose, will be again enjoying the products of Teltower.

Towards Christmas, I shall probably send you the third volume of the thousand and one nights of my foolish life, which looks almost more indiscreet in the account given, than it actually was.

You will be amused, when you see that I have been plagiarizing from you. Were your *métier* not so utterly different from mine, it would happen oftener.

This note was written some time ago, but the turnips have not yet arrived, and as I expected them from day to day, I did not seal my letter. Lieutenant Mendelssohn wants to take a few words to you from me. Here, therefore, is the little I have written, with my best wishes and hopes. A parcel and a petition will soon follow. The nervous fever, if it has not actually depopulated our printing works, has at all events very much crippled them, otherwise you would have had the Third Part before this.

Let me hear from you soon. I have some merry songs in stock. We have also been singing your *Drei Könige* lately. In this way, we must drive away the bitterness of death.

GOETHE.

79.—GOETHE TO ZELTER.

Weimar, 29th December, 1813.

HARDLY had I given Lieutenant Mendelssohn the note, written long ago, with a complaint, that the turnips had not yet come, when they actually arrived, in excellent condition, and though—being very small—they certainly give the cook some trouble in dishing, still my guests relish them all the more. A thousand thanks, and look kindly upon the enclosed. The date will show you, how merrily I managed to get along, through the most anxious time. More anon!

G.

THE WADDLING BELL.

A child refus'd to go betimes
    To church like other people;
He roam'd abroad, when rang the chimes
    On Sundays from the steeple.

His mother said: "Loud rings the bell,
    Its voice ne'er think of scorning;
Unless thou wilt behave thee well,
    'Twill fetch thee without warning."

The child then thought: "High overhead
    The bell is safe suspended—"
So to the fields he straightway sped
    As if 'twas school-time ended.

The bell now ceased as bell to ring,
    Roused by the mother's twaddle;
But soon ensued a dreadful thing!—
    The bell begins to waddle.

It waddles fast, though strange it seem;
    The child, with trembling wonder,
Runs off, and flies, as in a dream;
    The bell would draw him under.

He finds the proper time at last,
    And straightway nimbly rushes
To church, to chapel, hastening fast
    Through pastures, plains, and bushes.

Each Sunday and each feast as well,
    His late disaster heeds he;
The moment that he hears the bell,
    No other summons needs he.

Töplitz, 22nd May, 1813.   (E. A. BOWRING.)

1814.

80.—GOETHE TO ZELTER.

Weimar, 23rd February, 1814.

.... FIRST of all, I must tell you that our little Sing-song Society has been feeding upon you, and living upon you alone, and after a melancholy pause, has risen again upon you. We offered the transfiguration of *Johanna Sebus*, as a sacrament of our rescue from the broad, never-ending floods.

I could also tell you a long story about the *In te, Domine, speravi*, how I composed these words in my Bohemian solitude, amidst peculiar embarrassments from within and without; they had neither rhythm nor resonance, though meant for four persons—I might say, four voices—and I had no dearer wish, than to hear these beautiful words, musically commented on by you. I was tempted into drawing four lines, one below the other, in order to make the way I understood it, clear. Now that I hear your composition, I find in it a pleasant experience, and want no more instruction. The Dilettante is only touched by that which is easily comprehensible, and by that which has an immediate effect; this is also characteristic of his own productions, wherever he ventures tentatively upon any one of the arts. My composition, which is fairly rounded and definite, resembles one of Jomelli's, and it is curious and funny enough, to catch oneself accidentally upon such paths, and for once to become aware of one's own somnambulism. In order to get clear about this, in another branch of Art, to which I have devoted myself more seriously, I am examining some old landscape sketches, and perceive that it is much the same here.

Surely there must be some magic sounds in *Die wackelnde Glocke*, for, as a matter of fact, I wrote it in Töplitz, whither it seemed to call you. The fact of my *Verliebte*

*Launen** still interesting the Berliners, after a lapse of forty years, leads me to suppose that it must contain some freshness, which does not yield to time. . . . .

As a merry bit of padding, I enclose a few rhymes out of the wallet of the World's Course † (*aus der Tasche des Weltlaufes*).

> The years are jolly folk, I say!
> They brought us plenty yesterday,
> And still they bring us gifts to-day,
> And so we younger ones get through
> A jolly life of Nothing-To-Do;
> Till suddenly the years are struck,
> They've brought us quite enough good luck;
> No more they give, no more we borrow,
> They take to-day, they take to-morrow.
>
> Age is quite the gentleman.
> He knocks as often as he can,
> But no one says: "Come in! Good-day!"
> And at the door he will not stay,
> Lifts the latch,—and wellaway!
> "Rude old fellow!" now we say.

GOETHE.

81.—ZELTER TO GOETHE.

Berlin, 9th March, 1814.

. . . . *Die wackelnde Glocke* should, I think, be sung by a good Contralto, such as I have often heard among elderly Bohemian women. There are too, in Bohemia, mountains shaped like bells, and driving past them at a certain distance, they seem, to a fantastic eye, to wander after you. Thus, once a child, always a child. . . . .

Whilst re-reading your letter, I am again reminded of what I really wanted to say before, viz. that I should like to see your Composition for four persons, or your Scheme, be it what it may. We are such slaves to the current forms, the subject or image of which our fathers had before them, that we cannot go beyond them, without losing our identity. Were the opportunity, or the image to confront us

---

* *Die Laune des Verliebten*, a pastoral, the first piece that Goethe wrote for the stage.
† These poems are contained in the cycle headed *Epigrammatisch*.

again, through which form becomes definite and necessary, no one would have to strain every nerve to seem original. If we only lived nearer each other, no doubt many difficulties on this point would be cleared up, as certain things cannot be illustrated by words, and are only plain through the medium of Art. I well remember, that the music of the Leipzig Bach, and his son, the Hamburg Bach, who are both quite new and original, seemed to me in their day almost unintelligible, though I was attracted also by a dim perception of their genuineness. Then came Haydn, whose style was blamed, because it, so to speak, travestied the bitter earnestness of his predecessors, so that good opinion reverted back again to them. At last Mozart appeared, who enabled us to understand each of the three men, whom he had for his masters.

Z.

82.—Goethe to Zelter.

Weimar, 22nd April, 1814.

To-day but a word or two, dear Friend, to tell you, that to my great delight, your last consignment reached me safely; the parts are copied out, and so far prepared, that my compendious household-Choir can soon give me a treat.

To be sure, a special art is requisite to keep alive this heterogeneous body, from which now this, now that member drops off. The *Ruhelied* is admirable, our Tenor sings it very well, and in these restless times, it is all the happiness we get.

Eight days ago, I had a special bit of good luck. Professor Sartorius of Göttingen,* an old friend, avails himself of the communication re-opened between the Germans, and is paying me a visit. What at present is more desirable, than the conversation of a man, whose business it is, to be acquainted with, and to balance the strength, and the relations of states, one against the other, up to our own time? We get the greatest tranquillity from surveying this huge Whole, and from founding our

---

* Hofrath Sartorius of Göttingen, the only man with whom Goethe would discuss politics at this time.

hopes of future circumstances upon it, instead of finding ourselves, as formerly, in the sad plight of being carried away by the moment, puzzled by newspapers, and perhaps utterly confounded by gossip,—all the more, as the question may now be said to involve, not only the future destiny of Europe, but that of the whole world. . . . .

G.

>   Bloomed a little flower,
>   Like a bell,
>   In a springtide hour,
>   As it fell.
>   Came a little bee,
>   Sipped the dew;
>   " Why, you must be for me,
>   And I for you."
>
>   You never long the greatest man to be ;
>   No! All you say is : " I'm as good as he."—
>   He's the most envious man beneath the sun,
>   Who thinks that he's as good as everyone.
>
>   I am forced to hide from men,
>   Keep my treasure in my den,
>   For it puts the others out,
>   That I know what I'm about.

83.—GOETHE TO ZELTER.

Weimar, 4th May, 1814.

. . . . I HAD a friend, who used to say, that only under two circumstances, would he wish to be a king, namely, at dinner, when fresh herrings, or English beer were handed round, in order that he might help himself to the middle slice of the fish, and have the first glass of the beer. I had a similar feeling, when you told me of those aristocratic visitors, who enjoyed your grand and unique representation. Here, to be sure, it is easier not to grudge the distinguished guests the rest of their kingly fate. I should have gladly joined in the revel at that great table, which admits so many sympathetic guests. . . . .

The most laughable scenes in *Wilhelm Meister* are serious in comparison with the tricks I have to resort to, in contriving that your music shall be no longer visible only, but audible as well. . . . .

When an opportunity offers, I shall send you a full score by Christoph Kaiser, some of whose things you know, especially a Christmas Cantata. He was with me in Italy, and is still leading an abstruse life in Zürich; I should like to hear in detail, what you think of his style. What I shall send you is the Overture, and the first Act of *Scherz, List und Rache*, the whole of which he has set to music. He is in my thoughts just now, as I am working at my *Italiänische Reise*, and should like to be as clear about his art, as I am about his studies and his character.

Briefly and hurriedly, let me thank you for the great pleasure, which your parcel gave me. I succeeded, this time, in getting the variable Choir that meets at my house, very well organized.

G.

84.—ZELTER TO GOETHE.

Berlin, 15th May, 1814.

. . . . YOUR last letter of the 4th May, from Weimar, arrived safely. Please let me have Christoph Kaiser's score as soon as possible, as I am already busy preparing for my journey to the Baths, though for the rest of this month, at least, I remain where I am. As yet I do not know a note of Kaiser's music, and if you should chance to have his Christmas Cantata at hand, please send that also. Reichardt wrote to me the day before yesterday, that he expects a lasting improvement in his painful condition. The Abbé Vogler* died suddenly at Darmstadt, on the 6th of this month. Art would lose an excellent man by his death, had he not wasted the best time of his life in ploughing foreign acres, dissecting organs, and furbishing up old trash. . . . .

Z.

85.—ZELTER TO GOETHE.

Berlin, 8th November, 1814.

. . . . ON the 11th of October last, Prince Blücher paid our *Singakademie* a visit, and I thought I could not

---

* The master of Weber and Meyerbeer. See J. P. Simpson's Translation of *The Life of Weber*, written by his son.

do better than greet him with the little song, *Vorwärts Hinan!* They sang it with such truthfulness and delicacy, that he was delighted. The 181 voices sounded so fresh and spirited; the old fellow could not help crying. . . . .

Z.

86.—GOETHE TO ZELTER.

Weimar, 27th December, 1814.

. . . . My kindest regards to Herr Staatsrath Schulz; my delight in his essay will be plain from the appended copy of a passage in a letter, which I sent to a friend, immediately after reading through his pamphlet; perhaps it will better express all that I feel towards him, than I could have done directly. . . . .

G.

COPY.

. . . . After all this, I cannot conceal from you, dear Friend, that a great gratification has of late befallen me. I have known for some time past, that Herr Staatsrath Schulz * of Berlin—a superior man in every way—was keenly interested in my *Farbenlehre*, and that he had specially worked out the physiological part, though he only jotted down his remarks, without thinking of immediate publication, because he wished first to go deeper into the matter. Now, at my earnest request, he has been kind enough to put forward with great clearness, as a clever man of business, his view of the question, as it now is, and to collect, and make an inventory of the results, as well as of the individual experiences. This is the first time I have happened to see such a superior man agreeing with my fundamental principles, extending them, building up upon them, adjusting a good deal, supplementing them, and opening up new views. His admirable *aperçus* and deductions, which many a one might envy, justify our entertaining great hopes. The transparency of his course

---

* "This was the beginning of an interesting friendship, though letters between Goethe and Schulz did not become frequent until the year 1816." See Lyster's Translation of Düntzer's *Life of Goethe*, vol. ii. p. 312.

is just as clear as the ramification of his method. His close observation of the most subtle phenomena incidental to the subject, his acuteness, without hair-splitting, and, in addition to this, his extensive reading, make it dependent upon himself only, to enrich and enhance in value the historical part of my work. If I get his consent to the printing of his essay, it will be certain, even in its present shape, as a mere sketch, to produce great effect.

1815.

87.—ZELTER TO GOETHE.

Berlin, 11th April, 1815.

. . . . I AVAIL myself of the opportunity, to send you some autographs of remarkable people. And even if you should already have something of theirs in your collection, the compositions are, from a historical point of view, important in themselves; particularly those of Sebastian Bach, and Kirnberger.* In the life of Fasch, you will find an explanation of the piece, headed *La Coorl*.† . . . .

Z.

88.—GOETHE TO ZELTER.

Weimar, 17th April, 1815.

As you, my dear, silent Friend, have opened your mouth at exactly the right moment, I will gladly pardon your remissness hitherto, and send you my best thanks into the bargain. I had already received some intelligent and detailed reports of the performance of *Epimenides*,‡ but now, in you come with your bold pen, and by dotting the *i* and crossing the *t*, for the first time make the writing perfectly legible.

Everything depends on a play of this kind being given a dozen times in succession. Do but realize the elements, which go to make up such a representation, and you will almost despair of a happy result.

---

* Johann Philipp Kirnberger, one of Sebastian Bach's pupils, author of *Die Kunst des reinen Satzes*. He taught both Fasch and Zelter.

† One of Emanuel Bach's character-pieces, so called after Karl Fasch, whose name was mispronounced, " Coorl," by an Austrian friend.

‡ An allusion to Zelter's graphic account of the performance of *Des Epimenides Erwachen* at Berlin. Goethe wrote this short play, by Iffland's desire, in honour of the return of the King of Prussia to Berlin. It symbolizes Goethe's apathy, at a time which called forth an outbreak of patriotic feeling in Germany.

1. The work of the Poet. . . .
2. The Composer. . . .
3. The Orchestra. . . .
4. Actors and Singers. . . .
5. Costumes. . . .
6. Sundries. . . .
7. Scenery. . . .
8. A Public. . . .

How many dozens of tin plates would be wanted, to fuse together the refractory ingredients of such bell-metal! (See *Cellini*, Part II. p. 176.)

When the play is frequently repeated, it is quite a different matter. Without bellows and flames, without art and intention, there arise the most delicate elective affinities, which, in the pleasantest way, unite those seemingly isolated members into a whole; on the actors' side, more certainty and pliability, acquired by practice, strengthened by applause, supported by an animated insight into, and a general survey of the whole; on the spectators' side, acquaintance, custom, favour, prejudice, enthusiasm, and whatever may be the names of all the good spirits, without which, even the *Iliad* and *Odyssey* would remain to us but a lifeless frame-work.

Hence it is, that with more light-hearted nations, when any piece has once taken hold of them, it can be repeated *ad infinitum*, because the actors, the play, and the public come to understand each other, better and better; and then too, one neighbour stirs up another to go to the Theatre, and the general, everyday talk at last makes it a necessity for everyone to see the novelty. I saw an instance of this in Rome, when an Opera, *Don Juan*, (not Mozart's,) was given every evening for a month, an event which so stirred the city, that the humblest shopkeepers, with kith and kin, kept house in pit and boxes, and no one could exist, without having seen Don Juan roasting in Hades, and the Commendatore floating heavenwards, as a blessed spirit. . . . . It pleased me greatly, that you should have held so firmly to the pivot upon which my play turns, (but, as I hope, without creaking and jarring,) and that you felt it so deeply,—although it is quite in accordance with your nature. Without these fearful chains, the whole thing would be a folly. The fact that this instance is proved in women, makes the thing more pardonable, and draws it into the domain of emotion; however, we will say nothing further about the matter, and leave the result to the gods.

I will look through Catel's book, one day soon. Give my kindest regards to the author. At present, however, I guard myself as much against architecture, as against fire. The older we get, the more must we limit ourselves, if we wish to be active. If we do not take care, owing to the multitude of external claims, our mind, and our physical powers will evaporate in empty smoke, out of pure sympathy, and the necessity of criticism.

I doubt not you have succeeded in clothing *Hans Adam's** body in a tight-fitting jacket; and I look forward to seeing him parade about in it. I will look out one of my later things for you. I find Orientalizing very dangerous work, for before one is aware of it, the most solid poem slips out of one's hands, like a balloon, and vanishes into air, merely from the rational and spiritual gas with which it fills itself. . . . .

Just as I was considering, what to fill up my remaining space with, Herr Mendelssohn came in, bringing with him your kind greeting and gift,—both of them most welcome; I received him cheerfully, but absently, for just when he came in, I was more than a hundred miles away from the house. The manuscript music is delicious! I had no specimen of either of the three masters in my collection. My very best thanks! As we have brought the Berliners to reflect and to make puns, let us stick to it for a time. Remember me very kindly to Herr Staatsrath Schulz. I have studied his treatises again lately; both they and he have become so much the dearer to me. Now adieu! May this letter happily inaugurate the communications we have just re-opened !

G.

* The first lyric in the *Divan*.

89.—GOETHE TO ZELTER.

(End of May.)

I SHALL send you a few words at once, in return for your dear letter, so that you may be kept in the humour to write now and again. First and foremost then, pray let me have some theatrical news, from time to time; for as I am on good terms with Count Brühl, whom I knew as a boy, and as the success of *Epimenides* was owing to his exertions, I should like to do him a favour, and in a general way, to remain on good terms with the Berlin Theatre. If there were only some incitement, very likely I should work again at play-writing for a time, and then, Berlin is, after all, the only place in Germany, for which one has the courage to undertake anything. Owing to the numerous journals and daily papers, the whole of the German stage lies bare before our eyes, and whither can one turn confidingly, when one looks close? Only speak out, in your own blunt way, as you were always wont, that I may not go on in the dark, and squander my good intentions on false undertakings.

I have made my *Proserpina** the vehicle for everything which modern criticism finds and favours in works of Art: (1) Heroic and landscape decoration; (2) heightened recitation and declamation; (3) Hamiltonian-Handelian † gestures; (4) change of costume; (5) play of drapery; and—(6) even a *tableau* for a Finale, representing the realm of Pluto; all this, accompanied by the music you know of, which serves as welcome spice for this immoderate feast of the eyes. It was received with great applause, and when foreigners come to us, it will be a useful little sample, to show what we can do.

For some time past, I have had just enough inclination, to contribute articles to the *Morgenblatt;* and that I may save you from wasting time, looking for them, I will mark the numbers, and should like you to hunt them up.

---

* A lyric monodrama, introduced into *Der Triumph der Empfindsamkeit.*

† Goethe had seen Lady Hamilton at Naples in 1787. See *Die Italiänische Reise.*

No. 69. Account of some old treasures of German Art, discovered in Leipzig.

75
& } Account of *Epimenides Erwachen*.
76.

85
& } Articles upon the German Theatre.
86.

They are about to publish *Don Ciccio*, famous in the secret literature of Italy for the 365 libellous sonnets, written upon him by a clever adversary, and published daily throughout a whole year.

Then Shakespeare is to be discussed: (a) considered generally as a Poet; (b) compared with the ancient and with the most modern Poets; (c) regarded as a Poet for the stage.

I shall then discuss the Festival, in commemoration of Iffland and Schiller, as arranged by us for the 10th May.

Also I shall give an account of the *Proserpina*, and explain more in detail, what I briefly touched upon above, so that a similar, nay, better representation of this little play, may be given in several different Theatres.

I have been looking over my *Orientalischer Divan*, in order to send you a new poem, but I now see clearly for the first time, how this kind of poetry drives one to reflection; for I did not find anything vocal in it, especially for the *Liedertafel*, for which, after all, it is our main business to provide. For what cannot be sung in company, is in reality no song, just as a monologue is no drama.

I have hidden the *Gastmahl der Weisen;* if it were to become known, it could not but deeply wound certain individuals, and after all, it is not worth while quarrelling with the world, simply to afford it some amusement.

I am just now busy with my *Italiänische Reise*, and particularly with Rome. Fortunately I still have diaries, letters, remarks, and notes of all kinds, so that I can give a perfectly true description, and a graceful romance as well. In this I am greatly assisted by Meyer's sympathy, for he saw me arrive, and start off, and he stayed in Rome, the whole time that I was in Naples and Sicily. Had I not these notes and this friend, I should not dare undertake this work; for, when once we have become clear about anything, how are we to call to remembrance the sweet delusion in which, as in a mist, we hoped and searched, without knowing what we should attain to, or what we might find. Meanwhile I am reading Winckelmann in the new edition by Meyer and Schulze, who have immensely enhanced the value of his works, inasmuch as here we see what the author has actually accomplished, and also exactly what it is, which after so many years is found to require correction and supplement. Meyer's merits, as editor, are incalculable, and if he makes this work a foundation, and all through his life continues to add to it what he learns, he will have done a great thing for Art and its preservation, for in its present state, it is daily becoming more insecure, owing to the perpetual talking to and fro, and the way in which people bungle.

His own History of Art, from the earliest, down to the most recent times, has already been sketched from beginning to end, and some portions have been worked out in a masterly style. The merits of such men as Rubens, Rembrandt, &c., have never yet been expressed by anyone with so much truth and energy. One fancies oneself in a gallery of their works: the effects of light and shade and colouring in these admirable artists, speak to us from the black letters.

Now do make up your mind to write a History of Music in the same sense! You would hardly be able to resist doing so, were I to read out Meyer's work to you, for only a quarter of an hour. From your letters and conversation, I have already become acquainted with many of your firstrate masters. With the same intelligence, and with the same powers, you would have to begin with an important period, and work forwards and backwards, for the True can be raised and preserved only by its History, and the False can be lowered and destroyed only by its History.

As for what is false, I met with a remarkable instance lately. A quotation from Winckelmann referred me to the homilies of Chrysostom, for I wanted to see what that Father of the Church had to say about beauty, and what did I find? A Pater Abraham à Sancta Clara,* who

* The name in religion of Ulrich Megerle, born in Swabia, 1642, and Chaplain to the Imperial Court at Vienna, 1669-1709. The Capuchin's

has the whole of the grand culture of Greece behind him, lives amidst the most abject surroundings, and with a "golden mouth," tells his bad public the stupidest stuff, in order to edify them, by means of degradation. Yet how great is one's admiration of the Greek language and form, even in this repulsive reflection! I now, however, for the first time understand, why our good Christians of modern days prize him so highly: they themselves have to repeat the same twaddle perpetually, and everyone feels that he cannot attain that eloquence. . . . . G.

Before I closed this, I again looked through my *Divan*, and find a second reason, why I cannot send you any poem out of it; this, however, speaks in favour of the collection. For every individual member is so imbued with the spirit of the whole, is so thoroughly Oriental, referring to Eastern customs, usages, and religion, that it requires to be explained by one of the preceding poems, before it can produce any effect upon the imagination, or the feelings. I did not myself know, in what a strange way I had made the whole thing hang together. The first hundred poems are nearly complete; when I have finished the second, the Collection will look graver. . . . .

G.

90.—GOETHE TO ZELTER.

Weimar, 29th October, 1815.

. . . . I HAVE not returned empty-handed from my crusade, and ere long, you will receive my printed observations upon Art and Antiquity, in the districts about the Rhine and Maine,* with incidental remarks on Science. To be sure, it is not my way to work for the day, but in this instance, I have been so loyally and earnestly challenged to such a duty, that I cannot shirk it. In reality, too, I only

Sermon in *Wallenstein's Lager* was modelled upon a sermon of his. Goethe had sent a volume of his works to Schiller, which accounts for the report that Goethe wrote the Sermon in *Wallenstein*. See Buchheim's Introduction to *Wallenstein*.

* These observations were contained in a Memoir, written for his old Leipzig fellow-student, Hardenberg, and called *Von Kunst und Alterthum am Rhein und Main*.

play the editor, inasmuch as I express the sentiments, wishes, and hopes of intelligent and worthy men. In these departments, as in every other, there is as much goodwill, as confusion and mistrust; everyone would like to do something, and of course the right thing, and no one understands, that this can only happen when we work unitedly, and all together.

Now I must tell you, that my *Divan* is larger by several members, some of them of the freshest and most youthful kind. It can now be divided into books, according to the different contents; and there are several vocal things among them, though—in accordance with their Oriental style—reflection prevails in most of them,—as moreover befits the years of the poet.

Further, the account of my stay in Naples and my journey through Sicily has been pretty thoroughly revised, by means of diaries, letters, and my own memory, and is just going to be copied. The journey as far as Rome was already in train before I left. No one will learn very much from this little volume, but the reader will have a vivid picture of districts, objects, people, and travellers.

I heard no public musical performances on my journey, that gave me any pleasure. I met with some sympathetic voices, which sounded very agreeable, when accompanied by piano and guitar. I heard *Gott und die Bajadere*, given with all imaginable beauty and feeling.*—But is the first number of your engraved Songs no longer to be had? I could not get it in Frankfort, though the others were there. They know nothing about you on the Maine, and the Rhine is not acquainted with you, so we have been preaching your Gospel in these districts. In Heidelberg, on the other hand, you are held in the freshest remembrance. You will, no doubt, allow me to send some of your Canons and Part-Songs there; I should also like to

---

* One of these "sympathetic voices" was that of Marianne von Willemer, the poet's favourite and correspondent. Her singing of the Air from *Don Giovanni*, *Gib mir die Hand, mein Leben*, so bewitched Goethe, that he said, she was herself "a little Don Juan." He used to read aloud to her the Persian love-poems, in which he delighted, as well as his own *Westöstlicher Divan*, part of which she inspired. She could have been no mean poetess herself, since she wrote the famous Song, *Was bedeutet die Bewegung?* afterwards set by Mendelssohn.

forward the score of *Johanna Sebus*. They have a society of amateurs, under a clever and able conductor.* A well-intentioned young man has started a singing Academy in Frankfort, which I hope to be able to assist, and I wish you would test it. These musicians suffer from the same misfortune as poets, for each one brings forward only his own work; that which is like him, and within his reach. Fräulein Hügel plays Handel's and Bach's Sonatas most admirably, and unfortunately, neither in that province of Art, nor in any other, is there any central point, after which everybody is sighing, since people are only accustomed to revolve around themselves. . . . .

Brühl has taken the Wolffs away from us, which does not lead one to prejudge his directorship favourably. Of course you cannot prevent a man from trying to appropriate to his own use the services of cultivated artists, but it would be better and more profitable, if he would train them himself. Were I as young as Brühl, no chicken should be allowed on my stage, that I had not hatched myself. And now a kind farewell, and do send me a little Song or Canon!

G.

* The famous Thibaut, author of *Ueber Reinheit der Tonkunst*, an English version of which, (by Mr. W. H. Gladstone,) entitled *Purity in Musical Art*, appeared a few years ago.

1816.

91.—GOETHE TO ZELTER.
Weimar, 11th March, 1816.

You are probably right, my dearest Friend, in saying that there is no such thing as uninterrupted correspondence, unless one gossips; and as this is not our case, it is perhaps natural, that we should not hear from one another for quite a long time. Then too, the after-results are so hazardous, that one scarcely dares to give them expression, for only very seldom, may we venture to promise applause to conclusions without premises.

The presence of Messrs. Schadow and Weber has brought me into closer *rapport* with Berlin; for through personal intercourse and friendly talk, even distant conditions can be brought nearer to us. A thousand times have I thought of you, and how you sail, swim, bathe, and wade about in such a sea!

My little volume about the Rhine and the Maine, Art and Antiquity, will now soon reach you; I have broken off at the thirteenth sheet, like Scheherazade. Had I earlier recognized the importance of these pages, I should have refused the little job altogether; as it is, I was seduced into it only by degrees,—so let it go its ways! On the other hand, I must gratefully acknowledge, that had it not been for this pressing necessity, I should never have been able to direct my attention, either to the important question of the preservation of Art throughout the barbaric time, or to the peculiarities of national and provincial restoration. We find in it much that is opposed to our refined sensuality, and we can make nothing of it, unless we grasp the idea; even absurdities please us, when we are clear about them.

My *Divan* has grown in bulk and in strength. The style of poetry, which, without further reflection, I have adopted and made use of, has this peculiarity, that, like the Sonnet, it almost resists being sung; it is also notable enough, that the glory of Orientals is writing, not singing. However, it is a kind of poetry that suits my time of life, mode of thought, experience, and view of things, while it allows one to be as foolish in love-matters, as one can only be in youth.

Herewith a Song, that can anyhow be sung. And now, my kindest farewell.

G.

> Thy heart to fathom,
> My heart impels me!
> This is my longing,
> To tell, to tell thee!
> Sadly, how sadly,
> The world looks at me!
>
> In my thoughts ever
> My friend lives lonely—
> No foe, no rival,—
> His image only;
> Like lights of morning
> A thought rose on me.
>
> My life I'll give him,
> To-day, for ever,
> Its only service
> Henceforth to love him.
> I think upon him—
> My heart lies bleeding!
>
> Power,—I have no power,
> Only to love him,
> As now in silence.—
> What of the future?
> I would embrace him,
> And, lo I cannot!

92.—GOETHE TO ZELTER.

Weimar, 26th March, 1816.

INDEED you have had another hard task put upon you; unfortunately, it is ever the same old story, that to live long means as much as to outlive many, and in the end, what is the meaning of it all? A few days ago, the first edition of my *Werther* came accidentally into my hands, and this long since forgotten song began to resound again in me. But then one cannot understand, how a man could bear to live another forty years in a world, which already, in his early youth, appeared so absurd to him.

One part of the riddle explains itself by the fact, that every one has some peculiarity in himself, which he proposes to develop, whilst allowing it to work on continuously. Now this strange Nature makes fools of us day by day, and so we grow old, without knowing why or wherefore. When I look closely into the matter, it is only the talent implanted in me, that helps me through all the unsuitable conditions, in which I find myself entangled, by false tendencies, accident, and the adoption of foreign elements. . . . .

The course of Art during the Middle Ages, and certain luminous points at the reappearance of pure natural talents, have, I hope, gained through my work. But unfortunately, the legions of scribblers in Germany will very speedily thrash out my harvest, whatever it may be, and swagger along to the patriotic harvest-home, with bundles of straw, as though they were rich corn-sheaves. . . . .

GOETHE.

93.—ZELTER TO GOETHE.

Berlin, Sunday, 31st March, 1816.

AFTER several rehearsals with Orchestra and Chorus, there was a reading rehearsal with music, yesterday evening.

Prince Karl of Mecklenburg read the part of Mephistopheles, and the actor Lemm, provisionally, that of Faust; the rehearsal was at Prince Radzivil's,* in the midst of his family-circle. The Princess and her children were present, the Crown Prince, with his brothers and sisters, Prince George of Mecklenburg, Frau von der Recke, with

* Prince Radzivil was one of the seven people, who answered Beethoven's invitation to subscribe for the publication of the Mass in D. His music to *Faust* was brought out by the *Singakademie* in 1833, shortly after his death; it was afterwards frequently given at Berlin, and elsewhere in Germany.

her friend Tiedge, Frau von Humboldt, and several artists, who are to take part in the representation.

As a beginning, only those scenes were read, in which none but Faust and Mephistopheles appear. Prince Karl reads this character in a way that leaves little to be desired—voice, tone, rhythm, figure, and appearance—all is congruous, even to the cloven foot; what is wanting in modulation and *tempo* will, I hope, arrange itself; his delivery too, won quite universal applause, and the actor jogged by his side, like a donkey next to a horse.

The effect of the poem upon an almost entirely youthful audience, to whom everything was new and strange, is very remarkable, and they are never tired of wondering that all that is in print; they go and consult the book, to see if it really stands so. That it is true, they all feel, and it is as if they were inquiring, whether the truth is true. The composer has hit off much to admiration; the defect consists in this, that he, like all artists at the outset of their career, makes main points of what should be secondary. .... The play is to be given in three Parts. The Second Part, which we shall soon rehearse, begins with Auerbach's cellar; I shall continue to let you know all about it.

Z.

94.—ZELTER TO GOETHE.

Berlin, 4th April, 1816.

.... THE bearer of this letter is the banker, Abraham Mendelssohn.* He is the second son of the philosopher, and from the first years of his youth, after his father's death, he has been attached to my house and all its inmates. He is one of the right sort, and as such you will receive him. He has amiable children, and his eldest little daughter could let you hear a thing or two of Sebastian Bach. The wife is also a most excellent mother and manager, though unfortunately she is not very strong. The husband is very fond of me, and I keep open bank with him, for in times of universal want, he has grown rich, without damage to his soul. Farewell, my ever be-

---

* Father of Felix Mendelssohn.

loved! I shall soon see you again, even if it should be only for a day.

Z.

95.—Zelter to Goethe.

Berlin, Sunday, 7th April, 1816.

.... Yesterday we had a reading rehearsal of *Faust*, and just as we were about to begin, all the young Royalties announced themselves..... Count Brühl played the poet quite decently. Lemm, the actor, has improved, and came gradually into his part. Prince Karl, however, has deteriorated, and fell into the preaching tone. We had finished the first Act, when the King unexpectedly arrived; most likely he could not endure home any longer, as his children had all gone off.

The whole of the first Act was repeated, and the King, who at first, as of old, kept quiet and in the background, after two hours of silence, became sociable, chatty, and really amiable.....

Z.

96.—Goethe to Zelter.

Weimar, 14th April, 1816.

Your letters, dearest Friend, surprised me most agreeably in my garden,—gave me much to think about,—nay, incited me to a rambling conversation in the Faraway. Then came Mendelssohn, and as I was just in the humour, and he was recommended by you, I told him what I should probably have told you; this I think he deserved, as he talked very intelligently, and in the course of his conversation, discussed many important points in Science, Art, and life. Unfortunately I did not see his people, they stayed only one afternoon; I should have liked to invite them to breakfast to-day, and to have shown them my goods and chattels.

I have had a most delightful letter from Staatsrath Schulz. When the Germans study to be more and more universally unsympathetic, and gracelessly reject what they should grasp with both hands, that individual is in truth celestial, who shows a faithful and honest sympathy, and joyfully co-operates with others. Remember me to him most kindly, when you see him. Seebeck of Nürnberg holds his own admirably, and I must own, that I am greatly delighted, that an old and faithful fellow-labourer should win the prize in Paris, whilst the Germans behave towards us, as if they were staring ghosts. But they shall not get off scot-free; I am only waiting for a fitting opportunity to give it them pretty soundly.

Amongst our new arrangements in Jena, I intend setting up a complete prismatic apparatus; no Academy of Sciences has ever thought of doing this hitherto, and I shall take the opportunity of letting them hear plenty about it. Still, in matters of this kind, nothing is to be done with violence; one must wait till an opinion, like an epidemic, fastens on mankind.

Be sure to go on with your theatrical criticisms. Things must indeed be in a strange state with you in Berlin, if the people cannot master so plain and conventional a play as *Clavigo;* besides, it is a thoroughly German way of doing things, to seek the entrance to a poem or any other work, everywhere, except through the door. I have, throughout my life, had plenty of opportunities for wondering, how it happens, that thoroughly educated persons are absolutely incapable of recognizing æsthetic, or higher moral aims. I had rather not have written a single verse, if hundreds of thousands did not read the production, reflect upon it, enlarge upon it, elucidate it, understand it.

Faust may, in future months, give you many a confused hour. If you go on being as rude as you were to the gloomy Count, that will be something of itself; people are far too often apt to be callous and stupid in such cases. The incredible conceit, in which young people nowadays grow up, will, in a few years, manifest itself in the wildest follies.

Look into the *Morgenblatt* occasionally; you will there find different contributions of mine, that go into the whole matter, and a good deal you can certainly claim as your own. The fact is, I have a great number of essays lying by me, and I have found some amusement this spring, in touching them up and publishing them it is the first

K

spring—after a long interval—that we have seen approaching, without horror and alarm.

Last Sunday we celebrated the grand *Huldigung's Fête*. The honours, distinctions, and compliments bestowed on us, told every sensible man among us very plainly, that he must give himself up for the time being. However, the task allotted to me is the most pleasant one; I have nothing to do, except what I thoroughly understand, and I have only to continue doing what I have done for the last forty years, with ample means, great freedom, and without worry or hurry. . . . .

My last empty page I shall fill with a few verses; you can use them, if you feel inclined.

G.

THE PUBLIC.

Gossip and gossip, and no redress,
   None at all.
We've got you into a pretty mess,
   In you fall!
To us it's all play,
Get out as you may,
   Adé!

MR. EGO.

Talking and talking to set it right,
   Makes it worse.
Twaddle and twaddle! Life so bright
   Is a curse!
I'm out and away,
To me it's all play,
   Adé!

97.—GOETHE TO ZELTER.

Weimar, 3rd May, 1816.

I ANSWER your dear letter at once. I am glad that Wolff* has given satisfaction, and glad to know through you, why and wherefore. The Weimar actors are at their

---

* Pius Alexander Wolff was one of Goethe's favourite actors. It was he who brought out *Tasso* in 1807, when, by Goethe's desire, a bust of Wieland, instead of Ariosto, was crowned on the stage. Goethe wrote the lines, beginning *Mögt zur Gruft ihn senken*, for his funeral.

best when they work together, but I am glad to hear, that even the individual carries away with him something of the whole.

In August, 1803, two young people, Grüner and Wolff, came here, our company being then absent in Lauchstädt; I had time and inclination, and felt disposed to make an effort, to bring these two up to a certain point, before the others returned. I dictated to them the first elements, which, as yet, no one else has thoroughly mastered. Both studied them attentively, and Wolff has never wavered nor swerved from them, so that his hold on Art is secured to him for life. Grüner, at Vienna, has hoisted himself up to the position of a powerful actor, nay, director, and this shows that he too has clung to a certain foundation. Both had come to me with faith and affection, the one abandoning a military career, the other, mercantile pursuits, and neither of them fared badly. A few days ago, when I was sorting some old papers, I found the draft of a letter to Wolff's mother, which has a nice look about it even now. At the same time, I came upon the draft of that catechism, or *a b*, ab, which, with more pretension, one might also call Euclidic elements. Perhaps these papers may seduce me into thinking the matter over again. They do not go far into the subject, for the company returned, and then everything had to become practical.

In those days, however, we enjoyed our life and our theatrical doings so much, that a part of the company paid me a visit in Jena during the winter, in order to continue our rehearsals. Owing to the snow, the *Schnecke* was impracticable, and Grüner lost the pamphlet, which he carried about in his pocket as a talisman, but he recovered it some days later, for he sounded an alarm about it in all the pothouses, and luckily a driver had picked it up.

When you see Mademoiselle Maas, remind her in a friendly way, of these adventures, for she was one of the party, and got some little amusement out of them. She was a favourite of mine, on account of her great self-possession, and charmingly clear recitation; for that very reason, I was, on one occasion, terribly angry with her, during a rehearsal of *Tell*, because, Heaven knows why, she fell into a lazy way of talking. You see, your friendly gossip has made me turn back to earlier times, when the system which in after times worked on of itself, was worked ont purely and correctly. So just now I am living my life in Sicily over again, in my own way, and now I see for the first time, how a ten weeks' sojourn in that country affected me.

And now, to another text. If, in future, people tell you that I am ill, do not believe them; if they tell you I am dead, do not think so. As for the last news you heard, no doubt there is something rather odd about it; therefore give heed.

The *Huldigung's Fête* was to have taken place on Palm Sunday, the 7th of April, and thus the key-stone of a new arch was to be laid, after many destructive troubles. On the 2nd of April, I was seized with a strange rheumatic attack, not dangerous, but still very severe, and I was obliged to take to my bed. As far as I could see, it appeared almost impossible for me to be in my place on the 7th. But happily I recalled to mind one of Napoleon's maxims—*L'Empereur ne connoit autre maladie que la mort,*—and so I said that unless I were dead, I would appear at Court at noon on Sunday. It seems that the doctor and Nature took to heart this despotic saying, for on Sunday, at the given hour, I was standing at my place, on the right, next to the throne, and even at dinner, I was able to do all that was expected of me. Afterwards, however, I retired again, and went to bed, to wait until the categorical Imperative should send me a mortal challenge again. As yet, all has gone well. I had before this made up my mind to stay at home till Midsummer, as you also are obliged to; for the empirical forces, which have for long been directed to things without, will now, if God wills, be turned to things within, only empirically too, but we must thank God that it is so.

But what will you say now, when I tell you, that I too have lately had a severe blow? Pretty Berka on the Ilm, where we spent such a delightful time, in many different ways, with Wolf and Weber and Duncker! Picture to yourself, first of all, that pretty Viennese piano, belonging to the Organist Schutz, with the music of Sebastian, Philip Emmanuel Bach, &c. Well, Berka was burnt to the ground, between the 25th and 26th of April. By dint of extraordinary presence of mind, and the help of kind people, the piano was saved, as well as many other things in the house, in at most seven minutes' time, which is astonishing; for a tremendous fre, which began at a baker's house, had, by half-past eleven, spread the flames far and wide. All the organist's old pieces by Bach and Handel, which he had got from Kittel of Erfurt, are burnt, and that, merely owing to a stupid accident or arrangement, by which he had transported them from the untidy chamber, in which they had hitherto lain, to a rather distant room, where he could put them in order.

Of course, all these things are already engraved; let me know how I could get them from Härtel's in Leipzig, or elsewhere, for I should be glad to give him a little pleasure in this way. Heaven bless copper plate, type, and every other means of multiplying things, so that a good work which has once existed, can never again be destroyed. If you should see Geheimrath Wolf, give him the kindest messages from me, but tell him also that the accursed little *Trompeterstückchen* escaped being burnt by the strangest chance, as I happened to have it in the Town; like a good many other things, it was saved by dispersion.

Tell me calmly and quietly, what you think of Madame Wolff, when you see her in some new part, or when you have seen her more frequently; do the same with regard to him. I cannot be content with any other report but yours; I myself do not see it so well, for I am either in a productive state, *i.e.* I insist that he who does not do things quite rightly shall do better, and I feel convinced that he will do better,—or my case is exactly the reverse; disbelief steps in, and I curse what is done, because I feel ashamed of being able to expect that it might be any better.

May the moral order of the world preserve you!

G.

98.—ZELTER TO GOETHE.

Berlin, 8th May, 1816.

.... BEETHOVEN has composed a Battle Symphony,* as deafening as he himself is deaf. Now women know to

* " 'This Orchestral programme-music,' says Sir G. Grove, ' entitled

a nicety what happens in a battle, though the time has already long gone by for anyone to understand what music is. . . . .

On Sunday evening, the Battle Symphony was given in the Theatre, and I heard it from the very farthest end of the pit, where all the deafening effect is lost, and yet I was overwhelmed, nay, shattered. The piece is a real whole, the parts of which can be intelligibly divided and connected. The English advance from afar, drums beating; as they get nearer, *Rule Britannia* tells us who they are. Similarly, the opposing army moves forward, and is immediately recognized by *Marlborough s'en va t'en guerre*. The fire of cannon and small arms is clearly distinguished on both sides, the orchestral music, which consists of harmoniously connected thoughts, and interests the ear of the listener, works like the storm and tumult of battle. The armies seem to be engaged hand to hand; furious onslaughts on the squares and such-like incidents,—the excitement growing. One army yields, the other pursues, now vehemently and close at hand, now at a distance. At last there is a lull. Then, as though issuing from the ground, muffled and mysterious, the *Air de Marlborough* echoes sorrowfully in the minor key, interrupted by the failing accents of lament and woe. Then the victory of the conquerors is made known by the air of *God save the King*, and at last, by a complete, vivid, triumphal movement. All this hangs really well together, though it cannot be taken in at once, even by a good ear, for yesterday I thought it a rare joke. The performance too was splendid, although twenty additional violins would not have been too many. *Vivat* Genius! and the devil take all criticism! . . . .

Z.

Wellington's Victory, or The Battle of Vittoria, is a work conceived on almost as vulgar a plan as the *Battle of Prague*, and contains few traces of his (Beethoven's) genius. This however is accounted for by the fact that the piece was suggested by Maelzel the mechanician, a man of undoubted ability, who knew the public taste far better than Beethoven did."

99.—GOETHE TO ZELTER.

Jena, 21st May, 1816.

.... I AM very glad that you approve of my Epilogue to *Essex*.* Madame Wolff begged me for a conclusion; I did not wish to get rid of it with mere phrases, and so I made a study of the history and the novel, upon which the play is founded. I might certainly just as well have written a new tragedy, as this Epilogue; so no wonder, if it was full of matter. And if you bear in mind, that it was written during the three days of the battle of Leipzig, many a prophetic line will seem to you of deeper significance. . . . .

A strange confusion presents itself, when one looks into the political and moral imbroglio of the world of Art, manufactures, and science: all sorts of advantages and disadvantages in the various branches, at one and the same time. Everything that is undergoing extension and enlargement, excellent! Everything that requires depth and unity, near its destruction.

I was very glad to get your report of Beethoven's Battle. Those are the advantages of a large city, which we go without. . . . .

G.

100.—GOETHE TO ZELTER.

Weimar, 6th June, 1816.

.... WHEN I tell thee, thou sterling, and much-tried son of earth, that my dear little wife has in these days left us, you will know what this means.†

G.

* A play by Banks and Dyk. The lines in Goethe's Epilogue :—
"Man must experience, be he who he may,
One last success and one last fatal day."
seem to point to Napoleon.
† On the day of his wife's death, Goethe wrote these lines :—
"O Sun, that striv'st in vain
Dark clouds to cross!
This is my life's whole gain,
To weep her loss."

101.—GOETHE TO ZELTER.

Weimar, 22nd July, 1816.

. . . . BEFORE leaving, I shall send a copy of your songs to Offenbach, for André. I am greatly pleased, that my sombre Byzantine derivation * could attract you; without some such foundation and derivation, all criticism is tomfoolery, and even with it, nothing is done, for it still requires a whole lifetime of observation and action; therefore, to no one would I more willingly hand over the surface of the earth, than to the bungler, who with complacent cheerfulness *demands indulgence*, with apparent earnestness, *desires a candid criticism*, and with modest pretension, *wants to be thought a good deal of*. May my Commentary show its gratitude to your text!

I have lately met with much kindness and affection. Friends of my youth, not seen for twenty-five years, and now elderly men, came unexpectedly to see me, and were glad to find many things in their old places, and much that had progressed, progressing further. On the evening of the 20th, when I was repelled with a protest, I found Chladni, who is gaining great credit, by his thorough and arduous study of meteoric stones and figures of sound. He is working for a time, when men will once more rejoice to learn from others, and gratefully make use of what they, by the sacrifice of their lives, have gained, more for others than for themselves. Nowadays, when one speaks, even to eminent men, of something which they ought to learn through tradition, they assure us, that they have not yet had time to examine it.

May God grant you less learned scholars, so that something of your virtues may remain upon the earth; but the others, who place themselves on a level with the highest, while in reality they are grovelling on the lowest steps, worshipping the semblance—leave them, I beseech you, in their self-complacency, for it would be a sin to break up their world.

Properly speaking, one ought not to return, after having

* See Letter 102.

departed this life; however, this time I succeeded in doing it again, the difference being only that of a few hours. Still it is strange, how once more life clutches hold of one instantly, and—just because time was so urgent, and they thought to lose me again directly, I experienced and effected as much as I usually do in weeks.

Things are looking quite cheerful in my household. August, as you know, enters very intelligently into everything, and we have, in a few hours, laid the foundation for our next winter's entertainments. I have been so helped with my chemistry and physics, that I do not know whether I ought to regret not being able to get to Würzburg this evening. . . . .

G.

102.—GOETHE TO ZELTER.

Tennstedt, 9th August, 1816.

. . . . OUR *Rochus Fest* * of 1814 is as good as finished; it is to enliven the second number. I should like to submit it to you, that it may be quite complete. Some few things may have escaped me.

I am very glad you adopt so cordially my derivation of modern from ancient Art. I am myself convinced that I have laid a good foundation; your parallel with music is very welcome. . . . .

G.

103.—GOETHE TO ZELTER.

Tennstedt, 28th August, 1816.

YOUR dear letter came yesterday at the right time, that I might enjoy it to-day, and have a chat with you. I am keeping this birthday in special solitude. Hofrath Meyer, who stayed with me for a month, and Geheimrath Wolf, who looked in for a day and a half, went away early this morning, and so I am left to myself.

---

* A sketch of the Festival of St. Rochus at Bingen, which Goethe had witnessed, in company with Zelter, and Cramer, the famous mineralogist.

These two men, each with great gifts, are widely different to live with. The former, though quite as certain of his subject as the latter, will never spoil a party, because he knows how to keep silence, and how to lead; the latter, on the other hand, is, in the strangest way, given to contradiction, for he obstinately gainsays every remark that is made, nay, every established fact, which puts one into a state of desperation, even though one is prepared for it. This ungracious manner grows upon him, year by year, and makes his society, which might otherwise be so instructive and profitable, useless and intolerable; nay, one ends by becoming infected with the same madness, and thinking it pleasant to say the reverse of what one believes.

One can readily imagine, how admirably this man must have acted as a teacher in former years, when he rejoiced in being thoroughly positive about things. . . . .

I have read with pleasure your article on Mesdames Catalani, Milder, and Mara; people never understand, that beautiful hours, like beautiful talents, must be enjoyed on the wing.

You will already have seen from the newspapers, how absurdly the Leipzigers have behaved at this juncture.* I think we shall be driven to preserve God's gifts in spirits, for such an accursed set of people, in order that when an opportunity occurs, they may compare and classify them.

The ancient Art of the Netherlands, as you have seen it at Heidelberg, will be a great gain to you, just because you do not wish to master it. Read my pamphlet again, and yet once again, now that you have seen the thing itself. I did not wish to settle the matter; for who can and dare do this? I know too, that no one is altogether satisfied with me; but this I know also, that the understanding can here find a way into the wood.

I have had reason lately to look into Teutonic poetry, and, as is my wont, I cannot resist taking some steps at once. If in doing this, I can seize upon any ballads for you, that will be my greatest reward. I would also gladly

---

* Referring to a scandalous criticism on Catalani, which appeared in the Leipzig newspaper.

render some service to the subject itself, but to me, the most sorrowful part of it is, that the Germans do not always clearly know, whether they are carrying home full wheat-sheaves, or bundles of straw.....

G.

104.—GOETHE TO ZELTER.

Weimar, September, 1816.

LAST time you found me in a melancholy state, and now I must sadden you. The enclosed letter contains the news of a great misfortune,* and my only comfort is to know you near me, and to feel that I am prepared to share your troubles with you.

G.

105.—GOETHE TO ZELTER.

Weimar, 14th October, 1816.

.... HEREWITH the new copy of my *Pflanzen-Metamorphose;* the missing part I have had written out, for it might probably be difficult to find it in Berlin. If, in your leisure hours, you should read the little work again, look upon it merely as symbolical, and always imagine to yourself some other kind of vitality, developing progressively out of itself. I have again looked into Linnæus' writings lately, in which he founds the science of botany, and I now see very clearly, that I too have used them only symbolically, that is, I attempted to transfer the same method and style of treatment to other subjects, thereby acquiring an organ, with which a great deal may be done.....

G.

---

* This refers to the death of Zelter's little daughter, Clärchen, which took place at Berlin, during Zelter's absence at Weimar.

106.—Goethe to Zelter.

Weimar, 7th November, 1816.

.... Truly not till we are old, do we know what we met with in youth. Once for all, we learn and comprehend nothing! All that affects us is but incitement, and, God be praised, if anything does but stir in response! I have again been reading Linnæus lately, and am amazed at this extraordinary man. I have learned any amount from him, only not botany. Barring Shakespeare and Spinoza, I do not know that any dead writer has had such an effect upon me.

It is strange, but quite natural, that people should speculate on our last days as on Sibylline leaves, having coldly and impiously allowed a bonfire of the time that went before.—I have pressing and tempting invitations to the Rhine, of which you have probably heard, as people there seem to consider it quite a settled matter. But what is all that to me? I own to perceiving the good effect of my few summers on the Rhine and Maine, for, after all, I merely preached St. John's Epistle, "*Little children, love one another*," and that failing, "*Live and let live.*" And you will approve of my saying, that if this heavenly message should to some extent take hold of your Nineveh, you would become quite different people, without being more or less than you are.

But to what end is the outlay of days and hours in direct personal exertion? I will rather, from my quiet, unmolested abode, dictate and copy so much, and print, and let things lie, for publication abroad or for keeping at home, so that everyone, as you very rightly feel, may be silent as to the source from whence he gets them, and that anyhow the whole of humanity may be bolstered up a little.

All the tomfooleries about pre- and post-occupations, plagiarisms and half purloinings, are perfectly clear to me, and I think them silly. For what is in the air, and what the age demands, may suddenly enter into a hundred people's heads at once, without anyone having borrowed from the other. But here let us stop, for in the dispute about priority, as in that about legitimacy, no one possesses a prior claim, nor one that is more rightful, than he who can preserve himself.

If Isegrimm * goes on telling of his absurd behaviour towards me, it points to a bad conscience; he will not report, how bestially I replied to it. Luckily or unluckily, I had taken more glasses of Burgundy than I ought to have done, so that I too went beyond bounds. Meyer, who is always composed, was sitting near, and felt rather uneasy at the affair.

It was on the night of the 27th of August, and I had already formed a friendly plan of celebrating my birthday on the 28th with this friend, who had arrived unexpectedly. It chanced that Meyer had to leave in the morning, and, although unwillingly, I allowed that excellent unbearable to drive off, and spent the 28th of August pleasantly, alone. That man, steeped in contradiction, would, in honour of my fête-day, have ended by maintaining that I had never been born.

All this, however, will come home to him, and in the end, he will not know what to do with himself. Herder, too, was presumptuous enough to carry youthful follies of this kind over into old age, and at last became almost desperate about it. Examine yourself, and see if such stuff is to be found in you; I do so every day. One must not swerve in oneself, not even a hair's breadth, from the highest maxims of Art and life; but in empiricism, in the movement of the day, I would rather allow what is mediocre to pass, than mistake the good, or even find fault with it. . . . .

I have again revised my *Rochus-Festival*, and had it copied out; it has gained in definiteness and brilliancy. Unless one imitates the painters, who put on more washes again, the more they stipple, detaching and once more re-uniting the objects, nothing can come of such things.

The first essay of the second issue will create a mighty noise; it is called *Neu-Deutsche, fromm-patrictische Kunst.*

Yours,

G.

* F. A. Wolf. See Note to Letter 121.

Weimar, November 7th, 1816.

.... Please send me the books unfranked. In fact no one need scruple to send me anything in this way, as I have the freedom of the post, which I prefer to the freedom of the press, though I occasionally avail myself of that also.

More ere long! Generally speaking, goodness and excellence may accrue to many things, if cultivated men club together, to act constitutionally. We Germans stand pretty high, and have no reason whatever for allowing ourselves to be driven about, hither and thither, by the wind.

All good spirits praise the Lord God!

GOETHE.

107.—GOETHE TO ZELTER.

Weimar, 14th November, 1816.

IN order that our friendly and animating discussion may not come to a standstill, I send you a few words, with reference to your proposal to write a Cantata for the Reformation Jubilee. It would, I suppose, best shape itself on the lines of Handel's *Messiah*, a work into which you have penetrated so deeply.

As the leading idea of Lutheranism rests on a very dignified foundation, it gives a fine opportunity for poetical, as well as musical treatment. Now this basis rests on the decided contrast between the *Law* and the *Gospel*, and secondly, upon the accommodation of such extremes. And now, if in order to attain a higher standpoint, we substitute for those two words, the expressions *Necessity* and *Freedom*, with their synonyms, their remoteness and proximity, you see clearly, that in this circle is contained everything that can interest mankind.

And thus Luther perceives in the Old and New Testaments, the symbol of the great and ever-recurring order of the world. On the one hand the Law, striving after love, and on the other, love, striving back towards the Law, and fulfilling it, though not of its own power and strength, but through faith; and that too, by exclusive faith in the Messiah, proclaimed to all,—all powerful.

Thus briefly, we are convinced, that Lutheranism can never be united with the Papacy, but that it does not contradict pure reason, so soon as reason decides upon regarding the Bible, as the mirror of the world; which indeed it should not find difficult.

To express these ideas in a poem, adapted to music, I should begin with the thunder on Mount Sinai, with the *Thou shalt*, and should conclude with the Resurrection of Christ, and the *Thou wilt!*

For the further illustration of my plan, I will add the successive order, in which the whole should be arranged.

First Part.

1. The giving of the Law on Mount Sinai.
2. The warlike, pastoral life, as described in the Books of Judges, Ruth, &c.
3. The consecration of Solomon's Temple.
4. The break up of the worshippers, who are driven to the mountains and hill-tops.
5. The destruction of Jerusalem, followed by the Babylonish captivity.
6. Prophets and Sibyls, announcing the Messiah.

Second Part.

1. St. John in the wilderness, taking up the Proclamation.
2. The recognition by the Three Kings.
3. Christ appears as a Teacher, and draws the multitude to Him. Entry into Jerusalem.
4. At the approach of danger, the multitude disperses; His friends fall asleep; His sufferings on the Mount of Olives.
5. The Resurrection.

On comparing these two parts, the first seems to be intentionally longer, and has a decided central point, which however is not wanting in the second either.

In the First Part, numbers 1 and 5 are parallel with each other; Sinai and the Destruction, the time of the Judges, and the service of Baal; numbers 2 and 4, idyllic, enthusiastic, the consecration of the Temple as the highest climax, &c.

In the Second Part, in numbers 1 and 5, the dawn preceding the sunrise would be expressed in gradually ascending strains. Numbers 2 and 4 stand in contrast. Number 3, the entry into Jerusalem, might express the unconstrained and pious joy of the people, in the same way as the consecration of the Temple expresses the princely, priestly limitation of the Divine worship.

Thousands of other situations will occur to you at the first glance. These things must not be connected historically, but lyrically; everyone knows the whole, and will gladly allow himself to be transported from one region into the other, on the wings of poetry.

The text should consist of passages from the Bible, well-known evangelical hymns, interspersed with what has been written in later times, and whatever else can be found. Luther's own words could hardly be made use of, as the good man is thoroughly dogmatic and practical; so also is his enthusiasm. But, after all, it is your business to look into the writings themselves. Above all things, read his preface to the Psalms, which is quite inestimable. Further, his prefaces and introductions to the other Biblical books. Probably you will there come across applicable passages, and at the same time, succeed in thoroughly grasping the meaning of the whole doctrine, the gift of which we propose to commemorate.

Perhaps after what has been said above, this is the place to add a few words concerning Catholicism. Soon after its first origin and promulgation, the Christian religion lost its original purity through heresies, rational and irrational. But as it was called upon to check and control barbarous nations, and morally corrupted people, harsh means were necessary; they did not want doctrines, but service. The one Mediator between the Highest God of Heaven and earthly men was not enough, &c. as we all know; and thus there arose a kind of heathenish Judaism, which exists, and makes its influence felt, up to the present day. All this had to be revolutionized in men's minds, for which reason Lutheranism refers itself solely to the Bible. Luther's conduct is no secret, and now that we are about to commemorate him, we cannot do so in the right way, unless we acknowledge his merits, and describe what he achieved, both in his own day, and for those that came after him. This Festival should be given in such a manner, that every right-minded Catholic should be able to join in its celebration. Of this, however, more anon. If my plan pleases you, erect something for yourself, and tell me about it, and I will join. So much, if it be not too much, for to-day! The Weimar Friends of Art are similarly actuated, in their preparations for the monument they have already designed. We are making no secret of the matter, and hope at all events to contribute our share.

G.

108.—GOETHE TO ZELTER.

Weimar, 10th December, 1816.

YOUR little Song has arrived; we thank you heartily for what you have done so well. If the melody is varied to suit the text, as you have indicated, it cannot fail to be very effective. In return, I send you the scheme for the grand Cantata, further developed; may it come into full flower with you! I have kept a copy of it. . . . .

The composer must accurately weigh the relations of all the different parts to one another, and reserve for himself continuous *Crescendos*, which he can get by variation, starting from the thunderings on Mount Sinai.

Taking Handel's *Alexander's Feast* as my guide, instead of giving but the one character of Timotheus, as he appears in that work, I have introduced several speakers, who may be imagined, now merely reciting, now singing, now competing with the Chorus, just as may be considered fit in the course of the action.

The speakers are mostly men, but should it be necessary, women may be substituted. What I particularly wish to know is, how the leading parts are to be distributed, and in what passages one should introduce regular Airs, for which Biblical and other pious sayings might then be adapted, in such a way, as to be recognizable, and yet at the same time more convenient rhythmically.

First Part.

Symphony.
At the end, thunder on Mount Sinai.
An eager semi-chorus, (the people,) is bent on seeing closely what goes on.
The Levites, (a semi-chorus,) restrain them.
The people are thrust back from Sinai, and worship their God.
Aaron, in his speech on the apostacy to the golden calf, inaugurates the scene.
The people humble themselves, and receive the Law.
Speaker. (Joshua.)
March through the Wilderness.
Conquest of the land.
Warlike Shepherd-Choruses, similar to those in my *Pandora*.
Speaker, (Samuel,) explains the fluctuation of the people, between Priesthood and Monarchy.
Steadfastness of the king and nation in their conception of the only national God.
Solomon's accession to the throne.
Choruses of women.
The Shulamite, the best beloved, in the distance.
Choruses of Priests.
Consecration of the Temple.
Choruses of all kinds.
Speaker. (Elijah.)
Preparing the way for the apostacy to Baal.
Service on Mountain-heights, and in the open air.
Choruses of the people, who are returning to the pleasantness of their earlier and freer open air life.
Mirthful festivity, less religiosity.
Choruses of priests of the Baal type, imposing from their harshness and roughness.
Speaker. (Jonas.) Threats, prophesying the coming of great hordes of enemies.
Approach of the enemy.
Anxiety.
Downfall of the kingdom, violent.
Captivity. Lovely and melancholy.
Speaker, (Isaiah,) predicting salvation and future happiness.

Choruses, accepting the prediction gratefully, but in an earthly sense.
Choruses of Prophets and Sibyls, pointing to the spiritual and eternal.
Triumphant Finale.

Second Part.

Symphony.
Sunrise.
Loveliness of the early morning.
Rural, not pastoral.
Expanse of solitude.
Speaker. (St. John.)
He receives the promise.
He beholds the star of the Nativity.
As the morning star.
Ushering in the approach of the Three Kings.
Procession of the Three Kings.

There is nothing contradictory in Janissary music being used here, for of course it came to us from the other side of the Oxus. It would be specially appropriate on the arrival of the Third King, who is always represented as something of a barbarian.

(This scene must needs be decidedly dramatic, for the sake of variety.)

The Kings vanish in the distance.
Speaker. (Christ.)
He appears as a Teacher.
Chorus attentive, but hesitating.
His teaching becomes more elevated.
The people throng around Him and applaud, but always in an earthly sense.
Christ elevates His teaching to the spiritual level.
The people misunderstand Him more and more.
Entry into Jerusalem.
Speakers. (Three Apostles.)
Fear of danger.
Christ consoling, strengthening, and admonishing.
Alone, in anguish of soul.
The extreme agony.

Speaker. (Evangelist.)
Brief mention of the physical suffering.
Death. Resurrection.
Chorus of Angels.
Chorus of the terrified watchmen.
Chorus of women.
Chorus of the disciples.
Everything earthly dies away, and the spiritual rises higher and higher, until it reaches to the Ascension, and Immortality.

1817.

109.—GOETHE TO ZELTER.
Weimar, 1st January, 1817.

.... WITH the New Year comes the announcement of my son's marriage with the elder Fräulein von Pogwisch;* it is the wish of both the young people, and I have nothing to say against it. Court and Town sanction their union, which will found some very pleasant social relations. . . . .

Farewell, and do not omit, from time to time, to set your swan and bustard quills in motion for my sake.

G.

110.—ZELTER TO GOETHE.
Berlin, 8th January, 1817.

.... YOUR letter of New Year's Day contains delightful New Year's news. The marriage of your good August with a girl, who is popular and beloved, both at Court, and in the country, may and must make you happy too.

Here comes the young wifeling, and strokes the old gentleman's beard, and tickles him behind the ear, slinks off at the right moment, and tastes the soup, peeps into corners, and flicks away the dust with her finger, looks out for the weather, goes to the stable, orders the carriage to be brought round, turns the old fellow out into the sunshine, gives him a good airing, packs him back again into the chaise, and settles his cloak straight, while at home— there stands the soup in friendly expectation, and it's "Papa" here and "Papa" there, and wherever things go

---

* Ottilie von Pogwisch had, as a child, delighted Goethe with her singing, at his private concerts, and he hoped by this marriage to reclaim his son, who already showed signs of the dissolute tendency, which eventually ruined him. Goethe was very fond of Ottilie; "when he was in Jena, she had to write to him every week; so too he wrote to her." (See Düntzer's *Charlotte von Stein*.)

a little bit wrong or awry, there she steps quietly in, once more restoring the magnetic force of happy union.

My love to your dear boy, and his darling; he may reckon on my warmest sympathy. His happiness is in his own hands, and for his prosperity—may the gods be favourable, and no demon disturb it. . . . .

Z.

111.—GOETHE TO ZELTER.

Weimar, 23rd February, 1817.

. . . . PRAISE and gratitude to you for the good words, with which you so loyally honour *Iphigenie!* * My *Italiänische Reise* shows how strangely the second edition came about. It is there noticed, that the ancient Tragedians have treated this subject, and it could not fail to charm me, when I had become so much at home in the house of Atreus.

A cyclical treatment has many advantages, only we moderns do not know exactly how to manage it. . . . .

I have again brought *Mahomet* † upon the stage, as a means for practising our first grammatical exercises. Things look strange enough,—as regards myself, they are as favourable as possible. In the actual artistic, technical, and economical details, the arrangement could not be better; but at the end, a stupid piece of mismanagement excited general indignation, and an explosion was inevitable.‡ I expected it, and thought I should get quit of the whole business; instead of which, I felt myself bound to help in supporting the rotten edifice. This is quite possible, and easy for me, as my son has been associated with me in the Management, and I exercise unlimited power in the art-department, without being worried by collateral matters. In a short time, everything will look different, and if I continue up to Midsummer, doing what I have done during the last three weeks, I shall be able to go forth into the wide

---

* In a previous letter, Zelter had praised the altered version of *Iphigenie.*
† Goethe's Translation of Voltaire's *Mahomet.*
‡ See the end of this Letter.

world, and the Theatre will gain more from this, than the Athenians did, from Solon's laws and departure. . . . .

To fill up the empty space, I will tell you in confidence, that for quite a fortnight, day and night, (when the latter means a great deal with me,) I have been busy with a piece of work, which you would not credit me with. It is this. I am revising Kotzebue's *Schützgeist.* They had very stupidly given the piece *in extenso,* on the Grand Duchess's birthday. It lasted till half-past ten o'clock; the Court and the Town protested against its reproduction. But as the motives of this piece of patchwork are still interesting to some extent, and exactly what the people like, I set to work at it, and became the protecting spirit of *The Protecting Spirit.* It now holds its place in our *répertoire,* and by this alone I feel myself richly rewarded for my trouble.

Farewell, and write soon.

Yours,
G.

112.—GOETHE TO ZELTER.

Jena, 29th May, 1817.

. . . . SINCE Jena revived again, I have had many interesting experiences in the natural history department, and, like Ezekiel, I am utterly amazed to see the old bone-field suddenly stirred up to life. Before Midsummer, I expect to be able to publish a Number, consisting of twelve sheets, and shall let my old guards of the sovereignty of Nature march up in a series of columns. All this I could do the more calmly, that the Second Part of my *Rhein und Main,* which is worth some fugitive productions, was on its way to you.

The manifestos of war and peace therein contained will be ceaselessly attacked. I have not much more time to be sincere,—therefore let us make use of it; the aspect of things is really too foolish, when we, from our own standpoint, distinctly see what incredible advantages and privileges the century has, what admirable individuals are at work in it, and how, nevertheless, everything is in a state of confusion, one sphere of activity destroying the other, so that every person I speak to individually, seems reasonable, but when regarded relatively, mad This goes so far, that I sometimes seem to myself to have two natures, and do not rally from this feeling of doubt, till I converse with persons, who are at home in their own province, both theoretically and practically. And in an Academy such as ours was and is, these are always to be found.

As I have now moved into a pretty, cheerful Gardenhouse, the second Part of my *Italiänische Reise* will be taken in hand next, of course with the old motto, "I too was born in Arcadia." This Italy is so hackneyed a country, that were it not that I see myself reflected in it, as in a youth-restoring mirror, I would rather have nothing at all to do with it.

These are my present pursuits, though at the end of May, and in this loveliest of garden-dwellings, I am freezing in a comfortless fog, and for the first time thoroughly understand a huge stove of the year 1661, in a fairly sized room. After all, what clever fellows our ancestors were! . . . .
G.

113.—GOETHE TO ZELTER.

Jena, 16th December, 1817.

. . . . I AM living between Weimar and Jena; at both places, I have work which gives me pleasure. In Jena, I can actually work and learn at the same time; natural science, especially chemistry, is so vigorous, that one gets young again most pleasantly, seeing that one finds one's earliest forebodings, hopes, and wishes realized, and at the same time, vouchers for the best and highest to which one can raise oneself in thought. My next number of *Naturlehre* will, I hope, supply you with much that is symbolic of your own kind and benevolent intentions.

In this innocent way, I live my quiet life, and allow the horrible smell of the Wartburg fire,* at which all Germany is taking offence, to pass off; it would, by this time, have evaporated here, had it not been driven back by the North East wind, and smothered us a second time.

* An allusion to the patriotic Festival, celebrated in 1817, by the *Burschenschaftler*, at the Wartburg. (See Buchheim's edition of Heine's *Rosa*, pp. 180, 294.)

In such cases, the individual person who suffers from the universal folly, must be allowed to say with some self-complacency, that even if he did not foresee, he felt all this beforehand, and that, with regard to those points, which had become clear to him, he not only advised against, but also advised in favour of, advised indeed the very things which everyone wishes he had done, when the business goes wrong. This justifies my impassibility, for which reason, I have—like the Epicurean gods—enveloped myself in a quiet cloud; would that I could draw it more closely about me, and make it more and more dense and impenetrable. . . . .

A work which the Grand Duke brought with him from Milan, with reference to the *Last Supper* of Leonardo da Vinci, has taken great hold of me. The engraving by Morghen is of course often to be met with in Berlin; and even though you should happen to know it already, take another look at it, and examine it with respectful attention. You will then find it deeply affecting, when you hear from me all the particulars,—what was the origin of the picture, how it was thought out, composed, elaborated, and finished, as a wonder of the world; again, how it faded away at once, was neglected, injured, restored, and by this very restoration, utterly destroyed. Further, you will be glad to find, that the Milanese are still deserving of honour, for their veneration of this corpse, and the way in which they preserve and keep alive the traces of its remembrance. And having got thus far, and hoping for a speedy reply, I will only add kind greetings to friends.

G.

114.—GOETHE TO ZELTER.

Jena, 31st December, 1817.

AT your suggestion, I have been looking through the few scraps of poetry I have by me, and find only the enclosed, which may perhaps come in useful for your Society. It was an extemporary offering to my very old friend, Knebel, on his seventy-third birthday. Good luck to the Society, which may also sing it at certain epochs! . . . .

G.

Lustrum hath a foreign sound!
Lustra then express it!
Eight or nine, on this same ground,
We have borne, confess it!
Laughed and lived, and as it came,
Loved perhaps another;
He that strives to do the same,
He shall be our brother,—
Say, 'Tis much. Life strews our way,
Not with thornless flowers!—
But the goal's the goal to-day,
And rejoicing ours!

30th November, 1817.

G.

1818.

115.—ZELTER TO GOETHE.

11th January, 1818.

.... SHOULD you be willing to send me your explanatory poems, please do so as soon as possible, as I am rather in the humour just now; I always want more time for freeing myself from my usual surroundings, than I do for the actual work. I could not help smiling, any more than you could, when I heard you had read Mattheson's* *Vollkommene Capellmeister*. That man was Secretary of Legation for Great Britain up to the time of his death, and an eminently useful statesman at the same time. By the the time he had reached his seventy-second year, he had written the same number of works, mostly musical, which cut a strange figure nowadays. I am very fond of dipping into them, for they always help me to thoughts for which I should have to seek far enough, Heaven knows, but for him! Some time ago, I sent you a good manuscript copy of *Das Wohltemperirte Clavier*, so you ought not to have been forced to buy it. . . .

Z.

116.—GOETHE TO ZELTER.

Jena, 20th January, 1818.

.... ROSSINI was once asked, which of his Operas pleased him best? His answer was—"*Il Matrimonio Segreto*."†

---

* Johann Mattheson, better known as an author than as a musician, was one of Handel's earliest friends at Hamburg. Their dispute and consequent duel, so nearly fatal to the great composer, are well known to the students of Handel's biography. His versatility was wonderful. At different times of his life, he was an operatic singer, an organist, a tutor, a Cantor, and the caron of a cathedral, besides which, he wrote and composed. Perhaps *Der Vollkommene Capellmeister* is the most valuable of his numerous works.

† This seems to be a mistake; the Opera cited by Rossini was, according to his latest biographer, *Don Giovanni*.

In the second Act of *Elena*, an Opera by old Mayer of Bergamo,* there is said to be a very effective Sestett; a popular Bohemian melody, a sort of Notturno, is said to be the principal theme. Would it be possible to get hold of the score of this Sestett?

For several years past, your *Fasch* has been lying among a number of papers in Jena; I found it lately, and read it at one sitting, with great edification. How it transports one into another world! And how passing strange is that old item, out of the catalogue of universal history,—the King! I say "old," and he has not yet been dead forty years, but his deeds of commission and omission are already antiquated,—though this may perhaps be ascribed to the hurry of these last days. Now farewell! and let me soon have some cheerful tidings. . . . .

G.

117.—GOETHE TO ZELTER.

Jena, 16th February, 1818.

. . . . You know Jena too little for it to mean anything to you, when I tell you, that on the right bank of the Saal, close to the Camsdorf bridge, above the ice-laden waters, which are dashing violently through the arches, I have taken possession of a tower, (*vulgo Erker*,) which has for many years past tempted me, my friends, and my own people to live there, though not one of us would ever have given himself the trouble to mount the staircase. Here I while away the happiest hours of the day, looking out on the river, the bridge, the gravel-walks, meadows and gardens, and then upon the dear funny nest itself, with the hills and mountains, and heights, famous in battle, rising beyond. When the sky is clear, I can, day by day, see the sun setting somewhat later, and more to the north; by this I regulate my return to town.†

In this state of almost absolute solitude, the Third Part of my *Kunst und Alterthum* has been prepared for the

---

* Johann Simon Mayer, the composer of no less than seventy Operas. His fame in Italy was only eclipsed by that of Rossini, who, it is said, borrowed from him his well-known orchestral *Crescendo*.

† Goethe occupied rooms on the top-story of the Inn *Zur Tanne*, where he remained till the end of June.

press. The Second Part of my *Morphologie* is likewise progressing. I hope to get the upper hand of my *Entoptische Farben*, in connection with my *Farbenlehre*, before Easter. Let friend Schulz know of this, if you chance to meet him anywhere.

Further, I should not forget to tell you, that we have the most complete arrangements for observing atmospheric changes, while I, on my part, try to interweave the *forms of the clouds*, and the *colours* of the sky, with words and images.

But as all this, except for the whistling of the wind and the rushing of the water, runs off absolutely without a sound, I really want some inner harmony, to keep my ear correct; and this is possible, only by my faith in you, and in what you do and what you value. Therefore I send you only a few fervent prayers, as branches from my Paradise. If you can but distil them in your hot element, I suppose the drink can be swallowed comfortably, and the heathen will be made whole!

Apocalypse—last chapter! Verse 2.

That joke I told you of, you did not understand. Someone, talking to that composer, named several of his works, and asked him which he thought the best; he replied— *Il Matrimonio Segreto*, meaning the composition of Paesiello. I need not further explain the neatness and ingenuity of his answer. . . . .

G.

118.—GOETHE TO ZELTER.

(Not dated.)

As our correspondence is only by fits and starts, now that the flood-gates have once been opened, I may as well tell you this, that, and the other.

First then, with regard to your question about Leonardo's *Last Supper*. Of this priceless work, the first complete fugue of a painter, surpassing all that had preceded it, and yielding to none that came after it, a mere shadow is all that remains in the place where it was painted, the approximate position in which the figures stood to one another.

But we can form a certain idea of it, from several copies that were made of it, of which I can only mention three specifically.

1500—1512.

One by Marco d'Oggionno, at Castellazzo, in the refectory of a deserted convent; it is a little smaller than life, highly characteristic, and smacks of Leonardo's teaching and example.

1565.

One at Ponte Capriasca, weaker than the above, though on the same lines; very useful for comparison.

1612—1616.

One in the Ambrosian Library at Milan, the upper part of the figures painted by Andrea Bianchi, called Vespino; the figures life-size like the original, very good and effective, but without a trace of Leonardo. The faces are already passing into empty generalities, such as one sees in drawing-books.

It is from these three copies, that the drawing for Morghen's engraving was made, as well as Bossi's cartoon and his life-size paintings, an enormous mosaic of which was constructed at Milan, by command of the Viceroy.

But I can tell you thus much by way of consolation, that for Morghen's engraving, the old genuine copy in Castellazzo was invariably consulted with scrupulous care, so that, after all, a great deal more has remained to us, than we suppose.

But meanwhile, until you learn circumstantially what I have to say about it, as you very likely will at Easter, through my pamphlet upon *Kunst und Alterthum*, look up the Heidelberg *Jahrbücher* for December, 1816, in which Müller of Rome, otherwise called "*Maler* (Painter) Müller," has given a clever illustration from Bossi's work, with some thoughtful notes, from which alone you may gain a great deal. The gaps which he leaves, I fill up.

As soon as you again come across the engraving, apply your laws of counterpoint to it; it will be a great delight to you.

G.

119.—ZELTER TO GOETHE.

Berlin, 1st March, 1818.

.... MAYER'S Opera of *Elena* was destroyed by fire; worse still, the music is unknown, but in spite of that, I have commissioned them to get the Sestett you want. I suppose it is the well-known Simon Mayer? You did not write his Christian name, and here, no one knows of any other Mayer among composers. Stop! One of my earlier disciples, Meyer-Beer by name, created a *furore* in Padua last year with one of his Operas,* and he might be the *younger*, as you speak of the *old* Mayer. . . . .

Z.

120.—GOETHE TO ZELTER.

Weimar, 8th March, 1818.

MY best thanks for your midnight souvenir.† Here is something about the old Mayer, which will amuse you. How I wish I could be borne upward, on Faust's cloak, and let myself down in your Opera-house, at your grand function. Earthly means and ways will hardly bring me to Berlin. More in my next.

G.

Enclosure.‡

"At Bergamo, Church-music is still all the rage. I thought I saw before me the Italians of 1730.

"The beauties of the Church-music are nearly all conventional, and although a Frenchman, I cannot reconcile myself to furious chanting. The Bergamese spare no pains to satisfy their passion, which is favoured by two circumstances: the famous Mayer lives at Bergamo; so does old David. Marchesi and David seem to me the Berninis of vocal music, great talents, destined to usher in the reign of bad taste. They were the precursors of Madame Catalani, and of Pachiarotti, the last of the Romans.

* *Romilda e Costanza*, in which Pisaroni had the leading part.
† The Song, *Um Mitternacht*.
‡ Translated from the French.

"Mayer might have wooed a more brilliant fate, but gratitude attaches him to this country; born in Bavaria, he came accidentally to Bergamo, and the *chanoine*, Count Scotti, sent him to the Naples Conservatoire, and supported him there for several years; after that, he was offered the choir of Bergamo, and although the post was not worth more than twelve or fifteen hundred francs, the most brilliant offers could not attract him elsewhere. I have heard it said at Naples, where he wrote the Cantata of *St. Charles*, that he would not travel any more; if that is so, he will write no more music. In Italy, a composer must always be on the spot, to study the voices of his singers, and write his Opera. A few years ago, the managers of La Scala offered Paesiello ten thousand francs; he answered, that at eighty years of age, people no longer ran about the country, and he would send his music; they declined with thanks.

"It is plain, that we owe Mayer to the generosity of a rich amateur; so also Canova and Monti. When Monti's father refused to send him any more money, he was about to quit Rome in tears, and had already engaged his *vetturino*. Two nights before starting, he happened to read aloud some verses at the *Académie des Arcades*. Prince Braschi sends for him—'Remain at Rome; go on composing fine verses; I will ask my uncle for a post for you.' Monti became private secretary to the Prince. Somewhere or other, he unearthed a monk, the General of his order, a clever, philosophical man. He proposed to introduce him to the Prince-nephew, but the monk refused. Such singular modesty piqued the Prince; stratagems were used to bring the monk to him, and soon afterwards, he became the Cardinal Chiaramonti.

"Patriotism is common in Italy; see the life, (related to me at Bergamo,) of that poor Count Fantuzzi of Ravenna. This patriotism is discouraged in every way, and forced to lose itself in *niaiseries*.

"At Bergamo, when Mayer and David conduct the Church-music, they get an *oro*, *i.e.* a piece of gold.

"They are now reviving an Opera of Mayer's—*Elena* —which was played before *La Testa di Bronzo;* what languishing music! The transports at the Sestett in the second Act! that is the *musique de nocturne*, gentle, melting, the true music of melancholy, which I have so often heard in Bohemia. This is a bit of genius, which the veteran Mayer has kept from early days, or else, somebody gave it him; it supported the entire Opera. There's a people for you! Why, they are born for *the beautiful!* An Opera, two hours in duration, is sustained by one delicious movement, which lasts hardly six minutes; people come fifty miles to hear this Sestett, sung by Mademoiselle Fabre, Remorini, Bassi, Bonoldi, &c., and through the forty performances, six minutes make them forget two hours of *ennui*. There is nothing shocking in the rest of the Opera, but there is simply nothing at all."

The above are extracts from a curious book, entitled, *Rome, Naples et Florence, en* 1817. *Par M. de Stendhal, officier de Cavalerie. Paris* 1817. which you must certainly get. The name is an assumed one; the traveller is a gay Frenchman, an enthusiast for music, dancing, and the Theatre. These few specimens will show you his free-and-easy style. He both attracts and repels, interests and annoys the reader, so one cannot get rid of him. One reads the book over and over again with renewed pleasure, and would like to learn certain passages by heart. He seems to be one of those clever fellows, whom the besom of war has driven hither and thither, an officer, *employé*, or spy, by turns,—or perhaps all at the same time. He has been in a number of different places, and knows how to use the traditions of others, and generally, how to appropriate a good deal to himself. He translates passages from my *Italiänische Reise*, and maintains that he heard the little story from a Marchesina. Enough, one must not only read the book, but possess it.

G.

121.—GOETHE TO ZELTER.

(Written in the little room above the Saal, amid wind and rain.)

19th March, 1818.

.... You have been a great benefactor to m^e lately, for the *Midnight Song* has been sung to me, properly and sympathetically, by a gentle, sweet creature, whose energy only partially failed her in the last strophe. Once again, you have right loyally and well set a seal on your love and regard for me. My son, who is not easily moved, was beside himself, and I fear that out of gratitude, he will ask you to stand godfather.

I am back again in my turret, over the bridge, and the roaring waters; the stout wooden rafts, trunk to trunk, doubly bound, are being steered carefully through, and pass safely down the stream; one man is sufficient for this duty, the second seems to be there, merely for the sake of company.

The logs of firewood follow after, in dilettante fashion; some, as Heaven wills, come to land somehow, others are carried away in the whirl, whilst others, at intervals, are pushed up on to the gravel and sand banks. To-morrow, perhaps the water will rise, lift them all up, and carry them miles off to their destination, the fireside. You see I have no need to trouble myself with the daily papers, as the most perfect symbols come to pass before my own eyes.

However, if I am to be candid, this peacefulness is only apparent; for I had long wished to do honour to, and enjoy the musical doings of your Passion-week, with you, whereas now, my eye and spirit are hovering over the anarchy of the wood-rafts.

But if I am to be perfectly sincere, let me comfort myself by telling you, that if you are quite honest in your feelings towards me, you will not invite me to come to Berlin; and in this, Schulz, Hirt, Schadow, and all who really wish me well, agree. To our excellent friend, Isegrimm,* (pray remember me to him,) it is all one and the same; in me, he would merely have one person the more to contradict. I care as little to hear about the hundred hexameters, as about the hundred days of Bonaparte's last administration. God keep me from German Rhythmicism, as from French change of dynasty! The 6/8 time of your *Midnight* exhausts everything. Such quantities and quali-

---

* F. A. Wolf, the author of *Prolegomena ad Homerum*. In a former letter, Zelter asks, " Has not our Grimmbart sent you his hundred hexameters ? " See Letter 106.

ties of tone, such variety of movement, of pauses, and drawings of breath!—ever equal, ever changing! The gentlemen with their longs and shorts (— ᴗ ᴗ —) may talk each other into agreement for a long time, before they produce such work as yours.

They always forget that they used to assure us, till we were weary of it, that a poet is no grammarian! Homer, Homerides, rhapsodists, and all the motley throng, prattled on, as God willed, until at last they were fortunate enough to have their stupid stuff copied, when the grammarians took pity on them, and after a lapse of two thousand years of turning and twisting, at last brought matters so far, that with the exception of the priests of these mysteries, no one knows, nor can know, anything further about the subject. Someone assured me lately, that Xenophon wrote just as bad prose as I do; this surely should be some consolation to me.

To fill up my remaining space, let me tell you a good joke. Our Milanese friends,* whom the Grand Duke learnt to know on his travels, men of rare value, knowledge, activity, and practical wisdom, whom I have every reason to cultivate, do not understand a word of German.

I am having my essay on the *Last Supper* translated into French, by a clever Frenchman, who came to us, as an emigrant, and endured with us, during the time of the invasion, the visits of his blessed compatriots, and the consequences thereof. It is a most curious experience, to see oneself reflected in the mirror of a foreign language. I have never troubled myself about the translations of my works; this however goes into the life of the matter, and is therefore very interesting to me. If I am to find again in the French that description, which I merely wrote down in German, just as I felt it, I must here and there come to the rescue, but this will not be a difficult matter, as the translator has succeeded in giving evidence of the logical flexibility of his own language, without injuring the impression on the senses.

---

* People who were anxious to patronize Goethe, but had never read any of his works in the original.

In spite of having perhaps bored you, at the beginning of this letter, with my account of the rafts, made of large trunks of trees, I must end by telling you, that to-day— Holy Thursday—the day of your festival—the great timber Fair is being held at Kosen on the Saal, above Naumburg, where future town and country edifices are floating about by the hundred, in the rough; the Architect of all the worlds grant that they and we may prosper!

Tui amantissimus,
G.

122.—ZELTER TO GOETHE.

Berlin, 7th April, 1818.

.... A NEW Tragedy has sprung upon us—*Die Ahnfrau,* by a gentleman calling himself Grillparzer,— trouble and woe from first to last. .... There is unmistakable talent, though it is all lost; the light is wanting, and where that is not, I am much obliged to you for the shadow. .... What beautiful soul then was German enough to sing you that song, (*Um Mitternacht,*) without Italianisms, and with such animation, that you could not help being pleased? ....

I have set for you *Kennst Du das Land,* for the sixth time, so as to satisfy myself once at all events; the best specimen shall migrate to Weimar. .....

Z.

123.—GOETHE TO ZELTER.

Jena, 28th June, 1818.

.... IF not disagreeable to you, I should like to send a copy of your Motett to Thibaut of Heidelberg; although a jurist, he has a sensitive musical temperament, and has, as I hear, gathered about him a circle of resolute friends, who perform the compositions of the older masters lovingly, zealously, and carefully. It is a reflex of light called forth by you; I cannot say indeed, how clearly it shines, but people who know were very much pleased.

Ten sheets of my *Divan* have been printed, nine of my

Kunst und Alterthum, and four of *Morphologie*. Some, if not all, must reach you by Michaelmas. There is no more company, at least not for me, so I am entertaining myself at present, by dictating, with a hope that, at some future time, the influence of my work will be felt at a distance.

It seems so strange to one, when one contemplates gravely and benevolently the doings of men—(speaking merely with regard to Plastic Art, in which I am most interested.) The most gifted people come to me, urging me to tell them what they are to do, and when I tell them my honest opinion, and they, having been convinced, take the first steps, they immediately slip back again from the silliest conventionalism into the most commonplace bungling, and are as well satisfied, as if it could not have been otherwise. Meantime I keep to my old maxims, while they behave, as though I had said nothing whatever. If I am not mistaken, you masters of the art of music have a great advantage over us here, in so far as you can, at the very outset, compel your pupils to accept what is recognized as law. I will not stay to examine, how arbitrary may be the proceedings of one individual after another, in after days. And so I will inclose in this packet some preliminary fragments, in regard to which, you anyhow have this advantage, that you need not summon Herr Sickler to roll them up. I have written all this in the midst of a heavy thunderstorm, which is driving straight against my windows from the West. It began by stirring up the dust, and was more remarkable for a general downpour of rain, from every quarter of the sky, than for thunder and lightning. My turret is admirably situated for watching all this, and I do not know how I shall be able to give up this commanding view. There is still a great deal to say, but I have no more room on this sheet.

And thus, henceforth and for ever,

G.

Morgenblatt, 1818, No. 240.
A man severe, with wrinkled brows,
("Herr Doctor Müllner, I, Sir!")
And out of window all he throws,
Yes, even *Wilhelm Meister*.

> Your only connoisseur, in brief,
> To doubt it were uncivil:
> For if his heroes come to grief,
> He sends them to the devil.

124.—ZELTER TO GOETHE.

Berlin, 27th August, 1818.

.... As soon as I am well again, I am off to Darmstadt, to wait upon my Grand Duke of the Orchestra, who has twisted a new Opera out of Spontini. In Cassel, I heard a capital performance of Rossini's world-famous Opera, *Tancredi*. The music is charming, which means, it is of the genuine Italian kind, *chiaro, puro e sicuro*. Flowing melody, grace, and freedom, in every number; even the Symphony is pretty, although it has nothing to do with the piece. ....

They have left an empty space round Lessing's grave in Brunswick, near old Campe's garden; no stone, no nothing. I think it quite grand, after seeing the silly monument, scribbled over with wretched verbiage, which they have put up to Klopstock, in Wandsbeck, and which the wind has made away with once already. You are quite right: those who come after us are no longer like our contemporaries. What we have is not much, and what we had, we know not. ....

Z.

1819.

125.—GOETHE TO ZELTER.
Weimar, 4th January, 1819.

.... SINCE you left, I have done next to nothing of what I had resolved to do. When the Dowager Empress of Russia came here, I could not refuse to assist in some festivities, so I undertook to furnish a masque; herewith the programme,—the explanatory poems shall be sent you later.

The procession consisted of nearly 150 persons;—to dress them characteristically, to group them, to range them in rank and file, and lastly, when they appeared, to explain what they were meant to represent, was no small task; it took me five weeks and more. In return however, we obtained universal applause, which certainly was dearly enough purchased, by the great outlay of imagination, time, and money. Those who took part, spared no expense in decking themselves out; yet all this vanished at last in a few moments, like a firework that explodes in the air.*

I, personally, have least to complain of, for the poems, with which I took a great deal of trouble, remain; and a costly present from the Empress, enhanced by her friendly, gracious, and confidential reception, repaid me beyond all expectation. . . . .

I must tell you, by the way, that I spent three consecutive weeks in Berka, writing the poems for the procession; the Inspector played to me every day for from three to four hours, and at my request, in historical order, selections from Sebastian Bach to Beethoven, including Philipp Emanuel, Handel, Mozart, Haydn, Dussek too, and others like him. At the same time, I studied Marperger's † *Vollkommene*

---
* This was the last and most important of all Goethe's masques.
† Goethe means Marpurg, but there would seem to be a confusion, for the author of *Der Vollkommene Capellmeister* was Mattheson. See Letter 127.

Capellmeister, and could not help smiling, while learning my lesson. Yet how earnest and thorough those days were, and how such a man must have felt the trammels of the Philistinism that held him captive!

I have bought the *Wohltemperirte Clavier*, as well as Bach's *Chorales*, and have presented them to the Inspector as a Christmas gift, with which he may refresh me when he comes here on a visit, and edify me, when I go back to him again.

I should indeed like, holding your hand, to sink myself into the essence of the Chorale, into that abyss, where one does not know how to help oneself alone. The old intonations, and the fundamental musical movements, are constantly applied to modern songs, and imitated by younger organists of more recent times; the ancient texts are set aside, and inferior ones substituted, &c. How different is the sound of the proscribed song, *Wie schön leuchtet der Morgenstern!* to that of the chastened version now sung to the same melody; and yet the genuine, and oldest version of all, probably a Latin one, would be still more suitable and appropriate. You see I am again hovering about on the borders of your territory, but owing to my fishy surroundings, nothing can come of it. This, however, is not the only point, about which one must learn to despair.

And thus, henceforth and for ever,

G.

126.—GOETHE TO ZELTER.

Weimar, 29th May, 1819.

IT is a matter of course that you should like my *Festgedichte*, for while in Berka, where I wrote them—reading Marperger and listening to Schütz playing—I thought of you incessantly, and wished we were nearer one another. You have already got more than I can say, out of this little series. Variety and freedom of metre came undesignedly, whilst I was at work, and contemplating the many different subjects. I scarcely touched the more modern artificiality; the eight-line strophe was my final object, and it is most curious, that not one sonnet would fit into the cycle; even your instinct will hardly be able to suggest, where it could have been introduced.

Thank you heartily for the kind reception you have given the children ;* I shall be able, through them, to enjoy what you had long since so kindly prepared for me. I can no longer feel happy anywhere, except in my own house, which, in summer especially, has every advantage, and where the possessions I have been accumulating for so many years past, are at my disposal, and are both a pleasure and a profit to me, although in comparison with Nagel's treasures of art, they would fade into nothing. . . . .

Yours,
G.

127.—Zelter to Goethe.

Berlin, 2nd June, 1819.

. . . . You speak in your letter † of having read Marperger. Do you not mean Marpurg? Marpurg is one of the best, for his style of writing is the best, but here too, as in Plastic Art, words fail to explain the spirit, and what one wants to know, one can only learn by setting to, oneself. He has written much, and was constantly at issue with Kirnberger about matters in which, in my judgment, Kirnberger was right; although the latter, when it came to writing, could not compare with the former, and consequently was always at a disadvantage before the world. I knew both these men, personally and intimately, and learnt most of what I wished to know from their conflicting opinions. . . . . Farewell, best beloved! The children will have plenty to tell you about the performance of the two scenes from *Faust;* it was a beginning, anyhow, and there was no want of goodwill.

Z.

128.—Zelter to Goethe.

Vienna, 20th July, 1819.

I ARRIVED here last Saturday, after a six days' voyage down the Danube from Ratisbon. The Danube

* August Goethe, and his wife, Ottilie.
† See Letter 125.

flows so rapidly, especially from Linz, that the vessel would, at the utmost, require three days for the whole of the sixty German miles, even if it stopped to rest at night. The usual passage-boat is detained for several days, on account of the various dues and customs. From Linz onward, we did thirty miles in the two half days, but I was all the more pleased, at having more opportunity to look about, and enjoy myself quietly. The number of whirlpools, the most splendid of which is the Saurüssel, make the voyage a perfect festival, with sailors who know what they are about, and I enjoyed myself like an emperor.

The construction of the ordinary passage-boat is so absurdly slight, that one goes on board, just for the fun of the thing, before one is aware of the danger. The boat consists of nothing but planks of pinewood, sawn and hewn into shape; a kind of model, in fact, without iron, cables, hemp, tar, pitch, anchor, or any other requisite for a navigable ship. There is only one single rope on board for anchoring the vessel; of course such things as masts and sails are out of the question, for the progress of the machine is like that of the Israelites into the Promised Land. The joints are stopped out with moss, and actually sewn together by means of wire; the tonnage is 2,000 *Centner*, the boat is 120 feet long, from sixteen to seventeen broad, and there is no leakage.

My fellow voyagers consisted of an Irish doctor, a German engraver, who made the strangest remarks about Art and wore a kind of mediæval beard, an apothecary, a butcher, a sword maker, a Capuchin friar, women, children, journeymen, and your humble servant. The journeymen, who pay little or nothing for their passage, bind themselves to labour at the oar, turn and turn about, for two hours, a duty they performed on this occasion rather lazily. In the cool morning and evening hours, I took my share of the labour; this expedited matters, and during the latter part of our voyage, even the women and girls shared in the arduous task. A tailor received dispensation, and in consideration for this, was obliged to sew on buttons to our coats and trousers, and mend the linings of our pockets, whilst some of the girls on board washed our stockings and pocket handkerchiefs.

This motley company was soon in such boisterous spirits, that the six days flew past like six hours. The crew had on board the best Bavarian beer; every morning we could buy fresh meat, bread and wine, and in fact could have gone the whole way in this fashion, as far as Peterwardein, without experiencing any want. As regards myself, I had to put up with very little from the Custom-house officers.

On the Saturday, after my arrival, I went straight to the Kärntner-Thor Theatre. The Opera, that of *Othello*, by Rossini, is a new and bright composition, which, for the first time, I heard admirably well done here. The composer has let the poet go, and set to music some sort of poem, which one can very easily make out from the music itself. Rossini is without doubt a man of genius, and knows how to use the means at his disposal, without first thinking, like Gluck, how he can invent the instruments which are to play his music. There are in the music *crescendos* which border on the grand,—he can let himself go, and in the end, the thought comes out effectively. He plays with the tones, and so the tones play with him.

On Sunday I went to the Marinelli Theatre. Three pieces were given: (1) *Die Werber;* (2) *Die Damenhüte im Theater;* (3) A Pantomime—*Schulmeister Beystrich*, or *Das Donnerwetter.* My ribs still ache from laughing. The pieces are more than vulgar. Actors and public together make up the comedy; the faintest hit that succeeds is loudly applauded, and any failure passes unnoticed. The actors are in constant movement, and enjoy the whole thing just as much as, if not more, than the audience. Such a Bohemian kind of pleasure defies all description; the children begin to scream and clap their hands, and all the rest scream and clap their hands too. After the piece, everyone with legs to stand on is called forward, and then a new farce begins. The actors express their thanks, still keeping up their characters in the play, and then, and not before, their individuality is prominently brought forward. The Theatre is always full, if not at the beginning of the evening, at all events toward the end, when everybody returns from the Prater.

The first comedian, Ignaz Schuster, is a regular genius from top to toe; there is nothing unreal in this fellow, his voice is as broad as a board, as sharp as vinegar, and as glib as an eel. One understands here, why the people of Vienna do not care about politics; they want to live and enjoy every minute, that is the reason; politics come from boredom and go to boredom. After the play, they go to supper; of a morning, to mass—each man to his own business, each man his own way, from one spectacle to another. Let them live on! they never will become wiser, they never were wise at all; they only understand themselves, and they may be right, because, after all, they assert their rights.

Wednesday, 21st July.

I passed last night in the village of Hitzing, close to Schönbrunn, where from a height, (*Die Gloriette*,) one can see the whole of the *Wiener Thal*. Schönbrunn is laid out in excellent French taste, and reminded me of Sans Souci. The Botanical Garden is much spoken of. In the ménagerie, I saw an enormous elephant—a splendid beast! —an ostrich, and a titmouse, all the very finest specimens. Several cages, however, are empty, for the Institution is not kept up. I was stongly advised to see a second play at the Marinelli Theatre, (*Der Lustige Fritz*,) but it was a failure. It is a pet piece with the public, but in spite of mutual goodwill between actors and audience, the play would not go down.

Thursday.

Yesterday evening, I heard Rossini's fourth Opera, *La Gazza Ladra;* the subject is very pleasing, and something very good might have been made of it; properly speaking, there should be a Merry-Andrew—this however, the poet has forgotten; on the other hand, the emotional element preponderates, and of this again, the composer has forgotten to make the most. Altogether, however, the music is intellectual and wanton, even to licentiousness, and in this respect, it borders on Mozart, though he has greater dash and depth. The singing was not much to speak of, but the audience was determined to be pleased with everything, as everyone palpably did his best.

The Prater is a large *Lustgarten*, (pleasure-ground,) for which one must have one's own private carriage, but then the whole of the country here is a pleasure-garden. People tell me things are no longer what they were, but where are they so ? The stranger does not care about this change of ideas; I am only too glad if I can shake off the Berliner; nay, one often regrets things which were formerly oppressive.

The *fiacres* are among the greatest conveniences of this Imperial City. I lose myself daily in the perpetual labyrinths of streets, but thanks to them, I can easily get home, especially of an evening, when coming from the Theatres, which are miles apart from one another. In the place of a higher, worshipful, spiritual police, which seems formerly to have been represented by images of saints, and chapels, there is now to be seen, at every corner in Vienna, a policeman, and one must allow that these people understand their duty; they appear to move, whilst they are always on the same spot, and step out of the way of the passers-by, in whose way they really are.

I was told that I should meet the young Napoleon, taking an airing in the garden at Schönbrunn, but I never saw him there. We soon observed, whilst pacing up and down the beautiful walks, that we were being constantly watched from a distance; this continued, until the evening put an end to our stroll.

The church of St. Stephen, which I visit daily, more than once, is a first-rate building, and the interior is remarkably fine, apart from the patches and restoration, which are easily distinguishable from the old part, and far less desirable. One cannot properly criticise the tower, for in strictness, there ought to be two; the present one has a spigot-look about it, and fails to make a good impression. The completeness of the details surpasses all belief, and the pulpit is an admirable piece of workmanship. I did not go to the top of the tower; the heat is so great, that the least exertion throws me into a perspiration.

Salieri,[*] who has written more than forty Operas, is the

---

[*] Antonio Salieri, a pupil of Gluck's, and an intimate friend of Haydn's; Beethoven dedicated to him three Sonatas for Pianoforte and Violin, and would sometimes call himself, " Salieri's pupil."

most honest fellow in the world; he is busy as ever, in the most childlike way. He is now sixty-nine years old, and considers himself out of fashion; this he need not do, for his talent still flows, and none of his pupils surpass him.

Evening.

I have just seen and heard a performance of Mozart's *Titus*, which, I dare affirm, was given more successfully at Weimar. All the ladies, (there were four of them,) were old enough to have been grandmothers, but all are well trained. Campi must have been excellent in her young days; now however, she looks as if she had never been young at all. Such a Titus as that has still to be born, if he is to be in love with all young women, who all want to kill him.

Saturday, 24th July.

Yesterday evening—I mean, yesterday morning—I paid twenty-six florins for an umbrella; believing I had it with me, I walked in the Prater after dinner, and got as wet as a poodle, for I had left the machine at home. Then I went to the Marinelli Theatre, to laugh myself dry again. Now just imagine my despair! *Der Verlorne Sohn*, (that was the name of yesterday's play,) thought I, would be able, both to laugh himself, and to make others laugh: a great mistake! This "lost" (*verlorne*) or rather "frosty" (*verfrorne*) Son, is a moral melodrama, with Chorus and dances; the Son, who is a great scamp, has a wife; having learnt absolutely nothing, he accordingly loses everything; the piece concludes with the fourth Act, in which the Son becomes happy once again, instead of reaping what he really deserves.

The poet Carpani * is one of my old acquaintances, whom I first learnt to know at Töplitz, in the year 1810; as this good old gentleman does not speak a word of German, I am obliged to talk Italian to him, and I find it comes more glibly to my tongue, than I had expected, after so many

---

* A poet and writer on music, known chiefly by his work, *Le Haydine*, an enthusiastic eulogy on Haydn. Later on, he also published *Le Rossiniane*, a similar eulogy on Rossini.

years of disuse. You will remember Carpani, when I remind you of a little book of his, *Le Haydine*, which contains some very pretty stories about old Haydn.

Weigl* has told me a great many interesting things about Mozart's youth, and later years. Weigl is a fine stately man of the world; his works are chaste, natural, and full of character; he succeeds best with what is secondary, and the results he achieves produce an immediate effect.

The double-bass is placed in a standing position, so that the player must sit beside it. I have not noticed any diminution of effect, and should like to see this method universally adopted. Those confounded goose-necks offend my eyes with their spikes; on the other hand, the prompter's boxes here are as large as in other parts of Germany, and prevent the eye from finding a centre for itself, and in addition to this, there is the ridiculously high seat of the conductor, conspicuous with all his dodges, —one can hardly understand, why such anomalies are allowed to exist.

The Burg Theatre is in high repute here, but the actors are away on their holidays, until next month. I intend now and then to take a trip from Baden to Vienna, and hope it will agree with me. The *Theater an der Wien* is a pretty house, roomy enough, with five rows of boxes, exclusive of the pit-boxes. One can see and hear there very comfortably. The Marinelli or Casperl Theatre, (Leopoldstadt,) is also a good one, but the seats are so extremely narrow, that I can hardly find room for my knees. The Kärntner-Thor Theatre is the best; the music is pretty, appropriate, and good throughout, but the singers and players are dreadfully fatigued and weary, for every day, they have an Opera and a rehearsal, and frequently two rehearsals on the same day. The instruments can stand it still less than the men. The players in the Orchestra are too shamefully treated; several of them eat their dinner and supper in the Theatre, because they have no other time for it. Weigl, too, complained of the hardship of his duties, and he has to compose at the same time.

* Author of the Opera, *Die Schweizerfamilie*.

Monday, 26th July.

Yesterday was Sunday, and I saw the Prater in its Sunday dress. Four rows of sturdy old chestnut-trees form three avenues, which begin at the Leopoldstadt, and continue for half a mile, in a direct line, to the Danube. The middle one, forty-five feet wide, is for carriages and horses; the two side avenues, twenty-four feet wide, are for pedestrians. Several hundred carriages are to be seen on the move, very splendid, some of them; the *fiacres* turn out too; close at hand are the foot-passengers, alone, in couples, or in groups. The variety is charming; it is delightful to see a promenade of so many men and women, beautifully dressed, in every kind of costume, flitting about like shadows. On either side, cafés and resting places are set up, under the shade of noble groups of trees; everything is a pattern of neatness and cleanliness. We sit down; music, issuing from the wood, echoes in our ears on all sides; now we are at the Opera, now at the ball, or parade. Coffee and cakes are served. A child presents me with a nosegay, a pretty girl offers me water as clear as crystal, an old woman hands me a toothpick; all this is paid for by copper *kreutzers* only, a good riddance of bad rubbish, for they are as heavy as the conscience, and drag one's pockets down to the ground. This avenue however, is not the only thing that forms the Prater. A second and third, just like it, extend in a fan-like shape, from the Leopoldstadt towards the Danube, (*i.e.* an arm of the Danube.) Here we see, as it were, the opposite pole of the planet, I mean the real people. The wider spaces of ground, towards the Danube, are occupied by refreshment stalls, where you can get beer, wine, meat, ices, and drinks of all kinds, coffee excepted. The three single cafés in the great avenues, monopolize the privilege of selling coffee. These second-class places of refreshment are so numerous, and close to one another, that the guests of one host are indistinguishable from those of another, and one is in danger of consuming a feast, which somebody else has paid for. . This is Vienna proper; between these tables and chairs, and drinking booths, smokers, bands, and merry-go-rounds, a happy crowd moves to and fro. People jog along, stop, meet a friend; it is a constant rest, and bustle at the same time.

Nothing is fenced off, and there is no obstacle; for although the owners of houses are landlords, yet the ground and soil belong to the Emperor, and must not be enclosed in any way. The impression produced on the mind by the behaviour of the people—I will not call it, the mob,—is one of careless oblivion. I could not remember that I thought or observed anything, and what I now write, strictly speaking, I invent, without being able to say, thus it is, and thus it was. What gives a really sunny aspect to the whole, is the large crowd of happy faces, belonging to all sorts of people, who, reconciled to-day with their God, see the world as they would like it to be. Neither men, nor women, nor old age, nor youth, is here as it ought to be. There is an idea in existence, as there is an existence in the idea. The first day I went into the Theatre, a violinist was tuning his instrument. A waiter came into the pit, and sang in the same key as the violin:

Chocolade,   Limonade,   Bavaroise,   Punsch.

Then another followed with:

Chocolade,   Limonade,   Bavaroise,   Punsch.

And then the whole Orchestra tuned upon this melody; I laughed so loud at this, that everyone looked at me as if I were a lunatic. Let them think of me as they please, the things I don't like here I can get just as well at home, and I hope to find them again there.

Tuesday, 27th July.

Yesterday evening, there was a splendid display of fireworks in the Prater, in honour of St. Anne. The worthy pyrotechnist, as a rule, has the misfortune to have bad weather; the public, one and all, take the deepest interest in the matter, for the people like to see such a spectacle, just as much as the artist likes to produce it. Yesterday we had the finest weather imaginable. It had rained itself out; there was no dust, no dewy mist, no breeze, but a dark evening sky. The rockets shot up straight as arrows, and everything went off successfully. There were two principal *tableaux*—the first in honour of beautiful women, and the last adorned with the name of St. Anne. The thing had something grand about it, unlike ordinary fireworks, on account of the spacious darkness of the night. The scaffolding which is always erected for such occasions, is from eighty to ninety feet high, and from a hundred and sixty to a hundred and eighty feet in length; there are three rows of boxes around it. The Imperial box, holding easily more than a thousand spectators, is in the centre. The pit, which was densely crowded, held probably some thirty thousand spectators; the ladies are always beautifully dressed, for the fair sex here is distinguished for its good taste. The charm of the scene is enhanced by the general satisfaction with everything, the way everyone quietly takes it to heart, if there is a failure, and the way they all rejoice, when it rights itself again.

This seems to me the only pleasure, in the enjoyment of which the Austrians are willing to do without their music, which persecutes us here in every direction. I was assured by a musician in Carlsbad, that music was a hard profession. I replied, that the musicians are better off than the visitors. "How so?" said he. "Why, surely," (I answered,) "they can eat without music." The good man went away ashamed, and I felt sorry for him, although my speech was quite in point, for it is really cruel to worry patients and convalescents in this manner. I certainly can stand a good deal, but when I come away from the Opera and sit down to supper, and am choked directly by the strains of some harpist or ballad-monger, which jar cruelly with what I have heard and enjoyed at the Theatre, it is really too much, and—wretch that I am—I quite forget that this scribbling is also a great deal too much; so farewell—with kind regards and greetings to all your circle. From yours eternally,

Z.

The Danube is now looking quite splendid. It has risen so high from the constant rains, and the melting of the snow upon the hills, that it rushes by, like an arrow. I am just off for a drive with Salieri. God bless you!

Thursday, 29th July.

The day before yesterday, I had the most charming walk to Schönbrunn and back, with Salieri. The old fellow is still so full of music and melody, that he speaks, as it were, in melodies, and he is, as it were, only understood in that way. It is the greatest enjoyment to me, to play the spy upon this genuine character, and to find him always truthful, always cheerful. I come back to this thought, now that I have examined the score of the new *Requiem* by Cherubini. This is a composition which, in these out of joint days, must needs please everywhere, and does please, just because there is no true word in it, and though everything is thought out and brought out in a most delightful manner, there is not the faintest feeling of a *requies æterna*. The composer has only cared to look up those passages in the poem, where he can be boisterous— *dies iræ—mors stupebit—rex tremendæ majestatis—flammis acribus*—and to fill out the intervals with measured restlessness; in short, the secondary matter is here made the principal thing, and the whole work appears as if one were constantly and passionately saying, "No," nodding one's head all the time. A review of this work, which now lies before me, is just as confusing and mendacious as the work itself; the composer is exalted into the seventh heaven, and then dragged down again, as one who has dared to enter the lists with Mozart, and wishes to rival him, when Mozart has done it much better; as if nobody else were allowed to compose, or die, or find rest, after Mozart! All the newest books of instruction are based upon this view, the old ones are thrown aside, and that is the present form of Art.

Amidst all this, it is quite touching to observe the goodnatured Salieri, who venerates this state of things, without any sorrow, and looks at it as an advance in Art, which is quite necessary, but unattainable by him. At the same time, he goes on writing, after his usual fashion, in a style full of unconscious irony and humour, and spins his own cocoon like a silkworm. He speaks with delight of a *Requiem* which he wrote, under the notion that he would soon follow his wife, who died in 1807; but as this has not yet taken place, he has now written a much shorter one, thinking it was good enough for him. He has allowed me to copy a Mass and an Offertorium, written by him in the year 1766. The latter is in no way inferior to the very best Italian works of the seventeenth century, produced in this style. It is devotional, pure, and elevating, written in conformity with the practical requirements of Art and the Church. You should have seen his childlike delight, when I, at the very first glance at this music, made some intelligible remarks about it; he knows the whole thing from tradition, whilst I have only acquired it by observation and study, and have had to make it clear to myself, for the theory of an ecclesiastical style of music has disappeared with the Church herself.

Beethoven, whom I should like to have seen once more in this life, is living in the country, and no one can tell me where. I was anxious to write to him, but people told me he was hardly approachable, on account of his almost complete deafness. Perhaps it is better that we should remain as we are, since it might make me cross to find him cross. . . . .

The articles in the Berlin papers are now a common topic of conversation; I also read the Viennese journals, which are written in a very chaste style. By to-morrow I shall have been here a whole fortnight, without once entering a Museum or Gallery, or examining any one of those Institutions, through which Art and Science are bounded in space. After my everyday wanderings along the Danube, and through this endless city, I have had enough, and feel so weary, that I could sleep on the hardest bed. Vienna is in truth a magnificent city, and her suburbs are splendid The knowledge of this fact makes one warm, in warm weather. Of course you can and do take a carriage, but it is not instructive, and as a rule, very expensive for one, who like me, does not understand the art of making bargains. The Austrian people have the most pleasing *naïveté*, which places them at such a distance from the so-called higher classes of society, that the latter really appear at a disadvantage. Thus, for example, if the Austro-German dialect is not good German, it is still a language, in which one moves with the same ease, as a fish swims in the water, whilst the higher classes always seem to be uncertain, what and how they should speak; doubtless, however, a great deal of good Italian and French is spoken here; this is very natural, considering the great conflux of nationalities, Viennawards.

Much importance is attached here to music, and this in contrast to Italy, who is, according to her own estimate, "the only saving Church;" the people here, however, are really thorough musicians. It is true they are pleased with everything, but they only retain what is first-rate. They are glad to listen to a mediocre Opera, which is well cast, but a first-rate work, even if not given in the best style, remains with them for ever. Beethoven is extolled to the heavens, because he works very hard, and is still alive; but it is Haydn, who presents to them their national humour, like a pure fountain, which does not mingle with any other streams, and it is he who lives in them, because he proceeds from them; they seem to forget him every day, and daily he rises to life again amongst them.

Baden, 2nd August.

Yesterday evening, the Emperor came to Vienna, and I arrived at Baden, looking like a miller's apprentice, for this dusty country perfectly answers to the description people gave me of it.

How am I sufficiently to thank you for your *Morphologie*, which I am devouring with the greatest interest, applying it to the Theory of Sound, and hence arriving gradually at the Theory of Thought and Invention? How naturally all this comes, and what will your honoured friend, F. A. Wolf, say, when he comes to read the first lines in Hafis (*Divan*, p. 379)? I jumble up one thing with another, reading now here, now there, and just enjoying myself, to the top of my bent; in the harum-scarum life here, everything comes into my head all at once.

On Sunday I visited the Picture Gallery of the Prince Esterhazy, which contains many fine things by Leonardo da Vinci, Raphael, Titian, Dürer, Eyck, Rubens, Bellini, Poussin; the works of many first-rate artists adorn the walls of whole suites of rooms. Some statues by more modern artists, such as Canova and Schadow, are interspersed with other marbles, and majestic vases. It is my own fault, that I have not seen more of such things. I have not looked at a single engraving; it makes me quite dumb and stupid to see such wonders, all at once, merely in passing through so hurriedly,—nay, I feel ashamed of my own ignorance, and yet quite angry, when my bear-leader says, "Just look at those beautiful heads! What hands! What a lovely landscape, &c."

To-day—the 3rd of August—is the anniversary of the death of my noble friend, Fasch. Having lived with him for many years, without one word of difference, I rejoice to be able to say, after a period of nineteen years, "Look, old friend and master! your work still abides; it is encouraged, it encourages others, they value it, and—Heaven be thanked!—it fell to my lot to preserve it for you, myself, and Art!" It is only after the lapse of years, that we see the soundness of a good thought.

9th August.

To give myself something new, I went, the day before yesterday, to Ulrich's, the local bookseller, where I found a pirated edition of your works, and amongst them, the Biography of P. Hackert,* which forms the eighteenth volume of the edition of 1811. The way in which you have put together this little work out of mere fragments, is so characteristic, and so easy, that it did my very heart good to read it. It was as good as new to me, for in the year 1811, at Schweidnitz, I had only time to skim through it; if you should still have a copy by you, be so good as to send it to me, at your convenience, and address it to Berlin. Hackert's youngest brother, George, the engraver, was my most intimate school-fellow at the Drawing Academy in Berlin, the Director of which in those days was the excellent Lesueur. Had I, at that time, been

---

* Philipp Hackert, an artist, with whom Goethe spent many pleasant hours in Italy, and from whom he had lessons in landscape-painting. See Letter 130.

my mother's less obedient son, I should have gone with George to Naples. God knows how I envied him, for having a brother who could invite him. The times were quite different to the present, and the consciousness of my inferior talent lay so heavily on my youth, that I did not understand, how to work myself forward out of it. The book has vividly recalled that time to me, and makes me feel at this moment forty years younger.

If I measure this harmless story of a fruitful, artistic life, with other pretentiously got-up biographies, in which the great appears small, and truth incredible, I see clearly, how much it takes, not to soar too high.

Baden, 12th August, 1819.

Yesterday morning, I read your Translation of *Mahomet* and *Tancred*. If I am to judge by the first impression, I must say, it quite surprises, nay, astounds me, to see what can be accomplished by a certain talent, practice, and mastery; yet I felt no comfort, when I closed the book. The reading of *Mahomet* almost broke my heart, and in the *Tancred*, I can't quite make out why the lovers must perish. They do not seem to me to be in the least tragic, at all events they do not act tragically, and the misfortune falls, like a bomb out of the clouds, upon wandering men, who in consequence suddenly acquire importance. I remember what you once said about this poet, that no talent was wanting to him, except depth. Mahomet is an undignified tyrant, and out of proportion to his antagonist, Sopir.

The minor characters in *Tancred* seem to be there, merely to make beautiful speeches; everything is thought out, devised, spun out, distorted: the father is supposed to have no presentiment, that the mother has approved of an alliance of her daughter with Tancred; the daughter, a brave, truthful creature, ought she, under these circumstances, to make a secret of her lover? How tormenting is all this! In short, had I been Voltaire, or his opponent, I should have undertaken to make a merry wedding comedy out of *Tancred*, and have introduced a fool, who would laugh at them all round.

What you say on page 377 of the *Divan*, under the heading, *Verwahrung*, as to the difference between poetry and the elocutionary arts, seems to me to apply here: these are tales, and a man who does not choose to believe them, can let them alone.

Voltaire's beautiful French seems purposely constructed, in order to give colour and shape to certain unreal beings, in order to enliven streets and promenades with painted corpses. It has often vexed me, to think how German critics have attacked French compositions, which, to my thinking, seem, in the language, and form of the whole, and of the details, undeniably smooth and mannerly, and when this impression has descended, by inheritance, to their nation, for several centuries, how should not the foreigner —I mean the German—who has no old traditions, be carried away by it?

This enables me to see clearly the merit of your Translation, which so aptly naturalizes the characters, without deviating from the original.

You must excuse this scribbling of mine, for, like a half mathematician, I write down equations, pen in hand, in order to make them intelligible to my understanding, by putting them in black and white before me. Here however, I have nothing else to do but to kill time. The music here, mingled as it is with the eternal jingling of bells, entirely distracts my thoughts.

The country about here produces abundance of corn, wine, fruit, and provisions of all sorts. I hear landowners in Baden grumbling about the fall in the price of corn; after that, loud abuse of Prussia; after that, gentler abuse of Russia. An intellectual conversation is out of the question. . . . .

16th August.

Yesterday, I heard some more vocal music, Italian, of course, for German is not spoken here by choice, much less sung. There is nothing but Rossini; that man rules, whether he chooses or not; there's Freedom for you! And the Italians are right. The voice will sing for her own sake, and whoever complies with her demands, he is her man. Now however, criticism is beginning to settle here, and it will lay hold of the nearest thing first; it might fare hard with Rossini, if he tried to do more than he can. Two young girls sang the music very prettily and neatly; the silliest stuff sounds well, as long as it goes off smoothly.

Beethoven is gone into the country, but no one knows whither; he has just written a letter from Baden to one of his lady friends *here*, and he is not at Baden. He is said to be intolerably *maussade;* some say he is a fool,—that's easily said. Heaven forgive us all our sins! The poor man, they say, is hopelessly deaf. I know how I feel, when I look at the fingering here, and I—poor devil! —one finger of mine after the other gets useless. Quite lately, Beethoven went to an eating-house, where he sat down at the table, and after an hour's meditation, called out to the waiter, "How much do I owe you?"—"Why, your honour has not eaten anything; what shall I bring you?"—"Bring what you like, and leave me alone!" His patron is said to be the Archduke Rudolf, who allows him 1,500 *Gulden* (paper money) a year. With this he must try to manage, like all other musicians in Vienna. They are kept there like cats, and any one who does not understand the art of mousing, will hardly save anything, and yet, in spite of this, they are all as round and jolly as weasels.

The adjoining park close to my lodgings, which are at the foot of the Calvarienberg, looks on Sunday, like a Turkish Paradise. All the prettiest women in Vienna turn out on a Sunday, after two o'clock, dressed so charmingly and looking so nice, that one would like to be nothing but eyes. There are many handsome women here, especially middle-aged women, and their complexions and figures are equally charming. Modest behaviour, even amongst those of doubtful virtue, is surprisingly universal, and those who do not understand the language of the eyes, would think they saw before them, forests of Madonnas. The park itself is not large, and may contain over a thousand square roods; it is intersected by broad walks, which are kept so clean, that one can walk there in shoes, after heavy and continuous showers of rain. The park faces the middle of the mountain-chain, crowned by San Calvario, which is easily ascended in half an hour, and from which one looks, to the left, upon the whole Baden Valley, while eastward, towards Vienna, straight in front of one, lies fruitful Hungary. On the right, half an hour off, is the village of St. Elena, in a cleft, through which runs a pretty river, like the Tepel at Carlsbad, or the Neckar at Heidelberg, but more graceful than either. The Archduke Anton has had fine walks made for the accommodation of the public, altering fields, and making bridges and resting-places, all at his own expense. The stone, as far as it can be seen, is limestone, sandstone, and a durable grey granite, which takes a fine polish, and of which the baths here are partially constructed. The bath water is from a sulphur spring, which steams all the country through which it percolates; the horses seem to dislike it, and it is with difficulty that they can be made to go into it; some of them seem maddened by it.

I have in vain tried to find the Opera of *Elena e Costantino*, in Vienna; Salieri and Weigl knew nothing about it. The Opera is by Simon Mayer, and was given at Milan, in the month of August, 1816. The Baroness von Pereira has promised me that she will write to Milan and get the Sestett; the Opera itself is not popular, the Sestett is said to give life to the whole work.

I do not think I have yet told you anything about the statue of Joseph II in Vienna. Whenever I look at it, the figure seems to me too thin; I may however be mistaken, having in my eye the statues of Marcus Aurelius, and of our Electoral Prince, at Berlin. People like myself can only make comparisons. The pedestal is of the finest grey granite.

19th August, 1819.

I may well say that I regarded Vienna with a kind of awe; why? I cannot tell you the reason, otherwise I should have been here long ago. I planned therefore to go straight to Baden, and from thence, to make an occasional excursion to the Imperial City. I do not think this was a mistake, although I began, first of all, by spending a fortnight in Vienna. I say this merely for your sake. If you ever felt inclined, you might, in the month of May, go straight to Baden, before the crowds of people have arrived. A lodging, with from four to five rooms, cannot, at the most, cost more than twelve *Gulden* (paper money); that is, a little more than a ducat, and everything else is comfortable, cheap, and good. Only foreign articles, such as coffee, tobacco, tea and the like, are dear, although not much dearer than elsewhere; anyhow they are to be had. A *fiacre* takes two hours to drive from here to Vienna; there are two halting places. I did it in two hours yesterday, and paid the fare, twelve *Gulden*, there and back. You can be absolutely solitary here, if you do not live in the Landstrasse, where there are no end of carriages. The best lodgings are to be found in the street facing the park, the Renngasse, where I am living, and the Alleegasse. The baths are close at hand. At the Frauenbad, people bathe in company; at the Theresienbad, which I have now changed to, because I get a *douche* there, you bathe alone. The attendants at the baths are well looked after, and therefore obliging. Warm towels and all kinds of bathing apparatus, I have never found so ready to hand as here. The little town was burnt down in the year 1812, and has been solidly and handsomely rebuilt. The environs for three or four miles round are highly interesting. Vösslau is pleasant and unpretending, Schönau, the same, and still more to my taste, Merkenstein, large and cheerful, the Brühl and Mödlingen, spacious and solemn, Sparbach, Johannisstein, as well as Laxenburg, truly imperial. Nature has here combined everything that can make a neighbourhood perfect, though Art has striven hard to hinder her.

28th August.

Well, what am I to write about to-day, my own heart's brother, blessed a thousand times over! Thanks be to all the gods, that wherever I go, wherever I live, I have thee, and carry thee with me in my heart. Health and every blessing to thy dear life, thy powers, thy will, thy work! May thy life bring forth fruit in patience, from one generation to another!—But you know all this better than I do.

> "As with an angel's wing, in the hot glow
> Of summer, thou hast gently cooled my brow;
> Through thee earth's noblest gifts were made my own,
> And every joy I feel in thee alone."

31st August, 1819.

I have now finished the music to a little poem, *Gleich und Gleich*, and should like you to listen to it, and see, if I have been able to conjure up a little flower, that would make a tiny bee hungry.* I serve you, as people sacrifice to the gods, by bringing to them their own gifts. Take, old fellow, mine, which is all thine, and give me all the credit as usual!

1st September, 1819.

To-morrow, I go from here to Presburg, that I may see something of Hungary, and then return home. For a long time, I have not read so much as I have in four weeks here, for I have been subscribing to the library. This too was of service to me; hitherto I had only seen Kotzebue's pieces acted; here I have read eleven plays of his in succession, which were before unknown to me, and many other dramatic works at the same time. I stuck fast at length in Klopstock's tragedies. I began the *David*—no go—so I passed on to *Solomon*—which also I failed to finish. Next winter, I will make another bite at it, even if my teeth stick fast; one should be at home for such undertakings as these.

The day before yesterday, I went to Mödlingen, to pay Beethoven a visit. He was just driving to Vienna, and meeting each other on the road, we got out of our carriages, and embraced each other most cordially. The poor man is so deaf, that I could hardly restrain my tears, when I saw him; then I drove on to Mödlingen, and he to Vienna. The country is inexpressibly charming; the Brühl, and the Castle-fortress of Prince Lichtenstein, which is still in a fair state of preservation, were worthy a closer study. We found there beautiful Gobelin tapestry, some fine old household furniture, and some remarkable family portraits, which still keep their colours.

I must tell you a joke, that tickled me uncommonly. My travelling companion on this occasion was Steiner, the music publisher, and as one does not get much talk with a deaf man, on a public highway, it was arranged that

---

* See the little poem, dated 22nd April, 1814, in Letter 82; it was afterwards called *Gleich und Gleich*.

Beethoven and I should meet properly, at four o'clock in the afternoon, in Steiner's music-shop. Directly after dinner, we drove back to Vienna. Full as a badger, and dog-tired, I lay down, and slept so soundly, that I forgot everything. Then I strolled away to the Theatre, and when I saw Beethoven in the distance, I felt quite dumbfoundered. He was evidently undergoing the same process, in discovering me, and this was not the place to come to an explanation with a deaf man. But the point of the story is yet to come.

In spite of all kinds of blame, to which Beethoven, rightly or wrongly, is here exposed, he enjoys that respectful consideration, which is only given to distinguished men. Steiner had immediately given out, that Beethoven would appear in person, at four o'clock, for the first time, in his narrow shop, which holds some six or eight people, and he had also asked guests, so that fifty clever men, crowded out into the street for want of room, were waiting there in vain. I myself only learnt the real state of things next day, when I got a letter from Beethoven, in which he excused himself, (in a way that suited me admirably,) because like myself—he had happily slept away the time of the *rendezvous!* . . . .

Here I have found my old idea realized—that of making the Orchestra so deep, that one does not see the untidy heads of the musicians; the music, too, which is not nearly so well organized here, as in Weimar, comes out clear and distinct. I cannot imagine anything less becoming on a stage, than to see the fine forms of well-dressed actors, and all that goes to make up a brilliant scene, fluttering between the confounded mops of the fiddlers in front.

15th September, 1819.

Yesterday, I made the acquaintance of Grillparzer, a well-grown young man, twenty-six years of age, quiet, invalidish, very taking. We had a country drive together, and got on very well. The old Abbé Stadler was with us, a bright, merry companion; he told us a great deal about the little Napoleon, on whom the Emperor lavishes all kinds of paternal worship.

He is now about eight years old, and, so long as four years back, he took his chief delight in soldiers, who like him in return. He invents long stories, and tells them to those around him;—one of these caused a serious investigation. Afterwards, he laughs at everybody. He is very curt with women and children, and likes learning languages. A little while ago, he asked the Emperor, " Where then is my father?"—" Your father is locked up."—" Why is he locked up ?"—" Because he did not behave well, and if you do not behave well, you will be locked up also." . . . .

Yours,
Z.

1820.

129.—GOETHE TO ZELTER.

Weimar, 12th April, 1820.

I WANT a genuine Zelterian composition for the enclosed hymn, which might be sung in Chorus every Sunday, before my house. If some such thing could reach my daughter-in-law during the month of May, she would have it rehearsed, so as to give me a solemn and kindly welcome, on my return, at the beginning of June. May the Paraclete watch harmoniously over my friend, now and everlastingly!

G.

130.—GOETHE TO ZELTER.

Weimar, 14th April, 1820.

IT is good for us to be forced, from time to time, to get quit of all our surroundings; this is the origin of our making interim-wills, in the course of our lives. In a fortnight's time, I intend to go to Carlsbad, so I have looked up another *Hackert* for you, and will send it, properly bound. You instinctively felt the care which I bestowed upon, and the meaning I gave to the little volume; it is obsolete in our dear Germany, and is now, together with many other good and useful things, covered by the sand-webs of the day, though like amber, it will inevitably be washed clean, or dug up again. Thank you for reminding me of it. . . . .

G.

131.—GOETHE TO ZELTER.

Carlsbad, 2nd May, 1820.

. . . . LET me congratulate you on your Raphael Festival;* it was well planned, and I feel certain, was

---

* Zelter had described in a previous Letter, a Festival held at Berlin, in commemoration of Raphael's birthday. The programme of the music selected by Zelter was remarkable; it included the *Crucifixus* by Lotti, a *Gloria in Excelsis* by Haydn, and a *Requiem* of Zelter's own

carried out equally well; you Berliners are inimitable in such things. May it ever be the custom, to commemorate all heroes, who are raised above the atmosphere of envy and opposition!

I should like to have heard the music, though I can form some idea of it, from what you say. The purest and highest style of painting in music is that which you yourself also practise; the object is, to transport the listener into that frame of mind, which the poem itself suggests; the imagination will then picture to itself figures, in accordance with the text, without knowing how it comes to do so. You have given instances of this in your *Johanna Sebus, Mitternacht, Ueber allen Gipfeln ist Ruh*, and what not? Tell me of anyone who has accomplished this, except yourself! The painting of tones by tones—thunder, crash, splash and dash are detestable. The minimum of this is wisely used, as you also use it, as a dot over an *i*, in the above examples. So I, bereft of sound and hearing, though a good listener, transform that great enjoyment into ideas and words. I know very well, that on account of this, I lose one third of life, but one must adapt oneself to circumstances. . . . .

G.

THE PROFITS OF YESTERDAY'S FAIR.
A Parable.

To the apple-woman's stall
Came the children flying,
Everyone for buying!
Seized the treasure, one and all,
"Apples! apples!" crying.—
The price they learnt,
And let them fall,
As though they burnt!—
How many buyers would there be,
If everything were sold cost-free!

132.—GOETHE TO ZELTER.

Carlsbad, 11th May, 1820.

. . . . EBERWEIN has been composing several songs; tell me your opinion of them. I feel at once that your compositions are identical with my Songs; the music,—like the gas which is pumped into the balloon,—merely carries them up aloft. In the case of other composers, I must first make sure of the way in which they have understood the Song, and ascertain what they have made out of it. . . . .

Meantime, new poems are being collected for the *Divan*. This Mahommedan religion, its mythology and customs, give scope for a style of poetry that is suitable to my years. Unconditional submission to the unfathomable will of God, a cheerful survey of the earth's varying activities, which are ever recurring like circles and spirals, love, an inclination that wavers between two worlds, all realism purified, and dissolving itself symbolically. What more can Grandpapa want?

It is strange enough that my *Prometheus*, which I had myself given up and forgotten, should crop up again just now. The well-known Monologue, which is included among my poems, was to have opened the third Act. I dare say you have all but forgotten, that the worthy Mendelssohn died from the consequences of an over-hasty publication of the same.* Be sure you do not allow the manuscript to become too public, lest it should appear in print. It would be very welcome, as a Gospel, to our revolutionary youth, and the High Commissions of Berlin and Mayence might make a serious face at my youthful caprices. It is remarkable however, that this refractory fire has been smouldering for fifty years, under the ashes of poetry, till at last it threatens to break out into destructive flames, the minute it can seize on really inflammable materials.

Now that we are speaking of old, though not old-fashioned things, let me ask, have you attentively read the *Satyros*, as it occurs in my works? The thought struck me, because it rises up in my remembrance simultaneously with this very *Prometheus*, as you will feel, so soon as you examine it from that point of view. I abstain from making any comparison, and merely remark that an important part of *Faust* also belongs to this period.

* This was in 1774. The Monologue called forth declarations from Lessing and Moses Mendelssohn, against Jacobi's book, *Ueber die Lehre des Spinozas*, and Mendelssohn's mortification at the public disclosure of the fact, that his own knowledge of Spinoza's ethics was deficient, is said to have hastened his death.

And now about the weather, a *sine quâ non* of the season for bathing and travelling. The dry upper air has prevailed; every cloud has disappeared, and this year's Ascension Day is a true heavenly Festival.

Generally speaking, a very late spring, with a high solstice, affects us palpably and agreeably. It is as if the trees, on awakening, were surprised at finding themselves already so far on in the year, and yet, on their own part still so far behindhand. Each day, fresh buds are opening, and those already open are developing further.

It is delightful to walk down the Prager Strasse towards sunset. All the leafless trees, hitherto unnoticeable, at all events unnoticed, are gradually becoming visible, as they unfold their leaves, and when the sun shines upon them from behind, they stand out clearly, so marked in their peculiar forms as to be recognizable. The green is so young, so yellow, so perfectly transparent. This enjoyment growing before our eyes, will be a feast to us, for yet another fortnight. For this first green will not be fully developed, even by Whitsuntide.

The day grows, and so everything is beautiful and good. May what is brightest and best fall to your lot!

G.

133.—ZELTER TO GOETHE.

Berlin, 13th May, 1820.

.... As your letter speaks of musical painting, shall I tell you of some who have done such things? ....

Haydn, in *The Creation* and *The Seasons*,—Beethoven, in his *Character-Symphonies* and the *Battle of Vittoria*, have drawn the most curious pictures. .... The Overture to Haydn's *Creation* is the most marvellous thing in the world, for by the ordinary, methodical, conventional resources of Art, a Chaos is produced, which converts the feeling of fathomless disorder into one of delight. In the Symphony which represents Winter, in *The Seasons*, I freeze in comfort at my warm stove, and for the moment, know not whether there is anything more delightful in the world. What old Bach and Handel achieved is quite measureless, especially in quantity, for every occasional transitory circumstance becomes in their hands an abyss of sensation, which they denote by the familiar black points. Nay, were there no limit to human things, and were the external resources rich enough, one would recognize, in the belly of the earth and the bosom of the stars, the life of Omnipotence. . . . .

Z.

134.—ZELTER TO GOETHE.

Berlin, 25th May, 1820.

. . . . . YESTERDAY was Princess Radzivil's birthday, and at last, our *Faust* was smoothly and fairly launched. The King was so pleased with us, that his praises seemed sweet as honey to me, and I too can say I was satisfied. . . . . The Duchess of Cumberland again was full of your praises, and regretted she had not been able to attend *all* the rehearsals, as the piece is really a *unique* thing, so that you cannot see it too often to probe its depth. "Long live Goethe!" was shouted at supper by one and all. It was a threefold cry from a hundred voices. Even if Radzivil's music had no merit at all, he is entitled to great praise, for having brought to light a poem hitherto concealed in darkest shadow, which everyone, after reading and feeling, thought himself obliged to withhold from his neighbour. I, at all events, know no one else enthusiastic and innocent enough, to put such a banquet before such people, as enables them for the first time to learn German. Just think of the circle in which all this goes on; a Prince, Mephisto, our first actor, Faust, our first actress, Gretchen, a Prince for the composer, a downright good King as foremost listener, with his youngest children and all his Court about him, as good an Orchestra, as can be found, and lastly, a Chorus of our best voices, the singers consisting of well-born ladies, (beautiful girls, most of them,) and men of position, —amongst them a Consistorialrath, a clergyman, a Councillor's daughter, Court-Councillors and high officials,— all these directed by the Royal *General-Intendant*, combining the offices of scene-shifter, stage-manager, prompter, in his own person,—in the Palace, in a Royal Castle;—you cannot blame me for wishing we had had you amongst us. . . . .

Z.

135.—GOETHE TO ZELTER.

Carlsbad, 24th May, 1820.

As a parting gift, I send you a little Song, which you may lovingly decipher and becipher. I have had a healthy, happy time. Now I am about to hasten homewards, where I hope to hear from you.

G.

ST. NEPOMUC'S EVE.*

Carlsbad, 15th May, 1820.

Little lights upon the broad stream quiver,
Children's voices on the bridge are singing,
Great and little bells above the river
Join, in rapturous devotion ringing.

Little lights must vanish, stars are dying;
So our sainted spirit gently glided
From the mortal body, still denying
He could tell the sin to him confided.

Quiver, little lights! Ye voices ringing
With the childlike laugh to childhood given,
Still remember, to the wide world singing,
What impels the star to stars in heaven.

136.—GOETHE TO ZELTER.

Jena, 6th June, 1820.

. . . . BUT now what am I to say to your representation of my *Faust?* The faithful account of it which

---

* St. John Nepomuc, the confessor of Queen Joanna, is said to have been thrown into the Moldau by order of King Wenceslaus (1378-1418), after he had tortured him in vain, in the hope of extracting from him the secrets of the Confessional, and finding matter of accusation against his virtuous wife, whose reproaches had goaded him to fury. The body of the Saint rose to the surface of the water, and was discovered by means of the unearthly lights which flickered round it. The last two lines of the Song :—

*Und verkündiget nicht minder
Was den Stern zu Sternen bringe.*

are somewhat obscure. Düntzer, who denies that "the star" means the soul of the Saint, thinks that they allude to the magical power of love, "which even in Heaven guides the course of the stars." The maidens of Prague honoured St. John Nepomuc, as the guardian of lovers.

I owe to you, transports me into the strangest region, and I see it quite clearly. After all, Poetry is really a rattlesnake, into the jaws of which one falls against one's own will. Certainly, if you keep together as you have hitherto, it will be, become, and remain the most out of the way work that the world has seen. . . . .

To fill up my remaining space, let me add as follows: About a year ago, when I happened to be sitting alone with my daughter-in-law, I told her a little story, like many you know, and many that I still have in my mind. She wanted to read it, but I had to tell her, that it only existed in the power of my imagination. Since then, I have scarcely ever thought of it again. On coming to Schleitz rather early and feeling the time hang heavy, I took out of my travelling-bag a quire of writing-paper, and a Viennese black chalk pencil that writes easily, and began the story. I am now dictating it, and as there is very little to alter, I find I have got about half way through it. The rest will no doubt follow in due course.

G.

137.—ZELTER TO GOETHE.

Berlin, 7th June, 1820.

. . . . SPONTINI, whose acquaintance I made yesterday, is just having his last Opera, *Olimpia*, translated into German. For this work, he wants forty violins in his Orchestra, (we have about half that number,) and an enlargement of the space for the Orchestra in the Opera House. If the rest of the band is to be arranged in this proportion, the pit may go and look for places outside. I for my part, will take a hint from this experience, although I see clearly enough, how and where it must end, if we are to extract the pith, and get at the root of the matter. . . . .

With the exception of the King and Crown Prince, who are not in Berlin, the Court was again present at the second performance of *Faust*, and they tried beforehand to make Spontini acquainted with the poem, by means of Madame de Stael's explanations. What the Italian Frenchman will learn from the devil, remains to be proved. He is treated by the whole Court with the distinction he deserves, when one considers the toilsome labour expended on his works, and the readiness with which he submits to alterations, which can hardly benefit the form of the whole. . . . .

Z.

138.—GOETHE TO ZELTER.

Jena, 9th July, 1820.

I FINISHED my last with a story, and begin this with another. You will perhaps remember, that my *Prometheus* * was first published in Vienna, in a pocket edition form; at the time, when we were in Töplitz together, I was still brooding over it, in the true sense of the word, and you took an equal share in it. The Duchess of Cumberland, who was recovering from a severe illness, wished to have something read aloud to her, so I took this very *Prometheus*, as my nearest and dearest; she was greatly pleased with it, and I let her keep the pocket edition copy.

Well, at our last interview, she talked about those days, and about the poem, and said she would like to have another small copy for a lady-friend of hers, but of course I had no more. Now I have been fortunate enough to find a small stray lamb in Carlsbad, and at once determined to send it to her; but I must first get it bound, that it may to some extent be worthy of passing through the fairest of fair hands. As she has so often spoken of me to you, I think it will be nice to send it to her through you. Say nothing about it, but let me know what you think and wish. . . . .

With regard to the picture of St. Cecilia,† I can only say, that the saint stands in the centre, and the small organ she holds in her hands, she has allowed to droop in such a way, that the pipes are slipping out, indicating that she is losing hold of earthly music, whilst she looks upwards, listening to the heavenly; the other saints do not stand in any relation to her; besides these, there are patron saints, of the city, the Church, and of him for whom the picture was

* Under the title of *Pandorens Wiederkunft*.
† Zelter had asked the question, "In what relation to Saint Cecilia do Paul and the Magdalen stand, as they are represented in Raphael's picture?"

painted, and these have no connection with one another, except that which the painter's art contrived to give them. The *Madonna del Pesce* is composed exactly in the same manner. The man who ordered the picture was probably called Tobias. . . . .

G.

139.—ZELTER TO GOETHE.

Berlin, 21st July, 1820.

. . . . I HAVE now heard Spontini's *Cortez* twice. The text is by De Jouy, and much better than the very bad German translation given here. I am inclined to prefer the music to that of the *Vestalin*, but I ought to hear it much more often, as I have got a kind of general view, but as yet, no firm point of observation. There are certainly admirable passages, and the dances throughout are quite excellent. My great puzzle is, that a highborn Italian, proved in high things, should clothe high heroic subjects with small melodious forms, whilst these again are strongly prejudiced by the musical accompaniment. But we shall see if we can find a firm point. For the rest, as an artist, I am on very good terms with this composer; he approached me voluntarily, and very confidingly, as no Italian or Frenchman has ever done before; he has four times visited the *Singakademie*, and 1 gladly acknowledge the interest he appears to take in it. . . .

Z.

140.—GOETHE TO ZELTER.

Jena, 20th September, 1820.

. . . . IT is to my absolute state of solitude and my habit of dictating, that you are indebted for this letter, which I am finishing on the evening of the arrival of yours. But that you, who have been rocking on the waves, sniffing up sea smells, and longing for the shore, may enjoy some happy hours this winter in peace and quiet, while remembering the perilous grandeur of the sea,* let me

* In a previous letter, Zelter had described his voyage to Stralsund, Putbus, and Rüden.

advise you to get a poem called *Olfried und Lisena;* it consists of ten Cantos, and over six hundred stanzas, and is written by one August Hagen,* a youngster in Königsberg.

Even though the food may occasionally seem too light for your strong palate and good powers of digestion, you are sure to be charmed, when you feel the very breath of your own Baltic through the whole of the little volume. It is a rare phenomenon, and has given me a great deal of pleasure.

But now, to a subject with which I ought to have begun, were it not that the joyful melodies of this world must so frequently be played *con sordini*. My daughter-in-law has given birth to another fine boy; but owing to her delicate constitution, she suffered fearfully, and to say the truth, I am still anxious about her. I can say no more, except that here too, I try to keep myself in Islam. . . . .

G.

141.—Zelter to Goethe.

Berlin, 23rd October, 1820.

YESTERDAY for the second, and to-day for the third time, I have been looking at your bust by Rauch. Clinging as I do to the first impression, I still choose to compare it with later ones, and find myself pretty well satisfied. Anyhow, our artist, at very first sight, saw deeper into you than any of his predecessors, who are known to me. . . . . The most pleasing picture of you is an original black chalk drawing by G. M. Kraus, of the year 1776; I recognize you completely in it, although it no longer resembles you now. Forehead, eye, nose, mouth, chin, and hair, all come from one centre, as the abode of what is in you and of what goes

---

* "There is August Hagen, in Königsberg, a splendid talent; have you ever read his *Olfried und Lisena?* There you may find passages which could not be better; the situations on the Baltic, and the other particulars of that locality, are all masterly. But these are only fine passages; as a whole, it pleases nobody. And what labour and power he has lavished upon it; indeed, he has almost exhausted himself. Now, he has been writing a tragedy." In *Kunst und Alterthum* Goethe had advised Hagen to treat only small subjects. See *Conversations of Goethe with Eckermann,* translated by Oxenford, p. 17.

forth from you. I coaxed this drawing out of old Nicclai's heir; he himself would never have given it to me. As I write this, it hangs before my picture of Sebastian Bach; I copy their features, and it seems to me just as if we had been young together. ....

Z.

142.—GOETHE TO ZELTER.

Weimar, 9th November, 1820.

.... I AM very well satisfied with Rauch's bust. If he had kept it concealed, and not exhibited it, till he had worked it out in marble, what is at present still problematical in it would never have come to be discussed.

Meyer also gives excellent testimony in favour of the picture after Albertinelli; an artist who quitted this earthly ball in 1520 may even then have left a good thing behind him. For the rest, this affair shows us, that our worthy Berlin friends boast of no firmly established Biblical standpoint; we have often enough seen the Visitation of the Blessed Virgin dated the 2nd of July, and marked as a redletter day in the Calendar, but we thought it meant, that she had received a visit from Elizabeth, whereas the reverse is really the case, for this Blessed Mary, being with child, had gone over the hills to visit her friend. All this is stated in detail, in the first chapter of St. Luke. Unquestionably the value of the picture is enhanced, when one carefully examines, and has thoroughly mastered the passage mentioned. . . .

G.

1821.

143.—GOETHE TO ZELTER.

Weimar, 18th February, 1821.

.... At Easter, I propose to offer my friends a fresh budget of *Kunst und Alterthum*, as well as a volume of *Wilhelm Meisters Wanderjahre*.

After all, the greatest charm of an author's otherwise hazardous life is, that while one is personally dumb to one's friends, one is meanwhile preparing a great conversation with them in all parts of the world.

It is the same with the musician, but he must act differently from certain friends, who do not allow their silent and absent acquaintances to benefit by the penitential tones of gentle Magdalenes, or by an appeal to the universal genius of the world.....

Most sincerely yours,
GOETHE.

144.—ZELTER TO GOETHE.

Berlin, 30th April, 1821.

Your Alexander Boucher,* or Alexander the Great, played here yesterday, with great applause. He reminds me of Baron Bagge, with this difference, that when the fool is subtracted from Boucher, a rare violin-player is left.....

His likeness to Napoleon, which was advertised beforehand, attracted several people, although the room was not full.....

---

* Spohr, who met this well-known French violinist at Brussels in 1819, says of him, "His face bore a remarkable likeness to Napoleon Bonaparte's, and he had evidently carefully studied the banished Emperor's way of bearing himself, lifting his hat, taking snuff, &c." He traded upon this resemblance, and on one occasion, advertised a Concert in these terms, "Une malheureuse ressemblance me force de m'expatrier ; je donnerai donc avant de quitter ma belle patrie, un concert d'adieux." He called himself " L'Alexandre des Violons."

Madame Boucher was even more applauded. Her playing on the piano and harp at the same time, shows her power over both instruments, a power which demands long practice, on account of the contrary motion of arms and fingers, queer as the whole thing is in itself. The composition of the Concerto which she played, pleased me more than that of her husband. Capellmeister Hummel has had a rare ovation : to-day he gives his second concert, and if he does not return to Weimar in a pulpy condition, the heat is not guilty of it, for it is exceptional.

The King has been to hear my Passion-music this year, and sent me twenty *Friedrichsd'or*, which I gladly welcomed, as the little yellow discs are rare with me. Besides this, he has been so gracious as to give me a site near the University Garden, upon which I mean to build a hall for my *Singakademie*. . . . .

Yours everlastingly,

Z.

145.—ZELTER TO GOETHE.

Berlin, 20th August, 1821.

I MUST communicate to you an old discovery, which I am now making for the second time. Turning over the leaves of my Lessing, I stumble, in the twenty-third volume of the *Theatrical Remains*, on the *Hercules Furens* of Seneca; herein I find the happiest of subjects for an Opera, and what is still more, towards the end, Lessing himself is of the same opinion. . . . . I have a young pupil,* now at work upon his third comic Opera, to whom I should like to give a serious subject. The boy's talent is sound, his work flows spontaneously, and he is industrious from love of the thing. In due time, I think of sending him to Italy, so that he may make his own way. . . . . A new Opera, *Der Freischütz*, by Maria von Weber, is making a *furore*. A silly huntsman, the hero of the piece, lets himself be enticed by necromancers, equally silly, into casting so-called magic bullets, by means of sorcery, at midnight; if

---

* Felix Mendelssohn.—The three Operas were, *Soldatenliebschaft*, *Die Beiden Pädagogen*, and *Die Wandernden Comödianten*.

he makes the best shot, he is to win the bride, who has already plighted her troth to him, whom he at last—shoots with this bullet? Not a bit of it! He does not even hit her. She only falls down at the report, springs immediately to her feet again, and marries him like a shot. Whether the hitter hits off marriage any better, history sayeth not. The music is greatly applauded, and is really so good, that the public puts up with all the coal and gunpowder explosion. With all the forge-bellows, I trace but little genuine passion. The women and children are crazy about it; the devil is black, virtue white, stage animated, Orchestra lively, and that the composer is no Spinozist, you may gather from this, that he has created so colossal a work out of the aforesaid Nothing. . . . .

Z.

146.—Goethe to Zelter.

Jena, 28th September, 1821.

. . . . I wish you would occasionally, with a few strokes of your pen, which are so easy to you, lay hold of the passing moment, and send it on some thirty miles further. I should have thought that my efforts for you, O ye Athenians! though they were not directed to each individual, but to the dear community as a whole, deserved some return.

I have spent my summer happily, undergoing my "cure:" the Carlsbad catastrophe was a bad after-cure, for I have so grown to the place, that I cannot bear to think of its being destroyed. From the heights above Franzenbrunnen, on that very 9th of September, I saw that mischievous flood roll down upon the Töpel region I know so well, and but for strange chances, I should have been involved in the calamity. In the days following, I had neither courage nor call to go there, so the horses, which had been ordered to drive me there, brought me home instead.

On arriving here, I find your dear letters and parcels, for which my best thanks; I have now got one of Streicher's many-octaved pianos, and I am told it is a success, so I hope my winter will thereby become a little more musical. . . . .

G.

147.—GOETHE TO ZELTER.

Jena, 14th October, 1821.

..... EBERWEIN is making arrangements for me to hear, instead of only looking at, some of the music you kindly intended for me, but if in the Chorus, *Dichten ist ein Uebermuth*, I restore the author, contrary to your emendations, without injuring the musical rhythm, you will perhaps pardon me. The poet feels strange, when he discovers that he has been tricked, like the old gentleman, fifteen hundred years ago.

I am much delighted with your kind words about the Prologue;* it chimes in with everything I have heard and am still hearing. It adds very much to my peace of mind, that in the quietest hermitage, far apart from the centre of busy life, I could produce something, which at a most important moment, was there found to be suitable and pleasing. I hope that, by degrees, people will learn to value the occasional poem, for those who know nothing about the matter, and who imagine that such a thing as an independent poem exists, are still for ever nagging at it. Among the tame *Xenien* you will, in future, find the following:—

> Wouldst thou thyself a poet prove,
> From heroes and shepherds hold aloof;
> Here is Rhodes, man! Dance away!†
> And to the occasion tune thy lay!

I write these lines, dearest Friend, on the 14th of October, in Jena, on the very spot, where so many years ago everything was a mere ruin; to-day, however, there is a Sunday quiet here, so that were it not for the sponsors and other witnesses, who have come to assist at the state-christening, one would suppose all the inhabitants had died off. However, the old limes, the very trees which calmly looked on at the tumult of the battle and the fires, still clothe themselves in a glorious foliage of green; and I

---

* A Prologue written by Goethe for the opening of the Berlin Theatre.

† An allusion to the well-known saying, *Hic Rhodus, hic salta.* See *Æsop's Fables.*

still occasionally creep out of my most insignificant cottage, into the botanical garden, where, it is true, I miss your fair pupil; you can give her another kind message from me.

I am glad that Boucher and his wife are doing so well; for that is industry and practice, backed by natural talent. I entirely approve of what you say about the human voice. When I heard Catalani in Carlsbad, I said, very appropriately, on the spur of the moment:—

> In drawing-room as in lofty hall,
> Never enough one hears;
> Now first we learn, and once for all,
> The reason we have ears.

.... A copy of my *Wanderjahre* will follow shortly. If you should happen to meet Carl Ernst Schubarth of Breslau, be kind to him for my sake; he has written something on my *Faust*, and is now publishing his *Ideen über Homer und sein Zeitalter*, a little book that I can greatly praise, for it puts one into a good humour. Those who are fond of pulling things to pieces, will not like it, because it reconciles and unites.

Very truly yours,

G.

148.—ZELTER TO GOETHE.

Berlin, 26th October, 1821.

.... To-morrow early, I, with my Doris, and a pupil of mine, Herr Mendelssohn's son, a lively boy of twelve years old, start for Wittenberg, to attend the *fête* there. You shall hear from Wittenberg, if I am coming—three strong—to Weimar. As your house is full enough, I shall put up at my good "Elephant," where I have always been treated thoroughly well; only let me see you again; I thirst to be near you. I should like to show your face to my Doris, and my best pupil, before I leave this world,—in which however, it is my desire to remain as long as possible. The pupil is a good and pretty boy, lively and obedient. To be sure, he is the son of a Jew, but no Jew himself. The father, with remarkable self-denial, has let his sons learn something, and educates them properly; it would really be *eppes Rores,* (something rare,) if the son of a Jew turned out an artist. . . . .

Z.

1822.

149.—GOETHE TO ZELTER.

Weimar, 5th February, 1822.

. . . . My kind greetings to Dorchen, and thanks for her kindness to Ulrike*; say a good word for me to Felix and his parents too. Since you left, my piano has been dumb; one single endeavour to re-awaken it was next door to a failure. However, I hear a great deal of *talk* about music,—which is always a poor sort of amusement.

Farewell! In your Berlin glory think of me who, in my sunny little back-room, think of you only too often.

Most truly yours,
G.

150.—GOETHE TO ZELTER.

Weimar, 13th March, 1822.

. . . . My best thanks for your affection and hospitality to the good child, Ulrike; she has returned home safely, and has a great deal to tell us. In her nice natural way, she sees things very clearly and plainly, and they stand before her, even as though they were present; one cannot say that she criticises, but she compares, with great insight. I am surprised that she did not write at once, for she is still perpetually with you in thought. . . . .

Of our Grand Duchess, I can only say that one's admiration and respect for her are ever on the increase; she has had two falls, both times hurting herself considerably, but she is always equal to herself, never wavering, nor swerving from her line of conduct; besides this, she makes it her business to keep the young people who like dancing and *fêtes*, on the move, and although a sufferer herself, to make

---

* Ulrike von Pogwisch, the younger sister of Goethe's daughter-in-law, Ottilie. Dorchen is Zelter's daughter, Doris.

others happy. She generally comes to see me once a week; so I always have ready something of interest to lay before her, and the calm and thorough interest she takes in all kinds of subjects, is a most delightful recompense. . . . .

All my belongings are well and happy, the grandchildren in particular are faultless; the life that is newly springing up is still in its first bloom, when the very defects of our nature seem graceful. . . . .

My opponents do not mislead me; has not everyone in the world, and more especially in Germany, to get accustomed to this sort of thing? My noble opponents, in physics especially, seem to me like Catholic priests, who would fain refute a Protestant by the Council of Trent.

Schubarth is a remarkable man; it is difficult to foretell in what direction he can succeed. Indeed, as literature now stands, especially German literature, which grasps and overgrasps at everything, clever young men work their way up to a clear survey more quickly, and perceive only too soon, that there is no special satisfaction in *criticising*. They feel they must *produce*, so as in some measure to satisfy themselves and others. This, however, is not given to everyone, so I have seen the best heads at variance with themselves. . . . .

G.

151.—ZELTER TO GOETHE.

Berlin, 17th March, 1822.

. . . . FELIX is well and industrious. His third Opera* is finished and written out, and will soon be performed among his friends. After his return from Weimar he also finished a Gloria, besides writing more than half a pianoforte Concerto for his sister; he has begun a Magnificat too. Even if I myself fail to do anything much, anyhow I keep my boys to it, and half-a-dozen of these positively delight me. . . . .

ZELTER.

* See note to Letter 145.

152.—GOETHE TO ZELTER.

Weimar, 31st March, 1822.

IF you wish to understand and explain problematical pictures, such as the one in question by Titian, the following considerations must be borne in mind. Since the thirteenth century, when people began to abandon the Byzantine style, which was still indeed respectable, but ended by being quite dry and mummified,—and to turn to nature, the artist considered nothing too high, nothing too deep for him to try and represent directly from reality; nay, the demand by degrees went so far, that pictures had, like a kind of paper of patterns, to include everything within the range of the eye. A picture of this kind had to be filled to the very edge with important and detailed matter; hence the inevitable result was, that figures foreign to and in no way connected with the main subject, together with other objects, were introduced, as proofs of the general skill of the artist. In Titian's day, the painter still willingly yielded to such requirements.

Now let us turn to the picture itself. In an open varied landscape, and almost at the edge of the picture, on the left hand, with rocks and tree adjoining, we see the loveliest nude maiden, resting herself as comfortably, composedly, and quietly, as on a lonely bed. If she were cut out, we should have a perfect picture as it is, and want nothing more; in the present masterpiece, however, the first intention was to represent the glory of the human form in its outer manifestation. Further, behind her stands a high narrow-necked vessel, probably for the sake of the metallic sheen; a soft wreath of smoke issuing from it. Can this be meant to indicate the piety of the beautiful woman, a silent prayer, or what?

For we are soon aware, that this is the picture of a notable person. To the right, on the opposite side, lies a skull, and out of the cleft close by, appears the arm of a man, not yet bared of flesh and muscle.

We soon see the connection; for between those bones, and that divine form, wriggles a small active dragon, greedily eying the tempting prey. But lest we should be somewhat anxious on her account, lying so quietly, as she does, whilst she seems to hold back the dragon by a spell, there rushes forth from the darkest of thunder-clouds an armed knight, mounted on a strange fire-breathing lion; these two will probably soon make an end of the dragon. And thus we see, although in rather an odd way, that it represents St. George threatening the dragon, and the lady whom he is to rescue.

Now on examining the landscape, we find that it is not in any way in keeping with the incident; on the principle stated above, it is merely as remarkable as possible in itself, and yet the figures described are happily placed there.

Between two rocky banks, a steeper one thickly wooded, and a flatter one with less undergrowth of vegetation, a river runs towards us, at first rushing, then gently flowing along; the steep bank on the right is crowned by a mighty ruin, huge shapeless masses of masonry, still remaining, indicate the power and strength displayed in their construction. Single pillars, nay, a statue left in its niche, indicate the grace of a royal residence such as this was; the force of time, however, has made all the efforts of human skill useless and futile.

On the opposite shore, we are reminded of more recent times: there stand mighty towers, fortifications that have been newly erected, or perfectly restored, newly made embrasures and battlements; far in the background, however, the two banks are connected by a bridge, which reminds one of the *Ponte degli Angeli*, in the same way as the tower behind it suggests the Castle of *St. Angelo*. From the prevailing love of truth and reality, such confusion of place and time was not laid to the account of the artist. But leaving the strictest congruity out of the question, we could not alter a single line, without injuring the composition.

We greatly admire the exquisitely poetical thunder-cloud which brings in the knight; but without having the picture before one, it is impossible to discuss such points in detail. On the one side, it seems to disengage itself from the ruin like a dragon's tail, but in spite of all Zoomorphism, one cannot interpret the whole into any special form; on the other side, between the bridge and the fortifications, a fire breaks out, the smoke of which is rising in gentle wreaths up to the fire-breathing jaws of the lion, and comes into contact with him. Enough, although at first we spoke of this composition as collective, we cannot but reflect that it has been woven into unity, and prize it accordingly.

In haste, yours truly,

G.

153.—ZELTER TO GOETHE.

Berlin, 7th April, 1822.

YESTERDAY, Saturday, Madame Mara came to me of her own accord, on foot too, to help me, she said, to count my well-deserved fees. Just think of this seventy-two-year-old matron, this demon of a singer, being touched by our *Messiah*. The pain and the bliss, she declares, carried her quite away; the audience must have thought her silly. The Fugues went so smoothly, an organ of living voices. She has often enough sung in this Oratorio in London; she summed up by confessing that our performance might vie with those in London, of which the English are sufficiently proud.

9th April.

Yesterday evening came Professor Hegel, to tell us that our friend Isegrimm was seriously ill, and inquiring for me. I was with him this afternoon. I found him in bed, and really very weak. He asked me to see that he was buried before sunrise, to a good blast of trumpets. I said Yes, and he should have a good dead march besides, provided he would so manage his decease, that I should be at hand. He has forbidden a post-mortem examination, shaving, shrouds and all such things; whoever is ignorant shall learn nothing through him. The worms will be hungry enough without all that; he is not so proud as to let himself be served up daintily for unfamiliar guests. It seems he wishes to outlive the executors of his last will, and I am glad not to make one of the worms, which are to hunger for his corpse. He was just then asking the doctor, whether he might eat sausage or maccaroni, and such things. He has begun to dictate a farewell letter to you, which perhaps he means to finish, when he is completely recovered. I doubt his being so bad; I should be sorry to lose him, for I learn from him; so he may just as well live till he is dead. . . . .

Z.

154.—GOETHE TO ZELTER.

Eger, 8th August, 1822.

IT was quite right of you to open up a conversation with me again, whilst you were in those outlandish, pious countries;* in return for it, you shall soon have back again a clean copy of your letter. If I continually thought of you all last winter, while I was drawing up in manuscript, and correcting in proof what you are now devouring,† I am well rewarded by your welcome pages, which have for ever set at rest my wish to see Moravia in its own individuality. So be it then! The beautiful *white* hall (washed clean in the blood of Christ, according to Zacharias Werner's priceless *Fool's Sonnet*), shall now never be entered by me, were I ever so well able to get about. . . . .

Nor am I anxious on your account: your nature knows how to assimilate, and after all, everything depends upon this. If people understood their own advantage, they would not blame anything traditionally handed down; what does not please us we should let alone, in order to take it up at some future time perhaps. Mankind does not understand this, and treats an author like the master of a cookshop; in return for that, they are served with sausages bought at the fairs, to their heart's content:—

> " Boys read their Terence with a different joy
> To that of Grotius, when he reads him too."
> The saying made me angry as a boy,
> Though now I cannot choose but own it true.

If I read Homer now, he seems different to what he was to me ten years ago; if one lived to be three hundred years old, he would always seem different. To convince oneself of this, one need only look backwards; from the

---

* Zelter had written at length to Goethe, about his religious experiences in Moravia.
† Vol. ix. of *Aus meinem Leben.*

Pisistratidæ to our own Wolf, what different sorts of faces does the old father make!

I am overjoyed that Wolf, (the friend in question,) has not been burnt, or eaten up by the fever, for I should not willingly miss him above-ground. We shall not see his like again. Would that God had willed him friendly, in addition to so many other qualities! And yet, how can all these contradictory things be reconciled?

I am very pleased that you approve of my treatment of that dirty Campaign ;* to play Grazioso in such a tragedy is always something of a part. . . . .

My greatest gain of late is the personal acquaintance of Count Caspar Sternberg, with whom formerly I corresponded. Having from early days been consecrated to the priesthood, he finally became Canon of Ratisbon; when there, he acquired, in addition to his knowledge of secular and state affairs, a love for the study of Nature, more especially the vegetable kingdom, for which department he has done a great deal. When driven from his post by the subversion of Germany, he returned to Bohemia, his native country, and now lives partly in Prague, partly on estates inherited from his elder brother. Here Nature once more kindly comes to his aid. He possesses important coal mines, in the roof of which the rarest kinds of plants have been preserved, and inasmuch as they show forms analogous only to the vegetation of the most Southern regions, they point to the remotest epochs of the earth. He has already published two books of them; when you have an opportunity, get some naturalist to show them to you. . . . .

Very truly yours,
G.

ENCLOSURE.

HE.

I thought that in myself I felt no pain,
Yet hollow were the chambers of my brain,
And at my heart a silent terror hung,
And round my brows th' enchaining darkness clung,

* The *Campagne in Frankreich*, which Goethe had just published as the Fifth Part of the Second Division of *Aus meinem Leben*.

Until the tears are flowing thick and fast,
And the restrained Farewell pours forth at last,—
Tranquil and full of cheer was *her* Farewell,
Yet now, perchance, I think *she* weeps as well.

SHE.

It must be. Ay, and he is gone!
My dear ones, leave me but alone,
The secret of my strangeness keeping.
It will not last for ever and a day;
But now that he is gone away,
I have no choice but weeping.

HE.

I am not in the mood for sorrow,—
What are the mellow gifts to me,
That we may pluck from every tree,
Since joy from none of them I borrow!
The day is wearisome and vain,
Tedious it is, when night lights up her fires,
Thy gentle image to renew again
Is now the only end of my desires.
And didst thou feel this longing as I feel it,
Thou'dst come half-way to meet me, nor conceal it.

SHE.

Since I appear not, thou far off art grieving,
Fears lest I prove untrue thy heart deceiving,
For else the image of my soul were here.
Doth Iris then adorn the blue of heaven?—
Let the rain fall, flesh out the colours seven;
See, thou art weeping! I again appear.

HE.

Most like indeed to Iris' heavenly bow,
My tender miracle of beauty, thou!
Bending in splendour, bright with harmony,
Ever the same and ever new, as she.

The Present of itself knows nought,
The Parting feels itself with terror duly,
Distance behind thyself will drag thee caught,
Absence alone knows how to value truly.

Weimar, 14th December, 1822.

1823.

155.—GOETHE TO ZELTER.

Weimar, 18th January, 1823.

. . . . ONE can never acquire any cheerful relationship with philologists and mathematicians. The handicraft of the former is to *emend*, of the latter to *define;* now there are in life so many defects (*mendæ*) to be found, and every single day has enough in itself to define, so that into our intercourse with such men, there enters a certain lifelessness, which brings death to all communication. Were I obliged to think that a friend to whom I dictate a letter, would formulate over the use and position of words, nay, even over the punctuation, which I leave to my amanuensis, I should instantly feel paralyzed, and there could be no sense of freedom. . .

Yours eternally,
G.

156.—AUGUST VON GOETHE TO ZELTER.

Weimar, 26th February, 1823.

HONOURED FRIEND,

We have lately passed a very sad and anxious time; on the 17th of this month, my poor father was suddenly attacked by inflammation of the pericardium, probably too, of a part of the heart itself; this was accompanied by inflammation of the pleura, which brought him, during this week, to the point of death. Fortunately on the 24th, the ninth day, came the crisis so earnestly desired by the doctors, and at the present moment, all danger seems to have passed away. We hope that my father's naturally strong and good constitution, which has enabled him, at his great age, to overcome this serious illness, may also help him to get the better of any of the consequences that may ensue. I send these lines to relieve your mind, with the request that you will communicate the news to Staatsrath Langermann, Count Brühl, and other sympathetic friends. Farewell, and remember me kindly to Doris. The enclosed letter is from Ulrike to Doris, and was written long ago.

Faithfully yours,
AUGUST V. GOETHE.

157.—AUGUST VON GOETHE TO ZELTER.

Weimar, 16th March, 1823.

HONOURED FRIEND,

I gladly take up my pen again to tell you, that the improved state of my father's health has continued, and that his recovery is steadily progressing. He is again at work with his *Kunst und Alterthum* and *Morphologie*, and thus by degrees, we are getting back into our old ways; one of these is that we are dining together again.

With what strange joy do we again look into the future! And how does the immediate past lie, like a hideous dream, behind us!

Please let Staatsrath Langermann see these lines, and give him our kindest greetings; my kind remembrances also to our friend Doris. I received a very sympathetic letter from Herr Mendelssohn, and must beg to be kindly remembered to him. Your dear Songs came safely, and greatly delight my father, like everything else that comes from you.

Yours very faithfully,
AUGUST VON GOETHE.

(Enclosure written in pencil, in Goethe's own hand, on a separate leaf.)

The first evidence of my renewed life and love, from
Yours gratefully and affectionately,
J. W. V. GOETHE.

158.—ZELTER TO GOETHE.

Berlin, 7th March, 1823.

My Felix has entered his fifteenth year; he grows under my eyes. His marvellous pianoforte playing I may look upon as quite a secondary matter; he may just as easily become a master on the violin. The Second Act of his fourth Opera * is finished. All he does becomes more solid, strength and power are scarcely wanting now; everything comes from within, he is only touched externally by things external. Imagine my joy, if we should live to see the boy live, and fulfil the promise of his innocence. He is healthy. I should like his very beautiful Pianoforte Quartett to be dedicated to your Grand Princess. Tell me how we ought to set about it? And tell me soon. It is quite new, and still better than the one he let you hear in Weimar.

Yours everlastingly,
Z.

159.—GOETHE TO ZELTER.

Marienbad, 24th July, 1823.

. . . . This place as a whole, and especially the part where I reside, is favourable enough for company; it is a terrace of handsome houses, flanked by two large buildings of equal size, which would make a figure in any town. The Grand Duke lives in the centre, and fortunately the whole neighbourhood is occupied by pretty women and intelligent men. Older associations become blended with new ones, and a past life makes one believe in a present.

As I have perhaps been more occupied with the science of the earth than was fair, I am now beginning on the atmospheric kingdoms; and were it only to learn the process of one's own thinking and ability to think, that is already a foretaste of reward. We know very well that man must attract and assimilate everything to himself, God Himself and the God-like; but this very attraction has its degrees,—it may be either lofty or commonplace.

* See Note to Letter 162.

However, my most prosperous work is the revision of the chronicles of my life. After various attempts, I have finally started from the latest period, for, my memory being fresh about this, I do not need to trouble myself long as to material; finally I perceive—thus working backwards—that what is familiar and present recalls the past, the forgotten.

In this sense, it must be of great moment to me, if distant friends regard what goes forth from me in print as addressed to them; for I see the time close at hand, when my voice will no longer be directly heard in writing. It is therefore very comforting to me, that you have all given my last number a kindly welcome: in each of those numbers, there is more life stowed away, than one would imagine from the view of it. Unfortunately, people nowadays read only for the sake of getting through the pages, therefore a still greater capability is required in the writer, that he may leave behind him a witness that he has not laboured in vain.

If you should find the pages of this letter in harmony with the most solemn, pine-clad peaks, seen from on high, consider my surroundings, where a thunderstorm, broadening out far away from the mountains, is sending down lightnings, thunder, and rain over the whole country. All our neighbourly world is away, and I am as good as alone on this wonderful spot. . . . .

Most truly yours,
J. W. von GOETHE.

159A.—ZELTER TO GOETHE.

Berlin, 17th August, 1823.

. . . . To-DAY, being the 17th of August, Rosenmeier, (an old military surgeon,) was talking to me about his old King, Frederick the Great, whose last hour he vividly described to me. When Hertzberg, the Minister, came into the sick-room on the day of the King's death, the King called out to him, "If you want a watchman, apply to me; I can serve you, so that you shall praise my vigilance." The Minister brought papers with him, and the King stretched out his arm to receive them. "Give me them! So long as the little lamp glimmers, it must be used; hurry everything up, life is short." After the death, women came, who were already prepared to wash the corpse; Rosenmeier forbade them. The King had always shown, even in illness, an insuperable modesty.* Consequently Rosenmeier was there at once to undress the corpse, to wash and examine it, and he declares on his honour, that he found the whole body perfectly natural and sound. I observed, that my father had already contradicted a certain rumour, saying, "It is incredible; so healthy a spirit and so sickly a body could not get on together for so long." . . . .

Z.

160.—GOETHE TO ZELTER.

Eger, 24th August, 1823.

IN reply to your welcome letter, dearest Friend, which reached me at a very fortunate moment, I shall—in accordance with my promise—before quitting the charmed circle of Bohemia, again address a letter to you, which you will welcome the more kindly and affectionately, as I have nothing but good news to communicate.

To begin with then, let me say that during the time I lately spent in Marienbad, I met with no disagreeables of any kind, nay, was cheerful as though returning to life again, and am now feeling better than I have done for long.

Further I must tell you, that after receiving that kiss, the bestower of which you probably guessed, I was favoured by another splendid gift from Berlin; for I have heard Madame Milder sing four little Songs, which she contrived to make so great, that the remembrance of them still draws tears from my eyes. So the praise I have heard bestowed upon her for so many years past, is no longer a cold historical word, but awakens true and deeply-felt emotion. Give her my kindest remembrances. She asked me for something from my own hand, and will receive through you the first leaflet, that is not absolutely unworthy of her.

* See Preusz's *Friedrich der Grosse*, vol. i. p. 364.

Madame Szymanowska,* an incredibly fine pianiste, affected me just as powerfully, though in quite a different way. I fancy she might be compared to our Hummel, only that she is a lovely and amiable Polish lady. When Hummel ceases playing, there rises up a Gnome before us, who, by the help of powerful demons, has performed such wonders, that one scarcely dares thank him for them; but when *she* stops playing, and comes and looks at us, we do not feel sure, whether we may not consider ourselves fortunate, that she has stopped. Give her a friendly welcome, when she comes to Berlin, which will probably be before very long; remember me to her, and help her when you can. . . . .

Forgive this,† and let me be silent, for too much has been said already; however, to an honest and penetrating thinker, it is revolting to see a whole generation—and one that is not quite to be despised—irretrievably involved in ruin. The older ones are already aware of it, but they can neither save themselves, nor do they care to warn others: for they are already a sect, which must keep together, if it is to be of any importance,—a sect, in which the incomer deceives himself, and the outgoer deceives the rest. Again I ask your pardon, for I ask it of myself; one always spoils an hour, by raking up such fruitless sorrows.

It is comfortless too, to listen to political discussions, from whatever quarter. To get quit of all such things, as well as of æsthetic conversations and lectures, I devoted myself for six weeks to a very pretty child, ‡ and was thus perfectly secured against all outward disagreeables.

But now for the strangest thing of all! The immense power that music had over me in those days! Milder's voice, the rich sounds of Szymanowska, nay, even the public performances of the local Jägerscorps untwisted me, just as

* Pianiste to the Empress of Russia. Goethe acknowledged his debt to her in the poem *Aussöhnung*.

† A tirade against the shallow dilettantism of the day, as illustrated in the case of Hensel, and other young painters.

‡ Ulrike von Levezow, Goethe's "Stella," daughter of the lady who was the original of "Pandora." The affair became so serious, that marriage was talked of, and the mother broke off everything, by suddenly leaving Marienbad. Goethe commemorated his resolution to give up Ulrike in the *Elegie*.

one lets a clenched fist gently flatten itself out. By way of partially explaining this, I say to myself—" For two years and more, you have not heard any music at all, except Hummel, twice, and therefore this faculty—so far as it exists in you—has been lying shut up and apart; now, all of a sudden, the Heavenly One falls upon you, and through the intervention of great talents, exercises her full power over you, claims all her rights, and awakens all your dormant recollections." I feel perfectly convinced, that I should have to leave the hall, at the first bar I might hear from your *Singakademie*. And when I now consider, what it is, to hear an Opera, as we give them, but once a week, (a *Don Juan*, or a *Matrimonio Segreto*,) renewing it within oneself, and assimilating this feeling with the others that form part of an active life, then, for the first time, do I understand what it is, to have to dispense with such an enjoyment, which, like all the higher enjoyments of life, takes a man out of and above himself, and lifts him, at the same time, out of the world and above it.

How good, how imperative then, it should be for me, to have an opportunity of spending some time by your side! By gently guiding and directing me, you would cure my morbid irritability, which, after all, must be regarded as the cause of the above phenomenon, and you would, little by little, enable me to take into myself the whole wealth of God's fairest revelation. Now I must see, how I can get through a dumb and shapeless winter, which in some measure, I look forward to with horror. However, we must endeavour, with good humour and courage, to turn the black days to account, for ourselves and our friends. A thousand times, my sincerest farewell!

G.

1824.

161.—GOETHE TO ZELTER.

Weimar, 9th January, 1824.

.... I ENCLOSE one of my mother's letters, as you wished to have it; throughout, as in every line she wrote, there speaks the character of a woman who—God-fearing as she was, in the Old Testament way—led a good life, full of confidence in the unchangeable God of nations and families, and who—when herself announcing her approaching death—made all the arrangements for her funeral so precisely, that the kind of wine and the size of the cracknels on which the mourners were to feast, were accurately fixed. . . . .

Ottilie is now in Berlin, and will flit about there from hour to hour, till she is obliged to pause now and then; perhaps after attaining her object of being again driven through the Brandenburg Gate, there may be at least some diminution of the hurry, without which, indeed, one can scarcely imagine her. You will, I know, be all kindness to her. Nothing very good can happen, without exciting her lively temperament.* . . . .

Do you know the following lines? They have grown to my heart; you really must draw them off again, by winning tones :—

> Most like indeed to Iris' heavenly bow,
> My tender miracle of beauty, thou!
> Bending in splendour, bright with harmony,
> Ever the same and ever new, as she.

Commending you to all good spirits,

G.

---

* Ottilie and her husband had begun to be on bad terms with each other, and she had joined her mother in Berlin, where she made the acquaintance of a young Englishman, whose attentions to her met with only too much encouragement.

ENCLOSURE.
FROM GOETHE'S MOTHER TO HER SON.

1st October, 1802.

DEAR SON,

My best thanks for your willingness to give a helping hand to Herr Schöff Mellecher, with his hobby-horse. I am always pleased, when you can show a Frankfurter any kindness, for you are with us still, and live in our midst—are a citizen—share in everything— your name stands in Barrentrap's Calendar, amongst the advocates; *summa summarum*—you still belong to us, and your compatriots esteem it an honour to themselves, that they can reckon so great and famous a man, among their fellow-citizens. Eduard Schlosser brought me your welcome greeting. I hope he is doing well, and Fritz Schlosser also, but I am often anxious about Christian. That young man is so very conceited—fancies he knows more than almost all his contemporaries, has extraordinary ideas, &c. He has a great opinion of you; if you can cool him down, pray do so. In that you are willing to send me some of the fruits of your mind, you do a good work; there is a great unfruitfulness amongst us—and your little brook, which has water in abundance, will do my thirsty soul good. I have plans in my head for your coming next year, and one plan is always brighter than the other— that will right itself. Please God, we all keep in good health, and we shall be able to manage the rest. Farewell! Greet my dear daughter, and our dear August, from

Your faithful old Mother and Grandmother,

GOETHE.

162.—ZELTER TO GOETHE.

Berlin, Sunday, 8th February, 1824.

.... YESTERDAY evening, we had a private performance of Felix's fourth Opera,* complete with Dialogue. There are three Acts, which, with two ballets, occupy some two hours and a half; the work had its due meed of applause.

* *Die Beiden Neffen, oder Der Onkel aus Boston,*—still in manuscript.

The text, too, by Dr. Casper, is clever enough, as the poet is musical. From my weak side I can hardly master my surprise, at a lad, just fifteen years old, progressing with such great strides. I find everywhere novelty, beauty, perfect originality; there is mind, flow, calm, sonority, completeness, dramatic force. The "Ensemble" shows an old hand. Orchestration interesting, not oppressive, nor wearisome, not mere accompaniment. The musicians enjoy playing it, and yet it is not so easy after all. Familiar things come and go past, not as though they were borrowed, but rather welcome and appropriate, each in its own place. Liveliness, exultation, no over-hurry, tenderness, elegance, love, passion, innocence. The Overture is a strange thing. Imagine for yourself a painter, who smudges a cake of paint on the canvas, picking out the mass with finger and brush, until at last, to our increasing astonishment, he ends by producing such a group that we cast about for the actual occasion of it, since what is true must really have happened. To be sure, I speak like a grandfather, who spoils his grandchildren. Never mind. I know what I say, and insist that I have said nothing but what I can prove. First of all, by unstinted applause, paid most sincerely by Orchestra and singers; it is easy to see from them, whether coldness or repugnance, whether love and favour, move their fingers and throats. You must know all about that. . . . .

Z.

163.—GOETHE TO ZELTER.

Weimar, 8th March, 1824.

. . . . FIRST of all, please give my kind remembrances to Herr Streckfuss; I have always followed his literary progress, poetical and otherwise, with great respect, though I have not earlier acknowledged his letter and parcel. This—situated as I was and feeling as I did—was often impossible: for as I could not reply to any confidence reposed in me with empty or specious phrases, and yet was incapable of always appreciating at the moment everything put before me, I got into arrears with many eminent men, and have done so more and more of late. So give him my kindest remembrances, and thank him for the souvenir. The little Book of *Ruth* * works in rattlesnake fashion upon all poetically productive minds; one cannot refrain from rearrangement, paraphrase, and enlargement of the subject-matter, which is certainly very pleasing, but nevertheless lies very far out of our way. I am anxious to see how the poet has acted in this instance.

Now I must tell you that the library here has purchased at a Nüremberg auction, a manuscript bearing the title, *Tabulatur-Buch geistlicher Gesänge* Dr. Martini Lutheri *und anderer gottseliger Männer, sammt beygefügten Choralfugen durchs ganze Jahr. Allen Liebhabern des Claviers componiret von Johann Pachelbeln, Organisten zu St. Sebald in Nürnberg*, 1704. If it would interest you, I could send it to you, at all events, to look at. It is bound in leather, has been gilt-edged, and looks exactly like an old piece of church furniture, although in a good state of preservation; it contains two hundred and forty-seven melodies.

Your report of Felix is all that could be desired, and is touching when considered as text and commentary; would that I could give you a similar account of one of my scholars! but unfortunately Poetry and Plastic Art have no recognized basis like yours. The most absurd empiricism is met with everywhere—artists and amateurs are equally insufficient; the one creates, the other criticises without any reason; consequently we have to wait till a man of decided talent steps forth, and perceives what is rational outside himself, because it lies concealed within him.

The Carnival gaieties ended badly for my household; in the last Cotillon—that mischievous dance of which boys and girls can never have enough—Ulrike had a bad fall on the back of her head, and her brain has not yet recovered from the shock. The Doctors make the best of the matter, but I do not know what will come of it.

Ottilie was met by this trouble, on her return, and after all the pomp and gaiety in Berlin, she will have to help us to pay for it. . . . .

* " Streckfuss has been incited by you yourself to turn the Book of Ruth into four metrical Songs," writes Zelter to Goethe, in a previous letter.

I have again been strangely attracted by Handel; Rochlitz's *Entwickelung des Messias*, (in his first volume, *Für Freunde der Tonkunst*, page 227,) has induced me to take up the Handel-Mozart score, from which, it is true, I can only pick out the rhythmical motives; I hope soon to become better acquainted with the harmonic ones as well, through Eberwein's performance. This would have been an interesting topic for our meeting, which, compared with former ones, would have turned out badly, had it not been for the good influence of the principal subject of our conversation. Here's to our early meeting!

G.

One word more! Have you seen the pictures by Schadow and Begas, that are being exhibited in the Pfeilersaal in the Royal Schloss? If not, go and look at them, and give me your candid opinion about them. Then get Nos. 56 and 57 of the *Haude und Spenersche Zeitung*, and read the critique upon them. It is written by a discerning person, but how he turns and twists himself about, in order to veil his conviction, which we could summarize in a few words! They are both talented and highly cultivated artists, who however are losing their best years in the modern German tomfoolery, sanctimoniousness, and affected fondness for antiquarianism: they satisfy nobody, and will probably go to the bad, because they will either come to their senses too late, or will never come to them at all.

Now and for ever,
Your faithful friend.

164.—GOETHE TO ZELTER.

Weimar, 11th March, 1824.

AFTER a short interval, my good Friend, I again come forward, and this time with desire and design; listen then to my story.

I enclose a poem, in explanation of which it may be necessary to state the following. Staatsrath Thaer, of whom you are sure to know something in general, as well as in particular, attains his seventy-third year on the 14th of May. On that day his pupils, from far and wide, are going to meet at his house in Mögelin, where they intend to give him a splendid *fête*. Now they want to have some brand-new Drinking-Songs for the occasion, and so have addressed themselves in neat and suitable petitions to Weimar, as the actual emporium of poetic art in Germany. Their friends too are not disinclined to help them. Thus the enclosed poem came into my head; for the preliminary understanding of it, I annex the following commentary:—*

Strophe 1.

Thaer, a physician, esteemed both as a practitioner and theorist, is looking around him in search of cheerful occupation in the field of Nature—he gets fond of gardening.

Strophe 2.

But he soon finds his powers cramped, and longs for a wider sphere of activity; he turns his attention to agriculture.

Strophe 3.

He pays attention to the English system of husbandry, and the very simple maxim, that with more activity and more intelligent farming, a far greater advantage may be gained than by following the old beaten track.

Strophe 4.

And thus he manages to stir up landowners to change their crops, gains pupils and followers, who approve of his teaching and leading, and propose now to give him, in his advanced years, a loud and public acknowledgment of their gratitude.

I hope that this poem, which is meant to be sung by a great number of landowners, seated at a banquet, may incite you to set it to some bright music; it is a *fête* that will not occur again, and I should like our two names to be mentioned together on the occasion. The man belongs first of all to Prussia, but after that to the world at large

* See *Goethe's Werke*, vol. xv. page 30, in Cotta's edition, 1866.

as well; his fame and reputation are thoroughly genuine, and so one may surely undertake something in which one can rejoice with him and his friends.

I trust you will be able soon to send me a successful score, which I will then attend to further. In the first instance, I should like to keep it to ourselves. If you have heard but little of the man, you need only ask those immediately about you; they will tell you enough to further your co-operation. Perhaps some one of his pupils, travelling to and fro, will join your *Liedertafel*, at any rate at a later period, in which case you could not better entertain such a guest. I go on daily in the old routine, and am glad I keep myself upright in it. Farewell, and love me.

I am on my legs again.*

G.

165.—ZELTER TO GOETHE.

Berlin, 20th March, 1824.

. . . . Your mention of Handel reminds me that I must thank Rochlitz; he sent me his book too, and said plenty of friendly things about Handel and myself. Herder somewhere calls Handel's *Messiah* a Christian Epic; in that one word he has hit the right nail on the head, for in fact this work contains in its fragmentary arrangement the whole convolution of his (*i.e.* Handel's) Christianity, as truly and honourably, as it is rationally poetical. The intention of the whole, viewed as a work, I have always considered accidental in origin, and I cannot rid myself of that opinion. . . . .

In Rochlitz's book, p. 76, Mara is said to have three times petitioned the King (Frederick the Great) for permission to marry Mara, and to have obtained it the third time. That, begging his pardon, is not true. The King roundly refused. When Mara ran away on the first occasion, and what is more, ran away from her engagement as first Singer to the King, she was still Mademoiselle Schmeling. Herr Mara was engaged at a good salary, as a virtuoso in the band of Prince Henry; so he was to be

* Written in Goethe's own hand.

punished as an eloper. The King would have liked to keep Mara, but she had not wished to engage herself for life. Now, however, she offered herself to the King, if the King would allow Mara, now advanced to the post of drummer, to go free, and give her permission to marry him. Consent was given, and now for the first time as a married couple, they ran away again. That was in the year 1778, after Mara had sung in January the part of Handel's "Rodelinda." When they had caught her again all right, the King ordered them to let her go. The King hated Mara, who was much more than a member of Prince Henry's band; the high and mighty Prince did more than that for his favourite, in spite of its being impossible to get at his heart by a secret staircase, and thousands of good deeds, for Mara was the commonest scamp, and maltreated his master outrageously. He sulked at him for weeks on end, and behaved impiously, disturbing the Sunday services and the sermon in Rheinsberg. He would go to the kitchen and eat up the dishes ordered for the Prince, and he got dead drunk when he ought to have been playing. All this was forgiven, year after year. The King knew of it, but was unwilling to spoil his brother's game. At last there was a catastrophe. At the Carnival-time, Prince Henry with all his Court was in Berlin, and gave masquerades, which far outshone the King's masked balls and all the other Court entertainments. On one occasion the whole of the King's Court had been invited to a Concert given by Prince Henry, to hear the wonderful Mara upon the violoncello. Everyone appeared, Mara likewise—drunk—and the one who did not play, was—Mara. Prince Henry in despair at such an affront, commanded, begged, entreated. Mara did not play, and this laid the foundation of the King's hatred. I tell you this story, based on authentic chronicles, because, according to Rochlitz's book, the King appears as a tyrant, who practised his revenge upon Mara, and cruelly separated a married couple. At that time they were not yet engaged. Mara's relation to Reichardt, too, who had just then become the King's Capellmeister, is not made clear, to Reichardt's prejudice.

Z.

166.—GOETHE TO ZELTER.

Weimar, 27th March, 1824.

. . . . Thus you have opportunely enlightened mo by your analysis of Handel's *Messiah*. Moreover, your view of the rhapsodical origin of this work is quite in accordance with my own opinion : for it is quite possible for the mind to raise up out of fragmentary elements a funeral pile, and finally, to point its flame, pyramid-wise, to Heaven.

One evening lately I heard the *Messiah*; I shall some day or other say a few words on the subject myself, but meanwhile advance, following your lead. The impulse given by Rochlitz I am grateful for, though I find him here as elsewhere : his honest intention and even work are patent, and one can only wish that he possessed the power of taking a firmer grasp of the subject, and of more definitely carrying through what he has recognized. . . . .

The chronicle-like notices of the adventures of Schmeling-Mara certainly have the true character of an empirical world; so it is that everything historical is surrounded with a strange uncertain being, and it really gets comical, when we reflect how we are determined to be convinced with certainty about what is long past. We possess here a pretty, old, silver bowl, which—as is proved by the engraving and inscription—dates from the time of the Emperor Frederick the First. It is unquestionably a christening gift, and yet the *savants* cannot agree as to who was really the baptized, and who was the witness of baptism. We already have five different opinions on the subject, and these may be reckoned as models of acuteness and nonsense ; only one of them is straightforward and plausible. . . . .

Yours truly,
G.

167.—ZELTER TO GOETHE.

Sunday, 4th April, 1824.

. . . . I RETURN you with many thanks the Pachelbel Chorale-Book. . . . . This Pachelbel is a representative

man of his kind, and has been eulogized by the best of his
colleagues, for he lived in the midst of the best Chorale
writers, from Luther up to Sebastian Bach, in genuine
possession of the traditional Church-modes. . . . .

Konrad Rumpf	Born 1530.	
Ludwig Senfel	„ 1530.	Died 1555.
Walter	„ 1538.	
Heinrich Schütz	„ 1585.	Died 1672.
Schein	„ 1586.	
Scheidt	„ 1587.	
Rosenmüller	„ ——	Died 1686.
Caspar Kerl	„ 1625.	„ 1690.
Froberger	„ 1635.	„ 1700.
Caspar Prinz	„ 1641.	„ 1717.
Theile	„ 1646.	„ 1724.
Dan. Vetter	„ ——	„ 1730.
Aless. Scarlatti	„ 1650.	„ 1730.
Pachelbel	„ 1653.	„ 1706.
Telemann	„ 1681.	„ 1767.
Seb. Bach	„ 1685.	„ 1750.

This may be a proximate, imperfect list of the names which
cannot be eliminated from the history of Art, and no doubt
there are several more. The above-named Heinrich Schütz,
Schein, and Scheidt are also styled the Trinity of the
Three Great S's. . . . . In former times, when an Organist
or Capellmeister was examined for official duty in Church,
a theme was given to him, (*Dux*,) for which he himself was
obliged to find, and *extempore* too, the *Comes* (*i.e.* the answer
to the subject of the Fugue); a similar task he had to work
out on paper in a room by himself; that done, the exercise
was judged by the Committee of Examiners, and such a
fugal work then received the name of *ricercata*.

So farewell, and pray for me, and help me to sing:

> Easter eggs, with joy they cry,
> The Quasimodogeniti.*
> Amen!

Yours,
Z.

* **Quasimodogeniti** is Low Sunday, the first Sunday after Easter.

168.—GOETHE TO ZELTER.

Weimar, 28th April, 1824.

. . . . I HOPE the *Tod Jesu*, (Graun's,) has this year too prepared a joyful Easter for you; that most lamentable of all events has been turned to such profit by the priests, and the painters too have fattened on it; why should the musician alone go empty away?

My *Messiah* brings me profit too, not at full length, but still "*in nuce;*" * the idea at all events is quickening, and this is a good deal for one like me. I am not disinclined to the thought that it is a collection, a compilation from a large stock of items, for it is in reality quite one and the same, whether the unity forms itself at the beginning or at the end; it is always the mind that produces it, and moreover the unity was implied in the Christian-Old-New Testament sense. In the end this very thing may hold good for Homer, only one must not say so to Wolf, who, when people admit that he is in the right, assures them they do not understand it. . . . .

G.

169.—GOETHE TO ZELTER.

Weimar, 26th June, 1824.

I AM very glad you have succeeded with *Troilus and Cressida*, or rather, that it has succeeded with you. I never made a secret of my deadly hostility to all parodies and travesties; but my only reason for it is that that horrid brood pulls down the beautiful, noble, and grand, in order to destroy it; nay, I do not like even the semblance of such things to be driven away by this.

The ancients and Shakespeare, when they seem to be robbing us, give us instead something to be esteemed, something worthy and enjoyable. The play in question captivated you in this way, it charmed and satisfied you, and certainly in quite the right sense.

Among my papers is a short essay on the *Cyclops* of Euripides, which certainly requires to be worked out

* This alludes to a performance of parts of Handel's *Messiah* in Goethe's house, on the 14th of April.

further and to be more accurately defined; perhaps you may encourage me to make the effort. Not long ago I heard a very charming performance of the Thaer Cantata, and was again delighted with the appositeness of the music, which rises with the feeling expressed in each strophe.

Rauch * is now going to leave; I would gladly have kept him a few days longer, especially as society—in true Berlin fashion—spoilt a great deal of my time. However, we have become of one mind about the picture and the likeness; do you look kindly upon what has been begun, and give him a helping hand.

The last number of *Kunst und Alterthum*, which is now in the hands of a bookbinder, will soon be sent to you.

Yours ever,
G.

170.—GOETHE TO ZELTER.

Weimar, 25th August, 1824.

A MIGHTY eagle, of the times of Myron or Lysippus, holding two serpents in his claws, is just lighting upon a rock; his wings are still moving, his spirit restless, for the struggling prey threaten him with danger. They are coiling themselves round his feet; their forked tongues are suggestive of deadly fangs.

In contrast with this, a screech-owl is perching upon a stone wall, its wings are closely folded, it is holding fast with feet and claws; it has seized some mice, which, half dead, wind their little tails round its feet, hardly able, by a faint squeak, to give a sign that they are still just alive.

Think of these two works of Art in juxtaposition! Here is neither Parody nor Travesty, but something that by nature is *high* and something that by nature is *low*, both worked out in an equally sublime style by an equally great master; it is a parallelism in contrast, which in each instance ought to give pleasure, and when combined, must create astonishment; the young sculptor might find here a task full of meaning.

(This would be the proper place for what I ought to say about the *Cyclops* of Euripides.)

* Rauch, the sculptor of the well-known statuette of Goethe.

Equally remarkable is the comparison of the *Iliad* with *Troilus and Cressida*. Here too is neither parody nor travesty, but as above we had two natural subjects contrasted with one another, so here we have a twofold spirit of the different ages. The Greek poem in the lofty style, representing itself, introducing only what is necessary, and even in its descriptions and its similes discarding all ornamentation, being based upon the grand mythical traditions of the remote past; on the other hand, the English masterpiece may be regarded as a happy transformation, a transposition of that great work into the romantico-dramatic style.

At the same time, we must not forget that this play, with many others, is indisputably derived from traditionary narratives, which had been already reduced to prose, and were only half poetical.

Yet even so it is perfectly original, as though the antique had never existed; and again, it required as much thorough earnestness, and as decided talent, as that of the grand old master, to make a feint of amusing us with similar personalities and characters, of slight significance, whilst all the time more modern phases of humanity were being made transparent to a later race of men.

G.

171.—GOETHE TO ZELTER.

Weimar, 30th October, 1824.

. . . . I AM now finishing my pamphlet on Natural Science, which this year was unfortunately delayed, and I am revising my correspondence with Schiller from 1794 to 1805. It will be a great gift to the Germans, nay, I dare say, to mankind. Two such friends, who, while laying bare their minds to one another, were constantly inciting each other to further progress! While revising this, a strange feeling comes over me, for I learn what I once was.

But what is really the most instructive part of all is that which shows the condition in which two men, who urge on their aims, as it were, *par force*, fritter away their time by excess of mental activity, by incitement and dissipation from without, so that in truth there comes forth nothing fully worthy of their powers, natural gifts, and intentions. It will be highly edifying, for every man worth his salt will be able to find comfort in this work.

Besides, it will help a great deal that is coming to life again, animated by the stirring impulses of that epoch. . . . .

G.

172.—ZELTER TO GOETHE.

Berlin, 27th November, 1824.

. . . . Once more we have with us a pair of Virtuosi-killers: Madame Grünbaum, (formerly Wenzel-Müller,) and Herr Moscheles, the pianist. The former sings our Milder and Seidler clean off the earth, and Moscheles really plays in such a fashion, that he makes one take a draught of Lethe, and forget in it all who went before him. Why, the fellow has hands which he turns inside out like a shirt, and even his nails can play. His compositions too I like next best to Hummel's, amongst the more modern writers. I had heard of him some time ago, and in the year 1819, went, on his account, by way of Prague, to Vienna; there I missed him, though he was expected at both places.*

Z.

173.—GOETHE TO ZELTER.

Weimar, 3rd December, 1824.

. . . . *Die Mitschuldigen* † produces quite the right effect. A so-called educated public wants to see itself on

---

* Referring to *The Life of Moscheles*, we read in his diary: " On the 23rd November, I heard a Psalm by Naumann at the *Singakademie*, afterwards went to the Mendelssohns'. . . . . Dec. 3rd. Music at Zelter's. Fanny Mendelssohn played the D minor Concerto by S. Bach, which I saw in the original manuscript. . . . . My musical conversations with Zelter were extremely interesting to me. He is the man who corresponds so much with Goethe on Teltower turnips and other better things."

† One of Goethe's earliest plays, written when he was under the combined influence of Molière and Lessing. He afterwards acted in it himself, when the play was produced at Weimar. Bertuch, Musäus, and Corona Schröter also took part in the performance. The passage referred to by Goethe is to be found in *Aus meinem Leben*, Part II.

the stage, and demands about as much from the drama as from society; *convenances* arise between actor and spectator; the people, however, are content that the clowns up there should amuse them with jokes which they have no desire to share in. Moreover, if you could read what I have said about the piece—I don't know where—you would find it accord perfectly with the sentiments of the first row of boxes. I will look up the passage and let you know of it.

Your musical gossip has been simply of incredible service to me; as far as it is possible to comprehend music ideally, you have enabled me to do so, and I now, at all events, understand why, of all Rossini's works, *Il Barbiere di Seviglia* is the one most generally praised. One evening recently I heard *Tancredi;* it was a very meritorious performance, and I should have been well satisfied, if only no helmets, armour, weapons, and trophies had appeared upon the stage. However, I got out of the difficulty immediately, and transformed the performance into a *favola boscareggia,* something like the *Pastor Fido*. Also I adorned the Theatre so as to have graceful Poussin landscapes; I peopled the scene with actors of my own, so that there was no want of ideal shepherds and shepherdesses, and even fauns, as in *Daphnis und Chloe;* and then there was nothing to find fault with, because the hollow pretension of a heroic opera fell away. . . . .

G.

174.—ZELTER TO GOETHE.

Berlin, 10th December, 1824.

. . . . FELIX is still the head-lad. His admirable industry is the fruit of a healthy root, and his sister, Fanny, has completed her thirty-second Fugue. The young people are wide awake, and when they have picked up anything for their own beak, you see it in their work; they are as pleased as if they had taken Mexico, and they are fond of me, just as they find me, and come and go like bees about a flower. . . . .

Z.

175.—ZELTER TO GOETHE.

Berlin, 22nd December, 1824.

.... To-day my Felix is to let us hear his latest Double Concerto.* The lad stands upon a root, which gives promise of a healthy tree. His individuality becomes more and more evident, and amalgamates so well with the spirit of the age, that it seems to look out of it like a bird from the egg. . . . .

Z.

176.—ZELTER TO GOETHE.

Berlin, 24th December, 1824. (Christmas Eve.)

Yesterday, Maria von Weber's latest Opera, *Euryanthe*, was given in our grand Theatre with most decided applause. In Vienna, Dresden, and elsewhere, the work failed to impress; this may be accounted for by a hundred reasons. The poem will not explain itself. Count Brühl has put the work imposingly on the stage, as befits the friend and *Intendant*, and in a style suitable to the historical romantic Opera.

Everybody was called for after the Opera. The composer first, who was obliged to show himself after the first Act, and deserves every encouragement for his intense industry, which is made doubly burdensome by his feeble health.

Afterwards there was plenty of feasting and revelry; such things bring about perfect satisfaction, nay, in the end, reconciliation. Several of his friends carried the composer away with them, Choruses of Singers and Horns followed, and the jubilee lasted into the small hours. You need not wonder that an old piece of goods like myself must always be at hand on these occasions, for I am not such a fool as to go into a corner with detractors, or worry myself at the prosperity of anyone in this world. . . . .

Z.

* For two Pianos and Orchestra; the work is still in manuscript.

1825.

177.—GOETHE TO ZELTER.

Weimar, 27th March, 1825.

. . . . LET me tell you, in good earnest, dearest Friend, that I am well in body, but so so in spirit; only I keep to myself, as everyone, without knowing it, is over-excited, for ever harping on the misfortune,* and whereas people, by their own exertions, might assist in the restoration, which would be praiseworthy on their part, they now besiege one, in an intolerable fashion, with their advice, their proposals, and their plans.

I think, however, that the one most to be pitied is the Grand Duke, who, in his fine, princely way, listens to everyone, and has to stand so much useless talk, which he can neither reject nor rectify. . . . .

Hitherto I have looked to Berlin with bright and friendly feelings, now I shall have to do so with the utmost gratitude; you will have heard of and rejoiced in the inestimable favour conferred on me by the Diet.†

I could tell you much; from time to time you will hear many a pleasant piece of news. This year, as regards myself, is as good as past, meanwhile I cling to each moment.

May the new building, and all else besides, succeed with you!

G.

* The burning of the Weimar Theatre on the 22nd of March. "The fire is the grave of my memories," said Goethe. This letter is a commentary on his feelings at the time.

† Goethe had formally petitioned the German Diet to make any piracy of his works a punishable offence.

ENCLOSURE.
[*Explanatory.*]

Weimar, End of March, 1825.

When clearing away the *débris* of the Theatre, they discovered among the ruins of the library the following passages from a manuscript of *Tasso*, which I had myself revised; the pages were burnt at the edges.

FIRST FRAGMENT.

When the unthought-of comes across our path,
When something monstrous interrupts our gaze,
Silent a while and still our spirit stands,
Nor is there aught we may compare with this.

SECOND FRAGMENT.

And now if all, if everything were lost?
If, on a sudden, thou shouldst find the friend
A beggar, whom thou thoughtest rich erewhile?

THIRD FRAGMENT.

The helm is broken in pieces, and the ship
Cracks upon every side; beneath my feet
The ground bursts open, gaping! In both arms
I clasp thee! So at length the sailor clings
Fast to the rock, on which he should have foundered.

178.—ZELTER TO GOETHE.

1st April, 1825.

.... Professor Cousin,* of whom you will have heard, has been liberated discretionally; he is received everywhere as a man of mark. He was not satisfied with your praise of *Don Alonzo*.† I told him frankly that he did not understand you. He speaks of you with the greatest veneration, but he is a Frenchman, and must become a very old man, before he finds, behind your peculiar

---

* Victor Cousin, the head of the Eclectic School, in France, author of *Histoire de la Philosophie au XVIII*ᵉ*. Siècle*, &c. &c. He was arrested in Dresden, on a charge of Carbonarism, and sent to Berlin, where he was detained for six months.

† *Don Alonzo, ou L'Espagne*, an historical novel by N. A. de Salvandy.

forms, the spirit which dwells in them, as in a comfortable citizen's house. One always get to = O with the liberality of the Liberals; they have no root, so height is wanting too. . . . .

Z.

179.—GOETHE TO ZELTER.

Weimar, 11th April, 1825.

WE too, my good Friend, have been suffering from the worry of deliberation, but happily only for a short time. Two architects stood opposed to one another; the one wanted to erect a *quasi*-People's Theatre, (*Volkstheater*,) the other a regular Court Theatre, (*Hoftheater*,) so here also the two parties of the day appeared in opposition, and actually balanced one another. It was only the Grand Duke's determination that put an end to the indecision; he went over to the majority, so that about sixteen days after the fire, we made up our minds what was to be done, and as we have a Court ready made, we are to have a Court Theatre too.

To be sure, we were helped in the matter, as the two plans aforesaid have been lying ready for years, and I will not deny that the one which carried the day originated with me, and with the chief architect, Coudray;* strangely enough, what induced us to draw it up, was the burning of your Theatre, since which time we have constantly thought of it, and worked at it for practice; thus one thing exercises its influence through and upon the other.

My new part of *Kunst und Alterthum* will soon be published; my letters to Schiller do not look amiss. The remark you made, that he is not of the same mind as myself on certain subjects, as for instance, on the question of Furies within and without,† you will find repeated in a

---

* Goethe was a great friend and admirer of this architect, who, with Von Müller and Schwabe, undertook to carry out his design for a "Twin-Monument" to himself and Schiller, over their common grave in the neighbourhood of the Fürstengruft.

† See *Schiller and Goethe Correspondence*, vol. ii. pp. 396, 397, Letter 836. Zelter had been reading Schiller's remarks on *Iphigenie*,—"Orestes himself is the most doubtful part in the whole; without Furies there can be no Orestes," &c.

remarkable manner, when the entire correspondence makes its appearance. Even during the course of this year, many such differences are to be found, and I see with pleasure that very many vote for me, as I never contradicted him, but let him have his way in all things; hence also in matters that were peculiarly my own.

I particularly recommend to your notice the Essay on Servian poetry,* as well as the poems themselves; should the subject not attract you at once, try to work your way into it. I have treated it carefully; my general remarks on National Songs are brief, but well considered. When, by degrees, I come to speak of the Songs of other nations, specifically, in the same way, I hope people will get a proper insight into something, round which hitherto they have only hovered vaguely with gloomy prejudice.

I enclose for you the last number of my *Morphologie*. Those who think analogously understand each other, even though the subject discussed or criticised is foreign to one or the other party. Have I not introduced into my pamphlets many things which can never be grasped, even by professional men, just because they think differently? I shall continue to do so as long as I am spared, quarrelling with no one, but not concealing my opinions and convictions, to please anyone.

The newspapers will by this time have informed you and my Berlin friends of the favour of the Diet; we will wait and see the upshot of the matter.

The French occupy a strange position with regard to German literature; their case is precisely that of the cunning fox, who could not manage to get anything out of the long-necked vessel; with the best intentions, they do not know what to make of our things, they treat all our art-products as raw material, which they must first manipulate for themselves. How pitiably they have disfigured and jumbled up my notes to *Rameau!* Not a single thing has been left in its proper place.

---

* This Essay was published in *Kunst und Alterthum*. The Servian poems, which were written by a young lady at Halle, interested Goethe greatly. "These are excellent," he said. "There are some among them, worthy of a comparison with *Solomon's Song*, and that is saying something."

Do write to me oftener! When you walk through Berlin, imagine that you are travelling, and tell me your thoughts about this, that, and the other; I too will let you hear how things are with me. In our later years let us do by letter, what in earlier years we did by personal intercourse; a little talking to and fro, even gossip if you will, can do no harm.

G.

180.—ZELTER TO GOETHE.

Berlin, 19th April, 1825.

. . . . I could have foreseen long ago, that you are not the man to build a Theatre for the People in Weimar. Him that makes himself green, the goats will eat.* Other high folk, who want to cork their wine, while it's fermenting, would do well to consider this. "Friends, we have lived to see it,"—nay, we are living to see it.† . . . .

Z.

181.—GOETHE TO ZELTER.

Weimar, 21st May, 1825.

I send you herewith a small volume which you are called upon to criticise before anyone else. The author, as it seems to me, aspires to what you have been doing all your life long, and are still doing; he is endeavouring to make that universal which, if it could become common, would instantly be annulled, and in fact, he appears to me like a physician, who is attempting to describe accurately an

---

* The German proverb of which this is a literal translation, corresponds to the French saying, *Qui se fait brebis, le loup le mange.*

† Goethe, commenting on this letter, once observed, "Zelter is a capital fellow, but sometimes he does not quite understand me, and puts a false construction on my words. I have devoted my whole life to the People and their improvement, and why should I not also found a Theatre? But here in Weimar, in this small capital, which, as people jokingly say, has ten thousand poets and a few inhabitants, how can we talk about the People, much less a Theatre for the People? Weimar will doubtless become, at some future time, a great city: but we must wait some centuries before the people of Weimar will form a mass sufficient to be able to found and support a Theatre."

incurable disease, and to distinguish its different effects. All this, however, I leave you to deal with.

Herr Mendelssohn stayed with us too short a time on his return journey; Felix produced his last quartett,* which astonished everyone. This personal dedication, audible and intelligible as it is, has greatly pleased me. I could only get a few hurried words with his father, for I was prevented and distracted by the music, and by a large concourse of people. I should so have liked to hear some Paris news from him. Felix told the ladies something about the state of musical affairs there, which is very characteristic of the day. My kind greetings to all the family, and keep me in the remembrance of that circle also.

I must further tell you that time and circumstance seem to favour the new edition of my works; I am just now working industriously at the annals of my life, a great mass of the materials for which, partly in preparation, partly finished, is lying before me. Now I find that our intimacy, from the year 1800, is interwoven with everything, and therefore I should like it to appear, as a perpetual testimony, and in pure gradation upwards, the truth of which can only be signified by giving the fullest details. I am at this moment studying your letters, which are lying before me neatly arranged, and now I am going to ask you to let me have mine for a short time, in batches of five years. I am just now working at the period, beginning with the opening of the century, and ending with Schiller's death; if you have the letters in order, pray send me them as soon as you can; I will return them soon, and as I proceed, I shall beg for the others. I should like to spin the whole length of this noble thread in and out, tenderly and carefully; it is worth the trouble, and really it is no trouble at all, but the greatest satisfaction, and I am already looking forward to seeing the great gap, from the beginning of the century up to the present day, continuously filled up.

Another thing just happens to strike me! There is in

---

* This was the B minor quartett, the dedication of which Goethe soon after acknowledged, in what Zelter calls, " a beautiful love-letter."—" I regard it," said Goethe to the young Mendelssohn, " as the graceful embodiment of that beautiful, rich, energetic soul which so astonished me when you first made me acquainted with it."

such matters a certain feeling which I cannot blame, that one likes to keep documents of this kind entirely to oneself. So the letters shall not be copied, without your express permission; what I extract, I shall mark with pencil in the margin.

Farewell! I am looking forward to living the past over again; this can only make the present time all the more precious.

Most truly yours,
G.

182.—ZELTER TO GOETHE.

23th May, 1825.

.... ONCE, several years ago, you wrote to me, that it is only possible to understand the works of Nature and of Art by tracing them to their origin; once they are ripe and complete, let him look to it, who would comprehend them.....

Felix has returned from Paris, and has made rare good progress in these few months. There he composed for Cherubini a *Kyrie** that will stand examination, all the more as that capital fellow, following his clever instincts, has taken up the piece almost ironically, in a spirit which, if not the right one, is at any rate very much what Cherubini has always been on the look out for, and if I am not much mistaken, has never found..... Abraham Mendelssohn has brought his younger sister back with him from Paris; for some twenty years she lived there as governess to General Sebastiani's daughter, who has just been married, and having realized a considerable pension, she now intends to reside in Berlin, her native place. One cannot but praise

---
* After hearing the B minor quartett, Cherubini remarked, "Ce garçon est riche; il fera bien; il fait même déjà bien, mais il dépense trop de son argent, il met trop d'étoffe dans son habit. Je lui parlerai, alors il fera bien." Felix compared Cherubini to an extinct volcano, still throwing out occasional flashes and sparks, but quite covered with ashes and stones. *A propos* of the *Kyrie*, Felix wrote to his parents, "I have been busy these last days making a *Kyrie à 5 voci* and *grandissimo* orchestra; in bulk it surpasses anything I have yet written. There is also a tolerable amount of *pizzicato* in it, and as for the trombones, they will need good windpipes."

the free and amiable disposition which this girl has kept from childhood—all through the *Inferno* of Paris—and it is enough to reconcile one again to the Prophets, that the old and failing father should see the promise of Abraham fulfilled in all his children. Farewell, my dearest! The prospect of your new edition rejoices heart and soul.

Your
Z.

183.—GOETHE TO ZELTER.

Weimar, 6th June, 1825.

.... If you come across a translation of *The Last Days of Lord Byron*, by William Parry, be sure you pounce upon it; so high and clear a standpoint is not easily attained. All that has been said about him hitherto falls away and vanishes like a mist of the valley.

The Servian *Volkslieder* too have just been published at Halle, in a pretty octavo volume. The Introduction, a short sketch of the history of the fallen Servian kingdom, is an extremely able and satisfactory, though unsatisfying account, showing a considerable wealth of knowledge. To have all the National Songs before one in a mass—just as I wished to—is extremely delightful and instructive; one knows at once what they are and what they are meant to be.

I cannot conclude without again referring to that overcharged music;* but everything, dear Friend, nowadays is *ultra*, everything perpetually transcendent in thought as in action. No one knows himself any longer, no one understands the element in which he moves and works, no one the subject which he is treating. Pure simplicity is out of the question; of simpletons we have enough.

Young people are excited much too early, and then carried away in the whirl of the time. *Wealth* and *rapidity* are what the world admires, and what everyone strives to attain. Railways, quick mails, steamships, and every possible kind of facility in the way of communication are what the educated world has in view, that it may over-educate

---

* Alluding to Zelter's criticism of Spontini's *Alcidor*, which had recently been performed in Berlin. See Note to Letter 184.

itself, and thereby continue in a state of mediocrity. And it is, moreover, the result of universality, that a mediocre culture should become common; this is the aim of Bible Societies, of the Lancasterian method of instruction, and I know not what besides.

Properly speaking, this is the century for men with heads on their shoulders, for practical men of quick perceptions, who, because they possess a certain adroitness, feel their superiority to the multitude, even though they themselves may not be gifted in the highest degree. Let us, as far as possible, keep that mind with which we came hither; we, and perhaps a few others, shall be the last of an epoch which will not so soon return again.

G.

184.—ZELTER TO GOETHE.

Berlin, 19th June, 1825.

. . . . COUNT BRÜHL is in despair about the new Opera.* The uninterrupted rehearsals of the numerous scenic effects, for two or three months past, have so monopolized the Theatre, that nothing else of any consequence could be undertaken. This wonder-work is launched at last, and the house so crammed, that the audience chokes and faints from the heat; directly after the first performance, Spontini makes the treasurer pay out to him the regulation 1,050 *Reichsthaler*, which he gets for every new work, and there they are, bankrupt again. People now say, Spontini pockets the money, while the others have to sweat for it.

Yours,
Z.

* This was *Alcidor, eine Zauberoper*, (magic Opera,) jestingly called *Allzudoll, eine Zauderoper*, (Quite too mad, a slow Opera,) on account of its length. Zelter thus alludes to it in a former letter,—" The libretto was written by Théaulon in French, and set to music accordingly; so at last we possess a Berlin original—that is, a new coat turned. . . . . Spontini seems to me like his own Gold-King, who smashes the heads of his people, by flinging gold at them." The Opera never made its way beyond Berlin. See also Letter 183.

185.—Zelter to Goethe.

Berlin, 26th June, 1825.

Our *Herr Generalmusikdirector, Ritter Spontini,* asks me for a recommendation to the great Goethe; this, between brothers in Art, such as you and he, should hardly be necessary.

Yet, as I cannot help wishing all my friends to be acquainted with each other, and I have an opportunity of sending you one more hearty greeting, don't let it bore you, to see face to face the composer of the latest and greatest Opera. He is going to Paris, returning thence about the time of our next Carnival.

Yours eternally,
Z.

Here comes my coffee. Good morning!

186.—Zelter to Goethe.

Berlin, 1st July, 1825.

.... I end by thanking you for your beautiful love-letter to my Felix. Any good that comes to him, I enjoy tenfold. He is close upon finishing his fifth Opera,* and I rejoice to see that it sparkles with real life, and does not rest upon mannerisms. He seizes the age by the ears, and carries it along with him, so let it pass! ....

Z.

187.—Goethe to Zelter.

Weimar, 3rd July, 1825.

.... Herr Spontini passed through in haste. It so happened that I was not at home, and yet I managed to get a quarter of an hour's conversation with him. How well we get on together, you may guess from the fact that we embraced before parting, which was the best acknowledgment of your introduction. ....

Yours,
G.

* *Die Hochzeit des Camacho.*

188.—GOETHE TO ZELTER.

Weimar, 6th July, 1825.

THE enclosed extract should have been sent in my last packet. . .

G.

ENCLOSURE.

Major Parry on Lord Byron.

"It will doubtless be obvious to every plain man like myself, that Lord Byron's greatest misfortune was his distinguished birth, and the neglect of moral education that followed upon it. He never overcame the mischievous prejudices and still more mischievous habits to which they led him. He was a nobleman, an only son, and a spoilt, neglected child. He was the victim of all these circumstances, and could set down to each of them a considerable part of his misfortunes. He was exposed in early days, and unfortunately for a long time, to almost everything which is calculated to foster vice in the human heart. His rank lifted him above all restraint; he had money, and no father to control him. Then came fame, not gained laboriously by little and little, but at once, and in overwhelming measure; an inordinate recompense for that which he had thrown off at ease, in a few bright, cheerful, and radiantly happy moments. He was so happy in his language, and so quick in thought, that writing was no labour to him, but a pleasure. He was not merely a poet, but for several years, like other young noblemen, what people call a man of fashion; the sentiments he then imbibed, and the habits he then adopted were never afterwards laid aside. He paid homage to them even in his conversation and behaviour, long after he had learnt to despise them in his heart. Like most men of extraordinary talents, he was naturally disposed to reflection, and preferred solitude to society; at all events, in all the conversations I had with him, he was earnest and thoughtful, although wonderfully quick, sharp, and decisive. With others, as I have already said, he was light, volatile, and sportive. He was always the man of the world. In such moments, the sentiments and habits of his earlier days acquired all their former power over his mind. His imposing talents, his noble natural gifts, and fine rare culture, were then all sacrificed upon the altar of fashionable trifling. He had felt how awfully boring all serious worldlings are, and as his associates were incapable of understanding his higher thoughts, he condescended to exchange thoughtless gossip with them. To use an old proverb, 'he howled with the wolves,'—and people have pictured him vain, presumptuous, boastful, unrestrained, thoughtless, whimsical and heartless, because these are too much the attributes of the class to which he belonged, and of the men with whom he consorted, and who discussed his character. His noble enthusiasm, devoted to the cause of freedom, his courage, which won for him the esteem even of the rough Suliotes, his generosity, which never allowed him, when he had the power, to leave a want or a sorrow unrelieved, his philanthropy, which led him to sacrifice time, money, and ease, to lighten the miseries of unhappy prisoners, have been invariably forgotten, and he has been exposed to the world's blame by heartless and insincere friends, who were utterly incapable of appreciating the high nobility of his character."

189.—ZELTER TO GOETHE.

6th November, 1825.

.... My Felix gets on and works hard. He has just finished an Octett for eight *obligato* instruments; it has hands and feet. Besides that, a few weeks since, he gave his worthy tutor, Heyse, a nice birthday present,—namely, a metrical translation of *Andria*, a comedy by Terence; it is entirely his own doing, and they say it contains really good verses. I have not seen it yet. He plays the piano like the deuce, and he is not behindhand with stringed instruments; besides this, he is healthy and strong, and is a rare good hand at swimming up stream. In the musical paper they have given rather a cold shower-bath to his Quartetts and Symphonies; that cannot hurt him, for these reviewers are but young fellows, looking for the hat which they hold in their hands. One might despair, if one did not remember how Gluck's and Mozart's compositions were criticised, forty years ago. These gentlemen drive slapdash over things that would never have occurred to them, and affect to judge of the whole house by a single brick. And I must give him credit for this, that he invariably works from the whole to the whole, finishing everything that he has begun, let it turn out as it will; this accounts for his showing no special affection for what is completed. To be sure, there is no lack of heterogeneous rubble, but that gets carried away by the stream, and conventional faults and weaknesses are rarities. . . . .

Z.

190.—GOETHE TO ZELTER.

Weimar, 26th November, 1825.

YOUR friend *Griepen-* * may be a very good *kerl* (fellow), but I cannot agree with him; he has studied the subjects which he discusses, but on the one hand, I think differently about them, and on the other, I think of them in a different connection.

I opened the volume, and found on page 336, paragraph 10, these words, "The usual classification into lyric, didactic, dramatic, and epic poetry," &c. Whereupon I closed the volume, and dictated the enclosed, which please keep to yourself. As this is the way I should have to treat the whole volume, I had better leave it alone.

Your aphorisms, on the contrary, I took up and took in with pleasure—you *have* what you *speak of*, and so we *have* it too, when we *hear* you; what you give here we understand, or think we understand, and at least we find an analogy in what we certainly do understand.

Let us stick to our old colours! let us feel and perceive, think and act; all the rest is of evil. The more modern world is given up to words, so let it go its own way.

Your bust has arrived uninjured, to our general satisfaction, and is worthy of all gratitude, because it brings you whom I long to see, so near me; but as with my own

---

* Professor Griepenkerl of Brunswick, author of a philosophical work on the ideas of Beauty and Perfection, which Zelter had sent to Goethe for his opinion.

bust, I find the features are somewhat exaggerated; this produces an unpleasant effect on nearer acquaintance. . . . .
                                                                G.

Enclosure.

It is not permissible to add to the three styles of poetry—the *lyric*, *epic*, and *dramatic*—the *didactic* as well. This will be understood by everyone who observes, that the three first differ in form, and that consequently the last, which takes its name from the subject-matter, cannot be classed in the same series.

All poetry should be instructive, but imperceptibly so; it should direct a man's attention to a sense of what it is worth while to instruct himself in; he must draw the lesson from it himself, as from life.

Didactic or schoolmaster poetry is and will ever be a half-breed between poetry and rhetoric; therefore at one time it tends towards the former, at another towards the latter, and may thus possess more or less poetical value, but like descriptive and satirical poetry, it is invariably a degenerate and secondary species, which, in a true system of æsthetics, should be classed between poetry and oratory.

The real value of didactic poetry—*i.e.* of a rhythmical work of Art, with embellishments borrowed from the imagination, and powerfully or gracefully introduced—is in no way impaired on that account. All may pass muster—from the rhyming chronicles, the short *versus memoriales* of the ancient pedagogues, up to the best works of this kind—but only in their own sphere, and respective order of dignity.

He who looks more closely into the matter, will at once be struck with the fact, that didactic poetry is valuable for the sake of its popularity; nay, the most gifted poet should consider, that if he has treated any chapter of what was worth knowing in this style, it redounds to his honour. The English have very estimable works of this kind; they first of all ingratiate themselves with the multitude, both seriously and in jest, and then, in explanatory notes, discuss what one must know, so as to be able to understand the poem.   Yours ever,
                                                                G.

191.—ZELTER TO GOETHE.

Berlin, 16th December, 1825.

.... YESTERDAY we had Spiker's brand-new version of *Macbeth* for the first time at our Theatre. .... The special novelty was a new, incidental Overture, with choruses and dances for the Witches. Kapellmeister Spohr of Cassel, the composer, is a clever man, and were it not too much of a good thing, the whole might be better. I have nothing to say against the idea, for the Orchestra once there, it may just as well play what is appropriate. But the question is, what is appropriate? No one need blacken the night,—and that's the cause of the mischief. The play is full of coarse company, and requires a downright style. That was wanting, and so the audience rejoiced, when the murderers up above took up their work again.

Z.

192.—GOETHE TO ZELTER.

Weimar, 30th December, 1825.

.... YOUR Sibylline leaf about *Macbeth*, I think I can explain tolerably well in my own fashion; anyhow it suggested to me these reflections.

These efforts are of the kind which King Saul demanded of the Witch of Endor, summoning forth the great dead, when we are unable to help ourselves. Shakespeare bristles up, even more repulsively than that dead prophet, and if they try to conjure him back again in all his integrity, that is worst of all. Such a mish-mash of very ancient and very modern will always be startling, as you have quite correctly felt.

How does all this costume help? Looked at attentively, it is evident that actors and dresses, decorations and ghosts, musicians and spectators are, after all, not in harmony with one another. This was what distracted you in so important a performance. To many others too it is revolting, though they do not confess it; many tolerate it, because it happens to be so; they have paid their money and sat out their time.

The *Sieben Mädchen in Uniform* delighted the Weimar public as well, for it is in keeping with the spirit of the age.

Everyone welcomes that mock-soldiering, turned into a half-licentious farce, when the public is groaning under the weight of a Shakespearian nightmare, and longing to escape from an oppressive dream of seriousness into the free atmosphere of folly.

Now that I no longer go to the Theatre, and have nothing further to do with it, but only watch my children, and the other generation that is growing up around me, curious lights dawn upon me. They are always taking sides; at one time I find them correct in their judgment, clear and intelligent, at another unfairly hampered by partiality and prejudice, with all the attendant consequences which we have known for long; only now do I understand the unsatisfactory nature of the Danaides-work of so many years, during which I endeavoured to realize the true and great advantages belonging to the stage, and to put them clearly before the public. It was your witches who bewitched me into making these observations; hence, you have yourself to blame for what you yourself called forth.

Yours unalterably,
GOETHE.

1826.

193.—GOETHE TO ZELTER.

Weimar, 15th January, 1826.

.... In my state of almost absolute solitude, I can scarcely imagine that all the gaiety and bustle which you let me see reflected in your mirror, should be going on close around you. However well *Macbeth* and *Euryanthe* may succeed, owing to what is expended upon them, to the influences of party spirit, and even to the recognition of what is excellent, neither of them can be really pleasurable on the stage, the former, on account of its excess of subject-matter, the latter, on account of its poorness and thinness of substructure. But as a fact, I no longer know what a theatrical public is, or whether, both in great and small things, it allows itself to feel satisfied, or perhaps merely silenced. I have, however, a reflex of it from yonder, as my children cannot do without the Theatre, and I have nothing to say against it.

I like reading the reviews in the *Haude und Spener-Zeitung;* for though we look into the daily papers but seldom, we come across much with good sound sense in it, which leads me to hope that the general tendency is good, and there is some chance of honest appreciation and recognition.

Personally I have grown accustomed to being howled at for many years past, and speak from experience, when I say, that for a long time to come, we need not be afraid of being outvoted, even though we may be contradicted. Only no impatience! go on undeterred, and talk betweenwhiles! In the end, plenty of people will be ready to declare themselves in favour of our way of thinking; nevertheless, we should not prevent anyone from forming his own circle, for in our Father's house, there is room for many families to dwell.

Art has been gracious to me, for I have received a

beautiful drawing of Giulio Romano's, and another by
Guercino. To be able to make a direct comparison between two such men, and to be delighted and instructed
by each in turn, is of the greatest value for one, who, to
be sure, makes conversation, now and then, out of Art and
works of Art, but nevertheless regards it merely as a necessary evil. If only I could from time to time be present at
your choral meetings, I would promise never to utter a
single syllable of criticism.
Try and get hold of a pamphlet, some fifty pages in
length, by Director Struve, entitled, *Two of Goethe's Ballads
compared with the Greek sources from which they are taken*,
Königsberg, 1826. The author, in leading his readers to
the fountain, whence I fetched the draught, is kind enough
to prove that I have presented the refreshing liquid in an
artistic vessel. What the poet wished for many years ago is
at last recognized. He discusses the *Zauberlehrling* and
the *Braut von Korinth*. My next shall be directly connected with this. . . . .

GOETHE.

194.—GOETHE TO ZELTER.

Weimar, 21st January, 1826.

"HE who has the will, must!"* and I go on to
say, he who understands, has the will. And thus, after
going round in a circle, we should land at the point from
which we started, namely, that one must be obliged
(*müssen müsse*) by conviction; hence we may hope, that
much good is in store for the time next ensuing.

So many things, relating to Art and Science, come
almost daily before my eyes, and there would be no in-
herent falsity, if man were not weak, and did not insist at
the same time on regarding that as final which he considers final. As a rule, however, I meet with many, whose
views are beautiful, clear, and lofty. People allow worth
in that which they cannot reach, they rejoice in that which
they would not themselves be in a condition to do; as in

---

* Goethe here quotes a comment of Zelter's on Lessing's axiom, *Kein
Mensch muss müssen.*

the end every able man must, if he would assert his own individuality, and work after his own fashion, whatever dilettantism and the levelling necessarily connected with it may, in the course of the day, corrupt or hinder. Everything will right itself in time, if only those who know what they want to do and can do, persevere unremittingly in work and action. You know this better than anyone, and experience it every day.

I feel I must tell you about some pieces of sculpture, which have lately arrived at my house, and on the value of which I now reckon. When in Rome, I lived in the Corso, opposite to Count Rondanini, who possessed, among other splendid works of Art, the face, the mask of a Medusa; it was larger than life-size, of white marble, and conspicuous for its excellence. We artists and connaisseurs often went to see it, nay, I actually had a good cast of this same work in my room. I have now had to dispense with the sight of it for forty years, as with much besides that is great and beautiful; it never petrified one, but informed one's feeling for Art with grand and glorious life. At length I hear it has come much nearer to me, having been moved to Munich, and I hazard the bold wish to possess a cast of it. This is not to be had, but an admirably preserved cast, ordered from Rome by command of his Royal Highness, your Crown Prince, has been promised to me, by the favour of His Majesty, the King.

Being forbidden to say anything about it, I will say only this much, that I am beyond all measure happy in the treasure I so earnestly longed for, and only wish we were allowed to look at it together.

Yet from one point of view it renews in me a painful feeling, for I cannot but reflect, that in those days, when I did not sufficiently understand the value of such treasures, they stood before my eyes, while now that I am to a certain extent able to appreciate them, I am separated from them by wide chasms.

However, it may be as well thus! For after all, when in the presence of such things, which were produced in a grander age, by men of greater capabilities, one loses all sense of proportion. And even the judicious effort not to let oneself be carried away thereby, into the path of false endeavour, awakens a painful feeling, if it does not end in actually hindering our life's activity. All good attend you!

G.

195.—ZELTER TO GOETHE.

19th January, 1826.

.... I REMEMBER in my younger days a Jew of the name of Michel, who appeared to be mad on all subjects, except two. When he spoke French, every word came trippingly from his tongue, and he was a first-rate chess-player. Now this "mad Michel" (as they called him), pays a visit to old Moses Mendelssohn, while he is sitting at chess with Abram, the old arithmetician, and begins to watch the game. Abram at last makes a gesture with his right hand, showing that he gives the game up for lost, and gets such a thumping whack on the head, that his loose wig tumbles off. Abram quietly picks it up, saying, "But, my dear Michel, how ought I to have moved then?" Lessing has copied the incident in *Nathan*, and now I am about it, I may as well tell you the rest. Abram, the aforesaid arithmetician, is the very man whom Lessing took as his model for Alhafi. He passed for a very great oddity, and a very great arithmetician, giving lessons for a few *Groschen*, or gratis, and he had a room in Mendelssohn's house, gratis too. Lessing highly esteemed him on account of his piety, and his innate cynicism. When Lessing went to Wolfenbüttel, Abram begged of him a rare book on mathematics from the local Library. Lessing found two copies, and sent one of them to Abram, to keep as a *souvenir*. Some time afterwards, Abram comes to Mendelssohn, bringing the book, and wants to present him with it. "Why, you surely do not want to part with that book; it's a keepsake from a friend." "I know that, but I do not want it any more; the examples are good, and I do not understand Greek." "Well, I see you want money; tell me, how much?" "No, no, I have money, and don't want any." "Well then, go, in God's name, and if you want anything, you know where I live!" A short time afterwards, Abram comes to Mendelssohn, who happens just then to have Professor Engel with him; he stands quite still, without uttering a word. "Well, Abram, how are you? Why are you so silent, and what do you mean by staring at me in that way? do you want anything?" "My wife has arrived from Hanover; I have but one chair,"—whereupon he seizes a chair and bolts with it out of the room. His wife lived in Hanover with her relations, for her husband never had a farthing.

It was good fun, hearing Professor Engel tell these stories, and others like them, he being a thorough cynic about good eating, drinking, and sleeping. . . . .

Now good-bye; may our little fish tickle your palate as pleasantly as your toothsome pheasants did ours!

Yours,
Z

196.—GOETHE TO ZELTER.

Weimar, 18th March, 1826.

I SHALL wait quietly to see how the enclosed poem, (*Charon*,*) upon which I set great store, will appear to our connaisseurs, and other congenial spirits. The lord of musical harmonies will be sure to find in it something Fugue-like, where manifold complications can be made to move, separate, meet, and answer one another. This illustration was distributed with the *Stuttgarter Kunstblatt*; but as it is folded together, it cannot be fully appreciated there. Take care of it, and think it over. . . . .

GOETHE.

197.—ZELTER TO GOETHE.

3rd April, 1826.

. . . . THE first comfort I got from your *Charon* was this, that our art of the Fugue is still living, and that what we build will not fall to ruins. To be sure, without your explanation, I should have had to reflect a long time, in order to get clear before me the beautiful contrasts, (counterpoint,) because here what is most serious stands

---

* The name of a modern Greek poem, translated by Goethe. It is one of the *Neugriechischen Heldenlieder*.

in delightful conflict with the most innocent love of life. And the poetry which you have put into him will be his delight as well as mine.

I had a similar experience with old Haydn. In reviewing his *Creation*, and particularly the Overture which is inscribed *Chaos*, I had remarked that such a theme was not permissible as a problem of Art; but that genius everywhere had triumphed over impossibilities, and therefore did so here,—giving my reasons for this statement. Old Haydn let me know, that with regard to this matter, he had never before expended a thought upon it, but that my construction squared with his imagination, now realized for the first time, and that he saw himself compelled to recognize the pictures I had suggested. Other critics had hopelessly condemned the musical paintings in the work, but now I was justified.

Yours, to-day and for ever,

Z.

198.—GOETHE TO ZELTER.

Weimar, 10th May, 1826.

.... PLEASE, dear Zelter, be kind to the bearers of this, (Mr. and Mrs. Bracebridge,) if it will not inconvenience you. I have nothing special to say about myself. I very narrowly escaped having to undertake the part of the Duke in my *Natürliche Tochter*. I have also enough to endure in the preliminary rehearsal. Think of me, and let me have some friendly sign from you.

Most truly yours,

G.

199.—GOETHE TO ZELTER.

Weimar, 20th May, 1826.

FIRST of all, my best thanks for the score of that truly enthusiastic song, *Weltseele*. It is now full thirty years old, and dates from the time, when a rich, youthful spirit still identified itself with the universe, in the belief that it could fill it out, nay, reproduce it in its various parts. That bold impulse has, at all events, left a pure and lasting influence upon life, and however much we may have advanced in philosophical knowledge and poetic treatment, still it was of importance *at that time*, and, as I can see, from day to day, it acted as a stimulus and guide to many. . . . .

We too had a passing visit from Matthisson; our disciples of the Muses gave him a friendly ovation, sang his poems, presented him with laurel wreaths, and did all this at a merry banquet, which went off fairly well. . . . .

When one thinks, how many men of mark just float about like drops of oil on water, and at most come in contact only at one point, one can understand how it is that so often in life one was thrust back into solitude. However, the fact of our having lived so long near one another as we and Wolf did, may have influenced and helped our endeavours, more than we know or are aware of.

You mention my *Phaethon*,[*] which I always think of with pleasure, although I regret that at the time I did not write down the two chief scenes. Even if it had fallen short of the mark, still it was always something, and no one now can form any idea of it.

I am again lured to those regions by a programme of Hermann's, which directs our attention to three antique Philoctetes', the first by Æschylus, the earliest; the second by Euripides, the latest; the third by Sophocles, between these two. I had soon to get quit of these reflections; they would have cost me four months of my time, which I can no longer afford to squander. Of the first two pieces there are only fragments and indications; the last we still have complete. Even here I dare not go further, as I am at once led astray; for I really could not restrain myself from thinking out this matter, which to me is so important, in preference to all besides,—the strangest things occurring in connection with it. Even a very ancient Latin author has written a *Philoctetes*, and moreover, in imitation of Æschylus, of which there are still some fragments left, and by which it is conceivable that the ancient Greek might in some measure be restored.

---

[*] A translation of the fragments of the *Phaëton* of Euripides, begun by Goethe in 1821.

You see, however, that this would be like trying to drink up an ocean, and our old throats would hardly be able to gulp it down.

To Zelter.

Weimar, 3rd June, 1826.
(Continuation of my letter of the 20th May.)

. . . . The manuscript of the new number of my *Kunst und Alterthum* is ready, and for the most part revised, so that the printing might be begun at once; however, I would rather let it rest, until the advertisement of my works is before the world. At my time of life, one has to lay down a law for oneself about such matters, and one must not imagine that one can, like Frederick the Great in the Seven Years' War, extemporize battle and victory on all sides. . . . .

I am chiefly concerned to hear that the good Bracebridges have attended and enjoyed your splendid choral rehearsals, as we hear from our last letters. Letters of introduction pull both ways, and remind me of a good story about an excellent lady, who, owing to her having received recommendations to the Montagues, as well as to the Capulets of a Swiss town, could scarcely venture to stir out of her house. It was exquisite to hear her account of the charming artifices she had to resort to, in order to make her way at all.

Thus anecdotes from private life as well as universal history prove, that in reality we wrestle and are wrestled with, for life and death, about utter absurdities. . . . .

And now I may tell you in confidence, that in order to give full weight to the first issue of my new edition, I have again undertaken the preliminaries of a work,* important not in extension, but in its poetical contents; it is one which I have not looked at since Schiller's death, and which would probably have remained *in limbo patrum*, but for the impetus it has now received. It is moreover calcu-

---

* This alludes to the *Helena*, afterwards introduced into the Second Part of *Faust*. As early as the year 1800, Goethe had read it aloud to Schiller, who "felt that in it breathed the lofty spirit of ancient tragedy."

lated to influence the latest style of literature, to an extent that nobody, whoever he may be, can have any idea of. I hope, as it is intended to settle a dispute, to see it create great confusion. . . . .

Truly yours,
G

200.—ZELTER TO GOETHE.

23rd May, 1826.

. . . . Hummel has given two successful concerts, although his arrival seemed hardly opportune. In my judgment, he is an epitome of contemporary pianoforte playing, for he combines what is genuine and new with feeling and skill. One hears music, one forgets fingers and keys; everything sounds as sure and easy, as it is really difficult. A vessel of the worst material, filled with Pandora's treasures. . . . .

Yours,
Z.

201.—ZELTER TO GOETHE.

Berlin, 25th May, 1826.

. . . . My Felix, when he was ten years old, discovered with his lynx eyes, in the score of a splendid Concerto by Sebastian Bach, six pure consecutive fifths, which I doubt I should ever have found out, as in the larger works I pay no heed to such things, and this particular passage is written in six parts. But the handwriting, as an autograph, is beautiful and clear, and the passage occurs twice. Now, is it an error or a licence? Either the composer has altered one part and forgotten to erase the other, or an accident, as I myself have experienced, may be the reason. I once asserted, when we were having an harmonic dispute, that I could let them hear *half-a-dozen* pure fifths, one after the other, and they would never find it out, and I won my point. It may have been so with old Bach, the purest, the most delicate, the most venturesome of all artists, *quo nihil sol majus optet*. . . . .

Yours,
Z.

202.—ZELTER TO GOETHE.

6th June, 1826.

.... FELIX has finished another quintett, which we are soon to hear. I do all I can to encourage him, as he urges himself on to experiment in the various forms, new and old. I am pleased too, that his music is really well paid by the publishers. In addition to this, he is very active, and cuts no bad figure at gymnastics, riding, and swimming; I had rather not advise him to fence, as he really *plays* well. Sufficient unto the day; you could not wish for anything better.....

Yours,
Z.

203.—ZELTER TO GOETHE.

Berlin, 11th June, 1826.

.... I GAVE young Bohn, lately married to a daughter of Seebeck, a short letter to that good creature, Ernestine (Voss), and a little Song, which Felix's sister has set very daintily to music. It is a poem by Voss on the death of our friend Schulz, and I set it to music for him, when I was in Heidelberg. By chance Fanny happens to have set it also, and as she has really hit off the spirit of it better than I have, I have sent it to Voss's widow, as it is equally applicable to his death.....

Even the day before yesterday people would have it, that Carl Maria von Weber had died in London, (like Achilles at the height of his glory,) but as the news is not confirmed, it only gains credit, on account of his frail condition. Owing to his judicious behaviour, he is a universal favourite, and, according to the measure of his talent, he has certainly worked hard enough; all his works, taken together, betray labour and toil, and he has had severe illnesses to fight against.....

Yours,
Z.

204.—ZELTER TO GOETHE.

28th July, 1826.

. . . . WILHELM VON HUMBOLDT, the Minister, sends you his affectionate greetings. . . . . He too is of opinion that the collection of Schiller's letters will be a welcome present to the world, as it will explain the origin of his best works, and show how he built himself up upon you. This is as certain, as that since Schiller's elevation to a higher sphere, the eagerness to understand your works has constantly gained ground. With Schiller everything works from without to within, with you it is the reverse; people want to understand what they feel,—deductions arise, in which Schiller is wealthy, and he turns our minds in the same direction.

I observe that it is the same in music. It is only since Mozart's time, that there has arisen a greater inclination to understand Sebastian Bach, for the latter appears thoroughly mystic, just where the former impresses us clearly from without, and we go along with him more easily, seeing that he collects terrestrial life around him. I myself was so circumstanced as to feel no pure pleasure in Mozart's works, because I had known Bach much earlier; compared with him, Mozart stood as the Flemish painters did to Italian and Greek artists, and it is only since I began to grow clearer and clearer on these points, that I esteem both at the highest value, without requiring of the one what the other achieves. The mystic must and will remain what it is, otherwise it would not be what it is; I can go quietly to sleep upon that, and leave the whole gang behind me to scream for an explanation in words, while it is stumbling over the sense. Mozart stands much nearer to Sebastian Bach than Emanuel Bach and Haydn, who are originals, and stand between the two first. The *Don Juan* and the *Zauberflöte* show plainly enough that Mozart had a mystic element in him, and that he is all the more secure of an easier effect, when he works from without inwards, where first there is light, and darkness follows very gradually. . . . .

Yours,
Z.

205.—GOETHE TO ZELTER.

Weimar, 12th August, 1826.

. . . . I MUST tell you another strange thing. A young porcelain painter from Brunswick inspired me with such confidence, and took my fancy so much, when he showed me his works, that I yielded to his pressing entreaty, and sat to him for several hours.* The picture proved a good one, to the satisfaction of everyone. If it gets safely through the firing process, it will, both on its own account, and for the sake of the beautiful ornamentation, be a good recommendation for him at home. His name is Ludwig Sebbers; he passed through here on his travels.

> Sibylline-like, of all its youth bereft,
> My face with vanity is yet acquainted!
> For still the less of it to paint is left,
> The oftener do the painters want to paint it!

I have had an honest laugh over these endeavours; but one must submit to it. .

Yours as ever,
GOETHE.

ENCLOSURE.

On again taking up Herr Streckfuss' translation of Dante, a few days ago, I admired the ease with which it moved within the given metre, and when I compared it with the original, and tried, after my fashion, to make some of the passages clearer and more flowing, I very soon found, that enough had already been done, and that nothing would come of finding fault with this work. Meantime it gave birth to the little poem, which I wrote in the accompanying book.

Let Herr Streckfuss keep Manzoni's tragedy, *Adelchi*, as a remembrance from me; if he does not know it, he will be pleased with it; if he is impelled to translate it, he

---

* This portrait was painted on a cup, and Goethe sat for it some twenty times; even after the second baking, he sat again for the finishing touches.

would render a service to German Iambics, as well as to the Trimeter, if he would, in like manner, follow the Italian style of writing, which would be all the easier, as the rhyme does not hinder him. What I think about this, is clearly seen from the monologue of *Swarto*, and without that, it would at once be apparent to so clear-sighted a man. The whole Tragedy may be resolved into a Recitative. I am most anxious to have your composition.

SECOND ENCLOSURE.

From God the Father Nature came.
Upon her track, the Human Mind
Fast following, caught the lovely dame,
A faithful wooer found her kind.
Nor yet unfruitful was their love:
A child of lofty thought and free
Was born, to all the world to prove,
" God's grandchild is—Natural Philosophy."

See *Dante's Inferno*, canto xi. line 98 (and Longfellow's translation).

Filosofia, mi disse, a chi l'attende,
Nota, non pure in una sola parte,
Come natura lo suo corso prende
Dal divino 'ntelletto, e da sua arte;
E se tu ben la tua Fisica note,
Tu troverai non dopo molte carte,
Che l'arte vostra quella, quanto puote,
Segue, come 'l maestro fa il discente :
Si che vostr'arte a Dio quasi e nipote.

" Philosophy," he said, " to him who heeds it,
Noteth, not only in one place alone,
After what manner Nature takes her course
From Intellect Divine, and from its art ;
And if thy Physics carefully thou notest,
After not many pages shalt thou find,
That this your art as far as possible
Follows, as the disciple doth the master;
So that your art is, as it were, God's grandchild."

206.—GOETHE TO ZELTER.

Weimar, 6th September, 1826.

.... FIRST of all, please read attentively to yourself the enclosed remarks on Dante. Had our excellent friend Streckfuss had my suggestions before him, when beginning his translation, he would, without additional trouble, have succeeded better in many points. So much has to be considered in connection with this original, not only what that extraordinary man had the power of doing, but also what it was that stood in his way, and what he strove to remove; only then does his nature, his aim, his art, shine out fully before us. Look at them carefully; if you are afraid they might hurt Streckfuss, you had better edify yourself with them, and conceal them. Still, as he is sure to be working at a new edition, it might be useful to him, in the whole and in details.

The enclosed table of the Theory of Sound, which is the result of many years' study, was written, as you may remember, somewhere about the year 1810, after I had discussed the subject with you. I did not at all want to satisfy the demand for a discourse upon physics, but to make the compass and substance of the subject clear to myself, and to point them out to others. I was prepared to systematize all the various departments of physics in this way. I found this table when clearing out the music-cupboard; I had not quite forgotten it, but did not know where to look for it, nor do I know whether I have ever shown it you. I have also lost in the same way several Essays, which some lucky chance may perhaps bring back again into my possession. . . . .

Come what may, Mademoiselle Sontag has passed through here, and made an epoch, with her wealth of sounds and tones.

Of course everyone says that such an artiste should be heard often, and the majority would like to be off to the Königstadt Theatre again, this very evening. And I agree with them. For in reality, one ought first of all to conceive of her and comprehend her as an individual, to recognize her in the element of the age, to assimilate oneself to her, to accustom oneself to her; then of course she would abide with us as an exquisite enjoyment. When heard in this off-hand way, her talent confused rather than charmed me. The good that passes by without returning, leaves behind it an impression that may be compared to a void, and is felt like a want. . . . . Most truly yours,

GOETHE.

ENCLOSURE 1.

In recognizing the qualities of Dante's great mind and spirit, our appreciation of his works will be greatly furthered, if we keep in view the fact, that just at his time, when Giotto was also living, Plastic Art reappeared in its natural strength. This genius of the time, working powerfully through sense and form, dominated him also. He comprehended subjects so clearly with the eye of his imagination, that he could reproduce them in sharp outline; consequently, we see before us what is most abstruse and most unusual, as if it were drawn from Nature. In the same way also, the *terza rima* seldom or never inconveniences him, but in one way or another assists him in carrying out his intention, and in limiting his forms. In this the translator has in most cases followed him, realizing for himself what is imaged before him, and striving to achieve what was requisite for its representation, in *his own* language and *his own* rhymes. If I had anything left to wish for, it would be in this respect.

G.

September, 1826.

ENCLOSURE 2.

The whole plan of the locality of Dante's *Inferno* has something minutely great (*Mikromegisches*) about it, and therefore bewildering to the senses. From above, down to the lowest abyss, one must imagine circle within circle; but this at once gives the idea of an amphitheatre, which, however enormous it may be, always appears to our imagination as something artistically limited, inasmuch as from above one overlooks everything down to the arena, as well as the arena itself. Let anyone look at Orgagna's picture,* and he will think he sees an inverted table of

* This painting, which has been ascribed to Bernardo, a brother of Andrea Orgagna, is on a wall of the Strozzi chapel in S. Maria Novella. According to Kugler, it is "a mere map, which scrupulously follows Dante's arrangement of the compartments or *bolge* of the infernal regions."—The table of Cebes of Thebes, the friend and disciple of Socrates, was a representation of "the whole of human life with its dangers and temptations." His only extant work, the Πίναξ, is an explanation of this table.

Cebes; the invention is more rhetorical than poetic, the imaginative faculty is aroused but not satisfied.

But though unwilling to praise the whole, still the rare wealth of individual localities takes us by surprise, astonishes, confuses us, and compels our veneration. Here also, with the clearest and most rigorous elaboration of the scenery, which stops our view at every step, the same style of description prevails, which, when applied to every condition and relation that appeal to the senses, as well as to the characters themselves, their punishments and tortures, is entitled to a like measure of our praise. We select an example out of the twelfth Canto:—

Inferno, canto xii. line 1.

> The place where to descend the bank we came
> Was alpine, and from what was there, moreover,
> Of such a kind that every eye would shun it.
> Such as that ruin is which in the flank
> Smote, on this side of Trent, the Adige,
> Either by earthquake or by failing stays,
> For, from the mountain's top, from which it moved,
> Unto the plain the cliff is shattered so,
> Some path 'twould give to him who was above; . . . .
> Thus took we down our way o'er that discharge
> Of stones, which oftentimes did move themselves
> Beneath my feet, from the unwonted burden.
> Thoughtful I went; and he said, " Thou art thinking
> Perhaps upon this ruin, which is guarded
> By that brute anger * which just now I quenched.
> Now will I have thee know, the other time
> I here descended to the nether Hell,
> This precipice had not yet fallen down."
> But truly, if I well discern, a little
> Before His coming who the mighty spoil
> Bore off from Dis in the supernal circle,
> Upon all sides the deep and loathsome valley
> Trembled so, that I thought the Universe
> Was thrilled with love, by which there are who think
> The world ofttimes converted into chaos;
> And at that moment this primeval crag
> Both here and elsewhere made such overthrow. . . . .

Now in the first place, I must explain the following, although in my copy of the original edition of Dante, (Venice, 1739,) the passage *e quel* down to *schivo* is also

---

* This alludes to the Minotaur.

made to refer to the Minotaur, in my opinion it applies simply to the locality. The place was mountainous, rocky (*alpestro*), but that does not say enough for the poet; the special thing about it (*per quel ch'iv'er'unco*) was so terrible that it bewildered eyes and sense. Hence, in order only to some extent to satisfy himself and others, he mentions (not so much by way of simile, as to give a concrete example,) a landslip, which probably in his time had blocked up the road from Tarentum to Verona; huge pieces of rock, and fragmentary wedges of the original mountain may have been lying there, one on the top of the other, still sharp and fresh in outline, showing no traces of the weather, united and levelled by vegetation, but in such a position, that the huge single fragments, poised lever-like, might easily have been made to totter by a mere kick. This happens here too when Dante descends.

But now the poet wants to go immeasurably beyond that natural phenomenon, he uses Christ's descent into Hell, so as to find a sufficient cause, not only for this wreck, but for many another which occurs in the kingdom of Hell.

The wanderers are now getting nearer and nearer to the trench of blood, which, bow-like, is surrounded by a level strand, which is also circular, where thousands of Centaurs are leaping about, and keeping their wild guard. Virgil, down on the plain, has already come near enough to Charon, but Dante is still tottering with uncertain steps among the rocks; we must refer to the passage again, for the Centaur speaks to his companions:—

> He said to his companions: "Are you ware
> That he behind moveth whate'er he touches?
> Thus are not wont to do the feet of dead men."

Now let anyone ask his imaginative faculty, whether this stupendous fall of rock and mountain has not become entirely present to his mind? In the other Cantos, with a change of scene, just the same tenacity and finish may be found and pointed out, through the recurrence of the same conditions. Such parallel passages make us familiar and thoroughly at home with the most intensely individual spirit of Dante's poetry.

The difference between the living Dante and the departed

spirits is also striking elsewhere, as for example, when the spiritual inhabitants of the *Purgatorio* are terrified at Dante, because he casts a shadow, by which they recognize his bodily presence.

G.

Weimar, 9th September, 1826.

Enclosure 3.
The Science of Music

Developes the laws of the Audible. This last arises from the vibrations of (various) bodies, and for us more particularly from the vibration of the air.

In the widest sense the Audible is infinite. But from this we set aside uproar, noise, and speech (*Geräusch, Schall, und Sprache*).

There remains that with which we have immediately to do, the musically audible, (Sound.) (*Der Klang.*)

This depends upon the purity of material, and the extent of the body that vibrates or causes vibrations.

In order to arrive at the measure of this extent, let us first regard the sounding body as a whole.

The distinct sound given by the whole, of itself, is called the Ground-tone.

The whole diminished gives a higher note,—enlarged, a lower.

We may diminish the whole gradually and without a break, but this gives no proportional parts.

We may divide the whole; this gives proportions.

The chief proportional parts are at some distance from each other (Chords).

The space between these is filled by intermediate proportional parts, resulting in a kind of gradual progression (Scale).

By these steps the ground-tone proceeds upwards and downwards, till it finds itself again (Octave).

More than this is not necessary at the beginning. What remains must be developed, modified, and explained by practical demonstration. The science is founded entirely on principles derived from experience, and is expounded in three divisions. The musically audible appears to us, (1) Organically (Subjectively); (2) Mechanically (partly subjectively, partly objectively); and (3) Mathematically (Objectively). All three are ultimately united, agreeably by the power of the musician, and in a more difficult manner, by scientific demonstration.

I. ORGANIC (SUBJECTIVE) MUSIC.

How the tone-world is revealed by and to mankind, appearing in the voice, received again by the ear, exciting the whole body indirectly, and necessitating a mental and moral inspiration, and a culture of the inward and outward sense.

Science of Singing.

Song is perfectly productive of itself. The natural gift of the outward sense, and the genius of the inward spirit, are absolutely required.

The Chest Voice.

The voices, varying in height and depth, are as follows, counting upwards:—Bass, Tenor, Alto, and Treble. Each is to be considered as a whole. Each comprises an octave and something over. They overlap one another, and contain together about three octaves. They are divided between the two sexes. Hence the significance of puberty, and the consequent change of voice, which can be prevented by castration.

Register.

I.e. the limit of the chest-voice.

The Head Voice.

Transition into the mechanical. Artificial union of both voices. Detailed explanation of the organization of the chest and throat.

Corollary, from the voices of animals, especially of birds.

Acoustics.

Receptivity of the ear. Its apparent passivity and indifference. Compared with the eye, hearing is a dumb sense; only part of a sense. We must ascribe to the ear, as to a highly organized entity, counter-effect and claim, whereby alone that sense is capable of taking up and grasping that which is presented to it from without. But in the case of the ear, special attention has always to be given to the medium of the sound, which operates actively on the effect. The productivity of the voice is thereby engendered, aroused, elevated, and multiplied. The whole body is set in motion.

Rhythm.

The whole body is incited to move in step (March), or in skips (Dance and Gesticulation).

All organic movements are manifested by means of pauses and resumptions of motion (*systole* and *diastole*).

At the one, the foot is lifted, at the other, put down.

Hence arise rhythmic weight and counterpoise.

Arsis, the up-beat.

Thesis, the down-beat.

Kinds of time: Even, and Uneven. These movements may be considered alone; but soon they are necessarily combined with Modulation.

II. MECHANICAL MUSIC. (Partly subjective, partly objective.)

Tones produced by various means, in accordance with musical laws.

Instruments.

Materials. Their tone, quality, purity, and elasticity.

Form. Natural, organic, and artificial. Metal, wood, glass. Reeds, length and evenness of surface.

Method of exciting vibrations.—Inflation; impact, horizontally or vertically applied.

Striking. Relation to Mathematics. The instruments result from knowledge of the proportions of measure and number, and increase this knowledge by means of variety.

Discovery of natural proportions of tones other than

those shown by the monochord. Relation to the human voice. These are a substitute for that, and inferior to it, but are raised to an equality with it, by treatment that is expressive and spiritual.

III. MATHEMATICAL MUSIC (OBJECTIVE).

How the elements of Music are shown in the simplest bodies outside us, and reduced in number, and in the proportions of their measure.

The Monochord.

Co-ordinate sounds of the harmonic tones. Different styles of sound-production, how they arise. Sympathetic vibrations. Organic demand for and subjective excitement of co-ordinate sounds.

Objective and material proof, by means of sympathetic vibrations of strings, tuned to these proportional parts.

Foundation of the simplest proportions of tone. Diatonic scales. The demands of nature not to be satisfied in this way. Practical exemplifications not to be accounted for, or shown in this way.—Reference to the minor mode. It is not generated in the first series of harmonic tones. It is manifested by means of less obvious conditions of numerical and commensurate proportions, and yet is perfectly suited to the nature of mankind, even more perfectly than the first, more obvious mode.

Objective proof (contrary to the usual order of things) in the sounding of tuned strings, for this tone, which is discovered by practical experiment. (Thus the ground-tone C gives, in the upward direction, the harmony of C major, and in the downward direction, that of F minor.)

The major and minor mode are the antipodes (polarities) of musical science. First principle of both—the major is generated from rising, the tendency to ascend, and to extend all intervals upwards; the minor, from falling,—its tendency is to descend, and to extend its intervals downwards. (The minor scale extended upwards becomes major.) Working-out of this paradox, as the ground of all music.

Origin and necessity of the leading note (*subsemitonium modi*) in rising, and of the minor third in falling.

Connection of the two modes by the dominant and tonic. (The former must always be major. Query, whether the latter must always be minor?)

Origin of *Arsis* and *Thesis* in all motion in this way, as also of the co-operation of material bodies, and of rhythm.

Artistic Treatment.

Limits of the octave. Concatenation of their identities. Definition of proportion of tone. With and against nature.

The art of rendering tones nebulous, and their outlines indistinct, in order to cause the approach of different keys to one another, and to make it possible to use one as well as another.

(*I.e.* Temperament.)

Instruction in singing. Exercises, to acquire the perception of what is easy and difficult, in the fundamental and derivative elements of vocalization. Grasp of genius and talent, and employment of all that has been said before, as material and instrument.

Union of speech with song, particularly in the *Canto fermo*, Recitative, and *Quasi parlando*.

Distinction (of song) from speech by a kind of register, and transition to this, and so to rational utterance.

Noise (uproar). Transition into the formless and the fortuitous.

207.—GOETHE TO ZELTER.

Weimar, 15th September, 1826.

HEREWITH, dearest Friend, the latest thing of the day, nay, of the hour! The poem has just been recited, but now we should like to sing it too. . . . .

With kindest greetings and good wishes,

G.

ENCLOSURE.

The Allied Brethren of the Amalia Lodge at Weimar to their Brother, His Most Serene Highness, Karl Bernhard,* Duke of Sachs-Weimar-Eisenach, on his return from a happy and profitable stay in America, on the 15th of September, 1826.

A freshening gale! Hoist, hoist the sail!
So dreamed the youth of late;
As man he sees his wish prevail,
Nor long had he to wait.
On, on he journeys, far away,
Through wind, and storm, and foam,
On alien soil scarce rests a day,
And sees again his home.

A humming, like a swarm of bees,
They build with all their might;
Empty and poor the morning sees
A state that's rich by night.
Submissive now the rivers trace
Their way through desert land,
The rock becomes a dwelling-place,
Flowers blossom in the sand.

Forthwith the princely pilgrim greets,
With manner firm and mild,
As brother, each good man he meets,
As father, every child.
He feels it beautiful to be,
Where God hath newly blessed;
With every honest fellow free,
And equal with the best.

Country and towns doth he survey,
Keen-sighted to compare;
Fond of his kind, at dances gay,
Beloved of ladies fair;
Both fight and victory to boot
He knows, among the brave;
The cannon fire a loud salute,
In recognition grave.

He feels that noble land's advance,
Her fortune is his own,
To her, ere now, full many a glance
Across the sea hath flown.

* The son of the Grand Duke, Karl August.

But let that be as it may be,
He dwells among us all!—
Earth's greatness is activity,
Love sets her free from thrall.

208.—GOETHE TO ZELTER.

Weimar, 11th October, 1826.

.... GRILLPARZER is an agreeable, pleasant man, and I dare say one may credit him with innate poetical talent; how far it reaches, and what it accomplishes, I will not say. It is natural that he should have appeared somewhat oppressed in our free life. . . . .

Do not delay to take up your paraЫe in writing, about the Table I sent you. You will see from it, how earnest was my endeavour, at least to define for Science the boundaries of that vast kingdom. Every chapter, every paragraph points to something pregnant; the method of arrangement may be allowed to pass; I chose it, because I thought of making it somewhat similar in form to my *Farbenlehre*. I intended to have done a good deal more, but it had to be set aside, owing to the hurry-scurry of my life. One ought to say to oneself betimes, that it is advisable, never to meddle with anything, that one cannot appropriate to oneself by enjoyment, nor energize productively, for one's own and other people's delight. . . . .

Now, in haste, let me ask you kindly to give my best thanks to our excellent and energetic Felix, for that splendid copy of his careful æsthetic studies; his work, as well as that of his master, will be instructive entertainment to our Weimar connaisseurs during the long winter evenings, which are now close upon us. . . . .

G.

1827.

209.—ZELTER TO GOETHE.

Berlin, 20th February, 1827.

.... MY Felix has accepted an invitation to Stettin, to conduct his latest works there; he left Berlin on the 16th. The lad reached his nineteenth year on the third of this month, and his work grows in ripeness and individuality. His last Opera, which it takes a whole evening to perform, has been now, for more than a year, travailing for birth at the Theatre Royal, and never reaches the light; whereas all manner of French rubbish and trash is on the stage, and hardly lives to the second representation. As we are young, and all other advantages are in our favour, for which many others have to wear away the best part of their life, it cannot do us very much damage,—if I did not wish, that with his industry, he might as soon as possible grow out and ahead of our time, to which we have to be civil, whether we like it or not. I dare say I might still be of some use to him, by making him fall back more and more upon himself. . . . .

Yours,
Z.

210.—GOETHE TO ZELTER.

Weimar, 2nd March, 1827.

YESTERDAY evening, (the 1st of March,) while Riemer and I were revising your letters of the year 1820, I really felt quite anxious about you, thinking over again your rash and dangerous voyage to Swinemünde. It is strange, that a danger long since past, appears in its peculiar form, far greater, and more real, than when we first hear of it, directly after its occurrence, for the mind struggles against it, as in the distress itself, striving to lessen its impression, and the joy of the escape passionately contributes to this feeling. In after years, all is different; we then have courage to look upon our terror, but for this very reason, it rises in the description to its real magnitude.

The account of your trip to St. Petersburg was welcomed with many thanks; the ladies of our court, who had seen the model on the spot, told us about it, but only incidentally. Since the great catastrophe* first gave clear proof of the bad situation of this huge city, whenever there is a fall in the barometer, especially at night, when the storm is raging among my fir-trees, I am forced to think of that locality.

If people are compelled—like the Venetians—to settle down in a swamp, or by chance, establish themselves in a most unsuitable locality, as did the first Romans,—well, it can't be helped; but deliberately to do the clumsy thing, like the great Emperor,† to the irreparable ruin of his own people, is surely too lamentable an expression of the principle of absolute monarchy. An old fisherman is said to have told him beforehand, that it was not a fit place for a city.

If I want to make an excuse for him, I am driven to say, that his great original genius was led astray by a fit of imitation. He had Amsterdam and the dyke-system of Holland in his mind, and did not perceive that it was wholly inappropriate here. The Dutch themselves made the same mistake, in the laying out of Batavia, inasmuch as they imagined, that people could live among marshes in the Torrid Zone, with as much impunity, as they could in the Temperate and the Frigid.

---

* The inundation of the Neva.

† "The situation of Petersburg," said Goethe to Eckermann, "is quite unpardonable, especially when we reflect that the ground rises in the neighbourhood, and that the Emperor could have had a city quite free from all this trouble, arising from overflow of the stream, if he had but gone a little higher up, and had only had the haven in this low place. An old shipmaster represented this to him, and prophesied that the people would be drowned every seventy years. There stood also an old tree, with various marks from times when the waters had risen to a great height. But all this was in vain; the Emperor stood to his whim, and had the tree cut down, that it might not bear witness against him."

Now for something more cheerful! as you are taking up French, I would advise you—if you have not already done so,—to read *Le Théâtre de Clara Gazul* and the *Poésies de Béranger*. In both you will very clearly recognize, what can be achieved by talent, not to say genius, when it appears at a pregnant point of time, and is perfectly reckless. Why, we began much in the same way. . . . .

A very favourable review of Ternite's* *Pompejana* is ready for the printer; we shall also make honourable mention of his Fra Angelico. Meyer knows the picture very well, having seen it in Florence. To be sure, if this heavenly life is to make any impression, we must purge our eyes to some extent of that earthly life, for, thank God, we have withdrawn ourselves quite as far from Priestcraft, as we have again drawn nigh to Nature; we cannot and must not renounce this inestimable advantage. . . . .

G.

211.—GOETHE TO ZELTER.

Weimar, 19th March, 1827.

How should the friend answer his friend in such a case? † A like calamity drew us so close to each other, that the bond between us could not be more intimate. The present sorrow leaves us as we are, and that of itself is a great deal.

The Fates are never weary of relating to one another the old myth of the Night, breaking in a thousand thousand times, and yet once more. To live long, means, to outlive many; such is the pitiful refrain of our vaudeville-like, listless life; it comes round again and again, fretting us, and yet goading us to fresh and earnest endeavour.

The circle of persons with whom I come most in contact, seems to me like a roll of Sibylline leaves, which, being consumed by the flames of life, vanish, one after the other, into the air, thus making those that are left more precious, from moment to moment. Let us work, until we, in our turn, either before or after one another, are summoned by

---

* The Inspector of the Royal Gallery at Potsdam.
† Alluding to the death of Zelter's only remaining son.

the Spirit of the Universe to return into other. And may the Eternally-Living not deny us new activities, like those in which we have already been put to the test! Should He, father-like, add to these the remembrance, and after-feeling of the rectitude and virtue we desired and achieved even in this world, we should assuredly but plunge all the more eagerly in amongst the wheels of this world's machinery.

The Entelechean * Monad must preserve itself only in restless activity; if this becomes its other nature, it can never, throughout Eternity, be in need of occupation. Forgive me these abstruse expressions! but people have from of old lost themselves in such regions, and tried to impart their meaning by this kind of speech, where Reason did not prove sufficient, and yet where one would not, by choice, allow Unreason to prevail.

That in the midst of your sorrow, you should remember that number of *Kunst und Alterthum*, pleased me very much, for even when we are suffering from the heaviest losses, we ought at once to begin looking about us, to see what is left for us to receive and to do. How often have we, in such cases, tested our activity with renewed eagerness, and thereby diverted our minds, and let in all sorts of consolation! The meaning I discovered in that passage from Aristotle was a great gain to me, as well on its own account, and for the sake of the æsthetic connection, as because a truth casts light around itself on all sides. . . . .

Ever and eternally yours,
GOETHE.

212.—GOETHE TO ZELTER.

Weimar, 29th March, 1827.

. . . . On a recent occasion, which I may perhaps ere long specify more particularly, I said, "*Il faut croire à la simplicité*," which means, one must believe in simplicity,

* From ἐντελέχεια, the actual being of a thing; Aristotle calls the soul the ἐντελέχεια of the body, that by which it actually is, though it had a capacity of existing before. The expression is also found in Leibnitz.

in what is simple, in what is originally productive, if one wants to go the right way. This however is not granted to everyone; we are born in an artificial state, and it is far easier to make it more artificial still, than to return to what is simple. . . . .

On Wednesday Krüger plays Orestes in my *Iphigenie;* but it is impossible for me to be present, as he would doubtless wish. What to me is the recollection of the days, when I felt, thought, and wrote all that!

And yet, quite recently, I have been tormented in the same kind of way. An Englishman,* who—like others—came to Germany, *not* to learn German, and was carried away by the stimulus of brilliant intellectual society, made an attempt to translate my *Tasso* into English. The first passages he tried his hand at were not so bad, and as the work progressed, it got better and better, not without the interference and co-operation of my domestic literary circle, which is always revolving, like a screw.

Then, as he wanted me to read through the whole piece with pleasure and comfort, he had his first copy very handsomely set up in grand octavo, and new type, so that of course I felt myself bound to go carefully and attentively through this strange work, which I have never re-read since it was printed, and have at most, heard imperfectly, when seated at a distance from the stage. Then, to my surprise, I clearly perceived what I had aimed at and what I had achieved in former days, and understood, how young people can find pleasure and consolation, by hearing, in well-set speech, that others have at one time tormented themselves, as they themselves are being tormented now. The translation is remarkable, some few mistakes have been altered, at my suggestion, the language becomes more and more fluent as one proceeds, and the last Acts, and the passionate speeches are extremely good. . . . .

The completion of a work of art in itself is the eternal, indispensable requisite! Aristotle, who had perfection before him, is said to have thought of the effect! What a pity!

* Probably C. Des Voeux, whose translation of *Tasso* was published in this year.

If, in these quiet days, I had at my command more youthful powers, I should give myself up entirely to the study of the Greek, in spite of all the difficulties I am conscious of. Nature and Aristotle would be the aims I had in view. We can form no conception of all that this man perceived, saw, noticed, observed, but he certainly was over-hasty in his explanations.

But do we not do the same, up to this very day? We have no lack of experience, we only lack calmness of mind, whereby alone our experience becomes clear, true, lasting, and of use.

See the Theory of Light and Colour, as interpreted before my very eyes, by Professor Fries * of Jena; it is a series of hasty conclusions, such as expositors and theorists have been guilty of, for more than hundreds of years past. I do not care to say anything more about these in public, but write it, I will; some truthful mind is sure to grasp it one day. . . . .

In my preface to Manzoni's works, (Frommann's edition,†) you will, as a fact, find only what you know already through my *Kunst und Alterthum*. But in connection with the Tragedy of *Adelchi*, and the choruses that occur in it, I have said some out of the way things, which you will be sure to welcome gladly.

What is excellent, (I say this here with reference to the beginning,) should never be carped at nor discussed, but enjoyed, and reverentially thought over in silence. However, as people neither apprehend nor comprehend this, let *us* do it, and be happy in so doing. . . . .

G.

213.—ZELTER TO GOETHE.

8th April, 1827.

. . . . OLD BACH, with all his originality, is a son of his country, and of his age, and could not escape French

---

* Jacob Friedrich Fries, Professor of Philosophy at Jena, author of *Julius und Evagoras, oder die Schönheit der Seele, Ein philosophischer Roman*.

† *Opere poetiche di Alessandro Manzoni, con prefazione di Goethe*, Jena, per Federico Frommann, 1827.

influence, especially that of Couperin. One wants to show one's willingness to oblige, and so one writes only for the time being. One can, however, dissociate him from this foreign element; it comes off like thin froth, and the shining contents lie immediately beneath. Consequently, I have arranged many of his Church compositions, solely for my own pleasure, and my heart tells me, that old Bach nods approval, just as the worthy Haydn used to say, " Yes, yes, that was what I wished! " .... The greatest stumbling-block in our time is certainly to be found in those utterly damnable text-books of the German Church, which cave in to the polemical earnestness of the Reformation, stirring up the unbelief, which no one wants, by means of the thick fumes of belief. The rarity of Bach consists in this, that a genius, in whom taste is innate, should, from such a soil, have conjured up a spirit, that must have sprung from great depths. He is most marvellous, when he is in a hurry, and not in the humour. I possess manuscripts of his, where he has thrice begun and then erased again ; he could not get it to go, but the music must be forthcoming, for next Sunday there was some inevitable wedding or funeral before him. Even the very worst foolscap paper seems to have been scarce at times, but the work had to be done; little by little he gets into the swing, and at last the great artist is there, Bach's very self. Afterwards he makes his improvements, quite as an afterthought, and with his cramped penmanship, becomes so dark, misty, and learned, using his own signs, which everyone is not acquainted with, that I have to refrain almost entirely from meddling with his manuscripts, because I find it no easy matter, to get away from them again. . . . .

Yours,
Z.

214.—GOETHE TO ZELTER.

Weimar, April 10th, 1827.

.... I CALL to mind an experience of mine in former days, when I had something to do with a man of real mark. The Prince Primate, our neighbour and constant companion, was Statthalter of Erfurt;* from his high and influential position, and still more as being himself an author, he had a fearful number of literary correspondents, to whom, as he was a man of rank, good breeding, and kindly disposition, he always sent some reply, however short. Now, it is true, he had knowledge extensive enough for such emergencies, but how could he have time to think over, and do perfect justice to each of his correspondents? So he adopted a certain style, which veiled the emptiness of his answers, and appeared to say something important to everyone, whereas in reality it was mere politeness. There must be hundreds of such letters lying about even now. I was often myself a witness of such replies; we used to joke about them, and as I was trying to maintain an unconditional love of truth, in dealing with myself and others, (which, as I too was often wrong, at times seemed like a kind of madness,) I took a solemn oath, never under similar circumstances—my celebrity at the time already threatened me with these—to give in to such a practice, since if I did so, all pure and sincere relations with my fellow men would in the end be dissolved and scattered to the winds.

The result of this was, that since that time, I have answered letters less frequently, and now, in my more advanced years, I observe the same practice, for a twofold reason: I do not care to write letters with nothing in them, and to write important letters, leads me away from my immediate duties, and takes up too much time. . . . .

Yours truly,
GOETHE.

215.—GOETHE TO ZELTER.

15th April, 1827.

. . . . MADAME CATALANI has scented out a few of our extra *Groschen*, and I almost grudge them to her. Too much is too much! She makes no preparation as yet for leaving us, for she has still to ring the changes on a couple

---

* Statthalter Dalberg, a Catholic prelate, and one of the most confidential friends of the Ducal family of Weimar.

of old-new transmogrified airs, which she might just as
well grind out gratis. After all, what are a few thousand
of our *Thalers*, when we get "God save the King" into
the bargain! It really is a pity! What a voice! A golden
dish with common mushrooms in it! And we—one almost
swears at oneself—to go and admire what is so con-
temptible! It is incredible; "a beast that wants discourse
of reason" would mourn at it. What an impossible state
of things! and yet it is a fact, that an Italian turkey-hen
comes to Germany—Germany with her Academies and
High Schools,—and old students and young professors
sit to listen, while she sings in English—let me write
angelically*—the airs of the German Handel. What a
disgrace, if that's to be reckoned an honour! In the heart
of Germany too! . . . .

Z.

216.—GOETHE TO ZELTER.

Weimar, 22nd April, 1827.

I WAS very much struck by your significant remark,
that Bach, who was so thoroughly original, had allowed
himself to be affected by a foreign influence; I immediately looked up *Franz Couperin* in the *Biographical
Dictionary*, and can understand how, owing to the great
activity of the Arts and Sciences in those days, some
Gallicisms may have been blown over hither. . . . .

But to return to Couperin and Bach. I do entreat you
to let me hear some of your thoughtful observations about
what you call French froth, as distinguished from the
German basis of the music, and thus, in one way or another,
to bring home to me, objectively and subjectively, this
instructive connection. . . . .

Now I must tell you, that yesterday evening, while revising our correspondence with Riemer, I was greatly
delighted with your splendid letter of the 20th of March,

---

* It is impossible to give the German play on the word *Englisch*,
with its double meanings, "English" and "angelically." Catalani's
Christian name was Angelica.

1824, where, whilst unravelling the course of Handel's *Messiah*, you so admirably trace the gradual development of the Chorale into four parts, out of the *Canto fermo*, with which it originated. This leads me to hope, that you will continue to think me worthy of enlightenment on similar subjects, and therefore that you will, as soon as may be, begin a friendly chat with me, by letter, about Couperin and Bach.

Pardon these fragmentary pages! there is such a hurly-burly around me, that I am in danger of being overtaken by the two greatest failings of human nature—*delay* and *over-haste*.

Yours unalterably,
G.

217.—ZELTER TO GOETHE.

22nd April, 1827.

.... THIS very week we are to have Felix's last Opera *—if it ever does come off,—we have yet to see. He has been obliged to alter a great deal, the book is not much to speak of, and even the improvements are not likely to be brilliant.

My Good Friday music was fairly successful. I am seven hundred *Thalers* to the good, and may rest content. . . . .

Yours,
Z.

218.—GOETHE TO ZELTER.

Weimar, 24th May, 1827.

.... THE second part of the *Wanderjahre* is finished; it needs only a few rushes to bind the whole garland of flowers together, and after all, any kind spirit, capable of grasping the separate parts, would do this just as well, and perhaps better than myself.

But now I mean to make a private confession to you, viz. that the encouraging sympathy of kind spirits has led me to take up *Faust* again, exactly at that point,

* *Die Hochzeit des Camacho.* See Letter 186.

where, on descending from the cloud of antiquity, he again confronts his evil genius. Do not say anything about this to anyone; I will however confide to you, that it is my intention to proceed from that point, and to fill up the gap between it and the final conclusion, which was ready long ago......

Yours, as of old,
GOETHE.

219.—GOETHE TO ZELTER.

Weimar, 9th June, 1827.

.... *A propos* of this,* some of my old reflections recurred to me, and I will write them down here. The musician, if he is in other respects a sentient, sensible being, moral and well-conducted, enjoys great advantages in the course of his life, because he can assimilate himself better than others to the current of life, and to every kind of enjoyment. For this reason, your accounts of your travels have quite a peculiar—nay, a twofold charm: the architect and musician are combined with the man of sterling worth, and the range of this society is practically infinite.

The English have introduced to us their *Living Poets,*—in two thick octavo volumes, more or less by quotations, and by short biographical notices. I have for some time past been studying this work very diligently; it suggests the most interesting comparisons. The decided merits of all these poets are the result of their *descent* and *position;* the least important of them has Shakespeare for an ancestor, and the Ocean at his feet.

Truly yours,
J. W. v. GOETHE

220.—ZELTER TO GOETHE.

9th June, 1827.

WHAT I called Sebastian Bach's French froth is not so easily skimmed off, that you can catch it in your hand. It is like the air, ever present, but impalpable. Bach

* Goethe had been reading an article by F. S. Kandler, on the condition of music at Naples.

passes for the greatest of harmonists, and rightly too. As yet one can scarcely venture to style him a poet of the highest order, although he belongs to those, who, like your Shakespeare, are far above childish playthings. As a servant of the Church, he wrote only for the Church, though not what you would call ecclesiastical music. His style is Bachish, like everything about him. He is necessarily obliged to use common signs and names, such as *Toccata, Sonata, Concerto,* &c., which is no more than saying, that a man is called *Joseph*, or *Christopher*. Bach's original element is solitude, as you actually admitted, when you once said, " I lie down in bed and make our *Bürgermeister-* organist of Berka play me *Sebastiana.*" That is just like him, you have to spy upon him.

Well, besides that, he was a man, a father, a godfather, nay a Cantor in Leipzig, and as such, no more than anyone else, even if not much less than a Couperin, who served two kings of France, for over forty years. In the year 1713, Couperin published and dedicated to his king this first bit of fundamental advice—Do not strike, but play (*touchez*) the piano.

A King of France is playing the piano, perhaps even the organ, pedals and all! Who would not immediately have imitated him? Couperin's new method particularly insisted on the introduction of the thumb, whereby alone even and sure execution becomes possible. (If I am not mistaken, in Carlo Dolce's picture of Saint Cecilia, the thumbs, if not hanging down, are at all events idle!) The more advanced Germans, and Bach, had long practised this method,* as is self-evident, but it was still limited to the

* " Some persons have pretended that Couperin taught this method of fingering before him, in his work published in 1716, under the title of *L'Art de toucher le Clavecin*. But, in the first place, Bach was at that time above thirty years old, and had long made use of his manner of fingering; and secondly, Couperin's fingering is still very different from that of Bach, though it has in common with it the more frequent use of the thumb. I say only, the more frequent: for in Bach's method the thumb was made the principal finger, because it is absolutely impossible to do without it, in what are called the difficult keys: this is not the case with Couperin, because he neither had such a variety of passages, nor composed and played in such difficult keys as Bach, and consequently had not such urgent occasion for it."—See J. N. Forkel's *Life of Bach*, p. 25.

right and left hand, whereby the latter is evidently spared. The Bach method claims the use of the ten fingers, which, with their different length and strength, are meant to perform every kind of service; to this method we are indebted for the incredible performances of the latest *toucheurs*. Now as all men must be French, if they mean to live, Bach made his sons practise the small, finnikin, dainty, Couperin notes, with their befrizzled heads; nay, he himself made highly successful efforts as a composer in this manner, and so the French frizzlings insinuated themselves into his style.

Bach's compositions are partly vocal, partly instrumental, or both together. In the vocal pieces, there is often much more than the words imply, and he has often enough been taken to task for this; nor is he strict in the observance of the rules of harmony and melody, over which he lords it with the greatest audacity. But when Biblical texts, such as "Break for the hungry thy bread," &c., "Ye shall mourn and lament," &c., "Jesus took unto himself the twelve," &c., "Then was our mouth filled with laughter," &c., are manufactured into Choruses, I am often inclined to admire in these very passages the sacred indifference, nay, the apostolic irony, with which some quite unsuspected effect is produced, without raising so much as a doubt of the sense and taste displayed in it. A *passus* and *sepultus* introduces the last pulsations of the silent powers,—a *resurrexit* or a *Gloria Dei Patris*, the eternal regions of sanctified suffering, in contrast with the hollowness of earthly things. This feeling however is, as it were, indivisible, and it might be difficult to carry away from it a melody, or anything materialistic. It only renews itself, strengthens itself, gathers up its strength again continually, by the repetition of the whole.

In all this, Bach is hitherto still dependent on some kind of theme; one should follow him upon the organ. That is his own peculiar soul, into which he breathes immediately the living breath. His theme is the feeling just born, which, like the spark from the stone, invariably springs forth, from the first chance pressure of the foot upon the pedal. Thus by degrees he warms to his subject, till he has isolated himself, and feels alone, and then an inexhaustible stream passes out into the infinite ocean.

His eldest son, Friedemann (of Halle), who died here, meant pretty much the same thing, when he said, "Compared with him, we all remain children."

I suppose that most of his grander compositions for the organ come to an end somehow, but they are never done. There is no end to them. Here I must stop, however, though much remains to be said. Weighing every possible testimony against him, this Leipzig Cantor is one of God's phenomena; clear, but we cannot clear him up. I might call out to him:—

> "You've made me work with might and main,
> And I've brought you to light again."

Z.

221.—GOETHE TO ZELTER.

Weimar, 17th July, 1827.

THE continuation of the fragment sent you on the 21st of June, through La Roche the actor, has been lying on my desk ever since, and I have not been able to make up my mind to send it off; I know not how, but some morose thoughts had got into it, such as one should never send to a distance, for by the time they give a friend a disagreeable hour, one has quite recovered from them oneself, and by means of happy and resolute activity, one has long since escaped from that gloomy condition, when vexation at being interrupted in one's work took one by surprise for the moment. . . .

The high pressure of musical, dramatic, literary, scientific, and other performances in Berlin, which are thrust before us in the papers, would wellnigh bewilder and overpower a distant recluse; however, I willingly believe that in the midst of all this bustle, one may well remain true to oneself, just as good inspirations are quite possible on the shore of the raging ocean, or elsewhere. . . . .

Your friend has moved up from his Garden-House, finding that he was too dependent upon artistic and literary surroundings, which up here are always to his hand, whereas, down yonder, he has them only partially at command. It was really funny to see the number of different things, which had been dragged down, during his four weeks' stay there. The greatest gain, however, that I realize from this experiment, is that I have again grown fond of that garden, to which I was almost a stranger, and that it has again become a necessity to me. The foliage there, and in the neighbourhood, especially on the old trees, is remarkably fine this year, and I therefore enjoy what has long been forgotten and neglected, still more than if it had been missed and longed for. I feel compelled to spend at least a few hours there every day.

As for the rest, I have much in my mind, and on hand, which ought to please you all, if it is realized; I certainly should like to surprise and astonish you again once or twice more; the plan for doing so is already complete.

Please ask any English friends of literature in your neighbourhood, if they know anything about Thomas Carlyle of Edinburgh, who deserves remarkably well for his services to German literature. . . . .

In haste, as in truth,
GOETHE

ENCLOSURE.

(Continuation of my last letter of the 21st June, 1827, sent through La Roche.)

Of course at this juncture, I thought of the worthy organist of Berka; for it was there, when my mind was in a state of perfect composure, and free from external distraction, that I first obtained some idea of your Grand Master, (Sebastian Bach). I said to myself, it is as if the eternal harmony were conversing with itself, as it may have done, in the bosom of God, just before the Creation of the world. So likewise did it move in my inmost soul, and it seemed as if I neither possessed nor needed ears, nor any other sense—least of all, the eyes.

As soon as music makes the first vigorous advance towards exercising an objective influence, it powerfully excites our inborn sense of rhythm, step and dance, song and rejoicing; by degrees, it runs off into the Transoxanic, (*vulgo* Janissary music,) or into the Jodel, into the love-cooing of birds.

Now however, a higher culture steps in; the pure *Canti-*

lena flatters and charms us; gradually, the harmonic *Chorus* is developed, and thus developed, the whole strives to return again to its divine origin. . . . .

I was very pleased to hear that you opened the wandering Buch,* and made friends with its contents. I am quite aware of what we owe to it, and to others of its kind; only it is a pity these gentlemen immediately set up a priesthood, and—in addition to what is worth our gratitude—endeavour to force upon us something which they themselves are not acquainted with, and perhaps do not even believe in.

Now as the human race invariably moves herd-like, they soon make the majority follow their lead, and an intelligent man, who is all for clear progress, and honours the problem itself, stands alone, before he is aware of it. As I no longer care to dispute, (and I never did like it,) I allow myself to deride and attack their weak side, which, I dare say, they themselves are quite well aware of.

Professor Fries,† who continues to hold forth in Jena upon the old Newtonian nonsense, did not venture, in his Compendium, to refer to the *little hole*, which I have made rather hard for them, but he now talks about a *narrow strip*, which is utterly senseless. But what is so stupid, that party-folk will not dare to bring it forward as hocus-pocus?

It is a subject that does not affect you in any way, and I should be sorry if you were to trouble yourself in the least about it, but having watched it now for nearly forty years, I may surely venture to tell you, how the mathematico-physical Leviathan conducts itself, with the harpoon which I thrust at it, sticking in its ribs.

It is no vain boast, if I assure you, that there is no one living, who has such a clear insight into these mysteries as I have, seeing forsooth how people drag along the true together with the false. Younger men indeed see and observe this, but they neither may nor can free themselves from tradition, as, of course, they would not have any

---

* A play on the name of Herr Leopold von Buch, (Book,) of Munich, a celebrated traveller and man of science, with whom Goethe differed, as to the progress of the formation of the earth.

† See note to Letter 212.

language, wherewith to express themselves, and it is in accordance with Nature, that one cannot speak the truth with false words.

Excuse these remarks, and think of some similar instance, that you may perhaps have met with in your own province.

What you say about diction, is not unknown to me. When, for instance, people want to praise a dramatic poem, they say that the language is very beautiful; but they seldom take cognizance of what is actually said. In the case of the *Helena* also, some very intelligent people have been chiefly pleased with the three or four new words introduced in it, and probably they have already considered in silence, how they would themselves make use of them. All this cannot, of course, affect an already celebrated author of sixty years' standing, but perhaps there has never been an instance of anyone who has had so few readers, and so many spies, pickers and stealers, who seize upon his diction, because they imagine, that if they could but speak in that way, it would be something done, even if they have nothing to say.

One *Xenion* touches upon this characteristic of our day. Unfortunately I withheld a good many of this kind, for the sake of blessed peace. A few days ago the following lines escaped me:—

> America, thy lot was cast by powers,
> Happier than those of our old Continent;
> Thou hast no ruined towers,
> No basalt monument.
> Thy heart endures no pain,
> In the heyday of life,
> From memories that are vain,
> Unprofitable strife.
> Then use the Present happily!
> And when your child thirsts for poetic glories,
> May some good genius keep him free
> From knights, from robbers, and from ghost-stories!

. . . . In return for your kind reception of my Scotch *Wanderer* * I send a ballad, (*Gutmann and Gutweib,*)

* A Highland Song, translated by Goethe. It is to be found in his works, under the title, *Hochländisch.*—*Gutmann und Gutweib* is a free translation of the humorous old Scotch Ballad, *Get up and bar the door.*

which I must not venture to praise; the original stands very high—the happy, animated blending of the Epic and Dramatic in this extremely laconic form, cannot sufficiently be admired. If I discover anything else of the kind, it shall follow forthwith. This is the fruit of my stay in the Garden-House, which I gave up, because Count Sternberg of Prague was paying us a visit; I have not been there again, owing to the misty rain, and the damp state of the valley resulting from it,—also on account of the difficulty of communication.

222.—ZELTER TO GOETHE

ENCLOSURE.

Berlin, 10th August, 1827.

.... At last we have in our hands the much disputed score of Mozart's *Requiem*,* corrected from manuscripts, and we know what we knew. As you see the periodical, *Cäcilia*, I suppose you are sure to have become acquainted with the bitter, sour jabbering of Herr Gottfried Weber of Darmstadt, against the authenticity of this posthumous work. There he affirms, that the *Requiem* is just as good as not Mozart's at all, and that if it be his, it is the weakest, nay, the wickedest thing, that ever came from the pen of that illustrious man. Enough, he says that Mozart left the work incomplete, but that after his death, Süssmayr interposed, and embezzled Mozart's thoughts, so that the work, owing to his completion of it, was corrupted, if not poisoned—that finally, since Mozart's death, the world has been living in an astonished and astonishing state of deception about this legacy, and that no one hitherto has had the heart to bring to light the blunders, spots, and faults of a spurious work of art. These are the humours of Weber. But we too have been in the world from our youth up; Mozart was born two years before me, (1756,) and we remember, only too well, the circumstances of his death. Mozart, I say, who had been so soundly taught, that he could compose off-hand, and

* The whole question of the authenticity of Mozart's *Requiem* has been ably summed up in a short treatise, by my friend, Professor Pole.

have time left for hundreds of things besides,—dallying with women, and the like,—had thereby run his good natural disposition too close. In this way he comes to have a wife and children, and falls into the extreme of poverty, in which his civic existence is lost. Lying on his sickbed, wretched in his home, worried, decried, with no helpful friends, in the end he is without even the commonest necessities of life. Some honest fellow orders any work Mozart may choose, so as to give him a little money in the most delicate way. An Opera-book is not forthcoming at the moment, and Mozart says, "I have a mind to write a *Requiem*, which you may use for my funeral." The weakness increases; he begins to care for his soul, and in solemn, solitary self-introspection, certain beginnings of single parts of the *Requiem* are unfolded, (as once, with so much truth, you placed them in the mouth of your Gretchen,) *dies iræ*—*tuba mirum*—*rex tremendæ*—*confutatis*—*lacrimosa*—and it is just these numbers which reveal the deepest contrition of a religious mind, showing at the same time, on one side, the last remains of a great school, and on the other, the passionate feeling of a dramatic composer. The style consequently is a medley,—uneven, nay, fragmentary,—and so arises that confusion, in which the criticism of to-day takes such delight. Thus tradition ran at the time, but no honest man would repeat it out loud.

After Mozart's death, worthy Süssmayr comes forward as the true friend, puts the *Requiem* together, and completes what is wanting, so that the suffering family gains thereby a sufficiency for its nakedness. The work is sold, and printed; Süssmayr makes as good an explanation as he can of his share in the work, and soon afterwards follows his friend into Eternity.

Now comes the aforesaid Hans Taps, accuses the friend of adulteration and lying, and talks in the most contemptuous tone about a well-meaning friend, without once suggesting any safe criterion, as to where we are really to look for Mozart, and where for Süssmayr, ascribing to Süssmayr, what he cannot possibly have written, and *vice versâ;* without reflecting, that if a clever man like Süssmayr puts forth all his powers, he can quite well avoid the *dormitat Homerus* part himself. And this really happened.

The *Benedictus* is as good as it can be, and cannot be Mozart, the School decides so much. Süssmayr knew Mozart's School, but it was not ingrained in him; he had not been through it in his youth, and here and there traces of this are found in the beautiful *Benedictus*. On the other hand, whatever is found fault with in Mozart's work, Süssmayr is said to have done. Thus the critic explains, that the first number in the *Requiem* has been borrowed from Handel, and consequently cannot be by Mozart,—who often and unquestionably attempted to write in the Handelian manner, in order to convince himself, that he too could do that kind of thing. In this piece, we have besides the choral music, a *Cantus firmus*, and an old melody too; guess what? It is the simple melody—(how comes the *Magnificat anima mea* into a *Requiem?*) in a word, it is the old *Cantus firmus* to be found in the Luther Chorale-Book up to this very day, *Meine Seele erhebt den Herrn*. I just now called the work fragmentary and uneven, by which I mean, that the numbers collectively are like chequer-work, and he who insists on considering them as a whole, is mistaken, as are several excellent composers; the whole *Requiem* consists of such numbers, and in spite of that, it is the very best I know of in the last century.

Before Mozart had taken a look round North Germany, Handel may have shone before him, as the most powerful intellect in Germany; some of his compositions bear the superscription *Nel Stilo di Haendel*. Then Mozart comes to Leipzig, while Hiller is yet alive, and splits his ears over Sebastian Bach, to the great astonishment of Hiller, who is trying to fill the *Thomaner* boys with horror at the crudities of that Sebastian. What does Mozart do? He proves himself in this style with a dexterity, which only such a School can give. Just listen to the music of the *schwarze Männer* in the *Zauberflöte*, (before the ordeal by fire). It is inlaid, it is the Luther Chorale, *Wenn wir in höchsten Nöthen*, interwoven with the orchestra in Bach's style,—and so on.

223.—GOETHE TO ZELTER.

Weimar, 17th August, 1827.

SCHLEGEL'S Lectures, extracts from which have reached me, deserve our best thanks; we recapitulate with an intelligent and well-informed man all those means of development, on the growth of which we throve successfully. The younger public, in particular, may well be satisfied with them, if they are inclined to take a rational view of the immediate past.

He is over sixty years of age, and knows how to estimate the trouble it cost him and others, to arrive at this point.

Here and there it would require a harder hit, to make the egg stand on its end. In the history of Art also, there are two considerations, that must never be lost sight of: firstly, that all beginnings cannot be regarded as too childlike and childish, and secondly, that in the sequel, the demand for reality is always in conflict with taste and meaning. . . . .

GOETHE.

224.—GOETHE TO ZELTER.

Weimar, 1st September, 1827.

. . . . MAKE my peace with the worthy F. Perhaps I might let him have a few lines from time to time—as, for example, I should have no objection to let Rösel print his little poem there, if he likes to—but these good people insist at once on our becoming associates, and we must be on our guard against that, because, now and then, they are wanting in tact and discretion. You will remember too, how Gleim,[*] in his old age, ended by frittering away his talent in this fashion; I remember in those days, writing on a page of the *Mercur*:—

> In the devil's name,
> What matters your name!
> In the *German Mercury*,
> Not a single trace I see

[*] Johann Wilhelm Ludwig Gleim, one of the so-called Anacreontic poets, author of the *Versuch in Scherzhaften Liedern*.

Of Father Wieland; yet, 'tis true,
He stands upon the binding blue;
And under the most execrable rhyme,
The name of Gleim.

My first and last topic is always your portrait. It is in itself a work of great merit, and has therefore been universally admired. If on looking at it, the educated connaisseur still finds it something of a problem, and upon closer examination, wanting in certain qualities, the reason is, that this eminently talented man,* like all our modern painters and sculptors, acknowledges no Sebastian Bach as an ancestor, whose teaching and practice must be respected. The result is,—with Begas, as with the others,—that they try their hand at all the different styles and manners, and therefore do not early enough succeed in developing the right style, and in coming to a perfect understanding with it. The consequence is, that the public does not know what to make of many honest efforts, be the work of art planned and executed in ever so careful a manner, for—whatever the artist may do—a false conception remains without effect on the natural man. . . . .

Your attached
GOETHE.

GOETHE TO ZELTER.

Weimar, 6th September, 1827.

(*Continuation.*)

.... BE sure to note down on paper your ideas about the minor scale; they would come just at the right moment for me, as I too have thought out something on the subject with Riemer; I will dictate it and seal it up, and wait until I hear from you, when I shall send it off immediately. It would be very pleasant to find that we had reached the same goal by different paths.

I think I shall now have to abandon Schlegel's Lectures to the Berliners; they certainly do not stand the test of a closer examination. On reading the first pages, I was content to hear what was old, for what is new too often proves

---

* Begas, the artist who painted Zelter's portrait.

vexatious to me. But, of course, one would like to have the old rendered ever more complete, better arranged, more concise, more readily surveyable; and this is not accomplished here. And then, how can a man write a history of anything that is not in his own line? I have often remarked, that if I had to write a criticism of anything I did not thoroughly understand, I was obliged to make mere phrases, however much in earnest I meant to be. . . . .

I got thus far before my birthday, when, as I well knew, my good friends were making preparations for the usual pleasant *fête;* but there was a surprise for me, which almost unnerved me, and left behind it a feeling, that I was hardly equal to such an event.

His Majesty of Bavaria arrived at night, on the 27th of August, declared next morning that he had come expressly for the day, honoured me with his august presence, just as I was in the midst of my friends and dear ones, presented me with the Grand Cross of the Bavarian Order of Merit, and, in fact, proved himself so thoroughly interested in and acquainted with my life hitherto, my work and endeavour, that I could not be sufficiently grateful in my expressions of admiration and esteem. His Majesty referred in a friendly, familiar way to my stay in Rome; this of itself would have led one distinctly to recognize the Princely Patron, who had there served his apprenticeship to Art. If I were to tell you more, it would fill several pages.

The presence of my most gracious Master, the Grand Duke, made this unexpected condition of things quite perfect, and now that it is all a bit of the past, I must really try for the first time to recollect how it all happened, and to think how one might have submitted more becomingly to such an ordeal.

But what we cannot experience twice in life, we must get through as well as possible *impromptu.* The delightful feelings, the significant proofs that remain, assure me that at any rate it was no dream.

So I dedicate this to you, now more than ever, my bosom-friend; your portrait was present always and everywhere.

GOETHE.

225.—ZELTER TO GOETHE.

Weimar,* 18th October, 1827.

. . . . OLD VOSS once said to me, when I had merely altered the position of a single word in his *Friedensreigen*, " You may as well let that alone ! "—and of course I might have done so, but it would have been all up with my love of the poem. I must be allowed to appropriate a part of it, in order to make it completely my own ; what do I care about the poet? His word is a stone, hurled into space, which I pick up, and how I pick it up, and how I look at it, recognize and interpret it, is *my* affair; and if he wants to be just, and if he has understood me, as I have understood him, he will remember that *his* word is printed, and remains his own. . . . . Naumann † of Dresden had not altered a single word in Schiller's *Ideal*, and Schiller scolded, like a reed-sparrow, at that famous man's composition, because it turned a beautiful poem into a throat-exercise for a *prima donna*. But with no words am I more chastely cautious than with yours. The very first time I read your poems, I grasp the sense, the feeling of the whole, and the melody comes at once ; I only stop short at a word, a phrase ; then I let it lie, until—Heaven knows how long afterwards—*my* word comes of itself, and then I finish. Numbers of your poems have been lying thus for years. . . . .

Z.

226.—GOETHE TO ZELTER.

Weimar, 24th October, 1827.

PLEASANT and creditable as is the meeting of old friends, and the renewal of old ties, still the influence of

---

* The date of this letter is somewhat puzzling, as Eckermann tells us that Zelter, who had been to Weimar on a visit, left Goethe on the evening of this very day, after a tea-party, given at Goethe's house, in honour of Hegel.

† Johann Gottlieb Naumann, a prolific writer of Operas, and of sacred music. His compositions are still performed occasionally in the Court Chapel at Dresden, but the only work known out of his native Saxony, is his setting of Klopstock's *Vater Unser*.

the present and the law of to-day apparently reassert themselves at once, so that these too are exposed to the nothingness of passing hours. I made these reflections after your departure, when I felt somewhat vexed, as the thought struck me, that I had neglected to tell you the most important things of all.

You were to have paid homage to Schiller's relics, and you ought to have read a poem which I wrote, when they were found again *al Calvario*,*—a novel too, which is quite peculiar in its style,†—several smaller poems, among them a collection, headed *Chinesische Jahreszeiten*,—and whatever else had any connection with these.

Perhaps it is not well to talk of and lament over such things afterwards, yet why should one not also take note of what has been neglected, when we have won and enjoyed so much? . . . .

Yours in haste, and sincerely,
GOETHE.

227.—GOETHE TO ZELTER.

Weimar, 27th October, 1827.

. . . . You did well to take a look at the world again, in its wild state of activity; it is always moving on, on—like a siege, no one troubles himself about any who chance to fall in the trenches, or in a *sortie*, and we will not be too particular about what is finally carried by storm.

I am very glad that my letter to Munich reached you; with regard to it, I will merely remark, that Schulze *on the Blood and Circulation* did not by any means find favour with me, for in referring to my earlier studies in the botanical field, he—in a very arrogant, youthful, and *gauche* way—calls me to account, for not having accomplished forty years ago what has not yet been achieved!

On the other hand, your Link, whom I will not reproach, because of your affection for him, lately had a certain opportunity, when he ought of necessity to have mentioned

---

* *Bei Betrachtung von Schiller's Schädel.*
† Was this *Die Novelle*, afterwards translated by Carlyle?

my *Metamorphose der Pflanzen*, and yet he carefully avoided alluding to it, whereas he brought forward again an old idea of Linnæus, which is no doubt ingenious, but still unsatisfactory. It seems to me, as if even good and eminent persons were on certain days, and under certain circumstances, doomed to be good for nothing.

Had I not gone in for the study of the Natural Sciences, I should never have gained this insight, for in ethical and æsthetic matters, the true and the false can never be driven into a corner in that way; in scientific matters however, if I am honest with myself, I must be so with others, and so I do not grudge the incalculable amount of time I have devoted to this branch of study; for now that I have treated the subject, every day must see my cause furthered, every friend and every foe, whatever attitude he chooses to assume, must help it on.

In haste,
Most truly yours,
J. W. v. GOETHE.

228.—ZELTER TO GOETHE.

Berlin, 28th October, 1827.

. . . . I HAVE twice enjoyed seeing Mdlle. Sontag at the Theatre Royal, as Myrrha in the *Opferfest*,* and as Susanna in Mozart's *Figaro*. Though I cannot particularize any special quality in her, take her for all in all, she is a joyful vision on the stage. She is a pretty darling, and always looks well, whether as third, fourth, or fifth in a great Theatre, surrounded by so much that is strange, and her vocalization and articulation are so perfect, that her voice shines out amongst much stronger voices, like a bright star. Her face moves with the melody, so the motions of her arms and hands, and all the rest of it are not repeated; it is always the same, and yet it is new. One duett was called for again; the two singers came back as they had gone off; first she had stood on the right side, now she stood on the left, and the whole duett seemed like

* *Das Unterbrochene Opferfest*, an Opera by Winter.

a new piece, which I, at all events, could have heard for the third time; some people too actually called out *Da Capo* again. . . . .

Z.

229.—GOETHE TO ZELTER.

Weimar, 6th November, 1827.

. . . . THANK you for having, by your graceful account, helped me to realize the gracefulness of that dainty songstress; my ears have long been unaccustomed to music, but my spirit is still susceptible. The recent performance of the *Zauberflöte* had a bad effect upon me; formerly I was more susceptible to such things, even though the performances may not have been better. Now two imperfections had to do with this, one external, the other internal, and the sensations produced were such as one experiences, on striking a bell with a crack in it. It is very strange! for even your much-loved songs, sung again and again, would not succeed. It is better to put up with such a state of things, than to talk, or even to write much about it.

On the other hand, the Art of Form, and especially Plastic Art, continue to give me as much pleasure as ever; the copies from Stosch's collection are keenly interesting to me; Herr Beuth's kind presents too supply me and Meyer with excellent subjects for instructive and edifying conversation. We are arranging a number of *Kunst und Alterthum*, in doing which, I always think that I am working first-hand for you.

You will be sure to gain pleasure and profit from a more intimate acquaintance with Zahn * and his works; as for me, I feel that the contemplation of antiquity, in its every relic, lifts me into an atmosphere, wherein I realize my humanity. . . . .

I have come into the possession of some very pretty drawings, for a moderate sum, and am expecting a con-

---

* Wilhelm Zahn, an architect, with whose tracings of the wall-paintings at Pompeii, Goethe had been greatly delighted. It was he, who afterwards wrote to Goethe, about the house that was called after him in Pompeii. See also Letters 340, 381.

signment of majolica from Nürnberg; this is a kind of folly, which my son shares with me. However, the sight of these dishes, plates, and vessels impresses us with the idea of a sturdy, bright kind of life, which is squandering an inheritance of grand and powerful Art. And as, after all, we like living with spendthrifts, who make life easy to themselves and us, without much enquiry, whence it comes, and whither it goes, in the same way, these objects, when seen in a mass before one, are full of bright meaning. How poor, in contrast to them, is our porcelain ware, on which you see flowers, landscapes, and heroic deeds; they give no impression as a whole, and never remind one of anything but botany, topography, and the History of warfare, things which I can only love in the garden, on a journey, and during my leisure hours. You see how one can gloss over one's own follies; but praised be every folly, that grants us innocent enjoyment like this!

And now let this letter set out upon the road, which I myself would so gladly take, and may it suggest a friendly meeting soon.

So be it!
GOETHE.

230.—ZELTER TO GOETHE.

Berlin, 16th November, 1827.

.... WHAT I wrote to you about Mdlle. Sontag was intended as a sort of epitome of the universal impression. One may well suppose that such a person, who in a few weeks can put by a sum of 11,000 *Thalers*—let alone valuable presents—provokes the envy of those immediately around her. Her fellows however confess, that they like to act and sing with her, and are always sure of happy co-operation. ....

In England they have made a pretty good translation into English of Schiller's Ballad, *The Glove*, with my music —I wish I got any benefit from it! Old Wieland may be right: it is not enough to live, one should also let live. *Addio.*

Yours,
Z.

231.—GOETHE TO ZELTER.

Weimar, 21st November, 1827.

I MUST tell you, that our wandering nightingale arrived on Sunday, the 11th of November, but owing to some undecipherable *brouillamini*, the result of misapprehension, neglect, ill-will, and intrigue, she has not appeared in public. She sang on Monday, at a *déjeûner*, given by the Dowager Grand Duchess, and was greatly applauded; afterwards, she paid me a visit, and gave us some little specimens of her extraordinary talent; these were enough for me, in so far as the idea I had entertained of her was confirmed and renewed. . . . .

I have felt, ever since it was first announced, what a great boon Walter Scott's *Life of Napoleon* would be to me, so I have let all sorts of people have out their tittle-tattle about it beforehand; but now I cannot refrain any longer, and I take up the book with confidence. Scott was born in 1771, just at the outbreak of the American Revolution; he was impressed, as a young man, by the throwing overboard of the tea-chests at Boston, as I was by the earthquake at Lisbon; how many strange things he—as an Englishman—must have had to look on at! I will tell you what I think about it, as I have opportunity. Even beforehand, I found the public true to its character. Customers, no doubt, sometimes allow the tailor to choose a particular stuff, but they insist upon having the coat fitted to their own bodies, and are highly indignant, if it proves too tight, or too loose; they are most comfortable, when wearing the loose dressing-gowns of the day and hour, in which they can feel as easy as they like; you may perhaps remember, that they treated my *Wahlverwandtschaften* as though it had been the garment of Nessus.

The Second Part of *Faust* is still shaping itself; the task here is the same as in the *Helena*,—so to formulate and arrange existing elements, that they may suit and accord with what is new; to accomplish this, much has to be thrown aside, and much to be remodelled. So it required resolution to begin the business; as I advance, the difficulties get less.

And now, with kindest greetings, let me exhort and cheer you on to persevere in that activity, to cultivate which—in the midst of peace—we are encouraged and compelled by the hostile pressure of the world. If we help ourselves, God will help us.

Ever truly and faithfully yours,
GOETHE.

232.—ZELTER TO GOETHE.

Berlin, 23rd November, 1827.

. . . . Our King occasionally takes the reins into his own hands: *e.g.*, he refuses to recognize any *virtuoso* as his *Kapellmeister*. Bernhard Romberg,* who as a composer is justly ahead of all *virtuosi*, only achieved that distinction through favouritism, and at the cost of a great deal of trouble, and he took his departure, when he learnt that the King had engaged Spontini at Paris. At that time I objected to him, that a king anyhow should be allowed to do, what the most ordinary person would—viz. to buy a *Kapellmeister* at his own price, wherever he liked. So Romberg bears me a grudge still, although he wants to be again what he refused to remain, and might have been still, had he followed my friendly advice.

Yours,
Z.

233.—GOETHE TO ZELTER.

Weimar, 4th December, 1827.

As for Walter Scott's *Napoleon*, I have thus much to say: if you have time and inclination, in your quiet

* Bernhard Romberg, who died at Hamburg in 1841, is always regarded as the head of the German School of violoncellists. Spohr met him at Berlin in the early part of the present century, and played in quartetts with him. One of these was by Beethoven, (Op. 18,) and Romberg asked, how Spohr could play "such absurd stuff?" This question squares with the well-known story of Romberg's tearing the copy of the first Rasoumowsky quartett from the desk, and trampling on it.

leisure at home, to harp back again in thought upon the significant course of the world's history, which has carried us hurriedly along with it during the last fifty years, I can give you no better advice, than to read tranquilly the aforesaid work, from beginning to end. Here you have an able, intelligent citizen, whose young days fell within the time of the French Revolution, who in his best years, and as an Englishman, watched, reflected upon, and doubtless discussed this important event in various quarters; besides which, he is the best narrator of his time, and takes the trouble to describe the whole series of events, in his usual clear and definite style.

The way in which—from his politico-national standpoint—he treats all this, and the way in which his view of this and that matter,—from the other side of the Channel—differs from ours, in our limited position on the Continent,—all this is a new experience to me, a new way of looking at and into the world.

The most remarkable thing however, is that he speaks like an upright citizen, endeavouring to judge of facts in a pious, conscientious spirit, and strictly on his guard against any Machiavellian views, which we should have thought, were inseparable from the treatment of universal history.

In these respects, I am very well satisfied with him as yet, having got to the fourth volume, and shall quietly go on with the book, looking upon him as a reporter, who has a right to submit his documentary extracts, his representation, and his vote, that he may then await the decision of the assembled judges.

Therefore, not until I have read the whole work through, the nine parts of which, by the way, have come just at the right time to cheer, and help in shortening the long, dreary evenings—do I intend to weigh, with equal interest, the objections that are brought against it. This cannot but prove interesting. It will then be seen, whether he has neglected to bring forward facts, whether he has distorted them, whether he looks at them as a partisan, whether he is prejudiced in judging them one-sidedly, or whether he must be acknowledged right. In the first place however, I say to myself, that in so doing, one will become more intimately acquainted with mankind, than with the subject, and on the whole one will, after all, have to acquiesce, for if one is not satisfied with history as with a legend, everything will finally resolve itself into doubt. . . . .

Your Lady correspondent * from *Sans Souci* may be an amiable girl ; at the same time she is a true German. This nation always fails to adjust things properly, they always stumble over bits of straw. You have answered the question very fully, kindly, and rationally ; you may look upon it too as an accident, that might easily occur amongst friends, who act and re-act so much upon one another. In like manner, they torment themselves and me about the *Weissagungen des Bakis;* they used to do so about the *Hexen-Einmaleins,* and many other bits of nonsense, which they think they can adapt to straightforward human intelligence. If only they would look for the physical-moral-æsthetic problems, which I have scattered so plentifully throughout my works, and apply these to themselves, and thus solve the enigmas of their own lives! However, many after all do this, and we will not grumble, because it is not done always and everywhere.

How much there is still, to say and to write! More anon. And herewith accept a store of sincerest good wishes.

G.

* A pupil of Zelter's, who had written to him, to know why two Distichs, published among Schiller's poems, had also appeared among Goethe's. Zelter told her that as they had been written by both poets together, they had appeared " under the firm of Goethe and Schiller."

1828.

234.—GOETHE TO ZELTER.

Weimar, 24th January, 1828.

. . . . . I HAVE kept tolerably well all this time, and have been able to devote my hours to a great deal of good and serious work. From three to four scenes of the Second Part of *Faust* have been despatched to Augsburg; I trust that when they appear in print, you and yours may, amid the streaming currents of life, be able to consecrate a little time to these pictures of mine. I am still engaged with this work, for I should very much like to finish the first two Acts, so that the *Helena* may be linked to them naturally, as a third Act, and thus adequately introduced, prove itself to be no longer a phantasmagoria and an interpolation, but an æsthetically rational sequel. We must wait and see with what success. . . . .

In my surroundings, as you know them, there has been no change; Ottilie's time is devoted to rearing her little daughter, who now looks quite pretty and pleasing. The world of young ladies here has been thrown into no slight commotion, by the recent arrival of some English recruits; they have been amusing themselves with all kinds of flirtations, so that there may be no lack of passion for capital, on which, when the time of leave-taking and final renunciation comes, they will have to draw abundantly for the interest of sorrow.

Yours unalterably,
G.

235.—GOETHE TO ZELTER.

20th February, 1828.

. . . . AND now, one word more about Walter Scott's much discussed, and still to be discussed *Napoleon*. Be the work what it may, I feel indebted to it, for it has helped me happily over the last six weeks of the past year; and that was no trifling matter, when you think of the solitary evenings, which people like us, are fain to pass in an interesting way, whilst everything that has but a spark of life in it, goes off to the Theatre, Court Fêtes, parties and balls. I found the work very convenient as a subject for thought, inasmuch as I took note, chapter by chapter, of everything that struck me as new, and of everything that was recalled to my remembrance; after that however, I immediately filled in, in their proper places, experiences of my own, that I had forgotten, and thus I no longer know what I found in the book, and what I added to it. Enough for me, that the long, ever important, and at the same time troublesome period from 1789 onwards, (when, on my return from Italy, the revolutionary nightmare began to oppress me,) up to the present time, has become perfectly clear and connected in my mind; besides, I can now bear to look at the details of that period again, because I see them in a certain connected order.

So here you have another example of my egotistical way of reading; I trouble myself less and less about what a book is; the main point is, what it brings me, what it suggests to me. I suppose you are not much better, and I hinder nobody from doing as he likes.

Walter Scott's confession that an Englishman will not budge a step, unless he sees some "English object" before him, is of itself worth many volumes. Quite recently we have seen, that the English can find no right *object* in the battle of Navarino. We will wait and see *in what quarter* it (the object) will really show itself. . . . .

Most truly yours,
G.

236.—GOETHE TO ZELTER.

Weimar, 28th February, 1828.

YOUR little letter has either come at a favourable hour, or it has made one, as it always does. I was busy at the time, arranging a number of simple, but genuine and masterly drawings and sketches, which I have bought at a reasonable price. This reminds me of a passage I dictated long ago, which I shall look up and have copied for you:—

"*Dilettanti*, when they have done their utmost, are wont to say, by way of excuse, that their work is not yet finished. Finished it certainly never can be, because it has never been properly begun. The master represents his work as finished with a few strokes ; whether worked out or not, it is already complete. The cleverest *dilettante* gropes about in uncertainty, and as the working out of the design proceeds, the insecurity of the first design becomes more and more apparent. It is only quite at the last, that the irreparable want is discovered, and of course the work cannot be finished in this way."

Our reader, (v. Holtei,*) does his work well; he has dined at my house, where he seemed pleasant company. Be he what he may, he has brought a certain kind of general intellectual stimulus into our circles. A really educated public should, I think, make a halt once in a way, listen to what it otherwise would have no chance of hearing, and thus gain new ingredients for its gossip about the town, the Court, and the English, and make the passing moment somewhat more significant.

Some private masquerades have afforded an opportunity for revealing a few of the truly astonishing poetic talents, that reign in silence among us here. Postmen, gipsies, and other messengers of the World and Fate, distributed to certain persons hundreds of little poems, many of which were distinguished by thoughts so appropriate as to make one envious. On inquiry it was found, that they had been written by persons whom one would never have thought of. . . . .

Yours unalterably,
G.

* A vaudeville-writer, whose Readings and Recitations made some sensation in Weimar. He threw such expression into his rendering of *Faust*, that August Goethe declared, he had never understood his father's work before. Goethe himself, however, disapproved of the adaptation. Von Holtei also contributed to a weekly periodical, started by Ottilie Goethe, called *Das Chaos*. See Letter 315.

237.—GOETHE TO ZELTER.

Weimar, 22nd April, 1828.

..... THE third issue of my new edition will appear at the Fair; some fresh things here and there in these little volumes I may perhaps recommend; the next issue has already been sent to Augsburg, and I now have on my conscience the fifth, in which the transformed *Wanderjahre* are to make their appearance. If man were not by nature damned to his talent, we should be forced to inveigh against the folly of burdening ourselves, throughout a long life, with ever fresh anxieties, and ever recurring toil.

A Number of *Kunst und Alterthum* is also coming to the front, and much else besides; meantime *Faust* is looking askance at me from one side, reproving me most bitterly, for not giving him the preference in my labour, him, the worthiest—and pushing all else aside.

I am also extremely inconvenienced by the wonderful influx of manuscripts, which I am asked to touch up, and of printed things, concerning which I am requested to say a few kind words—a trouble from which I have seen our impatient Wieland suffer grievously in his old age—for after all, the result is neither important nor encouraging. Every person, no doubt, is entitled to make and to think as much of himself as possible, only he ought not to worry others about this, for they have enough to do with and in themselves, if they too are to be of some account, both now and in future.....

My surroundings still continue tuneless and unmelodious; one day lately I tried the effect of an Opera, but the big drum, which made our whole wooden house quake to the rafters, frightened me off any further attempt. On the other hand, my garden at the Seven Cross Roads entices me at every favourable hour; there, I succeed in collecting my thoughts, and harmonizing and centralizing them to many a good issue (*zu manchem guten Hervorbringen mich zu einigen und zu innigen*)......

There have been many messengers, ascending and descending the heavenly ladder between this and Berlin, who have looked in upon me, so I am much nearer to you than you may suppose.

Thy very own,
G.

238.—ZELTER TO GOETHE.

Berlin, 26th April, 1828.

. . . . Our *Fête* in honour of Milder, celebrated in my house on the 9th, as well as the Dürer fête on the 18th, succeeded beyond expectation. For the latter occasion Felix wrote music,* which, in spite of the words, contains beautiful passages; the workmanship is masterly throughout. . . . .

Z.

239.—GOETHE TO ZELTER.

Weimar, 2nd May, 1828.

Enclosure sent by Goethe to Zelter, and headed,

For the Friends of Mademoiselle Sontag.

OLD and young are talking of Mademoiselle Sontag. She could not have been better received in Berlin or Paris, than she has been in London. She will undoubtedly carry away a good purse-full with her from here. Such facility and finish in singing have never been heard here before. I saw her on her first appearance, and shall never regret it. However, as all the papers are talking about Sontag's singing, I will merely add this. It was the French Ambassador, Prince Polignac, who introduced her at the Duke of Devonshire's, where, (Royalty excepted,) our great people here first made her acquaintance. At a ball given by the same Duke, Sontag was also among the guests, and she danced there with singular grace; everyone who managed to exchange a few words with her, seemed to

---

* *The Sons of Art*, a Cantata.

think himself very fortunate. Such distinction is without parallel in London. To-morrow a grand Drawing Room is to be held at Court, and it is thought, that the whole of the brilliant assemblage will attend the Opera in the evening, to hear Sontag again in the *Barbiere di Seviglia*. Should the King too intend to hear her one evening at the Opera—as no doubt he will,—the immense crowd will make it rather a dangerous affair.

To those who are interested in great Technical Enterprises.

In spite of all mishaps, the work in connection with the Thames Tunnel is being proceeded with. Not only the Company, but the nation itself seems to have made it a point of honour. You know what that means. An Englishman would rather become bankrupt, than allow himself to be disgraced. The whole nation acts in the same spirit. . . . .

G.

240.—GOETHE TO ZELTER.

Weimar, 21st May, 1828.

. . . . I MUST further remark, that like the Magician's Apprentice, I am threatened with drowning, by the flood of universal literature that I myself have called forth. Scotland and France pour themselves out almost daily; in Milan they are publishing a very important daily paper called *L'Eco;* it is in every respect admirable, reminding one of the familiar style of our morning papers, but it takes a broad intellectual view of things. Draw the attention of the Berliners to it; they may commendably season their daily dishes with it.

In consequence of this, I must tell you, that I now know what reception *Helena* met with in Edinburgh, Paris, and Moscow. It is very instructive, thus to become acquainted with three different modes of thinking: the Scotchman seeks to penetrate into the work, the Frenchman to understand it, the Russian to apply it to himself. Perhaps a German reader might combine all three endeavours. . . . .

Thy very own
GOETHE.

A graceful translation of my small poems * gave rise to the following parable, which I herewith send you, as a forerunner of the next Number:—

> I plucked some flowers, the meadow's bloom,
> And full of thought, I took them home;
> There, by my warm hand circled round,
> Their crowns were drooping to the ground.
> I set them in a fresh cool glass;
> And lo, a wonder came to pass!
> The little heads looked up so gay,
> The leafy stems in green array;
> And all as healthy, sweet and good,
> As though on Mother Earth they stood.

> So was it, when I heard my song,—
> And marvelled,—in a foreign tongue.

241.—ZELTER TO GOETHE.

27th May, 1828.

.... YESTERDAY, being Whit-Monday, Professor Hegel paid me an early morning call; then came Professor Wolff, and it was agreed to look up a fourth man for a rubber of whist this evening. That man turned out to be Wilken; so four German Professors were together in peace until midnight. *Cosa rara.* . . . .

Z.

242.—ZELTER TO GOETHE.

4th June, 1828.

SURELY it is a loss, that Lessing † did not have it out with you over *Götz von Berlichingen*, as he really would have enjoyed it, and he must have been sufficiently roused

---

* Goethe's poems were translated into French in 1825 by Madame Panckoucke, under the title, *Poésies de Goethe*. He could enjoy his *Faust* in Gérard's translation, when he no longer cared to read it in his own language.

† In a subsequent letter, Zelter thus alludes to Lessing's exclamation on reading *Werther*, "Lessing pleases me most, the earnest, severe, powerful Lessing, touched in spite of himself, tender, affectionate : ' Dear Goethe, one little chapter more!' "

for discussion. He was the man in defiance of whom, and for whose delight, you, in pure mischief, would have thrown off many a piece, and you might have shaken his over-firm faith in Aristotle, and made a breach in it here and there, for Lessing was an honest heart. He has done more than Aristotle; he has tried himself, and actually shown what cannot be done. Goethe's farce, satirizing Wieland,* doubtless gave him the greatest amusement. As a necessary consequence of his sentiments about Wieland, he must have envied you this farce, which he would much rather have written himself. Without this farce, the excellent Euripides would perhaps have long remained an unfamiliar friend to me, for at that time I thought very highly of Wieland, whom I only began to suspect, from his panegyric of Schweizer. Professor Engel too was of a similar opinion. As Schweizer's airs, especially those given to Hercules, the boastful, did not please me, I set the words to music for myself, and after singing them to Engel, he said, "Capital! but why will you wear yourself out with such a shabby Hercules? A calfskin is the proper thing for such a fellow."

Otherwise, Schweizer was not amiss, even if he was not on a level with his contemporary, Georg Benda of Gotha,† whose *Romeo and Juliet* I still affectionately remember, because his whole personality was thoroughly sympathetic to me. So true a musician I have never seen again; my darling wish was to become as *he;* he too was attached to me. With him all was truth and openness, and he had absorbed just so much of Italy as a clever German of his time could take in. With Naumann it was quite another thing, for he never knew where to stop, and so too he came to an end. But you, I expect, must have known these men yourself, for they were nearer to you. So too with *Götz von Berlichingen;* Lessing grudges it you, and cannot hide his

---

* *Götter Helden und Wieland*, a farce thrown off by Goethe one Sunday afternoon, in a fit of irritation at the Letters in *Der Deutsche Merkur*, comparing Wieland's Operetta, *Alceste*, to the Tragedy of Euripides.

† A famous clavier-player and oboist. His Duodrama, *Ariadne auf Naxos*, (1774,) was the first of its kind. His *Medea* was equally successful.

vexation. Just think a moment: is it not impertinent, that a stripling from Frankfurt should, like a second Prometheus, construct *such* beings out of *such* clay, whether you like it, or whether you don't, and pass by all the gods, without lifting his hat? . . . .

Z.

243.—GOETHE TO ZELTER.

Dornburg, 10th July, 1828.

SAD to the inmost heart, I was forced to spare my eyes and ears at least, so on the 7th of July I repaired to Dornburg, to escape those gloomy functions * through which—as is both right and proper—we give the multitude a symbolical illustration of its recent loss, which, in the present instance, it certainly feels in every sense.

I do not know if you are acquainted with Dornburg, a small town on the height in the Saale-valley, below Jena; in front of it, just on the slope of the Kalkflötz ridge, is a series of Castles, big and little, which have been built at widely different periods, and there are villas, surrounded by pretty gardens. I am occupying the little old Castle at the southernmost end, which has been newly done up. The view is glorious and inspiriting, the well-kept gardens are full of blooming flowers, the trellised vines are covered with rich clusters of grapes, and below my window I see a thriving vineyard,† which was planted on the most barren of hill-sides, only three years ago, by the Deceased, who loved to rejoice in the first green leaves of it, even so lately as last Whitsuntide. On the other side, the bowers of roses are quite fairy-like in their bloom, and the

---

* The funeral of the Grand Duke, Karl August. The news of his death, on the 14th of June, was broken to Goethe on the day following, by his son August. Goethe was inconsolable. "I thought," said he, "that I should depart before him; but God disposes as He thinks best; and all that we poor mortals have to do, is to endure and keep ourselves upright as well and as long as we can." See Eckermann's *Conversations of Goethe*, p. 322.

† " I . . . . bold spiritual communion with the tendrils of the vine, which say good things to me, and of which I could tell you wonders." See Eckermann's *Conversations of Goethe*, p. 323.

mallows, and I know not what besides, are blossoming and gay; to me all this appears in heightened colours, like a rainbow on a dark gray background.

For fifty years past, I have frequently enjoyed life on this spot with *him*, and could not at this time have stayed at any place, where the beautiful results of his activity could have been more strikingly brought before me. The more ancient part has been preserved and restored, the new bit, (I mean the little Castle I am living in, which was formerly private property,) has been suitably and carefully arranged, and connected with the old Castle gardens by lovely sloping walks and terraces. It is sufficiently spacious for a numerous household, if no exorbitant demands are made; there is no fuss nor pedantry, yet everything the gardener* is called upon to do, is perfect, the laying out of the grounds, as well as the flowers-beds.

And as it is, so it will continue, for the younger master and mistress can also understand what is good and suitable in these arrangements, and they have given proofs of this for several years past, when staying here on longer or shorter visits. It is a pleasant feeling too, that one about to leave the world, should give into the hands of the survivors, a kind of clue, by which they are enabled to guide their onward steps.

I too intend to keep the symbol granted to me, and to abide by it.

I want you to know, how your friend here, in his airy Castle, overlooking a pretty valley, with flat meadows, hilly fields, and vegetation reaching up to the steep, inaccessible edges of the forest, spends these long days from sunrise to sunset, so I will tell you in confidence, that for some time past I have been induced by foreign agencies, to take up again the study of natural science. Dear old Germany is quite unique in her peculiarity; I have been honestly on the watch to see, whether, among the results of the Scientific meetings, which have been going on for the last three years, I could find anything that might rouse, interest, and excite me, who for

---

* The Court-Gardener, Sckell, afterwards published a record of Goethe's stay in Dornburg.

the last fifty years have been passionately devoted to the study of Nature; but with certain exceptions here and there,—though even these, in truth, contributed only to my knowledge,—I have gained nothing, no new claim has been made on me, no new gift offered me, so I was obliged to turn the interest into capital, and now I am going to see what fruit the *summa summarum* produces abroad. Keep this to yourself, please, for I have just remembered, that the scientific world is again about to meet in Berlin, in great force.

May all good be with you!

G.

244.—GOETHE TO ZELTER.

Castle Dornburg, 26th July, 1828.

.... I REMEMBER well your telling me how delighted you were with the valley of the Saale, between Naumburg and Jena, and I thought of you affectionately from the very first. The terraces, like a Ducal garden, which expects its owner every moment, are in good order, and carefully attended to, all the summer flowers showing their gayest colours, and the vines hanging in such rich clusters, that the sight is quite amazing.

I send you a print, which, though I cannot exactly praise it, will at all events give you an idea of the place, more rapidly than any mere description would. The names below, referring to the letters above, will give you the necessary explanation. And your friend is dictating his present letter, behind the windows, (so far off, that they are almost invisible,) of the little castle, that stands on the edge of the rock to the left; this is the private property, lately acquired by their Royal Highnesses. . . . .

You will readily believe that during the last twenty days, I have got through a good deal of work, the outcome of *ennui*, unrest, and a feeling that work I must; unfortunately, it is so various in kind, that the publication will be no easy matter. My near hope of giving you all, the continuation of *Faust*, at Michaelmas, has also been frustrated by these events. If this continuation does not point to an extravagant condition of things, if too it does not force the reader to rise above his ordinary level, it is nothing worth. As far as it has gone, I think a good head will have enough to do, to master all that is hidden away in it. You are the very man for this, and consequently, the time before the continuation appears, will not hang too heavy on your hands.

The beginning of the second Act is successful; we will say this out with all modesty, because, were it not already in existence, we should not put it on paper. It now remains to link it to the first Act, the invention of which is completed down to the last detail, and which, but for this misfortune, would ere now have been ready, in a neat, clean copy. This too must be left to the uncertainties of time.

I can tell you thus much of the general state of feeling, that the first thought of every true heart is to continue on the path, marked out by the footsteps of the Departed; thereby those alterations which must be made, will at any rate become bearable, and in some points they may perhaps deserve applause. . . . .

Finally, as nothing essentially useful should be kept back from you, I must tell you that my table is well attended to, owing to the strange coincidence, that the Custodian of the Castle, my present host, was formerly employed in the Court kitchens, and is still able to do credit to his former vocation.

"That, at all events, sounds comfortable and pleasant!" you will say, and so it would, did not the gloomy catafalque appear at the same time in the background, exciting all those thoughts, which a man, in his cheerful moments, rightly lays aside. We might well be made dizzy by the rotation of human life, and the world around us.

Therefore keep firm on your feet, as far as you can, and I will endeavour to do the same.

Commending you heartily to all beneficent spirits,

Yours,
GOETHE.

Dornburg, 27th July, 1828.

245.—GOETHE TO ZELTER.

Dornburg, 27th July, 1828.

.... To turn to human affairs! I am glad you followed my advice, and directed your attention to Molière. Our dear Germans fancy they possess intellect (*Geist*), only when they are paradoxical, *i.e.* unjust. What Schlegel said about Molière in his lectures, wounded me deeply; * I kept silence for many years, but shall now bring forward one thing and another, with a view of exposing errors like these, for the comfort of many, who in our own day look before and after, and of many, who will do so in the future.

The French themselves are not quite clear about the *Misanthrope;* sometimes M. is supposed to have taken his model from a certain brusque courtier, sometimes to have described himself. Of course, he could not but draw it from his own heart, he had to delineate his own relations with the world; but what relations those were! the most universal that could possibly exist! I would wager you have caught yourself in the act of committing some folly, in more than one passage. And do you not play the same part towards your companions of the day? I am old enough by this time, yet hitherto I have not succeeded in going so far as to set myself by the side of the Epicurean gods. ....

As above, and ever,

Yours,

G.

.... I wish you could tell me of an author, from whom I could gain information, as to what kind of musical

---

* "To a man like Schlegel, a genuine nature like Molière's is a veritable eyesore; he feels that he has nothing in common with him, he cannot endure him. The *Misanthrope*, which I read over and over again, as one of my most favourite pieces, is repugnant to him; he is forced to praise *Tartuffe* a little, but he lets him down again as much as he can. Schlegel cannot forgive Molière for ridiculing the affectation of learned ladies; he feels probably, as one of my friends has remarked, that he himself would have been ridiculed, if he had lived with Molière." See Eckermann's *Conversations of Goethe*, pp. 230-231.

system was in vogue, during the first half of the seventeenth century, and how it could have been so expressed, that a Hamburg Rector, of that day, (Joachim Jungius,) was able to hand it down to his pupils in three printed sheets? I am just now occupied in studying that important epoch, to which we owe so much.

G.

246.—ZELTER TO GOETHE.

4th August, 1828.

You ask me—what kind of musical system was in vogue, during the first half of the seventeenth century, and how it could have been so expressed, that a Hamburg Rector of that day could hand it down to his pupils in three printed sheets? In the first place—so far as I can tell you,—there were many such treatises, partly copied by students of music, partly dictated by teachers; these take up very little room, inasmuch as they contain only single examples, or none at all. In Vienna I saw just such a treatise, the work of Wolfgang Amadeus Mozart; I myself have dictated several to my pupils—possibly Eberwein, your Musical Director, may have kept one of them. . . . . A relic of that time, still in much requisition, containing a collection of musical theories, is David Kellner's *True Instruction in Thorough Bass*, &c., a little tract consisting of less than a hundred pages, printed at Hamburg, in quarto, in the year 1732; this has outlived several editions. . . . .

Pietro della Valle, whom you know better than I do, places the music of his time high above that of the fifteenth and sixteenth centuries;* the chromatic scale had been smuggled in, and had given to music, character, suppleness, and freedom. . . . .

The subtler laws of harmony, by which a master in the art could be recognized, were already systematized at the end of the seventeenth century, although they were handed down only by tradition, to certain favoured persons. The product of that time appeared in a work by John Joseph

---

* *De musicâ ætatis suæ, in Joh. Bapt. Doni: de præstantiâ musicæ veteris libri III. Florentiæ*, 1647.

Fux, *Gradus ad Parnassum, sive manuductio ad compositionem musicæ regularem, nova ac certa nondum ante tam exacto ordine in lucem edita.* In accordance with this theory, the author had for years trained his illustrious pupil, Charles VI., who became a master in the art; and the cost of publishing the work in the Latin language, in a splendid folio edition, was defrayed by the Emperor, in the year 1725. The work has been translated into German;* the Latin edition is getting scarce, although I possess two copies.

The work is written, as all the educational works of Germany were in those days, in Question and Answer, between master and pupil, and people laugh at it now for that reason. The master was unwilling to appear before all the world, as superior to his illustrious pupil, and calls the pupil Joseph, (the author himself,) but the master, Aloysius, to wit Prænestinus, whose principles are here to be preserved for posterity, as being incomparable. Finally, these principles are the groundwork of all great and beautiful masterpieces of music, up to the present day; they are the manual of composition, and they leave to anyone who has mastered them, plenty of elbow-room to write what is beautiful correctly.

Yours,
Z.

247.—GOETHE TO ZELTER.

Dornburg, 9th August, 1828.

. . . . I FEEL twice as good-humoured with my old friend, Joachim Jungius, for having induced you to write those precious and instructive pages; they are just what I required, and something more; just as much as I understand, and in addition to that, something that I dimly feel. . . . .

If we want to get only half way to the proper understanding of a man, we must, before all things, study the age in which he lived, perhaps completely ignoring him the while; but finding, on our return to him, that we are fully satisfied with his conversation. Therefore I made it

* By Lorenz Mizler.

my business, to learn, if only imperfectly, what this thorough-going man might have dictated to his pupils, in the first half of the seventeenth century. Even at a very early age, he was Professor of Mathematics and Physics at Giessen, and later on, the practical part of the Theory of Sound could not have been a hidden or unfamiliar study to him.....

If, as I judge, Herr Mendelssohn practically influences Dr. Klöden's actions, he might perhaps try to further my wishes about the Fürstenwalder granite. I should, above all things, like to help the dear Prussians, on this side the Oder and the Spree, to a solid primeval mountain, so that we might not—as heretofore—have to borrow ignominiously from Sweden and Norway. Pardon me! but all these things amuse me. I know very well what I want, and I also know what the rest know, and how they would like to impose upon themselves and others. The greatest art of life, theoretical and worldly, consists in changing the *problem* into a *postulate;* by doing this, we gain our end. Whether your philosophers care to explain this to you, I do not know; my old Jungius, in his *Logica Hamburgensi*, has something to say about it.

I shall not trouble myself, as to the look of my scribble on paper. Glance now and again at the last tiny little Castle on the left of the engraving,* and take it kindly, that the friend, around whom an angry storm is raging, should turn his thoughts to you.....

Farewell! and in the midst of men, music, business, and diversion, think of me; take some passing moment by the wing, and compel it to let me have a good letter. Write as usual to Weimar,—although I have no intention yet of leaving this place, for where else should I find so much to look out upon and in upon? When I look down upon the slate-covered house, I think of you, my eyes resting on the little window, at which you may have sat in days gone by.

Yours ever,
G.

* See Letter 244.

248.—GOETHE TO ZELTER.

Dornburg, 26th August, 1828.

I AM asked to introduce and recommend to you Herr Chelard, *Maître de Chapelle de S. M. le Roi de Bavière*. He brings me this request from Weimar, whither he came with good letters of introduction; you will know him by his works. I do not quite understand his position; in Paris he wrote an Opera—*Macbeth*, with which he probably expected to open up a new path for himself; I fancy they never allowed it to be performed there, anyhow, I have never read anything about it in the Paris newspapers. Enough, it was either refused, or it failed; he took his score, went off to Germany, and came to Munich, where a German text was put to it, and the work was performed with great applause. The King conferred on him the above title. He is now going to Berlin, probably to make arrangements for a performance there, and if possible, to double the good reputation he has gained, and re-establish his celebrity in the Fatherland. He may, besides this, be looking about for other advantages, derivable from German music, for the furtherance of his own ends. All this you will soon see through and through for yourself; you will form your own opinion about it, and kindly assist him, as you think fit. . . . .

I have not yet seen Hegel's portrait, as they have not forwarded my boxes from Weimar. I dare say it is in one of them. I never doubted that you would all like Stieler's portrait of me. That excellent artist wrote about it to my son. You must, I think, have taken to the man himself. He is natural and truthful, and has developed his art in the right direction. . . . .

If you will bestow a few notes upon the enclosed verses, I should rejoice to get them back, and see them live anew.

Alas! I must once more revert to that desolating tempest; the furious storm and torrent of rain, which I drove through, in coming hither, on the evening of the 20th of July, was raging simultaneously from Havre de Grace and Nantes, across Lyons and Weimar, as far as Vienna, and who knows how much further eastwards? The very next day, it came upon you, and thus it has continued, alternating between you and us; I should be in utter despair, were it not that the vanity of having foretold it all is somewhat refreshing. And I cannot venture to hope for anything better, just at present. The misfortune is, that a high state of the barometer may—it is true—control the rain for the moment, but it cannot clear the atmosphere of clouds, nor rule the west wind; and thus, the moment it falls, incessant storm and rain set in, in full force. Do not quarrel with my way of expressing myself, for it will show you, just how I talk to myself. Those who have a professional knowledge of the weather, no doubt use other terms.

You are an admirer of old established laws. I will one day write down, what I think on the subject. These things are too great for us, merely because we always seek them, only in what is little. And so, ever in reverence for the all-prevailing powers,

Yours as of old,
G.

To the Rising Full Moon.

Dornburg, August, 1828.

Wilt thou suddenly enshroud thee,
  Who this moment wert so nigh?
Heavy rising masses cloud thee,
  Thou art hidden from mine eye.

Yet my sadness thou well knowest,
  Gleaming sweetly as a star!
That I'm lov'd, 'tis *thou* that showest,
  Though my lov'd one may be far.

Upward mount then! clearer, milder,
  Rob'd in splendour far more bright!
Though my heart with grief throbs wilder,
  Fraught with rapture is the night!

(Bowring.)

249.—Goethe to Zelter.

Dornburg, 7th September, 1828.

You, dearest Friend, have written often enough to please me, so I, at your request, make an effort to comply with your wish.

When I want to arrive at a partial explanation of the extremely various and irregular phenomena of the weather, I proceed thus: I assume the existence of *two* atmospheres, a lower and an upper one; the lower one does not extend particularly high, it really belongs to the earth, and has a violent tendency to carry itself and all that it contains from West to East; perhaps it may itself be obeying the diurnal movement of the earth. The peculiarity of this atmosphere is to generate water, especially when the barometer is low; the mists which rise from ponds, brooks, rivers, and lakes, then ascend, gather into clouds, and descend in rain, when the barometer falls still lower; when it is at its lowest point, raging storms are engendered.

The rise of the barometer however immediately effects a counterpoise; the wind blows from the East, the clouds begin to break, to contract, to be jagged at their upper ends, and gradually—in the form of mares' tails and of various light strips and lines, to rise into the upper regions, where, little by little, they lose themselves, so that when the barometer with us stands at 28 degrees, we can no longer see the smallest cloud in the sky, the east wind blows fresh and briskly, and it is only the *clearer* blue of the sky that still shows there is something overcast in the atmosphere, and that it is extended between us and the endless darkness.

What I have here stated is the pure law, eternally the same, in an alternation that cannot be further defined. This little bit of knowledge will enable one to judge of all other variations and contingencies, unless one allows oneself to be perplexed. But it is necessary to observe the following :—

I have only named *two* winds, the east wind and the west wind; the *north* in its operation is allied to the *east*, the *south* to the *west* wind, and thus we have two regions in the sky, opposed to each other, both as regards their position and their phenomena.

Let the above be borne in mind, and meanwhile assume it as a rule; then it will be easier to give some account of what follows.

For the last three or four years, the lower atmosphere has admitted an enormous accumulation of water, and the upper air cannot sufficiently maintain the balance. At a low state of the barometer, clouds accumulate upon clouds, the west wind drives them from the sea on to the Continent, where mists enough are rising over the watered surface of the earth, and clouds are forming, and constantly being driven forward towards the east. And even though the barometer should rise, and the passage towards the east be checked, still the quantity of water and cloud engendered, is so great, that the upper air cannot absorb and disperse it. In this way, for some days past, with a rise in the barometer, we have had a north wind, though the sky, especially towards the south, is heavily laden, and filled with masses of cloud. To the north-east, behind heaps of clouds, we see the blue sky peering through, and in it we trace an effort to produce streaks and lines of fleecy cloud; we may be sure that no rain will descend, but the sky does not clear, and when the barometer falls lower than the middle point, we have streams and torrents of rain. Thus during the whole of August, the sky was clouded, even if it did not rain, so our vintage, which promised so well, was spoilt. The vines below, above, and close to me, attached to stakes and trellises, display rich clusters of swollen grapes, which however, not being thoroughly penetrated with heat, cannot ripen. So of what use to us is the good sense and advice of your *connoisseur* of vines, Kecht? * If, according to his plan, the wealth of grapes were doubled, our despair at their failure would be doubled likewise.

Having, in all I say above, placed the barometer, from first to last, in relation with every phenomenon, I will now, in conclusion, state the main point, viz. that I ascribe that elasticity, heaviness, pressure, (or whatever that may be called, by which an otherwise unobservable peculiarity of the atmosphere is made observable,) to the increased or diminished state of the earth's power of attraction. If it increases, it dominates the moisture; if it decreases, the mass of moisture increases, and we see those effects as the consequence. Now, as for some years the formation of water in the lower atmosphere has been increasing, even a

* J. S. Kecht of Berlin, inventor of a new method in the cultivation of the vine.

high state of the barometer can scarcely overpower it, for even at 28 degrees, the sky does not become perfectly clear.

At present, I do not know what more to say; for all the experiences of these last three years, to my mind resolve themselves into these simple propositions. The fearful torrents of rain on mountain heights last year, such as that at the sources of the Neisse, as well as the late phenomena in level districts, the hailstorm in Hanover, the violent tempests in Germany, the awful rush of waters on the evening of July 20th, which extended from Havre de Grace and Nancy across Lyons, over Thuringia, as far as Vienna,—a taste of which you may have experienced on the 21st—all this, I think, I find explained by the above.

Now, if we think how—in the rapid rotation of the globe—this tendency to storm and moisture sets in violently from the Great Western Ocean, across England, where, during this very year, agriculture has suffered from the wet, we are certainly peering into an Infinity, for the penetration of which our mental organs are perhaps unequal.

Get yourself a good barometer, hang it up near you, compare its rise and fall with the physiognomy of the atmosphere, with the movement of the clouds, and whatever else may strike you; and as you do so, think of me, as I am thinking of you, at this moment, now that, towards noon, the sunshine is at last breaking through. The most wonderful massive clouds are forming and settling on a sky, here and there of a deep blue; they are still being carried about and held up by the elastic air; were the barometer to sink, they would fall. Glorious in very truth, and fearful, are these masses, illuminated by the sun.

Take from these general and special statements what may interest and be of use to you; I have adopted this method of looking at things, for the last forty years, and so I am able to be on good terms with Nature; of course everyone must know best, how to adapt his own difficulties.

Meanwhile evening has set in, so now I will bring this day of storms to a close, with only a few words more. The barometer kept steady, the sky cleared gradually, though not entirely; before sunset there were only a few strips of cloud, hovering low on the horizon; but over the range of hills to the east, a few shining clouds, like mountains, had settled gloriously, the light and dark sides of which, nay, the very cast shadows of projecting masses, indicated a perfectly substantial body. The illuminated portions appeared yellowish red, those in the shade, blue. And as they were not too high, and remained stationary for hours, they looked all the more deceptively like snowy Alps. The highest point at all events might have rivalled Monte Rosa.

Dornburg, 7th September, 1828.

Sunday morning, at half-past five o'clock, there is a perfectly unbroken, impenetrable fog, the barometer has risen, the wind is in the north-east, the windows are covered with moisture. Now this would be according to rule, and it would promise a beautiful, happy dissipation of the mist, for which spectacle I wish you could be here, as well as for the bright day which will follow it, of which more anon.

Evening.

And so it was too—a beautiful clear day, and by sunset, the sky was perfectly free from clouds; I drove down into the valley with a friend, and crossed over the bridge you know of, to the right bank. We ascended a hill between meadows, fields and vineyards, from which we could see the Saale below us, winding up and down the valley, through a fertile district. To the south, Jena was distinctly visible.

The whole scene was beautifully lit up. The chain of Castles about Dornburg, with the buildings at the back, and the town rising among the jagged masses of rock,—all this in shadow really looked quite solemn and dignified; whilst we up here in the sunshine, could view our territory to the right and left.

Monday, 8th September, 1828.

The barometer has gone up to 27″ 8‴ degrees; at six o'clock this morning, the fog was as thick as it was yesterday, yet we are sure to have a fine day, of which more by-and-bye.

And so the barometer has to-day uttered an emphatic

quos ego. It was just striking nine, the atmosphere had become perfectly clear, and the objects in the valley were peeping out from behind a faint mist. As everywhere else, so too it is in the World's history; as soon as Charles Martel appeared, the chaos which had enveloped Gaul and the rest of the world, disappeared. Happily Pepin and Charlemagne follow, but then again a long period of chaos.

Thursday, 11th September, 1828.

. . . . I drove back to Weimar, and thus my uninterrupted view came to an end at the same time with my contemplation of the heavens. Business had to be despatched, whatever the weather might be; the barometer moved up and down, the weather changed likewise, and there was nothing further to be said about it :—

> For with the heavenly bill of fare,
> The same old trumpery's always there.

. . . . As I am anxious to send off these pages to-day, and am prevented from filling them, though unwilling to leave them empty, I am going to have copied out for you, the contents of some leaflets, countless numbers of which are lying before me. I should like to classify them. Meanwhile take them unclassified, as they come into the writer's hands.

In the history of natural science one invariably remarks, that investigators hurry too quickly from the phenomenon to the theory, and thus become inadequate, hypothetical.

There is a delicate kind of empiricism, which identifies itself most intimately with the subject, and thereby becomes actual theory. This heightening of the intellectual faculty however, belongs to a highly cultivated age.

The most objectionable people are the quibbling investigators and the crotchety theorists; their endeavours are petty and complicated, their hypotheses abstruse and strange. Worthy Wünsch was one of this sort. Minds like his are easily satisfied with mere words, and they hinder the advance of science, for in point of fact one has to make after-experiments, and to clear up what they have obscured. Now, as there are not many, whose business it is to do this, the matter is allowed to rest, and some degree of value is ascribed to their endeavours, though no one is to blame for it.

Whole, half-, and quarter-mistakes are very difficult and troublesome to correct, and to sift, and it is hard to set what is true in them in its proper place.

It is not always necessary, that truth should be embodied, it is sufficient, if it hovers about in the spirit, producing harmony; if—like the chime of bells—it vibrates through the air, solemnly and kindly.

When one considers the problems of Aristotle, one is astonished at his gift of observation, and at all that the Greeks had an eye for; only they err in being over-hasty, for they go directly from the phenomenon to the explanation, thereby producing very inadequate theoretical conclusions. This however is a general mistake, that is still made, even in our own day.

In reality we only know, when we know a little; as we learn more, doubt gradually sets in.

No phenomenon can be explained by itself and of itself; only a number of them, when viewed collectively, and arranged methodically, end by yielding something that may pass for theory.

And yet Natural Science is as much in need of a categorical imperative as Moral Science,—only let it be borne in mind, that this does not bring us to the end, but merely to the beginning.

Yours ever,
G.

Weimar, 5th October, 1828.

(Forgive this more than casual communication.)

250.—Zelter to Goethe.

19th October, 1828.

. . . . Yesterday evening I went in a fit of despair to the Theatre—*Preciosa*. The story is illustrated by dance and choral music, with Recitatives spoken to music, so that you understand neither the one nor the other—they call it Melodrama, and it is described on the play-bill as *Schauspiel mit Gesang*, (a play with incidental music,) which means neither one thing nor the other, through four short Acts; even these are much too long, as really there is no action, and everyone is bored. The actors do not understand themselves, why they are all turned out so smartly; one is always waiting for the other to do something. The composer has taken the greatest pains, by strange modulation and all kinds of *tempi*, to produce a gloomily humouristic work, characteristic of a gipsy mob. The people in the Theatre and Orchestra do not know what they are listening to, nor what they are playing, and the public sits as quiet as a Church mouse, until it is all over.

A pretty stranger appeared for the first time as Preciosa. She is said to be her Prince's intimate friend. Who would like to see the object of his affections on the street like that? Were she mine, she should stay properly at home.

It now occurs to me for the first time, that poet and composer are no longer alive. *De mortuis nil.* I dare say you see what kind of humour I am in. Fling away my letter, and forgive

Yours,
Z.

251.—Goethe to Zelter.

Weimar, 30th October, 1828.

. . . . As you cannot be rid of the Theatre, get as much pleasure out of it as you can; but do not modify your criticism. Of what use is all the splendour of days gone by, if the nullity of the present is to be allowed to obtrude itself, simply because for the moment, it enjoys the privilege of being present and alive?

That worthy fellow, Oehlenschläger,* has given me personally a great deal of worry; he persisted, on his return from Italy, in wanting me to let him read aloud that same *Correggio;* this I obstinately declined, but offered to look at the play quietly by myself, whereupon he flew into such a passion, that at last he behaved quite like a madman. Indeed I have had to put up with a great deal from this brood.

He is one of those halves, that think themselves a complete whole, and something more. These sons of the North go to Italy, they get no further than to prop their bear upon his hind legs, and when he learns to dance a bit, then they think it is all right. . . . .

There are some Tyrolese here again, and I mean to get them to sing me their little songs, although I cannot stand their beloved *Jodeln,* except in the open air or in large rooms. . . . .

I have enjoyed some excellent talk with the returning Naturalists.† But when carefully considered, it will ever remain an established truth, that what I know well, I in reality know only for myself; as soon as I come out with it, conditions, definitions, and contradictions are immediately thrust upon me. This happens to you oftener than to me, as you come into contact, and have dealings with all sorts of people; and yet I am as certain to meet with opposition in my own house, as if I looked for it in the market-place. The safest plan is always to endeavour to change all that is in us and of us into action; then let others speak of it and treat it just as it pleases them.

G.

252.—Zelter to Goethe.

14th November, 1828.

Yesterday evening, we treated the public to Handel's *Samson.* . . . . We had just heard the sorrowful news of the death of the Dowager Empress of Russia; it was

---

* Author of *Correggio*, a Tragedy. Zelter had witnessed a performance of it in Berlin; Emil Devrient acted the part of the hero.

† There was a meeting of scientific men at Berlin in 1828, many of whom paid Goethe a visit on their way home.

a double loss to us, for the King sent an excuse. In other respects, we had an attentive and grateful audience. The Duke of Cumberland, who, as a rule, invariably complains of our having no organ, on this occasion declared himself fully satisfied.

Handel, who was a distinguished organist, wrote no organ-part for any of his Oratorios, though he looked after the Chorus most assiduously and artistically. Were he still alive, he must have said, "With such a Chorus as that, I will have no organ!" Even if he did not say it, he carried it out in practice. An organ may be necessary, either to veil, or to fill up the weakness of a Chorus. On the other hand, played neither wisely nor well, it may weaken and spoil the best choir. I was obliged to say as much to Cramer, the English king's *Capellmeister*, who was here a short time ago, for I know how it fared with the Choirs, throughout England, from the best source, (Handel himself,) and it is just the same now. Those people might confound us, but that we are old hands. If they are in love with themselves and their pit-coal, who shall blame us for loving what it is in our power to have? What business have they to talk about Handel?

Our knight, Spontini, was full of admiration, and said, "*Laissez-moi vos chœurs.*" Youth and beauty of every rank, disciplined, brought into order, and properly balanced, ought, it is true, to make an impression upon anyone, unless like me, he has had for years past to work from the centre of the organization outwards, and, all through the varying seasons of success and failure, to go on unweariedly accumulating fresh stores.

The cost of training the Choruses of the Theatre Royal amounts yearly to six thousand *Thalers*; for that sum they ought to be better, if the teachers realized even their most elementary duties. Many of the Chorus do not know their notes, and are tortured into them by a violin, badly played. *Our* Choruses are sung by all, *a prima vista*, and the most difficult music often goes as well as possible at the third rehearsal, for they pull themselves together, and talking is not the fashion. The late King of Saxony was the first and last, who spoke to me on the subject, like a man who understood it,—and he gave me the loveliest gold snuffbox. Farewell, and think of

Thy
Z.

253.—GOETHE TO ZELTER.

Weimar, 16th December, 1828.

ENCLOSED herewith, you have at last a transcript of the worthy Jungius' *Harmonie;* it was difficult enough to get this done,—a translation, such as you wished, could not be managed. Amongst your musical friends and pupils, there is sure to be someone, who understands Latin, and who would go through the work with you; afterwards, I should like to have your full opinion of it, for I am anxious to raise a solid memorial to that worthy man.

I enclose a transcript of the letter you despatched at my request; what you say refers more particularly to the close of the seventeenth, and the beginning of the eighteenth century; but with regard to the state of music in 1650, the most reliable information is probably to be got from the pamphlet in question, for though the man was a thorough mathematician and logician, he had of his own free will devoted himself to animated nature, and had issued works in advance of his time. As to the varied interests it awakened in me, you must remember that he was a contemporary of Lord Bacon, Descartes, and Galileo, and yet he managed to keep himself perfectly original, both in his studies and his teaching. You will pardon this new exaction! All good attend you!

Most truly yours,
G.

254.—ZELTER TO GOETHE.

22nd December, 1828.

. . . . You did well not to spare my idle modesty; I can read the work pretty fairly off-hand. As the contents are musical, I could spell out what is problematical in it more easily than many a Latin scholar could put it into German for me; for many a mistake has arisen from the Germanizing of Greek and Latin terms of Art. The fundamental principles of Harmony, here laid down, were carried out in practice by Hans Leo Hassler,* Palestrina, and others, as early as the beginning of the sixteenth century, and they still hold their ground, though the most modern theorists would fain persuade us, that it is all quite different now. This is so little the case, that even the old mistaken definitions, quite as mistakenly Germanized, pass muster, e.g. *Soni dissoni sunt, quorum mixtura auditui ingrata est*—which to this day still runs: *A dissonance is a cacophony*. But a dissonance, (if you do not mean by that something absolutely unmusical,) is no cacophony. As well in its origin as in its resolution, it is—more correctly speaking—consonant, and it does duty for the harmony, into which it must resolve itself. Similarly, *dur* and *moll* are neither hard nor soft, yet everyone knows what is meant by the terms, so long as people do not translate them into German.

Yours,
Z.

* A pupil of the famous Gabrieli. Proske, speaking of his style, says that he "imitates all the greatest beauty and dignity that can be found in both the Italian and German art of that day. The well-known chorale, *Herzlich thut mich Verlangen* or *Befiehl du deine Wege*, so much used by Bach in the Passion, was originally a love song, *Mein Gemuth ist mir verwirret*, in his *Lustgarten deutscher Gesänge* (1601)."

1829.

255.—GOETHE TO ZELTER.

Weimar, 2nd January, 1829.

.... My mother used to say, when she was overrun with visitors, "I could not get time to blow my nose"—I am glad to think of you in a similar predicament. ....

I could not possibly spare Herr Krüger even a few hours, though he deserved it, for I am deeply indebted to him for his portrait of Prince William. But no one can understand how I value *a succession* of hours, for the interrupted ones are, in my opinion, not only completely lost, but hurtful and disturbing into the bargain. It is the same with strangers, who do not understand what I am robbed of, just by an interruption.

And yet it is always disagreeable to me, when, in self-defence, I am obliged to refuse to see people, who have come from a distance.

You might complain much in the same way, but as a musician, you are forced to keep up with the world; of me the world has nothing, except what it can see in black and white.

When I have properly equipped my *Wanderers,** and sent them off, you light-minded people may receive them as you can; I, however, shall at once turn to Nature, and first of all, I shall try to further a French translation of my *Metamorphose der Pflanzen,†* with some additions. My two months' stay in Dornburg revived and encouraged my old reflections, most agreeably.

I must now really try and see, day by day, hour by hour, what can be done to make good the foundation of our principles, and practically to fortify it. There are some very clever youngsters, but every Tom-fool wants to begin from

---

* An allusion to *Wilhelm Meister's Wanderjahre.*
† The French translation was made by Soret.

the very beginning, to be independent, original, absolute, self-sufficient, to keep apart from others, to look straight ahead, and whatever else you may choose to call all those follies. I have been watching this course of things, since the year 1789, and I know what might have happened, had any one man cut straight in, without reserving a *peculium* for himself. Now, in 1829, it is my duty to become clear about what lies before me, and perhaps to give it expression, but even if I succeed in this, it will do no good, for truth is simple, and gives little trouble, but falsehood gives occasion for the frittering away of time and strength.

And now, accept what I have dictated for you in the solitary hour that I have gained, and give me an opportunity of being edified again by one of your welcome letters.

Yours unalterably,
J. W. v. GOETHE.

256.—GOETHE TO ZELTER.

Weimar, 6th January, 1829.

CANZONETTA NUOVA

sopra la Madonna, quando si portò in Egitto col bambino Gesù e San Giuseppe.*

ZINGARELLA.

Dio ti salvi, bella Signora,
E ti dia buona ventura!
Ben venuto, vecchiarello,
Con questo bambino bello!

MADONNA.

Ben trovata, sorella mia!
La sua grazia Dio ti dia;
Ti perdoni i tuoi peccati
L'infinita sua bontade.

---

* See *Egeria*. Raccolta di Poesie Italiane popolari, cominciata da Guglielmo Mueller e pubblicata da O. L. B. Wolff. Lipsia, 1829, p. 73.

ZINGARELLA.

Siete stanchi e meschini,
Credo, poveri pellegrini,
Che cercate d'alloggiare.
Vuoi, Signora, scavalcare?

MADONNA.

Voi, che siete, sorella mia,
Tutta piena di cortesia,
Dio vi renda la carità.
Per l'infinita sua bontà!

ZINGARELLA.

Son'una donna zingarella;
Benchè sono poverella,
Ti offerisco la casa mia,
Benchè non è cosa per tia.

MADONNA.

Sia per me Dio lodato,
E da tutti ringraziato!
Sorella, le vostre parole
Mi consolano il mio cuore.

ZINGARELLA.

Or scavalca, Signora mia;
Hai una faccia d'una Dia,
Ch'io terrò la creatura,
Che sto core m'innamora.

MADONNA.

Noi veniam da Nazaretto;
Siamo senza alcun ricetto,
Arrivati alla strania,
Stanchi e lassi dalla via.

ZINGARELLA.

Aggio qua una stallella
Buona per sta somarella;
Paglia e fieno ce ne getto,
Vi è per tutti lo ricetto.

Se non è come meritate,
Signoruccia, perdonate;
Come posso io meschina
Ricettare una regina?

E tu, vecchiarello, siedi,
Sci venuto sempre a piedi;
Avete fatto, oh bella figlia,
Da trecento e tante miglia.

Oh ch'è bello sto figliarello,
Che par fatto col pennello!
Non ci so dare assomiglio;
Bella madre e bello figlio.

Hai presenza di regina;
Lo mio core l'indovina,
Questo figlio è il tuo sposo;
Troppo è bello e grazioso.

Se ti piace, oh mia Signora,
T'indovino la ventura.
Noi, Signora, così sino
Facciam sempre l'indovino. etc etc.

The gipsy then modestly goes on to relate to the Virgin, what has happened since the Annunciation, and what will happen in the future. All this in rhymes so graceful, that you could not ask for better from a legend. It is thus that Italian children and women sing at their ease an artless harmony of the four Evangelists, and strengthen in their minds the Christian faith.

Anyone who recollects with pleasure the *Conversation between Christ and the Woman of Samaria*,* (which I published many years ago,) will be none the less delighted with this parallel.

I hope this poem, and the enclosed extract will divert you somewhat, until I get the better of my present, overworked condition, and am able to answer your friendly letters with something more than superficial words. . . . .

In haste, yours truly,

G.

ENCLOSURE.

On the Performance of Faust at the Théâtre de la Porte St. Martin, in Paris, 8th of November, 1828.

"It is Goethe's Faust; it is Gretchen, Mephistopheles, Martha, but travestied, materialized, confined to earth and hell,—all the spiritual part is effaced. We have every

* See *Ueber Italien*, a part of *Die Italiänische Reise*.

scene in the original, but all at cross purposes—the walk in the garden, the flaming wine, (though this is in a village alehouse,) the prison, the scene with the witches, even the Blocksberg. The arrival of Gretchen, the laugh of Mephistopheles, are true to Retsch's outlines. He has retained the laugh, but it is a wild, scoffing laugh, in everything else he is a Catholic devil. Faust's compact becomes valid at the first crime. Gretchen does not murder her child, but she poisons her mother with a sleeping draught, which Faust hands her, to secure a *rendez-vous,* when the devil increases the dose. For this, she is put upon the rack, and after she has been brought back, we see her cowering in horror, on her bed of straw, tearing at her chains, and pointing, mad with agony, to her wounds. Martha disguises herself, and comes to save her; Faust enters, fails to recognize her, and strikes at her. So passes the interval; Gretchen might but will not fly, and the executioner comes to fetch her. We have already seen the scaffold outside, and the crowd awaiting her. Scarcely has she come out, when a cloud descends, and as it rises again, we see Paradise above, in Bengal lights, Gretchen among the gods, kneeling at the feet of the Virgin, and Faust among the devils and the flames, in the usual style. All this allows of more than twenty different scenic decorations, many of which are brilliant surprises. The journals and daily papers have taken offence at it; even at this, the fourth representation, I heard a few pious hisses. However, the piece will pay its expenses. The common people will not find it wanting in interest; the contrast is what interested me.

"As Gretchen is kneeling before the image of the Virgin, the devil rises out of the earth, upon an enormous pedestal, formed of monsters and serpents, and thunders down his curses upon her, from this height; this is the way the people of Paris theatricalize the evil spirit, whispering into the ear! I must also mention a waltz, danced by Mephistopheles and Martha, which is really ingenious. The devil has her wholly in his power, as a magnetizer has the person who is being magnetized; with horrible energy she follows his gesticulations, her expression changing quickly from the coarsest, most abandoned sensuality, to an agony of pain and terror."

257.—GOETHE TO ZELTER.

Weimar, 18th January, 1829.

AFTER Easter, my readers will be good enough to make a walking-tour in the high Alpine valleys, with the familiar *Wanderers*,* (who will appear at that opportune season,) and there content themselves awhile, amongst the spinners and weavers. In case you like to prepare beforehand, listen to what follows.

A thoughtful and discerning friend, who undertook the business of looking over my manuscript, before it was sent to press, returned it to me with the following remarks:—

" It is pleasant to find oneself in the spinning-rooms of those simple, honest, mountain folk. Your description of these last in particular was doubly interesting to me, for I must confess that in former days I knew nothing more wretched, than the life of weavers and spinners in towns, and it was only on my last journey, that I had a very different experience, in the family life of an honest Swiss, at Leuk. I have observed that these weavers know how to express themselves better than other artisans, and I still remember my conversation with them. When I confessed my surprise, that with so large a family,—(four children were spinning beside their mother,)—he could live in so small a room, he answered quite cordially, 'And what will you say, when you hear that in addition to the weaver, two other labourers, a shoemaker, and a porkbutcher, live in this same nest, and that they all sleep in the same bed, and sit on the same chair? I am myself this Trinity, so you can understand, that we all get on very well together here, as I myself set so good an example.'"

I send the above to amuse you beforehand, asking you to keep the scene in your mind, when your friends, the Wanderers, introduce you to those regions.

At the same time, accept my best thanks for the kind reception you gave to my 'Holy Family in Egypt,† and their hostess. I own that when reading this and similar poems, I feel as if I were eating sweets, biscuits or the like;

* See Note to Letter 255.
† See the Italian poem, Letter 256.

food I admit, but a dainty morsel, such as women and children may find very toothsome in their native land. As a rule, Italian children have something inconceivably gentle, attractive, and graceful about them, which is in perfect harmony with this song.

A truce to these reflections, and let me beg you to tell me faithfully about Holtei's *Faust*,* as he appears to such a kindly disposed and well-meaning friend as you are. I no longer recognize my old theatrical friend in the newspaper; at one time it is all forbearance and hesitation, at another, enthusiasm got up to order.

"As it is constituted, so will it abide," says *Reineke Fuchs*.

To fill up the remaining space, let me tell you, that I have been presented with the portrait of a famous Frascate beauty; standing before her, one feels as though one were in the beneficent sunshine.

Yet it is somewhat strange! These regular features, this perfect health, this intensely self-complacent cheerfulness, has something offensive about it to us poor cripples of the North, and we can understand, why our works of art are sickly, because otherwise no one would look at them.

A few days ago, a very well-painted *Ecce Homo* stood in this place; everyone who looks at that will feel comfortable and at his ease, because he sees before him someone who is worse off than himself. Space compels me to finish at the right time; so be it ever!

G.

258.—ZELTER TO GOETHE.

24th January, 1829.

As, in your letter of the 18th of January, you talk of the pictures you have been lucky enough to get, I want to tell you, that Ternite made me a similar present on my birthday. It is a likeness of the botanist, J. Usteri. .... To me, the special charm lies in its exquisite resemblance to the face and figure of our Sebastian Bach, in his modest, grey-green cloth coat. I think I never yet

* See Note to Letter 236.

saw flesh and blood of the same colour. It reminds me of the following story.

Kirnberger had just such a portrait of his master, Sebastian Bach; it was my constant admiration, and it hung in his room, between two windows, on the wall above the piano. A well-to-do Leipzig linendraper, who had formerly seen Kirnberger, when he was a chorister at the *Thomas-Schule*, singing in a procession before his father's door, comes to Berlin, and it occurs to him, to honour the now celebrated Kirnberger with a visit. Hardly were they seated, when the Leipziger bawls out, "Why, good Lord! you've actually got our Cantor, Bach, hanging there; we have him too in Leipzig, at the *Thomas-Schule*. They say he was a rough fellow; why, the conceited fool did not even have himself painted in a smart velvet coat." Kirnberger gets up quietly, goes behind his chair, and lifting it up with both hands in the guest's face, exclaims, first gently, then *crescendo*, " Out, you dog! Out, you dog!" My Leipziger, mortally frightened, seizes his hat and stick, makes with all haste for the door, and bolts out into the street. Upon this, Kirnberger has the picture taken down and rubbed, the Philistine's chair washed, and the portrait, covered with a cloth, restored to its old place. When someone inquired, what was the meaning of the cloth? he answered, "Leave that alone! There's something behind it." This story was the origin of the report, that Kirnberger had lost his senses.

Z.

259.—GOETHE TO ZELTER.

Weimar, 26th January, 1829.

I WAS very much pleased to hear of your invitation to the *Ritterfest*, and it enhanced my satisfaction to find that you were No. 17 in the newspaper, and in such excellent company; now you yourself will give me the details, as between friend and friend.

Anything that lifts a man out of the common herd, always redounds to his advantage, even if it sinks him into a new crowd, in the midst of which his powers of swimming and wading must be put to the test again.

These marks of honour are really nothing but magnified encumbrances, upon which, notwithstanding, we must congratulate ourselves and others, because life—if it goes well—should ever be considered as a perpetual fight and a perpetual conquest.

Forgive these abstruse words, but I do not know how else to express myself; for in proportion as I think I understand myself better and better, I seem to become obscure to others. But you are such a queer fish, that nothing of that sort can fail to explain itself to you. . . . .

J. W. v. GOETHE.

260.—GOETHE TO ZELTER.

Weimar, 12th February, 1829.

. . . . I THINK I understand your complaints, or rather invectives against inadequate performances of music, prepared long beforehand. The tendency of the day to drag down everything, and make it weak and whining, is ever more and more prevalent. I could show you half a dozen poems, that have been written in my praise and honour, but in which I am actually treated as already one of the blest departed. It will end, according to the latest system of philosophy, in everything crumbling into *Nothing*, ere it has yet begun *to be*. . . . .

Now and then, by the wise management of our reigning Grand Duchess, I am called upon to attend to one or other piece of business, that may still be in keeping with my years and strength.

After as before, thy
GOETHE.

261.—ZELTER TO GOETHE.

14th February, 1829.

. . . . YESTERDAY, for the first time, I heard Auber's *Muette von Portici*. One may look upon the work as the beginning of a new *genre*, for it is neither an Opera proper, nor a Play, but a true Melodrama, only sung, instead of spoken. It is not inconsistent, and the interest is sufficiently sustained throughout the five Acts to give them real unity. Scribe's text is nothing particular. The leading character, a Neapolitan fisherwoman, has been seduced by the son of the Viceroy, who forthwith gets married to a Royal Princess. But why, and from what cause the lady is dumb, never appears. Running through all this, is a conspiracy of the Neapolitans against the Viceroy, who is inveighed against as a tyrant. The mounting of the piece is regal. Whoever has not seen Vesuvius in full action on the spot, let him come to Naples-Berlin, and we will show him a thing or two.

Yours,
Z.

262.—GOETHE TO ZELTER.

Weimar, 4th March, 1829.

IT is really for such old fellows as you, dearest Friend, that I have had the Schiller Correspondence printed now; the world of the present and the future, may make what they can of it. For them it is completely historical, and even so, it will be wholesome and serviceable to many intelligent readers; but to those who were living and working in those days, it will serve as a fuller and more convenient reference, should they wish to strike the balance of their lives.

But as a rule, it will interest every thoughtful person to look into the game, and see how the cards were dealt in those days, and with what various luck, skill, and ingenuity, every undertaking was carried on. . . . .

The exaggerations which are forced upon the Theatres of great, far-reaching Paris, injure us as well, for we have not got nearly far enough, to feel the want of them. But these are the consequences of the onward march of universal literature, and the only one comfort to be derived from it is, that even though the world in general is the worse for it, individuals are sure to reap the benefit; I have known very brilliant instances of this. For after all, what is truly rational and satisfactory is the inheritance of a few individuals, who work on quietly. . . . .

That very amusing anecdote of yours, about the servant,* who could not master the fact, that hot and cold water mixed produce tepid water, comes at the nick of time. It is rather like the Irish bulls, which are the result of a strange awkwardness of mind, and about which a good deal might be said from a physiological point of view. Here is one:—An Irishman is lying in bed; people rush in and call out, "Save yourself! the house is on fire!" "How so?" answers he, "sure, I am only a lodger here!" If you remember any others of a similar kind, or could tell me where to find them, you would be doing me a favour. I would let you know what I think about them.

The study of meteorological science, like so many other things, only issues in despair. The first lines of *Faust* are perfectly applicable here too. However, for the protection of truth, I must add, that he who does not ask for more than what is granted to man, will herein also be well rewarded for the pains he has taken. But it is not every man's way to be content. Here, as everywhere, people feel vexed at not obtaining what they want and expect, and then they fancy they have not received anything at all. For instance, you must, first of all, renounce foreknowledge and prophecy, and whom could we expect to do this? . . . .

Yours ever,
G.

263.—Zelter to Goethe.

9th March, 1829.

. . . . Your Irish Bull is worth as much as my story; I knew it partly in another form, though it is best as you have it. Passing into heroics, let me tell you the following:—Once, during the Carnival here, in the

---

* The passage referred to runs thus: "I knew Levin Markus, the father of Frau von Varnhagen, very well, as a humourist. On the day of his death, the cunning old fellow ordered his servant to bring him some water to wash in, and found fault with him, because it was as cold as ice, whereupon the servant fetched boiling water. 'You ox, am I a pig then, that you want to scald?' Back came the servant again. 'Not a drop of tepid water to be had, in the whole house!' L. M. gave a loud laugh, and expired."

middle of January, the lightning struck the King's Castle, and set it on fire. The hussar on guard rushes into Frederick the Great's Cabinet, "Your Majesty, it has come in. The Castle is on fire!" "Be off, and see that the staircase remains clear; I am busy," says Frederick.

One day, a drummer, who thought his honour insulted by the King, shot himself at the very door of the King's cabinet. "Bury him well!" said Frederick, "why was he only a drummer?" . . . .

You will already have seen from the paper, that we are going to perform *The Passion Music* of J. S. Bach. Felix has studied it under me, and is going to conduct it, so I give up my desk to him. One of these days I will send you the text, to which I have written a preface. Felix, owing to his friend Moscheles, has been invited to London, whence he may subsequently go to Italy. The lad is a joy to me, and it is good for him to get away from the parental roof. All that he wants intellectually, he takes with him, and I hope soon to hear more of him. *Vale!*

Yours,

Z.

264.—ZELTER TO GOETHE.

Berlin, 12th March, 1829.

OUR Bach music came off successfully yesterday, and Felix, without any fuss, held his forces well in hand. The King and the entire Court saw a closely packed house before them; I, with my score, posted myself in a small corner near the Orchestra, whence I could survey my little people and the public at the same time. About the work itself, I scarcely know what to say. . . . . Were it not that here and there a resemblance in melody to the more modern German operatic composers, such as Gluck and Mozart, reveals itself, bringing us back again for a moment to our own time, we should feel ourselves between heaven and earth, and thirty years older into the bargain. And it may be this, which makes the music in general scarcely practicable. But would that old Bach could have heard our performance! That was my feeling at every successful passage, and here I cannot but praise highly the whole body of my pupils at the *Singakademie*, as well as the Solo Singers, and the double Orchestra. You might say that the whole was an organ, in which every pipe was gifted with reason, power, and will,—nothing forced, no mannerism. There is no Duet, no Fugue, no beginning, no end, and yet all is as one, and everything in its place. A wonderful dramatic truth is followed out; one hears the False Witnesses, *i.e.* one sees them step forth; one sees the High Priests with their " What is that to us, &c. It is the price of blood; " and the *turba*, " Not on the feast-day, &c.," and the disciples, true, honourable followers, *bêtes*, " For what purpose was this waste? " They seem to be the very tones, which we knew not hitherto, but are now compelled to recognize. Then, after a while, the heartfelt lament for the glorious Son of Man, the Friend, the Councillor, the Helper, the Judge, &c. . . . . Stümer of the Theatre Royal, one of my former pupils, sang the narrative part so admirably, (especially at the performance,) that you heard the repetition of the Gospel words with delight. Before the performance, I had advised him not to hinder the progress of the story by sentimentality, and he did it as well as it could be done.

" Now, ye Muses, enough ! " Farewell, and " Know me, O my Shepherd ! "

Z.

265.—ZELTER TO GOETHE.

(Undated.)

IN compliance with a universal request, we have repeated the Passion Music before a full house. The old audience returned, and a new one came besides. The criticisms are tolerably different; and amongst many, one only shall be named, who has the right to judge,—a right as great as that of any other, and greater. Philosophers, who divide the Real from the Ideal, and throw away the tree, in order to recognize the fruit, are to us musicians, as we are with regard to their philosophy, of which we understand nothing, further than that we bring before their very door, the treasure which we have found. Hegel for instance! He is just now lecturing upon music ; Felix takes admirable notes, and—young rascal that he is—understands how to reproduce them very naïvely, with all his teacher's personal peculiarities. Now Hegel says, that Bach's is not the right kind of music; that now they are further advanced, although they are still a long way from the right thing. Well, that we know, or we don't know, as well as he, if he could only explain to us musically, whether he has already found the right thing. Meanwhile, let us go forward, *piano* and *sano*, as the God, whom we all serve, inspires us. For to be sure, we none of us know what to pray for, and yet we always pray for more and more; so let others do the same. . . . .

Yours,
Z.

266.—Goethe to Zelter.

Weimar, 28th March, 1829.

YOUR last letters, my dearest Friend, did me good, in jest and in earnest, for they came at a good time. The most recent, bringing news of the successful performance of that grand old musical work, has set me thinking. I seem to hear the distant roar of the sea. At the same time, I must congratulate you on such a perfectly successful rendering of that which it is wellnigh impossible to represent. I dare say, the connoisseur who is an associate of such an art, when listening to such works, has the same mental experience, that I myself had lately, when I set the legacy of Mantegna again before my eyes. It is Art already, Art in its entirety, its possibilities and impossibilities fully alive, and yet still undeveloped; were it not so, it would not be what it is here, not so venerable, not so rich in hope and in foundation. I heartily and ungrudgingly rejoice with you about Felix; among my many pupils, I have scarcely been so fortunate, even with a few. . . . .

Dr. Eckermann, whom I see daily, is by degrees cultivating purer and more sympathetic powers of criticism; with laudable patience, he is looking through an old and hopeless accumulation of manuscripts, tied up in bundles, and to my joy, he finds a good deal, worthy of being preserved and published; so the rest can now be safely burnt. . . . .

They want to give my *Faust* at the Theatre; with regard to that, I play a passive, not to say, a suffering part. However, on the whole, I need not feel uneasy about this piece, for Duke Bernard found it, in Upper Carolina, in the house of an Indian.

So much for to-day! All good wishes accompany this letter.

Your ever faithful
GOETHE.

267.—ZELTER TO GOETHE.

Berlin, 6th April, 1829.

. . . . I ENCLOSE you an extract about a similar little dispute,* which is just now to the fore; it will enable you to see what one has to contend with. In return, I present my adversary with a snare for so-called connoisseurs, and if he falls into it, he shall have it hotter next time. He is an earnest admirer of the compositions of W. Friedemann Bach, (eldest son of Sebastian Bach,) which I am not, and so he finds fault with me. *A propos* of this, he sent me an Organ Concerto by Friedemann Bach, and copied for me the saying of Quintilian, referred to in the letter. To save you the trouble of looking up chapter and page for yourself, here it is:—

"*Modeste tamen et circumspecto judicio de tantis viris judicandum est, ne, quod plerisque accidit, damnent quæ non intelligunt.*"

This Friedemann Bach of Halle was the most perfect organ-player, whom I have ever known. He died here in 1784, when I had already obtained my rights as a citizen, and had become Master-Mason. He was thought capricious, because he would not play for everybody; towards us young people he was nothing of the sort, and would play for hours together. As a composer, he had the *Tic douloureux* of being original, of separating himself from father and brothers, and consequently he sank into affectation, pettiness, barrenness, whereby he was as easily recognized, as one who shuts his eyes that he may be invisible. We

---

* Goethe had been irritated by some observations of Herr Bendavid, concerning the *Farbenlehre*, a subject on which he was unduly sensitive.

were always quarrelling about this, and as my æsthetic friend is still, to this very day, bitten with such original views, I cannot forbear to snub him. . . . .

Yours,

Z.

ENCLOSURE.

Passage from a Letter of Zelter's to Herr Bendavid.

. . . . The highest thing that I can say of the above work, (the Passion Music,) is, that I cannot express my delight in it. We were obliged to leave out some Chorales and Airs, and in spite of that, the performance takes some three hours. If you reflect that this music was given on Good Friday, and that the afternoon sermon intervened, five full hours must have been taken up in devotion. The good Leipzigers came and went as they chose, and so the music went its own way, and the world may thank its stars it is still there, for the worthy sons of old Bach, *tutti quanti*, took so little pains to keep together the works of their great father, that now even I, one born out of due time, deserve a little credit for picking up and admiring the crumbs, which they have left under his table; *they*, whose school exercises the loving father copied fair. In one word, dear friend, the above-named Organ Concerto, which you have so neatly copied from Sebastian Bach's own manuscript, and with which you have honoured me, is a painfully elaborated composition, with no mind in it! —How! No mind?—Yes, yes, and I am strongly tempted to think it even un-Friedemannic. Of course you know that old Bach copied his Concerto for four Claviers from honest old Vivaldi, note for note, only transposing it one tone lower. I too still possess twelve Organ Concertos* by Vivaldi, which Bach arranged for the organ in the same way, and I doubt my being mistaken, when I declare this Friedemann Organ Concerto to be just such a work, because there is not a claw of a single thought of Bach's in it, while on the other hand, there are whole handfuls of the fiddle-scrapings of those days. But you are not therefore to

* Zelter must have meant *Horn* Concertos.

call me ungrateful. For fifty years I have been wont to honour Bach's genius. Friedemann died here, Emmanuel Bach was *Kammermusicus* to the King, Kirnberger, Agrikola, pupils of old Bach, Ring, Bertuch, Schmalz, and others used to play hardly anything but old Bach's pieces; I myself have taught them for thirty years past, and have pupils who play every note of Bach well, and do you want to impose upon me, by saying, that such a bony canonic introduction, with a Fugue upon a succession of mere sevenths, (which old Bach called cobbler's patches,) is the genuine work of so noble a spirit as Friedemann Bach? Bach?—Not that I mean to run down Anton Vivaldi for it; only he is no Friedemann, just as Friedemann is no Sebastian, by a long way, whatever fuss Forkel may choose to make about him. What does Forkel mean, by saying, that Friedemann came next to his father in originality? Is that logic? What is originality? Either Friedemann was original, or he was not. If the first, he is what he is, first-hand from Nature, having none over him and none beside him; for the nearer he is to one before him, the less original is he. Explain your Forkel better to me, it will do you no harm. But who would think of saying old Bach was original, if he came near someone above himself? Would you say so of Homer, or Sophocles, or Shakespeare? I knew the greater part of Friedemann's compositions, and himself personally into the bargain; he himself unquestionably laid claims to peculiarity, which in his last years, became caprice, obstinacy, contradictoriness, nay, frivolity, for he had nothing to live upon, and preferred letting his wife and daughter starve, to earning anything,—though, with his great cleverness, this would have been an easy matter. The well-to-do and well-educated father of an only son sent me once, to offer Friedemann an important engagement, as a teacher. "I am no *Informator*," was his answer. He was highly honoured here in respect of his talents. His extemporary playing on the organ, especially when he was in the humour, was the admiration of such men as Marpurg, Kirnberger, Benda, Agrikola, Fasch, Bertuch, Ring, first-rate organ-players most of them, and yet they all felt, how far they were left behind by him. He played whatever first came into his head, and the longer he played, the more certain, magnificent, and overwhelming was the effect upon us youngsters. Still more often have I been compelled to recognize his superiority on the harpsichord, the grand piano, and the clavier, although I never heard him play a single note of his father's music, which everyone would have liked to hear.

268.—ZELTER TO GOETHE.

Good Friday, 17th April, 1829.

.... To-day, instead of the usual Passion Music, by Graun, I mean, by special request, to give another performance of Bach's *Passion*, bidding defiance to my old bent fingers, for my helper, Felix, is swimming on the high seas, past Heligoland, to England, whither he has been invited. As he plays the organ well, and there the organs are better than the organists, I think he may try his hand there too.
.... Paganini with his accursed Violin-Concertos is driving men and women mad here; I dare say he will once more carry off from Berlin 10,000 *Thalers*, if he does not once more lose them first at Faro. I have not money enough to give him two *Thalers* every time for his artifices, and have heard nothing of him, beyond seeing his portrait, which makes him very like the son of a witch. The real misfortune he brings upon us is, that he is the downright ruin of the young violinists in our Orchestra. *Vale!*

Yours,
Z.

269.—GOETHE TO ZELTER.

Weimar, 28th April, 1829.

.... In any case, it is our duty to look far afield, and to listen to voices that are powerful and convincing. The last quarterly issue of the *Edinburgh Review* on Foreign Literature has just arrived, and it is exceedingly curious to see what the leading men think of Continental authors. They are very conscientious about themselves, and respectful towards their public. Earnestness, thoroughness, moderation, and candour are their characteristics throughout, and the extent and depth of their insight is incredible.

The above was written some few days ago, and meanwhile I have been reading that remarkable piece in the seventh volume of Calderon's plays, translated by Gries, called *The Locks of Absolom*. Perhaps you may come across it at a fitting time, and have leisure to read it. The old truth reasserts itself in my mind, that in the same way as Nature and poetry have perhaps, in modern days, never been more closely united than in Shakespeare, so the highest culture and poetry have nowhere been more closely allied than in Calderon. We cannot expect our contemporaries to see this clearly. . . . .

A Frenchman* has set eight passages of my *Faust* to music, and sends me the score, very beautifully engraved; I should much like to send it on to you, for your friendly criticism.

This reminds me that you still have a score of my Cantata, *Rinaldo*,† composed by Winter, for Prince Frederick of Gotha; I still have the voice-parts, and many strange memories are associated with this *opus*. Let me have it back, therefore, if you can find it. . . . .

And thus for ever,
G.

270.—ZELTER TO GOETHE.

30th April, 1829.

LAST Tuesday, Paganini paid me a visit at the Academy, and listened to our performance; next day I at last heard one of his concerts. The man's achievements are marvellous, and I must say this, that though everyone would be glad to produce his effects, yet his method of producing them quite passes the comprehension of other *virtuosi* upon his instrument. His individuality is therefore *more* than music, though it is not higher music, and I expect I should be of the same opinion, if I heard him oftener. I was so placed, that I could see every movement of his hand and arm; as his figure is rather small, these members must be of rare flexibility, strength, and elasticity, for he is never

---
* Hector Berlioz.
† *Rinaldo* was written in 1811.

weary of conquering ever greater difficulties, in an ascending scale, with the same regularity as a clock with a soul inside it. The hundred artifices of his bow and fingers, to each one of which he has devoted thought and practice, follow each other in good taste and order, and distinguish him as a composer as well. But in any case, he is, in the *highest* potentiality, a perfect master of his instrument; that which, with the best will in the world, he does *not* succeed in, comes forth as a bold variation. . . . .

Please send your Frenchman's *Faust* one of these days; the subject is, as it were, specially devised for composers of our time.

Yours,
Z.

271.—Zelter to Goethe.

14th May, 1829.

. . . . Yesterday I heard Paganini again; the man is a rarity, and no mistake, a living violin. One starts, one laughs, one is in despair at the most hazardous antics; the difficulty is intelligible to all, for the effect is felt by all. Nor are grace and intellectual force wanting, and even that which is not perfectly successful, is still new and interesting.
Z.

272.—Zelter to Goethe.

May, 1829.

. . . . In Letter 345 of your Correspondence with Schiller, he writes that the melody for the *Bajadere* does not fit all the strophes equally well. Perhaps you will remember, that I sang it to the Dowager Duchess Amalie, and that Wieland told the Duchess, he had thought it impossible for one and the same melody to be so often repeated without becoming wearisome, whereas it really became more effective. My singing, to be sure, is not much to speak of, but then, as against that, many a singer cannot declaim. For the rest, Schiller was quite satisfied with my music to *Der Taucher*, and he railed at Naumann, who had just set *Die Ideale*. I had won a wager with the *Taucher* too. One of our friends was dissatisfied with the Ballad-forms, used by the poets, and exclaimed, "Who could think of setting such verses, such a Diver as this, to music?" Several of us were present, and I, who had been listening to the whole conversation in silence, called out, "I could! and Schiller himself shall praise it!" Then and there I wrote down the very notes, and so they have remained, however clumsy they may look. Immediately afterwards, when I gave them forth—for I had the poem on my lips,—an anything but musical matron, planted herself by my side, and kept beating time with her knitting-needle. Hardly was the last word over, when she exclaimed, choked with emotion, "Well, that was an infamous King!"

Yours,
Z.

273.—GOETHE TO ZELTER.

Weimar, 17th May, 1829.

FIRST of all, let me thank you heartily for your description of Paganini. .... I envy *him* such a listener, and *you* such a *virtuoso*. ....

I could not help being very much pleased to hear of the good old lady,* who treats my *Farbenlehre* as a sort of Bible. The little book certainly contains a good deal, which everyone can assimilate, even though a great deal that does not concern us is allowed to remain *in statu quo*. There is a very intelligent essay on colouring, which refers to this same *Farbenlehre*, in the January number of this year's *Morgenblatt*. The author is a practical artist, and all that he can make use of has become alive to him; he might go still further. For my own satisfaction I shall take up the subject again, from this point of view. Once you are penetrated by a fundamental maxim, you can begin to advance. Happily nothing in my work is in opposition to the artist, and what he acknowledges in me, he can at once make use of. But probably I shall never live to see a mathematician look at Nature, unaffected by the weird

---

* Zelter's sister-in-law, an old lady of seventy-six.

confusion of his formulæ, and use his common sense and understanding independently, like a sane person. Yet this alone will enable a young man of energy, before plunging into those labyrinths, to take the thread from the hands of kindly Nature, the true Ariadne, who alone blesses us, and to whom, all our life long, we cannot fail to be loyal. . . . .
So far to-day! With best wishes and greetings,
Faithfully yours,
GOETHE.

274.—ZELTER TO GOETHE.

21st May, 1829.

I AM reading, bit by bit, the Second Part of the Schiller Correspondence, about the original publication of *Wilhelm Meister*, which took place, just when I, for the first time, got through your outer skin. A new era had dawned for me out of the deepest affliction. I had just been happily married to my second wife, whom I had known from her childhood, (having been at the same *Gymnasium* with her brothers). Before this I had given her lessons in singing, or rather, through her crystal voice and transparent execution, I had felt for the first time, what no teaching can give. I could not help being pleased with my own Airs, when she sang them. People held their breath, so as not to let slip the smallest note. For her, I had already in early days written down my first fresh impressions of your Songs, on a series of leaves; I am sorry they are lost, for they marked the transition from my condition as a citizen, to my natural vocation.

I had so many children, so many mouths to feed, so much work, such delight in my strength, and then, I had another gentle wife, who kept the children in order, —and whenever the father came home, we had fine times of it. I built houses for people, who to this day owe me the money which I laid out, and when others bothered themselves about what it would all come to, I was as cheerful as possible. To be sure, there were difficulties now and then; I spoiled my customers, who had too good a time of it, and wanted to have what I myself had not got. That was the humour of the thing. Then enters to my household *Wilhelm Meister*, with his motley troop of rational and irrational cattle. People said, I had lost my wits—I saw only green meadows, and the sky full of fiddles. . . . .

Yours,
Z.

275.—GOETHE TO ZELTER.

5th June, 1829.

. . . . To-day the Princess Augusta* came to take a friendly leave of me; she is really as gifted as she is amiable. Good luck to her on that wide, tempestuous sea!

Do not put off writing. I am revising the account of my second stay in Rome, a curious little volume, which—however it may turn out,—will always encourage thought and feeling.

Your truly attached
J. W. v. GOETHE.

276.—ZELTER TO GOETHE.

Sunday, 21st June, 1829.

CERTAIN people can only show their presence of mind and their share of the business, by means of loud coughing, snorting, croaking and spitting; Herr Berlioz seems to be one of these. The sulphur-smell of Mephisto attracts him, and so he must needs sneeze and puff, till all the instruments in the Orchestra get the jumps— only not a hair of Faust's head moves. Thank you however for sending me the music. . . . . Worthy Winter's *Rinaldo*, on the contrary, has anyhow a human form of some kind, which is suitable for a Tenor; but now we are as far removed from that, as that so-called artificiality of tones is from music. . . . .

Ever yours,
Z.

---

* The present Empress of Germany, then on her way to marry Prince Wilhelm of Prussia.

277.—GOETHE TO ZELTER.

Weimar, 18th July, 1829.

.... HERE, in my little den on the ground floor, I have been arranging and hanging up in long rows, a series of pictures of ancient Latium and modern Rome. Besides that, I have collected around me a number of books on the same subject, thus reviving, as far as I can, the recollection of my second stay in Rome; I commend to your kind consideration the volume, which will contain these written reminiscences. ....

The Polish poet* paid me a visit, accompanied by the Princess Wolkonsky and a large suite; he did not utter a single word, and had not the good sense to present himself to me alone. One would feel inclined to inveigh against such behaviour, but that one has often been clumsy enough oneself.

Professor Rauch spent a day with us; he was pleasant, cheerful, active, just as of old. A young man whom he brought with him, and who may have a good deal of talent, showed us a design for a kind of frieze; the conception and the drawing were creditable, but the subject was Christ's entry into Jerusalem, which makes the rest of us feel vexed, at the trouble an able man takes, to look for motives, where there are none to be found. If people would only keep piety, which is so essential and lovable in life, distinct from Art, where, owing to its very simplicity and dignity, it checks their energy, allowing only the very highest mind freedom to unite with, if not actually to master it!

I am delighted at your return to the Second Part of *Faust;* that will urge me on to put aside various other things, and, at all events, to complete as soon as possible, the immediate work which touches upon it. The end is as good as quite finished, much that is important in the intervening passages is complete, and if some of the higher powers would only lay hold of me, and

* Adam Mickiewicz, who came to Goethe with a letter of introduction from Madame Szymanowska, the pianiste. Goethe, however, afterwards discovered, that on the occasion mentioned in this letter, his visitor was a Russian, and not the poet at all.

confine me in a high fortress, for three months, there would not be much left for me to do.* I realize it all so vividly in heart and mind, that I often feel quite oppressed.

And now, the sweetest thing last! It gives me heartfelt pleasure, to hear that the Princess Augusta impressed you so favourably with her many good qualities; she combines the characteristics of a woman and a Princess so perfectly, that one is really lost in admiration, which again gives rise to a feeling of deep respect, mingled with affection. I hope that you may in future have more frequent opportunities of convincing yourself of this.

Thus much from my quiet, and—now that the haymaking is over,—perfectly green valley. The calm is so great, that early this morning, a pretty roe came out of the bushes, and quietly began to eat the grass. I hope you are enjoying an equally pleasant morning in Berlin, with its abundant life, noise, and bustle.

Faithfully and ever diligently yours,
GOETHE.

278.—ZELTER TO GOETHE.

Berlin, 20th August, 1829.

. . . . FELIX is in Scotland, and has already written down to us here, from the Highlands. I have commissioned him to make a more accurate study of the national songs and dances, on the spot, than did those travelling amateurs, and uninstructed copyists, from whom we have hitherto derived our knowledge. The dear rascal has the luck of finding and making friends everywhere; he has seen Sir Walter Scott too. Then he found in London a young Hanoverian, who was attached to the English Embassy here, and who is now his companion on this instructive journey, whether they walk, ride, or go by water. Later on, he is to visit Ireland and Holland, coming home in the autumn for his sister's marriage with Hensel, the Court painter, and then starting for Italy. He is working hard, and trying to build himself up, where there is no lack of stone. . . . .

Z.

* Compare *Schiller and Goethe Correspondence*, Letter 480.

270.—GOETHE TO ZELTER.

Weimar, 20th August, 1829.

. . . . WE have just had with us an Englishman,* who, at the beginning of the century, studied in Jena, and who, since then, has followed up German literature, with a perseverance that is quite incredible. He was so well instructed in the *merita causæ* of our circumstances, that even had I wished to do so—and it is our usual way of treating foreigners—I could not have dared to try and humbug him with phrases. It transpired from his conversation, that for the last twenty years and more, very well-educated Englishmen have come over to Germany, and they have carefully studied the personal characteristics, as well as the æsthetic and moral relations of those men who may now be called our *ancestors*. He told strange stories of Klopstock's ossification.†

Then he proved himself a missionary of English literature, and read poems to me and my daughter, when we were together or alone. I particularly enjoyed following Byron's *Heaven and Earth* both with eye and ear, for I had a second copy in my hand. Finally, he drew my attention to Milton's *Samson*, and read it with me. It is curious to recognize in it Byron's ancestor; the latter is as grandiose and far-seeing as the former, but the descendant certainly runs off into the illimitable, into the strangest complexity, where the former appears simple and stately.

Our Polish poet has just presented himself; had he come a few days earlier, he would have been welcome to join our circle, but now I shall have to receive him alone, and that is a very difficult, almost an impossible matter. . . . .

On gloomy days and bright days,

Your truly attached,

G.

* Crabb Robinson.

† "I have not the slightest recollection of having mentioned Klopstock at all, and cannot think what he referred to. Voigt says he never knew Goethe forget anything, so perfect was his memory to the last, and that, therefore, I probably did speak about Klopstock."—*Crabb Robinson's Diary*, vol. ii. p. 240.

280.—GOETHE TO ZELTER.

Weimar, 10th October, 1829.

ONCE more I must entrust my affection and my thoughts to paper, and first of all, let me confess that since you left, I have felt quite down in the mouth. Any number of attractive and suggestive works of Art were lying and standing all around, everyone of which I might have shared with you! And what then did we share? Hardly anything worth mentioning.

There is really something absurd about the Present; all that people think of is, the sight, the touch of each other, and there they rest,—but it never occurs to them, to reflect upon what is to be gained from such moments. We should express our opinion on the subject thus. The absent one is an ideal person, those who are present, seem to one another to be quite commonplace. It is a silly thing, that the ideal is, as it were, ousted by the real; that may be the reason, why, to the moderns, their ideal only manifests itself in longing. However, we will not brood over this subject further, but let the matter rest, with this seemly and unseemly preface,—though no doubt I could spin out another long Litany, explaining the general style of more modern life.

Now however,—to pass from what is fanciful to what is pleasant,—I must tell you that Herr Ternite has proved himself truly generous; for while I already owe him my best thanks for the drawings and *fac-similes* he presented me with, he has shown the most flattering confidence in me, by entrusting me with his valuable traceries, which are now lying before me. I shall take the greatest possible care of them, and if there is anyone that deserves to see them, I shall show them to him myself.

Here now is the greatest marvel of antiquity; he that hath eyes to see, let him see, viz. let him see the healthiness of the moment, and what this is worth. For although by a most terrible calamity, these pictures were buried amongst ruins for nearly two thousand years, they are still just as fresh and as sound as they were in the happy, easy hour, which preceded their fearful entombment.

If we were asked, what they represent, it might perhaps be rather perplexing to give an answer; meantime I should say, that these forms give us the feeling, that the moment must be pregnant and sufficient to itself, if it is to become a worthy segment of time and eternity.

What is here said about Plastic Art, applies in reality even better to music, and you, old fellow, when you reflect upon your own work and your own Institution, will not dispute the strange words I have uttered above. Indeed, from this point of view, music fills up the present moment more decisively than anything else, whether it awakens in the tranquil mind reverence and worship, or whether it summons the active senses to dance and revelry. The rest I leave to a heart that is pious and reverential, and a mind that is full of discernment.

Now and ever yours,
J. W. v. GOETHE.

281.—ZELTER TO GOETHE.

27th October, 1829.

.... Mr Felix has met with an accident in London; he has been thrown out of a carriage, and prevented from coming to his sister's wedding in Berlin. I am afraid he may have broken something, for it is a long business, and he cannot write; still, they say he is getting better. He is expected to return by way of Calais, so I suppose he will come through France to Weimar, and pay you a call. ....

Yours,
Z.

282.—GOETHE TO ZELTER.

Weimar, 1st November, 1829.

.... ONE word about what I am reading! I have got as far as the eighth volume of Bourrienne's *

---

* Goethe observes that Bourrienne's History of Napoleon's campaign in Egypt "destroys the romantic cast of many scenes, and displays facts in their naked, sublime truth." See *Eckermann's Conversations with Goethe*, p. 391.

Memoirs. Recollection and illustration are here combined for us. The new view of an important point in history, here set before the reader, is noteworthy; the author makes it seem highly probable that Napoleon never meant to cross to England—that his real object was only, under this pretence, to form the nucleus of a great, active, military power, ready for all emergencies, and to arrange and locate a large body of troops round this centre, so that, at the shortest notice, he could bring them to and across the Rhine;* a plan in which he was so far successful, that (contrary to universal expectation) he surrounded Ulm, and got the place into his power,—to speak no further of the consequences of this expedition.

When we are challenged to turn our thoughts back to that period, we feel astonishment beset us afresh. It is fortunate, that at the time when we were living through all this, we could not clearly realize the immensity of such events. . . . .

I feel myself specially called upon to preserve what I have done for the study of Nature. Of the three hundred assembled Naturalists,† there is not one, who shows the faintest approximation to my way of thinking, and it may be, that is as well. Approximations only produce errors. If one wants to bequeath something useful to posterity, it must be confessions; one must present oneself as an individual, one's thought, one's opinions, and those who come after may pick out for themselves what suits them, and what will pass current universally. Our ancestors left us plenty of that kind of thing.

Herewith I close to-day's discourse.
I heard Paganini yesterday evening.

GOETHE.

---

* Zelter observes in his next letter, "If I am not mistaken, Las Cases has a passage, in which the hero reveals his intention at that time. The English alone were wise enough to make some use of such demonstrations, by exciting the whole of their Island, and so on."

† Goethe alludes to scientific meetings, one of which had been held some time before, in Berlin. See Letter 251.

283.—GOETHE TO ZELTER.

Weimar, 9th November, 1829.

.... I too have now heard Paganini, and immediately afterwards, on the very same evening, I opened your letter, which enabled me to fancy that my estimate of these marvels was fairly sensible. I thought there was something lacking to make up what we call enjoyment, which in me is always hovering between sense and understanding—a base to this pillar of flame and cloud.

Were I in Berlin, I should seldom miss the Möser Quartett evenings. I have always found performances of this kind more intelligible than other instrumental music; you hear four rational persons conversing together, and fancy you get something from their discourse, and learn to know the peculiarities of their different instruments. This time I felt the want of such a foundation, both mentally and orally; I only heard something meteoric, and could give no further account of it to myself. Yet it is curious to hear people, and especially women, talk about it; without the slightest misgiving, they gave utterance to what are really confessions.

And now I want to know, if you have good news of the worthy Felix; I take the greatest interest in him, for it is a very painful thing to see a person, who has become so famous, threatened in his onward course by a mean accident. Let me have a few comforting words about him. . . . .

I must own that the French entertain me more than anyone else; I follow with quiet thought the lectures of Guizot, Villemain, and Cousin. *Le Globe*, *La Revue Française*, and—for the last three weeks—*Le Temps*, introduce me to a circle we should look for in vain throughout Germany. But although I can give them the highest praise in all that touches immediately upon practical ethics, I am not equally well satisfied with their observations of Nature. Even granting that their method of experiment is fully entitled to our respect, still when it comes to reflection, they cannot rid themselves of mechanical and atomistic images, and once possessed of an idea, they want to bring it in by the back door, which, once for all, cannot be done.

In everything which is termed natural philosophy, I adhere to my own path, earnestly and attentively, step by step. Our contemporaries are really too odd, the more's the pity. The Milanese told me lately, with much astonishment, that Herr von B. was going to give them visible proof, that the Euganean range, which they had hitherto regarded as a natural offshoot of the Alps, had—some time or other—shot up out of the earth. They accept this, much in the same way as savages do a missionary's sermon. And a few days ago, I received a communication from the far North, to the effect that the Altai mountains also had once upon a time been heaved up out of the depths. And you may all thank God, if the earth's paunch does not some day think of relieving itself of its fermentation, in a similar fashion, between Berlin and Potsdam. The Paris Academy sanctions the idea, that after the earth's crust had been fully formed, Mount Blanc rose up out of the abyss at the very last moment. Thus, by little and little, nonsense is gaining the ascendancy, and will become the general belief of nations and scholars, just as in the darkest ages, people believed so firmly in witches and demons, and their doings, as actually to proceed against them with the most hideous tortures.

Herein I have always admired the great King Matthias of Hungary, who made a law forbidding all mention of witches—*inasmuch as there were none.* Without being a king, I—in a quiet way—act just in the same fashion towards these babblers, dabblers, and splutterers, by crediting Nature, in her great operations, with simpler and grander means. Meanwhile however, it is a pity, that from the Chinese boundary to this point, we are not allowed to announce anything but what holds good in Paris. Pardon me, if I continue to speak of things, which have no direct interest for you; I think you will find some echo of them in your own circumstances. Nothing draws me from my old, tried path, or hinders me from softly, softly, unveiling problems, as if I were peeling onions,—or from respecting every bud that shows real, though silent life.

I could say a great deal more about the way I am dealing

with the last things that have been sent to me. Here and there too, it is cheerful and pleasant enough, but in the end, I feel as if the roses are fading, though not without leaving offshoots and buds. The older I get, the more I rely upon *the law which bids the rose and lily bloom...*

Yours ever,
G.

284.—GOETHE TO ZELTER.

Weimar, 15th November, 1829.

LET me tell you a strange thing, that time has brought to light; it will amuse you to think about it. Your Frederick, who, I think, is justly called the Great, was in fact a regular King incarnate, and insisted that everything produced throughout the wide world, was also to be found in his kingdom. It is well known, that in consequence of this, the bread-eating people, served by patriotic millstones, had for some length of time, to swallow a goodly portion of clay and gravel with their food.

But never mind that; what I really wanted to tell you, is this. The King used to plague his Mining Department most dreadfully, to find him rock-salt in his dominions. For as it was found in Poland yonder, and in many other parts of the earth, he could see no reason, why it should not be met with in Prussia as well.

I have read several annual reports of the Mining Department, at the end of which, honest Count Heinitz states with all possible modesty, "that in accordance with our duty, the greatest pains have been taken, to find rock-salt in your Majesty's Dominions, but we have not yet been fortunate enough to attain this object, however, the investigations and examinations shall be continued with the greatest zeal." This phrase was traditionally repeated for several years. Many theories were discussed to and fro by the geologists of those days; many salt springs revealed themselves, but nobody hoped for blocks of mineral salt.

Now however, I am informed by the Superintendent of Salt Mines, Glenk, that in the night between the 22nd and 23rd of October, he sank a shaft to the depth of 1,170 feet, and came upon a perfectly pure form of crystal salt, which, judging by the fragments, was partly granular, partly laminated. He thought of sinking it another twenty feet deeper into this solid mass, and then taking further measures. The place is called Stotternheim, and it is situated behind the Ettersberg, in a great plain. I dare say you have a pleasant recollection of the mountain aforesaid.

I will say no more, yet it is strange that a royal magic wand could order beforehand that, which—after the lapse of so many years—is discovered in the lowest possible depths. To be sure, Prussia has no longer any need to trouble herself about salt at such a depth, but it is clear from the above, that such a thing might be obtained in the kingdom. Here therefore, let us make honourable mention of the fact, that during the last fifty years, our knowledge and technique have advanced so far, that a man is bold enough to bore down 1,200 feet into the earth, knowing and saying beforehand, what must be found there. This is much, but not enough; the treasure has then to be raised, and brought into common use, as one of the most essential needs of man and beast. Here however, we have the powerful assistance of Physics, Mechanism, and Chemistry.

If, before this, you have bestowed any attention upon the poem * sent you, (on the 29th of February, 1828,) which was printed in the Leipzig *Musenalmanach* (of 1830), you will forgive my being so explicit on the subject. The salt water then obtainable, came from a higher, and less favoured region. In earlier times, people were satisfied with a region that yielded little, but they feared to lose it, if they went deeper. Judgment and enterprise came in with later days, and thus we live to see, what Frederick the Glorious desired and commanded.

Be kind to this little story; it was interesting to me, one quiet evening, when the wish to tell it to someone made me turn to you. . . . .

G.

---

* *Die ersten Erzeugnisse der Stotternheimer Saline*, &c.

285.—ZELTER TO GOETHE.

15th November, 1829.

THAT fine word *Faustus, Fauste, Faust*, has been invested by you with such ominous importance, that by all laws, human and divine, you ought to be told of its further consequences. So listen! for the first time yesterday evening, I heard and saw, from beginning to end, *Faust*, the Grand Opera by J. C. Bernard and Spohr.

If I am not mistaken, the composer got together a Sanhedrim, or whatever they call it, in order that they might jointly sanction laws, which are to be universally current, alike for grand Opera and for light Opera, as is clear from the above stupendous work. In connection with this, he seemed especially to have reckoned on C. M. von Weber; whether an understanding was arrived at, I know not, nor have I asked.

Yesterday's performance of this full, highly wrought work, was worthy of the greatest praise, nor did the crowded house fail to applaud it. The Orchestra, the highest faculty of an Opera, was one man; the singers were as perfect as possible; machinery, decorations, witches, ghosts, and other monsters—all met with the fullest recognition and the best reception. . . . . Now, with regard to the work of the composer, who certainly merits more recognition as an artist in tones, than as a musician and melodist—everything—up to the smallest detail, is astoundingly worked out, with the greatest elaboration of art, so as to outwit, to outbid the most watchful ear. The finest Brabant lace is coarse work compared to it. . . . .

Z.

286.—ZELTER TO GOETHE.

17th November, 1829.

As you speak of Möser's Quartetts, it seems you must have heard them, even as far as Weimar. I must say, however rarely I go to hear them, they are the things I like best of their kind. I know not, if I ever wrote to you upon this subject, but I venture to doubt, if Haydn, Mozart, and

Beethoven ever enjoyed so pure, healthy, and sure a rendering of their Quartetts, as is given here, when Möser is at his best; for it would be too much to ask, that he should succeed every day. . . . .

To hear you praising my old Fritz is as valuable to me, as though I had discovered in my own cellar rock-salt enough for the whole monarchy. I certainly have read your poem in the *Leipziger Musenalmanach*, and I knew it even at the time, because you sent it to me, on the occasion of your Festival.

I am much amused with our " patriotic millstones," as you call them, when I see so many old gentlemen, between seventy and a hundred years old, doddering about me, who have held out for so long, on a diet of clay and silicious earth. The old King was also severely blamed, for forbidding the further import of Swedish iron into the country. Our cannon-wheels had to be covered with native iron, and when they were driven over our pavements, the tires snapped asunder, like the stems of tobacco pipes. At that time, people laughed at him; and never thought our iron could be utilized as it is now, when we make bracelets and chains of it. I pride myself not a little on having seen him so often; for when he died, I was already a citizen of Berlin, and had much more than I have now, because I spent less. . . . .

Yours,
Z.

287.—GOETHE TO ZELTER.

Weimar, 20th November, 1829.

IF we once let ourselves in for historical and etymological investigations, we almost always end in greater uncertainty than we began with. Your question as to the origin of the name of Mephistopheles, I cannot answer directly; but the accompanying pages may confirm your friend's surmise, which refers it to the same fantastic source and time, as the legend of *Faust;* probably, however, we must not assign it to the Middle Ages. It seems to have arisen in the sixteenth, and to have developed itself in the seventeenth century. The Protestant necromancers had no immediate need to fear ecclesiastical excommunication, and so there were all the more Cophtas, who knew how to profit by the stupidity, the helplessness, the passionate desires of mankind; for it was certainly easier to grow rich by means of a few cramped characters and senseless mutterings, than to eat one's daily bread in the sweat of one's brow. Have we not recently, among the Neustadt circle, unearthed a similar nest of treasure-diggers, and with them a dozen of the same sort of treatises on magic, none of which, however, is equal in value to the Codex, from which the accompanying extract has been made?

So much to begin with, together with my kindest greetings to Herr Friedländer, and pray pardon my elaborate reply. . . . .

May all good spirits follow in the train of so many devilish ones!

G.

1. ENCLOSURE.

The Romish Church always dealt with heretics and magicians, as belonging to the same class, and hurled the severest anathemas against them, as well as at everything connected with soothsaying and chiromancy. With the advance of knowledge, and a closer insight into the workings of Nature, the yearning after strange, mysterious powers seems to have increased. Protestantism freed men from all dread of ecclesiastical penalties; student life became more independent, and furnished opportunities for loose and impious tricks, and thus, in the middle of the sixteenth century, the belief in demons and magic seems to have assumed a more methodical form, whereas it had previously found followers only among the puzzle-headed vulgar. The scene of the story of *Faust* was laid in Wittenberg, and therefore in the heart of Protestantism, and certainly by Protestants themselves; for in all the writings relating to the subject, there is no trace of priestly bigotry, which, where it is found, is always obvious enough.

In order to give you a proof of the high dignity of Mephistopheles, I enclose the copy of an extract from a passage in *Faust's Höllenzwang*. This very remarkable work of closely reasoned nonsense is said to have been printed in Passau in 1612, after it had long been circulated in manuscript. Neither I, nor any of my friends, have seen an original, but we possess, (in the Grand Ducal Library,) a very neat and perfect copy, which—to judge from the handwriting, and other circumstances—probably belongs to the last half of the seventeenth century.

2. ENCLOSURE.

Praxis.
Cabulæ nigræ
Doctoris Johannis Faustii
Magi celeberrimi
Passau MDCXII.

SECOND TITLE.

D. Johannis Faustii
Magia
naturalis
et
innaturalis.

Or
The Inscrutable Book of Infernal Magic,
That is,
The Book of Wonders and Magic Arts,
Whereby
I have coerced the spirits of Hell, that they have been obliged perforce to carry out my will.
Printed at Passau Aō. 1612.
The First Part
of this Book
treats of the
Nigra mantia
Or
Cabula nigra
As also of
Magia naturali, et innaturali.

Cap. I.

Treats of the Classification of the Spirits, and their names, also of what assistance they can be to men.

Now in order, dear Descendant, that you may be made acquainted with the government and distribution of the Spirits into Satanic bands and princedoms, I will herewith, in this chapter, teach and show to you their names, one after the other, but in the following chapter, their division into bands and principalities.

Nadanniel is the Spirit, who is rejected of God, otherwise called Lucifer, also Bludohn, also Beelzebub.

There are also among the whole Hellish host seven Electors, as Lucifer, Marbuel, Ariel, Aciel, Barbiel, Mephistophiel, Apadiel.

But among these seven Electors, there are also counted four Grand Dukes—Lucifer, Ariel, Aciel, Marbuel.

There are also among the Lords of Hell seven Counts-Palatine, by name : Ahisdophiel, Camniel, Padiel, Coradiel, Osphadiel, Adadiel, Capfiel. All of these are very mighty spirits in the Army of Hell.

There are also among this Hellish host seven lesser Counts, by name: Radiel, Dirachiel, Paradiel, Armodiel, Ischscabadiel, Jazariel, Casadiel.

Ischscabadiel is a spirit of Pride.
Jazariel brings forth to men all those primeval Spirits, which hover about in mid-air, outside the Paradise of Joys.

There are likewise among the Hellish host seven Barons, by name:
1. Germiciel, a powerful Spirit of the air.
2. Adiel, a powerful fire Spirit.
3. Craffiel, a powerful war Spirit.
4. Paradiel. 5. Assardiel. 6. Kniedadiel. 7. Amniel.

There are likewise among the Hellish host seven Spirits of Nobility, by name:
1. Amudiel. 2. Kiriel; these two are mighty fire Spirits.
3. Bethnael. 4. Geliel. 5. Requiel. 6. Aprinaelis. 7. Tagriel.

These last four, 4, 5, 6, 7, are minor fire Spirits, and are numbered among the army of Hell.

There are likewise among the Hellish host seven *Civic Spirits*, by name:
1. Alhemiel. 2. Amnixiel. 3. Egibiel. 4. Adriel. These four also belong to the army of Hell.
5. Azeruel. 6. Ergediel. 7. Abdicuel.
These three are fire Spirits.

There are likewise among the Hellish host seven *Peasant Spirits*, which are named:
1. Aceruel. 2. Amediel. These two are fire Spirits.
3. Coradiel. 4. Sumnidiel. 5. Coachtiel. These three are Spirits of the air.
6. Kirotiel. 7. Apactiel. These two belong to the army of Hell.

There are likewise among the Hellish host seven *Wise Spirits*. These are the fleetest of all, and the head of the army of Hell, and they may be made use of for any Arts, whenever they are desired.
1. Mephistophiel. 2. Barbiel. 3. Marbuel. 4. Ariel. 5. Aciel. 6. Apadiel. 7. Camniel.

There are likewise seven *Foolish Spirits*, who have great power, and are also skilled in many artifices, but nevertheless are very foolish; they are fond of making compacts and agreements with mankind, so they can easily be eluded again by many artifices. These are by name:
1. Padiel. 2. Cafphiel. 3. Paradiel. 4. Casdiel. 5. Kniedatiel. 6. Amniel. 7. Tagriel.

There are likewise four *Free Spirits*, by name as follows:
1. Asmodiel is the Chief, and the Spirit of murder.
2. Discerdiel, the Spirit of contention.
3. Amodiel, the Spirit of harlots.
4. Damniel is the Spirit of theft, (a spirit of the air).

These four Free Spirits also belong to the army of Hell. Nadanniel is the Spirit bound and rejected of God.

Cap. II.

Treats of the Classifying of all Spirits into the bands of their Princes.

All the Spirits of the army of Hell are under Nadanniel or Lucifer, also called Beelzebub.

All Fire-Spirits under Ariel.

All the Spirits of the Earth and Air under Marbuel.
All the minor Dukes and Barons under Aciel.
All the Counts Palatine under Barbiel.

Under the seven Counts-Palatine are the seven Spirits of Nobility.

And Mephistophiel stands above Amudiel, for

N.B. Mephistophiel, instead of Lucifer, is placed at the head of all the Spirits.

Under the seven minor Counts stand the seven Spirits of Nobility, as they follow in order, for as the seven Spirits of Nobility follow in order, so also do the seven Civic Spirits follow in order.

Under the seven Spirits of Nobility stand the seven Civic Spirits, according to order, in the same way as the Spirits of Nobility follow in order.

Under the seven Civic Spirits stand the seven Peasant Spirits, in order, like the seven Civic Spirits.

Under the seven Peasant Spirits stand the seven Wise Spirits, according to order, as the Civic Spirits follow in order, and

Under the seven Wise Spirits stand the seven Foolish Spirits in order; as the Wise stand in order, so too the Foolish stand in order.

288.—GOETHE TO ZELTER.

Weimar, 16th December, 1829.

As I know it always puts you into the best of humours, when one introduces something creditable to your old King's memory, I send you herewith a good pinch of rock-salt, with the friendly request, that you will sprinkle it into your soup at the next opportunity, and when you feel the taste of it on your tongue, bear in mind that Frederick the Second could not easily have enjoyed a more delightful dinner, than if his food had been seasoned with this product of his own Kingdom, and he had seen his golden salt-cellars liberally filled with it. . . . .

G.

289.—ZELTER TO GOETHE.

17th December, 1829.

SMALL causes and great effects! A dumb fisher-maiden, seduced by the son of the Viceroy of Naples, is the heroine of the famous French Opera, *La Muette de Portici*. The maiden is dumb as a fish, but all the others, Mr. Auber at their head, make such a horrible shindy, five Acts long, that at last, even Vesuvius awakes, and feeling very uncomfortable in his interior, grumbling and roaring, spits at the sky. Our public is revelling in this dinner of the Titans, which it has now devoured for the twenty-seventh time, and yet it never cries, " Hold, enough ! " The singers and players are half roasted afterwards, but really I came away almost done to a turn. However there is no lack of talent, and it makes a precious pother. . . . .

18th December, 1829.

I have just heard Auber's Opera, *La Fiancée*. When you speak of a man, you should remember at least two of his actions. The lady is bent upon marrying an upholsterer, and gets a cavalry officer in his place ; a grand spectacle arises from this, which the band has to make, and does make, alone, for thunder and lightning are on this occasion engaged elsewhere. One is amused and interested, and there is some stuff in it, though the whole thing is a merry-go-round.

They have just brought me your letter of the 16th, in which you speak of the *Muette*, by this same composer. You are quite in your own way, which is also mine. All true music can only be *mental*, and work mentally ; what is beyond that, has been already forbidden by Lycurgus, and rightly, for it is of evil ! But in spite of that severe lawgiver, I must make an exception in favour of the organ, because that, from my youth upwards, has stirred my deepest conscience, like an earnest confessor, as you long ago showed quite involuntarily in *Faust*. That scene, in its place, is crushing in effect, and if no one knows how, I know it, for I have the whole Church before my eyes. . . . .

Salve!

Z.

290.—GOETHE TO ZELTER.

Weimar, 25th December, 1829.

.... THE reason why I mention the worthy name (of Dr. Primrose) here, and illustrate my circumstances, by the picture of his family circle, I will now briefly explain to you. I lately chanced to fall in with *The Vicar of Wakefield*, and felt compelled to read the little book over again, from beginning to end, being not a little affected by the vivid recollection of all that I have owed to the author, for the last seventy years. The influence Goldsmith and Sterne exercised upon me, just at the chief point of my development, cannot be estimated. This high, benevolent irony, this just and comprehensive way of viewing things, this gentleness to all opposition, this equanimity under every change, and whatever else all the kindred virtues may be termed,—such things were a most admirable training for me, and surely, these are the sentiments, which in the end lead us back from all the mistaken paths of life.

By the way, it is strange that Yorick should incline rather to that which has no Form, and that Goldsmith should be all Form, as I myself aspired to be when the worthy Germans had convinced themselves, that the peculiarity of true humour is to have no Form. . . . .

J. W. v. GOETHE.

291.—GOETHE TO ZELTER.

New Year's Eve, 1829.

I GATHER from your letter, dearest Friend, that it was Milton's tragedy that induced Handel to write his *Samson*. However, I should be curious to know, how he treated that glorious poetic work, and how he epitomized it. I read Milton's *Samson*, last summer, with an English man of letters, (Crabb Robinson,) who was staying with us, and my admiration of it was boundless. I could not mention any work, that approached so closely to the purport and style of ancient Greek Tragedy, nor one that deserved equal recognition, both as regards design and execution. Handel probably has dealt with it, as with the Bible, extracting, in accordance with dramatic rules, the most expressive, the most important, and at the same time the most vocal portions of the story. If any little book was printed for your performance, pray let me see it, or tell me, in what other way I can obtain the information I want. . . . .

The above has been lying by me for some time, and now at the end of the year, I will avail myself of the opportunity to add what has been occupying me for some time past. When at one with ourselves, we are so too with others. I have observed, that I regard *that* thought as true, which is fruitful to myself, which is connected with the rest of my thoughts, and at the same time, helps me on; now it is not only possible, but natural, that such a thought should not connect itself with the mind of another, nor help him on—nay, it may even hinder him, and consequently he will regard it as false. Once we are thoroughly convinced of this, we shall never enter upon controversies.

The belief that I had discovered Myron's cow * on the coins of Dyrrachium, gave me special encouragement, and it is still of use to me. The people of Leipzig and Göttingen would not hear of it; that does not affect me in the least, for I have my advantage from it. . . . .

GOETHE.

* For *Myrons Kuh*, see *Kunst und Alterthum.*

1830.

292.—GOETHE TO ZELTER.

Weimar, 12th January, 1830.

IT is both right and true, that every man has something to work at and to do, either in breadth or depth, even though he may not exactly aspire to height. I am delighted to find that you are firm and energetic, as of old, and actively interested in the doings of the world, which I indeed have long since given up. . . . .

The Schiller letters are another proof, that where friends are in earnest, each day brings its own gain, so that at last, the year, when summed up, is of incalculable advantage. Details, in reality, constitute the life; results may be valuable, but they are more surprising than useful.

Your dear letter of the 9th of January has just arrived; I well remember, that you had always rather a liking for the *Rogue of Timnath*, and that I admired your courage, in not hesitating to declare yourself Samson's rival.

In Milton, according to the way of the ancients, the lady should not have appeared again, after that scene of hatred and violence. I quite understand, that the musician would have further need of her; all the more so, because in our day, people demand a complete solution, whether for good or evil. I will inquire whether the score, left here in old days, may not possibly still be in existence, somewhere in the Chamberlain's office, and then amuse myself by making further comparisons. . . . .

Herewith, my kindest farewell!

G.

293.—Zelter to Goethe.

25th January, 1830.

.... From the enclosure, you will see again, how, often enough, I represent your Vicar or Chaplain. What a lot our Anglomaniac knows about his translation of *Macbeth!* Now as I consider this nothing but one translation the more, and do not conceal it from him, I had rather not disoblige my next neighbour.

Yours,
Z.

Enclosure.

18th January, 1830.

A special circumstance, my dear Zelter, makes it important for me to know, if Schiller understood English, or not? In his Correspondence with Goethe, they certainly discuss *Macbeth*, but not a word is said, as to whether Schiller had really mastered the English language. Herr von Goethe would be sure to know more exactly; in case you too are ignorant on this point, you would very much oblige me, if, when the occasion of your writing to him offered an opportunity, you could ask for more definite information.

Ever yours, &c.

Answer.

So far as I know, Schiller read English well enough, and even Goethe would not say more. But I should not like to swear, that both these men were not of opinion, that they understood Shakespeare the poet, better than his learned countrymen.

Surely Goethe's opinion must be known to you, that it is impossible to put that colossal man, skin, hair, and all, down upon a German table, like a live sucking-pig.

At Weimar too, (in his time,) they used so to manage at the little Theatre, that every week a really good piece was given in the best style, which, I suppose, necessitated the translation of French, Italian, and Spanish plays.

The spectator cares not a jot for historical accuracy; he wants to be carried away, edified, charmed. And the Theatre exists for the spectator, even if it is much too limited for a poet like Shakespeare, though up to the present time, he has shown himself unmistakable, in every dress that German tailors put upon him. Once for all, he will not let himself be killed.

"Take care of him," says Polypheme, "that I may eat him last of all!"*

Z.

294.—ZELTER TO GOETHE.

27th January, 1830.

YESTERDAY we had our first Carnival Opera, *The Siege of Corinth*, music by Rossini, whom the German critics, for the last fifteen years, have wearied themselves out with writing down. The story is a strange jumble. . . . . The music is fresh and dashing, with powerful passages, which go off like fireworks. . . . . The dance music is so charming, lively, and exciting, that it makes one want to dance too. . . . .

Yours,

Z.

295.—GOETHE TO ZELTER.

Weimar, 29th January, 1830.

As I now know that all Europe, as well as my cloister-garden, levelled by the snow, has to get on as best it may, I submit to it the more readily, that I am not called upon to set foot outside my door. So on this bright night, while Madam Venus is still clear, radiant, and lovely, shining in the Western heavens, above the horns of the young moon, and Orion with his dog and glittering necklace, is rising gloriously from the East, over my horizon of dark pine-trees,—inspired by all this, I will send you a cheerful, friendly word to your busy, lamp-lit city, and, before I do anything else, I will answer your last letter.

I observe that friends, particularly at our age, had better not let any external event, which may be made the subject

* This is a quotation from Goethe.

of controversy, fall at once into limbo; they ought rather
to go on considering it. For this reason, all that you say,
relating to the Aristotelian point in question,* is most
welcome to me, as it forms a most perfect commentary on
your and my own convictions. Moreover, differences like
these are important, if only, because when closely examined,
the dispute does not concern merely one individual case, but
two distinct factions which stand opposed to one another,
two kinds of representations, opposing one another at
particular points, because they would fain set each other
aside entirely. We contend that a work of Art should
be perfect, *in and of itself*; others think of the outward
effect produced by it—a point, which the true artist does
not trouble himself about in the least; as little as Nature
herself, when she produces a lion, or a humming-bird.
And even if we were only importing our own conviction
into Aristotle, we should be right, for it would be perfectly
correct, and proven, even without him; let him who
chooses to do so, interpret the passage differently.

Following on what went before, let me tell you in
fun, that in my *Wahlverwandtschaften*, I took care to round
off the inward, true Katharsis, with as much purity and
finish as possible, but I do not therefore imagine that any
pretty fellow could thereby be purged from the lust of
looking after the wife of another. The sixth commandment,
which seemed to the Elohim-Jehovah to be so necessary,
even in the wilderness, that he engraved it on granite
tables with His own finger,—this it will still be necessary to uphold in our blotting-paper Catechisms.

Pardon this! the subject is of such great importance,
that friends should ever take counsel with one another
about it; nay, I go so far as to add, that an incalculable
service has been rendered by our old Kant to the World,
and I may say, to my own self, in that he has, in his *Kritik
der Urtheilskraft*, placed *Art* and *Nature* side by side, and
admitted that both have the right to act from great principles, independently of any aim. In the same way,
Spinoza, in earlier days, confirmed me in my abhorrence
of those absurd final causes. Nature and Art are too

---

* This refers to a difference of opinion between Goethe and Professor
Raumer, as to the meaning of a passage in Aristotle's *Poetics*.

grand to go forth in pursuit of aims, nor is it necessary that they should, for there are relations everywhere and relations constitute life.

Hardly have I got so far, when another Berliner begins a quarrel with me. For it seems that Herr S―― too wants to win his spurs, by having a tilt at *me*. If only the good people, who generally ignore me, when they are making use of me, would also leave me in peace, when they cannot make use of me, they might express their opinions as powerfully and convincingly as they chose, and find as many followers as they could. I have found that idea absurd,* I have already said as much, and I shall say it again. However, we must not let this astonish or annoy us, for after all, there are still able ecclesiastics, who interpret *The Song of Solomon*,† of the sacred relationship between Christ and His Bride, the Church.

I had occasion lately to look at the original again; one is always glad to be led to it. I have dictated a few pages on this subject, which I shall probably send you, on condition that you do not show them to anyone. For who would care to let himself in further, for this feeble, poverty-stricken business?

I repeat what I said above: Let us become more and more convinced, that these differences indicate an immense chasm, which separates men from one another; nay, not one chasm, but many chasms, which in our younger days we leapt across, or bridged over, but which in maturer age, must be looked upon as given to us for the strengthening of our position.

I have—it is true—carefully to raise my drawbridges, and am constantly pushing my fortifications further forward; you, on the other hand, have to keep constantly on the field, and after your own fashion, to fight your way through in the given direction, and this suits you so well, that one cannot wish it were otherwise. And besides, you reap from it great and inestimable enjoyment, which the rest of us are unfortunately shut out from. . . .

* See *Goethe's Werke*, vol. xlv. p. 113.
† Goethe had made a free translation of *The Song of Solomon*, in his youth. In a letter to Merck, he calls it "the most splendid collection of love lyrics that God has made."

I have not been able to continue reading Bourrienne; he is always plucking at the freshly embroidered Imperial mantle, which was so soon cast aside, thinking to elevate himself thereby,—just as Böttiger rejoiced, when the Doge of Venice was deposed, as if his leader had died, and he were now to be promoted.

I would not exactly advise you to take in hand the more recent History of France, by Bignon, though the author is a genuine and thorough Napoleonist; as a diplomatist of many years standing, he has had the opportunity of seeing deeper than most men into the leading causes and effects. All this may pass muster, like the efforts of astronomers, whose observations and calculations we will not find fault with, inasmuch as, at all events, they bring us a little nearer to the idea of the Incomprehensible.

Thus ever, yours,
J. W. v. GOETHE.

296.—ZELTER TO GOETHE.

6th February, 1830.

.... I HAVE just read Corneille's *Cinna*, moved thereto by your last letter, and at the same time by Napoleon, who said, that he would have made Corneille a prince, had the poet lived under him. To be sure, *Cinna* is one of the crowns of French Tragedy. . . . .

Z.

297.—GOETHE TO ZELTER.

Weimar, 15th February, 1830.

" As to the title of my life's confidences—*Wahrheit und Dichtung*—which is certainly somewhat paradoxical, I adopted it, because my experience is, that the public always entertains some doubt as to the truthfulness of such biographical efforts. To meet this, I acknowledged to having written a kind of fiction, driven to it, to some extent unnecessarily, by a certain spirit of contradiction. For it was my most earnest endeavour, as far as possible, to represent and express the genuine, fundamental truth, which, as far as I could see into it, had prevailed throughout my life. But if such a thing is not possible in later years, without the co-operation of memory, and therefore of the imaginative faculty, so that in one way or other, we never fail to exercise the poetic gift, then it is clear, that we shall present, and bring into relief the *results*, and the past as it seems to us *now*, rather than the individual events, as they happened *then*. For does not the most ordinary chronicle necessarily embody something of the spirit of the time in which it was written? Will not the fourteenth century hand down the tradition of a comet more ominously than the nineteenth? Nay, in the same town you may hear one version of a striking event in the morning, and another in the evening.

Under the word *Dichtung*, I comprised all that belongs to the narrator and the narrative, so that I could make use of the truth, of which I was conscious, for my own ends. Whether I have attained them, I leave to the generous reader to determine, for then the question arises, Is what has been related consistent? Does it give an idea of the gradual development of a personality, already well known through his works?

In every History, even if it be written diplomatically, we always see the nation, the party, to which the writer belonged, peering through. The French speak of English History in a very different tone to that of the English themselves!

I was lately very much struck by this, in the memoirs of the Duc de St. Simon; you cannot fully enjoy the detailed reports of this highly educated and truth-loving man, unless you remember, that they are written by a *Duc* and a *Pair*. It is the reflection of a period, in which grand people find less to win, than they must fear to lose.

I felt it my duty to write the above, dearest Friend, in reply to a question very much like yours, which was put to me by one whom I highly honour; I give you the answer I gave him, as it is to the point in both instances. Remember that with every breath we draw, an ethereal stream of Lethe runs through our whole being, so that we have but a partial recollection of our joys, and scarcely any of our sorrows. I have always known how to value, profit by, and enhance the use of this precious gift of God.

Therefore, by the time it is a question of the cuffs and thumps, with which Fate, our lady-loves, our friends and foes have put us to the proof, the recollection of such things has—in the mind of a good and resolute man—long ago vanished into air.

It would be difficult, nay, impossible for me to specify any particular instance, as you request; * still, to please you, I bethink myself that our schoolmaster used to wield, as an emblem of majesty, a flexible ruler, which was otherwise not unserviceable, and with which he dealt occasional whacks, by way of punishment or encouragement. Yet even in those days of vigorous pedagogues, a humanizing means of information had been discovered, foreshadowing that, which since Beccaria's time, has had so gracious an influence on our Criminal Code,—for those who were to be punished, were made to hold out a hand, and submit again and again to canings more or less severe. This gave one an opportunity of boldly stretching out one's hand, like Mucius Scævola, and gaining an heroic martyr's wreath, without moving a muscle of one's face. Now, whatever may be the prospect of your winning or losing the dozen of champagne, I wish to bring forward my testimony, to the best of my recollection, with the greatest show of Truth (*Wahrheit*), and leaving Poetry (*Dichtung*) out of the account entirely.

We had got thus far, when a sorrow,† which indeed we had feared, though hope deferred it, came upon us; the news of this has already reached you, and my black seal, alas! confirms it. As you share in all our thoughts and feelings, it will give you much to ponder over. . . . .

Always your most constant friend,
J. W. v. GOETHE.

---

* Much discussion had been raised among some of Zelter's friends, about the interpretation of a passage in *Wahrheit und Dichtung*, which might, or might not mean, that Goethe himself had, as a boy, received "cuts and thumps" from the schoolmaster, in his own person. Zelter laid a bet of a dozen of champagne, that this was not so.

† The death of the Grand Duchess Luise.

298.—ZELTER TO GOETHE.

Berlin, 4th March, 1830.

.... ONCE more I sat out Spontini's Opera, *Olympia;* from first to last, it takes up nearly four hours. It is wearisome to endure so much in the enjoyment of so meritorious a work of Art; I cannot justify it, nor can I let it alone. What I learn from it is, that confessedly I cannot live without music. Your metaphor about the silkworm in *Tasso* * went right through me, each time I heard it. I recognize myself. . . . .

Yesterday evening I happened to pass by the Theatre, and went in, without knowing what the play was. It was *Emilia Galotti*. Now that is a Tragedy according to the rules of Aristotle. Father and mother wretched; bridegroom and bride wretched; a wretched prince; a love-lorn lady, cast off and wretched too; a wretched painter; Marinelli, a ragamuffin—all lying against one another and the world. There's the *thinking* artist for you ! . . . .

Farewell.

Z.

299.—GOETHE TO ZELTER.

Weimar, 7th March, 1830.

.... I HAVE laid aside the French Memoirs, for a time, as well as *Le Globe* and *Le Temps*. For it does strike one now and then, that all this does not concern one in the least, that about the past one probably knows as much as anyone else, and that one is neither the wiser nor the better for knowing what the day brings forth. . . . .

I have been unceasingly engaged for the last two months upon a work which gives me pleasure, and is meant to please you all as well; I am drawing fresh breath for it,

---

* Go tell the silkworm, he should cease to spin,
When ever nearer death he spins himself !
From his most secret being he unfolds
The costly woof, and never doth he rest,
Till in his coffin he himself hath sealed.
Torquato Tasso, act v. scene 2.

and hope to get it finished before Easter, so that I may once more burden myself with some new business.* . . . .

You are quite right not to give up your conception of Napoleon; it has cost us too much to get thus far, for us to abandon it for the sake of fools. It is therefore more interesting for us to read *Les Mémoires de Bignon*, an earnest diplomatist, who knows how to appreciate the hero and ruler, who worked in accordance with his great aims, and who remembers the achievements of the past in a proper spirit.

I am dictating this to the solemn tolling of bells, summoning people to the funeral service in the church; this is enough to make you realize my state of mind. The poetic confederates of Weimar too, have agreed to celebrate the event quietly, in their weekly paper (*Chaos*), which is familiar to you. I enclose you a copy; you will read it sympathetically. . . . .

Now and henceforward,
J. W. v. GOETHE.

300.—GOETHE TO ZELTER.

Weimar, 27th March, 1830.

. . . . Do not let your clear and peculiar affinity with *Emilia Galotti* be spoiled for you. This piece arose in its day, from out of the deluge of Gottsched, Gellert, and Weisse, as the island of Delos did, that it might compassionately receive a goddess in labour. We young folks took courage from it, and so became greatly indebted to Lessing.

In the present stage of culture, it can no longer be influential. If we look into it narrowly, we respect it, as we do a mummy, because it gives us a proof of the high and ancient dignity of the person preserved.

But now I should like to lead you into temptation, and recommend you to read a little book which you are sure to have heard of—*L'Ane mort et la Femme guillotinée*. The gay and talented young Frenchmen imagine that they can

---

* Goethe had been devoting himself entirely to the completion of *Die Classische Walpurgis-Nacht*.

fix a limit to the miserable *genre* of horrible, revolting plays and romances, by ingeniously outdoing them. Herein they fail to see, that they are whetting the public appetite for works of that kind, and making the need of them felt more vividly.

I will add nothing further, except my hope, that after reading this little volume, you will find your wild Berlin quite idyllic.

And so for ever.*

G.

. . . . My kindest remembrances to Felix, whose arrival you tell me of. I say nothing about it here, in order that the pleasure of seeing him again may be enhanced by the surprise.

As ever and everywhere,

G.

301.—ZELTER TO GOETHE.

12th April, 1830.

. . . . LAST week Mademoiselle Sontag made her first appearance as Desdemona, in Rossini's *Othello*, at the Grand Opera. I have already spoken highly of her to you, and I don't want to retract anything. . . . . In short everything about her, from head to foot—even her very dress—is song. This is Easter-tide, and as in the interim, on Palm Sunday and Good Friday, I have conducted two versions of the Passion Music, I have had plenty to do. Herewith I wished to satisfy, as far as I could, two sections of my good Berliners, by putting forward, within short intervals of one another, in one week, side by side, two genuine German, religious composers; J. S. Bach, whom people here compare to Calderon, and C. S. Graun, whom his friends compare to Tasso. Each performance had its special public. The *Tod Jesu* is especially dear to those, who have received the Communion on Good Friday, and Bach's *Passion* attracts persons, who understand something more than the general public; I wanted to show both parties the mutual relationship of two original German geniuses—

* These words are in English, in the original.

one of whom formed himself entirely upon Italian models, nay, generally worked upon Italian texts, while the other never went out of Germany, and as far as I know, never set any Italian piece;—naturally they are distinguished from each other, one by depth, another by clearness, while in fertility they are equal; both however, with regard to the *Cantilena*, where they speak to us on common ground, are genuinely Italian, *i.e.* natural.

Yesterday, after following to the grave my oldest friend, who died at the age of ninety, I went straight off to Mozart's *Figaro*, and found the charming Sontag as brilliant and delightful a Susanna as possible. . . . . Her special charm to me was this, that by her natural gift she divines, how this Opera, as I feel it, differs from Mozart's other works, by *the style of intrigue in the music*. One finds this style perhaps in the single pieces of any other Italian composer —Cimarosa, Grétry too, and others—but here it starts at once with the Symphony, pervading the whole action, and this seems to me to be new.

Felix had a letter from me to you, but the measles have detained him here; I commissioned him to let the letter go to you, and I hope it has arrived. They say here, that your son August is going with Eckermann to Italy; I wish him a safe arrival, lovely weather, and an eruption of Vesuvius. . . . .

Yours,
Z.

302.—ZELTER TO GOETHE.

16th April, 1830.

. . . . I HAVE just come back again from Rossini's *Othello;* Spontini took me to the Opera-house in his carriage. He too, (like all the critics,) is tooth and nail against this Opera. He affirms, that there are hardly six bars suitable to the action; that it is a *Charivari*, a *Galimathias*, no dignity, no strength, no sense, and all the rest of it. For his justification, I had again read right through Shakespeare's *Othello*, to stamp upon my mind the cruel effect of jealousy in a moral "depolarity," as I might call it, so I do not openly confute Rossini's enemies. ·I observe a discreet silence, for the thing is quite *sui generis*. . . . . In a word, I cannot find fault with it, even if I were forced to go yet again ; nay, if that most senseless play, the Opera, with its songs and dances, is to have its own place, in mirth and gravity, then is Rossini, to me alone, a born man of Operas, for I have been charmed, and—so have all the others too, against their will. The clapping, shouting, and calling went on and on, and the house was full, and beside itself with enthusiasm. Finally, I agree with Rossini himself, that he is a man of genius, and besides that, he handles his tools well. . . . .

Yours,
Z.

303.—ZELTER TO GOETHE.

18th April, 1830.

. . . . MADAME MILDER, on her journey to St. Petersburg, passed by Reval, and assisted at the celebration of the eightieth birthday of our Elizabeth Mara. That ancient nightingale still pipes, and cannot give it up; she teaches singing, and is true to the words she said to me, "I shall die, when I no longer sing." . . . .

Yours,
Z.

304.—ZELTER TO GOETHE.

22nd April, 1830.

THE following extract has, by way of justification, been reprinted in our paper, from the *Allgemeine Literaturzeitung* of Halle :—

" Herr von Goethe's dedication to the King of Bavaria,* which prefaced the last part of the Correspondence with Schiller, published by him, is an indirect reproach to those German Princes, who were Schiller's contemporaries ; it leaves us to infer, that that poet found amongst them no patron, through whose favour his existence might have been brightened, and his intellectual activity kept

---

* The King of Bavaria had been very kind to the poet, and had sent his own painter, Stieler, to take his portrait. Goethe naturally wished to express his feelings in poetry, but finding himself unable to do so, availed himself of the prose Dedication instead.

alive longer than it actually was, for the Fatherland. In order to remove this reproach, at all events from His Majesty, the King of Prussia, my most gracious master, and with a feeling, which all my compatriots will share with me, I venture to bring before the public the fact, only known to me in my official capacity, that our beloved King, when Schiller had expressed a wish to settle in Berlin, and had come to Potsdam for that purpose, assured to him of his own motion, a yearly income of three thousand *Thalers*, with free use of a royal carriage.* It was only the poet's subsequent illness, and early death, that deprived the generous Monarch, and our own more narrow Fatherland, of the distinguished honour of counting in Schiller one more illustrious Prussian."

"Berlin, 27th March, 1830."

"V. BEYME."

The thing was certainly known to me, and others besides, even though not officially, and if only out of respect for my dear patron, Beyme, then *Geh. Cabinetsrath*, I will testify, that he took up Schiller's cause zealously and provoked discussion about it. But obstacles were not wanting. The *Xenien* wrung the Academic withers of the gentlemen of the Guild. Hufeland and Fichte, honest and downright, had not yet taken root. Schiller was esteemed, and Kotzebue read, enjoyed, encored. Goodwill was to anticipate the deed; Schiller was to take it all on credit (*zu Gute*); money down (*schlechtweg gut*) would have suited him better, and—meanwhile the grass grows—well, that proverb one knows well enough!

Who that is living now can picture to himself the political-poetic-prophetic anarchy of that time,—the time of *Die Jungfrau von Orleans*? Each individual was then

* "A rich man, one day, threw from his window, a bank-note for a considerable amount, to a poet, who was passing that way, with the words, 'There, take it!' The note was immediately carried away by the wind. 'Many thanks, if only I catch it!' said the poet."

"*From the lap of the Immortals,—from the clouds doth fortune fall,
And the moment, now and ever, is the strongest lord of all.*"

This, (*Die Gunst des Augenblicks*, and Schiller's *Theilung der Erde* too,) I have, in its time, set to music, with bitter tears."—*Note by Zelter.*

an object of suspicion to his neighbour, and if men like Johannes Müller seemed to attract and repel at the same time, who then was to be trusted ? Why, the all-powerful Beyme even,—because he did not want the war, they did not want *him*. . . . .

Z.

305.—GOETHE TO ZELTER.

Weimar, 29th April, 1830.

I HAVE no reply to make to that publication. Alas! it only renews my old grief, that this most excellent man should, up to his forty-fifth year, have been left to himself, to the Duke of Weimar, and to his publisher,—whereby, no doubt, he was able to secure a moderate subsistence, though only a very limited one; only at the very last was a proposal made, to offer him a wider sphere, which would not even at an earlier date have been suitable, but when proposed, was hopelessly impracticable.

By the way, let me tell you a queer thing, viz. that after a severe but swift resolve, I have given up all newspaper reading, and am content with what I gather from social intercourse. This is of the greatest importance; for when carefully considered, it is mere Philistinism on the part of private individuals, to bestow too much interest upon matters that do not concern them.

During the six weeks that I have left all the French and German newspapers lying in their wrappers, it is incredible, what an amount of time I have gained, and what work I have got through.

The last volumes of my works are now in the hands of the printers, and the most urgent letters and the answers to them have almost all been attended to. And now I may whisper in your ear, that I have the happiness of finding that at my advanced age, thoughts arise within me, for the following out and practical realization of which, it might be well worth while, to live one's life over again. Therefore, as long as it is day, we will not occupy ourselves with *Allotria*.

One, Dr. Lautier, an able man, has sent me a little book, with a pamphlet and an explanatory letter, from which I can plainly see, that the good man has likewise bravely attacked the problems that have engaged the world, ever since it had any thoughts at all. As he refers me to you, pray give him my kindest regards. Unfortunately I dare not meddle with things in the abstract; I have so much of the concrete upon me, that I have to drag along anyhow. There is nothing more natural, than that such a man, who wants to penetrate into the depths that have to be fathomed, in his own way, should have to make his own language for himself. It will, at first, be a wearisome task for anyone else to understand it, although, if fortune be kind, he will be rewarded in the end. But now, have the goodness to send me the most realistic work in the world, the Red Book for the two Royal Residences—Berlin and Potsdam —the newest edition that can be got. I occasionally come across the local authorities, and after carefully attending to the contents of my letters, I do not want to neglect the proper formalities.

And thus ever,
G.

306.—ZELTER TO GOETHE.

28th April, 1830.

AGAIN we have finished off Haydn's *Creation*, and again we have not exhausted it. Everything that can be called a Musical Director by name, standing, and dignity, assembled upon this occasion, to solemnize the work, under Spontini, as chief commander. . . . .

As we are talking about Schiller, and I find, on my return from the Theatre, your letter of the 29th, I may as well tell you, that I have just seen *Cabale und Liebe* again. What electrical power that play had over me, and over all the impetuous youth of that time, fifty years ago, you can well imagine. He who can look back upon it from that time, will not reckon it so low as Moritz did in those days; he was right enough indeed, but he did not suspect the coming on of the Revolution. The play belongs to that time, and is so far an historical piece, full of power and mind, in spite of the low company at war with each other therein. This, and *Die Räuber*, it was reported had endangered Schiller's success, by the personal allusions contained in them. You might call these two plays the Chaos of the Schillerian Creation.

As you will hardly read to the two hundred and eighth page of Dr. Lautier's System of Thorough-Bass, let me recommend you to read the last fourteen lines of that page, for they say what the whole book means,—which indeed can be understood of itself. . . . .

Yours,
Z.

ENCLOSURE.

"On the conclusion of Haydn's Oratorio, *The Creation*, in which the respective members of the *Singakademie*, led by the excellent Zelter, especially distinguished themselves, Spontini, turning to the latter, addressed him warmly in these terms: ' Je salue avec respect le digne Nestor de la musique Prussienne et sa vaillante et unique Académie de chant, qu'il a bien voulu confer à ma direction et auprès de laquelle je le prie d'être l'interprète de mes sentimens pour elle.' Undoubtedly these few but earnest words do as much honour to the veteran of music, as, on the part of the speaker, they are in complete contrast to the rumours, constantly circulated by some persons, to the effect that Spontini has no reverence for what is great, and does not give it full recognition."—From the *Berliner Courier*, &c., by M. G. Saphir, 1830, No. 973, p. 4.

307.—ZELTER TO GOETHE.

10th May, 1830.

. . . . I HAVE now heard Mademoiselle Sontag three times in *Othello*. I wanted to see if she was *always* mistress of the situation. She was as different as three days of the week, and yet she was always Desdemona. . . . . Unhappily the sweet creature is about to become a countess; what a pity!

Felix, to whom I have given a letter for you, has been on the point of starting, from day to day. On Friday he played another Concerto of old Bach's at my house, like a true master; the Concerto is as difficult as it is beautiful, and it was good enough for old Bach himself to listen to. I am getting impatient for the time, when the lad will get away to Italy, out of the wild jingling of Berlin; in my judgment, he ought to have gone there at the beginning. There the stones have ears, here they eat lentils with pigs' ears! . . . .

Yours,
Z.

308.—GOETHE TO ZELTER.

Weimar, 3rd June, 1830.

A FEW minutes ago, at half-past nine this morning, the excellent Felix left for Jena, with Ottilie, Ulrike, and the children, favoured by the clearest weather, and the brightest sunshine, after having spent a happy fortnight with us, and delighted everyone with his finished, lovable art; there too he will charm his sympathetic friends, leaving behind in our neighbourhood, a remembrance which will ever be held in high honour. To me his presence was especially beneficial, for I found that my relation to music is still the same as ever; I listen to it with pleasure, and meditative interest, and I love the historical part of it. Who can understand any kind of phenomenon, if he is not thoroughly imbued with the course of its development down to the present time? The great thing for me was, that Felix understood this progressive advancement very commendably, and happily his excellent memory brings before him at will every kind of specimen. Beginning with the Bach epoch, he brought Haydn, Mozart, and Gluck to life again for me, gave me an adequate idea of the great masters of technique in more modern times, and lastly, made me feel and ponder over his own compositions; so he parted from me with my fervent blessing.

All this I have written off to you in hot haste, that I may challenge you to a fresh letter. Pray, say the very best you can, in words that mean something, to the worthy parents of this extraordinary young artist; give a kindly disposed botanical friend the enclosed note, and think of me as of a friend, who is not indeed always at his ease, though still ever earnestly, nay, passionately active and aspiring. He gladly edifies himself with the example that you give him.

And thus as ever, yours,

G.

309.—ZELTER TO GOETHE.

Berlin, 15th June, 1830.

THE tender, fatherly affection, with which you have honoured our Felix, has exalted his parents and brothers and sisters into the seventh heaven. I thank you as I can; it will be a lifelong joy to him. At times I grow frightened, when I look at the course of the boy's life. Up to the present time, he has met with scarcely a contradiction. As a pupil, I have not over-estimated him, nor found it necessary to praise him, although I can only view with complacency his natural obedience, and the instinct that he has, of busying himself mentally, when he is not forced to do anything; nay, I dare think of myself as having taught him the truth, as I recognize it in the second and third power, making up the full sum. He takes away with him from here a complete system, upon which he can build what genius inspires him with, and if he continues to develope in this way, he must think of his teacher. . . . .
A letter from Felix to his parents has just arrived from Munich, where he has had capital introductions. The lad still revels in the happiness that fell to his lot at Weimar and at Jena.

Farewell! Yours,

Z.

310.—GOETHE TO ZELTER.

Weimar, 8th July, 1830.

. . . . I MUST tell you, that Felix has recalled his delightful presence to our minds, by a very charming letter from Munich, in which he discusses that strange place with great judgment. His special friend there was the Court-painter, Stieler, who when painting my portrait, during a stay of more than eight weeks here, became quite one of ourselves. It is pleasant to learn, what such a man, at

such a time, and under such circumstances, regarded as
profitable. Furthermore, I suppose I must have told you
already, that my son and Dr. Eckermann started for the
South, the end of April. My son's journals on the way as
far as Milan, and thence to Venice, testify to his clear
views of worldly matters, his thoughtful activity in learning to know and to be friends with men and things. The
great advantage that this will be, to him and to us, is,
that he will get to know himself, and learn what he is
worth, far better than he was able to, in our simple and
limited surroundings. In all this you will give him your
blessing. . . . .

Most sincerely yours,

G.

311.—GOETHE TO ZELTER.

Weimar, 18th July, 1830.

. . . . ALL success to your Student Chorus! I can
quite imagine, that more modern listeners, who care for
nothing but sentimental drawling and murmuring, should
find a vigorous style of song which lifts the heart and
splits the roof, detestable; their Choral singing is never
anything else but *Ein laues Bad ist unser Thee*, (*Our tea is
all a lukewarm bath,*) and then they imagine nevertheless
that they have something of *eine feste Burg*, (*a Strong-
hold sure,*) and that a "God" of some kind or other is
troubling himself about them. . . . .

I should like to add thus much about my son: he is
looking about him with much quiet observation, and writing
diaries full of detail, which is after all the main thing, for
the objects themselves disappear, and impressions vanish.
He went from Milan, after he had thoroughly explored the
city and its environs, by way of Brescia, Verona, and
Padua, to Venice; there too he rummaged about famously,
and then went back to Milan, by way of Mantua, Cremona,
and Lodi. There he picked up what he had left behind
him, and made the acquaintance of your Professor Rauch;
they liked each other, and started together for Genoa, about
the 5th of July. Eckermann has accompanied him hitherto,
and will do so further. My son is truly the very model of

a realistic Traveller, and now he feels for the first time, how much knowledge he has sucked in. He has shown his judgment too in purchasing, at a moderate price, for my collection of medals,—especially those cast in the fifteenth and sixteenth centuries,—nearly a hundred very valuable specimens; these, to my great delight, have already reached me safely.

What I have promised you in the way of books and papers will be sent by coach, and herewith, *Herr Doctor*, I remain,

Your truly attached,

G.

312.—ZELTER TO GOETHE.

13th August, 1830.

.... To save the post, I will conclude, enclosing herewith an account of my installation as *artium liberalium magister*—a compliment not of my own seeking, but freely and ungrudgingly bestowed. Next day there was a banquet at Tivoli, every man paying for himself. There were plenty of toasts; at last it came to the turn of the newly-made Doctors. I was the only one present, the others had left Berlin, and I had to make the speech. In the ecstasy of my gratitude, and full of sweet wine, I must have expressed myself peculiarly, for everyone laughed through all the octaves; my speech was something like this: "In the name of my absent and worthy colleagues, I thank you sincerely; as regards myself, the honoured persons who have conferred on me such dignities as I now enjoy, will have to be responsible for it to God."

Yours,

Z.

313.—ZELTER TO GOETHE.

27th August, 1830.

.... For the first time for several months, I went yesterday to the Theatre. *Hans Sachs*,* a play by

---

* Two years before, Count Brühl had asked Goethe's permission to use his poem, *Hans Sachsens poetische Sendung*, as a Prologue to Dein-

Deinhardstein, is rather well given here; the poet has very cleverly contrasted the position of a mechanic, who, in addition to his craft, has acquired intellectual distinction, with that of other citizens and artisans. In the main, the ordinary citizen is quite right, and in particular instances, it is just the same with them, as with the higher and the highest classes. You too have expressed yourself satisfactorily upon the subject, and experience this more and more every day. But you must feel glad that you suggested this pretty play, by your honourable mention of the ancient father of German poets. The house was not full, but the play had a good effect—on me at any rate, if not to such an extent on any other of the audience.

One of our young musicians in the Orchestra had composed music for the *Entr'actes*, which seemed to me quite charming, if only because it does not attempt to say what it cannot. Many composers of this class will repeat after the end of an Act the very thing we are glad to be quit of, or else they betray beforehand, what is to come, tormenting the ear with strains which it cannot understand. Consequently, the value of a piece of music, which falls into its right place, and fills up the given time successfully, is untold.

Yours ever,
Z.

314.—ZELTER TO GOETHE.

26th September, 1830.

. . . . I have no comfort to give you about musical matters; I rub on in my old way, and let the rest of the world wag. Herr Marx or Markus, not the Evangelist, although in the *Musikalische Zeitung* he preaches the new doctrine of bunglers, brought me greetings from Felix, who is at Munich; this is understood of itself, as there is no good understanding between me and the bearer. This Marx has just published in quarto a *Kunst des Gesanges,*

---

hardstein's play. It may safely be conjectured, that the musical Hans Sachs of our day would make the revival of the Berlin play a hazardous scheme for an Impresario, but the comparison would interest the disciples of Wagner.

at which, by his own account, he has worked for nine years, that he may end by making Italian music a grief to the Germans. The work begins thus: "We now find ourselves at the outset of a period in the Art of music, in which Italian music fills all countries, Germany included, almost making us forget what German Art and German music are." If that were true, undoubtedly the best thing the Germans could do, would be to compose music, that would make us glad to forego the Italian. But the attack on the excesses of the Italian style, as exemplified in the once *salv. ven.* Castrati and other forgotten horrors, is as stale as the whole doctrine of Marx. Have but talent, my worthy Germans, and with that, go seek for ears and eyes, feeling and stimulus; foreign countries will do you no harm! Dürer, Hackert, Grothe, and many others besides, strengthened and confirmed their talent in Italy, and he who takes nothing thither, will bring nothing back. Handel, Graun, Hasse, Mozart, made music wherever they were, whether Scotch, Italian, Evangelical, it was all one to them,—and the world is filled with what they did, and did well. All honour to your German science—ye professorial gentlemen—if you will only let music be music still!

The quarrels over the new Berlin Hymn-Book are still going on; the truth may lie betwixt and between, though each faction may be far from it. The Porst Hymn-Book is certainly not enjoyable, unless one venerates the sentiment, the earnestness, and the truth contained in it; the new Book, on the contrary, is neither a new one, nor the old one,—nay, the very necessity of a new one just now would be open to attack, when the inability to make a new one is so candidly confessed. The cobbling and soling of the old ox-hide verses is—however brave a name one may attach to it—at best a green fig-leaf to the original sin. . . . .

To-day is the 5th of October, so I conclude in memory of the prophet of St. Helena.

Farewell, and let me soon hear your voice again.

Yours,

Z.

315.—GOETHE TO ZELTER.

Weimar, 5th October, 1830.

At a pleasant party lately, I compared you to a well-built mill, which requires water to turn its wheel-works, and must have plenty of corn, to prevent the stones from rubbing against each other. Now although, as an organic being, all this is your own, still you require a flood from without for your mill-stream, and many customers; the Theatre and the *ergo bibamus* may count among them. We wish you the choicest wheat in the shape of teachable pupils, whom you will not crush indeed, but—which is all the more desirable—grind and discipline. Take this simile in good part, for, according to Gall,* that sort of thing is innate in me.

Latterly I have again been looking into Sterne's *Tristram*, which made a great sensation in Germany, just at the time when I was a wretched little fellow at school. As years went on, my admiration for it increased, and it is still increasing, for who, in the year 1759, saw through Pedantry and Philistinism so well, or described it so cheerily? As yet I have not found his equal in the wide circle of letters.

Forgive me for thinking it important enough to tell you, that this is Sunday morning, and that nothing from without disturbs me; we have almost become accustomed of late to the wild excesses of masses of people and mobs, and marching bands too, we take for granted. It certainly seems strange to me, after the lapse of nearly forty years, to see a revival of the old uproarious tumults.

Since Herr von Henning was here, I have sent various things to the Berlin *Jahrbücher;* my contributions have been kindly received, and I recommend them to you, so that you may know what I am about. I am again taken up

---

* Johann Joseph Gall, the craniologist and phrenologist, whose lectures Goethe had attended in Halle. He was so much interested in the subject, that when prevented from attending by illness, he prevailed upon Gall to deliver the lectures, which he had missed, at his bedside. "Gall's assertion, that Goethe was born for political oratory more than for poetry, has much amused those who knew Goethe's dislike of politics." See Lewes's *Life of Goethe*.

with Nature, the best of all objects for a contemplative person like myself. The deeper one penetrates into her domain, the truer she becomes. She, no doubt, energetically resists awkward, incompetent persons, but in order to justify her sex, she yields to perseverance.

The *Campanella* was published in the *Chaos*;* if you were to send me the music for it, we should get a glimpse of flats and sharps again. The conclusion of the series for the year, *i.e.* fifty-two pages, is close at hand. I encourage them to go on; it gives our little society occupation, and is of some influence in many quarters. The title-page will have for a vignette a plan of Weimar, drawn like a compass, with points marking the places where the contributors reside.

My Frankfort patrons and friends sent me on my birthday a valuable silver goblet and several bottles of good wine, with some little verses, referring to the *General-Beichte*. Thus it resounds hither and thither, and in the end an echo comes back delightfully, now and again, to the sources amongst the rocks.

Remember me to your dear young people, and cheer them up as much as possible.

The above has been lying by me for several weeks past. The shocks of the Paris earthquake have branched out energetically through Europe; in Berlin too, you have experienced a fever fit. All the skill of those who are still proof, consists in making the single paroxysms harmless, and this gives us too plenty to do at every turn and corner. If we can manage this, we shall again be quiet for a time. I say no more.

Outside Troy mistakes are made, and inside Troy as well.
Reineke Fuchs.
G.

313.—ZELTER TO GOETHE.

Berlin, 26th October, 1830.

.... As a wind-up to the Royal wedding festivities (of Prince Albrecht), they gave us at the Opera a

* Ottilie's weekly paper, for circulation among friends. It came out every Sunday. See Letter 236, Note.

grand performance of *Wilhelm Tell, en masque*. The proper *Wilhelm Tell* was composed by Rossini for Paris; it gave offence however, on account of its revolutionary tendency, so they (h)offered (*hofirt*) us a completely new and altered text, and the Opera is now called *Andreas Hofer*. No one is supposed to notice this. Really they are just like little children, who fancy that no one can scent them out, if they keep their eyes shut.

What kind of a man Rossini is, will now be shown. My reputation is at stake. If however the work pleases, I have won, because I affirm, that no poet can do him any harm, nor make an end of him. One of these days some one will venture to adapt a *Figaro* to his *Semiramis*. . . . .

Z.

317.—GOETHE TO ZELTER.

Weimar, 29th October, 1830.

. . . . I AM glad you spoke kindly and gratefully to Herr von Humboldt, about his observations respecting my stay in Rome; it gave me much to think of and remember. He had a wonderful way of turning everything inside out, merging himself in the local conditions, and observing me as I then was. I found there was every reason to bring my inmost thought to bear on his remarks, and this has led me back to make all kinds of reflections on myself.

How I should like again to go over all I have recognized and known in your invaluable Museum, confess my ignorance, enrich and complete my ideas, but above all, gain for myself this once some free enjoyment, unspoilt by Criticism and History! Reflection on a work of Art is a fine thing, but praise must lead the way, and judgment follow.

Your Art Exhibition is also a living proof that everyone is busy and at work. Men with technical talent are always being born, and these are seldom without mind, even though it may not predominate. Pray let me have a few words about No. 392. It represents a royal pair in sorrow. That is a curious subject. I like the three Holy Kings adoring the Lord of the world, born in secret, and His mother and foster-father, better and better, the oftener they are painted. But I will not censure that which I have no conception of.

Limited as I am, I have been obliged to open up special paths, in order to get forward. Thus, for instance, I have been studying pearl fishery, *i.e.* trying to find out whether one could possibly obtain a jewel from gaping shells and half-decayed matter; and in this I succeeded. I have also come into the possession of such drawings as I am not likely to part with again all my life long.

6th November, 1830.

As to that branch of your *Liedertafel*,* you are not dissatisfied with it, and I should say that these excellent young people, in accordance with the advancing age, naturally want to go forward also; but whither? That is the question! We others, as all our Songs prove, required mirth within the bounds of sociability, and placed ourselves in innocent opposition to the Philistines. They, it is true, are neither conquered nor exterminated, but they no longer come into consideration. The more modern boon companions seek their opponents on a higher stage, and it would surprise me, if your pupils did not follow in Béranger's footsteps. That certainly is a field where there is still something to be done, and where they can outbid us, provided they have as much talent as the aforesaid. However, let us commend this, with much besides, to those demons who have their fingers in every pie of this kind.

It does not surprise me, that Bürger's talent is again a matter of discussion; he was decidedly gifted, and a thorough German, but he had no foundation, and no taste,

---

* A second *Liedertafel* had been started in Berlin, in imitation of the first, and the youthful members had come to Zelter, to ask him for the original Songs. "If you want to be a mere shadow of us, you are no good at all," said he, " but if you want to look upon your affair as a good sequel to a good thing, why then make your own Songs, or steal them, as you can."—"'This they did," (he continues;) "I myself wrote some completely new Songs for them, and some of their fellow-members have composed such good pieces, that one cannot but praise them. . . . . They are vigorous young fellows, somewhat inclined to anarchy, but really well-behaved, and well-disposed towards all that is beautiful, though they are like my barometer, which is always dancing up to, and down from Fair Weather, without ever coming to Settled."

and he was as flat as his public. Certainly, as a young enthusiast, I contributed much to his success before the world, but at last a shudder used to come over me, when a well-educated Court-lady, in the height of *négligé*, rapturously declaimed his *Frau Fips*, or *Faps*, or whatever the name may be. It became rather dangerous to continue the addresses one had begun to pay her, even though in other respects she seemed quite charming and seductive. Schiller indeed confronted him abruptly with his ideally polished mirror, and here we may take Bürger's part; yet Schiller could not possibly endure such commonplace near him, for his own aim was different, and moreover he attained it.

It cost me nothing to recognize Bürger's talent; it was anyhow remarkable in its day, and anything genuine and true in it will always be acknowledged, and mentioned with honour, in the History of German Literature.

It lies in the nature of the thing, that the contents of our six little volumes,* which you have been devouring, should delight as well as grieve you to the quick at the same time. Now if you consider that Schiller departed this life just at the right time, leaving us burdened with the period from 1806 onwards, you will have plenty of food for reflection, for it weighed heavily enough upon you also.

My *Farbenlehre* was printed up to about the tenth sheet; the papers belonging to it were the first that I saved. Strangely enough, it was found that someone else had also sought out the same asylum for important things, and removed what I had saved. So it was rescued over again. I found myself enabled, using my best judgment, to publish the entire work four years afterwards, and even now there is not much in it that I should care to alter. What had to be supplemented, I have inserted elsewhere; perhaps no one yet knows exactly what to make of it.

In giving those particulars, I expressed myself to the effect, that since Schiller's death we have not ceased to exert ourselves in a thousand different ways, up to the present day, which also, after its own fashion, brings its own burdens.

Forgive me this strange leap-frog manner; else there is

* The *Correspondence between Goethe and Schiller*.

no talk, no diversion. I let you do the same, without much deliberation. The great thing after all is only, Forwards!

G.

318.—ZELTER TO GOETHE.

2nd November, 1830.

.... A CERTAIN Madame Birch-Pfeiffer ingratiated herself with me the day before yesterday, by her acting as Countess Orsina (in Lessing's *Emilia Galotti*), and I shall be very glad to see her again. The objection I have never ceased to feel in my inmost heart, from old times, to the chief character in this well-known Tragedy, has now been brought into tragical agreement with the rest, by this Madame Birch-Pfeiffer aforesaid. From her first appearance in the Fourth Act, until she accompanies Claudia, the mother, to Guastalla, she makes herself an object of deep sympathy, as an Italian, as a lover,—nay, as almost lovable. A downright passion, disciplined by modesty and good breeding, must inspire respect. With all this, she is no beauty; her face scarcely pleased me—still she makes up for that by her deportment, her cleverness, and her clear elocution. In *her* version of it, the Prince is a murderer, and Marinelli, who is intended to be her counterpart, is a made-up, marred abortion. Madame Birch-Pfeiffer is also the authoress of a play, *Das Pfefferrösel*, which pleased me; I hope I shall get to know her personally. . . . .

Yesterday, I at length saw and heard the much-abused *soi-disant Andreas Hofer, ci-devant Wilhelm Tell*, and I think I have won my game.

This time the Composer has written an Opera for Paris, which has a capital Orchestra, and screamers for singers. I recognized the man himself in his complete individuality; still, his work is a novelty, as his ground is new, and I consider this Opera actually unfeasible in Italy, as the singers will decline to sing it, and the Orchestra cannot play it. The work is in four Acts, and throughout, all is spirit and life. Though in Rossini's Italian Operas we may have many a dreary moment, here there is nothing but continuous animation, fire, and variety. The poem is a ridiculous falsifica-

tion of the history of our time, and reminds one of the countless defeats of the triumphant party, nay, of the disgraceful fall of a brave patriot, about whom no one has troubled himself, except the enemy of the Fatherland. . . . .
The music so excited me, that I could not sleep that night; perhaps I may send you fuller details about the second performance. . . . .

Your account of your pearl-fishery is a second pearl. . . . .

Hegel and his wife have got the fever again, and I am anxious about both of them. Felix will, I expect, be in Rome now, whereat I greatly rejoice, as his mother was always opposed to Italy. I dreaded seeing him here, and in the country too, dissolving like a jelly under the corrupting influence of family gossip, for I consider him really a first-rate player, because he plays everything, and is a master of all styles. Let him go forth, therefore, into the world, and discover his masters, and awake them, and begin where the beginning is; the materials for that he brings with him. . . . .
Yours,
Z.

319.—GOETHE TO ZELTER.

Weimar, 9th November, 1830.

You have been good enough to send a silhouette of your world of wonders, deeds, and sounds into my cell here; here are *Cephalus and Procris* for you, with my interpretation of them.* Place yourself in front of it, stick in hand, thoughtfully, while you interpret it, as a ballad-singer does his song; anyhow it will satisfy you for the moment. But here where it ends, it ought properly to begin. Oh, the grandeur of the representation of a thing that can scarcely be represented at all!

Let me skip over to the *Woman of Samaria*!† Each of

---

* Appended to this letter is a long and minute description of Giulio Romano's picture.

† This refers to Hensel's picture of *Christ at the Well of Samaria*. The following quotation shows the impression that it made on Zelter's mind:—" In the distance, the Disciples are coming out of a wood, and the foremost of them, with arm uplifted, seems to say, 'There He sits again, talking with a maiden, while we must go and look for Him!'—

Christ's appearances, every one of His utterances tends to bring what is above us within the range of contemplation. He is always rising Himself, and raising others from what is low, and as this is most striking with sinners and transgressors, such instances occur very frequently.

This grand, moral, Prophet-like act cannot, however, be sensuously represented, and pictures of this kind are only painted, because they have often been painted before, and because artists like to repeat a seductive woman doing the devotional. When we consider the many husbands of the Samaritan woman, we certainly find it hard to conjecture what the meek prophet can be to her. It may be a good picture, but it says nothing. Modern artists have no idea of this, and in the end, they have to put up with your explanation of the minor details of the story. But herein lies the fundamental error of German artists for nearly forty years past. What have they to do with me? Have we not our Moses and our prophets?

I cannot forbear stating what has just occurred to me. Schiller had this same Christ-like tendency innate in him; he touched nothing low without ennobling it. It was the bent of his inward activity. Some manuscript notes are still in existence, written by a lady,* who lived for some time in his family. She jotted down simply and faithfully what he said to her, on leaving the Theatre, when she was making tea for him, and on other occasions; all was conversation in the higher sense, and his belief that this kind of thing could be taken up and made use of by a young woman, quite touches me. And yet it has been taken up and has been made use of; just as the Gospel was. "A sower went forth to sow," &c.

Now, let anyone paint Schiller at a tea-table, sitting opposite a young woman; what can possibly be expressed in that way? although a young, innocent child, confronting an eminent man, whose words she reverences, and would like to understand and preserve, is always a more

---

The painter appeared almost angry at this suggestion, for he answered, that he had never thought of such a thing. 'And what did you think of, then?' I said rather pettishly, 'if in looking at your work, one may not think the best that is possible of a man.'"

* Fräulein von Wurmb. See Letter 355.

commendable subject [than the Woman of Samaria],—only it is not a picturesque one.

Meanwhile, enough of this; turn back again to your *Giulio Romano*, where you will feel yourself fortified against all this twaddle. . . . .

Yours in haste,
G.

320.—ZELTER TO GOETHE.

• 13th November, 1830.

. . . . KRÜGER, the painter, whose fine large picture of the Military Parade has been so successful, has hurt his head, owing to a fall from his horse at a boar-hunt on St. Hubert's day,—but there was no further damage. I tell you this, merely because it was said, that his right hand had been severely injured—which is not the case, as I learn from his father-in-law. It would be an irreparable loss to Art, if this fine young fellow could no longer use his right hand. One may carry anything too far, and I say this, only because I happen to remember, that the excellent Mozart used to have his meat cut up for him by his wife, for fear of wounding himself with the knife. . . . .

To-morrow, Sunday, our Art Exhibition closes. The life-size marble statue of Hope, by Thorwaldsen, does not explain itself to me, although the individual parts are well worked out. The attitude seems to me paralyzed,—mummified,—and the drapery fits, or rather lies upon the figure, like a shroud. I do not understand this rightly, therefore forgive my mistakes; I cannot help doubting, whether it is possible to represent Hope in statuary. . . . .

Farewell; I think of you every hour, and feel you everywhere. Your bust, and those of Schiller and our King, in all shapes and sizes, stand on the chests and tables of the humblest abodes. The plaster-cast dealers carry them about all day long, shouting, through the streets. . . . . You can buy all three busts for six silver *Groschen*, and a bargain-driver can get them even cheaper, though one can hardly believe that it pays for the plaster; but the casts are so thin, that they must be handled very gently.

Yours,
Z.

321.—ZELTER TO GOETHE.

13th November, 1830.

WHAT I learn at third hand,* now that my last letter to you is already in the post, will be no secret to thee, thou best of men! This news opens up an old sore in me, which I thought had cicatrized at last. I had just begun to devour Thomas Carlyle's *Life of Schiller*, when the letter from Weimar, coming like a flash and a thunderbolt, dashed the book from my hand.

Our brotherhood, old friend, proves itself solemnly enough. Must we live through this, endure in silence, and be still!—Yes, with our own eyes we must see that perish, wherein we have no part. That is the only comfort we can feel. With pride I say "We," for I feel pain, if a needle pricks you. — —

I have now taken up the book again, and think to understand it better, nay, I find myself again in it. If you endured with Schiller two periods of distance and neighbourhood, there were three with me, though I do not therefore thrust myself either near or between you two, for each of you must have been conscious of his influence upon the world.

Die Räuber was a play which wounded me as deeply, as it delighted me greatly. If I was horrified at Franz Moor, and allowed there was something unpleasant about that old fool of a father, still I myself was a Karl Moor, like all the rest of us young people,—just that we might step forth as heroes, from our youthful commonplace.

Then appeared *Kabale und Liebe*, in which a musician was represented, in whom I recognized the exact counterpart of our *Stadtpfeifer*, George. This man was a first-rate hand at various instruments, a well-intentioned fellow, though of rough manners, and entirely devoted to me. Then there appeared a review of *Kabale und Liebe*, which made me angry;—I think Moritz was the author of it. I could have killed the reviewer; I declared so often and so

---

* This refers to the death of August Goethe at Rome, on the 27th of October, 1830. He was buried near the Pyramid of Cestius, where Goethe, many years before, had planned a grave. Thorwaldsen designed a monument, which he erected there, out of respect for Goethe.

loudly against him, that my father once said to me, "You seem to me like one who washes himself with dirty water, for you take pleasure in that which displeases you, you love going on about what vexes you; I think you can do something better than what you have never learnt to do, nor do I myself understand it." This—like everything that my father used to say—made me reflect; and when *Fiesco* appeared, and was played here by Fleck with great applause, there arose a coolness in me, which almost passed into coldness,—so that now, what I liked best, was to take my part as a player in old Döbbelin's Orchestra, let the Operas be what they might. This second epoch extended itself up to the time of *Wallenstein*. I had then become more intimately acquainted with Engel, Nicolai, Zöllner, Moritz, and others. Then I heard the faults of the play discussed:—it was not in harmony with history, it had cost eight years' work and was still so incomplete, &c.—I was obliged to hold my tongue, though I could not agree with them.

Fleck's acting of *Wallenstein* was masterly; the more I saw him, the more I was attracted. I summed up to myself all that I had hitherto heard about Schiller, and a deep desire arose within me, to make the personal acquaintance of the poet. Speaking sincerely, the chief inducement I had, in coming to you people in the first instance, was, that I might learn to know Schiller, and therefore I came by way of Jena, because I did not know, that Schiller had already settled in Weimar. He was not long back from Dresden. Naumann had composed music for his *Ideale*, and made a pupil of his, a Mdlle. Schäfer, sing it to the poet. The first thing that Schiller talked to me about was this composition, over which he got quite angry—that so illustrious a man could so belabour a poem, as to tear its soul to tatters with his vile tweedle-dee,—and so he launched out against composers as a body!

I need not describe the effect of so comforting an oration. I had brought Schiller's and your poems in my bag, and in one moment lost all desire to unpack them. This was before dinner. Schiller and I were to dine with you. His wife came and said, "Schiller, you must go and dress—time's up." So Schiller goes into the next room and leaves me alone. I seat myself at the piano, play a few chords, and hum the *Taucher* quite quietly to myself. Towards the end of the strophe, the door opens, and Schiller—only half-dressed—steals in. " Yes, that's right, that's as it ought to be," &c. Then the wife begins again ; " Dear Schiller, it is past two o'clock; do just dress first, you know Goethe does not like waiting too long."—And so it all came right.

You will remember, how often in those days I showed off my musical *divertissements* before him, and you, and all the rest,—how you used to send Ehlers* to my room, to practise the little pieces with me, and how well he did several of them.

Forgive me for being such a gossip. To-day is Sunday, (the 14th of November,) when one has an hour's peace, though I have already attended a stiff musical rehearsal, three hours long. I agree pretty well with what I find in Thomas Carlyle about Schubart. I too felt strongly about the violent treatment he met with, for he was a musician, though his music gave me no pleasure ; nor did his *Æsthetik der Tonkunst*, wherein he taught what I was just on the point of abjuring,—how to break through the wall, so as to penetrate into the Sanctuary, when the door is close by. He had learnt nothing, and is gone to the place from whence he came.

This letter was not intended to go, until I knew some more particulars about you, but to-day is the 18th, so I shall send it.

Felix arrived in Rome on the 1st of November, and has written to his parents from thence. Let me have a word from you ; I cannot set foot in the street, without being asked how you are.

Yours,
Z.

322.—ZELTER TO GOETHE.

Sunday, 21st November, 1830.

YESTERDAY, Prince Radzivil let me hear three new scenes from his *Faust*. I cannot sufficiently praise the

* Wilhelm Ehlers, actor, singer, and author of a volume of Songs, with guitar accompaniment.

care with which everything is thought out, even to the smallest details. . . . .

The Concert given by our Madame Milder went off successfully enough last Thursday, in spite of opposition from all quarters. In accordance with her wish and the first announcement, I had to conduct the music, though I only did so as a mediator, for without my presence, it would have been difficult to avoid a complete breach with friends and foes, who would not put up with her temper, caprice, bad behaviour, and so on. She likes having her own way. Her voice is even now a work of God.

Nothing is yet announced about the approaching Carnival. Spontini is looked for, if he is not hoped for. In Paris he is said to have praised Berlin, just as he praised Paris, when he was here. No new Operas have been heard of, and *Andreas Hofer* has not yet been given again. The Ballet is now the chief interest, and little Elsler really dances, or I should rather say, twists and pirouettes, marvellously. Madame Birch-Pfeiffer has not appeared again; she did not take. She could not get into the running, and tried it on with other Tragedies, which are no go here. The critics also did not exactly express themselves in her favour, and that goes for something; now and then too they are right. . . . .

Yours,
Z.

323.—Goethe to Zelter.

Weimar, 21st November, 1830.

Nemo ante obitum beatus is a phrase which figures in the world's history, but in reality means nothing. Had it any real meaning, it should be construed, "Expect trials up to the last." You, my good friend, have had no lack of these, nor I either, and it seems as though Fate were convinced that we are not woven together of nerves, veins, arteries, and other organs derived from them, but of wire.

Thanks for your dear letter: once before too I had to send you a Job's message* like that, as an hospitable greeting. Well, let the matter rest!

* See Letter 104.

The element in this trial that is really strange and significant is, that all those burdens which I thought to divest myself of immediately,—nay, with the New Year,—letting them devolve on one younger than myself,—I shall now have to drag on alone, and that too with more difficulty than ever.

In such matters, it is the grand idea of duty that can alone uphold us. I have no care but to keep myself in physical equilibrium; everything else will follow as a matter of course. The body must, the mind will, and he whose will can trace the inevitable path marked out before it, need not feel much anxiety.

I will not add more, but reserve for myself the privilege of advancing from this point, as occasion offers. My warm and grateful remembrances to all those, who have shown themselves so truly sympathetic.

Your faithfully attached
J. W. v. GOETHE.

324.—ZELTER TO GOETHE.

Berlin, 2nd December, 1830.

ECKERMANN's comforting letter of the 29th of November told us, that on that day you had left your bed, and that as you had ordered a calf's head for dinner, that showed you had a good appetite. This gave me the fancy to get Doris, to whom I read the letter, to order a calf's head that very evening, for supper after our concert, and as the daily inquiries after you at my house are many, sixty or more calves' heads may have been devoured here in Berlin, yesterday and to-day. . . . .

Sunday, 4th December, 1830.

. . . . The joy of my household, when they brought me yesterday evening your manuscript letter of the 1st of December,* was, you may well believe, very great. Dr. Vogel's fortune is made in Berlin. He can come when he

---

* Goethe had been seized with a violent hæmorrhage on the 25th of November, but owing to the skilful treatment of Dr. Vogel, he recovered so quickly, that on the 29th he wrote to Zelter in pencil, "The individual is still together, and in his senses. Cheer up!"

likes; although there is no lack of helpers' helpers here, we have plenty of patients too.

Yesterday evening, whilst I and two other friends were at Hegel's, his pupils brought him a gold medal, engraved with his portrait. He is not yet completely recovered, there are still remnants of the fever, but he reads at least once a day. We clinked glasses to your recovery. A thousand greetings from thousands; on such an occasion as this, many a little being turns up, that hardly ever let himself be seen before. On Wednesday my pupils chanted their "*Juvenes dum sumus*," in honour of your recovery, as if they wanted to sing the roof down on to their heads. *Vale!*

Yours,
Z.

My grateful thanks to Dr. Vogel. The lines of his bulletin are for me the whole of Hippocrates; I know them now by heart, and shall not forget them.

325.—Zelter to Goethe.

6th December, 1830.

. . . . The new Opera by Theodor Körner and J. P. Schmidt is called *Alfred the Great;* in the war against the Danes, the king loses his bride, but wins her back again intact. The poem may be a weak one, but the composer publishes its weakness so loudly, that I should gladly have gone to sleep, if the devil had not carried me straight away into the midst of the batteries, for I was in the Orchestra, having given up my stall to my daughter Rosamunde.....
It calms my mind, to know that Eckermann is with you again. Why cannot I too be to you, what after all no one else can be in the same way?

Yours,
Z.

326.—Goethe to Zelter.

Weimar, 6th December, 1830.

"I think we can manage that our communications shall not be interrupted. I write a good deal in pencil, which is afterwards copied out. All depends upon the proper economy of those faculties which still remain, and which are gradually strengthening; I have great need of them. The burdens imposed upon me do not diminish, but I distribute them among kindly-disposed persons, who prove their worth doubly in this instance. By degrees you shall hear the rest. For some time past I have distrusted peaceful appearances, and am engaged in putting my house in order; this, to my great comfort, is now going forward steadily, and without confusion.

"Arrangements have been made respecting our correspondence. If, as I suspect, you have determined that Doris also is in the future to enjoy the not inconsiderable profits, express this wish to me in a legal instrument, in order that it may be annexed in legal form to the other documents, by which I consider it my duty, as far as possible, to simplify the strangely complicated state of affairs, for my immediate successors.

"To be sure, you and I are on the same footing, as regards collections; we possess what to *us* is most precious, but it cannot be valued."

So much for to-day.

I enclose the original,* that you may see how we shift for ourselves.

Step by step!

As ever,
G.

327.—ZELTER TO GOETHE.

9th December, 1830.

YOUR truly kind offer of the 6th instant would leave me at a loss, how to express anew my gratitude for your love, if I could ever feel troubled about anything that you do.

If our collection of letters is some day or other to appear before the world, it is an honour for me to know, that the name of my worthy father will be kept for my posterity in

---

* Goethe wrote the first part of this letter in pencil, so that it had to be copied out.

alliance with yours. That is more than I, who can only take, and give nothing, thought to deserve.

So much you ought to know for your purpose, that I look upon four of my six living children, (daughters,) as provided for; I should like to see the two, who are still unmarried, Doris and Rosamunde, so well circumstanced, as not to be a burden to their sisters, who have several children of their own. Besides this, there is my grandchild, Louise, who also lives with me, the daughter of my unhappy Karl. I mean to leave this pretty, gentle girl, to the care of her benefactresses, Doris and Rosamunde. They have brought her up from childhood, and they may keep her. I have a little capital in ready money, to be invested for the child at interest, should she need a dowry. Now, as I gather from your letter, that you are making provisional arrangements, in respect of our correspondence, let me recommend to you, as entitled to equal shares, my unmarried daughters, Doris and Rosamunde, as they both have been devoted and good children to me. Neither of them is over strong. Good—honourable—excellent managers—and universally respected,—they bear with patience my advanced years, and I do not know how I could live more happily, were it not for my wish to leave these dear things rather more comfortably off. I write this with some emotion, as I cannot conceal from myself, that one of us two will find himself here alone, and I have no wish but to be with thee, where thou art, and to go whither thou goest.

Let me know now, if it would be agreeable to you, to make this legacy of love in favour of both my daughters, when you only know one of them personally, and I will at once give the necessary directions, through my solicitor.

Ever your most faithful
ZELTER.

328.—GOETHE TO ZELTER.

Weimar, 10th December, 1830.

YOU are perfectly right, my dear Friend. Did I not keep the clockwork of my life's activities in good order, I could scarcely continue to exist in so pitiful a condition. This time, however, the hand has only been put back a few hours, and now everything is going again in the old steady way.

However, since the expiration of November, I have another confession to make. The loss of my son weighed heavily upon me in more than one way, so I seized upon a piece of work that should completely absorb me. The fourth volume of my *Autobiography* had lain quietly aside, for more than ten years, in the form of sketches, only partially worked out; I had not ventured to take it up again. But now I laid hold of it with a will, and it has so far succeeded, that the volume might be printed as it is now, were it not that I hope to make the subject-matter fuller and more important, and the treatment of it still more perfect.

I got so far in a fortnight, and there can be no doubt, that the suppressed grief, and strenuous mental effort occasioned that shock, for which my body was predisposed. Suddenly, without any premonitory symptom, or any distinct warning, I broke a blood-vessel in my lungs, and the loss of blood was so great, that had not prompt and skilful help been at hand, the *ultima linea rerum* would, I suppose, have been drawn here. Ere long, I will write again about other things, which I worked at industriously, during the past sunless summer, in the hope that they would prove satisfactory, before and after. . . . .

The *faithful Eckart* * is a great help to me. Loyal, pure, and high-minded, he daily grows in knowledge, insight, and judgment, and is quite invaluable to me in the way of encouragement and sympathy ; Riemer too, on his side, makes my work and my life easier, by associating himself with me in correcting, amending, revising, and finishing off both manuscripts and proof-sheets. May we both have strength and consolation given us, to persevere actively unto the end.

Therefore, while often looking back, let us go bravely forward in this game of Goose !

J. W. v. GOETHE.

* Zelter's name for Eckermann.

329.—ZELTER TO GOETHE.

17th December, 1830.

. . . . I THINK I told you that we had a performance of Haydn's *Seasons*, with Thomson's words; this music ought to be esteemed one of our lost treasures, sung as it is by rustics, vine-dressers, and tillers of the soil,—countrified, yet with a brilliancy of its own,—so realistic, that I am always transported by it to a condition of innocence, and perfect mental equilibrium. . . . .

Your last of the 10th-14th instant was a great pleasure to me. My last could not yet have reached you, and I am now expecting your decision, as to the course to be adopted in the matter of our correspondence. I must confess too, that I cannot help feeling amused, for when I read Lessing's Correspondence with friend Nicolai, I could hardly get over the inclination to read Lessing's letters only,—and so people may feel about mine. At all events my letters have the merit of suggesting yours, and that is no slight consolation to me. . . . .

Yours,
Z.

330.—ZELTER TO GOETHE.

30th December, 1830.

. . . . A LETTER from Felix, dated Rome, 1st of December, tells me of the Pope's death, which occurred the evening before at the Quirinal. That lad came into the world at a happy hour. In Hungary he sees an Imperial head crowned, in Rome he finds a Conclave, and at Naples Vesuvius is getting itself ready for a performance. In Rome I gave him an introduction to the *Maestro di Capella del Sommo Pontefice*, Baini, and to the Abbate Santini. The latter, a musical antiquary and collector, writes to me, "Oh, what a brilliant youth that is! with what pleasure do I call him my friend; one may well say of him, as Scaliger used to say, when speaking of Pico della Mirandola, 'He is a monster without vice.'"

Santini has written an Italian version of Ramler's words to Graun's Passion Music, and they write to him from

Naples about it, "All our connoisseurs nowadays will listen to nothing else but the music of Graun and Handel, so true is it, that the truly beautiful can never be lost." To be sure, I knew what they are now learning in Italy, that there are people who live on the other side of their Alps. . . . .

Yours,
Z.

331.—GOETHE TO ZELTER.

Weimar, 28th December, 1830.

OUR business, my dearest Friend, has now been handed over to the juristical workshop, whence it is to be hoped, it will issue right and tight, fit to endure, and adequate for future times. . . . .

I will not conceal from you, that I have, in thought, compared your letters and Schiller's; when I tell you this, you will feel entirely satisfied. I only wish my thoughts had a shorthand writer, to save myself the trouble of expressing them. . . . .

For the last eight weeks, I have not read any newspaper, a habit I took up some years ago, and found beneficial. We other Philistines are, after all, much like the fly which, while sitting on the wheel of a coach that was travelling along, fancied it was stirring up clouds of dust. . . . .

Most truly yours always,
J. W. v. GOETHE.

1831.

332.—GOETHE TO ZELTER.

Weimar, 4th January, 1831.

TO-DAY *Falstaff* makes his appearance, and everyone has gone to the Theatre. The Weimaranians are fair and hospitable, and therefore deserve all the good things that are offered them. Devrient has the advantage of possessing a remarkable presence; of course it is now a wreck, but still it always commands respect, and one intuitively feels what he must have been, which is attractive to everyone who can still appreciate anything of the kind. Have we not sat and looked at old castles, to get artistic views of them?

Felix, whose successful visit to Rome you tell me of, cannot but be favourably received, wherever he goes: such great gifts, so young, so charming! . . . .

The two first Acts of *Faust* are finished. Cardinal von Este's exclamation,* which he meant as a compliment to Ariosto, might here perhaps be in place. Enough! Helena, without more ado, appears at the beginning of the third Act, not as a secondary character, but as a heroine. The course of this Third Part is well known; how far the gods will assist me in the fourth Act, remains to be seen. The fifth is likewise ready on paper, up to the end of the end. I should one day like to read this Second Part of *Faust* from the beginning, as far as the Bacchanal, straight through. But I usually guard myself against such a proceeding; others may do it afterwards, who come to it with fresh organs, and they will meet with many a knotty point.

And now a pregnant little word in conclusion: Ottilie says, that to a reader, our correspondence is still more intertaining than Schiller's. What she means by this, and

---

* On the first appearance of *Orlando Furioso*, Cardinal d'Este said to Ariosto, " *Dove, diavolo, Messer Lodovico, avete pigliate tante coglionerie?*"

how she explains it, you shall, if possible, hear one day soon, if Fortune favours.

And thus, as always,
J. W. v. G.

333.—ZELTER TO GOETHE.

7th January, 1831.

..... The day before yesterday I was again at the Opera, and heard a capital performance of the *Vestalin*. The work itself is a colossal nonentity, and at the same time, a perfectly reliable measure of the present condition of Art in Europe; for this Opera is on all sides considered as one of the better kind,—nay, as a work in the grand style. It is the clumsiest trifle I can imagine. The house was in raptures, and the Overture had to be repeated, which you may look upon as a sign of the hopes that are entertained of the Opera itself.

Yesterday, I saw for the first time, *Die Stricknadeln*, by Kotzebue. The play is really good, and the performance excellent. The character of the old Baroness is masterly. But as you, a short time ago, said of Schiller, that the commonplace became dignified in his hands, so Kotzebue degrades everything worthy of respect to commonplace, and so it is in this play. . . . .

Yours,
Z.

334.—ZELTER TO GOETHE.

Thursday, 10th January, 1831.

YESTERDAY evening, between six and eight o'clock, all the world here was admiring the most beautiful *Aurora Borealis*, in a perfectly clear, starry sky. The barometer had all at once risen extraordinarily high, and we had from seven to eight degrees of cold. I can't tell you anything further about it, except that our Professor Link, upon one occasion, when examining a young naturalist, gave him as a problem to solve, the origin of the *Aurora Borealis*. The youth, who had generally stood the test well, answered in confusion, that he did know it, and it had only just escaped him, but he would think it over. "Yes, please do so," said Link, " it's of great importance to me, for I don't know it, nor does anyone in the Academy."

20th January, 1831.

I reckon it no small matter, that you allow me to take a share in everything that interests you, in every kind of way. Personally I knew Niebuhr well, without knowing his many merits ; he too, though he could have known nothing more about me, than I did about him, would ask after you, when we happened casually to pass one another, and that alone gave him a value in my eyes. He seemed to me discontented with the world and with his lot, and it was just his luck, to be debarred the pleasure of hearing, shortly before his death, as you meant him to, how well pleased you were, with the Second Part of his Roman History. What does his rare talent avail a man, if it is to shrink up into itself, and if he finds no second person with the power of contemplating his hard-won treasure ? Wolf was not satisfied with the First Part of the Roman History, but what would *he* ever have been satisfied with ? . . . .

In re-reading your letter,* I stumble again on your view of Niebuhr's work, in relation to the individuality of the writer, and I enclose a book of the words of Handel's *Te Deum*, which we performed here last week, that you may see my preface. Strictly speaking, no one knows *how* a *Te Deum* ought to be, although thousands have written more than one. Here I wanted to explain how Handel treated it in this one instance, as a German in England, as a Lutheran German Christian, and as no other than Handel. Of course I have been familiar with the work for the last fifty years. Farewell !

Yours,
Z.

335.—GOETHE TO ZELTER.

Weimar, 17th January, 1831.

SOME three weeks ago, I received a beautiful letter from the inestimable Niebuhr, with a copy of the Second Part of his History of Rome ; it was written in the full

* See Letter 335.

confidence that I knew him, and should acknowledge his merits. This important book came to me just at the right moment, when I had given up all newspaper reading. So I was glad to transport myself into those ancient times, and read myself into the book uninterruptedly, an absolute necessity, if we would really steep ourselves in such an existence. Properly speaking, it is not my ambition to see clearly and definitely into the dark regions of history, except up to a certain point; but for the man's own sake, when once I had realized his endeavour, his views and method of research, his interests became mine also. It was in reality Niebuhr, and not Roman history that engaged my attention. It is the profound intelligence and industry of such a man, that really edify us. The agrarian laws, one and all, do not interest me in the least, but the way in which he explains them, the way in which he makes those complicated relations clear to my mind, this it is that helps me on, this it is that makes me feel that my duty is, to be equally conscientious with what I take in hand.

From early days he seems to have indulged in a peculiar kind of scepticism, not like one who acts from a spirit of contradiction, but like one who has a special faculty for discovering the false, while the truth itself is as yet unknown to him.

In this way I have been living with him for nearly a month, as with a living man. I have read through the work, which is really a terrible one to look at, and have wound my way through the labyrinth of the to be or not to be, of legends and traditions, stories and evidences, laws and revolutions, public offices, and their metamorphoses, and thousands of other contrasts and contradictions; I was just about to send him a friendly reply, such as he could not have expected to receive from any of his colleagues, near or far, nor from the initiated of any class.

For as I had read and studied his book, for his own sake, I was best able to say and to express what he had done for *me*, and that was just what he wanted to do, for I was satisfied with what he affirmed, whereas professional men, as is their wont, necessarily begin to doubt again at the very point, where he thought he had made an end of it.

This unexpected blow of Fate, in addition to my other

anxieties, is most untoward; and now I do not know of a
single soul, with whom I could confer on the subject. All
people of recognized position have their own method, and
anyhow, they look at the same things in a different association and connection, while the dear young people feel
their way about in the dark, and would, no doubt, like to
discover what is right in their own way too,—only, though
their intention is good, their means are inadequate. I
find no one who shares my own peculiar convictions; how
could I expect them to agree with me about the thoughts
of others? In this state of affairs, it must comfort me—
me, whom it in no way concerns to know how it fared in
Rome and Latium, with Volscians and Sabines, the Senate,
the people, and the *plebs*,—to think that I have thereby
won for my certain edification, principles of universal
human application, with which the memory of that excellent man is most closely interwoven.

Of least interest to you would be the most important part
of the work, which treats of the measurement of acres, for
you, and all other musicians, may thank God, that you have,
by means of an equable temperature, never attainable
there, succeeded in quietly turning your acres to profitable
account.

Thus always yours,
G.

336.—GOETHE TO ZELTER.

Weimar, 29th January, 1831.

YOUR document comes just at the right moment, for
I shall very soon have settled with the future, so that I can
live again in and for the present. My will, in which our
arrangement has been attended to in detail, was handed
over to the Grand Ducal Government, as early as the 8th
of January, and lately I have had a codicil added, in order
to make the extremely complicated state of my affairs clear
to those who come after me. In such things we ought to
do all we can, for if, as history teaches us, the very least
regard is paid to the last wills of kings, a private person
has all the more hope of influencing the future, especially
if he understands well the advantages of those who succeed

him. Party spirit, caprice, and unreasonableness, have less scope for action, and are less in their element in our legal status. . . . .

Your introduction to Handel's *Te Deum* is capital, and quite worthy of you. That precious public of ours always thinks nowadays, that it ought to be served with fresh, hot cakes from the pan. They have no idea, that one has first to be educated up to anything new or any really antique novelty. But how should they know this? Why, they are always being born anew.

I have all my life long heard it said by scientific people, incidentally to many an important production, that *what is true in it, is not new, and what is new, is not true;* which means nothing more than—*What we have learnt, we fancy we understand, and what we have still to learn, we do not understand.*

Had I not taken up the study of Natural Science, I should never have got to know mankind. In matters æsthetic and philosophical, it is difficult to distinguish benevolence from malevolence; but in Natural Science, earnest and honest men very soon see distinctly, what sort of people those are, who blame Nature, when she expresses herself distinctly, and even when she has found expression through man.

But now let me confess, that I was very wrong the other day, when, in my vexation at Niebuhr's death, I presumed to say, it was Niebuhr alone, and not the Roman affairs, so ably discussed by him, that interested me; that is in no way correct. For when a man versed in his subject treats any topic lovingly and thoroughly, he gives us a share in his interest, and forces us to enter into his topics. And this is my experience just now, since the Roman Antiquarian Society continues to send me the report of its proceedings, which are quite in the spirit of Niebuhr, were suggested by him, and are now being carried on in the very way he would himself have chosen, so that they really make him live again after his death. He still goes about and works. . . . .

G.

Weimar, 1st February, 1831.

.... ECKERMANN, who like a true Ali, is penetrated with the noble idea, that light and darkness in shadow produce colour, has brought me a small bust of Napoleon,* made of opal glass, which of itself is worth a journey round the world. It stands facing the rising sun, and when the first beam strikes it, it rings all the precious stones together, gleaming and shining with a blaze of colour. If I continue to turn it towards the sun, it does the same all day long. This, then, is the hermit's privilege over all those who have so much and think so much of themselves. One can be very happy without demanding that others should agree with one; for this reason, both the happiness and unhappiness of you musicians is carried to an extreme. Of actors I will not speak at all; they dance on the razor edge of the moment.†

Pardon such life-disturbing reflections; it is these which preserve my life for me. . . . .

As I have still time and space, I will give you the following piece of news, which I hope you will be gratified to hear. Our good Mara, whom you justly love and admire, is celebrating somewhere in the *ultima Thule*—I believe at Reval—her birthday-fête,—which is an old story. The people there—wishing to pay her a compliment—applied to Hummel for some music, and to me, through him, for some poetry. And so it was pleasant to remember, that in the year 1771, when I was an excitable young student, I had enthusiastically applauded Mademoiselle Schmeling; this furnished me with a good parallel contrast, and I easily threw off a few stanzas. To be sure—had a genial, musical combination been possible—we might here too

---

* This bust had been bought at Geneva by Eckermann, and presented by him to the Poet, who records in a letter to his friend, the fascination which it exercised over him:—

"If your Dæmon again brings you to Weimar, you shall see the image standing in a strong, clear sun, where beneath the calm blue of the transparent face the thick mass of the breast and the epaulettes go through the ascending and descending scale of every shade from the strongest ruby red. As the granite head of Memnon utters sounds, so does this glass figure produce a coloured halo. Here we see the hero victorious, even for the theory of colours." See Eckermann's *Conversations of Goethe*, p. 494.

† A transcript of the Greek proverb, ἐπὶ ξυροῖ ἀκμῆς.

have given the lady endless pleasures of recollection, if the first strophe had been furnished with the once famous motives of the *Sta. Elena al Calvario,* which would have painfully, yet gracefully, led her mind back to the days of her youth. I had already thought out the programme, but it remained locked in my own bosom. What occurred, I do not know. I shall keep the two stanzas secret from you; most probably they will come to light from that quarter, or from elsewhere, but I will not anticipate. . . . .

Yours,

G.

337.—ZELTER TO GOETHE.

Berlin, 12th February, 1831.

. . . . YESTERDAY a new Opera by Ferdinand Ries * was given for the second time, with the applause of his friends, myself included. The technical part is admirable, and the Orchestra, though it had hard work, kept an artistic fête-day, and covered itself with glory. The piece is called *Die Raüberbraut.* . . . . Madame Schröder-Devrient made a very dainty bride, and her singing left nothing to be desired. In my judgment, she is superior to her illustrious mother, inasmuch as she combines this gift with smooth acting, dignity, and womanliness. . . . .

Yours,

Z.

338.—GOETHE TO ZELTER.

Weimar, 19th February, 1831.

. . . . I GO on collecting in a quiet way, and have acquired some works of the greatest value, which fortunately, no one else was on the look-out for. One of Annibale Caracci's drawings is fine beyond all conception,

---

* The pupil of whom Beethoven said, " He imitates me too much." His works are learned, but they have no vitality or real genius in them. He is best remembered by his *Biographical Notices of Ludwig van Beethoven,* parts of which were translated into English by Moscheles.

being as it is, the successful achievement of a complete
man, who has thrown his whole soul into the picture; I
want nothing higher or better.

This is not understood by our latest aristocrats of Art,
who assume an absurdly high and mighty attitude towards this most estimable and influential family; and yet
they are just the very Leos and Durantes of their Art and
time.

You do well to live and let live in your Art; I too in
the long run, do the same,—for where a human spark
glimmers but half-way up the horizon, I am glad to be in
the way.

I do not care to trust individual instances of my blessing
and cursing, even to this sheet of paper; let them wander
up or wander down, as they may.

But as in general I can refuse you nothing, the stanzas
on Mara's fête shall follow. I do not know what Hummel
has done. According to my idea, the first verse ought to
have recalled the echoes of Hasse's *Sta. Elena al Calvario*;
the second might be as original and modern as it chose.

Let me add a further point to my own credit! I have
now by degrees come to see, that I must submit to living
without my son, and the enforced attempt at again acting
as *paterfamilias* is not succeeding badly; but that the echo
of that impressive nature may not die away too abruptly
for those who befriended him, I have jotted down for his
Italian friends in the first place, a very brief sketch of his
travels, a transcript of which I shall send you one day soon.
After all, that is something. His diaries are certainly
most interesting, but owing to the continual prominence of
those characteristics, to which you were no stranger, they
cannot be made public in their own energetic and pointed
style. They would be reading for us some day, if things
could be so happily arranged, that you came to pay us
another visit; the "Swan" would spread out its wings for
you. . . . .

Always yours,
G.

To MADEMOISELLE SCHMELING.

After a Performance of Hasse's *Sta. Elena al Calvario.*

Leipzig, 1771.

Clearest notes, the heart to stir.
Youthful gladness owing,
To the Holy Sepulchre,
With the Empress going;

Pure and true, no shade of wrong.
Heaven hast thou brought me!
Thither, O thou Queen of Song,
Did thy voice transport me!

To MADAME MARA.

On the happy occasion of the Anniversary of her Birthday.

Weimar, 1831.

Rich in song, thy honoured way!
All rejoiced in hearing.—
I too sang, a rougher day,
Toilsome journeys cheering.
Now—when I am near the goal—
Ancient charms confessing,
Would that thou couldst feel my soul
Greet thee, with a blessing!

339.—ZELTER TO GOETHE.

Undated.

THANK you for sending those two glorious little poems, which, across an interval of sixty years, have a double value, illustrating as they do, two characters, both full of life and action. Our lady is about a year younger than you, and throughout her long career as an artist, has retained her special characteristics, independence and individuality. She wrote to me two years ago, to say that she was on the point of writing her Biography, as people knew only one half about her, and by no means the right half,—which we may now hope to get. Even up to the last, she has nobly ignored the original source of her many sorrows, and that was her husband, the most abandoned of all Greeks.

She came to us from Leipzig, as Mdlle. Schmeling, in the year 1771, and made her *début* in Hasse's *Piramo e Tisbe*, with Concialini, to the admiration of the King, who would hardly listen to her before, perhaps because he thought her paternal name sounded so dreadfully German. From that time up to 1773, she sang here in the Carnival Operas, *Britannico, Iphigenia, Merope.* Then she fell in love with Mara, a violoncello-player and a favourite of Prince Henry, (the brother of the King,) and as neither of these gentlemen would permit a marriage between Berlin and Rheinsberg, the lovers ran away, taking French leave. They were caught, and Mara was transferred to a regiment at Cüstrin, where he was obliged to play a fife in the band. Mdlle. Schmeling was re-engaged, and for life. Mara came back to Berlin, and was allowed to marry her. From December, 1773, onwards, she sang in the following Carnival-Operas, as Madame Mara:—1. *Arminio.* 2. *Demofoonte.* 3. *Europa Galante.* 4. *Partenope.* 5. *Attilio Regolo.* 6. *Orfeo.* 7. *Angelica e Medoro.* 8. *Cleofide.* 9. *Artemisia.* 10. *Rodelinda.* In the year 1779 there was no Carnival, on account of the Bavarian War of the Succession, and in the following year, 1780, after a revival of the Opera, *Rodelinda*, man and wife, for the second time, absconded secretly. A second time they were detained, but the King ordered them to be let go, because, even at that high price, he wanted to get rid of the husband. We have documentary evidence of this, but our friend declines to recognize it, and it is quite possible, she might complain of force. She became the rage everywhere, from the moment of her first appearance in the Opera of *Britannico*, in which, when as Agrippina, with a voice of thunder, changing into maternal tenderness, she sang the air, "*Mi paventi il figlio indegno!*" addressing someone behind the scenes, she made me weep streams of bitter tears every time I heard her. The air is the orthodox bravura air of those days; it seemed as if a thousand nightingales were shouting for vengeance. In all tragic parts, she looked a head and shoulders taller than other people. I have heard nothing grander than her Queen Rodelinda. Connoisseurs blamed her for being too quiet in passionate parts. "What!" she exclaimed, "am I to sing with my hands and legs? I am a singer: what I can't do with my voice, I don't choose to do with anything else." The relations between such a person and her husband were a subject of general concern.* .... I don't say this for the pleasure of being unkind, although Mara was no friend of mine, but in justification of the great King, who got as little praise for this, as for the Miller Arnold trial,† since people praise no one who does the right thing, and indeed, would rather not know what the right thing is. There was a good deal besides: beautiful Rheinsberg, close to the Mecklenburgh country, was a nest of banditti, upon whom, as they were under the protection of the favourite, no one who valued his life, ventured to lay a hand. The King, however, knew perfectly well, where the smuggler's thread began, which twined itself as far as Berlin, by means of the Court carriages of Rheinsberg. Mara ended his days here in utter sottishness, although his wife never completely forsook him. I once confessed to her my admiration of her noble behaviour to him, whereupon she remarked, "But you must own, he was the handsomest man you could find." Reichardt too had perpetual quarrels with him, because Mara wanted to mix himself up with the affairs of the Royal Opera. The King let him sleep, all through the Carnival time, in the Watchhouse, on a bed of boards, where the common soldiers were allowed to indulge in their coarse jokes with him. That gave Reichardt the upper hand, and now, as a young *Capellmeister*, enjoying protection, he wrote a great many letters to the King, complaining about the old musicians. Thereupon the King said, "I thought I had quite got rid of the Opera, and now I have the old worry, and one fool more into the bargain." Had Reichardt pitched Mara into the Spree, he would have been punished, but it would have been a gain to him in the end. The King was just like that,—but Reichardt made himself unpleasant.

* Here follows the story of Herr Mara's refusal to play, already given in Letter 165.
† For an account of the celebrated Miller Arnold case, which attracted the notice of all Europe, even in the early days of the French Revolution, see Carlyle's *Frederick the Great*, vol. x. bk. xxi. cap. 7.

I have begun to gossip. Forgive me, these are common topics, but I cannot forget them; people were frivolous, I dare say, but I never could endure unfairness, especially when it had to do with my Fritz. My father could not stand an unjust word about the King. His brother, who used to visit us periodically, nearly every year, was always very well received, but when he began to speak of the behaviour of the King in Dresden, my father used to say, "My dear brother, when are you going back? At home, in your straggling Gros-Röhrsdorf, you are in your element, and if I come back to you again for another visit, I will praise your Saxons, till they blush up to the roots of their hair."

I do not know whether I told you, that it was the elder Schmeling who denounced me to my father, as a composer. Of an evening, my father used to frequent a select circle of citizens, clergymen, musicians, &c., who talked together over their beer and tobacco. On one occasion, when they were reading the newspaper, they lit on a composition of mine which was announced in it,—I think it was my Pianoforte Variations on an air of Cherubino's, in Beaumarchais' *Figaro*. My father said, it was the first time he had ever found mention of his own name, unconnected with himself, whereupon Schmeling said, "It is your son too; why, I know him." Next day at dinner my father asked me, what that meant? did I know the man? "Oh, yes," I answered, "and you, dear father, know him also." "Then it's you they are complimenting. Take care that they compliment you on your drawing and geometry,"—which, so far as I know, never did happen.

I wonder if Hummel knows Hasse's *Sta. Elena al Calvario*. These spiritual Dramas, (the result of which was the Opera,) are now crowded out by the Cantata. The Cantata belongs to Chamber-music, but the Oratorio, even if it is no part of the Liturgy, belongs to the Church, like the musical vespers, &c. Hasse twice set to music this Oratorio of Metastasio's—once for Dresden, and afterwards for Vienna. Possibly what you heard in Leipzig in the year 1771, was the first composition. I was fortunate enough to come across the arrangement for Vienna, just as you came across your Annibale Caracci; I got it from eminent connoisseurs, for people fancy the one is better than the other, because it is the other. Hasse wrote about a hundred Operas, if not more, without counting his sacred compositions. Each of his works contains powerful passages, such as only a German genius, cultivated in the better times of Italy, could produce. In spirit, energy, grace, and fertility, he outstripped the Leos, Durantes, Vincis, and Pergoleses, as also the master, whom he extolled, Alexander Scarlatti. If you discard the Italian mannerism, universally adopted in those days, you have an original, in all its German strength and glory. Besides that, he was a universal favourite, so that, having full confidence, both in the world and in himself, he could give the world what it will have, and at the same time smuggle in, as it were, his own most marked individuality; hence, if regarded too superficially, he is not assessed at his true value. . . . .

I prize those passages in your letter about our August, for in answer to repeated questions, I boldly ventured to give the same answer, founded, after my custom, on your earlier letters, and daily and yearly records; Felix's letters from Rome too agree beautifully with your narrative. That dear lad has never given me anything but pleasure. Art goes on crutches in Italy. Outsiders, whether voluntarily or involuntarily, dominate it; still the Italians continue working, and if they hold out to sea, I dare say they may expect good sailing weather again. They say the new Pope is a worthy man, and if he only proves himself a man, the worthiness is sure to follow. . . . .

Yours,
Z.

340.—GOETHE TO ZELTER.

Weimar, 23rd February, 1831.

In memoriam—to a sympathetic friend.

MY son was travelling for the recovery of his health. His first letters from beyond the Alps, were a great comfort and pleasure to me; he had seen and visited, with real, bright sympathy, Milan, and the fertile plains and glorious lakes of Lombardy, returning thither, after he had been to Venice. The unbroken narrative of his diary bore witness to his open, unclouded views of Nature and of Art, and he was happy in applying and extending the varied knowledge he had formerly acquired. So it continued up to Genoa, where, to his great pleasure, he fell in with an old friend, a Mr. Sterling, through whom I was made acquainted with Lord Byron. Thereupon he parted with Dr. Eckermann, who had accompanied him so far, and who now returned to Germany.

The fracture of his collar-bone, which unhappily occurred when he was on his way from Genoa to Spezzia, kept him there nearly four weeks, but even this accident, and a skin disease that attacked him at the same time, (and was also very troublesome in the great heat,) he endured manfully, and with good humour; he continued writing his diary, and did not leave the place, till he had seen all the country round about, and even visited the quarantine establishment. He knew how to make the very best of his short stay in Carrara, and his longer visit to Florence, always paying due attention to things in their proper order; his diary might serve as a guide to any like-minded person.

After leaving Leghorn by steamer, and encountering a heavy storm, he landed at Naples on a fête-day. There he found the able artist, Herr Zahn,* who had become very intimate with us, during his stay in Germany; he received him in the most friendly way, and now proved himself a most desirable guide and assistant.

His letters from this place, however, I must confess, did not altogether satisfy me; they showed a certain haste, a morbid state of exaltation, although, as regarded the record of his careful observations, he remained fairly equal to himself. He felt quite at home in Pompeii; his thoughts, observations, and doings in that city, show that he was cheerful,—nay, in high spirits.

A rapid journey to Rome did not calm his already overwrought nerves, and he only seems to have enjoyed with a kind of feverish haste, the honourable and friendly reception given him by the Germans, and the distinguished artists residing there. After a few days he was carried to his rest near the Pyramid of Cestius, at the spot for which

---

* See Letters 229 and 381.

his father used to long, in poetic dreams, before he was born. Perhaps his diaries will give us an opportunity, in future days, of reviving and recommending to sympathetic friends the memory of a youth so exceptional.
And thus, over graves, forward!

G.

341.—ZELTER TO GOETHE.

Monday, 14th March, 1831.

. . . . I have only just read for the first time, about L. da Vinci's cartoon, and am all the more eager to have the print before my eyes; meanwhile, an anyhow kind of composition dances before my imagination. It is all very well for you to talk, my beloved, about my explaining your Fugues!* You have grown up from childhood, surrounded, and inspired by such treasures. To be sure, we saw old Fritz on horseback, lifting his hat to the passers-by,—and that was good too. There were Collections here also, but a dragon always sat at the door, stretching out his claw for a ducat. One had to struggle, to submit, if not to be refused. Princess Amalie once let me see her music books, —the titles,—through a glass door. Then she took out a work, held it in her hands, turned over the leaves, and let me have a peep at them. Then I made a dart, and seized the folio volume out of her hands. She stepped back, and made eyes like carriage-wheels; they were the eyes of her great brother. Had I known Homer in those days, she would have been my ox-eyed goddess. . . . .

Yours,
Z.

342.—GOETHE TO ZELTER.

Weimar, Holy Thursday, 31st March, 1831.

FIRST of all I must tell you, that I have received a delightful and circumstantial letter from Felix, dated

* In a previous letter, Goethe had promised Zelter an engraving of a picture by Leonardo da Vinci, adding, " Frame it and glaze it at once, —keep it before your eyes, all your life long,—refresh and edify yourself with it. Really—by way of analogy—you should be able to explain to me, better than anyone else, this leading Fugue of the power of Art over Form."

Rome, the 5th of March; it gives me a transparent picture of that rare young fellow. His parents and friends in Berlin will no doubt receive similar accounts, written with the same disciplined freedom. For him we need have no further anxiety; the fine swimming-jacket of his talent will carry him safely through the waves and surf of the dreaded barbarism.

Now, I dare say you will remember, that I have always passionately adopted the cause of the minor third, and was angry that you theoretical cheap-jacks of music would not allow it to be a *donum Naturæ*. Of course a piece of gut or wire is not so precious, that Nature should exclusively confide her harmonies to it alone. Man is worth more, and Nature has given him the minor third, to enable him to express with cordial delight to himself, that which he cannot name, and that for which he longs. Man belongs to Nature, and he it is, who can take up into himself, control, and modify the tenderest relations of all the elementary phenomena combined.

Why, chemists make use of the animal organism as a Reagent, and shall we persist in sticking to mechanically definable relations of sound, while we are driving the noblest of gifts out of Nature into the domain of arbitrary artificiality?

You will pardon me. My interest in the subject has been excited lately, and I should like above all things to let you know *where* I obstinately insist, and why. . . . .

Ever yours indefatigably,
GOETHE.

343.—ZELTER TO GOETHE.

Wednesday, 6th April, 1831.

. . . . SPONTINI, who is full of your praises, let me know at once that you were in good case. He is going to send you his *Athenienserinnen;* you have promised him good advice, which will, I hope, meet with an equally good reception. . . . .

I have heard Beethoven's *Fidelio* again, with great pleasure. The composer has been admirably successful, just in those parts where the poem is weak to a degree; he has breathed such life into one sad, dreary scene in particular, that I marvel again and again, when I hear it. This is the advantage we derive from genius: it offends and reconciles, it wounds and heals; one must go along with it, there is no use stopping and loitering.

Yours,
Z.

344.—ZELTER TO GOETHE.

14th April, 1831.

I HAVE lately heard *Der Gott und die Bajadere*, a new opera by Scribe, with music, songs, and ballet, by Auber..... The music is not to be despised, and has many happy passages, though it is much criticised, and so am I, for trying to discover a good vein in it. On the other hand, Madame St. Romain, the Bajadere elect, was incessantly applauded, though here and there, individuals objected. . . . . Your honest, sympathetic interest in my music is ever present with me; just so, I think of you as one of our audience, especially when everything is in good trim, and goes off slick. Schale, our late Cathedral organist, Graun's most devoted worshipper, told me as far back as six-and-thirty years ago, how he wished his departed friend, Graun, could have heard his music performed in that way. I need not feel ashamed of that, when I have earned already close upon twenty thousand *Thalers* by this work, though to be sure they have all gone in dinners. Who knows, how else I should have been forced to earn the money? . . . .

Dr. Seebeck has sent me your two poems on the birthday-festival of our old friend, Mara; they were printed in Reval, with another, by a local poet. I suppose you have seen them.

Yours,
Z.

345.—ZELTER TO GOETHE.

19th April, 1831.

. . . . YESTERDAY, thanks to Möser, we had an extraordinarily good performance here of Beethoven's

Oratorio, *Christ on the Mount of Olives*. The work appears to be a fragment, and it seems as if the composer had adapted his own text. Witness the following:—

1. In the Introduction, we recognize the deep, sorrowful, heartfelt prayer of a soul in the keen agony of a fresh grief. The full Orchestra is like an overcharged heart, a pulse of superhuman power. I was deeply moved. After the Introduction, Christ sings (upon the Mount of Olives) :—

> "*Jehovah*, Thou my Father, *O send
> Comfort, power*, and *strength* to me!
> *It is now at hand*, the hour of my *sufferings*,
> Chosen by me already, ere yet the world
> At Thy *command*, from *Chaos did emerge*," &c.

The underlined words stand in the happiest connection, employed with marvellous art, simply as picturesque *motifs*,—something like an exercise in sketching, when, between five or more given points, chosen at random, a beautiful form, or group, has to be drawn in by a masterhand. The nonsense of the words vanishes, familiar tones appear as if we had never heard them before,—we are carried away.

No. 4. The soldiers, who are to seize Jesus, march like regular troops to the attack, and sing, first softly, and then more loudly :—

> "We have seen Him
> Going to the mountain,
> He cannot escape,
> Judgment awaits Him."

The music of the march is beyond all praise, and if the Russians have anything like it, God help their enemies! At last the disciples are aroused, and sing, still half asleep :—

> "What means the noise?
> How will it fare with us?" &c.

And now a Trio begins: Peter wants to interfere, Jesus commands submission, and a Seraph, who at an earlier stage was already conspicuous, like Saul among the prophets, now joins with them, each keeping his own style. Meanwhile, the soldiers are at their work, and coarse enough:

"Up! Seize the betrayer!
Tarry here no longer!
Drag Him hastily to judgment!"

and so on. Thereupon peals forth a final chorus of angels only, "*Worlds unborn shall sing His praise*," &c. Even if the work has no style as a whole, yet all is dissolved and fused into the most refreshing forms, with so beneficial and happy an effect, that it is like a pleasant summer night's dream. Viewed critically, the work is a fragment, parts of which are wanting, and one could dispense with a book altogether. Still one must have it close at hand, if only to convince oneself with surprise, of the truth of what Ramler tells me about Graun, incidental to the *Tod Jesu*, "Only words, my dear Ramler! Only give me words, I will make the rest." The rest!—is not that nice? . . . .

Z.

346.—GOETHE TO ZELTER.

Weimar, 24th April, 1831.

. . . . I have received a very graceful autograph letter from Madame Mara, to the effect that the poet deserves all praise, for the pretty and transparent manner in which he recognized and clearly expressed a connection, which spun its invisible threads through many a year. . . . .

A passage in one of your earlier letters, which I came across, whilst reading them over again, brought my thoughts back to the minor third; your last explanation has completely set my mind at rest, for what exists in Nature, must after all one day be avowedly taken up in theory and practice.

Your friend Graun, who only requires words, in order to make music, reminds me of Telemann with his playbill. Those good people respect neither the value of words, nor the powerful variety of their art. Bad thoughts, bad verses, they can make use of, and perhaps they prefer these, as it enables them to act with perfect freedom. You have given an admirable sketch of the opportunities, which significant words, even in an absurd connection, afford the musician. . . . .

The *Vampyr* * has been repeated here; the subject is detestable, but, from all I hear, the piece, as an Opera, is very well thought of. There you are! Significant situations arranged in an artful succession, and the musician is sure of applause. Words, in a rational, sensible connection, afford the same opportunity, as you have so often proved in the case of my poems.

Commending you to the best spirits of earth and air!

G.

347.—ZELTER TO GOETHE.

10th May, 1831.

.... FELIX—so his father tells me—has arrived in Naples; I have not heard from him.

I suppose you would like to have my version of the *Campanella*, which I enclose for you in score. The solo-singer must fix the *tempo*, in accordance with his own well-regulated feeling, and the movement must then be kept going evenly, up to the end. I hate the chronometer, and still more the man who is nowhere without it. The theorists would make an end of me; why, they actually misled the excellent Beethoven into putting *tempi* to his works, which do not bear it in the least. What can't go and stand by itself, to the devil with it! ....

Yours,

Z.

348.—ZELTER TO GOETHE.

19th May, 1831.

OLD KÖRNER † died last Friday, and yesterday evening, his body was taken to Wöbbelin, to be buried beside his children. There was a great gathering in the house of mourners, speeches were made, and hymns sung; he was a zealous member of the *Singakademie*. I was not present, and at my time of life, I must decline such emo-

---

* An Opera, written by Heinrich Marschner in 1828. It had a great success in London, the following year, and ran for sixty nights at the Lyceum Theatre.

† Father of Theodor Körner, the poet.

tions. We shall follow soon enough, if not by way of Wöbbelin.

A young actor, Emil Devrient, is starring here; I have seen him twice, and like him. Figure, voice, elocution, and stage-business are fairly in keeping; he actually reminded me of our Wolff, who left a considerable gap, when he was lost to our stage. West's *Donna Diana* is a most charming play, a true comedy; Devrient played Don Cäsar, and was quite up to the mark, for the play is always a favourite here.

Our Opera too is a sickly body; they are obliged to come to the doors of pensioned-off members, and submit to their rather arrogant demands. Madame Milder gets, over and above her pension, a hundred and fifty *Thalers* for every Opera, and for one of Spontini's, she asks fifty *Louis d'or*, because he is guilty of her being pensioned off. This I had from Spontini himself.

Demoiselle Schechner of Munich asks five thousand *Thalers* yearly, two thousand five hundred as a pension for life, and three month's leave every year; further, her own choice of parts, and full pay, when absent from sickness. So says Count Redern, our present *Intendant*. . . . .

Yours,
Z.

349.—GOETHE TO ZELTER.

Weimar, 1st June, 1831.

Do not fail, my good Friend, to continue sending me, from time to time, a few sheafs from the rich harvest of the outer world, to which you are sent, unlike myself, who am confined wholly to the inner life of my garden-hermitage. In one word, let me tell you, that I submit to this, in order to finish the Second Part of my *Faust*. It is no trifle, in the eighty-second year of one's age, to represent objectively, that which was conceived at the age of twenty, and to furnish a living skeleton, like this, with sinews, flesh, and skin; probably also, I shall cast over it, when finished, some folds of drapery besides, so that the whole may be an open riddle, to delight mankind for ever and aye, and give them something to think of. . . . .

Have you seen the four series of marginal drawings, by Neureuther, for my Parables and Poems? They are not regularly out for sale, but I do not know who is to blame for it.

He has honoured me with a most charming illustration, in large folio, admirably drawn with the pen. His text is the Parable, *I stood at my garden gate.* His penetration into the meaning is really wonderful; nay,—and this is most remarkable,—his modest courage has set forth what is arrogantly mysterious in the poem. . . . .

I often feel inclined to draw up the noteworthy results of my silent, solitary reflection, but then I give up the idea again. For, after all, these things might occur to anyone, if he entered into certain relations, where he cannot dispense with what is rational. . . . .

Yours ever,
J. W. v. GOETHE.

350.—GOETHE TO ZELTER.

Weimar, 9th June, 1831.

. . . . THE first important thing I take in hand is the discussion about your coat-of-arms. I am sending back the model, made by our excellent Facius,* together with another, made by a clever young fellow here; at the same time, I am telling her what else she ought to consider, so that our good little artist may, with ease and freedom, attain the end she has in view. I shall be pleased if it has a cheerful look about it; a light little cross of honour is always rather enjoyable. No rational man ought to trouble himself to unearth and set up the wretched wood of torture, the most repulsive thing under the sun. That was work for a bigoted Empress-Mother †; we ought to be ashamed to carry her train. Pardon me! but were you here, you would have to put up with even more. At eighty-two years of age, we are, in fact, more serious in and with ourselves, but we let the poor dear world wander on, in God's name, in the fool's life it has led for many

---

* Angelica Facius, daughter of an engraver in Berlin.
† Helena, mother of Constantine the Great.

thousand years. It is frightful to see, how it prides itself over and over again upon its errors!

I find, on reading this over again, that I should like to withhold it; this is very constantly my feeling now, for as one does not even like to say what one thinks, why should it occur to one to write thus?

After all these somewhat Timonian utterances,—which one should not always deny oneself,—I may, I think, tell you in confidence, that since the beginning of the year, many efforts of mine have proved successful; I hold to this, since I at least, could not improve upon them. Now you will have learnt all about my literary bequests. . . . .

In the *Revue de Paris*, No. 1, the 1st of May, in the third year's issue, there is a curious article on Paganini. It is written by a doctor, who knew and attended him for many years; he shows in a very able manner, that the musical talent of that remarkable man was influenced by the conformation of his body, and by the proportions of his limbs, which helped, nay, compelled him to do what seemed incredible,—impossible even. This leads the rest of us back to our former conviction, that the organic functions cause the strange phenomena of living beings.

As I have still some room left, I will here write down one of the greatest sayings, which our ancestors have bequeathed to us: "*Animals are instructed through their organs.*"

Now if we reflect, how much of the animal is still left in man, and that he is capable of instructing his organs, we shall always return willingly to these considerations. And now, into the envelope with all speed, before I repent of having put such strange things on paper!

Thus, as ever, yours,

J. W. v. GOETHE.

351.—GOETHE TO ZELTER.

Weimar, 9th June, 1831.

. . . . THE French Theatre will never cease to be instructive in the design, as well as in the execution of its bright, social comedies. Here, Art and technique are more than a hundred years old, it is a *métier* with an ancestry,—

while with us, one wearies oneself in vain. Our actors no longer know anything more about Art, and they have no idea whatever of the handicraft; everything still depends upon this and that individual person. But enough of this; I have long since turned my back upon that region. Still, the "pros and cons" about the shortcomings of the actors, the claims made upon them, and their feebleness of response, are being constantly poured into my ears, by those of my own household, and other intimate friends.

No more to-day; continue to write to me, and stir me up.

Thus, as ever!
G.

352.—Zelter to Goethe.

Berlin, 10th June, 1831.

.... I MUST save myself in my own way; otherwise it won't do. I should require a considerable time, before I ventured to say, whether *Sargines* * is a good Opera, or not. Hitherto, I had heard it without knowing the text, and could not enter into it. Paer, productive and instructive as he is, has been for a long time the pet of the singing tribe. He himself is said to have sung his own songs with so much grace, that such a man as Napoleon for instance, whom I consider genuine, as he was not in the habit of putting constraint upon himself, was enchanted with the performance; this kind of thing surprises me. So now I have given myself a libretto, and am beginning to use my eyes. ....

15th June.

.... The enclosed is a copy of an extract from one of our Felix's letters; I dare say he is back again in Rome by this time. His father positively refused to let him see Sicily. He may have his reasons, but the father of a dutiful son should know the limits of his power. I have taken care to point this out to the old gentleman.

* This Opera was written by Ferdinando Paer, at Dresden, in 1803. In 1806 Paer accompanied Napoleon to Warsaw and Posen, was made his *maître de chapelle* the following year, and subsequently took up his abode in Paris.

ENCLOSURE.

"7th May, 1831.

"Sterne has become a great favourite with me. I remembered that Goethe, when talking about *The Sentimental Journey*, once said, that the frowardness and despondency of the human heart could not possibly be better expressed, and when I chanced upon the volume accidentally, I thought I should like to make myself acquainted with it. I am delighted with the free handling of the subject throughout, and the sharp, incisive writing. Here I get very little German to read, so I am limited to Goethe's poems, which Hauser presented me with, and, by Heaven, there is enough food there for reflection ; they are always new. The poems that specially interest me here, are those which he evidently wrote in or near Naples, e.g. *Alexis und Dora;* for I see almost daily before my window, how that marvellous poem arose—nay, as happens with all masterpieces, I often think of it involuntarily, and without preparation, so that it seems to me, that the same thing must have struck me too under similar circumstances, and that it was only an accident, that he expressed it. I maintain that I have actually found the locality of the poem, *Gott segne Dich, junge Frau;* * I maintain that I have actually dined with the *Frau*, though naturally she must by this time have become quite an old woman, and the babe at her breast, a lusty vinedresser; there they were both of them. Between Pozzuoli and Baiæ lies her house, 'the ruins of a temple,' and to Cumæ ''tis a good three miles.' So you can imagine, how the poems are renewed for one, and how differently and freshly they affect one, on closer acquaintance. I really cannot speak of Mignon's Song. But seeing that Goethe and Thorwaldsen are alive, and Beethoven only died a few years ago,—what madness for H—— to maintain that German Art is as dead as a door-nail ! *Quod non.* . . . ."

CONTINUATION.

I could support in my own instance, your conviction of the effect of organism upon the intellectual nature. Morally

* *Der Wanderer.* See Letter 356.

too it has something to do with the most remarkable individuals of my personal acquaintance. One might say of old Bach, that the pedal was the ground-element of the developement of his unfathomable intellect, and that without feet, he never could have attained his intellectual *height*. Thus I fail to understand the strange question which Lessing makes his painter ask, Whether Raphael would have been just as great a genius, if he had been born without hands? Here is a man, (our painter Begas,) who can carry a pinch of tobacco to his nose, with his arm stretched round the back of his neck. Perhaps such elasticity belongs to a painter; but had I been so endowed, my talent, eagerness, and industry would have made me the best of violinplayers, for all my instincts drove me to that instrument, which I practised unweariedly,—and by so doing, helped on the gout in my hand. In spite of that, in earlier days, I played first-rate music on the violin, both in drawing-rooms and churches, and I was successful in public with Tartini's, Benda's, Celli's, and Corelli's concertos. To sum up—in the human organism there dwells a soul, which seeks for its fellow, as you long ago expressed it, when you said that one talent hinges on another. . . . .

Yours,

Z.

353.—GOETHE TO ZELTER.

Weimar, 18th June, 1831.

. . . . As the world is now, we are forced to say to ourselves, and to repeat it again and again, that good people have existed and will exist, and that we must not grudge them the expression of a kind word in writing, but bequeath it as a written legacy. This is the Communion of Saints, of which we confess ourselves members. With the lips I am but rarely willing to utter an absolutely truthful word; usually, people hear something different to what I say,— and that too is perhaps as well.

However, I have been rewarded for my patience and perseverance, by a drawing of Sachtleben's, an artist of the seventeenth century, a pupil and a master of the epoch in Art then flourishing. The little sketch is square, and slightly coloured. He had fallen in love with the country about the Rhine; his best pictures represent scenes of this description, and this is one of them.

The remarkable point about this little drawing is, that we see Nature and the artist on an equal footing, as peaceful friends together. It is he who perceives her advantages, and who acknowledges and tries most fairly to come to terms with them. Here there is already thought and reflection, a definite consciousness of what Art ought to and can accomplish,—and yet we see the innocence of never-changing Nature quite untouched.

The sight of this picture kept me upright, nay, so great was its influence, that when for the moment, I was out of sorts, and stepped in front of it, I really felt myself unworthy to look at it. The clever, courageous fellow, who, hundreds of years ago, wrote down this sort of thing amid the brightest surroundings, could scarcely tolerate such a pitiful spectator as I was, in the midst of the gloomy Thuringian hillocks. But when I wiped my eyes and got up again, why then indeed, it was cheerful day, as of old.

Now, however, I am moved to lead you into very different regions, for I must tell you briefly, that owing to the whirl of ephemeral publications, I have been dragged into the boundless horrors of the latest literature of French novels. In one word, *it is a Literature of despair*. In order to produce an immediate effect—just that one edition may follow on another, as quickly as possible—the opposite of everything that ought to be offered to man for his good, is so forced upon the reader, that in the end he no longer knows how to save himself. To outbid the hateful, the repulsive, the horrible, the worthless, and all that abandoned tribe, by the impossible, is their Satanic business. One ought to and must, I suppose, say *business*, for it is based upon deep study of olden times, of past conditions, of strange complications, and incredible facts, so that one ought not to call such a work either empty or bad. Moreover, it is men of marked talent who undertake this kind of thing, intellectually eminent, middle-aged writers, who feel condemned, throughout life, to occupy themselves with these abominations. . . . .

G.

354.—ZELTER TO GOETHE.

Wednesday, 22nd June, 1831.

.... I AM just skimming through the *Life of Schiller*, as told by his sister-in-law, Frau von Wolzogen. Such a collection of letters, each of which was despatched at its own time, to its own place, and under various circumstances, is an important item in the literary world. Anyone who knew Schiller in his best days, must wonder how such a fruitful tree could grow up, out of the philandering life he led for so many of the bright years of his youth. Comparing the women in his Tragedies with the race he was obliged to make shift with, one would suppose that education and culture worked their own opposites. I hope to find the second part more interesting, for barring the name of that noble poet, which is always dear to me, the long-drawn phrases devoted to the mutual billing and cooing are rather meagre food. . . . .

Yours,
Z.

355.—ZELTER TO GOETHE.

Undated.

.... AFTER all, the book, [Schiller's Life,] remains an historical document, on account of the original letters; J. Kant's and Herder's are a real ornament to it. The last days and hours of that noble man are very touching, and provoked me to weep hot tears. In one's old age, it is a glory to have seen such lights burning; everyone may pride himself to some extent, on having been a contemporary of such men as I have seen, the like of whom the world will not soon again be mistaken in.

The summary of thoughts at the end of the book, derived from Schiller's personal conversation, as recorded by Fräulein von Wurmb, might well have been omitted. According to her, Schiller is made to say, "One ought not to give children too early a conception of God; the demand ought much rather to come forth from within." As regards children, they understand well enough, if you only refrain from trying to tell them, what you do not know yourself.

On the other hand, it is quite another matter when Schiller himself says, "That at times he could have been unphilosophical enough to give up all he knew of Elementary Æsthetics for an empirical advantage, for the grip of a craftsman." . . . .

To-day, the 29th of June, I have received a letter from Felix, dated the 16th of this month, and written from Rome; I expect it is the last I shall get from that quarter, and it is damaged by the quarantine regulations. It contains an account of the Easter functions in the Sistine Chapel, during the Holy Week. The lad did not let a single note escape him; he looks at the whole thing historically, without betraying the foreigner and the heretic. It says something for him, that he can grasp the whole, which was well planned originally, though now worn away to rags, and also that he can recognize the hollow body behind the outward dignity and grandeur. . . . .

In setting your poems to music, I have been obliged to look around me for a locality, to see *how* and *where* they arose, and as many a one of my melodies has taken your fancy, the apple cannot have fallen so very far from the tree. I can boast of similar good fortune with several very different poets. Schiller, Voss, Matthisson, Tieck, Tiedge, and even Klopstock, have praised my melodies. When Naumann's eldest son was born, the Countess Eliza commissioned Himmel, myself, and others, to set to music a Cradle-Song she had written for him. Naumann, the father of the child, was himself to select the piece that pleased him most, without knowing the names of the authors. He said, that in the melody which he liked best, he recognized Himmel, his pet pupil—but that melody was mine.

7th July, 1831.

On Sunday, the 3rd of July, Schinkel's new Church was at last consecrated. . . . . The second and younger clergyman, who recited the Liturgy before the Altar, complained that preaching here must be a difficult matter, because of the height of the Church, and that if the Church was empty, there would be too much of an echo. For empty

Churches, I know no better remedy than full thoughts, clearly and purely expressed. On the other hand, if defrauded of its rights, the great building rears itself, resisting, and rings hollow.

Yours,
Z.

356.—GOETHE TO ZELTER.

Weimar, 28th June, 1831.

YOUR Potsdam expedition * gives the rest of us meditative people a fine opportunity of tracing out that egoism and anarchy, by means of which everyone forces his way in where he has no business, to some agreeable post, which he cannot properly fill. But after all, this much can be said in praise of anarchy, that when once it has a fixed aim in view, it looks about it for a dictator, and sees that that is the right thing.

The advantage, however, that you musicians have over all other artists is that a universal, universally-accepted foundation exists for the whole, as well as for the parts, so that anyone can write a score, with the full assurance of getting it performed, whatever it may be. You have your province, your laws, your symbolic language, which everybody must understand. Everyone of you, even though he had to perform the work of his deadly enemy, would necessarily, on this occasion, do what was required of him. There is no Art, —scarcely any handicraft even,—that can boast of the like. You may cling to what is oldest without pedantry, you can revel in what is newest without heresy and obstruction; and even if an individual of your circle produces something strange and unusual, still in the end it must be made to coincide with the totality of the Orchestra.

And now a word or two about the excellent Felix. Herr Papa was very wrong in not allowing him to go to Sicily; the young man will feel unsatisfied, and that might have been avoided. In one of my last letters from Sicily, or the subsequent one from Naples, there must be some traces of the

---

* Zelter had been summoned to Potsdam, to take the place of a Conductor, who was too ill to lead a performance of Haydn's Oratorio, *The Creation.*

unpleasant impression, left on my mind by that idolized island; I will not bore you, by returning to this subject.

In the second place, I must tell you—but in this you must not betray me—that that poem, *Der Wanderer*, was written in the year 1771, and therefore several years before my journey to Italy. But this is the poet's advantage, that he can feel beforehand the value of a thing, which the seeker of reality loves with a double love and greatly rejoices over, when he finds and recognizes it in actual existence.

In many an hour of quiet mental work, when you are continually in my thoughts, I too have been drawn towards modern French literature, and on such occasions, have been led to reflect on the *Religion Simonienne*. The leaders of this sect are very clever people, they know very accurately the defects of our time, and they understand too, how to bring forward a worthy ideal; but when they want to arrogate to themselves the power of removing what is unseemly, and promoting the ideal, they go dead lame. The fools imagine, that they can play Providence judiciously, and certify that everyone will be rewarded, according to his merits, if he joins himself to them wholly—body and soul—and becomes one of them.

What man, what society dare express such sentiments? seeing that we cannot easily know anyone from his youth up, nor criticise the rise of his activity. How else does character finally prove itself, if it is not formed by the activity of the day, by reflective agencies which counteract each other? Who would venture to determine the value of contingencies, impulses, after-effects? Who dare estimate the influence of elective affinities? At all events, he who would presume to estimate what man is, must take into consideration what he was, and how he became so. But such barefaced pretensions are common, and we have often enough met with them; indeed they are always recurring, and they must be tolerated.

These thoughts occurred to me in connection with St. Simonism, and no doubt it might suggest many other subjects for thought.

Of the latest productions in the way of French novels, and the literature nearest akin to them, I will only say thus much,—it is a literature of despair, from which by degrees everything true, everything æsthetic, is banishing itself. In *Notre Dame de Paris*, Victor Hugo allures the reader by the good use he makes of his earnest studies of old localities, customs, and events, but there is no trace whatever of natural life in the persons of the actors. These inanimate male and female lay figures are constructed according to very correct proportions, but except for their wooden and iron skeletons, they are absolutely mere stuffed puppets, which the author treats in the most merciless manner, turning and twisting them into the strangest positions, torturing and lashing them, lacerating them in mind and body—though indeed they have no real body—and mangling and tearing them to pieces, without pity. All this, however, is done with decided historical, rhetorical talent, and it cannot be denied, that the author possesses a vivid imagination, for without it he never could produce such abominations.

Your letters, including the announcement of the musical flower-fête, have arrived safely; I was specially glad to hear from you. So much for to-day.

Yours as ever,
G.

357.—GOETHE TO ZELTER.

Weimar, 13th August, 1831.

.... I HAVE lately been presented with some handsome elephants' teeth, dug out of our gravel-pits, which are being busily worked for the construction of roads. Just fancy! The outer part, with which the elephant chews, has roots, which however recede, and either chew likewise, or remain for ever unused.

Nature does nothing in vain is an old Philistine maxim. She works ever vitally, superfluously, and lavishly, so that the Infinite may be ever present, because nothing can last.

Herein I fancy I am actually approaching the philosophy of Hegel, which otherwise both attracts and repels me;—may a good Genius be gracious to us all!

As the Royal Theatre has found out the right way of filling its exchequer, I send you the latest antithesis, which the worthy descendants of the ancient Thespis have been able to arrive at. I enclose the original, as otherwise it would not be credited, but let me have it back.

"*Theatrical announcement.*

"*Carlstadt, the 10th of July, 1823, for the benefit of Herr Ignaz Viol and his daughter Ludmille:*
Menschenhass und Reue, (Misanthropy and Repentance,) a Tragedy never seen here hitherto; unfortunately it is by the fallen Kotzebue; it consists of six Acts, together with a Prologue, which will be recited separately, at the end of the piece, by Herr Viol.

"*Postscript. Many pressing debts place us in the agreeable dilemma of our creditors, so that we cannot travel further. I act the old man, my Ludmille plays Eulalia, therefore do not let us go to grief; Misanthropy is unknown to the inhabitants of this town, Repentance is unknown to us, for having wandered hither. Therefore we ask for encouragement, for we really are reduced to nothing.*"

But may all good spirits grant us ungrudgingly, what we have hitherto enjoyed. So be it!

J. W. v. GOETHE.

ENCLOSURE.

"London, 29th July, 1831.

"I have written to you so long and so often about political matters, that it is pleasant for once, to be able to begin a letter with something quite apart from politics, though it will certainly interest all your German readers. To-day a present was sent from England to your old master, Goethe, which does honour to those who give, as well as to the honoured man who receives it. It consists of a large seal for his writing-table. On a beautiful stone, greenish in colour, is engraved a serpent, biting its own tail; the motto is *Ohne Rast aber ohne Hast,* (*Without rest, but without haste,*) a simple and beautiful reference to the activity of the great man. The stone is set in a claw of pure gold, some two inches long, upon which are a number of allegorical ornamentations in relief, partially overlaid with coloured enamel. One of these is the horse, the emblem of England, and another is a wreath of oak leaves, which

is probably meant to represent Germany. There are
two masks, and two cornucopiæ, with the inscription,
'From Friends in England to the German Master.'
This beautiful work of art, (from the workshops of
the eminent goldsmiths, Salter, Widdowson, and Tate,)
is the gift of nineteen Englishmen and Scotchmen,
(each of whom subscribed two guineas,) admirers of
German literature, and of 'the German Master.' At the
head of the list stands *Thomas Carlyle*, the author of a
Biography of *Schiller*, that has been translated into German;
I expect his brother, *Dr. Carlyle*, suggested the undertaking.
Then follow the names of *W. Fraser*, the Editor of the
Foreign Review, *Dr. Magien*, a clever writer, *Herand*, the
author of the pithy article on Klopstock and the Stolbergs,
in the above Review, and the present Editor of that
excellent periodical, *Fraser's Magazine;* *G. Movi*, one of the
translators of Schiller's *Wallenstein*, and *Churchill*, whose
masterly translation of *Wallenstein's Lager* appeared in
Fraser's Magazine; *Jerdan*, the Editor of the *Literary
Gazette;* Professor *Wilson*, Editor of *Blackwood's Magazine;*
Sir *Walter Scott*, and his son-in-law, *Lockhard*, the present
Editor of the *Quarterly Review; Lord Francis Lewison Gower,*
the translator of *Faust;* the poets, *Southey*, *Wordsworth*,
and *Prorter*, (*Barry Cornwall*,)—a brilliant constellation,
whose friendly sign of recognition from the far-off northern
horizon cannot fail to touch the noble old man, and give
him pleasure." *

* This ill-spelt letter is from a London correspondent of Zelter's.
See Lyster's Translation of Düntzer's *Life of Goethe*, vol. ii. p. 472,
for an explanation, and Lewes's *Life of Goethe*, p. 559. For *Magein*
read Maginn; for *Herand*, Heraud; for *Movi*, Moir; for *Lockhard*,
Lockhart; for *Lewison Gower*, Levison Gower; for *Prorter*, Procter.
Carlyle himself conceived the idea of making this present to Goethe,
and the design of the seal,—the serpent of Eternity, encircling a star,—
was sketched by Mrs. Carlyle. The motto is a quotation from some
well-known lines of Goethe's, which Carlyle, in his Essay on *Goethe's
Works*, afterwards translated thus :

> Like as a star,
> That maketh not haste,
> That taketh not rest,
> Be each one fulfilling
> His god-given Hest.

358.—GOETHE TO ZELTER.

Weimar, 20th August, 1831.

.... As I connect your handsome present * with my approaching birthday, I must also tell you of the famous gift I have received from the other side of the Channel. *Fifteen English Friends,*† as they sign themselves, have had a seal made for me by the first goldsmiths in the country; it is something like an oblong vase in shape, so that you can hold it conveniently in the hollow of your hand. Its workmanship shows all that the united arts of the goldsmith and the enameller can achieve. One is reminded of the descriptions, in which Cellini is accustomed to praise his own works, and they have evidently aimed at an approach to the style of the sixteenth century. The English seem to have found the motto, *Ohne Rast, doch Ohne Hast,* full of significance, for in the main, it is a very good description of their own activity. The words are engraved round a star, within the well-known serpent circle, but unfortunately in old German capitals, which rather obscure the sense. The gift deserves my gratitude in every respect, and I have sent them a few friendly rhymes in return for it.

As the dear good Weimar folk will not let this festival pass without an *Ergo bibamus,* (the accompaniment of so many others,) and propose making capital out of various other incidental circumstances, I shall probably run away for a few days, even though I may not go far. It is becoming more and more impossible for me, to accept in person such acts of well-meant homage. The older I get, the more full of gaps do I perceive my life to be, whereas others like to treat it as a whole, and make merry over it. . . . .

I have received from England a *Review of German Literature,* written by W. Taylor, who studied in Göttingen forty years ago, in which he suddenly gives vent to theories, opinions, and phrases, which have been my aver-

---

* A present of engravings, from Zelter.
† There is a discrepancy in the number. Goethe's poem, *Worte die der Dichter spricht,* is dedicated to his *nineteen* friends in England. Only fifteen of the subscribers' names are known.

sion for the last sixty years. The ghostly voices of Messrs. Sulzer, Bouterwek, and the rest frighten us now, like echoes of the departed. Friend Carlyle, on the other hand, defends himself like a real master, and is making great advances, of which more anon.

And thus ever, yours,
G.

359.—ZELTER TO GOETHE.

Berlin, 28th August, 1831.

.... At the *Singakademie* yesterday evening, we began with Fasch's grand *Gloria in Excelsis Deo*, followed by the Chorus in sixteen parts, *Laudamus Te, benedicimus Te, adoramus*, &c. Afterwards, in unspoken honour of you,* we had old Bach's strong, sonorous Motett, *Sing to the Lord a new song, let the congregation of the Saints praise Him*. I knew by the performance that they had seen what I meant, and they asked for that great masterpiece over again, and sang it with such reverential joy, in accordance with my previous instruction, that old Bach, (who was still living when you were born,) must have quivered in his grave;—anyhow that was my feeling.

After the Academy, I went to the Festival, given by the Society of *Friends of The Poets*. I came a little late, and the proceedings had already begun. At that moment, Madame Wolff was reciting the Fourth Act of *Iphigenia*. Afterwards, Herr Schall read the principal Scene from *Clavigo* in a masterly fashion, and we ended with *Die Laune der Verliebten*, most charmingly read by two young beauties. Then we went to supper, and I was directed to take my place under your bust. What ought I to have said, and how ought I to have played the modest man? As long as you know who I am, that is enough for me. Between the courses at supper, poems were read; the best part of them was their brevity and the good intention of the authors. I was obliged to say something, not to appear a regular stick, and instead of a speech, after your health had been proposed, I read that passage in your last letter, describing the English

---

* The 28th of August was Goethe's birthday.

seal. The wine which they placed before *me* was most excellent, and I could not help noticing that I had the best. It was the hour of midnight, and the second half of it I can praise from my bed.

God be with you!
Yours,
Z.

360.—GOETHE TO ZELTER.

Weimar, 4th September, 1831.

FOR six days, and those too the gayest of the whole summer, I was absent from Weimar, having gone my ways to Ilmenau, where, in former years, I worked much, though a long time had elapsed since I last saw it. On a lonely little wooden summer-house, at the highest point of the pine forest, I recognized the inscription of that song, written on the 7th of September, 1783, which you have so lovingly and soothingly sent forth to all the world, upon the wings of music:

Ueber allen Gipfeln ist Ruh, &c.

So all these years afterwards, there lay before my view what abides, what has vanished. Success stood out in relief and was cheering, failure was forgotten and ceased to grieve. The people were all living on as before, in their own way, from the charcoal-burner to the porcelain manufacturer. Iron was being smelted, and manganese procured from the mines, though it is not now so much in request as formerly. They were boiling pitch, and collecting soot, in tubs, which were most artistically and elaborately finished. Hard toilers were bringing up coals to the pit's mouth. Gigantic, primæval trunks of trees had been discovered in the pit, whilst the men were at work; one of these I forgot to show you—it stands in the Garden-House. . . . .

The Forsters have probably told you of the fête in Weimar on my birthday;* it went off very successfully. The

---

* Though Goethe had escaped from the Weimar festivities, the people of Ilmenau would not let his birthday pass unnoticed. Early in the morning, they assembled in front of the Lion Inn, where he was staying, and sang the Chorale, *Nun danket alle Gott!* In the evening, they performed the miners' comedy, mentioned in *Wilhelm Meisters Lehrjahre*.

pretty little person, whom I was so glad to see at my table, made considerable effect. Ladies declare that her exquisitely tasteful bonnet had much to do with it. . . . .

You inquire about *Faust;* the Second Part is now complete in itself. I have for many years past known perfectly well what I wanted, but only worked out those particular passages which interested me at the moment. The consequence was that gaps became evident, and these had to be filled up. I firmly resolved to set all this to rights before my birthday. And so it was done; the whole work now lies before me, and I have only to correct a few trifles. So I shall put a seal on it, and then, it may add to the specific weight of the volumes that are to follow, whatever may come of it. . . . .

Now that these demands are satisfied, new ones immediately press forward from behind, *à la queue*, as at a baker's shop. I know well what is wanted; the future must show what can be done. I have planned far too many buildings, and in the end, I have neither means nor strength to finish them. I dare not think at all of *Die Natürliche Tochter;* how could I recall to memory the monstrous catastrophe, which is there forced upon one? . . . .

Yours always,
G.

361.—ZELTER TO GOETHE.

Sunday, 11th September, 1831.

. . . . ONE more recommendation! One of my young disciples, Otto Nicolai,*—this time, no relation to the Nicolai of the Universe,—has made himself a very cultivated singer; and besides that, he has set several of your poems to most graceful music. I have given him an introduction to our dear Ottilie, begging her to introduce the little man to you. I feel tolerably satisfied too with his singing of my trifles, and am glad to acknowledge this, as I know through him, that the fault does not lie at my door, if certain people

---

* In 1833, Nicolai was made organist of the Prussian Embassy at Rome, where he studied Italian music, and composed a series of Operas for Italian theatres. The later years of his life were passed at Vienna. The best of his works is *Die Lustigen Weiber von Windsor*, or *Falstaff*, as the Opera was called, when it was brought out in London, in 1864.

do not take to them. Now, if you could find a leisure hour, in which to hear this youth, that would be a lifelong joy to him. . . . .

Yours,

Z.

362.—GOETHE TO ZELTER.

Undated.

. . . . . THE Jackanapes of the day would like to see the Nobility abolished, as though it were possible for a man of worth to lose anything, by possessing worthy ancestors! Why, I suppose they will be taking away your great-uncle next. Instead of that they ought to ask God, daily and hourly, to let all that has stood the test of years be called legitimate, and to make it their prayer, that from time to time, a creature may be born, who shall stamp entire centuries with his name.

One quiet evening, I remembered that Cicero had left behind him a little work, called *De Senectute;* for the first time I felt inclined to apply it to myself, and I found it most charming.

As these ancient authors, for the most part, write in dialogue, it is only as if what one understands as a matter of course, were thrown off in conversation. He makes the elder Cato speak, and he—if you look into it narrowly —only gives a list of the excellent people in history, who have grown old, and describes how well old age agreed with them.

Then by way of illustration, he discusses the unreasonableness of wishing to recall anything, even the immediate past. Much else that does not concern me, I leave unnoticed, but I must tell you, how highly he esteems the honour, the respect, the reverence that are paid to old age, after a career worthily fulfilled. This comes with no uncertain sound from the lips of a first-rate Roman, who both thinks and speaks so finely about his ancestors, that we should be poor creatures indeed, were we not affected by it. . . . .

I have determined to bring Felix's most charming letter to light through the *Chaos,* when a fitting opportunity presents itself.

Your protégé shall be kindly received. Ottilie knows how to manage, so that a stranger, who may not happen to interest me at the moment, is brought to me in a happy hour. I must not omit to tell you, by the way, that she and the children behave most charmingly; about that a great deal might be said, though there is actually nothing to say, because so delicate a matter cannot be expressed in words.

I myself have been renewing my friendship with the twenty-four year old MS.,* (some sheets of which you have already seen.) I trust it will yet one day give you a cheerful, and even at your advanced age, an instructive hour. Herein I am confirmed by the words of the ancient sage, the force of which I have just felt anew: "I am ever learning, and only thus do I notice my increasing years." † . . . .

G.

363.—GOETHE TO ZELTER.

Weimar, 4th October, 1831.

. . . . ALL these circumstances considered, I cannot sufficiently prize the good fortune, that so early forced me to take an interest in Plastic Art. Having no talent for the practice of Art, I was obliged to take all the more pains to acquire theoretical knowledge, mastering just so much of it as would serve me for home use, *i.e.* would enable me to regulate my enthusiasm for any work, and make it permanent.

Now I very often become acquainted with eminent artists, whose names I never heard of, by means of the engravings sent me; and that makes the whole world rich to me, for their talent is absolute and tangible. With poetry it is quite different; there I have to make too many additions, and I never exactly know, if I am right in accepting this and rejecting that. Music, which is your

---

* Goethe alludes to the beginning of the Fourth Part of his Biography.
† A translation of Solon's line :—
γηράσκω δ'αἰεὶ πολλὰ διδασκόμενος.

life, is almost completely vanishing from my unpractised senses.

I have got a strange specimen of the newest school of German poetry, the Poems of Gustav Pfizer, which were sent me the other day; I read bits here and there in the little volume, but I have only half cut it. The poet seems to me to have real talent, and to be a good man besides. But while I was reading, it made me so wretched, that I quickly threw the book aside; when cholera is imminent, one ought to be most strictly on one's guard against all depressing and enervating influences. The little work is dedicated to Uhland, and the region over which he rules, is not calculated to produce anything exciting, excellent, or likely to conquer the destiny of men, so I will not find fault with it, though I shall not look into it again. It is strange, how cleverly these little gentlemen manage to wrap themselves up in a kind of beggar's mantle of moral and religious poetry, in such a way that even if it is through at the elbows, that defect must be regarded merely as a poetical intention. I will enclose the book for you in my next parcel, if only to get it out of the house.

So much for to-day. The continuation has already been copied.

G.

364.—GOETHE TO ZELTER.

Weimar, 5th October, 1831.

OTTILIE is reading Plutarch's *Lives* to me of an evening, adopting a new method, *i.e.* taking the Greeks first, for thus at all events, we remain in *one* locality, with *one* nation, and *one* way of thinking and acting. When we have done with these, we shall pass on to the Romans, and go through that series in like manner. We leave out the comparisons, expecting to learn from our own, unassisted impressions, how far the whole of the Roman part is comparable to the whole of the Greek. . . . .

I have been looking through two volumes, which I received lately, *Fragments de Géologie*, &c., *par A. von Humboldt;* I will tell you the strange thought, that they suggested to my mind. The extraordinary talent of this extraordinary man manifests itself in his *oral* delivery, and if we look at it carefully, all *oral* delivery aims at persuasion, at making the listener believe he is convinced. Few persons are capable of being convinced; the majority allow themselves to be persuaded, and hence the treatises here before us are genuine orations, delivered with great facility, so that at last one might fancy one had grasped the impossible. That the Himalayas have raised themselves 25,000 feet out of the ground, and nevertheless point heavenwards, as stiffly and proudly, as though it were a matter of course,—this is beyond the limits of my brain, in the dark regions where transubstantiation, &c. dwell, and my cerebral system would have to be completely reorganized, (which surely would be a pity,) if room had to be found for these marvels.

But there are minds which have compartments for such articles of faith, side by side with other quite reasonable *Loculamenta;* I do not understand it, but I hear of it, nevertheless, every day. But is it necessary then, to understand everything? Once more—with us the greatest rhetorician is perhaps the conqueror of the world. For as all facts are present to his vast memory, he contrives to use and apply them with the greatest skill and boldness. But he who belongs to the craft, sees pretty clearly, where weakness is intertwined with strength, and strength does not object to see itself somewhat dressed up, decked out, and toned down.

And so the effect is great, when such a paradox is delivered artistically and energetically, and for this reason many of our ablest physiologists plume themselves on being able to conceive the impossible. Consequently, I appear to them the most stiff-necked of heresiarchs, in which character may God graciously preserve and confirm me! Selah!
G.

365.—Zelter to Goethe.

Undated.

.... After the destruction of Troy—I mean the conquest of Paris—the victorious Blücher was received by us at the *Singakademie* with this Song,* and he compli-

* Goethe's *Vorwärts*, from the *Epimenides*. It will be remembered, that Blücher was nicknamed " General *Vorwärts*" by his soldiers.

mented me as a good general, adding that he never yet ventured an action with such a mass of pretty women, and that he doubted whether it would succeed with him; whereupon I replied, that his good sword was at home everywhere, and that he might surely be contented with his victory over our hearts.

9th October.

In return for your poetical testimony to my genealogical tree, I give you back an equivalent, which I had not forgotten:

"But he whom the poet praises, he hath received a form."
GOETHE'S *Euphrosyne.*

That poem left upon me an impression of undying happiness. During the first years of my frequent visits to Weimar, I used to be enticed away, as it were, by a Sibyl, in the earliest calm of the morning, to the monument in the Park, although I had never known the dear one. Once it was like a vision,—the stone had vanished,—it was as if I heard wafted towards me, "Avaunt! thou belongest to the earth." I tremblingly withdrew. On my return through the garden, I found you, standing at the open window of your room, and you sang out to me, " Good morning, old gentleman !" That was a good morning, and it remained with me, and ever since that time, my affection for you has been growing. When I heard people talking about you, with their so and so, and this and that and the other, it was like salt to my flame. I could not be angry with them, but I was forced to esteem myself higher, because I thought that I alone understood you and myself. So it is still, though we two are no longer children; and yet again we are as children, for we are still growing and exercising ourselves in the recognition of all that is true and right, owning our imperfection still, because we hope to be perfect. . . . .

We are far advanced in the improvement of our pianofortes. Comparing our Fortepiano with the first, made by Silbermann of Strasburg, it ought to be allowed, that he laid the foundation of a Babylonian building, *i.e.* of the confusion of tongues and the despair of musical sages, who lead the lives of dogs, trying to cram all that into their theory. French music may be compared to French politics; it is mongrel, effeminate tittle-tattle; their best writers cannot shake themselves free of it. A short time ago, I heard the *Wassertrüger* again, an estimable work, against which I have nothing to say. And yet the music in itself, in those parts where it aims at personifying the real earnestness of the poem, is about as good as a drum, covered with human skin,—and this is the best work of one of their best men. As to the *Medea* of this composer, I will not discuss it at all. Blows in the air, and fights in the looking-glass; too much of everything, in order to secure something. Let him who finds the confusion of sensations unedifying, keep away. Grétry is too soon forgotten; he does not fly into regions too high for him, but his feathers are his own. He lets himself down gently, and still keeps his wings moving, so that he can raise himself again at once.

Yours,
Z.

366.—Goethe to Zelter.

Weimar, 26th October, 1831.

. . . . The brothers Schlegel, in spite of their many fine gifts, were, are, and will be all their life long, unfortunate; they wanted to produce more than they were by nature capable of, and to effect more than was in their power; consequently they have done much mischief, both in Art and Literature. German artists and amateurs have not yet recovered from their false doctrines of Plastic Art, which proclaimed, taught, and disseminated egotism combined with weakness; nay—one must even leave them to their error for a time, for they would be in despair, if their eyes were opened. Meantime, we others have to suffer, we, whose business it is, to help forward artists, whose works there is no demand for after all, because they suit the taste of no one. So those amiable Societies honestly laugh at the public, instituting lotteries for articles which no one would buy, and on which the winner can scarcely be congratulated.

I would even love and encourage what is false, if only it were in request, and well paid for. So, let it be!

To return to those *Dioscuri*,—Frederick Schlegel, at all

events, choked himself, ruminating over moral and religious absurdities, which, in the course of his uneasy career in life, he would have liked to communicate to and disseminate amongst others; he therefore sought refuge in Catholicism, and in his downfall, drew after him a considerable, but over-rated man, Adam Müller.

Carefully considered, the Indian tendency too was only a *pis-aller*. They were wise enough to see, that they could not achieve anything brilliant in the field of German, Latin, or Greek Literature, so they threw themselves upon the far East, and here August Wilhelm distinguished himself honourably. All this and +, the time to come will evidence more clearly. Schiller did not love them,—nay, he hated them; I do not know whether it appears from our correspondence, that I endeavoured to bring about social intercourse at least, within our own circle. In the great revolution which they actually effected, they took little notice of me, to the annoyance of Hardenberg (Novalis), who wanted me to be extinguished too. I had enough to do with myself; why trouble myself about others?

Schiller was justly exasperated with them; as he stood in their way, he could not get in their way. He once said to me, when he was chafing at my habit of general forbearance, and even of promoting what I did not myself like.— " Kotzebue seems to me to be entitled to more respect, because of his fruitfulness, than that unfruitful race, which really and truly, does nothing but hobble along, calling back and checking anyone who is making rapid progress."

We must not bear August Schlegel a grudge, for having lived long enough to bring forward those disputes again. Envy at seeing so many more influential talents rising up, and vexation at having, as a youngster, cut so bad a figure, make it impossible for the good man, in his heart of hearts, to attain to a feeling of benevolence. . . . .

G.

367.—ZELTER TO GOETHE.

Berlin, Thursday, 27th October, 1831.

Our zealous theologian, Hengstenberg, is said to have delivered himself of a criticism on *Die Wahlverwandtschaften*, that is as heavy as lead. I do not know him, and if he does not understand you, you will not know him either.

This reminds me of a story about the Hamburg Bach, when Agricola asked him, "Have you read Marpurg's criticism of your new Fugue? He has taken you to task for it pretty sharply." "No," said Bach; "had he told one his criticism beforehand, one might perhaps have shaped one's ways accordingly; but if he likes his own Fugues, I do not see how mine are calculated to please him." . . . .

A new Opera by Scribe and Auber, *Le Philtre*, is so hopelessly weak and empty, that the house, on the occasion of the second performance, seemed as quiet as the grave.

On the other hand, the people of Königsstadt have arranged for themselves another new Opera by Rossini, *La Donna del Lago*, and very nicely too; it is pretty sure to last. Douglas, a Scottish knight, has promised his beautiful daughter to a Mr. Roderick; James V., King of Scotland, is also bent on having her, but she, come life or death, is bent on having a Mr. Malcolm Grame. That might happen anywhere, and the text is the most marvellous composition of everlastingly repeated, worn-out, Italian operatic tags;[*] yet the whole thing is as manageable and practicable, as a good-tempered girl. So there you have the Opera.

The absence of a long, broad, pathetic Symphony, so far from being regrettable, conciliated me at once. The Opera starts with itself; it has all the distinctive marks, which enable us to recognize at once the well-known composer, while at the same time, there are very evident signs, that his vein is far from being exhausted. The singers have enough to do, and yet they are spared, by means of the Orchestra, which Rossini handles as easily as if he were holding a bell firm in his hand,—weaving his instrumentation in as ingeniously, as if it were a natural growth. There is plenty to find fault with too, but he who sticks at that, is in danger of missing the boldest and most delicate passages, as they fly by, like game on the wing. The Chorus frequently attacks with such brilliancy and force, that for a moment

---

[*] The gems of the text of this Opera are to be found in a very humorous article in the *Cornhill Magazine* for November, 1885, called *With Some Librettists*.

one feels older by a few thousand years. The scene is, as I said before, in Scotland, and now and then I really fancied myself transported from the King's Bridge in Berlin, to a solemn Highland region, although the composer has not even been at the pains to look up so much as a single national Scotch song. . . . .

I told you before, that I had taken another turn at the Schiller Correspondence. The two Letters, numbered 389 and 390, have set me thinking again. Schiller says, "Can it really be, that Tragedy does not suit your nature, because of its pathetic force?" And again, "A certain reckoning on the spectators is a hindrance to you, and perhaps for that very reason, you are the less fitted to be a writer of Tragedy, because you are altogether created for a poet in the highest sense. Anyhow, I find in you all the poetic specialities of the writer of Tragedy, in their fullest measure, and if, notwithstanding this, you are really unable to write a perfectly genuine Tragedy, the reason must lie in the non-poetical requisites."

I, for my part, do not understand this *chiaroscuro*, and much I know about *writing* a Tragedy, or whether such things let themselves be written; when poetry bears about the same relation to the writing, as music does to the notes. It becomes somewhat clearer to my mind, when I remember, that Schiller was just then wrestling hard with his *Wallenstein*, and trying, as it were, to hook poetry on to it. Your answer, No. 390, contains all that Aristotle says, and something more besides. "For the rest," (you say,) "only go on without anxiety. The inner unity, which *Wallenstein* will have, must be felt, and you have great privileges in the Theatre. An ideal whole imposes on men, even if they do not know how to decipher it in its individual elements, nor how to estimate the value of the individual parts. . . . ."

Yours ever,

Z.

369.—GOETHE TO ZELTER.

Weimar, 31st October, 1831.

. . . . I AM glad to hear that you sometimes go back to the Schiller Correspondence; there you find two men of serious aim, at a fairly high standpoint; you are incited to the same intellectual activity, you seek to place yourself beside them, if possible above them; and that is all so much gain for the rising generation.

One day soon, you will receive the first numbers of the *Chaos;* it seems to me like the second year of a fairly happy marriage. But do give me leave to insert in it your delightful remarks about *La Donna del Lago* and the Königsstadt Theatre in general. . . . .

I have of old denounced the canting lot, and I have soundly anathematized the Berliners, as I know them, so it is but fair, that I should be excommunicated by them in their diocese. One of that tribe, wanting to have a fling at me lately, talked about *Pantheism;* he made a good shot there! I assured him with great simplicity, that I had never yet met with anyone, who knew what the word meant.

I had an interview the other day, with a very good-looking young fellow, a Prussian too, who, after some very proper talk, confided to me, that he also had taken up poetry as a profession, adding that he was trying to work against me and my followers. I assured him, that he was doing very wisely; for as no one could readily be of the same way of thinking as another, so nothing could be more natural, than for everyone, in verse or prose, to express himself differently also.

As regards Tragedy, that is a ticklish point. I was not born to be a tragic poet, for my nature is conciliatory; consequently, a purely tragic incident cannot interest me, for it must be essentially irreconcilable, and to me, in the exceeding flatness of this world, the irreconcilable seems an utter absurdity. I must not continue, for in the course of discussion one might go astray, and this one would rather avoid. . . . .

G.

369.—GOETHE TO ZELTER.

Weimar, 15th November, 1831.

As I know that one can ingratiate oneself with you, by thinking and speaking kindly of your Berlin folk, I may safely tell you, that yesterday we had a real fête, in honour of one of the most admirable of your heroes of peace.

It is really curious, that for the last 4,124 years, strictly calculated—that is, since Noah's experiment in getting drunk—though people have always gone on wishing for good wine, and as much of it too as possible, still no one has ever got to the bottom of the question, as to the greater or less amount of skill required in dealing with the details of vine culture, until at last, a plate-polisher in Berlin * made the egg stand on end, and gave us a standard, by which we can judge, how far people have hitherto approached the right treatment of the subject.

I dare say I wrote to you about this from Dornburg; since then, I have constantly devoted myself to it, as also to botany in general. In Weimar, Belvedere, Jena, and elsewhere, people caught up the published maxim at once, so I planted a few vines, which are now three years old, and have been pruned in that way. But in my garden, on the wall of the outhouse, there is a very old and healthy Hungarian vine, which bears very fine, large grapes, though you cannot rely on a regular crop. An experienced pupil and disciple of Kecht's has just been maiming it methodically, and he promises us eighty bunches of grapes for next year; you are invited to witness the vintage and to enjoy it with us. . . . .

You see that things with me go on after the old fashion. Amid the hundreds of subjects that interest me, one always constitutes itself the chief planet in the middle, and the remainder of the *Quodlibet* of my life revolves around it variously, moon fashion, until one or other of the satellites succeeds likewise in moving to the centre.

I should like to hear what news you have of our excellent Felix. I had an exceedingly interesting letter from Switzerland, part of which I confided to the *Chaos;* I wrote to him at Munich, but have not heard from him since.

My blessings on all that is good and beautiful!

J. W. v. G.

* J. S. Kecht. See Letter 249, Note.

370.—ZELTER TO GOETHE.

Sunday, 26th November, 1831.

THEY are just putting the worthy Hegel under ground; he died suddenly of cholera, the day before yesterday. On the Friday evening, he was actually at my house, and he gave a lecture the day afterwards. I ought to be one of the mourners, but I have got my Academy to attend to, and a cold besides. My house is open every week regularly to some four hundred people, and should anything happen to me, my Institution would suffer, and I should be reproached with having tempted Providence,—all the more, as contrary to universal custom, I neither fumigate nor *disinfect*, as it is called, clumsily enough.

Our University is so torn and divided, that I have not yet been able to make a fresh start. Now Hegel's death will give me an opportunity of rehearsing some music in memory of him, and we shall have a performance there. . . . .

The youngest daughter of Moses Mendelssohn was buried yesterday. She, of all the family, was most like her father, small and weakly,—a woman of delicate, fine intellect, and lovable beyond everything. She inherited very little from her father, and went away to Paris, where she made the acquaintance of General Sebastiani, and became governess to his only daughter. She educated this child up to the time of her marriage, and received a pension for the rest of her life, which she enjoyed in her native city of Berlin. It was a remarkable thing, to find no difference in language, manners, or habit of life, in the once Jewish maiden of Berlin, who, without the aid of an imposing presence, had become a lady in one of the first and most distinguished of Parisian houses. Since she came back to Berlin, ten years ago, though I have seen her frequently, (and always with pleasure,) I have scarcely heard her utter a word of French, English, or Italian; on the contrary, she spoke the most transparent. flowing German, with a brightness, which reminded me of your *schöne Seele*. Her vocation as a governess in Paris had made her turn Roman Catholic, but apart from her daily attendance at Mass, no appearance of positive religiosity would have been observable in her. Felix was her special favourite; she liked to have my letters to him, and copied them for herself. She was at my house only a short time ago, and now all that abides with me is her sweet memory. . . . .

Yours,
Z.

371.—GOETHE TO ZELTER.

Weimar, 23rd November, 1831.

. . . . FIRST of all, let me tell you that I have retired into my cloister cell, where the sun, which is just now rising, shines horizontally into my room, and does not leave me until he sets, so that he is often uncomfortably importunate,—so much so, that I really have to shut him out for a time. This reminds me of a little old verse, which, when translated, would run somewhat thus:

> Nay, not with love,—with bare respect,
> May we unite ourselves to thee:
> O Sun! couldst thou but take effect,
> And never shine,—how nice 'twould be!

I have further to tell you, that a new edition of the *Iphigenia in Aulis* of Euripides, edited by Hermann, *Knight* and *Professor* of Leipzig, has once more turned my attention to that incomparable Greek poet. His great and unique talent of course excited my admiration as of old, but what chiefly impressed me this time, was the element, as boundless as it is powerful, in which he moves.

Among the Greek localities, and their mass of primæval, mythological legends, he sails and swims, like a cannonball on a sea of quicksilver, and cannot sink, even if he wished it. Everything is ready to his hand—subject-matter, circumstances, connecting links; he has only to set to work to bring forward his subjects and characters in the simplest way, or to make the most complicated limitations even more complicated, and then at last, symmetrically, but entirely to our satisfaction, either to unravel or to cut the knot.

I shall not lay him aside the whole of this winter. We have translations enough, which well warrant our presumption in looking into the original; when the sun shines into my warm room, and I am helped by the stores of learning, acquired in days long gone by, I shall anyhow fare better than I should, at this moment, among the newly discovered ruins of Messene and Megalopolis.

As for the rest, you understand, that I am leading a testamentary and codicillary life, in order that the body of the property by which I am surrounded, may not be all too quickly dissolved into the meanest elements, like the individual himself. Yet even kings cannot accomplish anything a finger's-breadth beyond their earthly existence; so why should we other poor devils make a fuss about it? . . . .

G.

1832.

372.—GOETHE TO ZELTER.

Weimar, 14th January, 1832.

.... Jouy's libretto for Spontini's Opera, (*Les Athéniennes,*) is truly admirable. I have read it through once; there is great perception of dramatic effects, the treatment of such commonplace situations as are inevitable, is fresh and successful, there are pleasant resting places in the mid-current of the movement, (which is partly solemn, partly passionate,) where homely airs can be introduced, and the Finale is well-grouped, and full of life and movement. Let anyone who must sit out the third Act have at hand a cordial, both for heart and senses. Still, I do not know of any passage that I would omit or alter. I shall only be able to praise, and to give sound reasons for my favourable opinion, from the right point of view. ....

It will be all right for little Facius; her maintenance for one year more, is already as good as secured. The presence of Professor Rauch in Berlin will, in any case, be very advantageous to her. He who ceases to converse with the masters of his Art, will not make any advance, and will always be in danger of falling back. From every gifted person, we ought to demand unwearied endeavour,— a self-denial, which however, no one cares to form any idea of. Everyone would like to possess Art in his own fashion, but Art will be wooed and won only in her own way. How often I see gifted people conducting themselves like a wasp on a window pane; they want to force their heads through the impenetrable, fancying that they can do this, because it is transparent. . . . .

G.

373.—ZELTER TO GOETHE.

Berlin, 22nd January, 1832.

.... You need not trouble yourself about Jouy's operatic text; you have only to send it back to Spontini, who, I am sure, will be certain to put it before me, with his own casual observations. I too will let him know of your satisfaction with the poem. I am on proper artistic terms with him, and this he understands very well, as we don't force our opinions upon one another. We have often conducted important concerts, cheek by jowl, and at such a time, I have found myself between two forces. On the last occasion, in our largest Church, and in the presence of the whole of the Royal Orchestra and Chorus, he launched out very loudly in my praises; while I, in my turn, could not but admire his potential discretion, in letting things with which he was absolutely unfamiliar, take their own course. The most agreeable part of it was the universal sensation; I had not stirred, but everybody knew what was meant. . . . .

I enclose you another playbill. The Italian composer, Bellini, was till lately, unknown to me; Heaven only can say, whether I know him now. A Duke has forcibly stolen the lady-love of a Count, and made her his wife. The Count comes back six years afterwards, as a pirate, kills the Duke, and then comes to grief himself about it; the wife goes mad, and all that is left is a little rascal of five years old. The music is the most casual jumble of ideas, which purposely contradict every interpretation of what is going on. One is pitched and tossed between one's eyes and ears, one's feeling and one's reason, which are all biting and scratching each other. With all this, the fellow has talent and audacity, and lords it over the Orchestra and the singers, in the most impertinent fashion. Such stuff is now being carried off by a kind of virtuosity at the Königsstadt Theatre. Now and then I was in such despair, that I was on the point of running away, but before I could quite get up from my chair, something always pushed me back again. I felt at last, as if there was nothing left of me. . . . .

Tuesday, 24th January.

My brave *Concert-Meister*, Rietz,* died the day before yesterday. We are all very unhappy,—and there's an end of it. Now I shall have to roll the new stone up-hill again. There are some left to pick from still; they are all keen about it; tact and ability will come in time. Rietz had all those qualities, and the spirit of obedience besides. .... Help, ye Muses! And thou, Apollo forsake not
Thy
Z.

374.—GOETHE TO ZELTER.

Weimar, 27th January, 1832.

.... THE excellent Doris seems to be quite cheerful and at home here; she has come just at the right time, when we are all in full swing, and things are a little crazy, even in my house. A few days ago, they performed a *Quodlibet* of dramatic fragments, at a private house under the direction of Ottilie, who understands this sort of thing very well, and is therefore in great request as a manager. ....

I dare not say, how much I dislike the reverse side of Hegel's medal; one does not know in the least what it is intended for. I have proved in my verses, that I knew how to venerate and how to adorn the Cross, as a man and a poet; but it jars upon me, to see a philosopher leading his disciples by a round-about way over the primary and negative grounds of Being and not Being to that contignation. It can be had cheaper, and expressed better.

I possess a medal of the seventeenth Century, stamped with the likeness of a high dignitary of the Romish Church; on the reverse-side are figures of *Theologia* and *Philosophia*, represented as two noble women, facing each other, and the relation between the two is conceived with such exquisite purity, and is so entirely satisfactory, and

* Edward Rietz, an excellent violin-player, was the founder and conductor of an Orchestral Society at Berlin. His early death deeply affected his intimate friend, Mendelssohn, who inscribed the Andante in the String-Quintet, op. 18, with the words: "In memory of E. Ritz." The autograph is dated "Jan. 23, 1832," and entitled *Nachruf*.

gracious in expression, that I am keeping the medal to myself, so as to give it to someone worthy of it, if I can find him.

One lives, inwardly and outwardly, in a perpetual state of conflict, because of the young people, whose ways and doings one cannot approve of, and yet cannot altogether avoid. I often pity them, for having made their appearance in times that are so out of joint, when a stiff, unbending egotism hardens itself in ways that are half or altogether false, and hinders pure *Self* from working out its own development. The consequence is that when a free spirit perceives and expresses what admits of being clearly seen and expressed, very many good people must inevitably fall into despair. Now they entangle themselves in the old, conventional labyrinths, without noticing what stands in their way. I shall guard against expressing myself more definitely, but I know best what it is that keeps me young in extreme old age, and moreover in the *practical-productive* sense of the word, which after all is the main thing.

And thus ever,
J. W. v. GOETHE.

375.—ZELTER TO GOETHE.

1st February, 1832.

. . . . FELIX is now in Paris, and is making a stir, both as composer and performer. I enclose a short extract from his letter, by which you will see for yourself what else he is doing in a general way.

" Paris, 21st January, 1832.

"Yesterday, Rodriques was with me, talking of St. Simonism; he thought me stupid or clever enough, (I don't know which,) for him to make disclosures, which so enraged me, that I resolved not to have anything more to do with him, or any other of his accomplices. Early this morning, Hiller rushed into my room, to tell me how he had just been present at the arrest of the St. Simonians; he wanted to hear their sermon,—no Popes—soldiers suddenly appear upon the scene, and people are asked to be off as fast as they can, as Herr Enfantin and the others are arrested in the *Rue Monsigny*. National Guards and other soldiers are posted in the *Rue Monsigny*, every door is bolted, and now the trial has begun. It will go hard with them, for the new jury, consisting no longer of Odilon-Barrot candidates, is ministerial, and has already delivered some very stringent verdicts," &c.

376.—GOETHE TO ZELTER.

Weimar, 4th February. 1832.

. . . . A LITTLE while ago, you told me, that some cultivated Berliners rejoiced in the thought, that probably, with the exception of your copy of my *Farbenlehre*, there was no other in Berlin. If, by chance, there is one in the Royal Library, it will be locked up, and tabooed, as a forbidden work. Two octavo volumes, and one number in quarto, have been in print for three-and-twenty years, and it is one of the most important experiences of my old age, that since those days, the Guilds and Societies have always opposed it, and regarded it with grim fear. Right they are! and I praise them for it. Why should they not curse the broom, which threatens, sooner or later, to destroy their cobwebs? I kept quiet at the time, but now I will not spare a few words.

The circle you tell me of, is made up entirely of honourable, well-meaning people; but they certainly belong to a Guild,—a persuasion,—a party,—whose best part it undoubtedly is, to shelve, if it cannot annihilate, all the hostile elements that encroach upon it.

What is a Minister, but the head of the party, which he has to protect, and upon which he depends? What is the Academician, but an initiated and adopted member of a great Society? If he were not connected with it, he would be nothing; the Society, on the other hand, must carry out the traditions it has accepted, and must admit and assimilate only a certain kind of novelty, in the way of select observations and discoveries; everything else must be set aside as heresy.

Seebeck, an earnest man, in the highest and best sense

of the word, knew very well, in what relation he stood to
me, and to my method of thinking about Natural Science,
but, once received into the reigning Church, he would
have been considered a fool, had he shown the least trace
of Arianism. When the multitude is, once for all, satisfied
with words and phrases about certain difficult and doubtful
phenomena, we must not bewilder it. Judging by your
letter, the interlocutors themselves confess that he has been
moderate,—*i.e.* that he did not explain himself upon the
chief points, that he was able to listen silently to what
displeased him, and, while fulfilling his academic duties, to
conceal his sentiments behind palpable specialities,—I
mean, by remarkably successful experiments, in which he
showed great cleverness. His son, only a short time ago,
assured me of his excellent father's sincere appreciation of
me. . . . .

I must tell you of the strangest thing that has just
happened. . . . .

CONTINUATION.

Weimar, 20th February, 1832.

Whilst dictating the above, I get a dissertation from
Prague, where a year ago, under the auspices of the Arch-
bishop, my *Farbenlehre* was taken up regularly, in the series
of other physical subjects, and now looks very well on the
list. I am much amused by the paradox, that Catholic
countries should consider allowable, what in Calvinistic
countries is not only forbidden, but even discredited. I am
well aware, that one has only to live long, and try to get
breadth into one's work, and everything will lead to a
result of some kind in the end. . . . .

Doris will have many pleasant things to tell you about
Weimar; in Frau von Pogwisch, Frl. Ulrike, and Emma
Froriep, she found old and intimate allies, and her wise
and quiet, yet actively sympathetic ways won for her
many new and attached friends. She had an opportunity
too of getting to know, and up to a certain point, take
delight in my collections, so far as they can be seen and
enjoyed by the world. In our modest household, she could
be as comfortable as she liked in a quiet way, and no

doubt she will go back to her daily, domestic life, which is full of stir and activity, feeling refreshed and all the better for the change. . . . .

And thus ever,

G.

377.—ZELTER TO GOETHE.

7th February.

. . . . I AM just now reading Italian, and looking up a passage in *Benvenuto Cellini*. . . . . I still remember the first impression it made on me, thirty years ago, when you brought the book to my study. I have now begun it all over again, and am reading it through, from the first to the last chapter. The *naïveté* with which that young fellow describes his very just hatred of that accursed music, attracted me most powerfully, as I myself had endured the exact opposite. How often, with tears and earnest prayers, have I called on God to change that confounded taste of mine for the music that I loved, into a talent more befitting my condition, and more gratifying to my father. All that came before me, as vividly, as though the agony of my soul at that time were brought before my eyes in a vision. I dare say I have written to you about this ten times already, but the effect is always the same.

Young Friedländer, who has been appointed custodian of the Royal Library here, tells me that he has just discovered an hitherto unknown MS. of the life of Benvenuto Cellini, and besides that, a work upon the Goldsmith's Art. . . . . I told you, I was reading Italian; that reminds me, that the Italian Spontini has just been dissolving your little Mignon, like a pearl, in the river of German instrumentation. The little piece is pretty and effective, and Mignon plays with it, like a child among children; if it went on in this strain to the end, it would be a complete thing. But he lays the chief stress on his long-drawn, everlasting repetitions of *Kennst Du es wohl?* and I should like to see the man who would say, *Es muss wohl Itulien gemeynt seyn*, ("I suppose that means Italy.") It was given at yesterday's Concert, with full Orchestra, (drums excepted,) and with great applause. As the people were going out, someone exclaimed quite audibly, *Dahin! scheer' Er sich und lass uns ungeschoren.** . .

Yours,
Z.

378.—ZELTER TO GOETHE.

16th February, 1832.

. . . . I THINK I have already written to you about Auber's Opera, *Der Gott und die Bajadere*.† Yesterday's performance was so perfect in every respect, that I really quite revelled in the music. There is something Indian about it, quite different to anything we have had before. Brilliancy, novelty, easy flow,—and our star, Mdlle. Elsler, (the *Bajadere*,) not only dances, but acts more perfectly than anyone I have seen, since Vigano. The whole house was delighted. Her figure presents a mark for thousands of eyes. Every part of her face is a keyboard of colour, played upon with marvellous grace. . . . . . The vocal parts too were admirably cast. Mantius,‡ (the *God*,) is to be sure a beginner, and rather undersized, but his tenor voice is even in compass, and of the greatest beauty. He has made immense progress in a very short time. . . . .

Yours.
Z.

379.—ZELTER TO GOETHE.

Sunday, 19th February, 1832.

. . . . Now for another Opera, *Fra Diavolo!* . . . . This *Diavolo* is a handsome, young, long, thin, pale banditti-

---

* We give a literal translation of what is obviously meant for the parody of a line in Mignon's Song, " Be off with you thither, (*scheer' Er sich*,) and leave us unfleeced!" (*ungeschoren!*) in other words, " Be off with you, Spontini, to Italy,—you and your high prices!"—There is a similar play on the word *wohl* in the sentence above.

† See Letter 344.

‡ Edward Mantius, originally a legal student at Leipzig, was for some time a favourite Handelian singer at Berlin. He was greatly appreciated by Mendelssohn, and sang the leading tenor parts, during the career of Jenny Lind at Berlin. He was twenty-seven years on the stage, and appeared in no less than a hundred and fifty-two characters. He died at Ilmenau in 1874.

man, and sings tenor like all tenerinos, piping on in falsetto, for that is the fashion nowadays. .... Now about the action!

> The dragoons, they booze and sing;
> The banditti, they steal and sing.
> My lord is sulky and sings, how he loathes that confounded singing.
> The lovers worry each other and sing, and make it up, and sing again.

It takes a man like Auber, (and the critics are not agreed about his talent,) so to be-music three such Acts, as to prevent anyone dying of *ennui*, and for this, an Orchestra is wanted as good as the Parisian, and not worse than ours, for the difficult passages given to singers and Orchestra are the best thing about it, if all goes well. ....

I have received from Paris a letter from Felix, dated the 15th of this month. As he has often been there, new acquaintances have trodden on the heels of the old, and seemingly, the political, no less than the artistic life there, stimulates his love for the Fatherland. As regards the artistic life, his confession squares pretty tolerably with my prophecies to him, though I never was at Paris,—and to be sure, business-men or merchants, amongst whom he has lived from childhood, sniff out the places where there is most doing.— —Of late years, the activity of trade has been most dangerous for well-to-do people, though a sharp look-out in the market has often enough enriched the ragamuffin.—But I do not understand that. ....

Yours,
Z.

380.—GOETHE TO ZELTER.

Weimar, 23rd February, 1832.

.... I WILL insert here, what I found occasion to jot down, a few days ago.

"The consciousness of having effected the artistic development of an important natural taste abides with us, as one of our finest feelings; but at the present time, it is a greater merit than formerly, when every beginner still believed in schooling, in *régime*, and in masters, and modestly subjected himself to the grammar of his particular department, about which most of the young people of to-day decline to know anything.

"German plastic artists have, for the last thirty years, been under the delusion, that natural talent can develop itself, and a host of enthusiastic amateurs, who also have no fundamental principles, confirm them in this belief. A hundred times, I hear an artist boast, that he owes everything to himself alone! I generally listen to this patiently, but sometimes I am goaded into replying, 'It looks like it too.'

"For what then is man, in and through himself? When he opens his eyes and ears, he cannot avoid objectivity, example, tradition; he educates himself by these, according to his individual taste and convenience, as far as he can, for a time. But just when he reaches the highest point, he finds this fragmentary existence does not suffice; he feels that discomfort, which is the special trouble of practical men. Happy he, who is quick to grasp what Art means!"

Much as I have effected for the whole community, and much as has been set in motion by me, still I can name but one man, who has cultivated himself from the very beginning, in entire accordance with my ideas; this was the actor, Wolff, who is still held in honourable remembrance in Berlin. In the hope of receiving a friendly answer, more anon.

J. W. v. GOETHE.

381.—GOETHE TO ZELTER.

Weimar, 11th March, 1832.

THAT's right! After having built and established your citadel, at the expense of your whole life, you should not be without a trustworthy body-guard, and warlike allies; so you are laying about you manfully, to preserve what you have won, to promote your chief aim, and thus to lessen the burdens, which must necessarily accompany a position like yours.

Here there come across my mind all sorts of examples from Ancient History; these, however, I cast aside, for, as a rule, one does not find any comfort in the thought, that the greatest of one's ancestors must have fared much worse than oneself.

Fortunately, your individual gift has to do with sound, that is, with the moment. Now, as a series of consecutive moments is always a kind of Eternity itself, you have been allowed to remain firm and constant in the midst of what is transitory, and thus perfectly to satisfy my mind, as well as Hegel's, so far as I understand it.

Look at me, on the other hand! me, living chiefly in the past. less in the future, and for the moment, in the distance,—and remember, that in my own way, I am quite content.

I have received from Naples a very pleasant reminder from Zahn,* that good, energetic young fellow, whom I dare say you still remember. I am well pleased to find that they have given my name to the house, which has been recently discovered, though they have not yet completely unearthed it. This is an echo from afar, meant to commemorate my son's death. The house is admitted to be one of the most beautiful hitherto discovered, and remarkable for a mosaic, such as we have not yet met with in antiquity. This was announced in the newspapers long ago, so perhaps you have already heard something about it.

However, they are sending me a detailed drawing of the great, enclosed space, columns and all, as well as a small copy of the famous painting. We must take care that we do not behave like Wieland, who, owing to his great susceptibility, allowed what he read last to blot out, as it were, all that went before, for we might quite be tempted to say, that nothing has as yet come down to us from antiquity, equal to this in picturesqueness of composition and execution.

What would you say, were they to lay before you an intelligible page in musical type, belonging to that time,— a time suggestive of earlier Grecian models,—in which you were forced to recognize a master of the Fugue, with its inner and outer criteria?

The few, but really earnest *connoisseurs*, whom you know

---

* See Letters 229 and 340.

of, will find ample material for conversation and edification in this subject, for some days to come. Besides this, some perfectly different, yet equally interesting things have found their way to me,—namely, several specimens of an organic world, that disappeared before all historic times. Remains of fossil animals and plants are accumulating around me, but one must of necessity refrain from thinking of anything but the origin and position of the place of discovery, because to absorb oneself further in the contemplation of the ages, could only lead to madness. I should really like one day, as a joke, when you are rehearsing bright and lively Choruses, with your jovial youngsters, to place before you a primæval elephant's grinder, dug out of our gravel pits; you would feel the vivid and charming contrast.

But now, I beg of you to continue, as you did in your last, to express aphoristically the old eternal maxims of Nature, by which man makes himself comprehensible to man through language, in order that the decrees of Fate may one day be fulfilled in the Future. It is strange, that English, French, and now Germans too, like to express themselves incomprehensibly, just as others like to listen to what is incomprehensible. I only wish, that an Italian would occasionally step in, and let us hear his emphatic language.

So be it, then!

J. W. v. GOETHE.*

382.—ZELTER TO HERR GEHEIMRATH UND KANZLER VON MÜLLER, AT WEIMAR.

Berlin, 31st March, 1832.

I COULD not thank you, until to-day, honoured Sir, for your most friendly sympathy,—which is all the occasion allows of.

What we expected, what we dreaded, inevitably came.

---

* This is Goethe's last letter. Zelter wrote to Goethe for the last time, on the day of the poet's death, the 22nd of March; the letter reached Weimar on the day of the funeral.

The hour struck. The minute-hand stands still, like the sun at Gibeon; for see! the man lies overthrown, who bestrode the Pillars of Hercules, whilst under him, the powers of the earth contended for the dust beneath their feet.

What can I say of myself—to you, to all there, and everywhere? As he is gone before me, so daily do I draw nearer to him, and I shall find him again, and perpetuate that sweet affection, which, for so many successive years, cheered and enlivened the space of six-and-thirty miles that lay between us.

Now I have a request to make. Continue to honour me with your kindly letters. You will be able to judge, how far I may be trusted, as the undisturbed relations between two close friends, who were really one,—though judged by their capacities, far apart,—are well known to you. I am like a widow, who has lost her husband, her lord and guardian! And yet, I dare not grieve; I am forced to stand amazed, at the riches he brought me. It is my duty to preserve that treasure, and to turn the interest into capital.

Pardon me, noble friend! I surely ought not to complain, and yet the old eyes are disobedient, and must have their way. But once I saw him weep; that must justify me.

ZELTER.

INDEX.

A.

ABRAM, 258.
 Abschatz, 8.
Acoustics, 7.
Agrikola, 356, 472.
Ahnfrau, Die, 164.
Albertinelli, 201.
Albrecht, Prince, 407.
Alcestis, 99.
Aldobrandini, 17.
Alexander's Feast, 145.
Alfieri, 89, 95.
Allgemeine Literarische Zeitung, 18, 83.
Allgemeine Literaturzeitung, Die, 18, 395.
Aloysius, 325.
Amalie, Princess, sister of Frederick the Great, 441.
Amelang, Fräulein, 28.
America, 277, 295.
André, 136.
Angelico, Fra, 281.
Anton, Archduke, 186.
Apollo, 8.
Apostolo Zeno, 56.
Ariosto, 130, 426.
Aristarchus, 57.
Aristophanes, 28.
Aristotle, 282, 283, 284, 310, 334, 386, 391, 473.
Arnim, 63.
Arnim, Bettina von, 79.
Arnold, 437.
Æschylus, 13, 261.
Æsop's Fables, 205.
Artaserse, 99.
Ascanio in Alba, 98.
Auber, 348, 380, 443, 472, 486, 487.
Augereau, Marshal, 45.

Augusta, Princess, 362, 364.
Aus meinem Leben, 213, 214, 236.
Austria, Emperor of, 177, 181, 190.
Austria, Empress of, 77.
Austria, Joseph II., Emperor of, 186.

B.

Bach, E., 4, 110, 115, 132, 167, 265, 356, 472.
Bach, F., 292, 354, 355, 356, 409.
Bach, S., 99, 110, 115, 123, 127, 132, 133, 167, 168, 194, 201, 232, 236, 263, 265, 284, 285, 287, 288, 289, 290, 291, 292, 293, 298, 300, 339, 346, 347, 351, 353, 354, 355, 356, 357, 393, 399, 400, 452, 462.
Bacon, Lord, 338.
Baini, 424.
Banks, 135.
Bagge, Baron, 202.
Barabbas, 14.
Barrentrap, 224.
Bassi, 161.
Bavaria, 160.
Bavaria, King of, 301, 395.
Beaumarchais, 438.
Becarria, 390.
Beethoven, 4, 65, 73, 90, 91, 103, 126, 133, 134, 135, 137, 173, 180, 181, 185, 188, 189, 194, 308, 374, 433, 442, 443, 446, 451.
Begas, 227, 300, 452.
Bellini, 182, 480.
Benda, 318, 356, 452.
Bendavid, 354, 355.
Béranger, 281, 409.

Bernhard, J. C., 373.
Berlioz, 358, 362.
Bernini, 159.
Bertuch, 356.
Bertuch, Legationsrath, 18, 236.
Bethmann, 11.
Beuth, 305.
Beyme, 396, 397.
Bignon, 388, 392.
Blackwood's Magazine, 460.
Blücher, 112, 468.
Bohemia, 84, 109, 161, 214, 220.
Bohn, 264.
Bonoldi, 161.
Bora, Catherine von, 43.
Bossi, 158.
Böttiger, 18, 388.
Boucher, A., 202, 206.
Boucher, Madame, 203, 206.
Bourrienne, 367, 388.
Bouterwek, 462.
Bowring, E. A., 78, 107, 325.
Bracebridge, 260, 262.
Braschi, Prince, 160.
Brand, 9.
Braut von Messina, Die, 11, 12, 15.
Brentano, 63.
Brizzi, 73, 84.
Bruch, Max, 37.
Brühl, Count, 118, 123, 128, 217, 238, 247, 403.
Brun, Frau Friderike, 1.
Buch, 294.
Buchheim, Prof., 1, 121, 152.
Buchholz, 18.
Bürger, 409, 410.
Burney, Dr., 16.
Byron, 365, 440.

C.

Calderon, 85, 358, 393.
Campagne in Frankreich, Die, 214.
Campe, 166.
Campi, 174.
Canova, 160, 182.
Caracci, A., 433, 438.
Carlyle, Dr., 460.
Carlyle, Mrs., 460.

Carlyle, T., 293, 303, 417, 460, 462.
Carlyle's *Frederick the Great*, 437.
Carlyle's *Life of Schiller*, 415, 460.
Caspar, Dr., 225.
Castiglione, Duke of, 102.
Castle of St. Angelo, 211.
Catalani, 138, 159, 206, 286, 287.
Catel, 117.
Cato, 465.
Cebes, 269, 270.
Celli, 452.
Cellini, Benvenuto, 17, 19, 97, 116, 485.
Cervantes, 18.
Chaos, Das, 313, 392, 407, 465, 474, 475.
Charlemagne, 333.
Charles VI., 325.
Charles Martel, 333.
Charlotte von Stein, 149.
Chelard, 327.
Cherubini, 65, 179, 245.
Chiaramonti, 160.
Chinesische Jahreszeiten, 303.
Chladni, Dr., 7, 136.
Christ, 14, 143, 271, 343, 363, 412, 413.
Christus am Oelberge, 91, 444.
Chrysostom, St., 120.
Churchill, 460.
Cicero, 465.
Cimarosa, 394.
Cinna, 388.
Clavigo, 129, 462.
Clemenza di Tito, La, 174.
Concerts Spirituels, 16.
Concialini, 436.
Confessions of a Female Poisoner, The, 18.
Constant Prince, The, 75.
Constantine IX., 57.
Constantine the Great, 448.
Constantinus, 57.
Conversations of Goethe with Eckermann, 200, 319, 323, 367, 432.
Corelli, 452.
Corneille, 388.

Cornhill Magazine, 472.
Correspondence between Schiller and Goethe, 7, 9, 10, 16, 17, 18, 19, 32, 47, 100, 241, 349, 350, 361, 364. 383, 384, 395, 410, 473.
Cotta, 18, 45, 47, 228.
Coudray, 241.
Cousin, 240, 369.
Couperin, 285, 287, 288, 290, 291.
Cramer, 337.
Cramer, L. W., 137.
Creation, The, 398, 399.
Cumberland, Duchess of, 195, 198.
Cumberland, Duke of, 337.
Cuzzoni, 99.
Cyclops, The, 233, 234.

D.
Dalberg, 286.
Damenkalender, Der, 63.
Danaiden, Die, 5.
Dante, 267, 269, 270, 271, 272.
David, 159, 160.
Deinhardstein, 404.
Delilah, 88.
Denner, 98.
Descartes, 338.
De Senectute, 465.
Des Vœux, C., 283.
Deutsche Lyrik, 1.
Devonshire, Duke of, 315.
Devrient, 426.
Devrient, E., 336, 447.
Dichtung und Wahrheit, 85.
Die Lustigen Weiber von Windsor, 464.
Divan Westöstlicher, 117, 119, 121, 122, 124, 164, 181, 183, 193.
Döbbelin, 416.
Dog of Aubry, The, 40.
Dolce, Carlo, 290.
Don Ciccio, 119.
Don Giovanni, 91, 122, 155, 222, 265.
Doni, 324.
Dschinnistan, 5.
Duncker, 132.

Düntzer, 196.
Düntzer's *Life of Goethe*, 36, 40, 64, 113, 460.
Durante, 434, 439.
Dürer, 182, 315, 405.
Dussek, 167.
Dyk, 135.

E.
Early Letters, Goethe's, 36.
Eberwein, K., 54, 55, 58, 62, 64, 67, 69, 72, 81, 192, 205, 227, 324.
Eckermann, 5, 17, 21, 280, 302, 353, 394, 402, 419, 420, 423, 432, 440.
Edinburgh Review, 357.
Egeria, 341.
Egmont, 103.
Egypt, 367.
Ehlers, 417.
Eichstädt, 17.
Einsiedel, 82.
Elpenor, 46.
Elsler, F., 418, 486.
Emilia Galotti, 391, 392, 411.
Enfantin, 483.
Engel, J. J., 93, 259, 318, 416.
England, 39, 331, 357, 459.
Entoptische Farben, 157.
Epimenides Erwachen, Des, 115, 118, 119, 468.
Erwin und Elmire, 28.
Essex, 135.
Este, Cardinal d', 426.
Esterhazy, Prince, 181.
Eugenie, 17.
Eumenides, The, 13.
Euripides, 13, 233, 234, 261, 318, 477.
Euryanthe, 238, 255.
Eyck, 182.

F.
Fabre, Mdlle., 161.
Facius, A., 448, 479.
Fantuzzi, Count, 160.
Farbenlehre, Die, 44, 45, 67, 70, 75, 80, 81, 113, 157, 278, 354, 360, 410, 483, 484.
Farinelli, 99.
Fasch, 4, 115, 156, 182, 356, 462.

Faust, 47, 55, 73, 74, 126, 127, 128, 129, 159, 160, 193, 195, 196, 197, 206, 262, 288, 307, 311, 313, 314, 317, 321, 343, 344, 346, 350, 354, 358, 359, 362, 363, 373, 374, 375, 380, 417, 426, 447, 460, 464.
Faust's Höllenzwang, 375.
Faustina, 99.
Fichte, 15, 16, 17, 18, 396.
Fidelio, 73, 90, 442.
Fiesco, 416.
Figaro, 304, 394, 408.
Fleck, 416.
Fleck, Madame, 34.
Foreign Review, The, 460.
Forkel's *Life of Bach*, 290, 356.
Forster, 463.
France, 25, 316, 367.
Franklin, 75.
Fraser's Magazine, 460.
Fraser, W., 460.
Frederick I., Emperor, 231.
Frederick the Great, 4, 16, 28, 156, 219, 220, 229, 230, 262, 351, 371, 372, 374, 379, 437, 438, 441.
Freischütz, Der, 203.
Friedländer, 76, 79, 80, 81, 97, 100, 375, 485.
Friedrich, Prince of Gotha, 87.
Fries, 284, 294.
Froberger, 232.
Frommann, 284.
Froriep, 484.
Für Freunde der Tonkunst, 7, 227.
Fux, 325.

G.

Gabrieli, 339.
Galileo, 338.
Gall, 40, 406.
Gartenhaus, 18.
Gastmahl der Weisen, Das, 119.
Gaul, 333.
Gazza Ladra, La, 172.
Gellert, 392.
Gerard, 317.
Gerbert, 57.
Gerhard, 8.

Germany, 48, 59, 95, 96, 98, 99, 115, 118, 125, 126, 152, 191, 209, 214, 283, 287, 298, 320, 327, 331, 365, 369, 394, 405, 406, 440, 460.
George IV., 316.
George, St., 211.
Giotto, 269.
Gleim, 299, 300.
Glenk, 371.
Globe, Le, 369, 391.
Gluck, 90, 91, 98, 171, 173, 251, 351, 400.
Goethe, 1, 5, 6, 7, 10, 16, 17, 18, 19, 21, 24, 28, 29, 32, 36, 37, 40, 42, 45, 46, 47, 57, 59, 64, 76, 83, 85, 86, 91, 92, 100, 109, 110, 113, 115, 118, 121, 122, 130, 135, 137, 149, 150, 156, 163, 167, 182, 195, 200, 205, 208, 213, 214, 217, 221, 226, 228, 233, 234, 236, 239, 241, 242, 243, 244, 248, 251, 256, 259, 261, 262, 266, 280, 284, 289, 294, 295, 302, 305, 310, 313, 317, 318, 319, 320, 336, 343, 354, 363, 365, 368, 384, 385, 386, 387, 390, 392, 395, 403, 406, 410, 415, 417, 419, 421, 441, 451, 459, 460, 461, 462, 463, 466, 468, 469, 490.
Goethe, Christiane Sophie, 135, 224.
Goethe, Julius August Walther, 37, 41, 53, 137, 149, 169, 216, 217, 223, 224, 313, 319, 394, 402, 415, 439.
Goethe, Katharina Elisabeth, 223, 224.
Goethe, Ottilie (*née* von Pogwisch), 41, 149, 169, 200, 223, 226, 311, 313, 400, 407, 426, 464, 466, 467, 481, 484.
Goldsmith, 381.
Görres, 63.
Gotha, Prince of, 87, 358.
Gott und die Bajadere, Der, 122, 443, 486.
Götter Helden und Wieland, 318.
Gottsched, 392.

Götz von Berlichingen, 21, 23, 26, 27, 28, 32, 317, 318.
Gower, Levison, 460.
Graun, 233, 357, 393, 405, 424, 425, 443, 445.
Greece, 121.
Greek Tragedy, 5, 12, 14, 381.
Grétry, 394, 470.
Gries, 358.
Griepenkerl, 251.
Grillparzer, 164, 189, 278.
Grothe, 405.
Grotius, 213.
Grove's *Dictionary of Music*, 4, 91, 133.
Grünbaum, Madame, 236.
Grüner, 131.
Guercino, 256.
Guizot, 369.

H.
Hackert, G., 182, 183.
Hackert, Philip, 182, 191, 405.
Hagen, August, 200.
Hagen, Frau von, 350.
Hamilton, Lady, 118.
Hamlet, 86.
Handel, 123, 133, 142 145, 155, 167, 194, 227, 229, 230, 231, 233, 287, 288, 298, 336, 337, 381, 405, 425, 428, 431.
Handschuh, Der, 306.
Hardenberg, 121.
Härtel, 133.
Hasse, 98, 405, 434, 435, 436, 438, 439.
Hassler, 339.
Haude und Spenersche Zeitung, 227, 255.
Hauser, 451.
Haydn, 91, 110, 167, 173, 174, 175, 181, 191, 194, 260, 265, 285, 373, 398, 399, 400, 424, 456.
Hegel, 212, 302, 317, 327, 352, 353, 373, 412, 420, 424, 458, 476, 481, 489.
Heidelberg, *Jahrbücher* of, 158.
Heine, 152.
Heinitz, Count, 371.
Helena, 13.

Helena, mother of Constantine the Great, 435, 448.
Hengstenberg, 471.
Henning, 406.
Henry, Prince, brother of Frederick the Great, 229, 230, 436.
Hensel, 221, 364, 412.
Heraud, 460.
Hercules, Pillars of, 491.
Herder, 8, 9, 10, 141, 229, 454.
Hermann, 261, 477.
Hertzberg, 219.
Heyse, 250.
Hiller, 298.
Hiller, F., 482.
Himmel, 84, 455.
Hippocrates, 420.
Hirt, 68, 162.
History of Art, The, 17, 19.
Hochzeitlied, 6.
Holland, 280, 364.
Holtei, 313, 346.
Homer, 29, 30, 103, 213, 233, 356, 441.
Horen, Die, 93.
Hufeland, 396.
Hügel, Fräulein, 123.
Hugo, V., 458.
Humboldt, A. von, 467.
Humboldt, Frau von, 127.
Humboldt, K. W., 16, 66, 85, 265, 408.
Hummel, 203, 221, 222, 236, 263, 432, 434, 438.
Hungary, 186, 188, 424.
Hungary, Matthias, King of, 370.
Hymn-Book, Berlin, 405.
Hymn-Book, Porst, 405.

I.
Ideale, Die, 302, 359, 416.
Iffland, 11, 22, 32, 34, 44, 84, 100, 101, 115, 119.
Iliad, The, 116, 235.
Iphigenia in Aulis, 477.
Iphigenia, Opera, 90, 91.
Iphigenie in Tauris, 13, 150, 241, 283, 462.
Ireland, 364.

INDEX.

Italiänische Reise, Die, 112, 118, 119, 150, 152, 161, 343.
Italy, 4, 51, 56, 98, 99, 112, 152, 156, 160, 182, 312, 318, 336, 351 364, 394, 400, 405, 411, 412 439, 457, 485, 486.

J.
Jacobi, F. H., 36, 193.
Jagemann, Caroline, 40, 85.
Jassy, 48.
Jerdan, 460.
Joanna, Queen of Bohemia, 196.
Jomelli, 108.
Jordan, 460.
Journal of Fashion, The, 18.
Jouy, De, 199, 479, 480.
Judas Iscariot, 29, 31.
Jungfrau von Orleans, Die, 396.
Jungius, 324, 325, 326, 338.

K.
Kabale und Liebe, 34, 398, 415.
Kaiser, Christoph, 112.
Kandler, 289.
Kant, 386, 454.
Kappe, 48.
Karsten, 40.
Kecht, 330, 475.
Kellner, 324.
Kerl, C., 232.
Kiesewetter, 105.
Kirnberger, J. P., 115, 169, 347, 356.
Kittel, 133.
Klöden, 326.
Klopstock, 166, 188, 302, 365, 455, 460.
Knebel, 10, 153.
Körner, 446.
Körner, T., 420, 446.
Kotzebue, A. F. F., 23, 151, 188, 396, 427, 459, 471.
Kraus, G. M., 200.
Kritheïs, 29, 30.
Krüger, 283, 340, 414.
Kügelgen, 76.
Kugler, 269.
Kunst und Alterthum, 156, 158, 165, 200, 202, 217, 234, 241, 242, 262, 282, 284, 305, 314, 382.

L.
La Coorl, 115.
Langermann, 217.
Lannes, Marshal, 45.
Laocoon, 17.
La Roche, 292, 293.
Las Cases, 368.
Laune des Verliebten, Die, 109, 462.
Lauchery, 20.
Lautier, 397, 399.
Lehrjahre, Wilhelm Meisters, 1, 7, 35, 36, 111, 165, 361, 362, 463.
Leibnitz, 282.
Lemm, 126, 128.
Leo, 434, 439.
Leonardo da Vinci, 153, 157, 158, 182, 439, 441.
Lessing, 166, 193, 203, 236, 256, 358, 317, 318, 411, 424, 452.
Lesueur, 182.
Levezow, Frau von, 83.
Levezow, Ulrike von, 221.
Levin, 28.
Lewes's *Life of Goethe*, 16, 18, 36, 57, 64, 406, 460.
Lichtenstein, Prince, 188.
Liedertafel, 65, 66, 71, 73, 106, 119, 229, 409.
Lied von der Glocke, Das, 36.
Lind, Jenny, 486.
Link, 303, 427, 428.
Linnæus, 139, 140, 304.
Literarische Zeitung, 19.
Literatur Zeitung, 17, 33.
Literary Gazette, The, 460.
Lockhart, 460.
Longfellow, 267.
Lorenz Stark, 93.
Lorzing, 68.
Lotti, 191.
Ludwig, Carl, 29.
Lulu oder Die Zauberflöte, 5.
Luther, 42, 43, 44, 142, 144, 226, 232, 298.
Lützow, 105.
Lycurgus, 380.
Lysippus, 234.

M.
Maas, Mdlle., 87, 131.

Macbeth, 253, 255, 327, 384.
Maelzel, 134.
Magiuu, 460.
Mahomet, 150, 183.
Mantegna, 353.
Mantius, 486.
Manzoni, 266, 284.
Mara, 229, 230, 436, 437.
Mara, Madame, 7, 10, 12, 16, 138, 212, 229, 230, 231. 395, 432, 434, 435, 436, 443, 445.
Marchesi, 159.
Marcus Aurelius. 186.
Markus, Levin, 350.
Marpurg, 167, 168, 169, 356, 472.
Marschner, 446.
Martial, 1, 18.
Marx, 404, 405.
Mattausch, 34.
Mattheson, J., 155, 167.
Matthisson, 53, 261, 455.
Mayer, J. S., 156, 159, 160, 161, 186.
Mecklenburg, George Prince of, 126.
Mecklenburg, Karl, Prince of, 126, 127, 128.
Medea, 470.
Melancthon, 43.
Megerle, Ulrike, 120.
Meles, 29, 30.
Mellecher, 224.
Mendelssohn, A., 19, 117, 127, 128, 206, 207, 217, 236, 244, 245, 326, 450, 456.
Mendelssohn, F., 3, 16, 19, 122, 127, 203, 206, 207, 208, 209, 218, 224, 226, 237, 238, 244, 245, 248, 250, 263, 264, 278, 279, 288, 315, 351, 352, 353, 357, 364, 367, 369, 393, 394, 399, 400, 401, 404, 412, 417, 424, 426, 439, 441, 446, 450, 455, 456, 465, 475, 477, 481, 482, 485, 486, 487.
Mendelssohn, Fanny, 236, 237, 264.
Mendelssohn, Henriette, 245, 476.
Mendelssohn, Lieutenant, 106.
Mendelssohn, M., 19, 193, 258, 476.
Merck, 387.
Merkur, Der Deutsche, 299. 318.
Messiah, The, 212, 229, 231, 233, 288.
Metamorphose der Pflanzen, Die, 18, 139, 304. 340.
Metastasio, 56, 438.
Meyer, H., 17, 19, 83, 119, 120, 137, 141, 201, 281, 305.
Meyerbeer, G., 112, 159.
Michel, 258.
Mickiewicz, 363.
Milder-Hauptmann, P. A., 90, 91, 95, 117. 138, 220, 221, 236, 315, 395, 418, 447.
Milton, 16, 355. 381. 383.
Mirandola, Pico della, 424.
Misanthrope, Le, 323.
Mitschuldigen, Die, 236.
Mizler, 325.
Moir, 460.
Molière, 236, 323.
Monti, 160.
Moravia, 31, 213.
Morgenblatt, Das, 118, 129, 165, 360.
Morghen, 153, 158.
Moritz, 398, 415, 416.
Morphologie, 157, 165, 181, 217, 242.
Moscheles, 236, 351, 433.
Möser, 369, 373, 374, 443.
Mozart, 5, 10, 12, 91, 98, 110, 116, 167, 172, 174, 175, 179, 227, 251, 265, 296, 297, 298, 304, 324, 351, 373, 394, 400, 405, 414, 465, 475, 477, 481.
Muette von Portici, La, 348, 380.
Müller, A. E., 81, 471.
Müller, Cantor, 10.
Müller, F., 158.
Müller, J., 21, 22, 397.
Müller, Kanzler von, 241, 490.
Musenalmanach, 1, 2, 372, 374.
Musikalische Zeitung, 83.
Musäus, 236.
Myron, 234, 382.

N.

Nagel, 169.
Napoleon, 45, 64, 73, 79, 132, 135, 162, 202, 367, 368, 388, 392, 432, 450.
Napoleon, Duc de Reichstadt, 173, 189.
Naturlehre, 152.
Naturliche Tochter, Die (or *Eugenie*), 12, 16, 17, 23, 28, 260, 464.
Nathan der Weise, 258.
Naumann, 236, 302, 318, 359, 416, 455.
Navarino, Battle of, 312.
Nepomuc, St. John, 196.
Netherlands, The, 138.
Neugriechische Heldenlieder, 259.
Neureuther, 448.
Newton, 80.
Newtonians, 75.
Nicolai, 57, 201, 416, 424.
Nicolai, Otto, 464.
Niebuhr, 428, 429, 431.
Noah, 475.
Norway, 55, 326.
Novalis, 471.
Novelle, Die, 303.

O.

Odilon-Barrot, 483.
Odyssey, The, 116.
Oehlenschläger, 63, 336.
Oggionno, Marco d', 158.
Oldenburg, 74.
Olfried und Lisena, 200.
Orgagna, A., 269.
Orgagna, B., 269.
Orientalischer Divan, 119.
Orlando Furioso, 426.
Othello, 171, 393, 394, 399.

P.

Pachelbel, 226, 231, 232.
Pachiarotti, 159.
Paer, 73, 450.
Paesiello, 157, 160.
Paganini, 357, 358, 359, 360, 368, 369, 449.
Palestrina, 339.

Panckoucke, Madame, 317.
Pandora, 59, 74, 83, 221.
Parry's *Last Days of Lord Byron*, 246, 249.
Pastor Fido, 237.
Penelope, 26.
Pepin, 333.
Pergolesi, 439.
Periera, Baroness von, 186.
Peter the Great, 280.
Pfeiffer, Madame Birch-, 411, 418.
Pfizer, 467.
Pfund, 102.
Phaeton, 261.
Phidias, 39.
Philoctetes, 261.
Pilate, 14.
Pisaroni, 159.
Plotinus, 38.
Plutarch, 467.
Poems, 1, 6, 7, 8, 9, 26, 52, 53, 55, 57, 59, 67, 71, 72, 73, 77, 78, 81, 94, 104, 106, 107, 108, 109, 110, 111, 113, 117, 122, 123, 125, 130, 133, 154, 159, 161, 164, 165, 187, 188, 192, 193, 196, 205, 206, 213, 214, 215, 221, 256, 259, 260, 266, 277, 295, 299, 300, 303, 306, 317, 328, 341-3, 359, 360, 372, 396, 403, 407, 435, 446, 451, 457, 461, 468, 469, 477, 485.
Pogwisch, Ulrike von, 208, 217, 400, 484.
Poland, 371.
Pole, 296.
Polignac, Prince, 315.
Porpora, 98.
Poussin, 182, 237.
Prater, The, 172, 174, 176, 177.
Preciosa, 335.
Preusz's *Friedrich der Grosse*, 220.
Prinz, 232.
Procter, 460.
Prolegomena ad Homerum, 21, 162.
Prometheus, or *Pandorens Wiederkunft*, 59, 193, 198.
Propertius, 10, 28.

INDEX. 501

Propyläen, Die, 100.
Proserpina, 118, 119.
Proske, 339.
Prussia, 23, 184, 228, 371, 372.
Prussia, Crown Prince of, 197, 257, 340, 372.
Prussia, King of, 44, 65, 66, 115, 128, 195, 197, 203, 257, 308, 337, 351, 396, 414.
Prussia, Louisa, Queen of, 11, 12.
Pygmalion, 95.
Pythagoras, 96.

Q.
Quarterly Review, The, 460.
Quintilian, 354.

R.
Raphael, 182, 191, 198, 452.
Radzivil, Prince, 126, 195, 417.
Radzivil, Princess, 195.
Rameau, 87.
Rameau's Neffe, 35, 242.
Ramler, 424, 445.
Rasoumowsky, 308.
Raüber, Die, 34, 398, 415.
Rauch, 200, 201, 234, 363, 402, 479.
Raumer, 386.
Raynal, 28.
Recke, Frau von der, 126.
Redern, Count, 447.
Reichardt, J. F., 7, 16, 27, 33, 112, 230, 437.
Reineke Fuchs, 346.
Reinhard, 48.
Rembrandt, 120.
Remorini, 161.
Revue de Paris, 449.
Revue Française, La, 369.
Retsch, 344.
Richter, J. P. F., 63.
Riemer, 77, 85, 86, 279, 287, 300, 423.
Ries, F., 433.
Rietz, 481.
Righini, V., 91.
Rinaldo, 87, 88, 94, 358.
Ring, 356.
Rintel, 1.

Robert, 89.
Robinson, Crabb, 365, 381.
Rochlitz, 7, 227, 229, 230, 231.
Rochus Fest, 137, 141.
Rodriques, 482.
Romano, Giulio, 256, 412, 414.
Romberg, 37, 308.
Romeo and Juliet, 85, 86.
Rondanini, 257.
Rosel, 299.
Rosenmeier, 219, 220.
Rosenmüller, 232.
Rossini, 155, 156, 166, 171, 172, 174, 184, 237, 385, 393, 394, 395, 408, 411, 472.
Rousseau, 95.
Rubens, 120, 182.
Rudolf, Archduke, 183.
Rumpf, K., 232.
Russia, 55, 184.
Russia, Czar of, 40.
Russia, Empress of, 221.
Russia, Maria Feodorowna, Dowager Empress of, 167, 336.
Ruth, Book of, 226.

S.
Sachs, Hans, 403, 404.
Sachs-Weimar-Eisenach, Karl Bernhard, Duke of, 277, 354.
Sachtleben, 452, 453.
St. Cyr, General, 103.
St. Romaine, Madame, 443.
St. Simon, Duc de, 389.
Salieri, 91, 173, 179, 186.
Salis, 53.
Salter, Widdowson, and Tate, 460.
Salvandy, 240.
Salzmann, 16.
Samson, 87, 88, 89, 381.
Samson Agonistes, 365, 381.
Santini, 424.
Saphir, 399.
Sartorius, 110.
Satyros oder der vergötterte Waldteufel, 193.
Saxony, 302.
Saxony, King of, 337.
Scaliger, 424.
Scarlatti, 232, 439.

Scævola, Mucius, 390.
Schadow, 124, 162, 182, 227.
Schäfer, Mdlle., 416.
Schale, 443.
Schall, 462.
Schechner, Mdlle., 447.
Scheidt, 232.
Schein, 232.
Scherz, List und Rache, 112.
Schikaneder, 5.
Schiller, 1, 2, 8, 9, 10, 11, 15, 16, 17, 18, 19, 21, 22, 26, 27, 28, 32, 34, 35, 36, 40, 46, 47, 52, 53, 69, 92, 100, 119, 121, 235, 241, 244, 262, 265, 302, 303, 306, 310, 359, 360, 384, 395, 396, 398, 399, 410, 413, 414, 415, 416, 417, 425, 426, 427, 454, 455, 460, 471, 473.
Schinkel, 455.
Schlegel, A. W., 299, 300, 323, 470, 471.
Schlegel, F., 59, 470, 471.
Schleiermacher, 25.
Schlosser, E., 224.
Schlosser, F., 224.
Schmalz, 356.
Schmeling, 438.
Schmidt, 45.
Schmidt, J. P., 420.
Schopenhauer, 40.
Schriftproben, 63.
Schröder-Devrient, Madame, 433.
Schröder, F. L., 86.
Schröter, Corona, 236.
Schubart, 417.
Schubarth, 206, 209.
Schulz, 113, 117, 128, 157, 162, 264.
Schultz, Prof., 303.
Schulze, 120.
Schulze, Oberbaurath, 303.
Schuster, Ignaz, 171.
Schütz, 132, 168.
Schntz, H., 232.
Schutz, Hofrath, 18.
Schutzgeist, Der, 151.
Schwabe, 241.
Schweizer, 318.
Schweizerfamilie, Die, 89, 90, 175.

Sekell, 320.
Scotland, 55, 316, 364, 473.
Scott's *Life of Napoleon*, 307, 308, 311.
Scott, Sir Walter, 307, 312, 364, 460.
Scotti, Count, 160.
Scribe, 349, 443, 472.
Sebastiani, General, 245, 476.
Sebbers, 266.
Seebeck, 129, 264, 443, 483.
Seidler, 236.
Seneca, 203.
Senfel, 232.
Sentimental Journey, The, 451.
Seven before Thebes, The, 13.
Seviglia, Il Barbiere di, 237, 316.
Shakespeare, 86, 98, 119, 140, 233, 253, 289, 290, 356, 358, 384, 385, 394.
Sibbern, 104.
Sickler, 165.
Silbermann, 469.
Silesia, 83.
Singakademie, 4, 25, 49, 51, 73, 81, 112, 126, 199, 203, 222, 236, 352, 399, 446, 468.
Singe-Thees, 51.
Singschule, 50.
Singspielen, 16.
Söhne des Thals, Die, 42.
Solomon's Song, 242, 387.
Solon, 151, 466.
Sontag, Mdlle., 268, 304, 306, 315, 316, 393, 394, 399.
Sophocles, 13, 261, 356.
Soret, 340.
Southey, 460.
Spain, Philip V., King of, 99.
Spiker, 253.
Spinoza, 140, 193, 386.
Spohr, 202, 253, 308, 373.
Spontini, 79, 166, 197, 199, 246, 247, 248, 308, 337, 391, 394, 398, 399, 418, 442, 447, 479, 480, 485, 486.
Stabat Mater, 53.
Stadler, 189.
Stael, Madame de, 21, 197.
Stein, Charlotte von, 40.

Steiner, 188, 189.
Stendhal, de, 161.
Sterling. 440.
Sternberg, Count Caspar, 214, 296.
Sterne, 381, 406, 451.
Stieler, 327, 395, 401.
Stolberg, Count, 460.
Stosch, 305.
Streckfuss, 225, 226, 266, 267, 268.
Streicher, 204.
Struve, 256.
Stümer, 352.
Stuttgarter Kunstblatt, 259.
Suetonius, 94.
Sulzer, 462.
Supplices, The, 13.
Süssmayr, 296, 297, 298.
Sweden, 326.
Switzerland, 475.
Szymanowska, Madame, 221, 363.

T.
Tacitus, 23.
Tancred, 183.
Tancredi, 166, 237.
Tartini, 452.
Tartuffe, 323.
Tasso, 393.
Taucher, Der, 359, 417.
Taylor, 10, 461.
Teaching of Spinoza, The, 36.
Telemann, 101, 232, 445.
Temps, Le, 369, 391.
Terence, 213, 250.
Ternite, 281, 346, 366.
Thaer, 227, 334.
Thayer's *Life of Beethoven*, 91.
Théâtre de Clara Gazul, Le, 281.
Théaulon, 247.
Theile, 232.
Thibaut, 123, 164.
Thomas-Schule, 10, 347.
Thomson, 424.
Thorwaldsen, 414. 415, 451.
Tieck, 455.
Tiedge, 53, 127, 455.
Titian, 182, 210.

Torquato Tasso, 130, 240, 283, 391, 393.
Trent, Council of, 209.
Triumph der Empfindsamkeit, Der, 118.
Troilus and Cressida, 233, 235.

U.
Ueber Reinheit der Tonkunst, 123.
Uhland, 467.
Ulrich, 182.
Ulrike, 484.
Unger, 3, 18. 19.
Unger, Madame, 1.
Unzelmann, 19.
Unzelmann. Madame, 19.
Usteri, 346.

V.
Vallo, Pietro della, 324
Varnhagen, Frau von, 350.
Vespasian, 94.
Vespino, 158.
Vestalin, Die, 79, 199, 427.
Vetter, 232.
Vicar of Wakefield, The, 381.
Victor, General, 45.
Vigano, 486.
Villemain, 369.
Vinci, 439.
Viol, 459.
Virgil, 271.
Vivaldi, 355. 356.
Vogel, 419, 420.
Vogler, 112.
Voigt, 16, 365.
Volkommene Capellmeister, Der, 155, 167.
Volkslieder, 9.
Volkslieder, Servian, 246.
Voltaire, 75, 87, 150. 183, 184.
Von Kunst und Alterthum am Rhein und Main, 121, 124, 151.
Voss, 17, 21, 59, 72, 264, 302, 455.
Voss, Ernestine, 264.

W.
Wagner, R., 404.

Wahlverwandtschaften, Die, 67, 92, 307, 386, 471.
Wahrheit und Dichtung, 388, 390, 423.
Wallenstein, 17, 40, 121, 416, 460, 473.
Walpurgis Nacht, Die Classische, 392.
Walpurgis Nacht, Die Erste, 3, 95.
Walter, 232.
Wanda, 42.
Wanderjahre, Wilhelm Meisters, 202, 206, 288, 314, 340, 345.
Wassertrager, Der, 470.
Weber's *Life of Weber*, 112.
Weber, B. A., 124, 132.
Weber, C. M., 112, 203, 238, 264, 373.
Weber, G., 296.
Weigl, 175, 186.
Weihe der Kraft, Die, 42.
Weimar, Amalia, Dowager Duchess of, 28, 46, 85, 359.
Weimar, Constantine, Prince of, 10.
Weimar, Karl August, Grand Duke of, 16, 18, 40, 153, 163, 218, 239, 241, 277, 301, 319, 397.
Weimar, Karl Friedrich, Grand Duke of, 9.
Weimar, Luise, Grand Duchess of, 208, 390.
Weimar, Maria Paulowna, Grand Duchess of, 9, 348.
Weimar, Princess of, 362.
Weiss, 80.
Weisse, 392.
Weissagungen des Bakis, Die, 310.
Wenceslaus, King, 196.
Werneburg, 96.
Werner, Z., 42, 52, 63, 213.
Werther, 57, 93, 125, 317.
West, 447.
Wieland, 5, 18, 28, 130, 300, 306, 314, 318, 359, 489.
Wilhelm Tell, 21, 22, 26, 27, 131, 408, 411.
Wilken, 317.

Willemer, Marianne von, 122.
Wilman's Taschenbuch, 4.
Wilson, 460.
Winckelmann, 120.
Winter, 15, 87, 89, 304, 358, 362.
Wohltemperirte Clavier, Das, 155, 168.
Wolf, F. A., 21, 33, 36, 37, 45, 52, 64, 132, 133, 137, 141, 162, 181, 214, 233, 261.
Wolff, Madame, 123, 133, 135, 462.
Wolff, P. A., 123, 130, 131, 447, 488.
Wolff, Prof., 317.
Wolkonsky, Princess, 363.
Wolzogen, Frau von, 454.
Wolzogen, Geh. Rath von, 10, 12.
Wordsworth, 460.
Wranitzky, 5.
Wünsch, 333.
Wurmb, Fräulein von, 413, 454.

X.

Xenien, 1, 205, 295, 396.
Xenia, 18.
Xenophon, 163.

Z.

Zahn, 305, 440, 488, 489.
Zauberflöte, Die, 5, 15, 91, 265, 298, 305.
Zelter, Clärchen, 139, 198.
Zelter, Doris, 206, 208, 217, 419, 421, 422, 481.
Zelter, Georg, 281.
Zelter, K. F., 1, 2, 3, 4, 9, 15, 29, 32, 37, 42, 45, 51, 59, 76, 115, 137, 139, 150, 162, 191, 198, 199, 208, 213, 226, 236, 241, 243, 244, 246, 247, 251, 256, 281, 300, 302, 310, 317, 336, 355, 368, 390, 396, 399, 409, 419, 423, 441, 456, 460, 461, 490.
Zelter, Karl, 92, 422.
Zelter, Louisa, 422.
Zelter, Rosamunde, 420, 422.
Zenobius, 92.
Zinkgräf, 8.
Zöllner, 416.

CHISWICK PRESS:—C. WHITTINGHAM AND CO., TOOKS COURT, CHANCERY LANE.

CATALOGUE OF
BOHN'S LIBRARIES.
736 *Volumes*, £158 9s.

The Publishers are now issuing the Libraries in a NEW AND MORE ATTRACTIVE STYLE OF BINDING. The original bindings endeared to many book-lovers by association will still be kept in stock, but henceforth all orders will be executed in the New binding, unless the contrary is expressly stated.

New Volumes of Standard Works in the various branches of Literature are constantly being added to this Series, which is already unsurpassed in respect to the number, variety, and cheapness of the Works contained in it. The Publishers beg to announce the following Volumes as recently issued or now in preparation:—

Johnson's Lives of the Poets. Edited by Mrs. Napier. 3 Vols. [*See p.* 6.
The Works of Flavius Josephus. Whiston's Translation. Revised by Rev. A. R. Shilleto, M.A. With Topographical and Geographical Notes by Colonel Sir C. W. Wilson, K.C.B. 5 volumes. [*See p.* 6.
North's Lives of the Norths. Edited by Rev. Dr. Jessopp. 3 vols.
[*See p.* 7.
Goethe's Faust. Part I. The Original Text, with Hayward's Translation and Notes, carefully revised, with an Introduction and Bibliography, by C. A. Buchheim, Ph.D., Professor of German Language and Literature at King's College, London. [*In the Press.*
Arthur Young's Tour in Ireland. Edited by A. W. Hutton, Librarian, National Liberal Club. [*Preparing.*
Ricardo on the Principles of Political Economy and Taxation. Edited with Notes by E. C. K. Gonner, M.A., Lecturer, University College, Liverpool.
[*In the press.*
Schopenhauer's Essays. Selected and Translated. By E. Belfort Bax.
[*In the press.*
Edgeworth's Stories for Children. With 8 Illustrations by L. Speed.
[*See p.* 4.
Racine's Plays. Second and Concluding Volume. Translated by R. B. Boswell. [*See p.* 7.
Hoffmann's Works. Translated by Lieut.-Colonel Ewing. Vol. II.
[*In the press.*
Bohn's Handbooks of Games. New enlarged edition. In 2 vols.
See p. 21.
  Vol. I.—Table Games, by Major-General Drayson, R.A., R. F. Green, and 'Berkeley.'
  II.—Card Games, by Dr. W. Pole, F.R.S., R. F. Green, 'Berkeley, and Baxter-Wray.
Bohn's Handbooks of Athletic Sports.
[3 *vols. ready. See p.* 21.
  By Hon. and Rev. E. Lyttelton, H. W. Wilberforce, Julian Marshall, Major Spens, Rev. J. A. Arnan Tait, W. T. Linskill, W. B. Woodgate, E. F. Knight, Martin Cobbett, Douglas Adams, Harry Vassall, C. W. Alcock, E. T. Sachs, H. H. Griffin, R. G. Allanson-Winn, Walter Armstrong, H. A. Colmore Dunn, C. Phillipps-Wolley, F. S. Creswell, A. F. Jenkin.

For BOHN'S SELECT LIBRARY, see p. 23.

February, 1891.

BOHN'S LIBRARIES.

STANDARD LIBRARY.

336 Vols. at 3s. 6d. each, excepting those marked otherwise. (*59l*. 10s. 6d.)

ADDISON'S Works. Notes of Bishop Hurd. Short Memoir, Portrait, and 8 Plates of Medals. 6 vols.
This is the most complete edition of Addison's Works issued.

ALFIERI'S Tragedies. In English Verse. With Notes, Arguments, and Introduction, by E. A. Bowring, C.B. 2 vols.

AMERICAN POETRY. — *See Poetry of America.*

BACON'S Moral and Historical Works, including Essays, Apophthegms, Wisdom of the Ancients, New Atlantis, Henry VII., Henry VIII., Elizabeth, Henry Prince of Wales, History of Great Britain, Julius Cæsar, and Augustus Cæsar. With Critical and Biographical Introduction and Notes by J. Devey, M.A. Portrait.

— *See also Philosophical Library.*

BALLADS AND SONGS of the Peasantry of England, from Oral Recitation, private MSS., Broadsides, &c. Edit. by R. Bell.

BEAUMONT AND FLETCHER. Selections. With Notes and Introduction by Leigh Hunt.

BECKMANN (J.) History of Inventions, Discoveries, and Origins. With Portraits of Beckmann and James Watt. 2 vols.

BELL (Robert).—*See Ballads, Chaucer, Green.*

BOSWELL'S Life of Johnson, with the TOUR in the HEBRIDES and JOHNSONIANA. New Edition, with Notes and Appendices, by the Rev. A. Napier, M.A., Trinity College, Cambridge, Vicar of Holkham, Editor of the Cambridge Edition of the 'Theological Works of Barrow.' With Frontispiece to each vol. 6 vols.

BREMER'S (Frederika) Works. Trans. by M. Howitt. Portrait. 4 vols.

BRINK (B. ten). Early English Literature (to Wiclif). By Bernhard ten Brink. Trans. by Prof. H. M. Kennedy.

BROWNE'S (Sir Thomas) Works. Edit. by S. Wilkin, with Dr. Johnson's Life of Browne. Portrait. 3 vols.

BURKE'S Works. 6 vols.

— **Speeches on the Impeachment of Warren Hastings;** and Letters. 2 vols.

— **Life.** By Sir J. Prior. Portrait.

BURNS (Robert). Life of. By J. G. Lockhart, D.C.L. A new and enlarged edition. With Notes and Appendices by W. Scott Douglas. Portrait.

BUTLER'S (Bp.) Analogy of Religion, Natural and Revealed, to the Constitution and Course of Nature; with Two Dissertations on Identity and Virtue, and Fifteen Sermons. With Introductions, Notes, and Memoir. Portrait.

CAMOËNS' Lusiad, or the Discovery of India. An Epic Poem. Trans. from the Portuguese, with Dissertation, Historical Sketch, and Life, by W. J. Mickle. 5th edition.

CARAFAS (The) of Maddaloni. Naples under Spanish Dominion. Trans. from the German of Alfred de Reumont. Portrait of Massaniello.

CARREL. The Counter-Revolution in England for the Re-establishment of Popery under Charles II. and James II., by Armand Carrel; with Fox's History of James II. and Lord Lonsdale's Memoir of James II. Portrait of Carrel.

CARRUTHERS. — *See Pope, in Illustrated Library.*

CARY'S Dante. The Vision of Hell, Purgatory, and Paradise. Trans. by Rev. H. F. Cary, M.A. With Life, Chronological View of his Age, Notes, and Index of Proper Names. Portrait.
This is the authentic edition, containing Mr. Cary's last corrections, with additional notes.

CELLINI (Benvenuto). Memoirs of, by himself. With Notes of G. P. Carpani. Trans. by T. Roscoe. Portrait.

CERVANTES' Galatea. A Pastoral Romance. Trans. by G. W. J. Gyll.

—— **Exemplary Novels.** Trans. by W. K. Kelly.

—— **Don Quixote de la Mancha.** Motteux's Translation revised. With Lockhart's Life and Notes. 2 vols.

CHAUCER'S Poetical Works. With Poems formerly attributed to him. With a Memoir, Introduction, Notes, and a Glossary, by R. Bell. Improved edition, with Preliminary Essay by Rev. W. W. Skeat, M.A. Portrait. 4 vols.

CLASSIC TALES, containing Rasselas, Vicar of Wakefield, Gulliver's Travels, and The Sentimental Journey.

COLERIDGE'S (S. T.) Friend. A Series of Essays on Morals, Politics, and Religion. Portrait.

—— **Aids to Reflection. Confessions** of an Inquiring Spirit; and Essays on Faith and the Common Prayer-book. New Edition, revised.

—— **Table-Talk and Omniana.** By T. Ashe, B.A.

—— **Lectures on Shakespeare and** other Poets. Edit. by T. Ashe, B.A. Containing the lectures taken down in 1811-12 by J. P. Collier, and those delivered at Bristol in 1813.

—— **Biographia Literaria; or, Bio**graphical Sketches of my Literary Life and Opinions; with Two Lay Sermons.

—— **Miscellanies, Æsthetic and** Literary; to which is added, THE THEORY OF LIFE. Collected and arranged by T. Ashe, B.A.

COMMINES.—*See Philip.*

CONDÉ'S History of the Dominion of the Arabs in Spain. Trans. by Mrs. Foster. Portrait of Abderahmen ben Moavia. 3 vols.

COWPER'S Complete Works, Poems, Correspondence, and Translations. Edit. with Memoir by R. Southey. 45 Engravings. 8 vols.

COXE'S Memoirs of the Duke of Marlborough. With his original Correspondence, from family records at Blenheim. Revised edition. Portraits. 3 vols.

*** An Atlas of the plans of Marlborough's campaigns, 4to. 10s. 6d.

COXE'S History of the House of Austria. From the Foundation of the Monarchy by Rhodolph of Hapsburgh to the Death of Leopold II., 1218-1792. By Archdn. Coxe. With Continuation from the Accession of Francis I. to the Revolution of 1848. 4 Portraits. 4 vols.

CUNNINGHAM'S Lives of the most Eminent British Painters. With Notes and 16 fresh Lives by Mrs. Heaton. 3 vols.

DEFOE'S Novels and Miscellaneous Works. With Prefaces and Notes, including those attributed to Sir W. Scott. Portrait. 7 vols.

DE LOLME'S Constitution of England, in which it is compared both with the Republican form of Government and the other Monarchies of Europe. Edit., with Life and Notes, by J. Macgregor.

DUNLOP'S History of Fiction. New Edition, revised. By Henry Wilson. 2 vols., 5s. each.

EDGEWORTH'S Stories for Children. With 3 Illustrations by L. Speed.

ELZE'S Shakespeare.—*See Shakespeare*

EMERSON'S Works. 3 vols.
 Vol. I.—Essays, Lectures, and Poems.
 Vol. II.—English Traits, Nature, and Conduct of Life.
 Vol. III.—Society and Solitude—Letters and Social Aims—Miscellaneous Papers (hitherto uncollected)—May-Day, &c.

FOSTER'S (John) Life and Correspondence. Edit. by J. E. Ryland. Portrait. 2 vols.

—— **Lectures at Broadmead Chapel.** Edit. by J. E. Ryland. 2 vols.

—— **Critical Essays contributed to** the 'Eclectic Review.' Edit. by J. E. Ryland. 2 vols.

—— **Essays: On Decision of Charac**ter; on a Man's writing Memoirs of Himself; on the epithet Romantic; on the aversion of Men of Taste to Evangelical Religion.

—— **Essays on the Evils of Popular** Ignorance, and a Discourse on the Propagation of Christianity in India.

—— **Essay on the Improvemen of** Time, with Notes of Sermons and other Pieces.

—— **Fosteriana:** selected from periodical papers, edit. by H. G. Bohn.

FOX (Rt. Hon. C. J.)—*See Carrel.*

GIBBON'S Decline and Fall of the Roman Empire. Complete and unabridged, with variorum Notes; including those of Guizot, Wenck, Niebuhr, Hugo, Neander, and others. 7 vols. 2 Maps and Portrait.

GOETHE'S Works. Trans. into English by E. A. Bowring, C.B., Anna Swanwick, Sir Walter Scott, &c. &c. 14 vols.
Vols. I. and II.—Autobiography and Annals. Portrait.
Vol. III.—Faust. Complete.
Vol. IV.—Novels and Tales: containing Elective Affinities, Sorrows of Werther, The German Emigrants, The Good Women, and a Nouvelette.
Vol. V.—Wilhelm Meister's Apprenticeship.
Vol. VI.—Conversations with Eckerman and Soret.
Vol. VII.—Poems and Ballads in the original Metres, including Hermann and Dorothea.
Vol. VIII.—Götz von Berlichingen, Torquato Tasso, Egmont, Iphigenia, Clavigo, Wayward Lover, and Fellow Culprits.
Vol. IX.—Wilhelm Meister's Travels. Complete Edition.
Vol. X.—Tour in Italy. Two Parts. And Second Residence in Rome.
Vol. XI.—Miscellaneous Travels, Letters from Switzerland, Campaign in France, Siege of Mainz, and Rhine Tour.
Vol. XII.—Early and Miscellaneous Letters, including Letters to his Mother, with Biography and Notes.
Vol. XIII.—Correspondence with Zelter.
Vol. XIV.—Reineke Fox, West-Eastern Divan and Achilleid. Translated in original metres by A. Rogers.
—— **Correspondence with Schiller.** 2 vols.—*See Schiller.*
—— **Faust.**—*See Collegiate Series.*

GOLDSMITH'S Works. 5 vols.
Vol. I.—Life, Vicar of Wakefield, Essays, and Letters.
Vol. II.—Poems, Plays, Bee, Cock Lane Ghost.
Vol. III.—The Citizen of the World, Polite Learning in Europe.
Vol. IV.—Biographies, Criticisms, Later Essays.
Vol. V.—Prefaces, Natural History, Letters, Goody Two-Shoes, Index.

GREENE, MARLOWE and BEN JONSON (Poems of). With Notes and Memoirs by R. Bell.

GREGORY'S (Dr.) The Evidences, Doctrines, and Duties of the Christian Religion.

GRIMM'S Household Tales. With the Original Notes. Trans. by Mrs. A. Hunt. Introduction by Andrew Lang, M.A. 2 vols.

GUIZOT'S History of Representative Government in Europe. Trans. by A. R. Scoble.

—— **English Revolution of 1640.** From the Accession of Charles I. to his Death. Trans. by W. Hazlitt. Portrait.

—— **History of Civilisation.** From the Roman Empire to the French Revolution. Trans. by W. Hazlitt. Portraits. 3 vols.

HALL'S (Rev. Robert) Works and Remains. Memoir by Dr. Gregory and Essay by J. Foster. Portrait.

HAUFF'S Tales. The Caravan—The Sheikh of Alexandria—The Inn in the Spessart. Translated by Prof. S. Mendel.

HAWTHORNE'S Tales. 3 vols.
Vol. I.—Twice-told Tales, and the Snow Image.
Vol. II.—Scarlet Letter, and the House with Seven Gables.
Vol. III.—Transformation, and Blithedale Romance.

HAZLITT'S (W.) Works. 7 vols.
—— **Table-Talk.**
—— **The Literature of the Age of** Elizabeth and Characters of Shakespeare's Plays.
—— **English Poets and English Comic** Writers.
—— **The Plain Speaker.** Opinions on Books, Men, and Things.
—— **Round Table.** Conversations of James Northcote, R.A.. Characteristics.
—— **Sketches and Essays,** and Winterslow.
—— **Spirit of the Age;** or, Contemporary Portraits. New Edition, by W. Carew Hazlitt.

HEINE'S Poems. Translated in the original Metres, with Life by E. A. Bowring, C.B.

—— **Travel-Pictures.** The Tour in the Harz, Norderney, and Book of Ideas, together with the Romantic School. Trans. by F. Storr. With Maps and Appendices.

HOFFMANN'S Works. The Serapion Brethren. Vol. I. Trans. by Lt.-Col. Ewing. [*Vol. II. in the press.*

HOOPER'S (G.) Waterloo: The Downfall of the First Napoleon: a History of the Campaign of 1815. By George Hooper. With Maps and Plans. New Edition, revised.

HUGO'S (Victor) Dramatic Works. Hernani—Ruy Blas—The King's Diversion. Translated by Mrs. Newton Crosland and F. L. Slous.

—— **Poems**, chiefly Lyrical. Collected by H. L. Williams.

HUNGARY: Its History and Revolution, with Memoir of Kossuth. Portrait.

HUTCHINSON (Colonel). Memoirs of. By his Widow, with her Autobiography, and the Siege of Lathom House. Portrait.

IRVING'S (Washington) Complete Works. 15 vols.

—— **Life and Letters.** By his Nephew, Pierre E. Irving. With Index and a Portrait. 2 vols.

JAMES'S (G. P. R.) Life of Richard Cœur de Lion. Portraits of Richard and Philip Augustus. 2 vols.

—— **Louis XIV.** Portraits. 2 vols.

JAMESON (Mrs.) Shakespeare's Heroines. Characteristics of Women. By Mrs. Jameson.

JEAN PAUL.—*See Richter.*

JOHNSON'S Lives of the Poets. Edited, with Notes, by Mrs. Alexander Napier. And an Introduction by Professor J. W. Hales, M.A. 3 vols.

JONSON (Ben). Poems of.—*See Greene.*

JOSEPHUS (Flavius), The Works of. Whiston's Translation. Revised by Rev. A. R. Shilleto, M.A. With Topographical and Geographical Notes by Colonel Sir C. W. Wilson, K.C.B. 5 vols.

JUNIUS'S Letters. With Woodfall's Notes. An Essay on the Authorship. Facsimiles of Handwriting. 2 vols.

LA FONTAINE'S Fables. In English Verse, with Essay on the Fabulists. By Elizur Wright.

LAMARTINE'S The Girondists, or Personal Memoirs of the Patriots of the French Revolution. Trans. by H. T. Ryde. Portraits of Robespierre, Madame Roland, and Charlotte Corday. 3 vols.

—— **The Restoration of Monarchy in France** (a Sequel to The Girondists). 5 Portraits. 4 vols.

—— **The French Revolution of 1848.** Portraits.

LAMB'S (Charles) Elia and Eliana. Complete Edition. Portrait.

LAMB'S (Charles) Specimens of English Dramatic Poets of the time of Elizabeth. With Notes and the Extracts from the Garrick Plays.

—— **Talfourd's Letters of Charles Lamb.** New Edition, by W. Carew Hazlitt. 2 vols.

LANZI'S History of Painting in Italy, from the Period of the Revival of the Fine Arts to the End of the 18th Century. With Memoir and Portraits. Trans. by T. Roscoe. 3 vols.

LAPPENBERG'S England under the Anglo-Saxon Kings. Trans. by B. Thorpe, F.S.A. 2 vols.

LESSING'S Dramatic Works. Complete. By E. Bell, M.A. With Memoir by H. Zimmern. Portrait. 2 vols.

—— **Laokoon, Dramatic Notes,** and Representation of Death by the Ancients. Trans. by E. C. Beasley and Helen Zimmern. Frontispiece.

LOCKE'S Philosophical Works, containing Human Understanding, Controversy with Bishop of Worcester, Malebranche's Opinions, Natural Philosophy, Reading and Study. With Introduction, Analysis, and Notes, by J. A. St. John. Portrait. 2 vols.

—— **Life and Letters,** with Extracts from his Common-place Books. By Lord King.

LOCKHART (J. G.)—*See Burns.*

LUTHER'S Table-Talk. Trans. by W. Hazlitt. With Life by A. Chalmers, and LUTHER'S CATECHISM. Portrait after Cranach.

—— **Autobiography.**—*See Michelet.*

MACHIAVELLI'S History of Florence, THE PRINCE, Savonarola, Historical Tracts, and Memoir. Portrait.

MARLOWE. Poems of.—*See Greene.*

MARTINEAU'S (Harriet) History of England (including History of the Peace) from 1800-1846. 5 vols.

MENZEL'S History of Germany, from the Earliest Period to the Crimean War. Portraits. 3 vols.

MICHELET'S Autobiography of Luther. Trans. by W. Hazlitt. With Notes.

—— **The French Revolution** to the Flight of the King in 1791. Frontispiece.

MIGNET'S The French Revolution, from 1789 to 1814. Portrait of Napoleon.

MILTON'S Prose Works. With Preface, Preliminary Remarks by J. A. St. John, and Index. 5 vols. Portraits.
— **Poetical Works.** With 120 Wood Engravings. 2 vols.

MITFORD'S (Miss) Our Village. Sketches of Rural Character and Scenery. 2 Engravings. 2 vols.

MOLIÈRE'S Dramatic Works. In English Prose, by C. H. Wall. With a Life and a Portrait. 3 vols.
'It is not too much to say that we have here probably as good a translation of Molière as can be given.'—*Academy.*

MONTAGU. Letters and Works of Lady Mary Wortley Montagu. Lord Wharncliffe's Third Edition. Edited by W. Moy Thomas. New and revised edition. With steel plates. 2 vols. 5s. each.

MONTESQUIEU'S Spirit of Laws. Revised Edition, with D'Alembert's Analysis, Notes, and Memoir. 2 vols.

NEANDER (Dr. A.) History of the Christian Religion and Church. Trans. by J. Torrey. With Short Memoir. 10 vols.
— **Life of Jesus Christ, in its Historical Connexion and Development.**
— **The Planting and Training of** the Christian Church by the Apostles. With the Antignosticus, or Spirit of Tertullian. Trans. by J. E. Ryland. 2 vols.
— **Lectures on the History of** Christian Dogmas. Trans. by J. E. Ryland. 2 vols.
— **Memorials of Christian Life in** the Early and Middle Ages; including Light in Dark Places. Trans. by J. E. Ryland.

NORTH'S Lives of the Right Hon. Francis North, Baron Guildford, the Hon. Sir Dudley North, and the Hon. and Rev. Dr. John North. By the Hon. Roger North. Edited by A. Jessopp, D.D. With 3 Portraits. 3 vols. 3s. 6d. each.
'Lovers of good literature will rejoice at the appearance of a new, handy, and complete edition of so justly famous a book, and will congratulate themselves that it has found so competent and skilful an editor as Dr. Jessopp.'—*Times.*

OCKLEY (S.) History of the Saracens and their Conquests in Syria, Persia, and Egypt. Comprising the Lives of Mohammed and his Successors to the Death of Abdalmelik, the Eleventh Caliph. By Simon Ockley, B.D., Portrait of Mohammed.

PASCAL'S Thoughts. Translated from the Text of M. Auguste Molinier by C. Kegan Paul. 3rd edition.

PERCY'S Reliques of Ancient English Poetry, consisting of Ballads, Songs, and other Pieces of our earlier Poets, with some few of later date. With Essay on Ancient Minstrels, and Glossary. 2 vols.

PHILIP DE COMMINES. Memoirs of. Containing the Histories of Louis XI. and Charles VIII., and Charles the Bold, Duke of Burgundy. With the History of Louis XI., by Jean de Troyes. Translated, with a Life and Notes, by A. R. Scoble. Portraits. 2 vols.

PLUTARCH'S LIVES. Translated, with Notes and Life, by A. Stewart, M.A., late Fellow of Trinity College, Cambridge, and G. Long, M.A. 4 vols.

POETRY OF AMERICA. Selections from One Hundred Poets, from 1776 to 1876. With Introductory Review, and Specimens of Negro Melody, by W. J. Linton. Portrait of W. Whitman.

RACINE'S (Jean) Dramatic Works. A metrical English version, with Biographical notice. By R. Bruce Boswell, M.A. Oxon. 2 vols.

RANKE (L.) History of the Popes, their Church and State, and their Conflicts with Protestantism in the 16th and 17th Centuries. Trans. by E. Foster. Portraits. 3 vols.
— **History of Servia.** Trans. by Mrs. Kerr. To which is added, The Slave Provinces of Turkey, by Cyprien Robert.
— **History of the Latin and Teutonic Nations.** 1494-1514. Trans. by P. A. Ashworth, translator of Dr. Gneist's 'History of the English Constitution.'

REUMONT (Alfred de). –*See Carafas.*

REYNOLDS'(Sir J.) Literary Works. With Memoir and Remarks by H. W. Beechy. 2 vols.

RICHTER (Jean Paul). Levana, a Treatise on Education; together with the Autobiography, and a short Memoir.
— **Flower, Fruit, and Thorn Pieces,** or the Wedded Life, Death, and Marriage of Siebenkaes. Translated by Alex. Ewing. The only complete English translation.

ROSCOE'S (W.) Life of Leo X., with Notes, Historical Documents, and Dissertation on Lucretia Borgia. 3 Portraits. 2 vols.
— **Lorenzo de' Medici,** called 'The Magnificent,' with Copyright Notes, Poems, Letters, &c. With Memoir of Roscoe and Portrait of Lorenzo.

RUSSIA, History of, from the earliest Period to the Crimean War. By W. K. Kelly. 3 Portraits. 2 vols.

SCHILLER'S Works. 7 vols.
Vol. I.—History of the Thirty Years' War. Rev. A. J. W. Morrison, M.A. Portrait.
Vol. II.—History of the Revolt in the Netherlands, the Trials of Counts Egmont and Horn, the Siege of Antwerp, and the Disturbance of France preceding the Reign of Henry IV. Translated by Rev. A. J. W. Morrison and L. Dora Schmitz.
Vol. III.—Don Carlos. R. D. Boylan —Mary Stuart. Mellish — Maid of Orleans. Anna Swanwick—Bride of Messina. A. Lodge, M.A. Together with the Use of the Chorus in Tragedy (a short Essay). Engravings.
These Dramas are all translated in metre.
Vol. IV.—Robbers—Fiesco—Love and Intrigue—Demetrius—Ghost Seer—Sport of Divinity.
The Dramas in this volume are in prose.
Vol. V.—Poems. E. A. Bowring, C.B.
Vol. VI.—Essays, Æsthetical and Philosophical, including the Dissertation on the Connexion between the Animal and Spiritual in Man.
Vol. VII. — Wallenstein's Camp. J. Churchill. — Piccolomini and Death of Wallenstein. S. T. Coleridge.—William Tell. Sir Theodore Martin, K.C.B., LL.D.

SCHILLER and GOETHE. Correspondence between, from A.D. 1794-1805. Trans. by L. Dora Schmitz. 2 vols.

SCHLEGEL (F.) Lectures on the Philosophy of Life and the Philosophy of Language. Trans. by A. J. W. Morrison.
—— **The History of Literature, Ancient and Modern.**
—— **The Philosophy of History.** With Memoir and Portrait. Trans. by J. B. Robertson.
—— **Modern History,** with the Lectures entitled Cæsar and Alexander, and The Beginning of our History. Translated by L. Purcell and R. H. Whitelock.
—— **Æsthetic and Miscellaneous Works,** containing Letters on Christian Art, Essay on Gothic Architecture, Remarks on the Romance Poetry of the Middle Ages, on Shakspeare, the Limits of the Beautiful, and on the Language and Wisdom of the Indians. By E. J. Millington.

SCHLEGEL (A. W.) Dramatic Art and Literature. By J. Black. With Memoir by Rev. A. J. W. Morrison. Portrait.

SCHUMANN (Robert), His Life and Works. By A. Reissmann. Trans. by A. L. Alger.
—— **Early Letters.** Translated by May Herbert. With Preface by Sir G. Grove.

SHAKESPEARE'S Dramatic Art. The History and Character of Shakspeare's Plays. By Dr. H. Ulrici. Trans. by L. Dora Schmitz. 2 vols.

SHAKESPEARE (William). A Literary Biography by Karl Elze, Ph.D., LL.D. Translated by L. Dora Schmitz. 5s.

SHERIDAN'S Dramatic Works. With Memoir. Portrait (after Reynolds).

SKEAT (Rev. W. W.)—*See Chaucer.*

SISMONDI'S History of the Literature of the South of Europe. Trans. by T. Roscoe. Portraits. 2 vols.

SMITH'S (Adam) Theory of Moral Sentiments; with Essay on the First Formation of Languages, and Critical Memoir by Dugald Stewart.
—— *See Economic Library.*

SMYTH'S (Professor) Lectures on Modern History; from the Irruption of the Northern Nations to the close of the American Revolution. 2 vols.
—— **Lectures on the French Revolution.** With Index. 2 vols.

SOUTHEY.—*See Cowper, Wesley, and (Illustrated Library) Nelson.*

STURM'S Morning Communings with God, or Devotional Meditations for Every Day. Trans. by W. Johnstone, M.A.

SULLY. Memoirs of the Duke of, Prime Minister to Henry the Great. With Notes and Historical Introduction. 4 Portraits. 4 vols.

TAYLOR'S (Bishop Jeremy) Holy Living and Dying, with Prayers, containing the Whole Duty of a Christian and the parts of Devotion fitted to all Occasions. Portrait.

TEN BRINK.—*See Brink.*

THIERRY'S Conquest of England by the Normans; its Causes, and its Consequences in England and the Continent. By W. Hazlitt. With short Memoir. 2 Portraits. 2 vols.

ULRICI (Dr.)—*See Shakespeare.*

VASARI. Lives of the most Eminent Painters, Sculptors, and Architects. By Mrs. J. Foster, with selected Notes. Portrait. 6 vols., Vol. VI. being an additional Volume of Notes by Dr. J. P. Richter.

WERNER'S Templars in Cyprus. Trans. by E. A. M. Lewis.

WESLEY, the Life of, and the Rise and Progress of Methodism. By Robert Southey. Portrait. 5s.

WHEATLEY. A Rational Illustration of the Book of Common Prayer, being the Substance of everything Liturgical in all former Ritualist Commentators upon the subject. Frontispiece.

YOUNG (Arthur) Travels in France. Edited by Miss Betham Edwards. With a Portrait.

HISTORICAL LIBRARY.

22 Volumes at 5s. each. (5l. 10s. per set.)

EVELYN'S Diary and Correspondence, with the Private Correspondence of Charles I. and Sir Edward Nicholas, and between Sir Edward Hyde (Earl of Clarendon) and Sir Richard Browne. Edited from the Original MSS. by W. Bray, F.A.S. 4 vols. 45 Engravings (after Vandyke, Lely, Kneller, and Jamieson, &c.).

N.B.—This edition contains 130 letters from Evelyn and his wife, printed by permission, and contained in no other edition.

PEPYS' Diary and Correspondence. With Life and Notes, by Lord Braybrooke. 4 vols. With Appendix containing additional Letters, an Index and 31 Engravings (after Vandyke, Sir P. Lely, Holbein, Kneller, &c.).

N.D.—This is a reprint of Lord Braybrooke's fourth and last edition, containing all his latest notes and corrections, the copyright of the publishers.

JESSE'S Memoirs of the Court of England under the Stuarts, including the Protectorate. 3 vols. With Index and 42 Portraits (after Vandyke, Lely, &c.).

—— Memoirs of the Pretenders and their Adherents. 6 Portraits.

NUGENT'S (Lord) Memorials of Hampden, his Party and Times. With Memoir. 12 Portraits (after Vandyke and others).

STRICKLAND'S (Agnes) Lives of the Queens of England from the Norman Conquest. From authentic Documents, public and private. 6 Portraits. 6 vols.

—— Life of Mary Queen of Scots. 2 Portraits. 2 vols.

—— Lives of the Tudor and Stuart Princesses. With 2 Portraits.

PHILOSOPHICAL LIBRARY.

16 Vols. at 5s. each, excepting those marked otherwise. (3l. 14s. per set.)

BACON'S Novum Organum and Advancement of Learning. With Notes by J. Devey, M.A.

BAX. A Handbook of the History of Philosophy, for the use of Students. By E. Belfort Bax, Editor of Kant's 'Prolegomena.'

COMTE'S Philosophy of the Sciences. An Exposition of the Principles of the *Cours de Philosophie Positive*. By G. H. Lewes, Author of 'The Life of Goethe.'

DRAPER (Dr. J. W.) A History of the Intellectual Development of Europe. 2 vols.

HEGEL'S Philosophy of History. By J. Sibree, M.A.

KANT'S Critique of Pure Reason. By J. M. D. Meiklejohn.

—— Prolegomena and Metaphysical Foundations of Natural Science, with Biography and Memoir by E. Belfort Bax. Portrait.

LOGIC, or the Science of Inference. A Popular Manual. By J. Devey.

MILLER (Professor). History Philosophically Illustrated, from the Fall of the Roman Empire to the French Revolution. With Memoir. 4 vols. 3s. 6d. each.

SCHOPENHAUER on the Fourfold Root of the Principle of Sufficient Reason, and on the Will in Nature. Trans. from the German.

—— Essays. Selected and Translated by E. Belfort Bax. [*In the press.*

SPINOZA'S Chief Works. Trans. with Introduction by R. H. M. Elwes. 2 vols.
Vol. I.—Tractatus Theologico-Politicus—Political Treatise.
Vol. II.—Improvement o the Understanding—Ethics—Letters.

THEOLOGICAL LIBRARY.

15 *Vols. at* 5s. *each (except* Chillingworth, 3s. 6d.). (3l. 13s. 6d. *per set.*)

BLEEK. Introduction to the Old Testament. By Friedrich Bleek. Trans. under the supervision of Rev. E. Venables, Residentiary Canon of Lincoln. 2 vols.

CHILLINGWORTH'S Religion of Protestants. 3s. 6d.

EUSEBIUS. Ecclesiastical History of Eusebius Pamphilius, Bishop of Cæsarea. Trans. by Rev. C. F. Cruse, M.A. With Notes, Life, and Chronological Tables.

EVAGRIUS. History of the Church. —*See Theodoret.*

HARDWICK. History of the Articles of Religion; to which is added a Series of Documents from A.D. 1536 to A.D. 1615. Ed. by Rev. F. Proctor.

HENRY'S (Matthew) Exposition of the Book of Psalms. Numerous Woodcuts.

PEARSON (John, D.D.) Exposition of the Creed. Edit. by E. Walford, M.A. With Notes, Analysis, and Indexes.

PHILO-JUDÆUS, Works of. The Contemporary of Josephus. Trans. by C. D. Yonge. 4 vols.

PHILOSTORGIUS. Ecclesiastical History of.—*See Sozomen.*

SOCRATES' Ecclesiastical History. Comprising a History of the Church from Constantine, A.D. 305, to the 38th year of Theodosius II. With Short Account of the Author, and selected Notes.

SOZOMEN'S Ecclesiastical History. A.D. 324-440. With Notes, Prefatory Remarks by Valesius, and Short Memoir. Together with the ECCLESIASTICAL HISTORY OF PHILOSTORGIUS, as epitomised by Photius. Trans. by Rev. E. Walford, M.A. With Notes and brief Life.

THEODORET and EVAGRIUS. Histories of the Church from A.D. 332 to the Death of Theodore of Mopsuestia, A.D. 427; and from A.D. 431 to A.D. 544. With Memoirs.

WIESELER'S (Karl) Chronological Synopsis of the Four Gospels. Trans. by Rev. Canon Venables.

ANTIQUARIAN LIBRARY.

35 *Vols. at* 5s. *each.* (8l. 15s. *per set.*)

ANGLO-SAXON CHRONICLE. — *See Bede.*

ASSER'S Life of Alfred.—*See Six O. E. Chronicles.*

BEDE'S (Venerable) Ecclesiastical History of England. Together with the ANGLO-SAXON CHRONICLE. With Notes, Short Life, Analysis, and Map. Edit. by J. A. Giles, D.C.L.

BOETHIUS'S Consolation of Philosophy. King Alfred's Anglo-Saxon Version of. With an English Translation on opposite pages, Notes, Introduction, and Glossary, by Rev. S. Fox, M.A. To which is added the Anglo-Saxon Version of the METRES OF BOETHIUS, with a free Translation by Martin F. Tupper, D.C.L.

BRAND'S Popular Antiquities of England, Scotland, and Ireland. Illustrating the Origin of our Vulgar and Provincial Customs, Ceremonies, and Superstitions. By Sir Henry Ellis, K.H., F.R.S. Frontispiece. 3 vols.

CHRONICLES of the CRUSADES. Contemporary Narratives of Richard Cœur de Lion, by Richard of Devizes and Geoffrey de Vinsauf; and of the Crusade at Saint Louis, by Lord John de Joinville. With Short Notes. Illuminated Frontispiece from an old MS.

DYER'S (T. F. T.) British Popular Customs, Present and Past. An Account of the various Games and Customs associated with different Days of the Year in the British Isles, arranged according to the Calendar. By the Rev. T. F. Thiselton Dyer, M.A.

EARLY TRAVELS IN PALESTINE. Comprising the Narratives of Arculf, Willibald, Bernard, Sæwulf, Sigurd, Benjamin of Tudela, Sir John Maundeville, De la Brocquière, and Maundrell; all unabridged. With Introduction and Notes by Thomas Wright. Map of Jerusalem.

ANTIQUARIAN LIBRARY.

ELLIS (G.) Specimens of Early English Metrical Romances, relating to Arthur, Merlin, Guy of Warwick, Richard Cœur de Lion, Charlemagne, Roland, &c. &c. With Historical Introduction by J. O. Halliwell, F.R.S. Illuminated Frontispiece from an old MS.

ETHELWERD. Chronicle of.—*See Six O. E. Chronicles.*

FLORENCE OF WORCESTER'S Chronicle, with the Two Continuations: comprising Annals of English History from the Departure of the Romans to the Reign of Edward I. Trans., with Notes, by Thomas Forester, M.A.

GEOFFREY OF MONMOUTH. Chronicle of.—*See Six O. E. Chronicles.*

GESTA ROMANORUM, or Entertaining Moral Stories invented by the Monks. Trans. with Notes by the Rev. Charles Swan. Edit. by W. Hooper, M.A.

GILDAS. Chronicle of.—*See Six O. E. Chronicles.*

GIRALDUS CAMBRENSIS' Historical Works. Containing Topography of Ireland, and History of the Conquest of Ireland, by Th. Forester, M.A. Itinerary through Wales, and Description of Wales, by Sir R. Colt Hoare.

HENRY OF HUNTINGDON'S History of the English, from the Roman Invasion to the Accession of Henry II.; with the Acts of King Stephen, and the Letter to Walter. By T. Forester, M.A. Frontispiece from an old MS.

INGULPH'S Chronicles of the Abbey of Croyland, with the CONTINUATION by Peter of Blois and others. Trans. with Notes by H. T. Riley, B.A.

KEIGHTLEY'S (Thomas) Fairy Mythology, illustrative of the Romance and Superstition of Various Countries. Frontispiece by Cruikshank.

LEPSIUS'S Letters from Egypt, Ethiopia, and the Peninsula of Sinai; to which are added, Extracts from his Chronology of the Egyptians, with reference to the Exodus of the Israelites. By L. and J. B. Horner. Maps and Coloured View of Mount Barkal.

MALLET'S Northern Antiquities, or an Historical Account of the Manners, Customs, Religions, and Literature of the Ancient Scandinavians. Trans. by Bishop Percy. With Translation of the PROSE EDDA, and Notes by J. A. Blackwell. Also an Abstract of the 'Eyrbyggia Saga' by Sir Walter Scott. With Glossary and Coloured Frontispiece.

MARCO POLO'S Travels; with Notes and Introduction. Edit. by T. Wright.

MATTHEW PARIS'S English History, from 1235 to 1273. By Rev. J. A. Giles, D.C.L. With Frontispiece. 3 vols.— *See also Roger of Wendover.*

MATTHEW OF WESTMINSTER'S Flowers of History, especially such as relate to the affairs of Britain, from the beginning of the World to A.D. 1307. By C. D. Yonge. 2 vols.

NENNIUS. Chronicle of.—*See Six O. E. Chronicles.*

ORDERICUS VITALIS' Ecclesiastical History of England and Normandy. With Notes, Introduction of Guizot, and the Critical Notice of M. Delille, by T. Forester, M.A. To which is added the CHRONICLE OF ST. EVROULT. With General and Chronological Indexes. 4 vols.

PAULI'S (Dr. R.) Life of Alfred the Great. To which is appended Alfred's ANGLO-SAXON VERSION OF OROSIUS. With literal Translation interpaged, Notes, and an ANGLO-SAXON GRAMMAR and Glossary, by B. Thorpe. Frontispiece.

RICHARD OF CIRENCESTER. Chronicle of.—*See Six O. E. Chronicles.*

ROGER DE HOVEDEN'S Annals of English History, comprising the History of England and of other Countries of Europe from A.D. 732 to A.D. 1201. With Notes by H. T. Riley, B.A. 2 vols.

ROGER OF WENDOVER'S Flowers of History, comprising the History of England from the Descent of the Saxons to A.D. 1235, formerly ascribed to Matthew Paris. With Notes and Index by J. A. Giles, D.C.L. 2 vols.

SIX OLD ENGLISH CHRONICLES: viz., Asser's Life of Alfred and the Chronicles of Ethelwerd, Gildas, Nennius, Geoffrey of Monmouth, and Richard of Cirencester. Edit., with Notes, by J. A. Giles, D.C.L. Portrait of Alfred.

WILLIAM OF MALMESBURY'S Chronicle of the Kings of England, from the Earliest Period to King Stephen. By Rev. J. Sharpe. With Notes by J. A. Giles, D.C.L. Frontispiece.

YULE-TIDE STORIES. A Collection of Scandinavian and North-German Popular Tales and Traditions, from the Swedish, Danish, and German. Edit. by B. Thorpe.

ILLUSTRATED LIBRARY.

80 *Vols. at 5s. each, excepting those marked otherwise.* (19*l.* 17*s.* 6*d.* *per set.*)

ALLEN'S (Joseph, R.N.) Battles of the British Navy. Revised edition, with Indexes of Names and Events, and 57 Portraits and Plans. 2 vols.

ANDERSEN'S Danish Fairy Tales. By Caroline Peachey. With Short Life and 120 Wood Engravings.

ARIOSTO'S Orlando Furioso. In English Verse by W. S. Rose. With Notes and Short Memoir. Portrait after Titian, and 24 Steel Engravings. 2 vols.

BECHSTEIN'S Cage and Chamber Birds: their Natural History, Habits, &c. Together with SWEET'S BRITISH WARBLERS. 43 Coloured Plates and Woodcuts.

BONOMI'S Nineveh and its Palaces. The Discoveries of Botta and Layard applied to the Elucidation of Holy Writ. 7 Plates and 294 Woodcuts.

BUTLER'S Hudibras, with Variorum Notes and Biography. Portrait and 28 Illustrations.

CATTERMOLE'S Evenings at Haddon Hall. Romantic Tales of the Olden Times. With 24 Steel Engravings after Cattermole.

CHINA, Pictorial, Descriptive, and Historical, with some account of Ava and the Burmese, Siam, and Anam. Map, and nearly 100 Illustrations.

CRAIK'S (G. L.) Pursuit of Knowledge under Difficulties. Illustrated by Anecdotes and Memoirs. Numerous Woodcut Portraits.

CRUIKSHANK'S Three Courses and a Dessert; comprising three Sets of Tales, West Country, Irish, and Legal; and a Mélange. With 50 Illustrations by Cruikshank.

—— **Punch and Judy.** The Dialogue of the Puppet Show; an Account of its Origin, &c. 24 Illustrations and Coloured Plates by Cruikshank.

DANTE, in English Verse, by I. C. Wright, M.A. With Introduction and Memoir. Portrait and 34 Steel Engravings after Flaxman.

DIDRON'S Christian Iconography; a History of Christian Art in the Middle Ages. By the late A. N. Didron. Trans. by E. J. Millington, and completed, with Additions and Appendices, by Margaret Stokes. 2 vols. With numerous Illustrations.

Vol. I. The History of the Nimbus, the Aureole, and the Glory; Representations of the Persons of the Trinity.

Vol. II. The Trinity; Angels; Devils The Soul; The Christian Scheme. Appendices.

DYER (Dr. T. H.) Pompeii: its Buildings and Antiquities. An Account of the City, with full Description of the Remains and Recent Excavations, and an Itinerary for Visitors. By T. H. Dyer, LL.D. Nearly 300 Wood Engravings, Map, and Plan. 7*s.* 6*d.*

—— **Rome:** History of the City, with Introduction on recent Excavations. 8 Engravings, Frontispiece, and 2 Maps.

GIL BLAS. The Adventures of. From the French of Lesage by Smollett. 24 Engravings after Smirke, and 10 Etchings by Cruikshank. 612 pages. 6*s.*

GRIMM'S Gammer Grethel; or, German Fairy Tales and Popular Stories, containing 42 Fairy Tales. By Edgar Taylor. Numerous Woodcuts after Cruikshank and Ludwig Grimm. 3*s.* 6*d.*

HOLBEIN'S Dance of Death and Bible Cuts. Upwards of 150 Subjects, engraved in facsimile, with Introduction and Descriptions by the late Francis Douce and Dr. Dibdin.

INDIA, Pictorial, Descriptive, and Historical, from the Earliest Times. 100 Engravings on Wood and Map.

JESSE'S Anecdotes of Dogs. With 40 Woodcuts after Harvey, Bewick, and others; and 34 Steel Engravings after Cooper and Landseer.

KING'S (C. W.) Natural History of Precious Stones and Metals. Illustrations. 6*s.*

KRUMMACHER'S Parables. 40 Illustrations.

LODGE'S Portraits of Illustrious Personages of Great Britain, with Biographical and Historical Memoirs. 240 Portraits engraved on Steel, with the respective Biographies unabridged. Complete in 8 vols.

LONGFELLOW'S Poetical Works, including his Translations and Notes. 24 full-page Woodcuts by Birket Foster and others, and a Portrait.

—— Without the Illustrations, 3s. 6d.

—— **Prose Works.** With 16 full-page Woodcuts by Birket Foster and others.

LOUDON'S (Mrs.) Entertaining Naturalist. Popular Descriptions, Tales, and Anecdotes, of more than 500 Animals. Numerous Woodcuts.

MARRYAT'S (Capt., R.N.) Masterman Ready; or, the Wreck of the *Pacific*. (Written for Young People.) With 93 Woodcuts. 3s. 6d.

—— **Mission; or, Scenes in Africa.** (Written for Young People.) Illustrated by Gilbert and Dalziel. 3s. 6d.

—— **Pirate and Three Cutters.** (Written for Young People.) With a Memoir. 8 Steel Engravings after Clarkson Stanfield, R.A. 3s. 6d.

—— **Privateersman.** Adventures by Sea and Land One Hundred Years Ago. (Written for Young People.) 8 Steel Engravings. 3s. 6d.

—— **Settlers in Canada.** (Written for Young People.) 10 Engravings by Gilbert and Dalziel. 3s. 6d.

—— **Poor Jack.** (Written for Young People.) With 16 Illustrations after Clarkson Stanfield, R.A. 3s. 6d.

—— **Midshipman Easy.** With 8 full-page Illustrations. Small post 8vo. 3s. 6d.

—— **Peter Simple.** With 8 full-page Illustrations. Small post 8vo. 3s. 6d.

MAXWELL'S Victories of Wellington and the British Armies. Frontispiece and 4 Portraits.

MICHAEL ANGELO and RAPHAEL, Their Lives and Works. By Duppa and Quatremère de Quincy. Portraits and Engravings, including the Last Judgment, and Cartoons.

MILLER'S History of the Anglo-Saxons, from the Earliest Period to the Norman Conquest. Portrait of Alfred, Map of Saxon Britain, and 12 Steel Engravings.

MUDIE'S History of British Birds. Revised by W. C. L. Martin. 52 Figures of Birds and 7 coloured Plates of Eggs. 2 vols.

NAVAL and MILITARY HEROES of Great Britain; a Record of British Valour on every Day in the year, from William the Conqueror to the Battle of Inkermann. By Major Johns, R.M., and Lieut. P. H. Nicolas, R.M. Indexes. 24 Portraits after Holbein, Reynolds, &c. 6s.

NICOLINI'S History of the Jesuits: their Origin, Progress, Doctrines, and Designs. 8 Portraits.

PETRARCH'S Sonnets, Triumphs, and other Poems, in English Verse. With Life by Thomas Campbell. Portrait and 15 Steel Engravings.

PICKERING'S History of the Races of Man, and their Geographical Distribution; with AN ANALYTICAL SYNOPSIS OF THE NATURAL HISTORY OF MAN. By Dr. Hall. Map of the World and 12 coloured Plates.

PICTORIAL HANDBOOK OF Modern Geography on a Popular Plan. Compiled from the best Authorities, English and Foreign by H. G. Bohn. 150 Woodcuts and 51 coloured Maps.

—— Without the Maps, 3s. 6d.

POPE'S Poetical Works, including Translations. Edit., with Notes, by R. Carruthers. 2 vols.

—— **Homer's Iliad,** with Introduction and Notes by Rev. J. S. Watson, M.A. With Flaxman's Designs.

—— **Homer's Odyssey,** with the BATTLE OF FROGS AND MICE, Hymns, &c., by other translators including Chapman. Introduction and Notes by J. S. Watson, M.A. With Flaxman's Designs.

—— **Life,** including many of his Letters. By R. Carruthers. Numerous Illustrations.

POTTERY AND PORCELAIN, and other objects of Vertu. Comprising an Illustrated Catalogue of the Bernal Collection, with the prices and names of the Possessors. Also an Introductory Lecture on Pottery and Porcelain, and an Engraved List of all Marks and Monograms. By H. G. Bohn. Numerous Woodcuts.

—— With coloured Illustrations, 10s. 6d.

PROUT'S (Father) Reliques. Edited by Rev. F. Mahony. Copyright edition, with the Author's last corrections and additions. 21 Etchings by D. Maclise, R.A. Nearly 600 pages.

RECREATIONS IN SHOOTING. With some Account of the Game found in the British Isles, and Directions for the Management of Dog and Gun. By 'Craven.' 62 Woodcuts and 9 Steel Engravings after A. Cooper, R.A.

RENNIE. Insect Architecture. Revised by Rev. J. G. Wood, M.A. 186 Woodcuts.

ROBINSON CRUSOE. With Memoir of Defoe, 12 Steel Engravings and 74 Woodcuts after Stothard and Harvey.
—— Without the Engravings, 3s. 6d.

ROME IN THE NINETEENTH CENtury. An Account in 1817 of the Ruins of the Ancient City, and Monuments of Modern Times. By C. A. Eaton. 34 Steel Engravings. 2 vols.

SHARPE (S.) The History of Egypt, from the Earliest Times till the Conquest by the Arabs, A.D. 640. 2 Maps and upwards of 400 Woodcuts. 2 vols.

SOUTHEY'S Life of Nelson. With Additional Notes, Facsimiles of Nelson's Writing, Portraits, Plans, and 50 Engravings, after Birket Foster, &c.

STARLING'S (Miss) Noble Deeds of Women; or, Examples of Female Courage, Fortitude, and Virtue. With 14 Steel Portraits.

STUART and REVETT'S Antiquities of Athens, and other Monuments of Greece; with Glossary of Terms used in Grecian Architecture. 71 Steel Plates and numerous Woodcuts.

SWEET'S British Warblers. 5s.—*See Bechstein.*

TALES OF THE GENII; or, the Delightful Lessons of Horam, the Son of Asmar. Trans. by Sir C. Morrell. Numerous Woodcuts.

TASSO'S Jerusalem Delivered. In English Spenserian Verse, with Life, by J. H. Wiffen. With 8 Engravings and 24 Woodcuts.

WALKER'S Manly Exercises; containing Skating, Riding, Driving, Hunting, Shooting, Sailing, Rowing, Swimming, &c. 44 Engravings and numerous Woodcuts.

WALTON'S Complete Angler, or the Contemplative Man's Recreation, by Izaak Walton and Charles Cotton. With Memoirs and Notes by E. Jesse. Also an Account of Fishing Stations, Tackle, &c., by H. G. Bohn. Portrait and 203 Woodcuts, and 26 Engravings on Steel.

—— **Lives of Donne, Wotton, Hooker,** &c., with Notes. A New Edition, revised by A. H. Bullen, with a Memoir of Izaak Walton by William Dowling. 6 Portraits, 6 Autograph Signatures, &c.

WELLINGTON, Life of. From the Materials of Maxwell. 18 Steel Engravings.

—— **Victories of.**—*See Maxwell.*

WESTROPP (H. M.) A Handbook of Archæology, Egyptian, Greek, Etruscan, Roman. By H. M. Westropp. Numerous Illustrations.

WHITE'S Natural History of Selborne, with Observations on various Parts of Nature, and the Naturalists' Calendar. Sir W. Jardine. Edit., with Notes and Memoir, by E. Jesse. 40 Portraits and coloured Plates.

CLASSICAL LIBRARY.

TRANSLATIONS FROM THE GREEK AND LATIN.

103 *Vols. at 5s. each, excepting those marked otherwise.* (25l. 4s. 6d. *per set.*)

ACHILLES TATIUS.—*See Greek Romances.*

ÆSCHYLUS, The Dramas of. In English Verse by Anna Swanwick. 4th edition.
—— **The Tragedies of.** In Prose, with Notes and Introduction, by T. A. Buckley, B.A. Portrait. 3s. 6d.

AMMIANUS MARCELLINUS. History of Rome during the Reigns of Constantius, Julian, Jovianus, Valentinian, and Valens, by C. D. Yonge, B.A. Double volume. 7s. 6d.

ANTONINUS (M. Aurelius), The Thoughts of. Translated, with Notes. Biographical Sketch, and Essay on the Philosophy, by George Long, M.A. 3s. 6d. Fine Paper edition on hand-made paper. 6s.

APOLLONIUS RHODIUS. 'The Argonautica.' Translated by E. P. Coleridge.

APULEIUS, The Works of. Comprising the Golden Ass, God of Socrates, Florida, and Discourse of Magic, &c. Frontispiece.

CLASSICAL LIBRARY.

ARISTOPHANES' Comedies. Trans., with Notes and Extracts from Frere's and other Metrical Versions, by W. J. Hickie. Portrait. 2 vols.

ARISTOTLE'S Nicomachean Ethics. Trans., with Notes, Analytical Introduction, and Questions for Students, by Ven. Archdn. Browne.

— **Politics and Economics.** Trans., with Notes, Analyses, and Index, by E. Walford, M.A., and an Essay and Life by Dr. Gillies.

— **Metaphysics.** Trans., with Notes, Analysis, and Examination Questions, by Rev. John H. M'Mahon, M.A.

— **History of Animals.** In Ten Books. Trans., with Notes and Index, by R. Cresswell, M.A.

— **Organon;** or, Logical Treatises, and the Introduction of Porphyry. With Notes, Analysis, and Introduction, by Rev. O. F. Owen, M.A. 2 vols. 3s. 6d. each.

— **Rhetoric and Poetics.** Trans., with Hobbes' Analysis, Exam. Questions, and Notes, by T. Buckley, B.A. Portrait.

ATHENÆUS. The Deipnosophists. Trans. by C. D. Yonge, B.A. With an Appendix of Poetical Fragments. 3 vols.

ATLAS of Classical Geography. 22 large Coloured Maps. With a complete Index. Imp. 8vo. 7s. 6d.

BION.—See *Theocritus.*

CÆSAR. Commentaries on the Gallic and Civil Wars, with the Supplementary Books attributed to Hirtius, including the complete Alexandrian, African, and Spanish Wars. Portrait.

CATULLUS, Tibullus, and the Vigil of Venus. Trans. with Notes and Biographical Introduction. To which are added, Metrical Versions by Lamb, Grainger, and others. Frontispiece.

CICERO'S Orations. Trans. by C. D. Yonge, B.A. 4 vols.

— **On Oratory and Orators.** With Letters to Quintus and Brutus. Trans., with Notes, by Rev. J. S. Watson, M.A.

— **On the Nature of the Gods,** Divination, Fate, Laws, a Republic, Consulship. Trans. by C. D. Yonge, B.A.

— **Academics,** De Finibus, and Tusculan Questions. By C. D. Yonge, B.A. With Sketch of the Greek Philosophers mentioned by Cicero.

CICERO'S Works.—*Continued.*
— **Offices;** or, Moral Duties. Cato Major, an Essay on Old Age; Lælius, an Essay on Friendship; Scipio's Dream; Paradoxes; Letter to Quintus on Magistrates. Trans., with Notes, by C. R. Edmonds. Portrait. 3s. 6d.

DEMOSTHENES' Orations. Trans., with Notes, Arguments, a Chronological Abstract, and Appendices, by C. Rann Kennedy. 5 vols. (One, 3s. 6d; four, 5s.)

DICTIONARY of LATIN and GREEK Quotations; including Proverbs, Maxims, Mottoes, Law Terms and Phrases. With the Quantities marked, and English Translations. With Index Verborum (622 pages).

— **Index Verborum** to the above, with the *Quantities* and Accents marked (56 pages), limp cloth. 1s.

DIOGENES LAERTIUS. Lives and Opinions of the Ancient Philosophers. Trans., with Notes, by C. D. Yonge, B.A.

EPICTETUS. The Discourses of. With the Encheiridion and Fragments. With Notes, Life, and View of his Philosophy, by George Long, M.A.

EURIPIDES. Trans. by T. A. Buckley, B.A. Portrait. 2 vols.

GREEK ANTHOLOGY. In English Prose by G. Burges, M.A. With Metrical Versions by Bland, Merivale, and others.

GREEK ROMANCES of Heliodorus, Longus, and Achilles Tatius; viz., The Adventures of Theagenes and Chariclea; Amours of Daphnis and Chloe; and Loves of Clitopho and Leucippe. Trans., with Notes, by Rev R. Smith, M.A.

HELIODORUS.—*See Greek Romances.*

HERODOTUS. Literally trans. by Rev. Henry Cary, M.A. Portrait.

HESIOD, CALLIMACHUS, and Theognis. In Prose, with Notes and Biographical Notices by Rev. J. Banks, M.A. Together with the Metrical Versions of Hesiod, by Elton; Callimachus, by Tytler; and Theognis, by Frere.

HOMER'S Iliad. In English Prose, with Notes by T. A. Buckley, B.A. Portrait.

— **Odyssey,** Hymns Epigrams, and Battle of the Frogs and Mice. In English Prose, with Notes and Memoir by T. A. Buckley, B.A.

HORACE. In Prose by Smart, with Notes selected by T. A. Buckley, B.A. Portrait. 3s. 6d.

JULIAN THE EMPEROR. Containing Gregory Nazianzen's Two Invectives and Libanius' Monody, with Julian's Theosophical Works. By the Rev. C. W. King, M.A.

JUSTIN, CORNELIUS NEPOS, and Eutropius. Trans., with Notes, by Rev. J. S. Watson, M.A.

JUVENAL, PERSIUS, SULPICIA, and Lucilius. In Prose, with Notes, Chronological Tables, Arguments, by L. Evans, M.A. To which is added the Metrical Version of Juvenal and Persius by Gifford. Frontispiece.

LIVY. The History of Rome. Trans. by Dr. Spillan and others. 4 vols. Portrait.

LONGUS. Daphnis and Chloe.—*See Greek Romances.*

LUCAN'S Pharsalia. In Prose, with Notes by H. T. Riley.

LUCIAN'S Dialogues of the Gods, of the Sea Gods, and of the Dead. Trans. by Howard Williams, M.A.

LUCRETIUS. In Prose, with Notes and Biographical Introduction by Rev. J. S. Watson, M.A. To which is added the Metrical Version by J. M. Good.

MARTIAL'S Epigrams, complete. In Prose, with Verse Translations selected from English Poets, and other sources. Dble. vol. (670 pages). 7s. 6d.

MOSCHUS.—*See Theocritus.*

OVID'S Works, complete. In Prose, with Notes and Introduction. 3 vols.

PAUSANIAS' Description of Greece. Trans., with Notes and Index, by Rev. A. R. Shilleto, M.A., sometime Scholar of Trinity College, Cambridge. 2 vols.

PHALARIS. Bentley's Dissertations upon the Epistles of Phalaris, Themistocles, Socrates, Euripides, and the Fables of Æsop. With Introduction and Notes by Prof. W. Wagner, Ph.D.

PINDAR. In Prose, with Introduction and Notes by Dawson W. Turner. Together with the Metrical Version by Abraham Moore. Portrait.

PLATO'S Works. Trans. by Rev. H. Cary, H. Davis, and G. Burges. 6 vols.

—— **Dialogues.** A Summary and Analysis of. With Analytical Index to the Greek text of modern editions and to the above translations, by A. Day, LL.D.

PLAUTUS'S Comedies. In Prose, with Notes by H. T. Riley, B.A. 2 vols.

PLINY'S Natural History. Trans., with Notes, by J. Bostock, M.D., F.R.S., and H. T. Riley, B.A. 6 vols.

PLINY. The Letters of Pliny the Younger. Melmoth's Translation, revised, with Notes and short Life, by Rev. F. C. T. Bosanquet, M.A.

PLUTARCH'S Morals. Theosophical Essays. Trans. by Rev. C. W. King, M.A.

—— **Ethical Essays.** Trans. by Rev. A. R. Shilleto, M.A.

—— **Lives.** *See page 7.*

PROPERTIUS, The Elegies of. With Notes, translated by Rev. P. J. F. Gantillon, M.A., with metrical versions of Select Elegies by Nott and Elton. 3s. 6d.

QUINTILIAN'S Institutes of Oratory. Trans., by Rev. J. S. Watson, M.A. 2 vols.

SALLUST, FLORUS, and VELLEIUS Paterculus. Trans., with Notes and Biographical Notices, by J. S. Watson, M.A.

SENECA DE BENEFICIIS. Translated by Aubrey Stewart, M.A. 3s. 6d.

SENECA'S Minor Essays. Translated by A. Stewart, M.A.

SOPHOCLES. The Tragedies of. In Prose, with Notes, Arguments, and Introduction. Portrait.

STRABO'S Geography. Trans., with Notes, by W. Falconer, M.A., and H. C. Hamilton. Copious Index, giving Ancient and Modern Names. 3 vols.

SUETONIUS' Lives of the Twelve Cæsars and Lives of the Grammarians. The Translation of Thomson, revised, with Notes, by T. Forester.

TACITUS. The Works of. Trans., with Notes. 2 vols.

TERENCE and PHÆDRUS. In English Prose, with Notes and Arguments, by H. T. Riley, B.A. To which is added Smart's Metrical Version of Phædrus. With Frontispiece.

THEOCRITUS, BION, MOSCHUS, and Tyrtæus. In Prose, with Notes and Arguments, by Rev. J. Banks, M.A. To which are appended the METRICAL VERSIONS of Chapman. Portrait of Theocritus.

THUCYDIDES. The Peloponnesian War. Trans., with Notes, by Rev. H. Dale. Portrait. 2 vols. 3s. 6d. each.

TYRTÆUS.—*See Theocritus.*

VIRGIL. The Works of. In Prose, with Notes by Davidson. Revised, with additional Notes and Biographical Notice, by T. A. Buckley, B.A. Portrait. 3s. 6d.

XENOPHON'S Works. Trans., with Notes, by J. S. Watson, M.A., and Rev. H. Dale. Portrait. In 3 vols.

COLLEGIATE SERIES.
10 *Vols. at* 5s. *each.* (2*l.* 10s. *per set.*)

DANTE. The Inferno. Prose Trans., with the Text of the Original on the same page, and Explanatory Notes, by John A. Carlyle, M.D. Portrait.

—— **The Purgatorio.** Prose Trans., with the Original on the same page, and Explanatory Notes, by W. S. Dugdale.

DOBREE'S Adversaria. (Notes on the Greek and Latin Classics.) Edited by the late Prof. Wagner. 2 vols.

DONALDSON (Dr.) The Theatre of the Greeks. With Supplementary Treatise on the Language, Metres, and Prosody of the Greek Dramatists. Numerous Illustrations and 3 Plans. By J. W. Donaldson, D.D.

GOETHE'S Faust. Part I. German Text, with Hayward's Prose Translation and Notes. Revised, with Introduction and Bibliography, by Dr. C. A. Buchheim.
[*In the Press.*]

KEIGHTLEY'S (Thomas) Mythology of Ancient Greece and Italy. Revised by Dr. Leonhard Schmitz. 12 Plates.

HERODOTUS, Notes on. Original and Selected from the best Commentators. By D. W. Turner. M.A. Coloured Map.

—— **Analysis and Summary of,** with a Synchronistical Table of Events—Tables of Weights, Measures, Money, and Distances—an Outline of the History and Geography—and the Dates completed from Gaisford, Baehr, &c. By J. T. Wheeler.

NEW TESTAMENT (The) in Greek. Griesbach's Text, with the Readings of Mill and Scholz, and Parallel References. Also a Critical Introduction and Chronological Tables. Two Fac-similes of Greek Manuscripts. 650 pages. 3s. 6d.

—— or bound up with a Greek and English Lexicon to the New Testament (250 pages additional, making in all 900*l*.) 5s.

The Lexicon separately, 2s.

THUCYDIDES. An Analysis and Summary of. With Chronological Table of Events, &c., by J. T. Wheeler.

SCIENTIFIC LIBRARY.
50 *Vols. at* 5s. *each, excepting those marked otherwise.* (13*l.* 6s. 0d. *per set.*)

AGASSIZ and GOULD. Outline of Comparative Physiology. Enlarged by Dr. Wright. With Index and 300 Illustrative Woodcuts.

BOLLEY'S Manual of Technical Analysis; a Guide for the Testing and Valuation of the various Natural and Artificial Substances employed in the Arts and Domestic Economy, founded on the work of Dr. Bolley. Edit. by Dr. Paul. 100 Woodcuts.

BRIDGEWATER TREATISES.

—— **Bell (Sir Charles) on the Hand;** its Mechanism and Vital Endowments, as evincing Design. Preceded by an Account of the Author's Discoveries in the Nervous System by A. Shaw. Numerous Woodcuts.

—— **Kirby on the History, Habits, and Instincts of Animals.** With Notes by T. Rymer Jones. 100 Woodcuts. 2 vols.

—— **Buckland's Geology and Mineralogy.** With Additions by Prof. Owen, Prof. Phillips, and R. Brown. Memoir of Buckland. Portrait. 2 vols. 15s. Vol. I. Text. Vol. II. 90 large plates with letter-press.

BRIDGEWATER TREATISES. *Continued.*

—— **Chalmers on the Adaptation of External Nature to the Moral and Intellectual Constitution of Man.** With Memoir by Rev. Dr. Cumming. Portrait.

—— **Prout's Treatise on Chemistry, Meteorology, and the Function of Digestion,** with reference to Natural Theology. Edit. by Dr. J. W. Griffith. 2 Maps.

—— **Roget's Animal and Vegetable Physiology.** 463 Woodcuts. 2 vols. 6s each.

—— **Kidd on the Adaptation of External Nature to the Physical Condition of Man.** 3s. 6d.

CARPENTER'S (Dr. W. B.) Zoology. A Systematic View of the Structure, Habits, Instincts, and Uses of the principal Families of the Animal Kingdom, and of the chief Forms of Fossil Remains. Revised by W. S. Dallas, F.L.S. Numerous Woodcuts. 2 vols. 6s. each.

—— **Mechanical Philosophy, Astronomy, and Horology.** A Popular Exposition. 181 Woodcuts.

BOHN'S LIBRARIES.

CARPENTER'S Works.—*Continued.*

— **Vegetable Physiology and Systematic Botany.** A complete Introduction to the Knowledge of Plants. Revised by E. Lankester, M.D., &c. Numerous Woodcuts. 6s.

— **Animal Physiology.** Revised Edition. 300 Woodcuts. 6s.

CHEVREUL on Colour. Containing the Principles of Harmony and Contrast of Colours, and their Application to the Arts; including Painting, Decoration, Tapestries, Carpets, Mosaics, Glazing, Staining, Calico Printing, Letterpress Printing, Map Colouring, Dress, Landscape and Flower Gardening, &c. Trans. by C. Martel. Several Plates.

— With an additional series of 16 Plates in Colours, 7s. 6d.

ENNEMOSER'S History of Magic. Trans. by W. Howitt. With an Appendix of the most remarkable and best authenticated Stories of Apparitions, Dreams, Second Sight, Table-Turning, and Spirit-Rapping, &c. 2 vols.

HIND'S Introduction to Astronomy. With Vocabulary of the Terms in present use. Numerous Woodcuts. 3s. 6d.

HOGG'S (Jabez) Elements of Experimental and Natural Philosophy. Being an Easy Introduction to the Study of Mechanics, Pneumatics, Hydrostatics, Hydraulics, Acoustics, Optics, Caloric, Electricity, Voltaism, and Magnetism. 400 Woodcuts.

HUMBOLDT'S Cosmos; or, Sketch of a Physical Description of the Universe. Trans. by E. C. Otté, B. H. Paul, and W. S. Dallas, F.L.S. Portrait. 5 vols. 3s. 6d. each, excepting vol. v., 5s.

— **Personal Narrative of his Travels** in America during the years 1799-1804. Trans., with Notes, by T. Ross. 3 vols.

— **Views of Nature; or, Contemplations** of the Sublime Phenomena of Creation, with Scientific Illustrations. Trans. by E. C. Otté.

HUNT'S (Robert) Poetry of Science; or, Studies of the Physical Phenomena of Nature. By Robert Hunt, Professor at the School of Mines.

JOYCE'S Scientific Dialogues. A Familiar Introduction to the Arts and Sciences. For Schools and Young People. Numerous Woodcuts.

JOYCE'S Introduction to the Arts and Sciences, for Schools and Young People. Divided into Lessons with Examination Questions. Woodcuts. 3s. 6d.

JUKES-BROWNE'S Student's Handbook of Physical Geology. By A. J. Jukes-Browne, of the Geological Survey of England. With numerous Diagrams and Illustrations, 6s.

— **The Student's Handbook of Historical Geology.** By A. J. Jukes-Brown, B.A., F.G.S., of the Geological Survey of England and Wales. With numerous Diagrams and Illustrations. 6s.

— **The Building of the British Islands.** A Study in Geographical Evolution. By A J. Jukes-Browne, F.G.S. 7s. 6d.

KNIGHT'S (Charles) Knowledge is Power. A Popular Manual of Political Economy.

LILLY. Introduction to Astrology. With a Grammar of Astrology and Tables for calculating Nativities, by Zadkiel.

MANTELL'S (Dr.) Geological Excursions through the Isle of Wight and along the Dorset Coast. Numerous Woodcuts and Geological Map.

— **Petrifactions and their Teachings.** Handbook to the Organic Remains in the British Museum. Numerous Woodcuts. 6s.

— **Wonders of Geology; or, a Familiar Exposition of Geological Phenomena.** A coloured Geological Map of England, Plates, and 200 Woodcuts. 2 vols. 7s. 6d. each.

SCHOUW'S Earth, Plants, and Man. Popular Pictures of Nature. And Kobell's Sketches from the Mineral Kingdom. Trans. by A. Henfrey, F.R.S. Coloured Map of the Geography of Plants.

SMITH'S (Pye) Geology and Scripture; or, the Relation between the Scriptures and Geological Science. With Memoir.

STANLEY'S Classified Synopsis of the Principal Painters of the Dutch and Flemish Schools, including an Account of some of the early German Masters. By George Stanley.

STAUNTON'S Chess Works. — *See page 21.*

STÖCKHARDT'S Experimental Chemistry. A Handbook for the Study of the Science by simple Experiments. Edit. by C. W. Heaton, F.C.S. Numerous Woodcuts.

URE'S (Dr. A.) Cotton Manufacture of Great Britain, systematically investigated; with an Introductory View of its Comparative State in Foreign Countries. Revised by P. L. Simmonds. 150 Illustrations. 2 vols.

— **Philosophy of Manufactures,** or an Exposition of the Scientific, Moral, and Commercial Economy of the Factory System of Great Britain. Revised by P. L. Simmonds. Numerous Figures. 800 pages. 7s. 6d.

ECONOMICS AND FINANCE.

GILBART'S History, Principles, and Practice of Banking. Revised to 1881 by A. S. Michie, of the Royal Bank of Scotland. Portrait of Gilbart. 2 vols. 10s.

RICARDO on the Principles of Political Economy and Taxation. Edited by E. C. K. Gonner, M.A., Lecturer, University College, Liverpool. [*In the press.*

SMITH (Adam). The Wealth of Nations. An Inquiry into the Nature and Causes of. Edited by E. Belfort Bax. 2 vols. 7s.

REFERENCE LIBRARY.

32 Volumes at Various Prices. (8l. 18s. per set.)

BLAIR'S Chronological Tables. Comprehending the Chronology and History of the World, from the Earliest Times to the Russian Treaty of Peace, April 1856. By J. W. Rosse. 800 pages. 10s.

—— **Index of Dates.** Comprehending the principal Facts in the Chronology and History of the World, from the Earliest to the Present, alphabetically arranged; being a complete Index to the foregoing. By J. W. Rosse. 2 vols. 5s. each.

BOHN'S Dictionary of Quotations from the English Poets. 4th and cheaper Edition. 6s.

BOND'S Handy-book of Rules and Tables for Verifying Dates with the Christian Era. 4th Edition. 5s.

BUCHANAN'S Dictionary of Science and Technical Terms used in Philosophy, Literature, Professions, Commerce, Arts, and Trades. By W. H. Buchanan, with Supplement. Edited by Jas. A. Smith. 6s.

CHRONICLES OF THE TOMBS. A Select Collection of Epitaphs, with Essay on Epitaphs and Observations on Sepulchral Antiquities. By T. J. Pettigrew, F.R.S., F.S.A. 5s.

CLARK'S (Hugh) Introduction to Heraldry. Revised by J. R. Planché. 5s. 950 Illustrations.

—— *With the Illustrations coloured*, 15s.

COINS, Manual of.—*See Humphreys.*

COOPER'S Biographical Dictionary. Containing concise notices of upwards of 15,000 eminent persons of all ages and countries. 2 vols. 5s. each.

DATES, Index of.—*See Blair.*

DICTIONARY of Obsolete and Provincial English. Containing Words from English Writers previous to the 19th Century. By Thomas Wright, M.A., F.S.A., &c. 2 vols. 5s. each.

EPIGRAMMATISTS (The). A Selection from the Epigrammatic Literature of Ancient, Mediæval, and Modern Times. With Introduction, Notes, Observations, Illustrations, an Appendix on Works connected with Epigrammatic Literature, by Rev. H. Dodd, M.A. 6s.

GAMES, Handbook of. Edited by Henry G. Bohn. Numerous Diagrams. 5s. (*See also page* 21.)

HENFREY'S Guide to English Coins. Revised Edition, by C. F. Keary, M.A., F.S.A. With an Historical Introduction. 6s.

HUMPHREYS' Coin Collectors' Manual. An Historical Account of the Progress of Coinage from the Earliest Time, by H. N. Humphreys. 140 Illustrations. 2 vols. 5s. each.

LOWNDES' Bibliographer's Manual of English Literature. Containing an Account of Rare and Curious Books published in or relating to Great Britain and Ireland, from the Invention of Printing, with Biographical Notices and Prices, by W. T. Lowndes. Parts I.-X. (A to Z), 3s. 6d. each. Part XI. (Appendix Vol.), 5s. Or the 11 parts in 4 vols., half morocco, 2l. 2s. Also in 6 vols. cloth, 5s. each.

MEDICINE, Handbook of Domestic, Popularly Arranged. By Dr. H. Davies. 700 pages. 5s.

NOTED NAMES OF FICTION. Dictionary of. Including also Familiar Pseudonyms, Surnames bestowed on Eminent Men, &c. By W. A. Wheeler, M.A. 5s.

POLITICAL CYCLOPÆDIA. A Dictionary of Political, Constitutional, Statistical, and Forensic Knowledge; forming a Work of Reference on subjects of Civil Administration, Political Economy, Finance, Commerce, Laws, and Social Relations. 4 vols. 3s. 6d. each.

PROVERBS, Handbook of. Containing an entire Republication of Ray's Collection, with Additions from Foreign Languages and Sayings, Sentences, Maxims, and Phrases. 5s.
—— A Polyglot of Foreign. Comprising French, Italian, German, Dutch, Spanish, Portuguese, and Danish. With English Translations. 5s.

SYNONYMS and ANTONYMS; or, Kindred Words and their Opposites, Collected and Contrasted by Ven. C. J. Smith, M.A. 5s.

WRIGHT (Th.)—*See Dictionary.*

NOVELISTS' LIBRARY.

13 *Volumes at* 3s. 6d. *each, excepting those marked otherwise.* (2l. 8s. 6d. *per set.*)

BJORNSON'S Arne and the Fisher Lassie. Translated from the Norse with an Introduction by W. H. Low, M.A.

BURNEY'S Evelina; or, a Young Lady's Entrance into the World. By F. Burney (Mme. D'Arblay). With Introduction and Notes by A. R. Ellis, Author of 'Sylvestra,' &c.
—— Cecilia. With Introduction and Notes by A. R. Ellis. 2 vols.

DE STAËL. Corinne or Italy. By Madame de Staël. Translated by Emily Baldwin and Paulina Driver.

EBERS' Egyptian Princess. Trans. by Emma Buchheim.

FIELDING'S Joseph Andrews and his Friend Mr. Abraham Adams. With Roscoe's Biography. *Cruikshank's Illustrations.*
—— Amelia. Roscoe's Edition, revised. *Cruikshank's Illustrations.* 5s.
—— History of Tom Jones, a Foundling. Roscoe's Edition. *Cruikshank's Illustrations.* 2 vols.

GROSSI'S Marco Visconti. Trans. by A. F. D.

MANZONI. The Betrothed: being a Translation of 'I Promessi Sposi.' Numerous Woodcuts. 1 vol. 5s.

STOWE (Mrs. H. B.) Uncle Tom's Cabin; or, Life among the Lowly. 8 full-page Illustrations.

ARTISTS' LIBRARY.

9 *Volumes at Various Prices.* (2l. 8s. 6d. *per set.*)

BELL (Sir Charles). The Anatomy and Philosophy of Expression, as Connected with the Fine Arts. 5s. Illustrated.

DEMMIN. History of Arms and Armour from the Earliest Period. By Auguste Demmin. Trans. by C. C. Black, M.A., Assistant Keeper, S. K. Museum. 1900 Illustrations. 7s. 6d.

FAIRHOLT'S Costume in England. Third Edition. Enlarged and Revised by the Hon. H. A. Dillon, F.S.A. With more than 700 Engravings. 2 vols. 5s. each.
Vol. I. History. Vol. II. Glossary.

FLAXMAN. Lectures on Sculpture. With Three Addresses to the R.A. by Sir R. Westmacott, R.A., and Memoir of Flaxman. Portrait and 53 Plates. 6s.

HEATON'S Concise History of Painting. New Edition, revised by W. Cosmo Monkhouse. 5s.

LECTURES ON PAINTING by the Royal Academicians, Barry, Opie, Fuseli. With Introductory Essay and Notes by R. Wornum. Portrait of Fuseli. 5s.

LEONARDO DA VINCI'S Treatise on Painting. Trans. by J. F. Rigaud, R.A. With a Life and an Account of his Works by J. W. Brown. Numerous Plates. 5s.

PLANCHÉ'S History of British Costume, from the Earliest Time to the 10th Century. By J. R. Planché. 400 Illustrations. 5s.

LIBRARY OF SPORTS AND GAMES.

10 *Volumes at 3s. 6d. and 5s. each. (2l. 6s. 0d. per set.)*

BOHN'S Handbooks of Athletic Sports. With numerous Illustrations. In 7 vols. 3s. 6d. each.

Vol. I.—Cricket, by Hon. and Rev. E. Lyttelton; Lawn Tennis, by H. W. W. Wilberforce; Tennis, Rackets, and Fives, by Julian Marshall, Major Spens, and J. A. Tait; Golf, by W. T. Linskill; Hockey, by F. S. Creswell.

Vol. II.—Rowing and Sculling, by W. B. Woodgate; Sailing, by E. F. Knight; Swimming, by M. and J. R. Cobbett.

Vol. III.—Boxing, by R. G. Allanson-Winn; Single Stick and Sword Exercise, by R. G. Allanson-Winn and C. Phillipps-Wolley; Wrestling, by Walter Armstrong; Fencing, by H. A. Colmore Dunn.

Vol. IV.—Skating, by Douglas Adams; Rugby Football, by Harry Vassall; Association Football, by C. W. Alcock. [*In the press.*

Vol. V.—Cycling and Athletics, by H. H. Griffin; Rounders, Field Ball, Baseball, Bowls, Quoits, Skittles, &c., by J. M. Walker, M.A., Assistant Master Bedford Grammar School. [*In the press.*

Vol. VI.—Gymnastics, by A. F. Jenkin; Clubs and Dumb-bells, by G. T. B. Cobbett and A. F. Jenkin. [*In the press.*

Vol. VII.—Riding, Driving, and Stable Management. By W. A. Kerr, V.C., and other writers. [*Preparing.*

BOHN'S Handbooks of Games. New Edition, entirely rewritten. 2 volumes. 3s. 6d. each.

Vol. I. TABLE GAMES.

Contents:—Billiards, with Pool, Pyramids, and Snooker, by Major-Gen. A. W. Drayson, F.R.A.S., with a preface by W. J. Peall—Bagatelle, by 'Berkeley'—Chess, by R. F. Green—Draughts, Backgammon, Dominoes, Solitaire, Reversi,

Go Bang, Rouge et noir, Roulette, E.O., Hazard, Faro, by 'Berkeley.'

Vol. II. CARD GAMES.

Contents:—Whist, by Dr. William Pole, F.R.S., Author of 'The Philosophy of Whist, &c.'—Solo Whist, by R. F. Green; Piquet, Ecarté, Euchre, Bézique, and Cribbage, by 'Berkeley;' Poker, Loo, Vingt-et-un, Napoleon, Newmarket, Rouge et Noir, Pope Joan, Speculation, &c. &c., by Baxter-Wray.

CHESS CONGRESS of 1862. A collection of the games played. Edited by J. Löwenthal. New edition, 5s.

MORPHY'S Games of Chess, being the Matches and best Games played by the American Champion, with explanatory and analytical Notes by J. Löwenthal. With short Memoir and Portrait of Morphy. 5s.

STAUNTON'S Chess-Player's Handbook. A Popular and Scientific Introduction to the Game, with numerous Diagrams. 5s.

—— **Chess Praxis.** A Supplement to the Chess-player's Handbook. Containing the most important modern Improvements in the Openings; Code of Chess Laws; and a Selection of Morphy's Games. Annotated. 636 pages. Diagrams. 5s.

—— **Chess-Player's Companion.** Comprising a Treatise on Odds, Collection of Match Games, including the French Match with M. St. Amant, and a Selection of Original Problems. Diagrams and Coloured Frontispiece. 5s.

—— **Chess Tournament of 1851.** A Collection of Games played at this celebrated assemblage. With Introduction and Notes. Numerous Diagrams. 5s.

BOHN'S CHEAP SERIES.

Price 1s. each.

A Series of Complete Stories or Essays, mostly reprinted from Vols. in Bohn's Libraries, and neatly bound in stiff paper cover, with cut edges, suitable for Railway Reading.

ASCHAM (Roger). Schoolmaster. By Professor Mayor.

CARPENTER (Dr. W. B.). Physiology of Temperance and Total Abstinence.

EMERSON. England and English Characteristics. Lectures on the Race, Ability, Manners, Truth, Character, Wealth, Religion. &c. &c.

—— **Nature:** An Essay. To which are added Orations, Lectures, and Addresses.

—— **Representative Men:** Seven Lectures on PLATO, SWEDENBORG, MONTAIGNE, SHAKESPEARE, NAPOLEON, and GOETHE.

—— **Twenty Essays on Various Subjects.**

—— **The Conduct of Life.**

FRANKLIN (Benjamin). Autobiography. Edited by J. Sparks.

HAWTHORNE (Nathaniel). Twicetold Tales. Two Vols. in One.

—— **Snow Image,** and Other Tales.

—— **Scarlet Letter.**

—— **House with the Seven Gables.**

—— **Transformation;** or the Marble Fawn. Two Parts.

HAZLITT (W.). Table-talk: Essays on Men and Manners. Three Parts.

—— **Plain Speaker:** Opinions on Books, Men, and Things. Three Parts.

—— **Lectures on the English Comic Writers.**

—— **Lectures on the English Poets.**

—— **Lectures on the Characters of Shakespeare's Plays.**

—— **Lectures on the Literature of** the Age of Elizabeth, chiefly Dramatic.

IRVING (Washington). Lives of Successors of Mohammed.

—— **Life of Goldsmith.**

—— **Sketch-book.**

—— **Tales of a Traveller.**

—— **Tour on the Prairies.**

—— **Conquests of Granada and Spain.** Two Parts.

—— **Life and Voyages of Columbus.** Two Parts.

—— **Companions of Columbus:** Their Voyages and Discoveries.

—— **Adventures of Captain Bonneville** in the Rocky Mountains and the Far West.

—— **Knickerbocker's History of New York,** from the beginning of the World to the End of the Dutch Dynasty.

—— **Tales of the Alhambra.**

—— **Conquest of Florida under Hernando de Soto.**

—— **Abbotsford & Newstead Abbey.**

—— **Salmagundi;** or, The Whim-Whams and Opinions of LAUNCELOT LANGSTAFF, Esq.

—— **Bracebridge Hall;** or, The Humourists.

—— **Astoria;** or, Anecdotes of an Enterprise beyond the Rocky Mountains.

—— **Wolfert's Roost,** and other Tales.

LAMB (Charles). Essays of Elia. With a Portrait.

—— **Last Essays of Elia.**

—— **Eliana.** With Biographical Sketch.

MARRYAT (Captain). Pirate and the Three Cutters. With a Memoir of the Author.

Bohn's Select Library of Standard Works.

Price 1s. in paper covers, and 1s. 6d. in cloth.

1. BACON'S ESSAYS. With Introduction and Notes.
2. LESSING'S LAOKOON. Beasley's Translation, revised, with Introduction, Notes, &c., by Edward Bell, M.A. With Frontispiece.
3. DANTE'S INFERNO. Translated, with Notes, by Rev. H. F. Cary.
4. GOETHE'S FAUST. Part I. Translated, with Introduction, by Anna Swanwick.
5. GOETHE'S BOYHOOD. Being Part I. of the Autobiography. Translated by J. Oxenford.
6. SCHILLER'S MARY STUART and THE MAID OF ORLEANS. Translated by J. Mellish and Anna Swanwick.
7. THE QUEEN'S ENGLISH. By the late Dean Alford.
8. LIFE AND LABOURS OF THE LATE THOMAS BRASSEY. By Sir A. Helps, K.C.B.
9. PLATO'S DIALOGUES: The Apology—Crito—Phaedo—Protagoras. With Introductions.
10. MOLIÈRE'S PLAYS: The Miser—Tartuffe—The Shopkeeper turned Gentleman. Translated by C. H. Walt, M.A. With brief Memoir.
11. GOETHE'S REINEKE FOX, in English Hexameters. By A. Rogers.
12. OLIVER GOLDSMITH'S PLAYS.
13. LESSING'S PLAYS: Nathan the Wise—Minna von Barnhelm.
14. PLAUTUS'S COMEDIES: Trinummus — Menaechmi — Aululria — Captivi.
15. WATERLOO DAYS. By C. A. Eaton. With Preface and Notes by Edward Bell.
16. DEMOSTHENES—ON THE CROWN. Translated by C. Rann Kennedy.
17. THE VICAR OF WAKEFIELD.
18. OLIVER CROMWELL. By Dr. Reinhold Pauli.
19. THE PERFECT LIFE. By Dr. Channing. Edited by his nephew, Rev. W. H. Channing.
20. LADIES IN PARLIAMENT, HORACE AT ATHENS, and other pieces, by Sir George Otto Trevelyan, Bart.
21. DEFOE'S THE PLAGUE IN LONDON.
22. IRVING'S LIFE OF MAHOMET.
23. HORACE'S ODES, by various hands. [*Out of Print.*
24. BURKE'S ESSAY ON 'THE SUBLIME AND BEAUTIFUL.' With Short Memoir.
25. HAUFF'S CARAVAN.
26. SHERIDAN'S PLAYS.
27. DANTE'S PURGATORIO. Translated by Cary.
28. HARVEY'S TREATISE ON THE CIRCULATION OF THE BLOOD
29. CICERO'S FRIENDSHIP AND OLD AGE.
30. DANTE'S PARADISO. Translated by Cary.

THE NEW WEBSTER.

*AN ENTIRELY NEW EDITION,
Thoroughly Revised, considerably Enlarged, and reset in new type from beginning to end.*

2118 PAGES.   3500 ILLUSTRATIONS.

Prices: *Cloth*, £1 11s. 6d.; *Sheep*, £2 2s.;
Half Russia, £2 5s.; *Calf*, £2 8s.

Editorial work upon this revision has been in active progress for over **10 years.**
Not less than **100** editorial labourers have been engaged upon it.
Over **60,000*l.*** was expended in its preparation before the first copy was printed.
Webster is the Standard in our Postal Telegraph Department.
Webster is the Standard in the U.S. Government Printing Office.
The *Times* said of the last edition : ' It has all along kept a leading position.'
The *Quarterly Review* said : ' Certainly the best practical dictionary extant.'
The *Lord Chief Justice of England* said : ' I have looked, so that I may not go wrong, at WEBSTER'S DICTIONARY, a work of the greatest learning, research, and ability.'
The *Chief Justice of the U.S.A.* said : ' I have used and relied on WEBSTER'S UNABRIDGED DICTIONARY for many years, and entirely concur in the general commendation it has received.'

The only Authorised and Complete Edition.

LONDON: GEORGE BELL AND SONS.

www.ingramcontent.com/pod-product-compliance
Lightning Source LLC
Chambersburg PA
CBHW031946290426
44108CB00011B/691